Aviation Maintenance Technician Series

Airframe
Volume 1: Structures
Third Edition

DALE CRANE

TERRY MICHMERHUIZEN
Technical Editor

SCHOOL OF AVIATION SCIENCES
WESTERN MICHIGAN UNIVERSITY

LEARD WYLIE
Technical Editor

SCHOOL OF AVIATION SCIENCES
WESTERN MICHIGAN UNIVERSITY

ROBERT AARDEMA
Technical Editor

SCHOOL OF AVIATION SCIENCES
WESTERN MICHIGAN UNIVERSITY

EDITOR
FOR THE TH...

LINDA S. CLASSEN
MARY ANN EIFF
H.G. FRAUTSCHY
JERRY LEE FOULK
TERRY MICHMERHUIZEN

D1434612

Aviation Supplies & Academics, Inc.
NEWCASTLE, WASHINGTON

Aviation Maintenance Technician Series: Airframe
Third Edition
Volume 1: Structures

Aviation Supplies & Academics, Inc.
7005 132nd Place SE
Newcastle, Washington 98059-3153
Email: asa@asa2fly.com
Website: www.asa2fly.com

Cover photo courtesy Bombardier Aerospace, used by permission

Photo credits: p. 6—©iStockphoto.com/Dan Harmesan; p. 20—Raisbeck Engineering; p. 25—©iStockphoto.com/David Maczkowiack; p. 28—Cessna Aircraft Company; p. 28—Piper Aircraft; p. 29—Beech Aircraft Corporation; p. 158—Miller Electric Manufacturing Co.; p. 159—The Lincoln Electric Company; p. 235—Robert Scherer; p. 251—Heatcon Composite Systems; p. 424—Joe Finelli; p. 425—Cessna Aircraft Company; p. 451—Aircraft Braking Systems Corporation.

Illustration credits: pp. 41, 237—line drawings courtesy Grumman Corporation; p. 156—drawing source courtesy The Lincoln Electric Company; p. 314—illustration courtesy Chadwick-Helmuth Company, Inc.

Sections of some chapters are excerpted from previous publications, and have been used with permission: pp. 202–203, "Poly-Fiber Covering and Painting Material" courtesy Poly-Fiber Aircraft Coverings, Riverside, California; pp. 205–207, sections of the Superflite System manuals; pp. 205–207, Ceconite 7600 procedures provided by Blue River Aircraft Supply, Harvard, Nebraska.

ASA-AMT-STRUC-3
ISBN 1-56027-548-0
    978-1-56027-548-0

Library of Congress Cataloging-in-Publication Data
Crane, Dale.
      Airframe / Dale Crane; Terry Michmerhuizen, technical editor.
          p.   cm.   — (Aviation maintenance technician series)
      Includes index.
      1. Airframes—Maintenance and repair. I. Title. II. Series.
      TL 671.9.C663 1994
      629.134'6—dc20   94-22063
                                                  CIP

11

CONTENTS

PREFACE

Aviation maintenance technology has undergone tremendous changes in the past decades. Modern aircraft, with their advanced engines, complex flight controls and environmental control systems, are some of the most sophisticated devices in use today, and these marvels of engineering must be maintained by knowledgeable technicians. The Federal Aviation Administration, recognizing this new generation of aircraft, has updated the requirements for maintenance technicians and for the schools that provide their training. The FAA has also instituted an Aviation Maintenance Technician Awards Program to encourage technicians to update their training.

New technologies used in modern aircraft increase the importance of maintenance technicians having a solid foundation in such basic subjects as mathematics, physics, and electricity. The *Aviation Maintenance Technician Series* has been produced by ASA to provide the needed background information for this foundation and to introduce the reader to aircraft structures, powerplants, and systems.

These textbooks have been carefully designed to assist a person in preparing for FAA technician certification, and at the same time serve as valuable references for individuals working in the field. The subject matter is organized into categories used by the FAA for the core curriculum in 14 CFR Part 147, Aviation Maintenance Technician Schools, and for the Subject Matter Knowledge Codes used in the written tests for technician certification. In some cases in the ASA series, these categories have been rearranged to provide a more logical progression of learning.

This textbook is part of the ASA series of coordinated maintenance technician training materials. The series consists of the *General*, *Airframe*, and *Powerplant* textbooks with study questions, the *Fast-Track Test Guides for Aviation Mechanics*, exam software for Aviation Maintenance Technician tests, the *Oral and Practical Exam Guide*, the *Dictionary of Aeronautical Terms*, and the *Aviation Mechanic Handbook*.

Continued

To supplement this fundamental training material, ASA reprints the FAA Advisory Circulars AC 43.13-1B and 2A *Acceptable Methods, Techniques, and Practices—Aircraft Inspection, Repair, and Alteration*, and semiannually updated excerpts from the Federal Aviation Regulations that are applicable to the aviation maintenance technician.

Dale Crane

ACKNOWLEDGEMENTS

A series of texts such as this *Aviation Maintenance Technician Series* could never be compiled without the assistance of modern industry. Many individuals have been personally helpful, and many companies have been generous with their information. We want to acknowledge this and say thank you to them all.

Aeroquip Corporation, *Jackson, MI*

Aerostar International, *Sioux Falls, SD*

Airborne Division, Parker Hanniflin Corporation, *Elyria, OH*

Aircraft Braking Systems Corporation, *Massillon, OH*

American Avionics, *Seattle, WA*

Beech Aircraft Corporation, *Wichita, KS*

Biddle Instruments, *Blue Bell, PA*

Blue River Aircraft Supply, *Harvard, NE*

Cessna Aircraft Company, *Wichita, KS*

Chadwick-Helmuth Company, Inc., *El Monte, CA*

Christie Electric Corp., *Gardena, CA*

Dayton-Granger, *Fort Lauderdale, FL*

DeVilbiss Ransburg Industrial Equipment, *Maumee, OH*

Evergreen Weigh, Inc., *Lynnwood, WA*

General Electric Aircraft Engines, *Cincinnati, OH*

Grayhill, Inc., *La Grange, IL*

Grumman Corporation, *Bethpage, NY*

Heatcon Composite Systems, *Seattle, WA*

Hobart Brothers Company, *Troy, OH*

Lincoln Electric Company, *Cleveland, OH*

John Fluke Manufacturing Company, *Everett, WA*

Machida, Incorporated, *Orangeburg, NY*

Maule Air, Inc., *Moultrie, GA*

Micro-Surface Finishing Products, *Wilton, IA*

Miller Electric Manufacturing Company, *Appleton, WI*

Monsanto Chemical Company, *St. Louis, MO*

NASA Lewis Research Center, *Cleveland, OH*

Northrop Corporation, *Pico Rivera, CA*

Optronics Engineering, *Goleta, CA*

Piper Aircraft Company, *Vero Beach, FL*

Poly-Fiber Aircraft Coatings, *Riverside, CA*

Raisbeck Engineering, *Seattle, WA*

Randolph Products, *Carlstadt, NJ*

Simpson Electric Company, *Elgin, IL*

Superflite, *Elk Grove Village, IL*

Technical Chemical Company, *Dallas, TX*

Teledyne Battery Products, *Redlands, CA*

Zetec, Inc., *Issaquah, WA*

A special thanks goes to David Jensen and Pete Owsley of Heatcon® Composite Systems of Seattle, Washington, for their valuable input and their editing of the section on Composite Construction.

A very special thanks goes to Terry Michmerhuizen, Leard Wylie, and Robert Aardema of the School of Aviation Sciences of Western Michigan University for their careful editing, critiquing, and many suggestions in the first and second editions. Additionally, very special thanks to the members of the Editorial Board for the Third Edition (see Pages ix–x), for their valuable help in updating this new full-color edition of the *Structures* volume of *AMTS: Airframe*. The publisher would also like to thank Robert Scherer for the use of his "NC-51" Beech Starship photograph, Heatcon Composite Systems and Miller Electric Mfg. Co. for their contributions to the color photography added in this Third Edition.

AMT Airframe
Editorial Board

Third Edition, Volume 1: Structures

Linda S. Classen
Metro Tech, Instructor and Mechanic

Linda Classen is an Aviation Maintenance Instructor at Metro Technology Center in Oklahoma City. She has Private Pilot, Commercial, Instrument, and Certified Flight Instructor certificates. She holds a degree in journalism, and is a member of the Association for Women in Aviation Maintenance (AWAM), and the Professional Aviation Maintenance Association (PAMA).

Mary Ann Eiff
Human Performance and Safety Consultants

Mary Ann Eiff designs maintenance and management courses and teaches aircraft mechanics, managers and supervisors for airlines and MROs. She developed courses and taught aviation maintenance at Purdue University.

Mary Ann has a Master's in Adult Education, an A&P, Private Pilot, and loves to encourage young people into aviation careers. She was on the founding Board for Women in Aviation International and for the Association for Women in Aviation Maintenance (AWAM). In 2001, AWAM awarded her the Mary Ann Eiff Teacher of the Year Award for encouraging people into aviation careers. She was also awarded the Women in Aviation Educator of the Year Award by WAI. In 2004 she was awarded the PAMA Award of Merit, and the Phillips 66 Aviation Leadership Award.

Henry (H.G.) Frautschy
Executive Director, Vintage Aircraft Association; and Editor,
Vintage Airplane Magazine

H. G. Frautschy was named Executive Director of the Experimental Aviation Association (EAA)'s Vintage Aircraft Association division in March 2000, after serving as the Editor of *Vintage Airplane* magazine and Associate Editor of both *Sport Aviation* and *Warbirds* magazines since October 1990. Prior to joining the EAA staff, Frautschy was Publications Manager for Air Wisconsin, a regional airline based in Appleton, WI. He also served as Senior Technical Writer for Sikorsky Aircraft.

A 1980 graduate of Parks College of St. Louis University with a bachelor of science degree in aircraft maintenance management, Frautschy also holds a private pilot certificate (with a seaplane rating) as well as airframe and powerplant mechanic certificates, and he currently holds an FAA Inspection Authorization. He currently maintains a 1948 Aeronca 15AC Sedan, and is restoring a 1947 Aeronca 11CC Super Chief. He was also actively involved in the construction of the EAA's Stoddard-Hamilton GlaStar aircraft. An active Young Eagles pilot, Frautschy has flown over 125 missions in support of EAA's program intended to give the gift of flight to one million young people.

Jerry Lee Foulk
LeTourneau University Instructor, FAA Designated
Mechanic Examiner
Jerry Foulk has been an instructor of aviation maintenance since 1976, first at the Pittsburgh Institute of Aeronautics in Pittsburgh, PA, at Moody Aviation in Elizabethton, TN, and currently at LeTourneau University's School of Aeronautical Sciences, Longview, TX, starting in 2003. He earned his Bachelors of Science degrees in Bible and in Aviation Technology from LeTourneau in 1976, and has also been an FAA Designated Mechanic Examiner since 1993. Jerry also was Technical Editor for the Second Edition of ASA's *AMTS Powerplant* textbook by Dale Crane.

Terry Michmerhuizen
Owner, Mitch's Aero Services LLC, Brenco IA Training
Terry is an A&P, IA, ASC, a Designated Airworthiness Representative (DAR) with 10 years experience teaching aviation maintenance at the university level. He holds a private pilot certificate, was a U.S. Army Helicopter Mechanic, and was a chief inspector at an FAA-certified Repair Station. He is a member of the American Society for Quality (ASQ), Society of Automotive Engineers (SAE), PAMA, and has a Masters Degree in Management. He also conducts IA initial training courses preparing A&Ps to obtain their IA certificate.

EDITORIAL NOTE
to the Second Edition

This *Aviation Maintenance Technician Series, Airframe* textbook is now comprised of two volumes, entitled *Volume 1: Airframe Structures,* and *Volume 2: Airframe Systems.*

The previous edition of Airframe has been separated into two volumes for this Second Edition. The large amount of material required by the Federal Aviation Administration in the Airframe section of the curriculum creates large reference textbooks that can sometimes be unwieldy. This division will make it easier for readers to use and study the required material in sections.

Volume 1 contains the material concerned with aircraft structures, including: a study of aerodynamics as it relates to aircraft structures; also, hydraulic and pneumatic systems as they relate to the landing gear. Both metallic and nonmetallic structures as well as assembly and rigging are covered in this volume.

Volume 2 covers the various systems that include electrical, fuel, cabin atmosphere control, instruments, communications and navigation, ice and rain control, and fire protection systems. The subject of aircraft inspections is also included in this volume.

Volume 1:
Airframe Structures

BASIC AERODYNAMICS

1

Continued

Basic Aerodynamics

Basic Fixed-Wing Aerodynamics

The Beginnings of Flight

People have dreamed of taking to the air since the earliest observers watched the graceful flight of birds. It was only natural the first thoughts of flight assumed a need for flapping wings. In Greek mythology, Daedalus and his son Icarus escaped from Crete by making wings of feathers held together with wax. Icarus was so enamored of flight, he flew too close to the sun. The wax melted, and he plunged into the sea and drowned.

The earliest experimental flying machines emulated the bird, using flapping wings for propulsion. These machines, or "ornithopters," were unsuccessful. The first successful heavier-than-air flying machines were built and flown by the Chinese centuries before Christ, kites held in the air by the same aerodynamic forces that sustain modern airplanes and helicopters.

ornithopter. A heavier-than-air flying machine that produces lift by flapping its wings. No practical ornithopter has been built.

Two Types of Lift

Two types of lift raise aircraft against the force of gravity: aerostatic and aerodynamic. Aerostatic lift is produced when the weight of air displaced by the aircraft is greater than the weight of the aircraft. Aerodynamic lift is produced when movement of the aircraft through the air forces down a weight of air greater than the weight of the aircraft.

Aerostatic Lift

While the Chinese were flying kites and raising objects with the kites' aerodynamic lift, most experiments in Europe were of an aerostatic nature. In November of 1783, the Montgolfier brothers launched a manned hot-air balloon from Paris, France. Between the two world wars of the twentieth century, huge lighter-than-air flying machines carried aloft thousands of persons and transported tons of cargo, and in 1929 the German *Graf Zeppelin* made a round-the-world flight of more than 21,000 miles.

During the 1920s and 1930s, the U.S. Navy experimented with several huge lighter-than-air flying machines, using two of them, the *USS Akron* and the *USS Macon*, as flying aircraft carriers. Interest in lighter-than-air craft was dealt a serious blow on May 6, 1937, when the German airship *Hindenburg* burned as she docked at the U.S. Naval Air Station in Lakehurst, New Jersey. Strained diplomatic relations between the ruling parties in

Zeppelin. The name of large rigid lighter-than-air ships built by the Zeppelin Company in Germany prior to and during World War I.

Germany and the United States meant the Germans did not have access to helium gas (only found in commercial quantities in the United States). They used the extremely flammable hydrogen gas to lift the Hindenburg.

Experimental work with large lighter-than-air machines continues today, and gas-filled blimps frequently advertise above our cities. The most common lighter-than-air aircraft, though, are hot-air balloons. Made of modern high-strength synthetic fabrics, these aircraft use propane burners to heat the air.

blimp. A cigar-shaped, nonrigid lighter-than-air flying machine.

Figure 1-1. *The modern hot-air balloon uses the same type of aerostatic lift that carried two aeronauts aloft in France more than two centuries ago.*

Aerodynamic Lift

Most modern aircraft employ aerodynamic lift, which requires relative movement between the air and the aircraft.

To create aerodynamic lift, a specially shaped surface, called an airfoil, is moved through the air. A low pressure is produced above its surface, and a relatively high pressure is produced below it. This pressure differential deflects the air downward, and the mass of the air forced down is balanced by an equal force that pushes upward on the airfoil. This upward force is the aerodynamic lift.

aerodynamic lift. The force produced by air moving over a specially shaped surface called an airfoil. Aerodynamic lift acts in a direction perpendicular to the direction the air is moving.

airfoil. Any surface designed to obtain a useful reaction, or lift, from air passing over it.

Properties of the Atmosphere

The atmosphere is the layer of gases that surrounds the earth from its surface to a height of about 22 miles. These gases consist of a mixture of nitrogen and oxygen with a small percentage of other gases, including water vapor.

In the troposphere, the lowest layer of the atmosphere, all our weather exists. The troposphere extends from the surface to about 36,000 feet, and in this layer, the temperature and pressure decrease steadily as the altitude increases.

Immediately above the troposphere is the stratosphere, which extends to the upper limit of the atmosphere. The temperature in the stratosphere remains constant at -56.5°C (-69.7°F), but the pressure continues to decrease. The boundary between the troposphere and the stratosphere is called the tropopause.

Standard Atmospheric Conditions

The ICAO (International Civil Aeronautical Organization) standard atmosphere, also known as the International Standard Atmosphere (ISA), is a hypothetical condition whose parameters have been accepted by international agreement as representative of the atmosphere surrounding the earth for the purposes of aircraft design and performance calculations, and for the calibration of aircraft instruments.

ICAO Standard Atmosphere		
Parameter	**British Units**	**Metric Units**
Pressure, P_0	2116.22 lb/ft^2 29.92 in. Hg	$1.013250 \cdot 10^5$ N/m^2 760 mm Hg
Temperature, T_0	518.67°R 59.0°F	288.15°K 15.0°C
Acceleration due to gravity, g_0	32.1741 ft/sec^2	9.80665 m/sec^2
Specific weight, $g_0\rho_0$	0.76474 lb/ft^3	1.2230 kg/m^3
Density, ρ_0	0.0023769 lb-sec^2/ft^4	0.12492 kg-sec^2/m^4

Figure 1-2. *Conditions of the standard ICAO atmosphere*

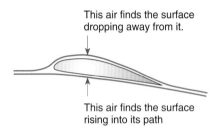

This air finds the surface dropping away from it.

This air finds the surface rising into its path

Figure 1-3. *The air flowing over the upper surface of this airfoil finds the surface dropping away, and is forced to speed up. The air flowing below the airfoil finds the surface rising into its path, and is forced to slow down.*

In practical flight conditions, air pressure is measured in terms of altitude rather than inches of mercury or pounds per square inch. The altimeter is an absolute-pressure gage, or barometer, that measures the pressure of the air and indicates the altitude at which that pressure exists.

When the barometric scale of the altimeter is set at the standard sea-level pressure, 29.92 inches of mercury, the indication is called pressure altitude.

Density altitude, used to determine the amount of lift produced by an airfoil and the amount of power produced by an engine, is found by correcting pressure altitude for nonstandard temperature.

Bernoulli's Principle

Aerodynamic lift is produced by the relative movement between an airfoil and the air. Air is a viscous fluid: it "wets," or tends to adhere to, any surface over which it flows.

An airfoil like the one in Figure 1-3 is shaped in such a way that the air flowing over its upper surface finds the surface dropping away from it, and it must speed up. The air flowing below the airfoil finds the surface rising into its path and it is forced to slow down.

In 1738, the Swiss physicist Daniel Bernoulli explained the relationship between potential and kinetic energy in the air as it flows over an airfoil. Air's potential energy relates to its pressure, and kinetic energy to its velocity. The sum of potential and kinetic energy in the air is its total energy.

Bernoulli's principle explains that if the total energy in the air flowing over an airfoil remains constant, any increase in its velocity will cause a corresponding decrease in its pressure.

Since the air flowing over the top of the airfoil speeds up, its pressure decreases, and air above it flows down to fill the low pressure. The air flowing under the airfoil is slowed down and its pressure increases. Air is forced away from the high pressure. The net result is that the air flowing around the airfoil is forced downward. (*See* Figure 1-4.) The weight of forced-down air is exactly balanced by the force pushing upward on the airfoil, aerodynamic lift.

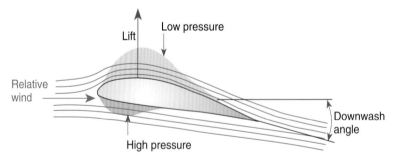

Figure 1-4. *Aerodynamic lift is produced by a relatively low pressure above the airfoil surface pulling air down to the surface, while a relatively high pressure below the surface forces the air away. The mass of the air deflected downward is balanced by an equal upward force on the airfoil.*

Axes of an Aircraft

An aircraft in flight is free to rotate about three axes: the longitudinal, or roll axis; the lateral, or pitch axis; and the vertical, or yaw axis. *See* Figure 1-5.

Forces Acting on an Aircraft in Flight

Four basic forces act on all aircraft in flight. During straight and level, unaccelerated flight, these forces are balanced and act through the aircraft's center of gravity. *See* Figure 1-6.

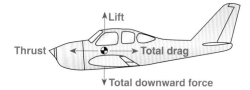

Figure 1-6. *Four basic forces act on an airplane in flight: a forward force of thrust, an upward force of lift, a rearward force of drag, and a downward force made up of weight and an aerodynamic down load on the tail.*

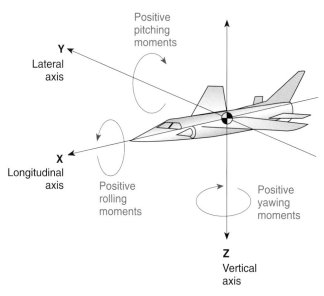

Figure 1-5. *An airplane in flight is free to rotate about its longitudinal, lateral, and vertical axes. These three axes are mutually perpendicular, and all pass through the aircraft's center of gravity.*

Thrust

The propeller or jet stream of an airplane, and the forward vector of the lift produced by a helicopter's rotor, provide thrust, or a force that causes forward movement. Thrust for a glider and for an airplane under reduced power, is produced by the forward component of lift and weight caused by the aircraft's downward flight path. *See* Figure 1-7.

When the thrust line is above the center of gravity, an increase in thrust rotates the airplane nose-down about its lateral axis. A decrease in thrust lets the airplane rotate nose-upward.

Lift

Lift is the total upward force produced by the aerodynamic reaction of the air flowing over the airfoil-shaped surfaces of the aircraft. The lift force is perpendicular to the relative wind, and may be tilted by varying the amounts of lift produced by each wing panel. Lowering the left aileron while raising the right aileron changes the shape of the wing airfoil, increasing the lift on

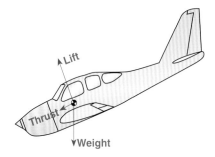

Figure 1-7. *When an airplane is in a power-off glide, the thrust is produced by the forward component of the lift and weight vectors.*

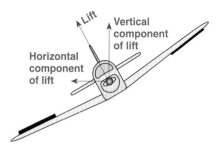

Figure 1-8. *Lift acts in a direction that is perpendicular to the lateral axis and may be tilted by rolling the airplane about its longitudinal axis. When the lift is tilted from its true vertical, it produces both a vertical and a horizontal component.*

induced drag. Aerodynamic drag produced by an airfoil when it is producing lift. Induced drag is affected by the same factors that affect induced lift.

parasite drag. A form of aerodynamic drag caused by friction between the air and the surface over which it is flowing.

angle of attack (α). The acute angle formed between the chord line of an airfoil and the direction of the air that strikes the airfoil.

trimmed flight. A flight condition in which the aerodynamic forces acting on the control surfaces are balanced and the aircraft is able to fly straight and level with no control input.

Figure 1-9. *Forces acting on an airplane in straight and level flight and turning flight.*

the left side of the airplane and decreasing the lift on the right side. The airplane rolls to the right and the lift tilts. Lift now has two components: one vertical and one horizontal. *See* Figure 1-8. It is this horizontal component of lift that causes an airplane to turn.

Weight

The weight of an airplane is the total pull of gravity. Weight acts through the center of gravity directly toward the center of the earth. Weight is the greatest part of the downward force on airplanes, but there are also other downward forces.

An airplane's downward tail load changes with its airspeed, and may be adjusted so all the downward forces are exactly equal to the upward forces. The combination of the downward forces moves the center of gravity to the same location as the center of lift, and the airplane balances about its center of gravity. *See* Figure 1-9.

For the airplane to remain at the same altitude, the total upward force must equal the total downward force. When the airplane is turning, centrifugal force causes a horizontal movement away from the center of the turn. This centrifugal force adds vectorially to the aircraft's weight to produce a resultant weight that is greater than the lift. If the lift is not increased as the airplane turns, the upward force will not equal the downward force, and the airplane will descend in the turn.

Drag

An airplane's drag is the sum of the forces that hold it back against the forward force of thrust. There are two basic drag forces: induced drag, which is produced by the same factors that produce aerodynamic lift, and parasite drag, which is caused by all factors not producing lift.

Induced drag, which is affected by the angle of attack, increases as the airspeed decreases. Parasite drag increases as the airspeed increases. The total drag is the sum of the induced and parasite drags. Total drag is least at the point where induced and parasite drags are equal.

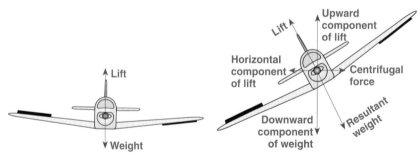

In straight and level trimmed flight, the lift exactly balances the weight.

In turning flight, centifugal force adds to the weight, and if the lift is not increased, the downward component of weight will be greater than the upward component, and the airplane will descend.

Development of the Aerodynamic Forces

Five factors affect aerodynamic lift and induced drag:

- Shape of the airfoil section

- Area of the airfoil

- Air density

- Speed of the air relative to the airfoil surface

- Angle between the airfoil and the relative wind (the angle of attack)

Notice that two of these factors relate to the airfoil, two to the air, and one to the relationship between the two. The direction of the lift produced by the wing is always perpendicular to the direction of the relative wind.

relative wind. The direction the wind strikes an airfoil.

Airfoil Sections

Aerodynamic lift depends on the shape of the airfoil section and on the airfoil surface area. Figure 1-10 shows a typical subsonic airfoil section and some of the more important terms related to its shape.

The mean camber (H) is a line drawn midway between the upper and lower cambers, and its curvature is one of the most important factors in determining the aerodynamic characteristics of the airfoil. The maximum camber (F) of a typical low-speed airfoil is about 4% of the length of the chord line, and is located about 40% of the chord length behind the leading edge. The maximum thickness (E) is about 12% of the chord length and is located about 30% of the chord length behind the leading edge.

mean camber. A line that is drawn midway between the upper and lower camber of an airfoil section. The mean camber determines the aerodynamic characteristics of the airfoil.

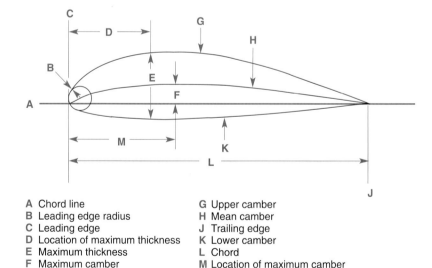

A Chord line	G Upper camber
B Leading edge radius	H Mean camber
C Leading edge	J Trailing edge
D Location of maximum thickness	K Lower camber
E Maximum thickness	L Chord
F Maximum camber	M Location of maximum camber

Figure 1-10. *Airfoil nomenclature*

The center of pressure is the point on the chord line of an airfoil at which all of the aerodynamic forces are concentrated. The lift vector acts from the center of pressure in a direction that is perpendicular to the relative wind, and the drag vector acts from this same point in a direction parallel to the relative wind.

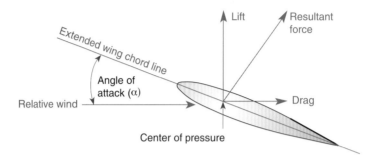

Figure 1-11. *The center of pressure of an airfoil is that point on the chord line at which the aerodynamic forces are considered to be concentrated.*

The center of pressure of a subsonic airfoil is typically located somewhere around 30% to 40% of the chord line back from the leading edge. On an asymmetrical airfoil, the center of pressure moves forward as the angle of attack increases, and backward as it decreases. On a symmetrical airfoil, the center of pressure does not move, but remains in essentially the same location as the angle of attack changes.

Figure 1-12 shows an evolution of airfoil shapes. The earliest airfoils were deeply cambered, and some were not even covered on the bottom. The shape was copied from a bird's wing. The next major step in airfoil development was the Clark-Y airfoil, the standard airfoil section through the 1920s and into the 1930s. The National Advisory Committee for Aeronautics (NACA), the ancestor of today's NASA, developed much more streamlined airfoils that allowed a smoother flow of air and greater lift with less drag. These airfoils included both symmetrical and asymmetrical sections.

When airplanes such as the Lockheed Lightning of World War II fame began flying in the transonic range, their subsonic airfoil sections left much to be desired. Shock waves formed, increasing drag and destroying control. Further study developed the supersonic airfoils, with their maximum thickness about midway back and their equally sharp leading and trailing edges. The supercritical airfoil evolved next, with its blunter leading edge and flatter upper surface. This airfoil section reduces the velocity of the air over the upper surface and delays the extreme drag rise that occurs as the airfoil approaches the speed of sound.

The NASA-developed GAW-1 and GAW-2 low-speed airfoils have the same downward cusp at the trailing edge that the supercritical airfoil has. These airfoils were developed for general aviation aircraft, and they give a wing a higher L/D ratio by increasing the lift and decreasing the drag.

cusp. A pointed end.

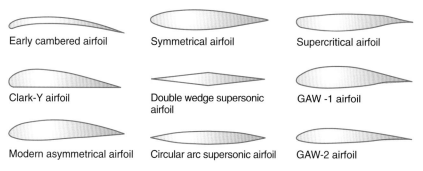

Early cambered airfoil   Symmetrical airfoil   Supercritical airfoil

Clark-Y airfoil   Double wedge supersonic airfoil   GAW -1 airfoil

Modern asymmetrical airfoil   Circular arc supersonic airfoil   GAW-2 airfoil

Figure 1-12. *Airfoil types*

symmetrical airfoil. An airfoil that has the same shape on both sides of its center line.

asymmetrical airfoil. An airfoil section that is not the same on both sides of the chord line.

Aerodynamic Lift

To find the amount of aerodynamic lift produced by an airfoil, use the formula in Figure 1-13. When the air density is expressed as a density ratio (σ) between standard air density at sea level and the density of the existing air, and the velocity of the air is expressed in knots, the dynamic pressure (q) of the air in pounds per square foot is found with the formula in Figure 1-14. Notice that the lift is affected by the square of the airspeed. Doubling the airspeed increases the lift four times.

density ratio (σ). The ratio of the density of the air at a given altitude to the density of the air at sea level under standard conditions.

dynamic pressure (q). The pressure a moving fluid would have if it were stopped. Dynamic pressure is measured in pounds per square foot.

$$L = C_L qS$$

L = aerodynamic lift in pounds
C_L = coefficient of lift from characteristic curve for the angle of attack specified
q = dynamic pressure in pounds per square foot
S = airfoil surface in square feet

Figure 1-13. *Formula for finding aerodynamic lift*

$$q = 0.00339\ \sigma\ V^2$$

q = dynamic pressure in pounds per square foot
0.00339 = a constant that allows knots to be used as the velocity
σ = density ratio as found in Figure 1-15
V = true airspeed in knots

Figure 1-14. *Formula for finding the dynamic pressure*

knot. A measure of speed equal to one nautical mile per hour.

Figure 1-15 is an excerpt from the International Civil Aeronautical Organization (ICAO) Standard Atmosphere Chart. As the altitude increases, the density of the air decreases, but the temperature and the speed of sound decrease only to an altitude of 36,089 feet, and then stabilize. This altitude is the beginning of the stratosphere.

Altitude feet	Temperature		Density Slugs / ft³	Density ratio	Speed of sound knots
	°F	°C			
Sea level	59	15	.002378	1.000	661.7
1,000	55.4	13	.002309	0.9711	659.5
5,000	41.2	5.1	.002049	0.8617	650.3
10,000	23.3	-4.8	.001756	0.7385	638.6
20,000	-12.3	-24.6	.001267	0.5328	614.6
30,000	-47.9	-44.4	.000890	0.3741	589.5
36,089	-69.7	-56.5	.000706	0.2971	573.8
40,000	-69.7	-56.5	.000585	0.2462	573.8
50,000	-69.7	-56.5	.000362	0.1522	573.8

Figure 1-15. *Excerpts from the ICAO Standard Atmosphere Chart*

coefficient of drag. A dimensionless number used in the formula for determining induced drag as it relates to the angle of attack.

coefficient of lift. A dimensionless number relating to the angle of attack used in the formula for aerodynamic lift.

L/D ratio. A measure of efficiency of an airfoil. It is the ratio of the lift to the total drag at a specified angle of attack.

stall. A flight condition in which an angle of attack is reached at which the air ceases to flow smoothly over the upper surface of an airfoil. The air becomes turbulent and lift is lost.

The information required about the airfoil is its shape and its area. Figure 1-16 shows a typical set of characteristic curves for a specific shape of airfoil. Such curves are available for every airfoil section.

The coefficient of lift (C_L), the coefficient of drag (C_D), and the lift over drag (L/D) curves are the most important characteristics. These curves let you find the appropriate coefficients, or dimensionless numbers, for the airfoil at each angle of attack.

Notice that the C_L curve increases steadily from 0 at 0° angle of attack until, at an angle of attack of 20°, it suddenly drops off. This is the critical angle of attack at which the air ceases to flow smoothly over the top of the wing, and the wing stalls.

The C_D curve is relatively flat from 0° up to about 3° and then turns sharply upward and continues to increase with the angle of attack. You can find the values for the L/D curve by dividing the C_L by the C_D for the particular angle of attack. For example, at an angle of attack of 6°, the C_L is approximately 0.5 and the C_D is 0.04. Divide C_L by C_D to find that the L/D ratio for 6° is 12.5. This is the high point of the L/D curve, or the L/D_{MAX}. *See* Figure 1-16.

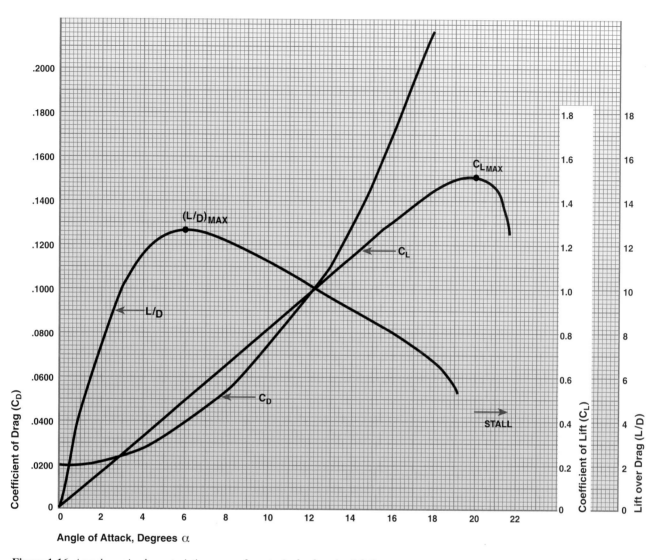

Figure 1-16. *Aerodynamic characteristics curves for a typical subsonic airfoil*

Find the amount of lift produced by a wing by following the steps shown in Figure 1-17.

Known values
Angle of attack = 16°
True airspeed = 60 knots
Density altitude = 1,000 feet
Wing area = 170 square feet

Find
Lift produced in pounds

Procedure
1. Find the coefficient of lift:
   In Figure 1-16, locate 16° along the angle of attack scale at the bottom of the chart. Follow this line upward until it intersects the C_L curve. From this point, follow a line to the right until it intersects the C_L index. This occurs at 1.3.
2. Find the dynamic pressure:
   Use the ICAO Standard Atmosphere Chart in Figure 1-15 to find the density ratio at 1,000 feet. Follow the horizontal line for 1,000 feet to the right to the density ratio column. = 0.9711
   Use the formula in Figure 1-14 to find the dynamic pressure:
   $q = 0.00339 \quad V^2$
   $= 0.00339 \times 0.9711 \times 60^2$
   $= 11.85$ pounds per square foot
3. Find the aerodynamic lift:
   Use the formula in Figure 1-13.
   $L = C_L q S$
   $= 1.3 \times 11.85 \times 170$
   $= 2,618.8$ pounds

Figure 1-17. *Finding the lift produced by a wing*

Induced Drag

Notice that the C_D curve in Figure 1-16 increases greatly with the angle of attack, but the angle of attack needed to produce a given amount of lift decreases as the airspeed increases. The induced drag, therefore, decreases with an increase in airspeed, as shown in the typical drag curve in Figure 1-19 on Page 18.

$D = C_D q S$

D = induced drag in pounds

C_D = coefficient of drag from characteristic curve for the angle of attack specified

q = dynamic pressure in pounds per square foot

S = airfoil surface in square feet

Figure 1-18. *Formula for finding the induced drag, in pounds, produced by an airfoil*

Parasite Drag

Parasite drag is caused by the friction of the air flowing over the surface of an aircraft, and it increases with the airspeed. Figure 1-19 shows the way induced drag and parasite drag change with airspeed. At low airspeed, such a high angle of attack is required that the induced drag is extremely high, but the air friction, or parasite drag, is low. As the angle of attack decreases and the airspeed increases, the induced drag decreases rapidly and the parasite drag increases. At the angle of attack that produces the maximum L/D ratio, induced and parasite drag are the same. The total drag, which is the sum of induced and parasite drags, drops until the drags become equal and then rises. As airspeed increases, the total drag increases just a little more slowly than the parasite drag until the airspeed reaches the transonic range. At this speed, the formation of shock waves on the surface, caused by compressibility, produces a rapid increase in the total drag. (*See* "Basic High-Speed Aerodynamics" beginning on Page 37.)

There are special forms of parasite drag. Profile drag is parasite drag produced by the skin friction as the air flows over it, and is present on an airfoil even when it is not producing lift. Form drag is the parasite drag caused by the form of the object passing through the air, and it is less a factor for streamlined bodies than for bodies that have other than streamlined shapes. Interference drag is the part of the parasite drag caused by air flowing over one portion of the airframe interfering with the smooth flow of air over another portion. Interference drag is minimized by the installation of fairings or fillets where the two surfaces or components join at an angle.

Flight at High-Lift Conditions

Airplanes need a high forward speed to produce enough lift to become airborne. Much research has gone into developing an aircraft that can maintain its lift at a low forward speed. This practical problem has, of course, been solved with the helicopter.

The coefficient of lift of an airfoil increases smoothly with the angle of attack until the critical angle of attack is reached. At this point, the air ceases to flow smoothly over the upper surface of the airfoil, and lift is lost. This condition is called a stall. *See* Figure 1-16 on Page 15.

An airplane stalls when it reaches its critical angle of attack, which can occur at almost any airspeed. If the airplane is heavily loaded, it requires such a high angle of attack for normal flight that there is very little margin left for the changes in angle of attack that occur while flying in turbulence.

Unintentional stalls and spins have plagued airplane operators since the beginning of flight. These can occur if an airplane is making a slow, high angle-of-attack approach for landing, and the pilot kicks the rudder to align the airplane with the runway. Both wings are operating at a high angle of attack, and when the rudder moves suddenly, the airplane yaws. The angle of attack of the wing moving forward is increased until this wing stalls.

compressibility effect. The sudden increase in the total drag of an airfoil in transonic flight caused by formation of shock waves on the surface.

profile drag. Aerodynamic drag produced by skin friction. Profile drag is a form of parasite drag.

form drag. Parasite drag caused by the form of the object passing through the air.

interference drag. Parasite drag caused by air flowing over one portion of the airframe interfering with the smooth flow of air over another portion.

fairing. A part of a structure whose primary purpose is to produce a smooth surface or a smooth junction where two surfaces join.

fillet. A fairing used to give shape but not strength to an object. A fillet produces a smooth junction where two surfaces meet.

spin. A flight maneuver in which an airplane descends in a corkscrew fashion. One wing is stalled and the other is producing lift.

The angle of attack of the wing moving backward is not increased and it continues to produce lift. The airplane enters a spin, and, if at low altitude, crashes.

Airplanes can also stall at high airspeeds. If an airplane is in a dive and the pilot tries to recover by pulling the control wheel back suddenly, the angle of attack will increase to the point that the airplane stalls.

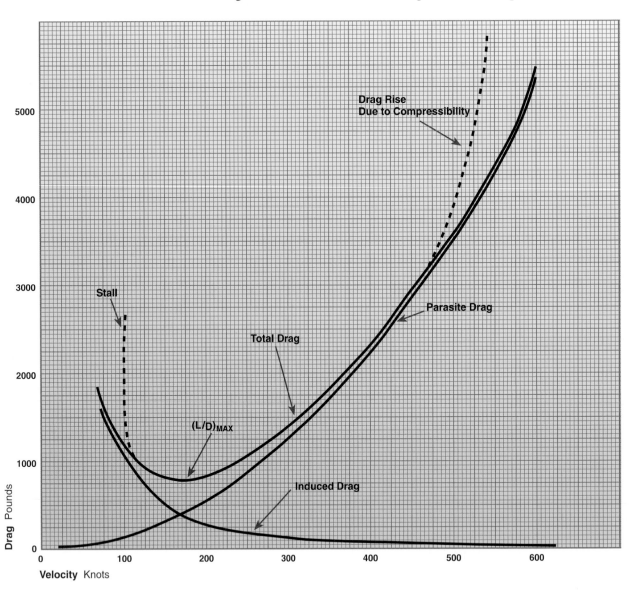

Figure 1-19. *Typical airplane drag curve*

Ground Effect

When an airplane flies at a height above the ground of less than one-half its wing span, the air forced down is deflected, which effectively increases the angle of attack without increasing the induced drag. This deflected air is called ground effect.

It is possible for the pilot to take off in a heavily loaded airplane at too low an airspeed. The decreased induced drag lets the airplane get airborne, but when the pilot climbs above the ground effect, the induced drag increases until the airplane drops back to a lower height. Pilots must drop the nose and pick up additional airspeed under these conditions, so the high angle of attack is not needed.

Effect of High-Lift Devices

An airplane can fly in a high-lift condition without stalling if the pilot can use wing flaps to modify the camber, or curvature, of the airfoil in flight. The various types of flaps are discussed in Chapter 4. The purpose of all flaps is the same: to increase the camber of the wing so it can operate with a higher angle of attack without the airflow over the top surface becoming turbulent and breaking away.

When the flaps are lowered and the camber is increased, both the lift and the drag are increased. Most flap installations are designed in such a way that the first half of flap extension increases the lift more than the drag, and partial flaps are used for takeoff. Lowering the flaps all the way increases the drag more than the lift, and full flaps are used for landing.

Boundary Layer Control

Air is viscous and clings to the surface over which it flows. At the surface, the air particles are slowed to near-zero relative velocity. Above the surface, the retarding forces lessen progressively, until slightly above the surface the particles have the full velocity of the airstream. The air immediately above the surface is called the boundary layer.

Air flowing over a smooth flat surface begins, as shown in Figure 1-20, by flowing in a smooth layer-like fashion with no air particles moving from one level to another. This is called laminar flow. Friction between the air and the surface uses part of the energy in the air, and the boundary layer thickens, becomes unstable and turbulent, and creates a great deal of drag. *See* Figure 1-20 on the next page.

ground effect. The increased aerodynamic lift produced when an airplane or helicopter is flown nearer than a half wing span or rotor span to the ground. This additional lift is caused by an effective increase in angle of attack without the accompanying increase in induced drag, which is caused by the deflection of the downwashed air.

boundary layer. The layer of air that flows next to an aerodynamic surface. Because of the design of the surface and local surface roughness, the boundary layer often has a random flow pattern, sometimes even flowing in a direction opposite to the direction of flight. A turbulent boundary layer causes a great deal of aerodynamic drag.

laminar flow. Airflow in which the air passes over the surface in smooth layers with a minimum of turbulence.

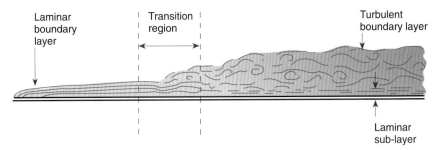

Figure 1-20. *Development of boundary layer on a smooth flat surface*

Boundary layer is studied by attaching hundreds of short tufts of wool yarn to the surface of a wing and photographing them in flight. At low angles of attack, most of the tufts lie flat against the surface and straight across the wing. But as the angle of attack is increased, some of the tufts behind the thickest part of the wing begin to wave back and forth and up and down. Some of them even wave around and point forward. These tufts show the turbulence in the boundary layer. *See* Figure 1-21.

Since a turbulent boundary layer causes a definite increase in drag and usually leads to airflow separation, much study has been made to find ways of minimizing it. Slots and slats force high-energy air from below the wing into the upper-surface boundary layer at high angles of attack. This allows for a higher angle of attack before the airflow separates. Slotted and triple-slotted flaps are used to duct high-energy air over the upper surface of the flaps when they are extended, which prevents the air separating from their surface.

A more extensive method of boundary layer control involves sucking the boundary layer from the surface so that the smooth air above it can flow nearer the surface. The wing surface has a series of small slots in its upper skin, and these slots open into a series of channels inside the wing that are connected to a suction pump. The turbulent air in the boundary layer is removed and the smooth air is pulled down to the surface.

slat. A secondary control on an aircraft that allows it to fly at a high angle of attack without stalling. A slat is a section of the leading edge of the wing mounted on curved tracks that move into and out of the wing on rollers.

slot. A fixed, nozzle-like opening near the leading edge of an airplane wing ahead of the aileron. A slot acts as a duct to force air down on the upper surface of the wing when the airplane is flying at a high angle of attack. The slot allows the airplane to fly at a high angle of attack before it stalls, and the slot is located ahead of the aileron, so the aileron will remain effective throughout the stall.

wing fences. Vertical vanes that extend chordwise across the upper surface of an airplane wing to prevent spanwise airflow.

Figure 1-21. *Tufts attached to the upper surface of these wings are used to study the boundary layer. Notice the wing fences, the dark objects parallel to the wing chord. These fences prevent the air from flowing spanwise.*

Vortex Generators

Vortex generators are small low-aspect-ratio airfoils such as those seen in Figure 1-22. They are installed in pairs on the upper surface of a wing, on both sides of the vertical fin just ahead of the rudder, and on the underside of the vertical stabilizer. They pull high-energy air down to the surface, which energizes the boundary layer and prevents airflow separation until the surface reaches a higher angle of attack.

Vortex generators are installed on the wing of an airplane ahead of the aileron in one row, about one-third of the way back from the leading edge. This is the point where the air begins to reach sonic velocity when the airplane is cruising in the transonic flight range. Another row is installed about one-third of the way forward of the trailing edge, where the air returns to subsonic speed. These generators are mounted in complementary pairs at such an angle that the vortex from one aids the vortex of its companion.

The pressure between the generators in a pair is higher than the pressure on the outside, and the air spills over and forms a tight swirl, or vortex. High-energy air is caught in the vortex and pulled down to the surface, where it energizes the sluggish boundary layer, delays the onset of shock-induced separation, and aids in maintaining aileron effectiveness at high speeds.

vortex generator. Small low-aspect-ratio airfoils installed in pairs on the upper surface of a wing, on both sides of the vertical fin just ahead of the rudder, and on the underside of the vertical stabilizers of some airplanes. Their function is to pull high-energy air down to the surface to energize the boundary layer and prevent airflow separation until the surface reaches a higher angle of attack.

vortex, *pl.* **vortices.** A whirling motion in a fluid.

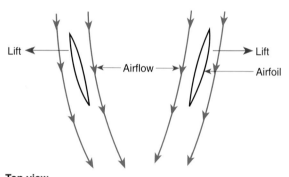

Top view

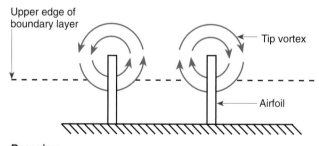

Rear view

Figure 1-22. *Vortex generators pull high-energy air down to the surface to energize the boundary layer and reduce drag.*

Vortex generators mounted on the wings improve flight characteristics at
high speed, but those on the empennage improve flight characteristics at low
speed. The generators mounted on both sides of the vertical fin prevent flow
separation over the rudder during extreme angles of yaw, as would occur if
rudder application was delayed after an engine failure at low airspeed. Vortex generators mounted on the lower surface of the horizontal stabilizer ahead
of the elevators prevent flow separation over the elevator at low airspeed.

Effect of Wing Planform

The planform of a wing is its shape as viewed from directly above, and it
affects the aircraft's flight performance. The two most important characteristics of wing planform are its aspect ratio and taper.

The aspect ratio is the ratio of the length, or span, of a wing to its width,
or chord. With all else equal, an increase in aspect ratio decreases the drag,
especially at high angles of attack. A sailplane is a high-performance glider
that operates at slow airspeed and high angle of attack, and all modern sail-
planes have very high-aspect-ratio wings.

The planform also has a pronounced effect on the stall progression. Figure 1-23 shows an exaggerated view of several basic wing planforms and
the way stalls progress on each. The rectangular wing has the most desirable
stall progression. The stall begins at the wing root and progresses outward,
so the air still flows smoothly over the ailerons when the wing loses enough
lift to cause the nose to drop. The elliptical wing has the most efficient planform, because it produces the minimum amount of induced drag for a given
aspect ratio. But it has two disadvantages that prevent its wide acceptance: it
is difficult and expensive to construct, and the stall progression is inferior to
that of a rectangular wing.

A wing with a moderate taper has many of the advantages of an elliptical wing, and is less costly to construct. Its stall characteristics are similar to
those of the elliptical wing. When the taper is increased, the stall characteristics become adverse, with the stall beginning near the tip and progressing
inboard. This progression causes the loss of aileron effectiveness, and thus
lateral control, while lift is still being produced by the inboard portion of
the wing.

Slots and Stall Strips

Some wings stall in such a way that the airflow breaks up ahead of the aileron while the wing is still producing lift. This causes a loss of lateral control.
Two methods of preventing this problem have been used on small- and me-
dium-size general aviation airplanes: slots and stall strips.

Some airplanes have a fixed slot just behind the leading edge of the
wing ahead of the aileron, like that in Figure 1-24. At a high angle of attack,
air flows through this slot and is forced down over the upper surface, letting
the wing reach a higher angle of attack before the area ahead of the aileron
stalls.

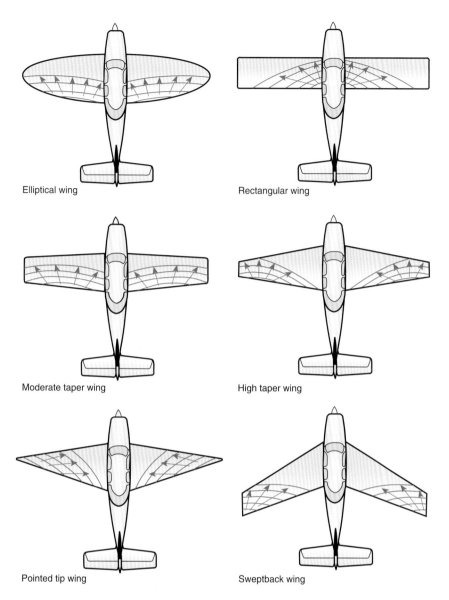

Elliptical wing

Rectangular wing

Moderate taper wing

High taper wing

Pointed tip wing

Sweptback wing

Figure 1-23. *Wing planforms and the progression of stalls*

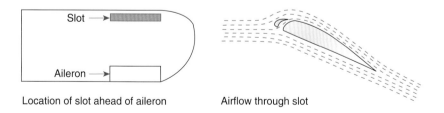

Location of slot ahead of aileron

Airflow through slot

Figure 1-24. *A fixed slot in the leading edge of the wing ahead of the aileron forces high-energy air down over the aileron and prevents this portion of the wing from stalling before the inboard portion of the wing stalls.*

A simpler fix for a wing that stalls in the aileron area before the root stalls is to install a stall strip, as in Figure 1-25. This is a small triangular strip of metal attached to the leading edge of the wing root. As the angle of attack increases, the stall strip disturbs the air and causes the root of the wing to stall before the tip stalls. The nose of the airplane drops before lateral control is lost.

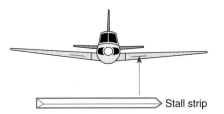

Stall strip

Figure 1-25. *A stall strip forces the root of the wing to stall before the tip area stalls. This allows the pilot to have lateral control during the stall.*

Wing-Tip Vortices

aspect ratio. The ratio of the length, or span, of an airplane wing to its width, or chord. For a nonrectangular wing, the aspect ratio is found by dividing the square of the span by the wing by its area.

Aspect Ratio = span² ÷ area

An airplane in flight has a low pressure above the wing and a high pressure below, and some of the high-pressure air flows from the bottom to the top around the wing tip and produces a strong swirl of air called a vortex. Energy is lost in the vortices, and steps have been taken to minimize them. One effective step is the use of a high aspect ratio. Figure 1-26 shows the planforms of three wings with the same area but different aspect ratios. The low-aspect-ratio wing is the least effective, because a large percentage of its surface is in the tip loss area.

External fuel tanks mounted on wing tips and tip plates on the ends of the wings prevent air spilling over the tip and causing vortices. Winglets minimize losses due to vortex generation. Winglets, small upturned vertical surfaces mounted on the wing tips, reduce drag by reducing the spanwise flow of air, therefore reducing vortices. *See* Figure 1-27.

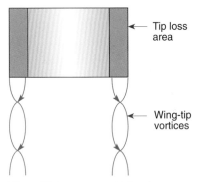

Tip loss area

Wing-tip vortices

Wing with low-aspect ratio has large percentage of its area in tip loss area, and produces strong wing-tip vortices.

Wing with medium-aspect ratio has less tip loss area and weaker vortices.

Wing with high-aspect ratio has the least tip loss area and weakest vortices.

Figure 1-26. *An increase in the aspect ratio of a wing decreases the amount of energy that is lost in wing-tip vortices.*

Figure 1-27. *Winglets extend upward from the wing tips of many modern airplanes to reduce drag and increase the L/D ratio by minimizing wing-tip vortices.*

Stability and Control

The development of the airplane was delayed by two problems: how to achieve stability and how to achieve control. Before the Wright brothers' successful flight in 1903, others had flown, but none had their success in controlling their aircraft.

"Stability" relates to maintaining the desired flight attitude with a minimum of pilot effort, and "control" involves rotating the airplane about one or more of its three axes.

Static Stability

The tendency of an aircraft to try to return to straight and level flight after it has been disturbed from this condition is called static stability.

If the nose of an airplane that has positive longitudinal static stability is forced up or down, and the controls are released, established forces bring the nose back to level flight. If the airplane has neutral static stability, the nose will stay displaced but will neither get further from its disturbed condition nor try to return to level flight. An airplane with negative static stability will deviate further from a condition of level flight and make no effort to return.

static stability. The characteristic of an aircraft that causes it to return to straight and level flight after it has been disturbed from that condition.

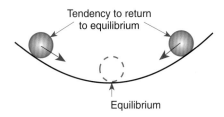

A ball has **positive static stability** when in a trough. If moved up the walls of the trough and released, it will roll back to the bottom, which is its position of equilibrium.

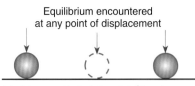

A ball has **neutral static stability** when on a flat plane. When moved from its position of equilibrium, it will not try to move farther away, neither will it try to return to its original position.

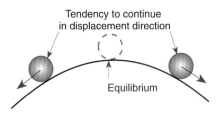

A ball has **negative static stability** when on a ridge. When released from its position of equilibrium (on the top), it will continue to move farther from its position with no added disturbance.

Figure 1-28. *Static stability*

damped oscillation. Oscillation whose amplitude decreases with time.

divergent oscillation. Oscillation whose amplitude increases with time.

undamped oscillation. Oscillation that continues with an unchanging amplitude once it has started.

Positive static stability about an airplane's lateral axis causes it to return to level flight after the control has been moved to drop a wing, and then released. Positive static stability about the vertical axis causes the airplane to straighten out and point into the relative wind after a rudder pedal has been depressed and then released. Neutral and negative static stability about these axes have the same effect as they have about the longitudinal axis. *See* Figure 1-28.

Dynamic Stability

Static stability is the production of a restorative force to bring the aircraft back to a condition of straight and level flight after it has been disturbed. Dynamic stability is the decrease of these forces with time.

For example, if the nose of an airplane that has positive static and positive dynamic longitudinal stability is forced down and the control released, the nose will rise, but will go beyond level flight into a nose-up attitude. From this position, static stability will cause the nose to drop, but again it will pass through level flight to a nose-down position, although not as low as the original displacement. The oscillations caused by these restorative forces will decrease, and the airplane will return to its level-flight attitude. These oscillations are plotted in Figure 1-29.

An airplane with positive static stability and neutral dynamic stability will continue to oscillate with the same displacement. One with positive static and negative dynamic stability will have divergent oscillations, and the intensity of the oscillations will increase with time.

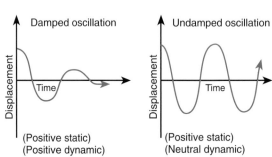
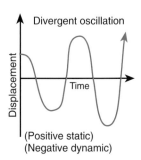

An airplane with positive static and positive dynamic stability will oscillate with damped oscillations if it is disturbed and the disturbance is removed.

An airplane with positive static and neutral dynamic stability will oscillate with an undamped oscillation.

An airplane with positive static and negative dynamic stability will oscillate with divergent oscillation when disturbed.

Figure 1-29. *Dynamic stability*

Longitudinal Stability

Longitudinal stability is stability along the longitudinal axis and about the lateral, or pitch, axis. A longitudinally stable airplane will maintain level flight without requiring the pilot to continually operate the controls.

An airplane has longitudinal stability because of the relationship between its center of gravity and center of lift. Figure 1-30 shows an airplane with its center of lift behind its center of gravity (CG). The nose-down rotation that would result is counteracted by a nose-up force caused by the downward aerodynamic load on the tail.

The nose-down force caused by the CG's position ahead of the center of lift is fixed and does not change with airspeed. But the tail load is speed dependent—the higher the airspeed, the greater the downward force on the tail. If the airplane is trimmed for level flight with the pilot's hands off the controls, and a wind gust causes the nose to drop, the airplane will nose down and the airspeed will increase. As the airspeed increases, the tail load increases and pulls the nose back to its level flight condition. If the nose is forced up, the airspeed will drop off, and the tail load will decrease enough to allow the nose to drop back to level flight. *See* Figure 1-30.

Flying wing airplanes usually have a large amount of sweepback, and since they have no tail, their longitudinal stability is produced by washing out the tips of the wing. The speed-dependent downward aerodynamic force at the wing tip is behind the center of lift, and it produces the same stabilizing force as that produced by a conventional tail.

Static stability causes an airplane to return to a condition of straight and level flight when it has been disturbed from this condition. This is good for most airplanes, but not for highly maneuverable military fighter aircraft. These aircraft are designed with what is known as relaxed static stability, and have little or no static stability. The airplane must be flown at all times, an almost impossible task for the pilot. To overcome this limitation, airplanes with relaxed static stability have sophisticated electronic stability augmentation systems that compensate for the lack of natural static stability.

Longitudinal Control (Rotation About the Lateral Axis)

When an airplane is trimmed for straight and level flight at a fixed airspeed, all the aerodynamic forces are balanced and no control forces are needed. But the airplane can be rotated nose upward about its lateral axis (pitch up) by increasing the downward tail load, or nose downward (pitch down) by decreasing the tail load.

The most generally used pitch control for an airplane is the fixed horizontal stabilizer with a movable elevator hinged to its trailing edge. When the control wheel or stick is pulled back, the trailing edge of the elevator moves up and increases the down load on the horizontal tail surface. The tail moves down and rotates the airplane nose-up about its lateral axis. *See* Figure 1-31 on the next page.

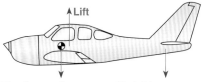

Lift

Fixed nose-down force independent of airspeed

Variable nose-up force dependent upon airspeed

Figure 1-30. *Longitudinal stability is produced by the relationship between the center of gravity and center of lift, and by the downward aerodynamic load on the tail.*

flying wing. A type of heavier-than-air aircraft that has no fuselage or separate tail surfaces. The engines and useful load are carried inside the wing, and movable control surfaces on the trailing edge provide both pitch and roll control.

stabilator. A flight control on the empennage of an airplane that acts as both a stabilizer and an elevator. The entire horizontal tail surface pivots and is moved as a unit.

Some airplanes use a stabilator for pitch control. *See* Figure 1-32. This is a single-piece horizontal surface that pivots about a point approximately one-third of the way back from the leading edge. When the control wheel is pulled back, the leading edge of the stabilator moves down and increases the downward force produced by the tail. This rotates the nose up. When the wheel is pushed in, the nose of the stabilator moves up, decreasing the tail load, and the airplane rotates nose down.

Figure 1-31. *This airplane uses a conventional horizontal stabilizer and elevators for longitudinal stability and control.*

Figure 1-32. *This airplane uses a stabilator for longitudinal stability and control.*

Longitudinal control is achieved on the V-tail Beech Bonanzas with two fixed and two movable surfaces arranged in the shape of a V. Moving the control wheel in and out actuates the movable surfaces together so they act as elevators and rotate the airplane about its lateral axis. When the rudder pedals are moved, the movable surfaces move differentially and act as a rudder to rotate the airplane about its vertical axis. The movable surfaces on this type of empennage are called ruddervators.

ruddervators. The two movable surfaces on a V-tail empennage. When these two surfaces are moved together with the control yoke, they act as elevators, and when they are moved differentially with the rudder pedals, they act as the rudder.

Beech Aircraft Corporation

dihedral. The positive angle formed between the lateral axis of an airplane and a line that passes through the center of the wing or horizontal stabilizer. Dihedral increases the lateral stability of an airplane.

Figure 1-33. *This airplane uses two fixed and two movable surfaces arranged in the form of a V for longitudinal stability and control*

Lateral Stability

Most airplane wings tilt upward from the fuselage, and this upward angle, called dihedral, gives the airplane lateral stability. If the airplane shown in Figure 1-34 is flying along with the pilot's hands and feet off of the controls, and a wind gust causes the right wing to drop, the air striking the descending right wing will increase its angle of attack, and the air striking the rising left wing will decrease its angle of attack. Since lift is determined by the angle of attack, the uneven lift will bring the airplane back to level flight.

Lateral Control (Rotation About the Longitudinal Axis)

Balanced aerodynamic forces cause a properly designed and trimmed airplane to fly straight and level with hands and feet off of the controls. The lift produced by the wings is equal.

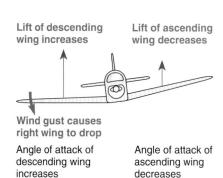

Lift of descending wing increases   Lift of ascending wing decreases

Wind gust causes right wing to drop

Angle of attack of descending wing increases

Angle of attack of ascending wing decreases

Figure 1-34. *Dihedral produces lateral stability. When the right wing drops in flight, its angle of attack increases, and the angle of attack of the left wing decreases. Increasing the angle of attack increases the lift, and the wings return to level flight.*

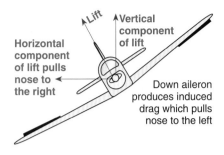

Figure 1-35. *The horizontal component of lift pulls the nose of a banked airplane around in a turn. When the bank is started, the down aileron produces enough induced drag to temporarily start the nose moving in the wrong direction.*

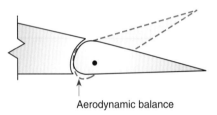

Aerodynamic balance

Figure 1-36. *A Frise aileron minimizes adverse yaw by extending the nose of the up-aileron below the lower surface of the wing to produce additional parasite drag. This counteracts the increased induced drag caused by the down-aileron on the opposite wing.*

adverse yaw. A condition of flight at the beginning of a turn in which the nose of an airplane momentarily yaws away from the direction in which the turn is to be made.

differential ailerons. An aileron system in which the aileron moving upward deflects more than the one moving down. The additional upward movement produces enough parasite drag to counteract the induced drag caused by the lowered aileron. Differential ailerons are used to minimize adverse yaw.

When you want to roll the airplane to the right, turn the control wheel to the right. The aileron on the right wing moves up, decreasing the camber, or curvature, of the right wing and decreasing the lift it produces. At the same time, the aileron on the left wing moves down, increasing the camber of the left wing and increasing the lift it produces. The difference in lift produced by the two wings rolls the airplane to the right.

Turning Flight

An airplane is turned by rotating it about its longitudinal axis. Look at Figure 1-35. When the airplane is rolled to the right, the lift produced by the wing, which acts perpendicular to the lateral axis, now has a horizontal component that pulls the nose around to the right.

But when the left aileron moves down to increase the lift on the left wing and start the bank, it also increases the induced drag that pulls the nose to the *left*. As soon as the wing rises, the lift tilts, and its horizontal component pulls the nose around to the right as it should.

The movement of the nose in the wrong direction at the beginning of a turn is called adverse yaw. It is minimized by the use of differential aileron travel. The aileron moving upward travels a greater distance than the aileron moving downward. The extra upward travel creates just about enough parasite drag to counteract the induced drag caused by the lowered aileron. Another way to minimize adverse yaw is to use Frise ailerons, as shown in Figure 1-36. The hinge of the aileron is set back from the leading edge so that when the aileron is deflected upward, its nose extends below the bottom wing surface and produces parasite drag.

At the beginning of a turn, the rudder is used to rotate the airplane about its yaw axis to start the nose moving in the correct direction. As soon as the bank is established, the adverse yaw force disappears and the rudder is neutralized.

Many large jet transport airplanes have two ailerons on each wing and flight spoilers to assist in roll control. The outboard ailerons are locked in their faired, or streamline, position when the trailing edge flaps are up. The inboard ailerons and the flight spoilers provide enough roll control for high-speed flight, but when the flaps are lowered, the inboard and outboard ailerons work together to provide the additional roll control needed for low-speed flight.

Flight spoilers are hinged surfaces located ahead of the flaps. They are used in conjunction with the ailerons to assist in roll control. When the ailerons are deflected, the flight spoilers on the wing with the up-aileron automatically extend to decrease the lift on the wing that is moving down and to produce additional parasite drag to overcome any adverse yaw. When a large amount of aileron is used, the spoilers account for about 70% of the roll rate.

Directional Stability

Stability about the vertical axis is called directional stability, and it causes the nose of the airplane to turn into the relative wind when it has been disturbed from this condition. Directional stability is achieved primarily by the weathervane tendency of the vertical fin. Figure 1-37 shows that when the airplane is flying straight into the relative wind, the air flows evenly around the fin, and there is no sideways force on the tail. But if a wind gust strikes the airplane and forces the nose to the right, the air striking the vertical fin gives it an angle of attack that increases the lift on the right side and pulls the tail around until the airplane is headed back into the relative wind.

An airplane's propeller forces the air to rotate around the fuselage in a corkscrew-like manner. This causes the air to strike the vertical fin in such a way that produces an angle of attack resulting in a sideways force to the right. To prevent this yawing force, most single-engine propeller-driven airplanes have the leading edge of the vertical fin offset a few degrees to the left. This places the fin directly into the relative wind when the airplane is flying at its normal cruising airspeed with the engine turning at a specific RPM.

The Effect of Sweepback

One of the problems with high-speed aerodynamics is the compressibility factor, which causes shock waves to form on the wing. With the leading edge of the wing swept back, compressibility can be delayed to a higher airspeed. But sweepback also has an effect on directional stability.

When an airplane with a swept-back wing is struck by an air gust that causes the nose to yaw to the left, as is shown in Figure 1-38, the right wing moves forward into the wind and the left wing moves back. More air is now flowing straight back across the right wing, producing more induced drag than the left wing, so the nose is pulled back to the right.

When airplane is flying straight into relative wind, air strikes both sides of vertical fin evenly and there is no force to the side.

When a wind gust forces the nose to rotate to the right, air strikes vertical fin in such a direction, it creates an aerodynamic force that pulls the tail to the right and corrects the yaw.

Figure 1-37. *Directional stability*

spoilers. Flaps that may be extended from the upper surface of a wing to destroy lift. Spoilers are used on some airplanes to assist the ailerons in providing roll control and to produce drag that allows the airplane to descend at a steep angle without gaining excessive airspeed.

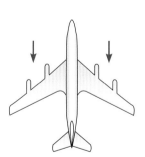

When an airplane with swept-back wings is flying straight into the wind, the lift and drag on both sides are equal.

When an airplane yaws to the left, the right wing produces more induced drag than the left, and the airplane tends to straighten into the relative wind.

Figure 1-38. *Effect of sweepback on directional stability*

Dutch Roll

Sweptwing airplanes sometimes encounter a condition in which the airplane oscillates about both its longitudinal and vertical axes at the same time. This is known as Dutch roll. When the airplane is disturbed in flight in such a way that a wing drops, both the dihedral and the sweepback work together to restore the airplane to straight and level flight. But if the dihedral effect is strong with respect to the static directional stability, an oscillation is set up that is uncomfortable to the occupants. Airplanes that have this problem are usually equipped with a yaw damper, a special automatic flight control device that senses the Dutch roll and applies corrective rudder action to prevent or at least greatly attenuate it.

Directional Control (Rotation About the Vertical Axis)

The rudder is used on an airplane only to rotate it about its vertical axis. An airplane is turned by tilting the lift vector with the ailerons and not by using the rudder. The rudder is used only at the beginning of the turn to overcome the adverse yaw and start the nose moving in the correct direction and for such flight conditions as crosswind takeoffs and landings.

Some airplanes have eliminated the movable rudder entirely, and others have connected it to the aileron controls through springs so that when a turn is started, the rudder automatically moves in the correct direction.

STUDY QUESTIONS: BASIC FIXED-WING AERODYNAMICS

*Answers are on Page 58. **Page numbers refer to chapter text.***

1. Lift produced by a body displacing a greater weight of air than its own weight is called
_____ lift. *Page 5*

2. Lift produced by the reaction caused when a mass of air is deflected downward is called
_____ lift. *Page 5*

3. The lowest layer of our atmosphere is called the _____ . *Page 7*

4. The layer of our atmosphere that is typified by the temperature of the air remaining constant as the pressure continues to drop is called the _____ . *Page 7*

5. The type of altitude measurement used to determine the amount of lift produced by an airfoil or the performance of an aircraft engine is _____ altitude. *Page 8*

6. The principle of physics that states that if the total energy in the air moving over an airfoil remains constant, any increase in its velocity will result in a corresponding decrease in its pressure, is called _____ principle. *Page 8*

7. The three axes about which an aircraft can rotate are:
   a. _____
   b. _____
   c. _____
      Page 9

8. The four basic forces that act on an aircraft in flight are:
   a. _____
   b. _____
   c. _____
   d. _____
      Page 9

9. If the propeller shaft is above the center of gravity of an airplane, addition of power will cause the nose to pitch _____ (upward or downward). *Page 9*

10. The total lift required by an airplane in a turn must be increased to compensate for the added _____ force caused by the turn. *Page 10*

11. There are two downward forces that act on an airplane in level flight. These are caused by the weight and by the _____ . *Page 10*

12. The center of pressure remains in essentially the same location as the angle of attack changes on a/an _____ (asymmetrical or symmetrical) airfoil. *Page 12*

13. Five factors that affect aerodynamic lift are:
   a. _____
   b. _____
   c. _____
   d. _____
   e. _____
      Page 11

14. The angle of attack at which the air no longer flows smoothly over the top of the wing and the wing stalls, is called the _____ angle of attack. *Page 14*

Continued

15. The point on the chord line of an airfoil at which all of the aerodynamic forces may be considered to be concentrated is called the _____ . *Page 12*

16. Find the number of pounds of lift produced by a wing with the airfoil shown in Figure 1-16, and an area of 200 square feet, when the angle of attack is 6° and the true airspeed is 150 knots while flying at 10,000 feet. Lift is _____ pounds. *Page 16*

17. If the airspeed is doubled, with no other variable condition changing, the lift produced by an airfoil will increase _____ times. *Page 13*

18. The direction of lift produced by an airfoil is _____ (parallel or perpendicular) to the direction of the relative wind. *Page 12*

19. Interference drag, profile drag, and form drag are all types of _____ (induced or parasite) drag. *Page 17*

20. Induced drag increases as the airspeed _____ (increases or decreases). *Page 16*

21. Parasite drag increases as the airspeed _____ (increases or decreases). *Page 17*

22. Three types of parasite drag are:
    a. _____ drag
    b. _____ drag
    c. _____ drag
       Page 17

23. The angle of attack at which the induced and parasite drags are the same produces the _____ (maximum or minimum) L/D ratio. *Page 18*

24. The total drag produced by an airplane in flight is _____ (least or greatest) at the point at which the induced and parasite drag are the same. *Page 18*

25. An airplane stalls only when it reaches a critically _____ (low flying speed or high angle of attack). *Page 17*

26. An airplane operating in ground effect has a/an _____ (increased or decreased) induced drag. *Page 19*

27. Wing flaps allow an airplane to fly at a high angle of attack without stalling. Flaps normally _____ (increase or decrease) the camber of the wing. *Page 19*

28. The random-flowing layer of air immediately adjacent to the surface of a wing is called the _____ layer. *Page 19*

29. Vortex generators mounted on the wings of an airplane improve flight characteristics at _____ (high or low) airspeed. *Page 22*

30. Vortex generators mounted on the empennage of an airplane improve flight characteristics at _____ (high or low) speed. *Page 22*

31. The two most important characteristics of a wing planform are its _____ and its _____ . *Page 22*

32. An airplane wing that operates most efficiently at a high angle of attack has a _____ (high or low) aspect ratio. *Page 22*

33. The stall begins on a rectangular wing at the _____ (root or tip). *Page 23*

34. Longitudinal stability is stability about an airplane's _____ axis. *Page 27*

35. Lateral stability is stability about an airplane's _____ axis. *Page 29*

36. Directional stability is stability about an airplane's _____ axis. *Page 31*

37. An airplane is rotated about its lateral axis by the use of its _____ . *Page 27*

38. The aerodynamic load on the tail of a longitudinally stable airplane acts _____ (upward or downward). *Page 27*

39. Dihedral is used to give an airplane _____ (lateral, longitudinal, or directional) stability. *Page 29*

40. Directional stability is achieved on an airplane by the use of the _____ . *Page 31*

41. An airplane has positive longitudinal static stability when its center of gravity is _____ (ahead of or behind) the center of lift. *Page 27*

Continued

42. An airplane is rotated about its longitudinal axis by the use of its _____ . *Page 30*

43. The aileron moving upward to begin a turn travels a _____ (greater or lesser) distance than the aileron moving downward. *Page 30*

44. The tendency of the nose of an airplane to start to travel in the direction opposite to that desired at the beginning of a turn is called _____ yaw. *Page 30*

45. A large airplane with two ailerons on each wing uses both ailerons in _____ (low- or high-) speed flight. *Page 30*

46. When an airplane uses spoilers to aid the ailerons in roll control, the spoiler will extend on the wing with the _____ (up or down) aileron. *Page 30*

47. An airplane is rotated about its vertical axis by the use of its _____ . *Page 30*

48. The leading edge of the vertical fin on most single-engine, propeller-driven airplanes is offset to the _____ (right or left). *Page 31*

49. A simultaneous oscillation about an airplane's longitudinal and vertical axes is called Dutch roll. It is minimized on many airplanes by the use of a _____ . *Page 32*

50. A horizontal tail surface that combines the functions of a stabilizer and an elevator is called a/an _____ . *Page 28*

51. A movable tail surface that combines the functions of a rudder and an elevator is called a/an _____ . *Page 29*

52. On a large aircraft that has two sets of ailerons on each wing, only the _____ . (inboard or outboard) ailerons are used when the trailing edge flaps are up. *Page 30*

53. The rudder on an airplane _____ (is or is not) used to cause the airplane to turn. *Page 30*

Basic High-Speed Aerodynamics

Compressibility

During the latter part of World War II, airplane design had advanced to the extent that a new problem arose. High-performance airplanes such as the Lockheed Lightning could attain such high speeds in a dive that, as they approached the speed of sound, the controls lost their effectiveness and in some instances developed flutter and vibration that caused the airplane to come apart in the air. There was thought to be an insurmountable sound barrier that prevented airplanes from flying faster than the speed of sound. But on October 14, 1947, Chuck Yeager, flying the Bell X-1, flew faster than sound and proved to the world that there was no such a thing as a true sound barrier.

At this speed, the air flowing over the airplane's surfaces no longer acts as an incompressible fluid, but it actually compresses and follows the laws of compressible flow.

Compressible and Incompressible Flow

When air flows at a subsonic speed, it acts as an incompressible fluid. Figure 1-39 shows the way air flowing at a subsonic velocity acts as it flows through a converging duct. The mass of air flowing through this duct remains constant at all locations. For the same mass of air to pass through the restriction in the tube, it must speed up, and as its velocity increases, its pressure decreases. As the air leaves the restriction and enters the diverging portion of the duct, it slows down to its original velocity, and its pressure rises to its original value. The density of this subsonic flow of air does not change.

converging duct. A duct, or passage, whose cross-sectional area decreases in the direction of fluid flow.

diverging duct. A duct, or passage, whose cross-sectional area increases in the direction of fluid flow.

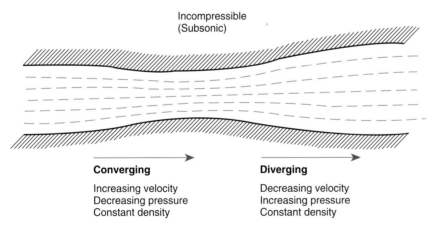

Incompressible
(Subsonic)

Converging
Increasing velocity
Decreasing pressure
Constant density

Diverging
Decreasing velocity
Increasing pressure
Constant density

Figure 1-39. *As air flows through a converging duct at speeds below the speed of sound, its velocity increases and its pressure decreases. As it leaves the restriction and enters the diverging portion of the duct, its velocity decreases and its pressure increases.*

When the air flows through this same converging duct at a supersonic velocity, shown in Figure 1-40, it behaves differently. It compresses and its density increases. Its velocity decreases and its pressure increases. As it flows into the diverging portion of the duct, it expands and its density decreases. Its velocity increases and its pressure decreases.

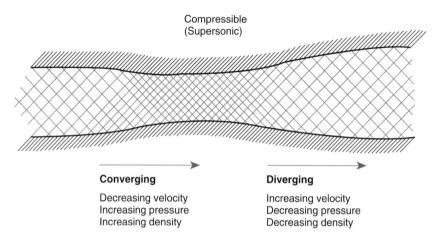

Compressible
(Supersonic)

Converging

Decreasing velocity
Increasing pressure
Increasing density

Diverging

Increasing velocity
Decreasing pressure
Decreasing density

Figure 1-40. *The flow of supersonic air through a convergent-divergent duct*

Altitude feet	Temperature		Speed of sound knots
	°F	°C	
Sea level	59.0	15.0	661.7
5,000	41.2	5.1	650.3
10,000	23.3	-4.8	638.6
15,000	5.5	-14.7	626.7
20,000	-12.3	-24.6	614.6
25,000	-30.2	-34.3	602.2
30,000	-48.0	-44.4	589.6
35,000	-65.8	-54.3	576.6
40,000	-69.7	-56.5	573.8
50,000	-69.7	-56.5	573.8
60,000	-69.7	-56.5	573.8

Figure 1-41. *The speed of sound in the air varies with the air temperature.*

Mach number. A measurement of speed based on the ratio of the speed of the aircraft to the speed of sound under the same atmospheric conditions. An airplane flying at Mach 1 is flying at the speed of sound.

The Speed of Sound

The speed of sound is the speed at which small pressure disturbances are able to move through the air. It is determined entirely by the temperature of the air, as indicated in the chart in Figure 1-41.

High-speed flight is measured in terms of Mach number, which is the ratio of the speed of the aircraft to the speed of sound. An airplane flying at a speed of Mach 1 at sea level is flying at the speed of sound, which, according to Figure 1-41, is 661.7 knots. When it is flying at a speed of Mach .75, it is flying at 75% of the speed of sound at the existing air temperature. Airplanes that fly at these speeds have Machmeters in the cockpit that automatically compensate airspeed for the air temperature and show the pilot the Mach number at which the airplane is flying.

Flight Speed Ranges

High-speed flight can be divided into four speed ranges:

Subsonic—Below Mach 0.75
   All airflow is below the speed of sound.
Transonic—Mach 0.75 to Mach 1.20
   Most of the airflow is subsonic, but in some areas, it is supersonic.
Supersonic—Mach 1.20 to Mach 5.00
   All of the airflow is faster than the speed of sound.
Hypersonic—Greater than Mach 5.00

Subsonic Flight

In low-speed flight, air is considered to be incompressible, and acts in much the same way as a liquid. It can undergo changes in pressure without any appreciable change in its density. But in high-speed flight the air acts as a compressible fluid, and its density changes with changes in its pressure and velocity.

An airplane passing through the air creates pressure disturbances that surround it. When the airplane is flying at a speed below the speed of sound, these disturbances move out in all directions and the air immediately ahead of the airplane is affected and its direction changes before the air reaches the surface. This subsonic airflow pattern is shown in Figure 1-42.

At speeds greater than the speed of sound, the disturbances do not spread out ahead of the airplane, and there is no change in flow direction ahead of the leading edge.

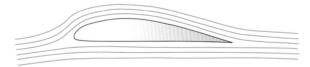

Air flowing around an airfoil at subsonic speeds deflects before it reaches the surface.

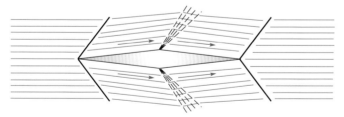

Air flowing around an airfoil at supersonic speeds is not deflected ahead of the leading edge.

Figure 1-42. *Air deflection around airfoil in flight*

subsonic flight. Flight at an airspeed in which all air flowing over the aircraft is moving at a speed below the speed of sound.

transonic flight. Flight at an airspeed in which some air flowing over the aircraft is moving at a speed below the speed of sound, and other air is moving at a speed greater than the speed of sound.

supersonic flight. Flight at an airspeed in which all air flowing over the aircraft is moving at a speed greater than the speed of sound.

hypersonic speed. Speed of greater than Mach 5 (5 times the speed of sound).

normal shock wave. A shock wave that forms ahead of a blunt object moving through the air at the speed of sound. The shock wave is perpendicular to the air approaching the object. Air passing through a normal shock wave is slowed to a subsonic speed and its static pressure is increased.

angle of incidence. The acute angle formed between the chord line of an airfoil and the longitudinal axis of the aircraft on which it is mounted.

wash in. A condition in the rigging of an airplane in which a wing is twisted so that its angle of incidence is greater at the tip than at the root.

wash out. A condition in the rigging of an airplane in which a wing is twisted so that its angle of incidence is smaller at the tip than at the root.

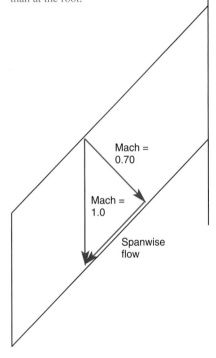

Figure 1-44. *By sweeping the wing back, the flight airspeed can be increased appreciably before the component of the air flowing directly across the wing reaches the speed of sound.*

Transonic Flight

When an airplane is flying below the speed of sound in the transonic range, some of the air flowing over the airfoil has accelerated until it is supersonic and a normal shock wave forms. Air passing through this normal shock wave slows to a subsonic speed without changing its direction. The shock wave can cause the air that passes through it to be turbulent, and to separate from the wing surface. Shock-induced separation can create serious drag and control problems.

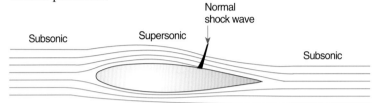

Figure 1-43. *When an airplane is flying in the transonic speed range, some air over the surface of the wing is speeded up until it becomes supersonic. A normal shock wave forms that slows the air behind it to a subsonic speed.*

Effect of Sweepback

One of the most common ways to prevent drag rise and control problems with an airplane flying in the transonic range is to sweep the wings back. Only the component of the air that flows across the wing surface perpendicular to the leading edge is involved in the production of lift. By sweeping the wing back at an angle, for example, 45°, when the airplane is flying at the speed of sound (Mach 1.0), the air flowing directly across the wing perpendicular to the leading edge is moving only at a speed of Mach 0.7. *See* Figure 1-44.

Notice in Figure 1-44 that there is a component of the air that flows in a spanwise direction. This airflow does not produce lift but it does cause problems. To minimize this spanwise flow, wing fences may be installed on the upper surface of the wing parallel to the line of flight. *See* Figure 1-21 on Page 20.

Forward-Swept Wing

The advantage gained by sweepback could also be attained by sweeping the wing forward. This has the additional advantage that the forward-swept wing stalls at the root first, eliminating the loss of lateral control experienced by a swept-back wing as it approaches a stall.

But forward-swept wings lack torsional rigidity. In other words, the wing tends to twist when high flight loads are applied. When a swept-back wing twists in flight, the wing tips wash out. Their angle of incidence, and thus the lift they produce, decreases. This decreases the load imposed on the wing. But when a forward-swept wing twists in flight, its tips wash in. Their angle of incidence increases and the loads imposed on the wing can increase until they destroy it.

The Grumman Corporation's research airplane, the X-29, uses high-tech composite construction to make the forward-swept wing lightweight and so rigid that it does not twist in flight.

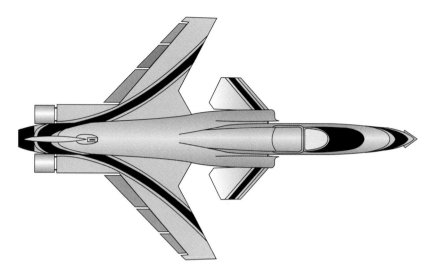

Figure 1-45. *The Grumman X-29 Advanced Technology Demonstrator exploits the advantages of the forward-swept wing because of the extensive use of composites in its aeroelastic tailoring of the wing to counteract undesirable bending stresses.*

aeroelastic tailoring. The design of an aerodynamic surface whose strength and stiffness are matched to the aerodynamic load imposed upon it.

Supersonic Airflow

When air flows over a surface at a supersonic speed, pressure waves form. There are three types of pressure waves, normal and oblique shock waves, and expansion waves.

Normal Shock Waves

Air flowing over an airfoil acts in the same way it does as it flows through a converging and diverging duct. Figure 1-46 shows that air approaching a relatively blunt-nose subsonic airfoil at a supersonic speed forms a normal shock wave, which wastes energy. When the supersonic airstream passes through a normal shock wave:

• The airstream slows to subsonic.

• The airflow direction immediately behind the wave is unchanged.

• The static pressure of the airstream behind the wave increases greatly.

• The density of the airstream behind the wave increases greatly.

• The energy of the airstream is greatly reduced.

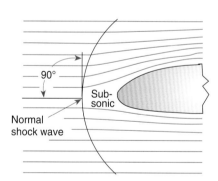

Figure 1-46. *When a supersonic airstream encounters a blunt object, a normal shock wave forms. The air immediately behind the wave is slowed to a subsonic speed.*

Oblique Shock Waves

When a supersonic airstream strikes a sharp-edged airfoil, the air is forced to turn, forming an oblique shock wave. *See* Figure 1-47. As the air passes through an oblique shock wave:

• The airstream is slowed down, but it is still supersonic.

• The flow direction changes to follows the surface.

• The static pressure of the airstream behind the shock wave increases.

• The density of the airstream behind the shock wave increases.

• Some of the energy in the airstream is converted into heat and is wasted.

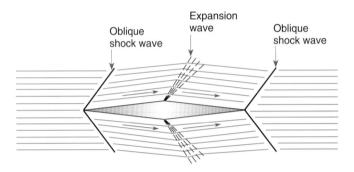

Figure 1-47. *When a sharp-edged, double-wedge airfoil moves through the air at a supersonic speed, the air is forced to turn, and oblique shockwaves form at the leading and trailing edges. At the center of the airfoil, the surface drops away from the airstream and an expansion wave forms.*

Expansion Waves

When air flows at a supersonic speed over a double-wedge airfoil like that in Figure 1-47, the air will turn to follow the surface and an expansion wave forms.

When supersonic air flows through an expansion wave:

• The airstream accelerates and the air behind the expansion wave has a higher supersonic velocity.

• The direction of flow changes to follow the surface.

• The static pressure of the airstream behind the wave decreases.

• The density of the air behind the wave decreases.

• There is no loss of energy in the airstream.

*Answers are on Page 58. **Page numbers refer to chapter text.***

54. The speed of sound in the air is affected only by the _____ of the air. *Page 38*

55. The ratio of the speed of an airplane to the speed of sound is called _____ .
    Page 38

56. When subsonic air flows into a converging duct, its velocity
    _____ (increases, decreases, or remains the same), its pressure
    _____ (increases, decreases, or remains the same), and its density
    _____ (increases, decreases, or remains the same).
    Page 37

57. When subsonic air flows into a diverging duct, its velocity
    _____ (increases, decreases, or remains the same), its pressure
    _____ (increases, decreases, or remains the same), and its density
    _____ (increases, decreases, or remains the same).
    Page 37

58. When supersonic air flows into a converging duct, its velocity
    _____ (increases, decreases, or remains the same), its pressure
    _____ (increases, decreases, or remains the same), and its density
    _____ (increases, decreases, or remains the same).
    Page 38

59. When supersonic air flows into a diverging duct, its velocity
    _____ (increases, decreases, or remains the same), its pressure
    _____ (increases, decreases, or remains the same), and its density
    _____ (increases, decreases, or remains the same).
    Page 38

60. The velocity of air that has passed through a normal shock wave is _____
    (subsonic or supersonic). *Page 41*

61. When air passes through a shock wave, its velocity is _____ (increased or decreased).
    Page 41

Continued

62. When air passes through an expansion wave, its velocity is _____ (increased or decreased). *Page 42*

63. Only the component of the air flowing across the wing _____ (parallel or perpendicular) to the leading edge is involved in the production of lift. *Page 40*

64. When a forward-swept wing flexes under flight loads, the lift produced at the wing tips _____ (increases or decreases). *Page 40*

Basic Rotor-Wing Aerodynamics

The concept of rotor-wing flight was proposed as early as 1500 by Leonardo da Vinci, who made drawings and models of a "helix." The late 1800s saw several small models of helicopters that did fly, and in 1907 the French engineer Louis Breguet built a man-carrying helicopter that actually rose from the ground, but was highly unstable and had no means of control. In 1921, the U.S. Army contracted with Dr. George de Bothezat to build a helicopter, and by the end of 1922, the large four-rotor machine did actually fly.

Throughout the 1920s and well into the 1930s, hundreds of experimental helicopters were built in America and abroad with varying degrees of success. In September of 1939 Igor Sikorsky flew his VS-300, with which he solved many of the control problems that had plagued other experimenters. The VS-300 made its first flights with a main rotor and three auxiliary control rotors, but this configuration soon gave way to one main rotor and a single tail rotor, which is standard today.

Development of the helicopter was assisted greatly by the autogiro. Stall and spin accidents in fixed-wing aircraft prompted much study and experimentation aimed at finding a "safe" flying machine, and in 1920, a Spanish engineer, Juan de la Cierva, began experimenting with a rotorcraft that had unpowered rotors. An aerodynamic force produced by air flowing upward through the rotor turns it, and as it turns, it produces lift that holds the machine in the air. Cierva's first autogiro was built from an airplane fuselage with its engine and propeller. For lift, it had a freewheeling four-blade rotor mounted on a pylon above the fuselage. The propeller provided thrust to pull the machine across the ground until there was enough air flowing upward through the rotor to start it spinning. When it spun, it produced enough aerodynamic lift to raise the autogiro into the air.

The primitive autogiro had a serious fault. It would roll over in flight. In 1922 Cierva discovered that by hinging the rotor blades and allowing them to flap up and down as they rotated he could eliminate this rolling-over tendency.

autogiro. A heavier-than-air rotor-wing aircraft sustained in the air by rotors turned by aerodynamic forces rather than by engine power. When the name Autogiro is spelled with a capital A, it refers to a specific series of machines built by Juan de la Cierva or his successors.

The autogiro met with limited success, but the knowledge gained from it, especially the knowledge of flapping rotor blades, was applied to helicopter development. Many of the patents held by the Autogiro Company of America were used in early helicopters.

Aerodynamic Principles

Rotor-wing aerodynamics are more complex than fixed-wing aerodynamics for such reasons as the speed variation along the length of the rotating rotor blade, the dissymmetry of lift caused by forward flight, and the problem caused by the helicopter flying in its own downwash.

Lift, or Rotor Thrust

The lift, or thrust, produced by a helicopter rotor is similar to the lift produced by the fixed wing of an airplane. It is affected by these factors:

solidity. The solidity of a helicopter rotor system is the ratio of the total blade area to the disc area.

- The density of the air

- The square of the rotor tip speed

- The blade-lift coefficient, which is a function of the shape of the airfoil section, the blade area, and the angle of attack

- The rotor solidity

The airfoil sections used on helicopter rotors are usually symmetrical, like the one in Figure 1-48. The location of the center of pressure of a symmetrical airfoil remains relatively constant as the angle of attack changes. This is important because as the blade rotates its angle of attack constantly changes, and if the center of pressure moved, it would cause undesirable stresses and vibration.

Figure 1-48. *Helicopter rotors typically use symmetrical airfoils because the center of pressure remains at a relatively constant location as the angle of attack changes.*

The area used for computing the lift of a helicopter rotor system is more complex than that for a fixed-wing aircraft. The spinning rotor creates a lift-producing disc, and there are three values that are used in computing the total amount of lift: the blade area, the disc area, and the solidity ratio.

- The blade area is the area in square feet of the actual rotor blade itself.

- The disc area is the area swept by the blade as it rotates.

    Disc area = 0.7854 · Blade span^2

disc area. The total area swept by the blades of a helicopter main rotor.

- The solidity ratio is the portion of the circular disc that is occupied by the blades, and is the ratio of the total blade area to the total disc area.

    Solidity ratio = Blade area ÷ Disc area

The solidity ratio for a typical rotor is between 4% and 7%.

The speed of a rotor blade through the air varies from its root to its tip, and it also varies with the speed of the helicopter through the air. When the helicopter is hovering in still air, the speed of the rotor blade through the air is the same on both sides of the disc.

Hovering blade tip speed = Tip speed

But when the helicopter is moving through the air, the blade that is moving in the same direction as the helicopter (the advancing blade) has a speed equal to its tip speed plus the speed of the helicopter.

Advancing blade tip speed = Tip speed + Helicopter speed

The blade moving in the direction opposite to that of the helicopter (the retreating blade) has an airspeed equal to its tip speed minus the helicopter speed.

Retreating blade tip speed = Tip speed – Helicopter speed

See Figure 1-49.

Dissymmetry of Lift

The tendency of the first autogiros to roll over when they were pulled through the air by their propellers was caused by dissymmetry of lift, which in turn was caused by the difference in airspeed between the advancing and retreating blades. Lift increases as the airspeed of the rotor increases, and the greater speed of the advancing blade gives the advancing half of the disc more lift than the retreating half. The most effective way of overcoming dissymmetry of lift is to mount the rotor blades on a hinge so they are free to flap up and down.

The advancing blade with its greater airspeed has more lift, so it flaps upward, and as it does, its angle of attack decreases and its lift decreases. The retreating blade with its lower airspeed has less lift, so it flaps downward. This increases its angle of attack and thus its lift. Rotor-flapping thus prevents dissymmetry of lift.

Torque

Newton's third law of motion states that for every action there is an equal and opposite reaction. The engine mounted in the fuselage of a helicopter drives the rotor, and the torque, or twisting movement, the engine imparts to the rotor has an equal but opposite reactive force that tries to rotate the fuselage. There are a number of ways the torque acting on the fuselage can be compensated. The engine can drive two rotors, one above the other, on concentric shafts with the rotors turning in opposite directions. The torque caused by the upper rotor is balanced by the opposite torque caused by the lower rotor. Other helicopters have two rotors mounted at an angle above the cabin and intermeshing with each other so that the torque from one rotor counteracts the torque of the other. Still other helicopters have two rotors, with one mounted on the forward end of the fuselage and the other at the aft end. By far the most popular configuration of helicopters uses a single main rotor,

advancing blade. The blade on a helicopter rotor whose tip is moving in the same direction the helicopter is moving.

retreating blade. The blade on a helicopter rotor whose tip is moving in the direction opposite to that in which the helicopter is moving.

torque. A force that produces or tries to produce rotation.

and its torque is counteracted by a small vertically-mounted rotor on the tail end of the fuselage. By changing the pitch of the tail-rotor blades with the foot pedals, the pilot can vary the amount of tail-rotor thrust to control the yaw of the fuselage about its vertical axis.

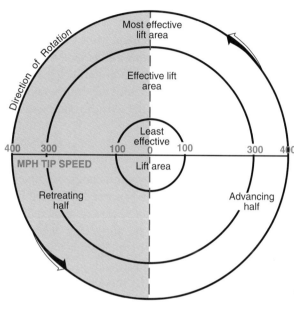

Hovering. When a helicopter is hovering, the rotor airspeed is the same on both sides of the disc.

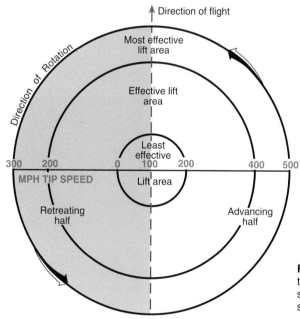

Forward Flight – 100 MPH. In forward flight the airspeed of the advancing blade is its rotational speed plus the helicopter speed, while the airspeed of the retreating blade is its rotational speed minus the helicopter speed.

Figure 1-49. *Production of dissymmetry of lift*

Autorotation

If the rotor of a helicopter is disengaged from the engine in flight, it will continue to turn and produce lift in the same way as the rotor of an autogiro. The aerodynamic force that causes this rotation is called the autorotative force, and it operates as shown in Figure 1-50.

Lift always acts perpendicular to the relative wind, and drag acts parallel to it. When air is flowing upward through the rotor of a helicopter or an autogiro, the lift vector is tilted forward, and the resultant lift is tilted ahead of the axis of rotation. The resultant lift has a horizontal component that acts forward in the plane of rotor rotation and produces an autorotative force that causes the rotor to spin. The rotor increases in speed until the drag becomes great enough to bring the resultant lift in line with the axis of rotation, and the rotor stabilizes at this speed.

Retreating Blade Stall

A rotor blade, like the wing of an airplane, stalls when its angle of attack becomes excessive. Low-speed flight of an airplane is normally limited by the stall, but the retreating blade stall of a helicopter occurs at high speed. When the helicopter is in high-speed forward flight, the advancing blade has a high airspeed and a low angle of attack, but the retreating blade has a low airspeed and a high angle of attack. When the forward speed is great enough, the angle of attack is so high that the rotor tip stalls. Increasing either the blade pitch or helicopter forward-speed causes the stall to progress inward toward the hub, and when approximately 15% of the rotor disc is stalled, the helicopter can no longer be controlled.

autorotation. Descent of a helicopter without the use of engine power. An aerodynamic force causes the rotors to rotate.

retreating blade stall. The stall of a helicopter rotor disc that occurs near the tip of the retreating blade. A retreating blade stall occurs when the flight airspeed is high and the retreating blade airspeed is low. This results in a high angle of attack, causing the stall.

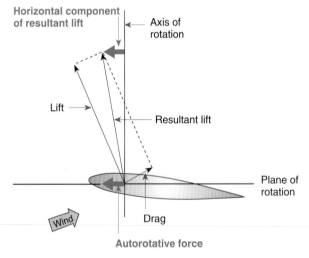

Figure 1-50. *When air flows upward through a rotor, the resultant lift has a component that acts forward in the plane of rotation and causes the rotor to spin.*

A retreating blade stall causes rotor roughness, erratic stick forces, and a stick shake whose frequency is determined by the number of rotor blades. *See* Figure 1-51.

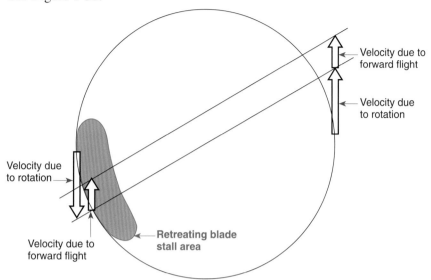

Velocity due to
forward flight

Velocity due
to rotation

Velocity due
to rotation

Velocity due to
forward flight

Retreating blade
stall area

Figure 1-51. *When a helicopter is flown at a high speed, the airspeed of the tip of the retreating blade is low and its angle of attack is high. The tip of the retreating blade stalls, as is indicated by the shaded area.*

Ground Effect

It requires less power for an airplane to fly very near the surface than it does higher up, and because of the same aerodynamic principles, a helicopter can hover near the ground with less power than it can a few feet higher. This increased efficiency near the ground is caused by the phenomenon called ground effect.

When a helicopter is hovering at a height well above the ground, the downwash is not affected by the presence of the ground, and there is a vertical velocity of the air moving through the rotor disc. This vertical component, V_V, and the rotational velocity of the rotor, V_R, produce an angle of attack like that in Figure 1-52 (on the next page). But when the helicopter is hovering at an altitude of less than one-half the rotor diameter, the air strikes the ground and flows outward. This decreases its vertical velocity, and the angle of attack of the blades increases. Increasing the angle of attack for the same rotor speed increases the lift, and because the lift always acts perpendicular to the relative wind, the lift vector tilts toward the vertical.

Since a lower blade angle is used to produce the lift needed to hover, the induced drag is decreased and less power is required for the helicopter to hover. Helicopter specifications list the hover ceiling for a helicopter both in ground effect (IGE) and out of ground effect (OGE). The hover ceiling IGE is always higher than it is OGE.

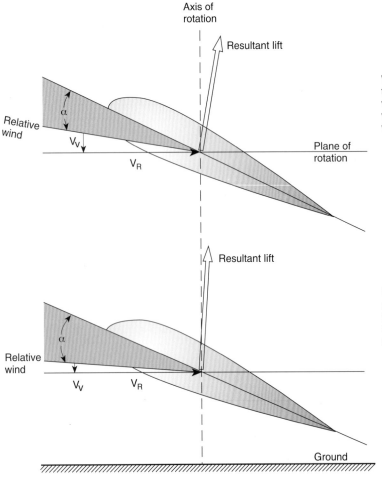

When the helicopter is hovering at an altitude of more than approximately one-half rotor diameter, the vertical velocity of the air through the rotor V_V and the rotational velocity of the rotor V_R combine to produce a relative wind that gives the angle of attack shown here.

When the helicopter hovers at an altitude of approximately one-half rotor diameter or less, the vertical velocity of the air through the rotor decreases, and since the rotational velocity remains the same, the relative wind changes and the angle of attack increases.

Figure 1-52. *Change in the angle of attack caused by ground effect*

translational lift. The additional lift produced by a helicopter rotor as the helicopter changes from hovering to forward flight.

Translational Lift

When a helicopter takes off, the pilot lifts it from the ground into a hover and then tilts the rotor disc forward with the cyclic control. The tilted lift has a horizontal component which pulls the helicopter forward. The forward motion increases the mass of air flowing through the rotor disc, and this increases the efficiency of the rotor system and the lift it produces. The increased lift caused by the beginning of forward flight is called translational lift.

Gyroscopic Precession

A gyroscope is a rapidly spinning wheel with the weight concentrated about its rim. Its spinning produces dynamic forces that are greater than the static force of gravity. One of the characteristics of a gyroscope is gyroscopic precession, which causes a force applied to the spinning wheel to be felt at a point 90° from the point of application in the direction of rotation.

The spinning rotor of a helicopter acts in the same way as a gyroscope. When the pilot wishes to tilt the rotor disc forward, the pitch of the retreating blade is increased and the pitch of the advancing blade is decreased, as shown in Figure 1-53.

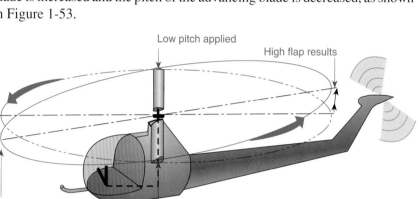

gyroscopic precession. The characteristic of a gyroscope that causes it to react to an applied force as though the force were applied at a point 90° in the direction of rotation from the actual point of application. The rotor of a helicopter and the propeller of an airplane act in the same way as a gyroscope and are affected by gyroscopic precession.

Figure 1-53. *The rotor of a helicopter acts as a gyroscope and is affected by gyroscopic precession. If the blade pitch is increased on the left side of the rotor, the disc will tilt forward.*

Transverse Flow Effect

In forward flight, air passing through the rear portion of the rotor disc has a higher downwash velocity than air passing through the forward portion. This is because the air passing through the rear portion has been accelerated for a longer period of time than the air passing through the forward portion. This increased downwash velocity at the rear of the disc decreases the angle of attack and the blade lift, so the lift on the rearward part of the disc is less than it is in the forward part. According to the principle of gyroscopic precession, maximum deflection of the rotor blades occurs 90° later in the direction of rotation than the force which caused it. The rotor blades will reach maximum downward deflection on the right (advancing) side and maximum upward deflection on the left (retreating) side. This transverse flow effect is responsible for the major portion of the lateral cyclic stick control required to trim the helicopter at low speed.

The unequal drag in the fore and aft portions of the disc also result in vibrations that are most noticeable at slow forward airspeeds.

coriolis effect. The change in rotor blade velocity to compensate for a change in the distance between the center of mass of the rotor blade and the axis of rotation of the blade as the blades flap in flight.

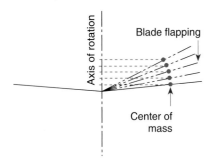

Figure 1-54. *The coriolis effect causes a rotor blade to change its velocity as its center of mass moves closer to the axis of rotation when the blade flaps in flight.*

Coriolis Effect

The effect that makes ice skaters spin faster when they pull in their legs or slower as they extend is called the Coriolis effect. This same effect causes a rotor blade to increase or decrease its velocity in its plane of rotation as it flaps in flight.

Figure 1-54 shows the way the center of mass of a blade of a three-bladed, fully articulated rotor moves closer to the axis of rotation as the blade flaps up. As the advancing blade flaps upward, its mass moves inward, and the blade accelerates—its tip moves forward. As it flaps down on the retreating side, it decelerates—its tip moves backward. Two-bladed rotors are not so affected by the Coriolis effect because they are typically under-slung, and the distance between their center of mass and the rotor shaft changes less than it does with a fully articulated rotor.

Settling With Power

If a pilot tries to hover a helicopter out of ground effect at an altitude above its hovering ceiling, the helicopter descends in the turbulent air that has just been accelerated downward.

In a normal hover, all of the airflow through the rotor is downward, as seen in Figure 1-55. When the helicopter is settling with power, some air flows upward through the rotor, and this upward flow causes two sets of vortices that destroy the lift produced by the rotor.

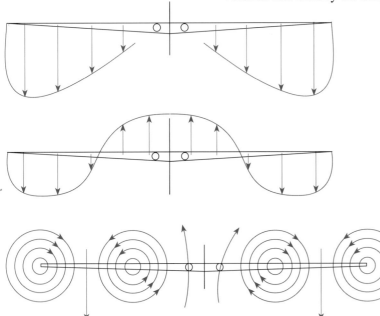

When the helicopter is hovering normally, all of the air flows downward through the rotor.

In power settling, some of the air flows upward through the center of the rotor while air is still flowing downward through the outer portion of the rotor.

The mixed airflow through the rotor causes two sets of vortices which destroy the lift.

Figure 1-55. *Airflow through a helicopter rotor during power settling*

Helicopter Flight Controls

A single-main-rotor helicopter's flight controls include the collective pitch control, the cyclic pitch control, and the antitorque pedals.

The collective pitch control changes the pitch of all rotor blades at the same time to change the total lift produced by the rotor disc. Engine power is coordinated with the collective control.

The cyclic control changes the pitch of the individual blades at a particular point in their rotation. It changes the lift around the rotor disc to tilt the disc and cause the helicopter to move forward, rearward, or to the side.

The antitorque pedals change the pitch of the tail rotor to increase or decrease its thrust to rotate the helicopter about its vertical axis.

Collective Pitch Control

The collective pitch lever is located by the left side of the pilot's seat and is operated with the left hand. This lever is moved up and down to change the pitch of all the rotor blades at the same time. Raising the collective control increases the blade pitch, the angle of attack, and the thrust, or lift, produced by the rotor disc. Increasing the angle of attack also increases the drag, and the rotor would slow down if engine power were not increased. The engine power is coordinated with the collective pitch control to increase the power when the collective pitch is increased.

Cyclic Pitch Control

The cyclic pitch control, located directly in front of the pilot and moved by the pilot's right hand, changes the pitch of the individual blades at a specific point in their rotation. This tilts the plane of the rotor disc, which gives the lift a horizontal component and pulls the helicopter in the direction the rotor is tilted. *See* Figure 1-56.

Because of gyroscopic precession, the blade pitch is actually changed 90° of blade rotation before the change is desired. For example, to tilt the rotor forward, the pitch is decreased on the advancing blade when it is at

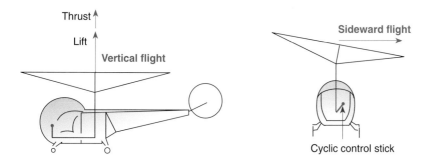
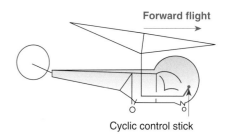

Figure 1-56. *Moving the cyclic control changes the pitch of the main rotor blades at a point in their rotation. This tilts the rotor disc and creates a horizontal component of lift that moves the helicopter in the direction the disc is tilted.*

right angles to the fuselage. On the opposite side of the helicopter, the pitch of the retreating blade is increased. These pitch changes cause the front of the rotor disc to lower and the rear of the disc to raise. *See* Figure 1-53 on Page 51.

Horizontal Stabilizer

Some helicopters have either a fixed or movable horizontal stabilizer near the tail, like the one in Figure 1-57, to hold the fuselage level in forward flight. When the cyclic pitch control is moved forward, the rotor tilts forward and the fuselage tries to follow it. Fixed horizontal stabilizers are set so that they provide the required downward force at cruise speed to keep the fuselage level and minimize the drag. Movable horizontal stabilizers are controlled by the pilot to allow the tail to rise on takeoff so the maximum amount of thrust can be used to increase the airspeed.

Antitorque Pedals

The rotor on most single-rotor helicopters rotates to the left as viewed from above. The torque reaction to this rotation causes the fuselage to rotate to the right. This torque force is compensated by thrust from the tail rotor that keeps the fuselage from rotating. The pilot controls tail rotor thrust by changing the pitch of the tail rotor blades with the antitorque pedals. *See* Figure 1-58.

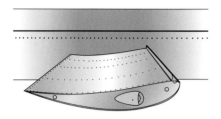

Figure 1-57. *A horizontal stabilizer on a helicopter provides a downward aerodynamic force to hold the tail down in forward flight.*

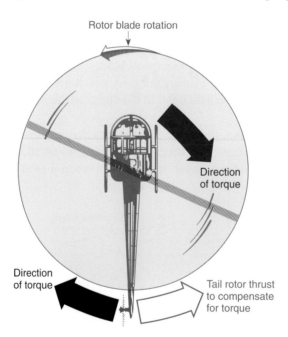

Rotor blade rotation

Direction
of torque

Direction
of torque

Tail rotor thrust
to compensate
for torque

Figure 1-58. *Torque of the engine driving the main rotor tries to rotate the fuselage to the right. This rotation is prevented by thrust from the tail rotor.*

When the pedals are in their neutral position, the tail rotor has a medium positive pitch, and the thrust from the tail rotor is approximately equal to the torque of the main rotor during cruising flight. This allows the helicopter to maintain a constant heading in level flight.

When the pilot moves the left pedal forward, the pitch of the tail rotor increases and produces additional thrust that rotates the nose to the left. When the pilot moves the right pedal forward, the pitch decreases until the tail rotor has a negative pitch. This assists the torque in rotating the nose to the right.

Sideways thrust from the tail rotor tends to pull the helicopter to the right, or causes it to drift. To counteract this tendency, the main rotor mast of some helicopters is offset to the left so that the tip-plane path has a built-in tilt that produces enough side thrust to the right to counteract the drift.

Stabilization Systems

A helicopter is statically stable, but dynamically unstable. When it is disturbed from a condition of level flight, a force is set up that tries to restore it. But this restorative force, instead of decreasing with time, increases and causes the helicopter to develop divergent oscillation.

Several types of stabilization systems have been developed to prevent this. Three commonly used systems are the stabilizer bar, the offset flapping hinge, and the electronic stability augmentation system.

Stabilizer Bar

The stabilizer bar, used for helicopters with two-blade rotors, involves two long arms with weights on their ends, mounted on a center bar so that they rotate with the rotor mast. The bar is perpendicular to the rotor blades and free to pivot with respect to the rotor mast. The weighted bar acts as a gyroscope and remains rigid in space as the helicopter pitches or rolls. *See* Figure 1-59.

The stabilizer bar continues to rotate in its original plane when the helicopter pitches or rolls. The angular difference between the stabilizer bar and the rotor mast moves the pitch change linkage in the correct direction to change the pitch of the blades and bring the helicopter back to a level flight attitude.

Offset Flapping Hinge

Moving the flapping hinge of a fully articulated rotor out away from the rotor mast, as is shown in Figure 1-60, generates stabilizing forces when the helicopter pitches or rolls. The angle of attack of the descending blade is increased and a restorative force is produced, which acts from the offset hinge and restores the helicopter to level flight. *See* Figure 1-60 on the next page.

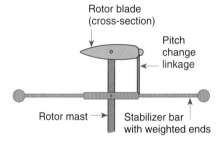

When the rotor mast is vertical, no corrective pitch change is made.

When the helicopter tilts, the stabilizer bar remains in a horizontal plane, and the blade pitch is changed to produce a force that restores the helicopter to level flight.

Figure 1-59. *Stabilization with a stabilizer bar*

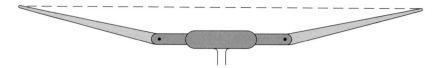

Offsetting the flapping hinge from the center of the mast increases the corrective action produced by the flapping rotor.

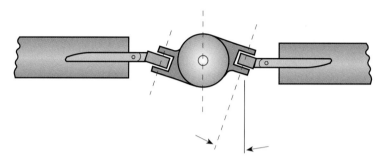

Angling the flapping hinge increases the stabilizing effect.

Figure 1-60. *Stabilization with offset and angled flapping hinges*

Electronic Stability Augmentation System

Many high-performance helicopters use an electronic stability augmentation system that senses any motion from the desired flight condition and feeds a signal back into the aircraft control system, restoring the helicopter to the desired flight attitude. A simplified block diagram of a stability augmentation system is shown in Figure 1-61.

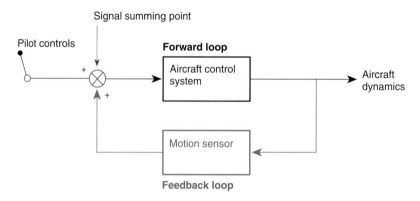

Figure 1-61. *Block diagram of a stability augmentation system*

Answers are on Page 58. Page numbers refer to chapter text.

65. The rotor blade on the side of a helicopter that is moving in the same direction the helicopter is moving is called the _____ blade. *Page 46*

66. The rotor blade on the side of a helicopter that is moving in the opposite direction to that of the helicopter called the _____ blade. *Page 46*

67. Helicopter rotor blades are mounted on flapping hinges to overcome the effect of _____ . *Page 46*

68. The retreating blade of a helicopter will stall when the helicopter airspeed is too _____ (high or low). *Page 48*

69. The stall of a helicopter rotor blade caused by the high angle of attack on the retreating blade begins at the _____ (hub or tip) of the blade. *Page 48*

70. When a helicopter is hovering in ground effect, the induced drag is _____ (greater or less) than it is when hovering outside of ground effect. *Page 50*

71. In order to tilt the rotor disc of a helicopter forward, the pitch of the _____ (advancing or retreating) blade is increased. *Page 51*

72. The coriolis effect causes the rotor blades to move _____ (back and forth or up and down). *Page 52*

73. The coriolis effect is most noticeable on _____ (two or three) -blade rotor systems. *Page 52*

74. When a helicopter hovers normally, the air flows _____ (upward or downward) through the rotor. *Page 52*

75. Drift caused by thrust of the tail rotor is compensated on some helicopters by tilting the main rotor a few degrees to the _____ (right or left). *Page 55*

76. The pitch of the rotor blades is changed at a particular point in their rotation by the _____ (collective or cyclic) pitch control. *Page 53*

Continued

77. The pitch of all the rotor blades is changed at the same time by the _____ (collective or cyclic) pitch control. *Page 53*

78. A helicopter usually has positive static stability and _____ (positive or negative) dynamic stability. *Page 55*

Answers to Chapter 1 Study Questions

1. aerostatic
2. aerodynamic
3. troposphere
4. stratosphere
5. density
6. Bernoulli's
7. a. longitudinal
   b. lateral
   c. vertical
8. a. thrust
   b. lift
   c. drag
   d. weight
9. downward
10. centrifugal
11. tail load
12. symmetrical
13. a. shape of the airfoil
    b. area of the airfoil
    c. air density
    d. speed of the air relative to the surface
    e. angle of attack
14. critical
15. center of pressure
16. 5,520
17. 4
18. perpendicular
19. parasite
20. decreases
21. increases

22. a. form
    b. profile
    c. interference
23. maximum
24. least
25. high angle of attack
26. decreased
27. increase
28. boundary
29. high
30. low
31. aspect ratio, taper
32. high
33. root
34. lateral
35. longitudinal
36. vertical
37. elevators
38. downward
39. lateral
40. vertical fin
41. ahead of
42. ailerons
43. greater
44. adverse
45. low
46. up
47. rudder
48. left
49. yaw damper
50. stabilator
51. ruddervator

52. inboard
53. is not
54. temperature
55. Mach number
56. increases, decreases, remains the same
57. decreases, increases, remains the same
58. decreases, increases, increases
59. increases, decreases, decreases
60. subsonic
61. decreased
62. increased
63. perpendicular
64. increases
65. advancing
66. retreating
67. dissymmetry of lift
68. high
69. tip
70. less
71. retreating
72. back and forth
73. three
74. downward
75. left
76. cyclic
77. collective
78. negative

2

METALLIC AIRCRAFT STRUCTURES

Continued

Continued

Aircraft Welding *138*

Continued

METALLIC AIRCRAFT STRUCTURES

2

Sheet-Metal Aircraft Construction

The first airplanes were made with a truss structure of wood or bamboo, and the lifting and control surfaces were covered with cotton or linen fabric. This structure was lightweight, but difficult to streamline. When aircraft speeds increased to the extent that streamlining became important, the structure had to be modified, and in the late 1920s the molded-plywood monocoque structure used on the record-setting Lockheed airplanes were state-of-the-art. The next logical step in the evolution of aircraft structure was to make the monocoque structure of thin sheet metal instead of plywood. This reduced the weight and allowed mass-production of aircraft.

Aluminum alloy was the logical choice of metal for this new type of construction. Pure aluminum is weak, but during World War I, the Germans discovered that by alloying aluminum with copper, manganese, and magnesium, they could increase its strength without increasing its weight. This new alloy was called Duralumin, and it was the forerunner of the high-strength and lightweight alloys that we use in aircraft construction today.

Types of Metal Structure

To take the maximum advantage of metal, most aircraft structure is of the stressed-skin type. There are two types of metal stressed skin: monocoque and semimonocoque.

Monocoque Structure

The name monocoque means single shell, and in a true monocoque structure, all the strength of the structure is carried in the outside skin. Figure 2-1 shows a simplified view of a monocoque structure. The bulkhead and formers give the structure its shape, but the thin metal skin riveted to them carries all the flight loads.

Semimonocoque Structure

Pure monocoque structure has the serious drawback that any dent or deformation will decrease its ability to carry the flight loads. To overcome this limitation, semimonocoque structure as seen in Figure 2-2 is widely used. In this type of structure, bulkheads and formers still provide the shape, and the

monocoque structure. A type of structure that carries all of the stresses in its outside skin.

Duralumin. The name for the original alloy of aluminum, magnesium, manganese, and copper. Duralumin is the same as the modern 2017 aluminum alloy.

stressed skin structure. A type of aircraft structure in which all or most of the stresses are carried in the outside skin. A stressed skin structure has a minimum of internal structure.

semimonocoque structure. A form of aircraft stressed skin structure. Most of the strength of a semimonocoque structure is in the skin, but the skin is supported on a substructure of formers and stringers that give the skin its shape and increase its rigidity.

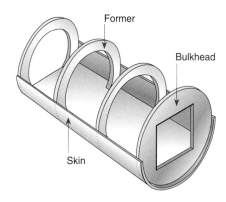

Figure 2-1. *A true monocoque structure has bulkheads and formers to give the structure its shape, but all of the flight loads are carried in the thin sheet metal skin.*

majority of the flight loads are carried in the skin, but stringers are installed across the formers to reinforce the skin and prevent its deforming under normal operational loads.

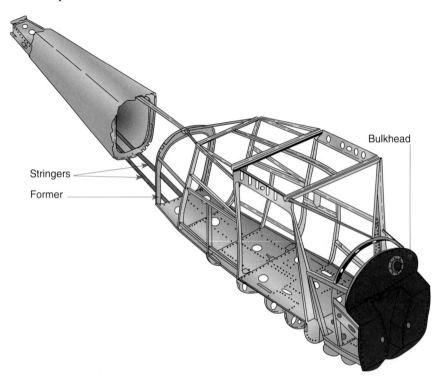

Figure 2-2. A semimonocoque structure carries the flight loads in its outer skin, but this thin skin is backed up with stringers that extend across the formers.

Reinforced Shell Structure

The reinforced shell structure such as the one in Figure 2-3 elaborates on the semimonocoque structure. This is the most commonly used structure in modern all-metal aircraft. The shape is provided by bulkheads, formers, and stringers, but this structure is reinforced with longerons that help carry the loads. A sheet-metal skin riveted over the structure carries a major portion of the flight loads.

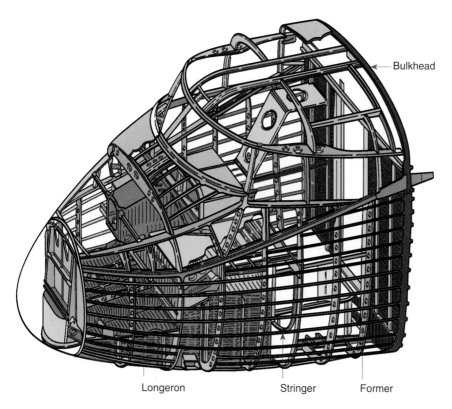

Longeron   Stringer   Former

← Bulkhead

Figure 2-3. *The reinforced shell is the most generally used type of construction for modern all-metal aircraft.*

Stresses Acting on an Aircraft Structure

Aircraft are unique in their structural requirements. They must be lightweight and at the same time withstand flight loads, landing loads, and a wide range of vibration. In this study of all-metal structure, we will consider the five basic stresses that act on all physical objects: tension, compression, torsion, bending, and shear. Tension and compression are the basic stresses and the other three are combinations of these two.

A stress is a force that is set up within an object that tries to prevent an outside force changing its shape. A strain is a deformation or a physical change caused by a stress.

A material that is strained within its elastic limit will return to its original size and shape after the stress is removed, but if it has been strained beyond this limit, it will be permanently deformed.

Tension (Tensile Stress)

Tension tries to pull an object apart. Consider the hoist in Figure 2-4. The chain is under tension, or more properly stated, it has a tensile stress in it.

stress. A force set up within an object that tries to prevent an outside force from changing its shape.

strain. A deformation or physical change in a material caused by a stress.

elastic limit. The maximum amount of tensile load, in pounds per square inch, a material is able to withstand without being permanently deformed.

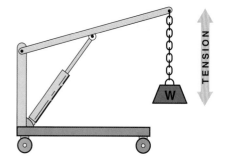

Figure 2-4. *The chain on this hoist has a tensile stress in it.*

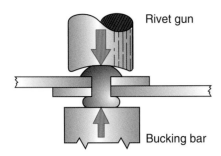

Rivet gun

Bucking bar

Figure 2-5. *The rivet shown here is strained by the compressive stress put into it when the rivet gun hammers it against the bucking bar.*

bucking bar. A heavy steel bar with smooth, hardened surfaces, or faces. The bucking bar is held against the end of the rivet shank when it is driven with a pneumatic rivet gun, and the shop head is formed against the bucking bar.

Compression (Compressive Stress)

Compression tries to squeeze the ends of an object together. The rivet in Figure 2-5 is distorted or strained by a compressive stress between the rivet gun and the bucking bar.

Torsion (Torsional Stress)

Torsion is a combination of tension and compression acting in the same object. The shaft in Figure 2-6 has a tensile stress and a compressive stress acting at 90° to each other, and they are both acting at 45° to the shaft. Propeller shafts and helicopter rotor shafts are both subjected to torsional stresses.

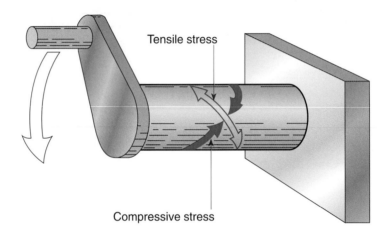

Tensile stress

Compressive stress

Figure 2-6. *This shaft is subjected to a torsional stress, which is made up of a compressive and a tensile stress.*

Bending

Bending is also made up of tension and compression. The wing of the airplane in Figure 2-7 is under a bending stress. When the airplane is on the ground, the top skin of the wing is under a tensile stress and the bottom skin is under a compressive stress. In flight these forces are the opposite. The top skin is under a compressive stress and the bottom skin is under a tensile stress.

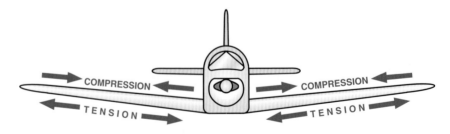

Figure 2-7. *In flight, the top of the wing of this airplane is under a compressive stress and the bottom is under a tensile stress. These two stresses make up the bending stress.*

Shear

A shear stress tries to slide an object apart. The clevis bolt in Figure 2-8 is subject to a shear stress. The force on the cable puts a tensile stress in the clevis bolt toward the right while the fixed fitting puts a tensile stress into the bolt toward the left. These two tensile stresses act beside each other rather than opposite each other, and the result is a force that tries to shear the bolt, or to slide it apart.

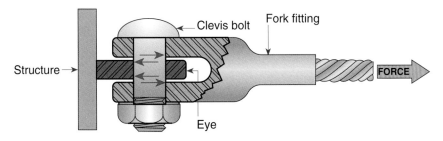

Figure 2-8. *A shear stress tries to slide the clevis bolt apart as a load is applied to the cable.*

STUDY QUESTIONS: SHEET-METAL AIRCRAFT CONSTRUCTION

Answers begin on Page 167. Page numbers refer to chapter text.

1. A stressed skin structure that is made in the form of a single shell with all of its strength in its outer skin is called a _____ structure. *Page 65*

2. A structure that has most of its strength in its outer skin, but supports this skin with stringers across the formers is called a _____ structure. *Page 65*

3. The five basic stresses to which a structure can be subjected are:
   a. _____
   b. _____
   c. _____
   d. _____
   e. _____
   Page 67

4. A force that is set up within an object that tries to prevent an outside force changing its shape is called a/an _____ . *Page 67*

5. A deformation within a material caused by a stress is called a/an _____ . *Page 67*

6. A material will return to its original size and shape after a stress is removed if it has not been stressed beyond its _____ . *Page 67*

Materials for Metal Aircraft Construction

The various metals used in aircraft construction are discussed in Chapter 7 of the *General* textbook of this *Aviation Maintenance Technician Series.*

Nonferrous Metals

Aluminum alloys are the most widely used nonferrous metal in aircraft construction. In this section, these alloys are discussed along with magnesium and its alloys, and titanium.

Aluminum Alloys

Aluminum is a lightweight metal, but it does not have sufficient strength to be used as a structural material. Pure aluminum alloyed with other metals is much stronger. Aluminum alloys are susceptible to corrosion, but their high strength and light weight make them a metal of choice.

Aluminum Alloy Designation and Characteristics

Copper was the first metal used as the primary alloying element for aluminum, and copper alloys are still the most widely used. Other elements are used, as in Figure 2-9. The alloy is identified by a four-digit number with the following significance:

> First digit—Alloy type
> Second digit—Modification of alloy
> Third and fourth digits—Purity of aluminum*

Alloy Type	Group
Aluminum 99+% pure	1xxx
Copper	2xxx
Manganese	3xxx
Silicon	4xxx
Magnesium	5xxx
Magnesium and silicon	6xxx
Zinc	7xxx

Figure 2-9. *Identification of aluminum alloys*

*The last two digits are also used for the old designation of alloys in use before the adoption of the four-digit system.

Alloy 1100 is a low-strength, commercially pure aluminum that can be used only in non-structural applications where strength is not important.

Alloy 2024 is the most popular structural aluminum alloy.

Alloy 3003 is similar to 1100 and is used for the same types of applications. It is non-heat-treatable, but can be hardened by cold-working.

Alloy 5052 is used for welded applications such as fuel tanks and rigid fluid lines.

Alloy 6061 is used in applications where heat-treatability, ease of forming, medium strength, and good corrosion resistance are needed.

Alloy 7075 is used for high-strength structural requirements.

Heat-Treatable Alloys

Aluminum alloys are divided into two basic categories, those that can be hardened by heat and those that cannot. Both can be softened by annealing. The most widely used heat-treatable alloys are 2024, 6061, and 7075 for sheet metal, and 2017, 2117, and 2024 for rivets.

Solution Heat Treatment

Heat-treatable alloys are hardened by heating them in a furnace until they have reached a specified temperature throughout and immediately quenching them in water. The metal gains hardness and strength over a period of several days through the process called aging.

During the aging process, some of the soluble constituents precipitate from the supersaturated solid solution, and the strength of the material increases. The submicroscopic particles that are precipitated act as locks between the grains that resist internal slippage and distortion when a load of any type is applied.

In the process of heat-treating, the grain size is reduced when the metal is hot, and it grows as the metal cools. For maximum strength the metal must be quenched immediately after it is taken from the oven so it will have the smallest grain size possible. If there is a delay between the time the metal is removed from the oven and the time it is quenched, the grains will grow large enough for the metal to become susceptible to intergranular corrosion that forms along the grain boundaries within the metal.

Precipitation Heat Treatment

When an aluminum alloy has been solution heat-treated, it gains its full hardness and strength by natural aging, but this strengthening process may be speeded up and increased by returning the metal to the oven and heating it to a temperature much lower than that used for solution heat treatment. It is held at this temperature for up to 24 hours and then removed from the oven and allowed to cool in still air. This precipitation hardening, or artificial aging, greatly increases the strength and hardness of the metal, but it decreases the ductility; the metal becomes more difficult to bend and form.

Figure 2-10 lists the heat treatment temperatures and times for the most popular aluminum alloys.

solution heat treatment. A type of heat treatment for nonferrous metals in which the metal is heated in a furnace until it has a uniform temperature throughout. It is then removed and quenched in cold water.

When the metal is hot, the alloying elements enter into a solid solution with the base metal to become part of its basic structure. When the metal is quenched, these elements are locked into place.

aging. A change in the characteristics of a material with time.

Certain aluminum alloys do not have their full strength when they are first removed from the quench bath after they have been heat-treated, but they gain this strength after a few days by the natural process of aging.

precipitation heat treatment. A method of increasing the strength of heat-treated aluminum alloy. After the aluminum alloy has been solution-heat-treated by heating and quenching, it is returned to the oven and heated to a temperature lower than that used for the initial heat treatment. It is held at this temperature for a specified period of time and then removed from the oven and allowed to cool slowly.

ductility. The property of a material that allows it to be drawn into a thin section without breaking.

Alloy	Solution Heat-Treatment			Precipitation Heat-Treatment		
	Temperature °F	Quench	Temper Designation	Temperature °F	Time of Aging	Temper Designation
2017	930-950	Cold water	T4			T
2117	930-950	Cold water	T4			T
2024	910-930	Water	T4			T
6061	960-980	Water	T4	315-325	18 hour	T6
				345-355	8 hour	T6
7075	870	Water		250	24 hour	T6

Figure 2-10. *Typical temperatures for heat treatment of various aluminum alloys*

Annealing

Some aluminum alloys can be hardened by heat treatment while others can be hardened only by cold-working. But both types can be annealed, or softened, by heating them in an oven to a specified temperature and then cooling them slowly in the furnace or in still air. Annealing leaves the metal soft, but in its weakest condition.

Aluminum Alloy Temper Designations

The temper of an aluminum alloy is noted by a letter that follows the alloy designation. *See* Figure 2-11.

F — The metal is left as fabricated. There has been no control over its temper.
T — The metal may be heat treated.
   T3 — solution heat treatment, followed by strain hardening. A second digit, if used, indicates the amount of strain hardening.
   T4 — solution heat treatment, followed by natural aging at room temperature.
   T6 — solution heat treatment, followed by artificial aging (precipitation heat treated).
   T7 — solution heat treatment, followed by stabilization to relieve internal stresses.
   T8 — solution heat treatment, followed by strain hardening and then artificial aging.
   T9 — solution heat treatment, followed by artificial aging and then strain hardening.
H — The metal cannot be heat treated, but can be hardened by cold working.
   H1 — strain hardened by cold working.
      H12 — strain hardened to its 1/4-hard condition.
      H14 — strain hardened to its 1/2-hard condition.
      H18 — strain hardened to its full hard condition.
      H19 — strain hardened to its extra hard condition.
   H2 — strain hardened by cold working and then partially annealed.
   H3 — strain hardened and stabilized to relieve internal stresses.
      H36 — strain hardened and stabilized to its 3/4-hard condition.
O — The metal has been annealed.

Figure 2-11. *Temper designations of aluminum alloys*

Nonheat-Treatable Alloys

Certain alloys, such as 3003 and 5052, cannot be hardened by heat treatment, but are hardened by cold-working. When these alloys are formed into sheets in the rolling mill, their strength and hardness are increased. The amount of this increase is indicated by their temper designation, as in Figure 2-11.

Nonheat-treatable alloys can be softened by annealing. When a sheet of 5052 aluminum alloy is formed by hammering or spinning, it gets hard and is likely to crack. If further working must be done, the metal may be annealed by heating it in an oven to a temperature slightly higher than is used for hardening and allowing it to cool very slowly.

Corrosion Protection of Aluminum Alloys

Pure aluminum is relatively corrosion resistant, but when it is alloyed with other elements to give it strength, it loses this resistance. The most efficient way to protect aluminum alloys from corrosion is to cover their surfaces with something that prevents air or moisture from contacting the alloy. There are three ways to do this: roll a thin coating of pure aluminum on the alloy sheet; form a hard, airtight oxide coating on the surface of the metal; or cover the surface with a film of enamel or lacquer.

Cladding

Aluminum alloy sheets to be used as the outside skin of an aircraft can be protected from corrosion and given an attractive finish by rolling a layer of pure aluminum on both of their surfaces. This resulting material is called clad aluminum and is available under such registered trade names as Alclad and Pureclad. The pure aluminum coating is about $2\frac{1}{2}$ to 5% of the thickness of the alloy sheet, and it decreases the strength of the sheet somewhat, as indicated in Figure 2-14 on Page 75.

Pure aluminum cladding does not corrode, but an airtight oxide film forms on its surface and prevents any oxygen or moisture from reaching the metal. The alloy sheet is protected as long as the cladding is not scratched through.

clad aluminum. A sheet of aluminum alloy that has a coating of pure aluminum rolled on one or both of its surfaces for corrosion protection.

Alclad. A registered trade name for clad aluminum alloy.

Pureclad. A registered trade name for clad aluminum alloy.

Oxide-Film Protection

A hard, airtight oxide film may be deposited on the surface of aluminum alloy sheets by either an electrolytic or a chemical action. The electrolytically deposited film is called an anodized film. The chemically deposited film is called a conversion coating, sometimes called Alodizing after one of the popular chemicals used to form the film, Alodine. These oxide films not only protect the metal, but provide a slightly rough surface that makes it possible for a paint film to adhere.

anodizing. The electrolytic process in which a hard, airtight, oxide film is deposited on aluminum alloy for corrosion protection.

Alodine. The registered trade name for a popular conversion coating chemical used to produce a hard, airtight, oxide film on aluminum alloy for corrosion protection.

Enamel or Lacquer Coating

Airplanes may be given an attractive and protective finish by covering the metal with a coating of enamel or lacquer. Before this type of finish will adhere to the metal, the surface must be prepared, usually with a primer. The most commonly used primers are zinc chromate, wash primer, and epoxy primer. All have special characteristics discussed in the section on "Aircraft Painting and Finishing," beginning on Page 212.

Magnesium Alloys

Magnesium alloys are lighter in weight than aluminum alloys and are used as structural materials when weight is a deciding factor. These alloys do have serious drawbacks, however. They are more reactive than aluminum alloys and are thus more susceptible to corrosion, and they are more brittle and thus more likely to crack. When a part is properly designed and the metal is protected against corrosion, it is useful as an aircraft structural material.

Titanium

Titanium is expensive and difficult to work, but its ability to retain its strength when exposed to high temperatures has made it a popular material for the construction of high-performance turbine-powered aircraft.

Titanium is heavier than aluminum, but is much stronger, and it is lighter than steel of equivalent strength. Special techniques must be used when forming, drilling, or cutting titanium.

Ferrous Metals

ferrous metal. Any metal that contains iron and has magnetic characteristics.

Metals that contain iron are called ferrous metals, and most ferrous metals used in aircraft construction are some form of steel, which is iron with a specific amount of carbon and other alloying elements added.

Alloy Steels

Steel alloyed with such elements as molybdenum, chromium, tungsten, nickel, and vanadium is used in aircraft engines and landing gears, and for fittings where high strength is needed.

Corrosion-Resistant Steel

Corrosion-resistant steel is sometimes called stainless steel, and is used in thin sheets for engine firewalls and exhaust system components. The main alloying elements in this steel are chromium and nickel.

Strength of Metal Structural Materials

The strength of a metal is measured in pounds per square inch of tensile strength, and there are several types of strength.

The elastic limit, or yield strength, of a material is the maximum amount of tensile load, in pounds per square inch, a material is able to withstand without being permanently deformed. Any time a material is loaded to less than its elastic limit and the load is released, it will return to its original size and configuration.

When a piece of metal is put into a tensile testing machine and a load is applied, the metal will stretch in direct proportion to the amount of the load until its elastic limit is reached. At this point it will continue to stretch without the load being increased. When the metal stretches, its molecular structure rearranges and it becomes harder and stronger, but it will not return to its original configuration after the load is removed. If the load is increased still further, the metal will pull apart when its ultimate tensile strength is reached.

The tensile strength of steel is directly related to its hardness, and can be determined by measuring its hardness with a Rockwell hardness tester, as is described in the *General* textbook of this *Aviation Maintenance Technician Series*. Figure 2-12 shows the relationship between the hardness and tensile strength of steel in the range that is normally used in aircraft structure.

Rockwell C-Scale Hardness Number	Tensile Strength 1,000 psi (approximate)
50	245
49	239
48	232
47	225
46	219
45	212
44	206
43	201
42	196
41	191
40	186
39	181
38	176
37	172
36	168
35	163
34	159
33	154
32	150
31	146
30	142
29	138
28	134
27	131
26	127
25	124
24	121
23	118
22	115
21	113
20	110

Figure 2-12. Relationship between hardness and tensile strength of steel

The strength of aluminum alloys does not relate directly to its hardness because of the effect of the alloys. But when you know the alloy and its hardness, you can determine its temper, and by reference to a chart such as the one in Figure 2-14, find its tensile strength.

For example, if a piece of 2024 aluminum alloy has a Brinell number of 120, a check of the chart in Figure 2-13 shows that this is the hardness of 2024 in its T3 state. The table in Figure 2-14 shows that 2024-T3 aluminum alloy has an ultimate tensile strength of 70,000 pounds.

yield strength. The amount of stress needed to permanently deform a material.

ultimate tensile strength. The tensile strength required to cause a material to break or to continue to deform under a decreasing load.

Alloy Number	Hardness Temper	Brinell Number 500 kg load 10 mm ball
1100	O	23
	H18	44
2014	O	45
	T6	135
2024	O	47
	T3	120
3003	O	28
	H16	47
5052	O	47
	H36	73
6061	O	30
	T4	65
	T6	95
7075	O	60
	T6	150

Figure 2-13. *Brinell hardness number for various aluminum alloys*

Alloy and Temper	Minimum Ultimate Tensile Strength psi
1100-O	13,000
1100-H18	24,000
2014-O	27,000
2014-T6	70,000
2024-O	27,000
2024-O Alclad	26,000
2024-T3	70,000
2024-T3 Alclad	65,000
3003-O	16,000
3003-H16	26,000
5052-O	28,000
5052-H36	40,000
6061-O	18,000
6061-T4	35,000
6061-T6	45,000
7075-O	33,000
7075-O Alclad	32,000
7075-T6	83,000
7075-T6 Alclad	76,000

Figure 2-14. *Minimum ultimate tensile strength of various aluminum alloys*

Bearing and Shear Strength

A riveted joint in a piece of sheet aluminum alloy must be designed so it will fail by the rivet shearing rather than the sheet of metal tearing. By using the charts in Figures 2-15 and 2-17 you can determine whether a riveted joint will fail in shear or bearing. When designing a riveted joint, always choose a rivet whose shear strength is near to, but slightly less than, the bearing strength of the metal sheet.

If two sheets of 0.040 aluminum alloy are riveted together with $\frac{1}{8}$-inch 2117T rivets, and the joint is loaded until it fails, it will fail in shear. The rivets will shear and the sheets of metal will be undamaged. We know this because the shear strength of $\frac{1}{8}$-inch 2117T rivets is 331 pounds, and the bearing

shear strength. The strength of a riveted joint in a sheet metal structure in which the rivets shear before the metal tears at the rivet holes.

bearing strength. The amount of pull needed to cause a piece of sheet metal to tear at the points at which it is held together with rivets. The bearing strength of a material is affected by both its thickness and the diameter of the rivet.

shear load. A structural load that tends to shear a rivet in the same way scissors shear paper.

strength for 0.040 aluminum alloy sheet for a $\frac{1}{8}$-inch rivet is 410 pounds. If the same size higher strength 2024T rivets were used in this joint, the sheet would tear at the rivet holes because the shear strength of the rivet is 429 pounds, which is greater than the 410-pound bearing strength of the sheet. *See* Figures 2-15 and 2-17.

Later in the chapter when we consider the actual design of a riveted joint, we will use the chart in Figure 2-81 on Page 118 to determine whether a joint will fail in bearing or shear.

Rivet Alloy	Diameter of Rivet (inch)				
	3/32	1/8	5/32	3/16	1/4
2117T	186	331	518	745	1,325
2017T	206	368	573	828	1,472
2024T	241	429	670	966	1,718

Figure 2-15. *Shear strength of aluminum alloy rivets in a single-shear joint. Double-shear strength is approximately twice that shown in the chart.*

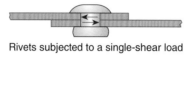
Rivets subjected to a single-shear load

Rivets subjected to a double-shear load

Figure 2-16. *Types of riveted joints*

Thickness of sheet (inch)	Diameter of Rivet (inch)				
	3/32	1/8	5/32	3/16	1/4
0.020	153	205	256	307	410
0.025	192	256	320	384	512
0.032	245	328	409	492	656
0.040	307	410	512	615	820
0.051	391	522	653	784	1,045
0.064	492	656	820	984	1,312

Figure 2-17. *Bearing strength of 2024-T3 aluminum alloy sheet*

STUDY QUESTIONS: MATERIALS FOR METAL AIRCRAFT CONSTRUCTION

Answers begin on Page 167. Page numbers refer to chapter text.

7. Identify the chief alloying agent in each of these aluminum alloys.
   a. 2024 _____
   b. 5052 _____
   c. 7075 _____
   Page 70

8. When a piece of aluminum alloy is heated in a furnace, then quenched in cold water, it is said to have been _____ heat-treated. *Page 71*

9. If there is a delay between the time the aluminum alloy is removed from the oven and it is quenched, the grains will grow to a size that makes the metal susceptible to _____ corrosion. *Page 71*

10. After a piece of aluminum alloy has been solution heat-treated, it gains strength over a period of days. This process is called _____ . *Page 71*

11. After a piece of aluminum alloy has been solution heat-treated, it can be returned to the oven and held at an elevated temperature for a period of time to increase its strength. This process is called _____ heat-treating. *Page 71*

12. Another name for precipitation heat-treating is _____ . *Page 71*

13. Aluminum alloy may be annealed by heating it in an oven and then cooling it _____ (slowly or rapidly). *Page 72*

14. An aluminum alloy that cannot be hardened by heat-treating _____ (can or cannot) be annealed by heating and controlled cooling. *Page 72*

15. An aluminum alloy that has been solution heat-treated and then strain hardened has the temper designation _____ . *Page 72*

16. An aluminum alloy that has been solution heat-treated and then artificially aged has the temper designation _____ . *Page 72*

17. An aluminum alloy that has been strain hardened by cold-working to its half-hard condition has the temper designation _____ . *Page 72*

18. An aluminum alloy that has been annealed has the temper designation _____ . *Page 72*

19. Aluminum alloy 3003 _____ (is or is not) heat-treatable. *Page 72*

20. If a nonheat-treatable aluminum alloy becomes too hard while it is being worked, some of the hardness can be removed by _____ . *Page 72*

21. Pure aluminum _____ (is or is not) susceptible to corrosion. *Page 72*

22. Aluminum alloy sheet that is protected from corrosion by rolling a coating of pure aluminum on its surface is called _____ aluminum. *Page 73*

23. Clad aluminum alloy is _____ (stronger or weaker) than a sheet of unclad metal of the same alloy and thickness. *Page 73*

24. A hard oxide film that is deposited on an aluminum alloy by an electrolytic process is called a/an _____ film. *Page 73*

25. A corrosion-protective oxide film may be deposited on aluminum alloy by a chemical called a/an _____ coating. *Page 73*

26. Magnesium alloys are _____ (more or less) susceptible to corrosion than aluminum alloys. *Page 73*

Continued

27. Titanium _____ (does or does not) retain its strength when it is exposed to a high temperature. *Page 74*

28. Metals that contain iron are called _____ metals. *Page 74*

29. Steel is iron with _____ and other alloying elements added in controlled amounts. *Page 74*

30. The main alloying elements for corrosion-resistant steel are _____ and _____ . *Page 74*

31. The load in pounds per square inch that causes a material to break is called the _____ tensile strength of the material. *Page 74*

32. The tensile strength of a piece of steel may be determined by measuring its _____ . *Page 74*

33. A piece of steel with a Rockwell-C hardness of 40 has a tensile strength of approximately _____ pounds per square inch. *Page 74*

34. The strength of aluminum alloy _____ (does or does not) relate directly to its hardness. *Page 75*

35. A piece of 2024 aluminum alloy with a Brinell hardness of 120 has a tensile strength of approximately _____ pounds per square inch. *Page 75*

36. A riveted joint should be designed so it will fail in _____ (bearing or shear). *Page 75*

37. A riveted joint connecting two sheets of 0.032-inch 2024-T3 aluminum alloy with $3/32$-inch 2117T rivets will fail in _____ (bearing or shear). *Page 76*

Aircraft Structural Fasteners

Sheets of metal must be fastened together to form the aircraft structure, and this is usually done with solid aluminum alloy rivets. This section of the *Aviation Maintenance Technician Series* covers both solid and special rivets.

Solid Rivets

When aircraft manufacturers started building all-metal aircraft in the 1930s, different manufacturers had different favored rivet head designs. Brazier heads, modified brazier heads, button heads, mushroom heads, flat heads, and 78°-countersunk heads were used. As aircraft construction standardized, four rivet head designs almost completely replaced all of these others. Rivets exposed to the airflow over the structure are usually either universal head MS20470, or 100°-countersunk head MS20426 rivets. For rivets used in internal structure, the round head MS20430, and the flat head MS20442 are generally used.

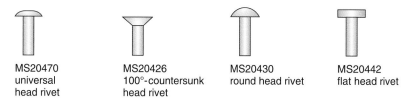

MS20470 universal head rivet	MS20426 100°-countersunk head rivet	MS20430 round head rivet	MS20442 flat head rivet

Figure 2-18. *Modern solid rivet design*

The material of which an aluminum alloy rivet is made is indicated by a mark on the manufactured head. Figure 2-19 shows the marks and indicates the metal or alloy of which the rivet is made.

A basic rule for rivet material selection is that you should use a rivet of the same material as the sheet metal you are joining, but this rule is not generally adhered to. Most aircraft structure is made of 2024 alloy, but 2024 rivets must be heat-treated and used shortly after they are removed from the quench. Because of this requirement, most aircraft are designed to use 2117 alloy rivets that can be driven just as they are received from the manufacturer.

When a higher strength rivet is required, use 2017 or 2024 alloy rivets. These are called "icebox" rivets, and they must be heat-treated before they are driven to prevent their cracking. Rivets of both of these alloys are heated to a specified temperature in an oven and are then quenched in water. They are soft when they are first removed from the water and may be driven immediately without cracking. But if they remain at normal room temperature for more than about ten minutes, they harden enough that they will crack. To prevent this hardening, they may be stored in a freezer at a temperature well below zero. They will remain soft enough to drive for several weeks if they are stored at a temperature of near -50°F, but they should be driven within 5 to 10 minutes after they are removed from the freezer.

Head Mark		Alloy	Code
Plain	○	1100	A
Recessed dot	⊙	2117T	AD
Raised dot	⊙	2017T	D
Raised double dash	⊖	2024T	DD
Raised cross	⊕	5056H	B
Three raised dashes	⊗	7075 T73	
Raised circle	◎	7050 T73	E
Recessed large and small dots	⊗	Titanium	
Recessed dash	⊖	Corrosion resistant steel	F
Recessed triangle	△	Carbon steel	

Figure 2-19. *Head identification marks for solid aluminum alloy rivets*

icebox rivet. A solid rivet made of 2017 or 2024 aluminum alloy. These rivets are too hard to drive in the condition they are received from the factory, and must be heat-treated to soften them. They are heated in a furnace and then quenched in cold water. Immediately after quenching they are soft, but within a few hours at room temperature they become quite hard. The hardening can be delayed for several days by storing them in a sub-freezing icebox and holding them at this low temperature until they are to be used.

Magnesium is a highly reactive metal and every reasonable precaution must be taken to prevent contact with other metals. For this reason rivets made of 5056 alloy are used to join magnesium alloy sheets. These rivets contain approximately 5% magnesium and create the least dissimilar metal problem of any of the rivets. These rivets may be driven as they are received without further heat treatment.

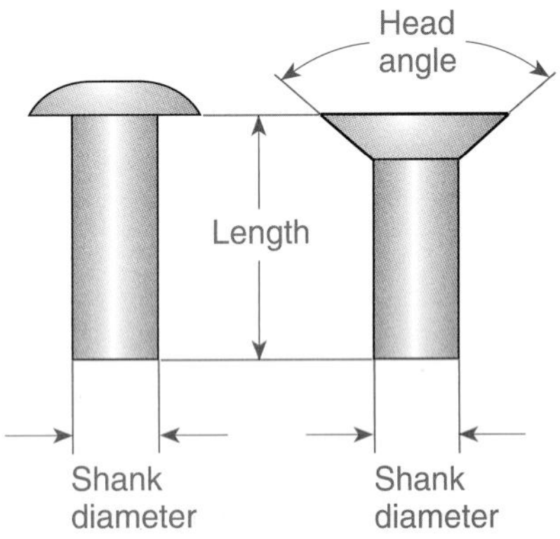

Rivet Dimensions

The diameter of a solid rivet is the diameter of its shank, as seen in Figure 2-20. In rivet specifications, the diameter is given in $\frac{1}{32}$-inch increments as the first dash number following the material code for the rivet.

The length of solid rivets is measured from the portion of the head that is flush with the surface of the metal sheet to the end of its shank. This length is measured in $\frac{1}{16}$-inch increments and is given in rivet specifications as the second dash number.

Rivet Identification

A solid aluminum alloy rivet is identified by a number that indicates its head shape, alloy, diameter, and length. The letters MS or AN identify the specifications under which the rivet is manufactured. The number indicates the shape of the head, the code that follows this number identifies the alloy, the first dash number is the diameter in $\frac{1}{32}$-inch increments, and the second dash number is the length in $\frac{1}{16}$-inch increments. This identification is shown in the example in Figure 2-21.

Figure 2-20. *Measurement of an aircraft solid rivet*

MS20470AD-4-6	
MS	Military Specifications
20470	Universal head rivet
AD	2117T alloy
-4	4/32 or 1/8-inch diameter
-6	6/16 or 3/8-inch length

Figure 2-21. *Meaning of rivet specification numbers*

Identification Number	Head Shape	Alloy	Diameter	Length
MS20426AD-4-4	100° Csk	2117T	1/8	1/4
MS20470DD-5-8	Universal	2024T	5/32	1/2
MS20430D-6-10	Round	2017T	3/16	5/8
MS20442D-4-6	Flat	2017T	1/8	3/8
MS20430A-3-4	Round	1100	3/32	1/4

Figure 2-22. *Examples of aluminum alloy rivet designation*

Solid rivets made of copper, stainless steel, and Monel are identified in a manner similar to that used for aluminum alloy rivets.

Monel. An alloy of nickel, copper, and aluminum or silicon.

Identification Number	Head Shape	Material	Head Mark
MS20427	100° Countersunk	Mild steel	Recessed triangle
MS20427M	100° Countersunk	Monel	Raised triangle
MS20427C	100° Countersunk	Copper	No mark
MS20427F	100° Countersunk	Corrosion resistant steel	No mark
MS20435	Round	Mild steel	Recessed triangle
MS20435M	Round	Monel	Raised triangle
MS20435C	Round	Copper	No mark
MS20435F	Round	Corrosion resistant steel	No mark
MS20441	Flat	Mild steel	Recessed triangle
MS20441M	Flat	Monel	Raised triangle
MS20441C	Flat	Copper	No mark

Figure 2-23. *Identification of solid rivets other than aluminum alloy*

Special Fasteners

There are many locations on an aircraft where it is not possible to reach both sides of the structure, and special blind rivets must be installed. In this section several types of blind rivets and other special fasteners that are used in place of solid rivets or bolts are discussed.

Friction-Lock Cherry Rivets

The Townsend Division of Textron, Inc., manufactures a series of blind rivets that are widely used in both civilian and military aircraft. Figure 2-24 shows two head styles of the self-plugging friction-lock Cherry rivet. The correct length of rivet is chosen and it is inserted through the holes in the sheets of metal to be joined. A special puller is clamped over the ridged stem and pulled. The tapered end of the stem is pulled into the hollow shank where it swells the shank and clamps the skins tightly together. Continued pulling breaks the stem and leaves part of it wedged tightly inside the shank. The stem should break off flush with the top of the rivet head. If not, a fine file may be used to make it flush, being careful to not scratch the surface of the metal being joined.

Friction holds the stem in the rivet shank, and it can vibrate out. Because of this possibility, friction-lock rivets are not approved to replace solid rivets on a size-for-size basis, but must be one size larger than the solid rivets they replace.

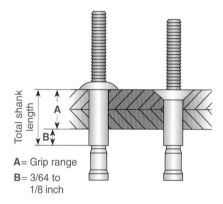

A = Grip range
B = 3/64 to 1/8 inch

Figure 2-24. *Self-plugging, friction-lock Cherry rivets*

rivet cutters. Special cutting pliers that resemble diagonal cutters except that the jaws are ground in such a way that they cut the rivet shank, or stem, off square.

Mechanical-Lock Cherry Rivets

A more secure rivet is the mechanical-lock Cherry rivet, as in Figure 2-25. A locking collar is swaged into the groove between the stem and the rivet head to prevent the stem from coming out of the installed rivet. A mechanical-lock rivet can replace a solid rivet on a size-for-size basis.

When the stem of this rivet is pulled, the end of the hollow stem is upset, which pulls the metal sheets tightly together and forms the upset head. Continued pulling shears the shear ring from the stem cone and allows the stem to pull up into the hollow shank enough for the stem break notch to be flush with the top of the rivet head. The puller forces the locking collar down tightly into the recess formed between the groove in the shank and the rivet head. This locks the stem in the shank, and further pulling snaps the stem off flush with the head of the rivet.

To remove a mechanical-lock Cherry rivet, follow the steps in Figure 2-26. File the broken end of the shank off smooth, and make a center punch mark in its center. Drill off the tapered part of the stem that provides the lock and, using a pin punch, pry out the locking collar. Use a drill that is slightly smaller than the rivet hole, and drill almost through the rivet head. Pry the head off of the rivet with a pin punch, and drive the rivet from the hole.

Other manufacturers produce mechanical locked rivets similar to these described. Most of them swage a collar into a groove between the stem and the rivet head to lock the stem in place as it is broken off by the pulling tool.

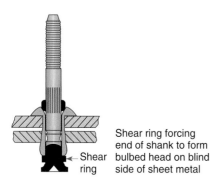

Rivet before stem is pulled

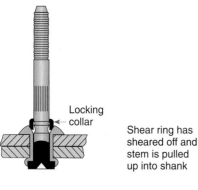

Shear ring forcing end of shank to form bulbed head on blind side of sheet metal

← Shear ring

Locking collar →

Shear ring has sheared off and stem is pulled up into shank

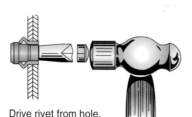

Collar has been forced down into groove in stem and stem broken off flush with rivet head

Figure 2-25. *Bulbed mechanical-lock Cherry rivets*

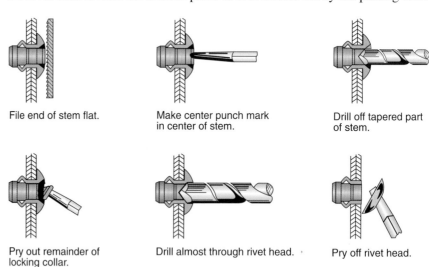

File end of stem flat.

Make center punch mark in center of stem.

Drill off tapered part of stem.

Pry out remainder of locking collar.

Drill almost through rivet head.

Pry off rivet head.

Drive rivet from hole.

Figure 2-26. *Removal of a mechanical-lock Cherry rivet*

Threaded Rivet

When the B.F. Goodrich Company conceived the rubber de-icer boot, it discovered a need for threaded holes in the thin sheet-metal skins of the wing and tail surfaces, and answered it with the Rivnut.

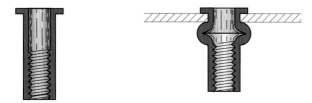

Rivnut before installation   Rivnut after it has been upset

Figure 2-27. *A Rivnut provides a threaded hole in a thin sheet metal.*

To install a Rivnut, drill the hole and cut the keyway with a special keyway cutter. Screw the Rivnut onto the threaded mandrel of a heading tool, such as the one in Figure 2-28. Insert the Rivnut into the hole with the key in the keyway and squeeze the movable handle. This upsets the Rivnut's shank, letting you turn the mandrel crank to remove the tool from the installed Rivnut.

High-Strength Pin Rivets

Modern aircraft construction techniques require as much automation as possible, and in locations where a high-strength fastener is required that is not likely to be removed in normal maintenance, a pin rivet such as the Hi-Shear rivet in Figure 2-29 may have been used. This fastener may be installed rapidly and has the same shear strength as an equivalent size structural steel bolt.

Pin rivets are installed by inserting the body of the rivet with the correct grip length through a hole that has been reamed to the correct size. The shank of these rivets does not expand to completely fill the hole as does the shank of a conventional solid rivet.

The correct grip length allows no more than $\frac{1}{16}$ inch of the straight portion of the shank to extend through the material, and the end of the unswaged metal collar should be slightly higher than the shearing edge of the pin. It is permissible to use a 0.032-inch steel washer between the collar and the material if necessary to position the collar.

To drive a pin rivet, hold a heavy bucking bar against the flat head and a Hi-Shear rivet set such as the one in Figure 2-30 against the collar. Impacts from the rivet gun swage the collar into the groove in the pin, and the shearing edge on the pin trims the top edge of the collar until it forms a smooth cone, as seen in Figure 2-31.

To remove a pin rivet, use a small, sharp chisel to split the collar and pry it off the pin. After removing the collar, tap the pin from the hole with a hammer.

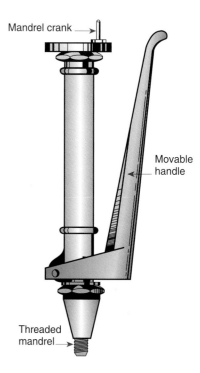

Mandrel crank

Movable handle

Threaded mandrel

Figure 2-28. *A Rivnut heading tool*

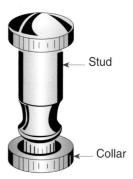

Stud

Collar

Figure 2-29. *High-strength steel pin rivets may be installed in an aircraft structure in locations that would normally use steel bolts loaded in shear.*

rivet set. A tool used to drive aircraft solid rivets. It is a piece of hardened steel with a recess the shape of the rivet head in one end. The other end fits into the rivet gun.

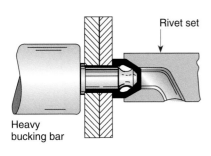

Heavy
bucking bar

Rivet set

Figure 2-30. *Hi-Shear rivet set in the correct position to swage the collar into the groove of the pin.*

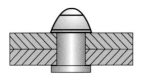

Correctly-driven pin rivet.

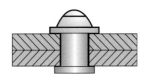

0.032-inch steel washer may be used to adjust grip length of pin.

Collar is underdriven. It may be driven more.

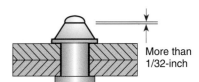

More than 1/32-inch

Collar is overdriven. If there is more than 1/32 inch between shearing edge of pin and top of collar, collar should be removed and a new one installed.

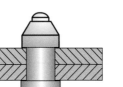

Pin is too long. Remove collar, install washer, or use shorter pin.

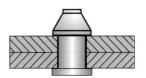

Pin is too short. Remove collar and use longer pin.

Figure 2-31. *Pin rivet inspection*

STUDY QUESTIONS: AIRCRAFT STRUCTURAL FASTENERS

Answers begin on Page 167. Page numbers refer to chapter text.

38. A solid aluminum alloy rivet with a dimple on its head is made of _____ alloy.
    Page 79

39. A solid aluminum alloy rivet with no mark on its head is made of _____ alloy. *Page 79*

40. A solid aluminum alloy rivet with a raised dot on its head is made of _____ alloy.
    Page 79

41. A solid aluminum alloy rivet with two raised dashes on its head is made of _____ alloy. *Page 79*

42. A solid aluminum alloy rivet with a raised cross on its head is made of _____ alloy.
    Page 79

43. Two solid aluminum alloy rivets that can be driven in the condition they are received without further heat treatment are coded _____ which is made of _____ alloy, and _____ which is made of _____ alloy. *Pages 79 and 80*

44. Icebox rivets must be heat-treated before they are driven. These rivets are made of either of two alloys; these are _____ and _____ . *Page 79*

45. The proper rivet to use for joining sheets of magnesium alloy is a rivet made of _____ alloy. *Page 80*

46. Identify the head style, alloy, diameter, and length of each of these solid rivets:
    a. MS20426AD-4-4   Head _____ , Alloy _____ ,
                        Diameter _____ , Length _____ .
    b. MS20470DD-6-8   Head _____ , Alloy _____ ,
                        Diameter _____ , Length _____ .
    Page 80

47. A rivet with a raised triangle on its head is made of _____ . *Page 81*

48. Friction-lock Cherry rivets _____ (are or are not) approved to replace solid rivets on a size-for-size basis. *Page 81*

49. Mechanical-lock Cherry rivets _____ (are or are not) approved to replace solid rivets on a size-for-size basis. *Page 82*

50. The stem of a mechanical-lock Cherry rivet is held in the hollow shank by a _____ that is swaged into a groove in the stem before the stem breaks off. *Page 82*

51. A special fastener that provides a threaded hole in a piece of thin sheet metal is the _____ . *Page 83*

52. High-strength pin rivets are designed to be used for _____ (shear or tensile) loads. *Page 83*

Tools for Sheet-Metal Construction and Repair

Aircraft manufacturing requires many exotic and sophisticated tools and fixtures that allow the structure to be built with the maximum degree of interchangeability of parts among aircraft of the same design. Repair of these aircraft requires relatively simple tools, which are described here, categorized according to their function.

Layout Tools

Aircraft drawings are discussed in the *General* textbook of this *Aviation Maintenance Technician Series*. In a detail drawing, all of the dimensions are given that are required to manufacture a part. This information, which includes all of the needed dimensions, angles, and radii, should not be scaled from the drawing because the paper stretches or shrinks, but should be laid out directly on the metal or on a template using the dimensions shown on the drawing.

Combination Set

The combination set in Figure 2-32 is a useful layout tool. When you place the stock, or square, head against the side of a piece of material, the blade extends across it at an exact 90° or 45° angle. Use the protractor head when you need an angle of other than 90° or 45°.

Use the center head to locate and mark the center of a round object. Notice that the head is in the form of two arms at right angles to each other, and the blade intersects this angle. To locate the center of a circle, lay the blade across it with the arms of the head tight against the outside edge and draw a line along the edge of the blade. Move the tool around about 90° and draw another line crossing the one just drawn. The intersection of these lines is in the center of the circle.

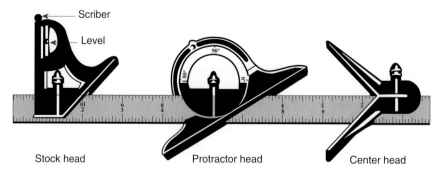

Figure 2-32. *The combination set is one of the most widely used tools for sheet metal layout.*

Steel Scales

The scale on the blade of the combination set is useful for layout work, but special scales are available in both flexible and rigid steel. One handy scale for sheet metal work is flexible and six inches long. One side is graduated in common fractions of an inch and the other is in decimal fractions. The common fraction side has graduations as small as $\frac{1}{64}$ inch, and the smallest graduation on the decimal side is one hundredth of an inch, or 0.01 inch.

When using a steel scale for making a measurement, do not use the end of the scale, but rather make the measurement between two marks on the scale away from the end.

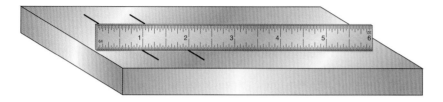

Figure 2-33. *When using a steel scale to determine the distance between two marks, do not use the end of the scale, but measure from one of its inch marks.*

One handy type of steel scale is the hook rule, seen in Figure 2-34. The inside edge of the hook is aligned exactly with the end of the scale. Place it over the edge of the object to be measured. You can make measurements quickly and easily from the edge to the marks on the scale. A hook rule is the most convenient way to get measurements from the edge when there is a radius involved.

Figure 2-34. *A hook rule is used for making measurements to the edge of a piece of material. It is especially helpful if the material has a radius or a bevel on its edge.*

Dividers

Dividers are used for transferring distances from a steel scale to the metal being laid out and for dividing a line into equal spaces, for example, when laying out a row of rivets. *See* Figure 2-35.

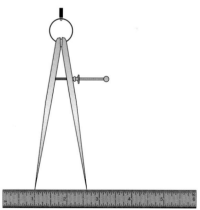

Figure 2-35. *Dividers are used to transfer distances from a steel scale to the metal being laid out.*

Marking Tools

When laying out a steel part for machining, it is acceptable practice to coat the surface of the metal with a dark blue opaque layout dye and scribe the marks with a sharp-pointed steel scriber. But this is not an acceptable practice for laying out parts on sheet aluminum or magnesium alloys. Any scribe marks in this thin sheet metal can cause stress concentrations that can lead to failure of the metal.

The best way to lay out thin sheet metal is to use an extra fine point Sharpie® permanent marker. This marking pen has a soft, sharp point and leaves a dark permanent mark on the sheet metal. These marks are considered permanent, but can be removed from the metal with a rag damp with alcohol.

Punches

Mark the exact location for drilled holes by holding the point of a prick punch at the location marked on the metal and tapping it lightly with a small hammer. The sharp point of the punch makes it easy to mark an exact location, but it does not indent the metal at the correct angle to start a drill.

After marking the locations of all drilled holes with a prick punch, enlarge the marks with a center punch. This punch is heavier than a prick punch, and its point is ground with a 60° angle, which is correct for making a twist drill start cutting. Center punches are available in sizes ranging from about three inches to five inches long. Be sure to use the punch that makes the appropriate starting indentation for the size drill you will be using.

Often when making a new piece of skin for an aircraft repair, you must use the original skin as a pattern. To do this, use a transfer punch to mark the center of the rivet holes. The end of the punch is the diameter of the rivet hole and has a sharp point in the center of its flat end. The metal sheets are held tightly together and the transfer punch is placed through a rivet hole and tapped lightly with a small hammer. The sharp point makes a small indentation like that produced by a prick punch, but at the location of the exact center of the rivet hole in the pattern.

Pin punches are used, not so much for layout, but for removing rivets after their heads have been drilled through, and for aligning sheets of metal by placing the punch through rivet holes in each of the sheets. These punches are available in sizes for most standard aircraft rivets, and all have straight shanks.

twist drill. A metal cutting tool turned in a drill press or hand-held drill motor. A twist drill has a straight shank and spiraled flutes. The cutting edge is ground on the end of the spiraled flutes.

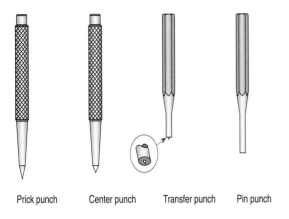

Prick punch   Center punch   Transfer punch   Pin punch

Figure 2-36. *Punches used for sheet metal layout and fabrication*

Cutting Tools

In both manufacturing and repair of sheet metal aircraft, some of the most important tools are those that cut the metal. It is extremely important to cut the metal at exactly the correct location, and to keep the edges free of cracks and burrs. This section discusses the cutting tools used in a shop first, and then the tools you as a technician will have in your personal tool chest.

Squaring Shear

The squaring shear in Figure 2-37 (Page 90) is one of the most useful tools in a sheet metal shop. These foot-operated shears normally accept a four-foot-wide sheet of thin sheet metal. The line on which the metal is to be cut is placed directly above the cutting edge of the bed of the shear, and it is held securely while the foot treadle is pressed down. Some squaring shears have a clamp near the cutting edge that allows you to clamp the metal so your fingers are not near the cutting edge when cutting small pieces of metal.

Large power-operated shears using energy stored in a flywheel to drive the cutting edge are used in steel fabrication shops to cut across sheets of heavy steel.

Throatless Shears

Throatless shears can cut across any size sheet of metal and can cut metal heavier than the foot-operated squaring shears. Their operation is much like a pair of heavy-duty, short-blade scissors. *See* Figure 2-38 on the next page.

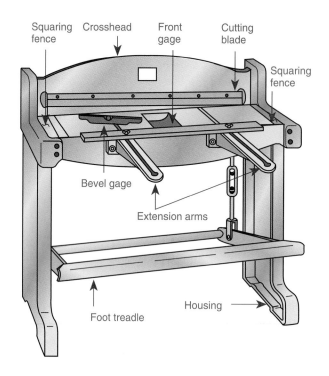

Squaring fence • Crosshead • Front gage • Cutting blade • Squaring fence • Bevel gage • Extension arms • Foot treadle • Housing

Figure 2-37. *A squaring shear for making straight cuts across sheets of thin metal*

Scroll Shears

Scroll shears are used to cut irregular lines on the inside of a sheet without cutting through to the edge. The upper cutting blade is stationary, while the lower blade is moved up and down with the handle. *See* Figure 2-39.

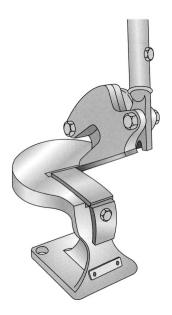

Figure 2-38. *Throatless shears cut metal in much the same way as scissors cut paper.*

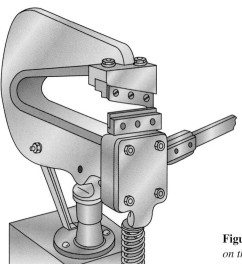

Figure 2-39. *Scroll shears are used to cut on the inside of a sheet of metal without cutting through to the edge.*

Bandsaw

Metal-cutting bandsaws are extremely versatile cutting tools. You can vary the speed of the blade to provide the correct cutting speed for the type and thickness of metal being cut. You can tilt the work table to allow the blade to cut the metal at an angle.

An especially useful feature is the butt welder and grinder built into this bandsaw. When it is necessary to cut on the inside of a piece of metal without cutting to the edge, the blade can be cut and inserted into a hole drilled in the metal, and then the ends of the blade can be welded back together and ground down smooth. The blade is then reinstalled on the saw and the metal is cut.

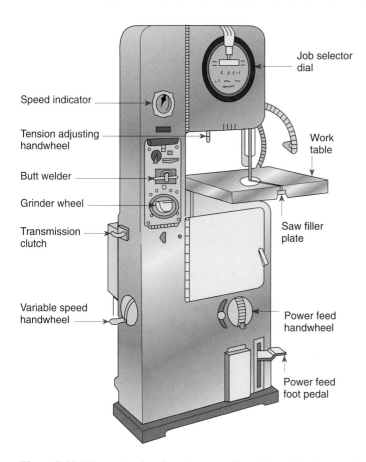

Figure 2-40. *The contour bandsaw is a versatile metal-cutting shop tool.*

Hacksaws

The most widely used metal-cutting saw is the hacksaw that holds a narrow, flexible steel blade under tension in an adjustable frame.

Hacksaw blades are about $\frac{1}{2}$-inch wide and are available in both 10- and 12-inch lengths. Blades are available with the number of teeth ranging from 14 to 32 per inch and may be made of either carbon steel or molybdenum steel.

Molybdenum blades are called high-speed blades and are considerably more expensive than carbon-steel blades, but they last so much longer that their overall cost is actually much less.

Determine how many teeth to use by the thickness of the material being cut. As a rule of thumb, there should always be at least two teeth on the material being cut. Figure 2-41 matches the number of teeth of the blade to the work.

The proper technique for using a hacksaw is to use as long a stroke as is convenient and to apply pressure on the forward stroke only. Lift the blade away from the metal on the return stroke to prevent dulling it.

Type of Material Being Cut	Recommended Teeth Per Inch
Material with large thickness and soft material where large chip clearance is needed	14
General shop use for cutting a variety of materials	18
Material with thicknesses between 1/16- and 1/4-inch	24
Material with thicknesses up to 1/16-inch	32

Figure 2-41. *Recommended teeth per inch for hacksaw blades*

Files

file. A hand-held cutting tool used to remove a small amount of metal with each stroke.

After cutting the metal to almost the correct size and shape, finish it by cutting the edges with a file. A file is so familiar to most of us that we often do not realize its importance or give it the care it deserves.

The teeth that cross the file at an angle are cutting tools and must receive the same care as any other cutting tool. The cut, or coarseness, of the teeth is designated by a series of numbers or by the name of the cut. The names, ranging from coarsest to smoothest, are: rough cut, coarse cut, bastard cut, second cut, smooth cut, and dead smooth cut. The designation of the cut is the same for all sizes of files, but the teeth on a small file are closer together than the teeth of the same-named cut on a larger file.

Files with a single set of teeth crossing the body at an angle of 65° to 85° are called single-cut files, and those with two sets of teeth, one crossing at an angle of 45° and the other crossing at an angle of 70° to 80°, are called double-cut files.

vixen file. A metal-cutting hand file that has curved teeth across its faces. Vixen files are used to remove large amounts of soft metal.

Vixen files are special cutting tools whose teeth are curved across the body of the file. These files are designed to remove a rather large amount of metal with each stroke and are used only on soft metal.

tang. A tapered shank sticking out from the blade of a knife or a file. The handle of a knife or file is mounted on the tang.

If you give files a reasonable amount of care they will give good service. Always match them to the work: use the right type and size of file, and choose the degree of coarseness to give the type of cut required. Never use a file without slipping a handle over the tang to protect your hands.

Never store files loose in your tool chest where they can be damaged by other tools. Store them in a rack or protect them in paper or plastic envelopes. They should never be oiled but should be kept clean and dry. When a file has been used to file soft metal, remove all of the metal that has remained between the teeth by brushing with a stiff brush or file card. Remove any stubborn metal with a sharp metal pick.

When filing hard metal, raise the file on the back stroke and apply pressure only on the forward stroke. Pressure on the back stroke will dull the teeth. It is a good practice, however, when filing very soft metals such as lead or soft aluminum, to apply some pressure on the back stroke to remove chips of metal from between the teeth.

Cross filing is done by moving the file lengthwise across the work, but when a very smooth surface is required, move the file sideways across the work. This is called draw filing.

Chisels

A chisel is a simple cutting tool made of a piece of hardened and tempered tool steel. The blade of the chisel is ground with a cutting edge, and is used to shear metal by driving it into the metal with a hammer.

There are a number of types of chisels in use. The most common is the flat chisel, the cutting edge of which is ground to an angle of approximately 70°, and into a convex shape. This convex shape concentrates the forces of the hammer blows in the center of the cutting edge. *See* Figure 2-43.

Cape chisels have a narrow blade and are used to remove the head of a rivet after it has been drilled through. *See* Figure 2-44.

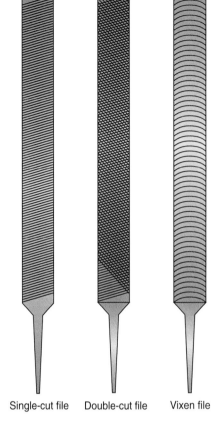

Single-cut file   Double-cut file   Vixen file

Figure 2-42. *Hand files*

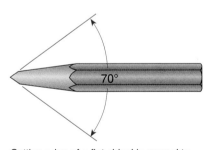

Cutting edge of a flat chisel is ground to an angle of approximately 70°.

Cutting edge is ground to a convex shape to concentrate hammer blows in the center of the cutting edge.

Figure 2-43. *A flat, or cold, chisel*

Figure 2-44. *A cape chisel may be used to remove the head of a rivet after it has been drilled through.*

burr. A sharp rough edge of a piece of metal left when the metal was sheared, punched, or drilled.

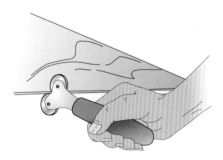

Figure 2-45. *A deburring tool used in production shops to deburr the edges of large sheets of metal.*

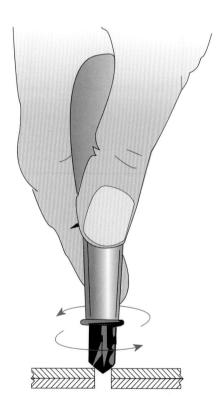

Figure 2-46. *A reamer or a large drill can be used to remove the burrs from the edge of a drilled hole.*

Deburring Tools

Any time metal is sheared or drilled, burrs are left on one side that must be removed. A smooth-cut file is a good tool for deburring, or removing these burrs, from the edges of sheets that have been sheared. A deburring tool used in production facilities uses two hardened, sharp-edged steel wheels mounted side-by-side with their edges almost touching. To deburr a piece of metal, pull the tool along the edge of the sheet with the wheels straddling the edge. The sharp edges of the wheels remove the burrs. *See* Figure 2-45.

You can make a handy deburring tool by grinding a sharp V-shaped notch in the end of a small flat file. Just pull this notch along the edges of the sheet that needs deburring and it will remove the burrs from both edges at the same time.

A countersinking tool or a drill a few sizes larger than the hole is good for removing burrs from the edges of a drilled hole. Be sure that you do not remove too much metal, just the burr. *See* Figure 2-46.

Drills

Twist drills are used in aircraft construction and maintenance to drill the thousands of rivet and bolt holes needed for the fasteners holding the aircraft structure together. Figure 2-47 shows the nomenclature of a typical twist drill.

Twist drill sizes are measured by three systems: numbers, letters, and fractions. The most popular drills used for aircraft sheet metal work are number drills. *See* the twist drill size chart of Figure 2-48.

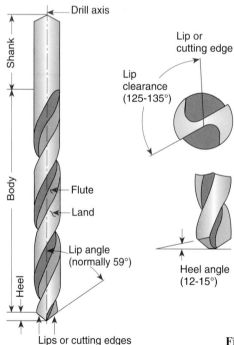

Figure 2-47. *Twist drill nomenclature*

Number or Letter	Fraction	Decimal Equivalent		Number or Letter	Fraction	Decimal Equivalent
80		0.0135		22		0.1570
79		0.0145		21		0.1590
78		0.0160		20		0.1610
	1/64	0.0156		19		0.1660
77		0.0180		18		0.1695
76		0.0200			11/64	0.1719
75		0.0210		17		0.1730
74		0.0225		16		0.1770
73		0.0240		15		0.1800
72		0.0250		14		0.1820
71		0.0260		13		0.1850
70		0.0280			3/16	0.1875
69		0.0290		12		0.1890
68		0.0310		11		0.1910
	1/32	0.0313		10		0.1935
67		0.0320		9		0.1960
66		0.0330		8		0.1990
65		0.0350		7		0.2010
64		0.0360			13/64	0.2031
63		0.0370		6		0.2040
62		0.0380		5		0.2055
61		0.0390		4		0.2090
60		0.0400		3		0.2130
59		0.0410			7/32	0.2187
58		0.0420		2		0.2210
57		0.0430		1		0.2280
56		0.0465		A		0.2340
	3/64	0.0469			15/64	0.2344
55		0.0520		B		0.2380
54		0.0550		C		0.2420
53		0.0595		D		0.2460
	1/16	0.0625		E	1/4	0.2500
52		0.0635		F		0.2570
51		0.0670		G		0.2610
50		0.0700			17/64	0.2656
49		0.0730		H		0.2660
48		0.0760		I		0.2720
	5/64	0.0781		J		0.2770
47		0.0785		K		0.2810
46		0.0810			9/32	0.2812
45		0.0820		L		0.2900
44		0.0860		M		0.2950
43		0.0890			19/64	0.2969
42		0.0935		N		0.3020
	3/32	0.0937			5/16	0.3125
41		0.0960		O		0.3160
40		0.0980		P		0.3230
39		0.0995			21/64	0.3281
38		0.1015		Q		0.3320
37		0.1040		R		0.3390
36		0.1065			11/32	0.3438
	7/64	0.1094		S		0.3480
35		0.1100		T		0.3580
34		0.1110			23/64	0.3594
33		0.1130		U		0.3680
32		0.1160			3/8	0.3750
31		0.1200		V		0.3770
	1/8	0.1250		W		0.3860
30		0.1285			25/64	0.3906
29		0.1360		X		0.3970
28		0.1405		Y		0.4040
	9/64	0.1406			13/32	0.4062
27		0.1440		Z		0.4130
26		0.1470			27/64	0.4219
25		0.1495			7/16	0.4375
24		0.1520			29/64	0.4331
23		0.1540			15/32	0.4688
	5/32	0.1562			31/64	0.4844
					1/2	0.5000

Figure 2-48. *Twist drill sizes*

Snake attachment

Right-angle attachment

Drill for right-angle attachment

Figure 2-49. *Attachments for drilling holes in hard-to-reach locations.*

Drill Motors

Most of the holes used for sheet metal repair work are drilled with hand-held pneumatic drill motors. These are superior to electric drill motors because they are lightweight, have excellent speed control, do not overheat when they are stalled, and they do not produce sparks which could serve as a source of ignition. Since rivet guns require compressed air, compressed air lines are usually available where sheet-metal repairs are being made.

Drill Attachments and Special Drills

Aircraft are noted for requiring work in hard-to-reach locations, and holes that need drilling are no exceptions. Fortunately, snake attachments and right-angle drill motors use very short twist drills, and right-angle attachments can be used in a conventional drill motor. *See* Figure 2-49.

You can use extension drills to drill in a location that cannot be reached with a conventional short drill. If the rigid extension drill is not available, use an extra-long drill. When using a long drill of a small size, it is a good idea to slip a piece of aluminum tubing over the drill to keep it from whipping.

Extension drill that uses a long, rigid shaft and conventional twist drill.

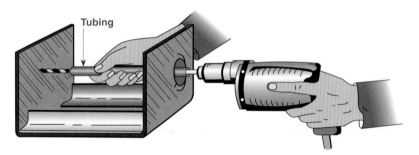

When using small diameter, extra-long drill, place piece of aluminum tubing around drill to prevent it whipping.

Figure 2-50. *Extension drills and extra-long drills*

Forming Tools

Large sheets of metal are formed in an aircraft factory with press brakes, drop hammers, hydropresses, and stretch presses. In the smaller maintenance shops the tools described here are used to form both straight and compound curves on thin sheet metal.

Cornice Brake

The cornice, or leaf, brake is one of the most familiar brakes in a maintenance shop. The metal to be bent is clamped between the bed of the brake and the top nose bar, with the sight line marked on the metal directly below the edge of the nose bar. (This is discussed in detail in the section on metal layout and forming beginning on Page 105.) The bending leaf is lifted, bending the metal against the radius on the top nose bar.

cornice brake. A large shop tool used to make straight bends across a sheet of metal. Cornice brakes are often called leaf brakes.

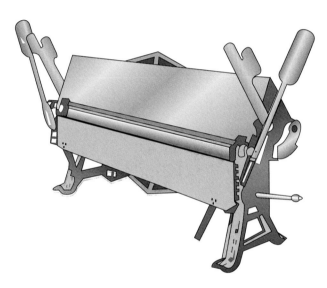

Figure 2-51. *A cornice brake is used for making straight bends across sheets of metal.*

Box Brake

A cornice brake can only bend the two opposite sides of a box, but a box, or finger, brake can bend up all four sides. A box brake is much like a cornice brake except the top nose bar is divided into sections called fingers. The brake is adjusted for the correct metal thickness and bend radius, and two opposite sides of the box are bent up. The metal is turned 90° and the fingers are adjusted so the two formed sides of the box fit between two fingers, and the final two sides of the box are bent.

Slip Roll Former

slip roll former. A shop tool used to form large radius curves in sheet metal.

You can bend large radius curves in a sheet of metal with a slip roll former, such as the one in Figure 2-52. These machines have three hardened steel rollers. The drive roller is rotated with a hand crank, the gripping roller is adjustable to clamp the metal between it and the drive roller so it will be pulled through the machine, and behind these two rollers is a radius roller that can be adjusted to force the metal into a curve as it is pulled through the rollers. The radius roller is adjusted to cause the metal to be slightly bent by the first pass, then the metal is passed through the rollers a second time with the radius roller moved up a bit. This makes the radius of the bend smaller. The metal may be passed through the rollers as many times as needed, and the radius roller adjusted each time until the metal has the desired bend. One end of the gripping roller can be lifted to remove the metal if it has been rolled into a complete cylinder.

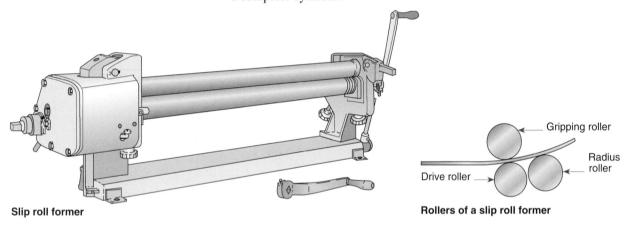

Slip roll former

Rollers of a slip roll former

Figure 2-52. *Slip roll formers are used for making large radius bends in sheet metal.*

Sandbag

You can form compound curves in a piece of sheet metal by bumping it with a soft-face mallet and a sandbag. The sandbag is made of canvas or leather and filled with clean dry sand. A depression is made in the bag and the metal is bumped into the depression. Always start at the outside edges of the bend and work toward the center. Continually check the work with a template to be sure the metal takes the desired shape.

Riveting Tools

Production riveting on an assembly is done with a high-tech riveting machine that drills the hole, countersinks it, drops the rivet in place, squeezes it to the proper compression, and automatically moves over to the location for the next rivet. The riveting done in maintenance shops is not so automated and is done with a rivet gun or a hand-held compression, or squeeze, riveter.

Rivet Gun

The typical rivet gun is shown in Figure 2-53. This is a pneumatic hammer that can drive a rivet set against the rivet head. The set is held in the gun with a beehive-shaped spring that screws over the end of the gun cylinder.

Rivet guns are available in several types and shapes, shown in Figure 2-54. These guns are classified according to the speed of the blows they deliver and the shape of their handle.

Use long-stroke, slow-hitting guns to drive large, hard rivets. These guns upset the rivet with a few blows without excessively work hardening them. Use fast-hitting guns to drive smaller rivets. They give you excellent control over the blows the gun delivers.

beehive spring. A hard-steel, coil-spring retainer used to hold a rivet set in a pneumatic rivet gun.

This spring gets its name from its shape. It screws onto the end of the rivet gun and allows the set to move back and forth, but prevents it being shot from the gun.

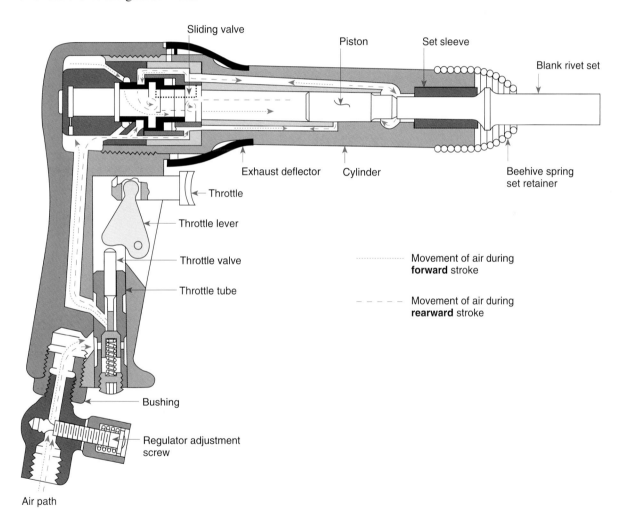

Figure 2-53. *A typical offset-handle pneumatic rivet gun*

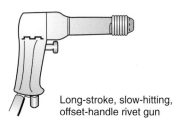

Long-stroke, slow-hitting, offset-handle rivet gun

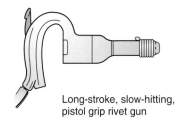

Long-stroke, slow-hitting, pistol grip rivet gun

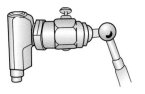

Fast-hitting, offset-handle rivet gun

Fast-hitting, pistol grip rivet gun

Fast-hitting, push button rivet gun

Figure 2-54. *Pneumatic rivet guns*

Rivet Gun Size	Maximum Rivet Diameter
1x	3/32 inch
2x	1/8 inch
3x	3/16 inch
4x	1/4 inch

Figure 2-55. *The rivet gun should match the size rivet being driven.*

Rivet guns are rated by size (*see* Figure 2-55), and all of these guns accept standard rivet sets that have a 0.401-inch shank.

Observe certain safety and operating rules when using a rivet gun:

• Never point a rivet gun at anyone at any time.

• Never depress the trigger of a rivet gun unless the rivet set is held firmly against the head of a rivet or against a piece of wood.

• Disconnect the hose from the rivet gun when it is to be out of use for an appreciable length of time.

Rivet Set

A rivet set is the device that actually drives the rivet. Standard rivet sets have a 0.401-inch shank that fits into the rivet gun and a cup in the end of the end of the shank that fits over the head of the rivet.

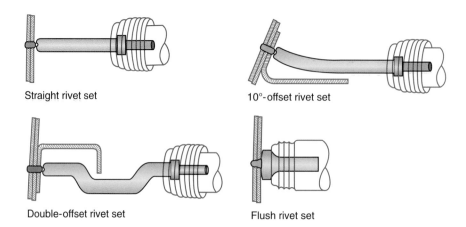

Straight rivet set

10°-offset rivet set

Double-offset rivet set

Flush rivet set

Figure 2-56. *Rivet sets*

The radius of the cup in the rivet set should be slightly greater than the radius of the rivet head. This concentrates the blows from the rivet gun and prevents the set from damaging the skin being riveted.

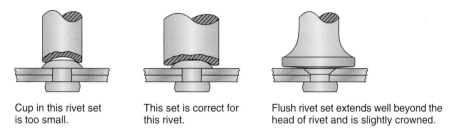

Cup in this rivet set is too small.

This set is correct for this rivet.

Flush rivet set extends well beyond the head of rivet and is slightly crowned.

Figure 2-57. *The radius of the cup in a rivet set is slightly greater than the radius of the rivet head. This allows the blows from the rivet gun to be concentrated on the rivet head.*

Bucking Bars

The rivet gun drives the rivet set against the manufactured head of a rivet, but it is the bucking bar that actually forms the shop, or bucked, head of the rivet. Bucking bars are made of hardened and polished steel and are available in many shapes and sizes. When choosing a bucking bar, match the weight of the bar with the size of the rivet.

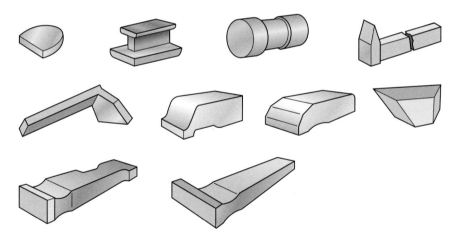

Figure 2-58. *Typical bucking bars*

Rivet Diameter (inch)	Bucking Bar Weight (pounds)
3/32	2 to 3
1/8	3 to 4
5/32	3-1/2 to 4-1/2
3/16	4 to 5
1/4	5 to 6-1/2

Figure 2-59. *Relationship between rivet size and proper bucking bar weight*

Compression Rivet Squeezers

You can use compression riveting to rapidly upset a large number of rivets reachable with a rivet squeezer. Rivets driven by this method are uniform and are not work-hardened by hammering.

The two most widely used pneumatically operated squeezers are the C-yoke and the alligator-yoke seen in Figure 2-60.

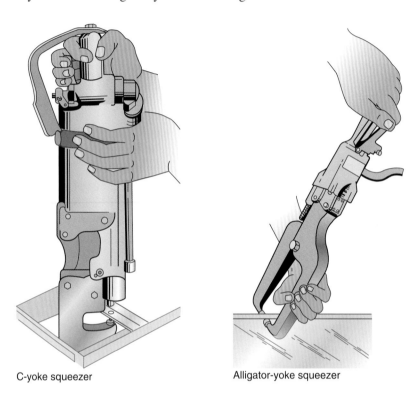

C-yoke squeezer

Alligator-yoke squeezer

Figure 2-60. *Compression rivet squeezers*

Sheet-Metal Assembly Tools

The actual riveting is a small part of the joining of sheets of metal. The layout, cutting, drilling, burring, and assembly must all be done carefully and accurately before the part is ready to be riveted.

When you have drilled, deburred and sprayed the mating parts with a corrosion-inhibiting primer, you must assemble them before riveting. You can hold the sheets together with sheet metal screws, but this is time consuming and damages the holes. It is best to use some form of patented fastener such as the Cleco fastener seen in Figure 2-61. These fasteners are quick and easy to install and remove, they hold the sheets tightly together, they are inexpensive, so an adequate number of them can be used, and they do not damage the rivet holes. They are available in sizes for all standard rivets and are color-coded to make selection of the correct size easy.

Cleco fastener. A patented spring-type fastener used to hold metal sheets together until they can be permanently riveted together.

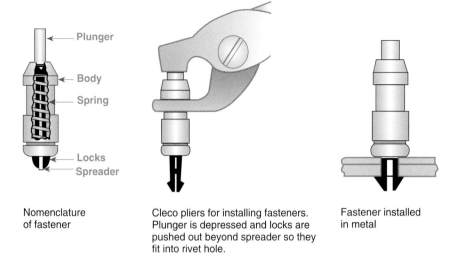

Nomenclature of fastener

Cleco pliers for installing fasteners. Plunger is depressed and locks are pushed out beyond spreader so they fit into rivet hole.

Fastener installed in metal

Rivet Diameter (inch)	Cleco Fastener Color
3/32	Silver
1/8	Copper
5/32	Black
3/16	Brass
1/4	Copper

Figure 2-61. *Cleco sheet metal fastener*

Figure 2-62. *Color-coding identifies the size of a Cleco fastener.*

Hole Finder

When replacing a piece of aircraft skin, you must drill the holes in the skin so they line up exactly with the holes in the structure beneath it. To do this, use a hole finder, or strap duplicator. This tool is made of two straps of metal spot-welded together at one end. The open end of one strap has a drill bushing that fits the proper drill for the rivet, and the open end of the other strap has a pin that fits into the rivet hole. This pin is exactly in line with the hole in the drill bushing. To use this tool, slip the hole finder over the new skin. The pin drops into the rivet hole in the structure below the skin. The drill bushing is now exactly over the hole and you can drill the skin through the bushing.

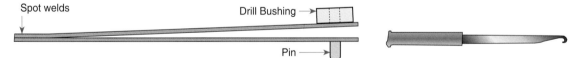

Spot welds   Drill Bushing   Pin

Figure 2-63. *A hole finder may be slipped over the edge of a new piece of aircraft skin to position the drill directly over the hole in the original structure. The chip chaser is a thin strip of metal with a hook in its end. It is inserted between the sheets of metal to capture and pull out any chips of metal left between the sheets when new rivet holes are drilled.*

Chip Chaser

When holes are drilled through partially assembled sheets of metal, chips are left between the sheets that can prevent the sheets from fitting tightly together. You must remove these chips with a chip chaser. These can be purchased, but you can make a good one with a worn-out hacksaw blade. Grind off the teeth and grind a notch into its edge at one end. Put a handle on the other end of the blade, and you have a very handy and effective tool. Slip the blade between the sheets and maneuver it until the chips are in the notch, then pull them out.

Answers begin on Page 167. Page numbers refer to chapter text.

53. Layout lines should be marked on sheet metal with a _____ .
    Page 88

54. Two things that determine the correct speed for a bandsaw blade are the type of metal being cut and its _____ . *Page 91*

55. When choosing the number of teeth for a hacksaw blade, choose one that will allow at least _____ (how many) teeth to be on the material being cut. *Page 92*

56. A flat chisel is ground so its cutting angle is approximately _____°. *Page 93*

57. Three ways of indicating the size of a twist drill are _____ , _____ , and _____ . *Page 95*

58. A number 30 twist drill is _____ (larger or smaller) than a number 50 drill. *Page 95*

59. Straight bends across a sheet of metal can be made with a _____ brake. *Page 97*

60. Straight bends with a large radius are made in a piece of sheet metal with a _____ . *Page 98*

61. Compound curves in a piece of sheet metal may be made with a soft-face mallet and a _____ . *Page 98*

62. A large-diameter hard rivet should be driven with as _____ (many or few) blows from the rivet gun as possible. *Page 99*

63. The radius of the cup in a rivet set should be _____ (greater or smaller) than the radius of the rivet head it fits. *Page 101*

64. The proper bucking bar used to drive a ⅛-inch rivet should weigh between _____ and _____ pounds. *Page 101*

65. The Cleco fastener to use in a hole for a ³⁄₃₂-inch rivet is colored _____ .
    Page 103

Layout and Forming

Laying out and forming sheet aluminum and magnesium require techniques and considerations quite different from those used in commercial sheet-metal work. Aircraft metals have high strength for their light weight, and their heat treatment makes them so brittle that they must be bent with a large enough radius that the metal is not excessively strained.

Grain of the Metal

When an ingot is rolled into a sheet of metal, the metal grains align in such a way that the maximum strength of the sheet is in a line parallel to the direction the sheet was rolled. This direction is said to be with the grain of the metal. If you look closely at the surface of a piece of aluminum alloy sheet, you can see lines that run the length of the metal. For the maximum strength of a formed, angled piece of sheet metal, make bends across the grain of the metal.

ingot. A large block of metal that was molded as it was poured from the furnace. Ingots are further processed into sheets, bars, tubes, or structural beams.

Bend Radius

When you bend a piece of metal, the material on the inside of the bend is subjected to a compressive stress and that on the outside is subjected to a tensile stress. There is a neutral plane, or neutral axis, within the metal that is not subjected to either a tensile or compressive stress. This plane lies at 44.5% of the thickness of the metal from the inside radius of the bend, but for practical purposes, the neutral plane can be considered to be in the middle of the metal thickness.

Figure 2-64 shows the minimum bend radius, measured on the inside of the bend, that can be used with the various aluminum alloys without weakening the metal.

bend radius. The radius of the inside of a bend.

neutral axis (neutral plane). A line through a piece of material that is bent. The material in the outside of the bend is stretched and that on the inside of the bend is shrunk. The material along the neutral plane is neither shrunk nor stretched.

Minimum Bend Radius for Aluminum Alloys								
Alloy	Thickness							
	0.020	0.025	0.032	0.040	0.051	0.064	0.072	0.081
2024-O	1/32	1/16	1/16	1/16	1/16	3/32	1/8	1/8
2024-T4	1/16	1/16	3/32	3/32	1/8	5/32	7/32	1/4
5052-O	1/32	1/32	1/16	1/16	1/16	1/16	1/8	1/8
5052-H34	1/32	1/16	1/16	1/16	3/32	3/32	1/8	1/8
6061-O	1/32	1/32	1/32	1/16	1/16	1/16	3/32	3/32
6061-T4	1/32	1/32	1/32	1/16	1/16	3/32	5/32	5/32
6061-T6	1/16	1/16	1/16	3/32	3/32	1/8	3/16	3/16
7075-O	1/16	1/16	1/16	1/16	3/32	3/32	5/32	3/16
7075-W	3/32	3/32	1/8	5/32	3/16	1/4	9/32	5/16
7075-T6	1/8	1/8	1/8	3/16	1/4	5/16	3/8	7/16

Figure 2-64. *Minimum bend radius for various aluminum alloys*

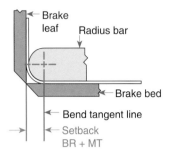

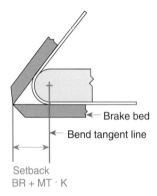

Setback
BR + MT · K

Figure 2-65. *Setback is the distance the bend tangent line is moved back from the brake leaf.*

mold line. A line used in the development of a flat pattern for a formed piece of sheet metal. The mold line is an extension of the flat side of a part beyond the radius. The mold line dimensions of a part is the dimension made to the intersection of mold lines and is the dimension the part would have if its corners had no radius.

setback. The distance the jaws of a brake must be set back from the mold line to form a bend. Setback for a 90° bend is equal to the inside radius of the bend plus the thickness of the metal being bent. For a bend other than 90°, a K-factor must be used. *See also* K-factor.

K-factor. A factor used in sheet metal work to determine the setback for other than a 90° bend.

Setback = K · (bend radius + metal thickness).

For bends of less than 90° the value of K is less than 1; for bends greater than 90° the value of K is greater than 1.

Setback

Setback is the distance the radius bar on the brake, such as in Figure 2-65, is moved back from the brake hinge line. For a 90° bend this is equal to the bend radius (BR) plus the thickness of the metal (MT). For a bend of more or less than 90°, the bend radius plus metal thickness must be multiplied by the K-factor from the table in Figure 2-66.

Degree	K-Factor	Degree	K-Factor	Degree	K-Factor	Degree	K-Factor
1	0.00873	46	0.42447	91	1.0176	136	2.4751
2	0.01745	47	0.43481	92	1.0355	137	2.5386
3	0.02618	48	0.44523	93	1.0538	138	2.6051
4	0.03492	49	0.45573	94	1.0724	139	2.6746
5	0.04366	50	0.46631	95	1.0913	140	2.7475
6	0.05241	51	0.47697	96	1.1106	141	2.8239
7	0.06116	52	0.48773	97	1.1303	142	2.9042
8	0.06993	53	0.49858	98	1.1504	143	2.9887
9	0.07870	54	0.50952	99	1.1708	144	3.0777
10	0.08749	55	0.52057	100	1.1917	145	3.1716
11	0.09629	56	0.53171	101	1.2131	146	3.2708
12	0.10510	57	0.54295	102	1.2349	147	3.3759
13	0.11393	58	0.55431	103	1.2572	148	3.4874
14	0.12278	59	0.56577	104	1.2799	149	3.6059
15	0.13165	60	0.57735	105	1.3032	150	3.7320
16	0.14054	61	0.58904	106	1.3270	151	3.8667
17	0.14945	62	0.60086	107	1.3514	152	4.0108
18	0.15838	63	0.61280	108	1.3764	153	4.1653
19	0.16734	64	0.62487	109	1.4019	154	4.3315
20	0.17633	65	0.63707	110	1.4281	155	4.5107
21	0.18534	66	0.64941	111	1.4550	156	4.7046
22	0.19438	67	0.66188	112	1.4826	157	4.9151
23	0.20345	68	0.67451	113	1.5108	158	5.1455
24	0.21256	69	0.68728	114	1.5399	159	5.3995
25	0.22169	70	0.70021	115	1.5697	160	5.6713
26	0.23087	71	0.71329	116	1.6003	161	5.9758
27	0.24008	72	0.72654	117	1.6318	162	6.3137
28	0.24933	73	0.73996	118	1.6643	163	6.6911
29	0.25862	74	0.75355	119	1.6977	164	7.1154
30	0.26795	75	0.76733	120	1.7320	165	7.5957
31	0.27732	76	0.78128	121	1.7675	166	8.1443
32	0.28674	77	0.79543	122	1.8040	167	8.7769
33	0.29621	78	0.80978	123	1.8418	168	9.5144
34	0.30573	79	0.82434	124	1.8807	169	10.385
35	0.31530	80	0.83910	125	1.9210	170	11.430
36	0.32492	81	0.85408	126	1.9626	171	12.706
37	0.33459	82	0.86929	127	2.0057	172	14.301
38	0.34433	83	0.88472	128	2.0503	173	16.350
39	0.35412	84	0.90040	129	2.0965	174	19.081
40	0.36397	85	0.91633	130	2.1445	175	22.904
41	0.37388	86	0.93251	131	2.1943	176	26.636
42	0.38386	87	0.80978	132	2.2460	177	38.188
43	0.39391	88	0.96569	133	2.2998	178	57.290
44	0.40403	89	0.9827	134	2.3558	179	114.590
45	0.41421	90	1.0000	135	2.4142	180	Infinite

Figure 2-66. *K-factor for finding setback for angles other than 90°*

Bend Allowance

Bend allowance is the actual amount of material used in the bend. Find it by using a chart such as the one in Figure 2-67. In this chart, the top number in each group at the intersection of the metal thickness and bend radius is the bend allowance for a 90° bend. The bottom number is the bend allowance for each degree of bend.

bend tangent line. A line made in a sheet metal layout that indicates the point at which the bend is started.

Figure 2-67. *Bend allowance chart showing the amount of material used in a 90° bend and in each degree of bend*

Metal Thickness	Radius of Bend (inches)													
	1/32	1/16	3/32	1/8	5/32	3/16	7/32	1/4	9/32	5/16	11/32	3/8	7/16	1/2
0.020	.062 .000693	.113 .001251	.161 .001792	.210 .002333	.259 .002874	.309 .003433	.358 .003977	.406 .004515	.455 .005056	.505 .005614	.554 .006155	.603 .006695	.702 .007795	.799 .008877
0.025	.066 .000736	.116 .001294	.165 .001835	.214 .002376	.263 .002917	.313 .003476	.362 .004017	.410 .004558	.459 .005098	.509 .005657	.558 .006198	.607 .006739	.705 .007838	.803 .008920
0.028	.068 .000759	.119 .001318	.167 .001859	.216 .002400	.265 .002941	.315 .003499	.364 .004040	.412 .004581	.461 .005122	.511 .005680	.560 .006221	.609 .006762	.708 .007862	.805 .008944
0.032	.071 .000787	.121 .001345	.170 .001886	.218 .002427	.267 .002968	.317 .003526	.366 .004067	.415 .004608	.463 .005149	.514 .005708	.562 .006249	.611 .006789	.710 .007889	.807 .008971
0.038	.075 .000837	.126 .001396	.174 .001937	.223 .002478	.272 .003019	.322 .003577	.371 .004118	.419 .004659	.468 .005200	.518 .005758	.567 .006299	.616 .006840	.715 .007940	.812 .009021
0.040	.077 .000853	.127 .001411	.176 .001952	.224 .002493	.273 .003034	.323 .003593	.372 .004134	.421 .004675	.469 .005215	.520 .005774	.568 .006315	.617 .006856	.716 .007955	.813 .009037
0.051		.134 .001413	.183 .002034	.232 .002575	.280 .003116	.331 .003675	.379 .004215	.428 .004756	.477 .005297	.527 .005855	.576 .006397	.624 .006934	.723 .008037	.821 .009119
0.064		.144 .001595	.192 .002136	.241 .002676	.290 .003218	.340 .003776	.389 .004317	.437 .004858	.486 .005399	.536 .005957	.585 .006498	.634 .007039	.732 .008138	.830 .009220
0.072			.198 .002202	.247 .002743	.296 .003284	.346 .003842	.394 .004283	.443 .004924	.492 .005465	.542 .006023	.591 .006564	.639 .007105	.738 .008205	.836 .009287
0.078			.202 .002249	.251 .002790	.300 .003331	.350 .003889	.399 .004430	.447 .004963	.496 .005512	.546 .006070	.595 .006611	.644 .007152	.743 .008252	.840 .009333
0.081			.204 .002272	.253 .002813	.302 .003354	.352 .003912	.401 .004453	.449 .004969	.498 .005535	.548 .006094	.598 .006635	.646 .007176	.745 .008275	.842 .009357
0.091			.212 .002350	.260 .002891	.309 .003432	.359 .003990	.408 .004531	.456 .005072	.505 .005613	.555 .006172	.604 .006713	.653 .007254	.752 .008353	.849 .009435
0.094			.214 .002374	.262 .002914	.311 .003455	.361 .004014	.410 .004555	.459 .005096	.507 .005637	.558 .006195	.606 .006736	.655 .007277	.754 .008376	.851 .009458
0.102				.268 .002977	.317 .003518	.367 .004076	.416 .004617	.464 .005158	.513 .005699	.563 .006257	.612 .006798	.661 .007339	.760 .008439	.857 .009521
0.109				.273 .003031	.321 .003572	.372 .004131	.420 .004672	.469 .005213	.518 .005754	.568 .006312	.617 .006853	.665 .007394	.764 .008493	.862 .009575
0.125				.284 .003156	.333 .003697	.383 .004256	.432 .004797	.480 .005338	.529 .005878	.579 .006437	.628 .006978	.677 .007519	.776 .008618	.873 .009700
0.156					.355 .003939	.405 .004497	.453 .005038	.502 .005579	.551 .006120	.601 .006679	.650 .007220	.698 .007761	.797 .008860	.895 .009942
0.188						.417 .004747	.476 .005288	.525 .005829	.573 .006370	.624 .006928	.672 .007469	.721 .008010	.820 .009109	.917 .010191
0.250								.568 .006313	.617 .006853	.667 .007412	.716 .007953	764 .008494	.863 .009593	.961 .010675

bend allowance. The amount of material actually used to make a bend in a piece of sheet metal. Bend allowance depends upon the thickness of the metal and the radius of the bend and is normally found in a bend allowance chart.

If a bend allowance chart is not available, use this formula:

Bend Allowance = $(0.01743 R) + (0.0078 T) \cdot$ degree of bend

R = Bend radius
T = Metal thickness

Layout of a Sheet-Metal Channel

In order to best understand the technique of sheet-metal layout, consider a channel such as that seen in Figure 2-68. This channel is made of 0.040-inch-thick 2024T4 aluminum alloy. The dimension across the bottom of the channel is 2 inches and each side of the channel is 1 inch high.

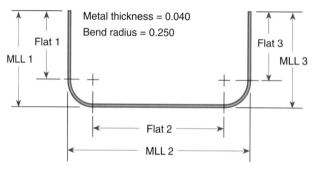

Mold Line Length 1 = 1 inch
MLL 2 = 2 inches
MLL 3 = 1 inch

Figure 2-68. *Sheet-metal channel used for explanation of layout*

To lay out this channel, follow these steps:

1. Choose the correct bend radius.
2. Find the setback.
3. Find the length of each of the flats.
4. Find the bend allowance.
5. Lay out the flat pattern.
6. Draw the sight lines on the flat pattern.

Choose the Correct Bend Radius

Use the chart in Figure 2-64 (Page 105) to choose the correct bend radius for the alloy and temper and the metal thickness. For 0.040, 2024T4 the minimum allowable radius is $\frac{3}{32}$ inch (0.094 inch). Since this is a practical problem, choose a radius of $\frac{1}{4}$ inch (0.250 inch).

Find the Setback

Since all of the angles in this channel are 90° angles, the setback is simply the bend radius of 0.250 plus the metal thickness of 0.040, or 0.290 inch. Move the radius bar of the brake back so the bend tangent is 0.290 inch back from the brake leaf hinge. *See* Figure 2-65, Page 106.

Find the Length of Each of the Flats

The flats, or flat portions of the channel, are equal to the mold line length minus the setback for each of the sides, and the mold line length minus two setbacks for the bottom.

Flat 1 = 1.00 − 0.29 = 0.71 inch
Flat 2 = 2.00 − (2 · 0.29) = 1.42 inch
Flat 3 = 1.00 − 0.29 = 0.71 inch

Find the Bend Allowance

Use the bend allowance chart in Figure 2-67, Page 107, by following a row of figures for 0.040-inch-thick material to the column for $\frac{1}{4}$-inch (0.250) bend radius. The bend allowance is 0.421 inch, which rounds off to the practical dimension of 0.42 inch.

Just to prove that the bend allowance formula on Page 108 works:

$$\text{Bend Allowance} = (0.01743\ R) + (0.0078\ T) \cdot \text{degree of bend}$$
$$= [(0.01743 \cdot 0.25) + (0.0078 \cdot 0.040)] \cdot 90$$
$$= 0.420\ \text{inch}$$

Lay Out the Flat Pattern

When you know the lengths of the flats and the bend allowances, you can lay out the flat pattern. Note that the metal needed to make the channel is less than the dimensions of the outside of the channel. This is because the metal follows the radius of the bend rather than going from mold line to mold line. The larger the bend radius, the less the material used for the channel. *See* Figure 2-69.

flat pattern layout. The pattern for a sheet metal part that has the material used for each flat surface, and for all of the bends marked out with bend-tangent lines drawn between the flats and bend allowances.

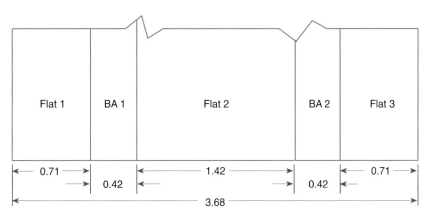

Figure 2-69. *Flat pattern layout of the channel in Figure 2-68*

sight line. A line drawn on a sheet metal layout that is one bend radius from the bend-tangent line. The sight line is lined up directly below the nose of the radius bar in a cornice brake. When the metal is clamped in this position, the bend tangent line is in the correct position for the start of the bend.

Draw the Sight Lines on the Flat Pattern

The pattern laid out in Figure 2-69 is complete, except for a very handy line you can draw to help position the bend tangent line directly at the point the bend should start. Draw a line inside the bend allowance that is one bend radius away from the bend tangent line for the sides of the channel. Put the metal in the brake with Flat 1, Figure 2-70, under the clamp and adjust the position of the brake until the sight line is directly below the edge of the radius bar, as is shown in Figure 2-71. Now clamp the brake on the metal and raise the leaf to make the bend. The bend will begin exactly on the bend tangent line.

Release the clamp and place Flat 3 under the clamp and repeat the process.

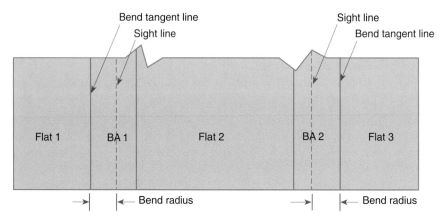

Figure 2-70. *Draw a sight line inside of the bend allowance area that is one bend radius from the bend tangent line that will be under the radius bar.*

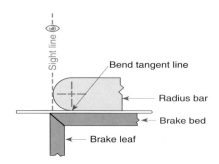

Figure 2-71. *Sight down over the edge of the radius bar and adjust the metal in the brake until the sight line is directly below the tip of the radius bar. Clamp the brake and make the bend.*

relief hole. A hole drilled at the point at which two bend lines meet in a piece of sheet metal. This hole spreads the stresses caused by the bends and prevents the metal cracking.

Folding a Box

You can form a box the same way as the channel just described, but you must also drill relief holes at the intersection of the inside bend tangent lines, and bend it in a box brake. The relief holes, whose diameter is approximately twice the bend radius, relieve stresses in the metal as it is bent and prevent the metal tearing. Two opposite sides of the box are bent first, and then the fingers of the brake adjusted so the folded-up sides will ride up in the cracks between the fingers when the leaf is raised to bend the other two sides. *See* Figure 2-72.

Forming Compound Curves

Large compound curves are formed in sheets of metal in the aircraft factories with drop hammers. The metal to be formed is placed over a heavy metal female die, and a matching male die is dropped onto the sheet metal. It drives the metal down into the female die and forms the compound curves with a minimum of work hardening of the material.

Smaller parts with more drastic curves are formed in hydropresses. The metal to be formed is cut to shape and all of the burrs are removed from its edges. This piece, called a blank, is then placed over a hard steel male die and is held in place by locator pins on the die fitting through index holes in the blank. The die with the blank is placed on the bed of the hydropress and a rubber pad in the ram of the press is forced down over the die with several thousand tons of pressure. The sheet metal is forced down into all of the recesses of the die and down along its sides.

Forming Small Compound-Curved Parts in the Maintenance Shop

It is often necessary to fabricate small compound-curved parts in the maintenance shop, for example, a reinforcing doubler to go inside a fuselage ring when splicing in a replacement section.

compound curve. A curve formed in more than one plane. The surface of a sphere is a compound curve.

doubler. A piece of sheet metal used to strengthen and stiffen a repair in a sheet metal structure.

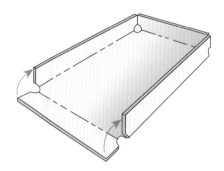

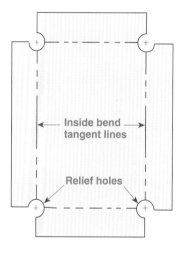

Figure 2-72. *When laying out a box, drill relief holes at the intersections of the inside bend tangent lines. These relief holes relieve stresses that could cause the box to crack in the corners.*

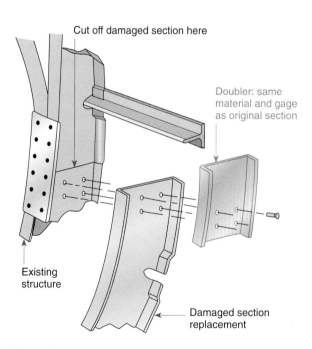

Cut off damaged section here

Doubler: same material and gage as original section

Existing structure

Damaged section replacement

Figure 2-73. *A formed reinforcing doubler is used when splicing a new section of a fuselage ring in place. This doubler has compound curves.*

concave surface. A surface that is curved inward. The outer edges are higher than the center.

extruded angle. A structural angle formed by passing metal heated to its plastic state through specially shaped dies.

convex surface. A surface that is curved outward. The outer edges are lower than the center.

lightening hole. A hole cut in a piece of structural material to get rid of weight without losing any strength. A hole several inches in diameter may be cut in a piece of metal at a point where the metal is not needed for strength, and the edges of the hole are flanged to give it rigidity. A piece of metal with properly flanged lightening holes is more rigid than the metal before the holes were cut.

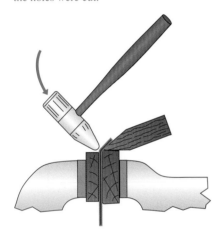

Figure 2-75. *Back the metal up with a piece of tapered hardwood to control the amount of bending done by each blow of the mallet.*

arbor press. A press with either a mechanically or hydraulically operated ram used in a maintenance shop for a variety of pressing functions.

joggle. A small offset near the edge of a piece of sheet metal. It allows one sheet of metal to overlap another sheet while maintaining a flush surface.

To form this reinforcement, first make a forming block of hardwood, such as birch or maple, that fits into the fuselage ring with enough clearance for the thickness of the doubler metal. The radius on the edges of the forming block should be the same as that inside the fuselage ring. The edges should taper back about three degrees so the metal will be bent more than 90° and will spring back to an exact right angle. Make a backup plate of hardwood, the same shape as the forming block, but just enough smaller that it comes to the edge of the radius on the forming block. Drill holes for bolts that are used as alignment pins. These bolts are not used to clamp the blocks together, but rather to keep them from shifting.

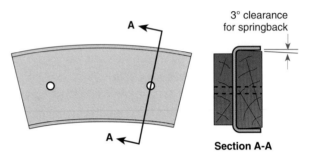

Figure 2-74. *A forming block and backup block used for forming compound curves in a piece of aluminum alloy.*

Cut the sheet metal blank from the same alloy and thickness as is used in the fuselage ring, and drill holes to fit over the alignment pins. Make the blank slightly larger than needed, as it can be trimmed to the exact dimensions when the forming is complete, but do not make it excessively large because one side has to stretch while the other side must shrink. Remove all burrs from the edges of the material, especially in the side that must stretch because a nick or burr could cause the material to crack.

Place the metal between the forming block and backup block and clamp them tightly in a large vise with the concave curve up. Use a soft-face mallet and begin working the metal down from near the ends, working toward the center. Hold a tapered wedge of hardwood behind the metal as is shown in Figure 2-75 and strike the metal as near the edge of the radius as you can. Fold the metal down against the forming block by bending it just a little with each blow of the mallet. As you fold it down, the metal will buckle, but keep these buckles small and they can be worked out by shrinking the metal. Make the bend using as few blows as possible to keep from work-hardening the material, while at the same time use enough blows to keep the buckles down to a size that can be worked out completely.

When you've finished the concave side of the reinforcement, turn the block over so the convex side is up and clamp it tightly in the vise. Begin working this side in the center of the bend and work toward the ends. The metal on this side must be stretched. Use the hardwood wedge behind the metal and form the curve with as few blows as possible, but with enough blows that the metal is stretched gradually so it does not crack and split.

It is often necessary to curve an extruded angle so it will conform to the shape of the structure. Gentle curves can be formed by shrinking or stretching one of the sides. To form a convex curve, stretch the side by hammering it with a soft-face mallet while holding it flat against a piece of steel. This thins and stretches the side and bends the angle. *See* Figure 2-76.

Form a concave curve in an extruded angle by shrinking one of the sides. Place the angle over a piece of hardwood that has had a V-shaped notch cut in it. Hammer on the standing side of the angle. The standing side of the angle must be shrunk to form the curve, and special care must be taken to prevent the material from buckling. It takes practice and skill to know exactly how hard to strike the material to form it without either excessively strain-hardening it or causing it to buckle. *See* Figure 2-77.

There is a commercially available tool for shrinking and stretching the metal. It is called a shrinker/stretcher. It has two pairs of smooth jaws that grip the metal and move toward each other to shrink the metal, or move away from each other to stretch the metal.

Flanging Lightening Holes

Thin sheet metal used for aircraft components usually has plenty of strength, but it often lacks stiffness or rigidity. To increase the stiffness of a part, the metal is often corrugated, and the edges of holes are flanged.

The web of a stamped metal wing rib does not carry an excessive amount of load, and the rib can be made much lighter by cutting large lightening holes that remove a considerable amount of metal. With these holes cut, the rib is still strong enough, but it lacks rigidity. If the edges of these lightening holes are flanged, the rib will be made stiff.

A set of flanging dies is used to flange the lightening holes. The hole is cut in the rib with a hole saw, a punch, or a fly cutter, and the edges are smoothed to prevent their cracking or tearing. The hole is placed over the tapered male die, which is placed in the female die. Pressure is applied with an arbor press that forces the dies together and flanges the edges of the lightening holes. *See* Figure 2-78.

Joggling

It is often necessary to install a doubler inside an aircraft structure and tie it to an extruded angle. In order for the doubler to lie flat against both the skin and the angle, its edges must be joggled, as in Figure 2-79.

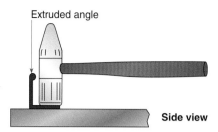

Figure 2-76. *A convex curve can be formed in an extruded angle by stretching one side of the angle.*

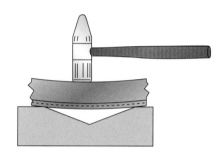

Figure 2-77. *A concave curve can be formed in an extruded angle by shrinking one side of the angle.*

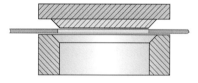

Figure 2-78. *A set of flanging dies is used to flange the edges of a lightening hole to give stiffness to thin sheet metal parts.*

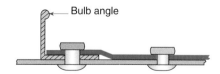

Figure 2-79. *A joggle allows a doubler to fit flat against the skin and also flat against the bulb angle.*

Answers begin on Page 167. Page numbers refer to chapter text.

66. The minimum bend radius for a piece of 0.040 2024T4 aluminum alloy is _____ inch. *Page 105*

67. The bend radius specified for a piece of aircraft sheet metal is the radius of the _____ (inside or outside) of the bend. *Page 105*

68. The metal on the inside of a bend is under a _____ (compressive or tensile) stress. *Page 105*

69. When making a bend in a piece of sheet metal, the metal will be the strongest if the bend is made _____ (with or across) the grain of the metal. *Page 105*

70. The minimum bend radius that should be used on a piece of 0.051-inch 7075-T6 sheet metal is _____ inch. *Page 105*

71. The setback required for making a 45° bend is _____ (more or less) than the setback for a 90° angle. *Page 106*

72. The correct setback for a 135° bend in a piece of 0.040 sheet metal with a ⅛-inch bend radius is _____ inch. *Page 106*

73. The bend allowance for a 90° bend in a piece of 0.051 aluminum alloy bent around a ⅛-inch radius is _____ inch. *Page 107*

74. The bend allowance for a 45° bend in a piece of 0.040 aluminum alloy bent around a ⅛-inch radius is _____ inch. *Page 107*

75. A channel using a ¼-inch bend radius will require _____ (more or less) material than one using a ⅛-inch bend radius. *Page 109*

76. Relief holes drilled in the corner of a pattern for a box should be drilled at the intersection of the _____ lines. *Page 111*

77. A sight line is drawn inside the bend allowance portion of a flat pattern a distance of one _____ from the bend tangent line that is clamped under the radius bar. *Page 110*

78. When forming a concave curve in a piece of sheet metal using a forming block, the forming should begin at the _____ (center or ends) of the curve. *Page 112*

79. When forming a convex curve in a piece of sheet metal using a forming block, the forming should begin at the _____ (center or ends) of the curve. *Page 113*

80. Flanging the edges of a lightening hole in a stamped sheet metal wing rib gives the rib added _____ (strength or stiffness). *Page 113*

Sheet-Metal Joints Using Solid Rivets

Riveted joints are an important part of an aircraft structure, and an aviation maintenance technician must know how to design a joint that will properly carry the stresses from one piece of material to the other. He or she must also know the proper way to install and remove rivets and know how to evaluate rivets.

Rivet Selection

When selecting rivets for a seam in an aircraft skin or for joining other pieces of aircraft sheet metal, take several things into consideration:

- If possible the rivet should not require heat treatment before it is driven. This means that if the required size is not excessive, AD (2117T) alloy rivets should be used rather than D (2017T) or DD (2024T) rivets.

- If magnesium sheets are to be joined, B (5056T) rivets should be used.

- Countersunk head rivets should be used in locations where smooth airflow is important. This essentially means at least on the forward half of the upper surface of the wing.

- Universal head rivets may be used for any location in which a protruding head rivet is required.

- The rivet size and material must be chosen so that the shear strength of the rivet is slightly less than the bearing strength of the sheets of material being joined. This allows the joint to fail by the rivets shearing rather than the metal tearing.

- Rivet size is chosen so the diameter of the rivet is approximately three times the thickness of the thickest sheet being joined.

Rivet Layout

When laying out the rows of rivets, the rivets should be close enough together to get maximum strength in the joint, but should not be so close that the holes weaken the material. The rivets must be placed far enough away from the edge of the metal that it does not tear. *See* Figure 2-80 on the next page.

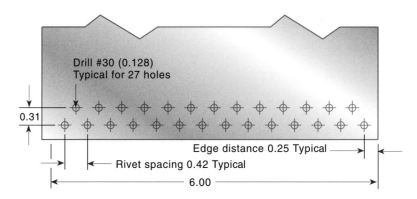

Drill #30 (0.128)
Typical for 27 holes

0.31

Edge distance 0.25 Typical

Rivet spacing 0.42 Typical

6.00

Figure 2-80. *Rivet layout for a two-row splice designed to carry 50% of the metal strength.*

pitch (rivet). The distance between the centers of adjacent rivets installed in the same row.

transverse pitch. *See* gage.

gage (rivet). The distance between rows of rivets in a multirow seam. Gage is also called transverse pitch.

edge distance. The distance between the center of a rivet hole and the edge of the sheet of metal.

Rivet Pitch

Rivet pitch is the distance between the center of adjacent rivet holes in a row. This should not be less than 3 rivet shank diameters, or more than 10 to 12 diameters.

Transverse Pitch

Transverse pitch, also called rivet gage, is the distance between rows of rivets in a multirow seam. Transverse pitch should be 75% of the rivet pitch.

Edge Distance

To prevent the rivets tearing the sheet at the edge, the center of the rivet holes should be no closer to the edge of the sheet than two diameters of the rivet shank for protruding head rivets, or two-and-one-half diameters for flush rivets.

Layout Practice

Consider this problem. We want to rivet together two pieces of 0.040 2024T3 material that are 6 inches wide so that the strength of the riveted joint will carry at least 50% of the strength of the metal. Protruding head rivets are to be used. Take these steps:

• Find the strength needed by the joint.

• Select the rivet.

• Lay out the rivet pattern.

Find the Strength Needed by the Joint

Refer to the chart in Figure 2-14 on Page 75 and find that the minimum tensile strength of 2024-T3 aluminum alloy is 70,000 psi. The sheets we are to join are 0.040 inch thick and 6 inches wide. This gives a cross-sectional area of 0.24 square inch.

$6 \cdot 0.040 = 0.24$ square inch

Find the full strength of this material by multiplying this area by the strength of the material in pounds per square inch.

70,000 psi $\cdot$ 0.24 sq. in. = 16,800 pounds

This joint is required to carry 50% of this strength, so it must carry 8,400 pounds.

$16,800 \cdot 0.50 = 8,400$ pounds

Select the Rivet

Protruding head rivets are to be used, so we will use universal head (MS20470) rivets. The thickest sheet to be joined is 0.040 inches thick, so the rivet diameter should be three times this, or 0.12 inch. The nearest standard diameter to this is $\frac{1}{8}$ inch (0.125). To prevent having to heat-treat the rivets before driving them, choose AD (2117T) rivets.

Refer to the chart in Figure 2-15 on Page 76 to find that each $\frac{1}{8}$-inch 2117T rivet has a shear strength of 331 pounds. The joint should fail in shear rather than in bearing, so check the bearing strength chart of Figure 2-17 on Page 76 and see that the bearing strength for 0.040 sheet with $\frac{1}{8}$-inch rivets is 410 pounds. This shows that the bearing strength and shear strength are reasonably close together, but the bearing strength is greater than the shear strength, so this is a good choice.

The joint must carry 8,400 pounds, so 25.4, or actually 26 rivets, are needed.

You can also select the rivet by using a chart similar to the one in Figure 2-81, which is excerpted from the Advisory Circular 43.13-1B. According to this chart, we will need 7.7 rivets per inch for 100% strength. But since we are only designing for 50% strength, we will need only 3.85 rivets per inch, or for the six-inch width, will need 23.1, or 24 rivets. The two-rivet difference found by the two methods is caused by the use of different sources of information for the strength of the aluminum alloy sheet. When a manufacturer's engineering data disagrees with the general information in AC 43.13-1B, always use the manufacturer's information.

Notice the line below the 4.9 in the $\frac{1}{8}$-inch rivet column in the chart in Figure 2-81. When a $\frac{1}{8}$-inch AD rivet is used in any sheet thicker than 0.025 inch, the rivet will shear. When used in 0.025 or thinner sheet, the metal will tear. *See* Figure 2-81 on the next page.

Number of Rivets or Bolts Required for Structural Repair of Bare 2024-T3 Aluminum Alloy						
Thickness of Metal (inches)	Number of AD Protruding-Head Rivets Needed Per Inch Width of Damage					Number of Bolts Needed
	3/32	1/8	5/32	3/16	1/4	AN-3
0.016	6.5	4.9				
0.020	6.9	4.9	3.9			
0.025	8.6	4.9	3.9			
0.032	11.1	6.2	3.9	3.3		
0.036	12.5	7.0	4.5	3.3	2.4	
0.040	13.8	7.7	5.0	3.5	2.4	3.3
0.051		9.8	6.4	4.5	2.5	3.3
0.064		12.3	8.1	5.6	3.1	3.3
0.081			10.2	7.1	3.9	3.3
0.091			11.4	7.9	4.4	3.3
0.102			12.8	8.9	4.9	3.4
0.128				11.2	6.2	3.4

Notes:
1. For stringers in the upper surface of a wing, or in a fuselage, 80% of the number of rivets shown may be used.
2. For intermediate frames, 60% of the number of rivets shown may be used.
3. For single-lap sheet joints, 75% of the number shown may be used.
4. Combinations of sheet thickness and rivet size *above the line* in each column will fail in bearing (the sheet will tear). Combinations *below the line* will fail in shear (the rivet will shear).

Figure 2-81. *Chart for determining correct number of rivets for a repair*

Lay Out the Rivet Pattern

You can make a good joint by using two rows of rivets. To stagger them, we must have an odd number of rivets, so use 27 rivets with 14 in one row and 13 in the other row. Figure 2-80, Page 116, shows the way this layout is made. The minimum edge distance is 2D, or $\frac{1}{4}$ inch. This leaves 5.5 inches between the two end rivets and we want 14 rivets in this row, so the rivet pitch will be 0.42 inch. This is greater than the minimum pitch, which is 3D or 0.375. The transverse pitch is 75% of the pitch, or 0.31 inch.

Use a fine Sharpie type permanent marker to draw a line 0.25 inch from the end of the metal. This line is the center of the rivets in the first row and is the proper edge distance from the end of the metal. Make a mark across this line 0.25 inch from each edge of the metal. These mark the centers of the end rivet holes. Divide the distance between the end rivets into 13 equal spaces. This is 0.42 inch, and to be sure the spaces are equal, set a pair of dividers to this distance and make a very small mark across your pencil line for the center of each rivet hole.

Draw a line 0.31 inch from the first row of rivets. This is the center line for the second row of rivets. Place a mark across this line midway between each rivet hole in the first row.

Mark the second sheet of metal with a line across its end 0.25 inch from the edge. This ensures that the rivet holes in the bottom sheet will have the proper edge distance.

Hole Preparation for Protruding Head Rivets

After laying out the rivet pattern, you are ready to drill the holes and get the material ready to rivet together. Make a slight depression with a prick punch at each location at which a rivet hole is to be drilled. The prick punch has a sharper point than a center punch, and it can be more accurately positioned at the center of the marks you have just made. Tap the prick punch lightly with a small hammer.

When you've marked all of the rivet holes with a prick punch, support the metal with a sheet of $1/4$-inch steel or a bucking bar and, using a center punch, make the prick punch marks slightly larger to enable the drill to start cutting without walking over the metal. Do not hit the center punch hard enough to distort the metal, but just hard enough to make a depression large enough for the drill point.

Choose the correct size drill for the rivet. The rivet hole must be large enough for the rivet to enter without scraping the sides, and it must not be too large for the rivet to completely fill when its shank is swelled by driving. Figure 2-82 shows the correct drill size to use for each of the most commonly used rivets.

Rivet Size (inch)	Drill Size
3/32	40 (0.098)
1/8	30 (0.128)
5/32	21 (0.159)
3/16	11 (0.191)
1/4	F (0.257)
5/16	O (0.316)
3/8	V (0.377)

Figure 2-82. *Drill size for solid rivet installation*

Drilling the Holes

With the correct-size drill installed in the drill chuck of an air or electric drill motor, drill a pilot hole, usually one rivet-size smaller than the one you will use for joining the metal. In this case, choose a number 40 drill.

Place the metal sheet on a piece of scrap wood so your work bench will not be damaged by the drill. If you are right-handed, hold the drill motor in your right hand and support it away from the metal with your left hand in such a way that your two hands are working against each other. The right hand is trying to force the drill into the metal and the left hand is forcing it back. This allows good control of the drill motor and allows you to drill holes that are straight and true.

When all of the pilot holes are drilled in one of the sheets, use two small C-clamps to clamp the sheets together. Protect the metal from the clamps with small pieces of $1/8$-inch or $1/4$-inch plywood, or use rubber-beaded spring clamps. The edge-distance line you have drawn on the bottom sheet should be visible through the center of the holes in the second row, and the edges of the two sheets should be aligned. Drill through the end holes in the second row and install silver-colored ($3/32$-inch) Cleco fasteners. Now the C-clamps can be removed and all of the other holes drilled with a number 30 drill. Install two copper-colored ($1/8$-inch) Clecos and remove the ones through the pilot holes and drill these holes through with the number 30 drill.

Remove the Clecos and deburr all of the holes by twisting a large drill, one about $1/4$ inch in diameter, in the hole by hand, just enough to remove the burrs from the edges. The holes are now ready for the installation of protruding head rivets.

drill motor. An electric or pneumatic motor that drives a chuck that holds a twist drill. The best drill motors produce high torque, and their speed can be controlled.

pilot hole. A small hole punched or drilled in a piece of sheet metal to locate a rivet hole.

countersinking. Preparation of a rivet hole for a flush rivet by beveling the edges of the holes with a cutter of the correct angle.

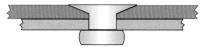

Desired: top skin thicker than head of rivet

Acceptable: top skin as thick as head of rivet

Not acceptable: top skin thinner than head of rivet.

Figure 2-83. *Countersinking*

Figure 2-84. *A countersinking tool has a threaded cutter with a pilot surrounded with an adjustable skirt. The amount the cutter protrudes from the skirt determines the depth the countersink will cut.*

radius dimpling. A process of preparing a hole in sheet metal for flush riveting. A cone-shaped male die forces the edges of the rivet hole into the depression in a female die. Radius dimpling forms a round-edged depression into which the rivet head fits.

Hole Preparation for Flush Rivets

If flush rivets are to be installed, the hole must be either countersunk or dimpled, depending upon the thickness of the metal.

Countersinking

The determination to countersink or dimple depends upon the thickness of the top sheet of metal. The metal must be thicker than the head of the rivet. *See* Figure 2-83.

Use a 100° countersink cutter with a $\frac{1}{8}$-inch pilot, such as the one in Figure 2-84. Use a piece of scrap metal of the same thickness as is being riveted and drill several number 30 holes in it. Use these holes to set the depth of the countersink tool. Adjust the countersink stop until it cuts a depression that allows the rivet head to be flush with the surface of the metal.

Dimpling

If the metal to be joined is too thin to be countersunk, you can dimple it. This is a process in which you press the edges of the rivet hole into a cone shape that allows the rivet head to be flush with the surface of the metal. There are two methods of dimpling a piece of metal: radius dimpling and coin dimpling.

Radius Dimpling

Radius dimpling is done by pressing a male die through the rivet hole and into a female die. The male die is struck a blow with a hammer that forms the metal into the recess that allows the rivet head to be flush with the metal. The edges of a radius-dimpled hole curve smoothly into the hole without any sharp edges. *See* Figure 2-85.

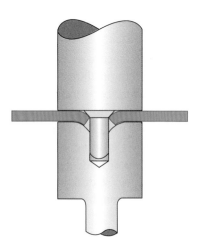

Figure 2-85. *Radius dimpling of a rivet hole*

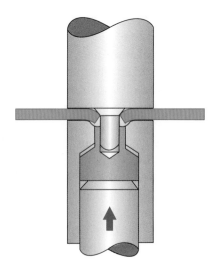

Figure 2-86. *Coin dimpling of a rivet hole*

Coin Dimpling

Coin dimpling is normally done with some type of pneumatic squeezer that exerts enough pressure to properly coin the material. The female die used for coin dimpling is considerably different than that used for radius dimpling. Figure 2-86 shows the dies used for coin dimpling.

To coin-dimple a hole, stick the male die through the hole to be dimpled and press it into the female die. Then force the coining ram up against the edge of the hole. This ram forces the metal tightly between the two dies and forms a dimple with sharp edges.

Coin dimpling can be done with the metal cold, or when dimpling hard metals such as 7075-T6 aluminum alloy, magnesium alloys, or titanium alloys, the dies may be heated with a built-in heater. This heat softens the metal enough that it can be dimpled without cracking. When the metal is heated for dimpling, it is said to be hot dimpled, or thermal dimpled.

When metals of different thicknesses are flush riveted together, a combination of countersinking and dimpling must be used. Figure 2-87 shows the procedure for three conditions.

Rivet Installation

Two methods of driving rivets are commonly used in aircraft construction and maintenance: compression riveting and gun riveting. Compression, or squeeze, riveting is often used when a large number of rivets must be installed in a location where both sides of the material are accessible to a clamp-type riveter. Gun riveting is used for all other locations.

Compression Riveting

When both sides of the material to be riveted are accessible to a rivet squeezer such as those seen in Figure 2-60 on Page 102, use compression riveting.

Set up the riveter for the chosen rivet and the thickness of material by installing the correct cupped set in the stationary jaw and a flat set in the movable jaw. Install washers between the jaws and the dollies, or sets, to adjust the distance they will be separated when the jaws are fully closed. This distance is equal to the total thickness of the materials being joined plus one half of the rivet shank diameter. This will allow the rivet to be upset with the proper size shop head. Squeeze a few rivets in a piece of scrap material of the correct thickness to check the adjustment of the sets. To use this type of riveter, just install the rivet in the hole, place the rivet head in the cupped dolly in the stationary jaw, and pull the trigger. Air pressure on a piston inside the squeezer forces the movable jaw toward the stationary jaw and squeezes the rivet, forming the shop head. *See* Figure 2-88 on the next page.

coin dimpling. A process of preparing a hole in sheet metal for flush riveting. A coining die is pressed into the rivet hole to form a sharp-edged depression into which the rivet head fits.

hot dimpling. A process used to dimple, or indent, the hole into which a flush rivet is to be installed. Hot dimpling is done by clamping the metal between heating elements and forcing the dies through the holes in the softened metal. Hot dimpling prevents hard metal from cracking when it is dimpled.

When top sheet is thick enough; it is countersunk and bottom sheet is left flat.

When top sheet is thin and bottom sheet thick, bottom sheet is countersunk and top sheet coin-dimpled.

When both sheets are too thin for countersinking, both are coin- or radius-dimpled.

Figure 2-87. *Hole preparation for flush riveting*

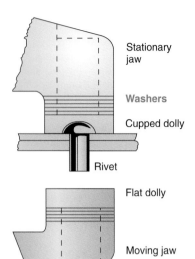

Stationary
jaw

Washers

Cupped dolly

Rivet

Flat dolly

Moving jaw

Figure 2-88. *Adjustment of the sets of a squeeze riveter is done by adding or removing washers between the jaws and the dollies.*

Gun Riveting

The greatest majority of rivets used in aircraft maintenance and repair are driven with rivet guns and bucking bars. Figure 2-89 shows the steps involved in properly driving a solid rivet. These steps are:

1. Install the correct rivet set.
2. Adjust the hitting force of the gun.
3. Install the rivet in the hole and position the rivet set against the rivet head.
4. Select the correct bucking bar and position it against the rivet shank.
5. Drive the rivet.
6. Evaluate the rivet.

   See Figure 2-89.

Install the Correct Rivet Set

Install the correct set for the rivet being driven in the rivet gun. The radius of the correct set is slightly larger than the radius of the rivet head, which allows the blows from the rivet gun to concentrate at the center of the rivet head. When the correct set is installed, screw a beehive spring onto the rivet gun to prevent the set dropping out of the gun.

Adjust the Hitting Force of the Gun

Hold the rivet set against a piece of scrap wood and pull the trigger. The set should hit the wood with a good solid blow, but not split it. Experience will give you the feel of the proper force the gun should have. If you are not sure of the adjustment, drive a few rivets in scrap material to get the feel of the proper adjustment.

Install the Rivet and Position the Set

The shank of the rivet chosen for installation should stick through the material by one-and-one-half diameters of the shank. Position the set so that it is exactly square with the material being riveted.

Select the Bucking Bar and Position It Against the Rivet Shank

Choose a bucking bar that is the proper weight for the rivet being driven and hold it absolutely flat against the end of the rivet shank. Figure 2-59 on Page 101 lists the correct weight of bucking bar for the rivet size.

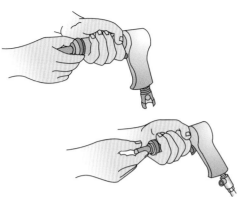

A Select and install correct rivet set in gun.

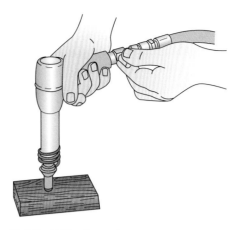

B Adjust hitting force of gun.

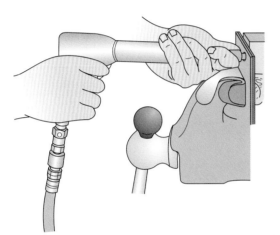

C Hold rivet set against rivet head.

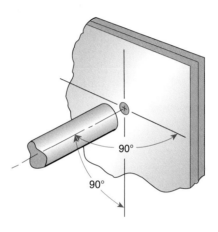

D Rivet set must be perfectly square with material being riveted.

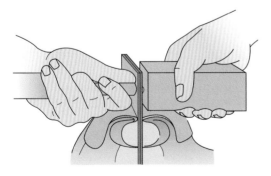

E Position bucking bar against end of rivet shank and drive rivet.

Figure 2-89. *Correct procedures for driving a solid rivet*

Drive the Rivet

Press the rivet set against the rivet head and the bucking bar against the rivet shank. Hold enough pressure on the bucking bar to try to force the rivet out of the hole, and just enough more pressure on the rivet gun that holds the rivet head against the metal. Holding this balance of pressure, pull the trigger of the gun, and drive the rivet with as few blows as possible.

Evaluate the Rivet

shop head. The head of a rivet which is formed when the shank is upset against a bucking bar.

A properly driven rivet should have a shop head that is round with slightly bowed sides. The head is flat and parallel with the material, and the diameter of the head is one and one-half times the diameter of the rivet shank, and its thickness is one-half the shank diameter.

Some of the more common problems with their causes and suggested remedies are listed in Figure 2-90.

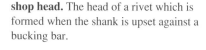
Correctly-driven universal head rivet.

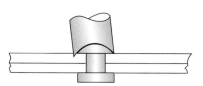
Skin marked by rivet set. Set not centered on head. Remove rivet and burnish skin.

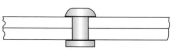
Rivet swelled between sheets. Parts not properly held together, or chips between sheets. Remove rivet, correct condition.

Formed head high on one side. Bucking bar held at angle when riveting. Remove rivet if head too thin on one side.

Correctly-driven 100°-countersunk rivet.

Thin head. Rivet too short or hit too hard. Remove rivet.

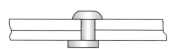
Rivet head clinched. Bucking bar held at angle when rivet was driven. Remove rivet.

Holes out of line. Redrill hole and install larger rivet.

Countersink too deep. Wrong rivet or wrong countersink. Remove rivet and replace with next larger size.

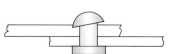
Open head. Set not held straight on head, or hole drilled at angle. "D" rivet remove; "AD" rivet drive more.

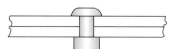
High head. Too long a shank, or not driven enough. "D" rivet remove; "AD" rivet drive more.

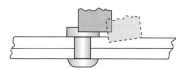
Cut formed head. Bucking bar did not cover entire end of rivet. Remove rivet.

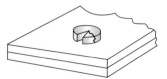
Cracked head. Hard rivet or hit too long. Remove rivet.

Figure 2-90. *Rivet evaluation*

Removal of Bad Rivets

To remove a rivet, follow the procedure in Figure 2-91.

1. Use a center punch to make a drill-starting indentation in the center of the manufactured head. AD rivets have a small dimple in the center of their head that makes this step easy.

2. Drill a straight hole in the center of the head with a drill that is one drill size smaller than the one used for the rivet. Drill this hole only through the head.

3. Knock the drilled head off the rivet shank with a cape chisel or pry it off with a pin punch.

4. Use a bucking bar to back up the skin around the rivet and punch the shank out of the skin with a pin punch.

NACA Method of Flush Riveting

The NACA (National Advisory Committee for Aeronautics) method of flush riveting uses a universal head or flush head rivet on the inside of the structure with the shop head formed in a countersunk hole in the outside skin. Drill the rivet hole and countersink the outside skin. Insert the rivet from

Make center punch mark in center of manufactured head.

Drill through head with drill one size smaller than used for rivet.

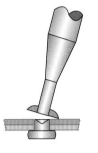
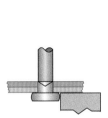

Use pin punch the size of hole, pry head off rivet.

Buck up metal with bucking bar beside shop head and use pin punch to drive shank from the metal.

Figure 2-91. *Procedure for removing a solid rivet*

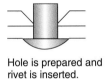

Hole is prepared and rivet is inserted.

Shop head is formed.

Shop head is trimmed flush with the skin with microshaver.

Figure 2-92. *NACA method of flush riveting*

the inside. The shop head is formed in the countersunk depression. Use either a squeeze riveter or a gun. After driving the rivet, mill off the excess portion of the shop's head flush with the skin with an air-driven microshaver. *See* Figure 2-93.

Team Riveting

Manufacturing and repairing an airplane often requires two people to drive rivets. The operator of the rivet gun is usually on the outside and the rivet bucker is on the inside. When the two cannot communicate directly, a code of taps may be used.

When the bucker is in position and ready for the rivet to be driven, he or she taps on the shank of the rivet one time. The riveter feels this tap through the rivet gun and knows to drive the rivet. If the rivet is driven correctly the

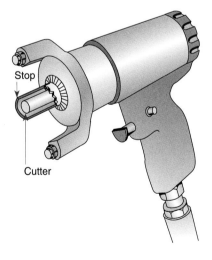

Stop

Cutter

Figure 2-93. *An air-driven microshaver*

bucker taps twice before the rivet set is removed. This is a signal that the rivet is good and they should proceed to the next rivet. Three taps on the rivet means that the rivet is bad and will have to be removed. The riveter marks the rivet for removal and goes on to the next one.

STUDY QUESTIONS: SHEET-METAL JOINTS USING SOLID RIVETS

Answers begin on Page 167. Page numbers refer to chapter text.

81. The solid aluminum alloy rivet recommended for magnesium skin is made of alloy _____ . *Page 115*

82. The rivet to use for joining two sheets of metal should have a diameter at least _____ times the thickness of the thickest sheet being joined. *Page 115*

83. The distance between the center of the rivet holes in a single row of rivets is called the rivet _____ . *Page 116*

84. When a single row of MS20470AD-4 rivets is laid out, the center of the holes should be no closer than _____ inch and no farther apart than _____ inches. *Page 116*

85. When laying out a two-row riveted seam, the rivet pitch is ½ inch, and the transverse pitch, or gage, should be _____ inch. *Page 116*

86. When making a rivet seam using MS20470AD-3 rivets, make sure that the center of the rivet holes is no closer to the edge of the sheet than _____ inch. *Page 116*

87. A riveted joint should be designed so it will fail in _____ (bearing or shear). *Page 117*

88. When a rivet pattern is laid out on a piece of aluminum alloy, the marks should be made with a/an _____ . *Page 118*

89. The correct size drill to use for a ⅛-inch rivet is a number _____ . *Page 119*

90. Pilot holes for ⅛-inch rivets should be made with a number _____ drill. *Page 119*

91. The determination to countersink or dimple a skin in preparation for flush riveting is determined by the _____ of the skin. *Page 120*

92. Two methods of dimpling are:
    a. _____
    b. _____
    Page 120

93. Hot, or thermal, dimpling is a form of _____ dimpling using heated dies. *Page 121*

94. The inside radius of a rivet set should be slightly _____ (larger or smaller) than the radius of the head of the rivet. *Page 122*

95. The shank of a rivet should stick out of the sheet by _____ times the rivet shank diameter. *Page 122*

96. A properly formed shop head on a rivet should have a diameter of _____ times the diameter of the rivet shank. *Page 124*

97. A properly formed shop head on a rivet should have a thickness of _____ of the rivet shank diameter. *Page 124*

98. The shop head of a rivet driven by the NACA flush rivet procedure is shaved flush with the skin with a _____ . *Page 125*

99. When riveting by the team method when it is impossible to see the person holding the rivet gun, the bucker indicates a good rivet by tapping on the rivet _____ time/times. *Page 125*

Repair of Sheet-Metal Structure

Aviation Maintenance Technicians repair damaged sheet-metal aircraft structures. All repairs must meet certain basic requirements:

- The repair must restore the structure to its original or equivalent condition of strength and rigidity.
- The repair must be as lightweight as possible, consistent with strength.
- The repair must not distort the aerodynamic shape of the aircraft.
- The repair must not change the weight of a component in such a way that it can cause flutter or vibration.
- The repair must be approved by the FAA.

Appraisal of the Damage

The first and perhaps the most essential step in repairing an aircraft structure is to carefully and accurately appraise the damage. Decide whether to repair or replace the damaged component, and if you decide to repair it, you must decide whether to repair it yourself or to remove it and have a repair station that specializes in this type of repair do the work.

Obvious damage is easy to appraise, but it is often the hidden damage that makes the difference between a profitable repair and one that loses money for the shop. You must consider the possibility that any visible damage may extend into the structure where it is not visible. Stresses that caused the damage may have deformed or broken structural components not visible from the surface.

Carefully examine all rivets adjacent to areas that have been strained. If you can slip a thin feeler gage between either rivet head and the skin, it's possible the rivet has been stretched. Remove the rivet and examine the hole for indication of elongation. Elongated rivet holes should be drilled out for the next larger size rivet if the edge distance and rivet spacing allows.

Sometimes a damaged aircraft has been allowed to sit in the open and collect water and dirt inside the structure or, even worse, to rest on bare concrete for a period of time. In these cases it is extremely important to examine carefully for evidence of corrosion. Corrosion can require replacement of skins or structural members that were not damaged in the original accident.

Modern aircraft are designed to have maximum strength and a minimum weight, and all repairs must be made so as not to compromise this strength. The manufacturers issue structural repair information for normal repairs, and their engineering departments are available to assist in designing repairs that are more complex than those shown in the repair manual.

Classification of Damage

Damage can be classified into three categories: negligible, repairable, and damage that requires replacement of the component.

Negligible damage is that which does not affect the airworthiness of the aircraft. Typical examples of negligible damage are smooth dents in the outside skin that are free of cracks and sharp corners, and that are not caused by stress wrinkles.

Repairable damage normally consists of the damage that can be repaired by the replacement of skins and repairs that are described in the structural repair manual.

Damage that requires replacement of a component is damage that involves extensive corrosion, or parts that are damaged beyond the limits specified in the structural repair manual.

Repair of Cracks in Noncritical Areas

Engine cowling and baffles are subjected to a great deal of vibration and often crack. If the crack is not stopped, it will grow until the component is seriously damaged and will require replacement or extensive repair.

When a crack is discovered, drill a small hole with a #40 or #30 drill slightly beyond the end of the visible crack. This hole distributes the stresses at the end of the crack so they will be less than the tensile strength of the metal. Install a patch over the crack to prevent vibration from causing further damage to the weakened component.

Surface Patch for Stressed Skin

One typical repair used as a practical project in many Aviation Maintenance Technician schools is a patch for a piece of stressed skin that carries all of the strength of the skin from one side of the damage into the patch, then from the patch into the skin on the other side.

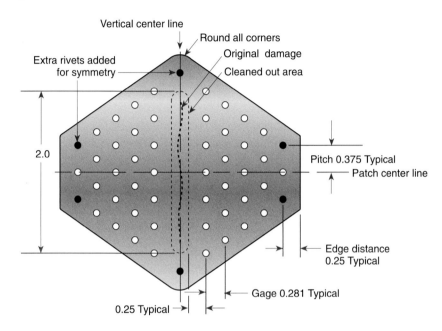

Figure 2-94. *Typical patch for a crack in a piece of stressed skin. This patch is designed to carry 100% of the strength of the skin across the patch.*

Assume the crack is in a piece of 0.032-inch 2024-T3 aluminum alloy skin, and can be cleaned out to a length of 2.0 inches with the ends rounded. The patch will be made of the same alloy and thickness as the original skin. For this repair determine the number of rivets by using the chart from Advisory Circular 43.13-1B that is shown in Figure 2-81 on Page 118.

Follow these steps:

1. Clean out the damage and round the ends of the cleaned-out area. Use a fine Sharpie-type of permanent marker, and mark a horizontal and a vertical center line across the hole.

2. Cut a piece of 0.032-inch 2024-T3 aluminum alloy about 5 inches square. Clean the surface and spray on a very light coat of zinc chromate primer. Using the fine Sharpie, draw a horizontal and vertical center line on the patch material. Hold the patch under the cleaned-out damage with the center lines crossing in the center of the hole. Trace the outline of the hole on the patch material.

3. Select the rivet. This repair does not require flush riveting, so an MS20470AD universal-head rivet will be used. For 0.032-inch skin use a $\frac{3}{32}$-inch rivet. Its diameter is approximately three times the thickness of the skin.

4. Find the number of rivets required. Use the chart in Figure 2-81. Follow the column for a $\frac{3}{32}$-inch rivet down to the row for 0.032-inch sheet. This shows that you will need 11.1 rivets per inch of cleaned-out damage. This will require at least 22.2, or actually, 23 rivets on each side of the damage.

5. Determine the rivet pitch. The minimum pitch for a $\frac{3}{32}$-inch rivet is 3D, or $\frac{9}{32}$ (0.28) inch, and the maximum pitch is 12D, or $1\frac{1}{8}$ (1.125) inch. A good choice is 4D, or $\frac{3}{8}$ (0.375) inch.

6. Decide on the edge distance. The recommended distance between the center of the rivet hole and the edge of the sheet is at least 2D. Using the minimum does not allow for ever having to use a larger rivet, such as would be needed if a hole were damaged. A good choice is $\frac{1}{4}$ (0.25) inch which is 2.7D, and it allows a $\frac{1}{8}$-inch rivet to be used if it is ever necessary. Draw a vertical line $\frac{1}{4}$ (0.25) inch from each edge of the damage outline on the patch.

7. Determine the number of rivets in each row. Twenty-three rivets are needed on each side of the patch, and the pitch is 0.375. This allows 7 rivets in the first row. To stagger the rivets, there should be 6 rivets in the second, 5 in the third, and 4 in the fourth row. This leaves 1 rivet for the fifth row.

8. Lay out the first row of rivets. Mark the center of one rivet at the intersection of the center line and the edge distance line. Mark the center of the other 6 rivets in this row. Space them at $\frac{3}{8}$ (0.375) inch intervals on both sides of the center rivet.

9. Choose the gage, or transverse pitch. This is 75% of the rivet pitch, or $\frac{9}{32}$ (0.281) inch. Draw 4 lines parallel to the first row of rivets on each side of the damage. The rows are separated by 0.281 inch.

10. Mark the location of the 6 rivets in the second row. These rivets are centered between the rivets in the first row and are on the first rivet gage line.

11. Mark the location of the 5 rivets in the third row. These rivets are in horizontal alignment with the rivets in the first row.

12. Mark the location of the 4 rivets in the fourth row. These are aligned with the rivets in the second row.

13. Mark the location of the single rivet in the center of the fifth row. This is all of the rivets needed to carry the load into the patch on one side of the

damage and out on the other side, but to make the patch symmetrical, place 2 more rivets in the fifth row.

Symmetry is important, not just to make the patch look good, but to avoid abrupt changes in the cross-sectional area and prevent stress risers that could cause structural failure.

14. Draw lines through the end rivets in each row and mark the location of a rivet at the intersection of these lines and the vertical center line. These two rivets do not carry any stress across the patch, but they prevent the edges of the patch curling up.

15. Draw lines for the outside of the patch 0.25 inch from the center line of all the outside rivets. Cut the patch along the outside lines, round all of the corners, and deburr the edges of the patch.

16. Mark the center of each rivet hole with a prick punch, and then make a drill-starting indentation at each mark with a center punch.

17. Drill all the rivet holes with a #40 drill, and deburr the edges of the holes on both sides of each piece of metal.

18. Mark the location of a rivet hole on the damaged skin 0.25 inch from the edge of the cleaned-out damage along the horizontal center line. Make a center punch mark at this location and drill a #40 hole.

19. Put the patch over the damaged area and hold it in place with a silver-colored Cleco fastener. Align the center line on the patch with the center line on the skin and drill a #40 hole through the patch along the center line on the opposite side of the damage. Secure this with a Cleco fastener.

20. With the patch in place, drill the rest of the rivet holes.

21. Remove the patch, deburr all the holes, and slightly crimp the edges of the patch as shown in Figure 2-95. Spray the skin where the patch is to be installed, and the inside of the patch with a light coat of zinc chromate primer.

22. Rivet the patch in place.

Flush Patch

When you must patch an aircraft skin in a location where a smooth surface is needed, a flush patch such as the one in Figure 2-96 is installed. The damage in this example is in a piece of 0.025-inch 2024-T3 aluminum alloy skin, and it is cleaned out to a 1.5-inch-diameter hole. The repair must be flush, so MS20426AD rivets will be used. *See* Figure 2-96 on the next page.

symmetrical. The same on either side of the center line.

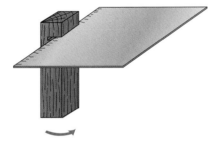

Figure 2-95. *Slightly crimp the edges of the patch by using a small hardwood stick with a saw cut across it at one end. There should be just enough crimp to prevent the edges of the sheet rising up.*

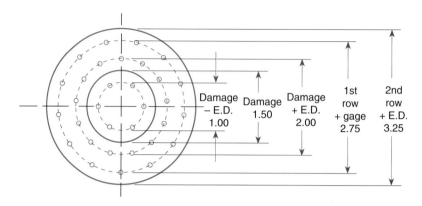

Figure 2-96. *Flush patch for stressed skin structure carrying 100% of the skin strength.*

Prepare the patch material of the same alloy and thickness as the original skin, and follow these steps:

1. Using a permanent fine-line marker, draw a horizontal and vertical center line across the damage, and clean it out to a circular hole.

2. Determine the number of rivets needed. Use the chart in Figure 2-81 on Page 118. For 0.025-inch skin and $\frac{3}{32}$-inch rivets, 8.6 rivets per inch are needed on both sides of the cleaned-out damage. The cleaned-out area is 1.5 inches in diameter, which requires 12.9, or 13 rivets on each side.

3. Plan the layout of the rivets. A total of 26 rivets is needed to carry 100% of the skin strength, and the layout can use the same minimums used in the previous repair:

    Edge distance — 0.25 inch

    Pitch — 0.375 inch

    Gage — 0.281 inch

4. Prepare the patch material using the same alloy and thickness as the damaged skin. Using a permanent fine-line marker, draw a horizontal and a vertical center line and a 1.5-inch-diameter circle representing the cleaned-out damage.

5. Lay out the first row of rivets. This row is laid out on a circle drawn one edge distance, or 0.25 inch, from the edge of the hole. The diameter of this circle is 2.0 inches and its circumference is $\pi \cdot D$, or $3.14 \cdot 2 = 6.28$ inches.

    In order to have 13 rivets in each row, the spacing of the inner row is $6.28 \div 13 = 0.48$ inch. This is slightly more than 5D which is well within the 3D to 12D range. Make a mark for the center of each rivet in this row.

6. Lay out the second row of rivets. The row is laid out on a circle that is 75% of the pitch from the first row. This circle has a diameter of 2.75 inches and a circumference of $3.14 \cdot 2.75 = 8.64$ inches. The 13 rivets in this row

therefore have a spacing of 0.66 inch, which is 7D, and is within the recommended range. Make a mark for each rivet in this row, placing it between the rivets in the first row.

7. Determine the outside diameter of the patch. An edge distance of 0.25 inch outside the second row of rivets gives the patch an outside diameter of 3.25 inches.

8. Lay out the rivets for the insert. Draw a circle one edge distance, or 0.25 inch, inside the circle that represents the cleaned-out damage. This circle has a diameter of 1.0 inch. Six rivets laid out around this circle will have a pitch of approximately 5.6D which is a good choice. Mark a rivet location every 60° around this circle.

9. Cut the patch along the outside diameter line and smooth its edges. Use a prick punch to mark each rivet hole and follow this with a center punch. Drill all of the holes with a #40 drill, and deburr their edges.

10. Drill a #40 hole one edge distance, or 0.25 inch, from the edge of the cleaned out damage on the skin along the vertical center line. Fasten the patch over the damage with a silver-colored Cleco fastener. Align the center line on the patch with that on the skin, and drill a hole through the skin across the patch from the first hole. Insert another Cleco fastener and drill all of the rest of the holes.

11. Mark, and cut out the insert from a piece of metal the same thickness as the original skin. Draw a circle one edge distance, or 0.25 inch, inside of the insert and drill six #40 holes to match the holes in the patch.

12. Dimple all of the holes in the original skin, the patch, and the insert with a 100° radius-dimpling tool.

13. Spray the skin, the patch, and the insert with zinc chromate primer and install the patch on the inside of the skin and hold it in place with Cleco fasteners. Install all of the rivets in the holes in the skin. Place the insert in the hole in the skin and rivet it to the patch.

Stringer Repair

Repair damaged bulb-angle stringers by removing the damaged section and inserting a filler, then reinforcing both sides with the same alloy and thickness of metal as the damaged stringer. *See* Figure 2-97 on the next page.

Follow these steps:

1. Remove the damaged portion of the stringer.

2. Cut a strip of aluminum of the same thickness and alloy as the bulb angle that is as wide as the distance between the bulb and the flat leg of the angle.

3. Cut and form an angle of this same material that has the same dimensions as the bulb angle.

bulb angle. An L-shaped metal extrusion having an enlarged, rounded edge that resembles a bulb on one of its legs.

4. Lay out a single line of rivets along the center line of the standing leg of the bulb angle and the filler. There should be at least 5 rivets on each side of the damage. Observe the minimum edge distance and the recommended pitch distance for these rivets.

5. Drill rivet holes through the stringer, the reinforcing angle, the filler, and the strip, and rivet the three sections of the repair together, using MS20470AD rivets.

6. Rivet the filler to the skin through the original rivet holes.

7. Rivet the reinforcing angle to the skin with the same rivet spacing as is used for the bulb angle stringer. Stagger these holes between those in the stringer.

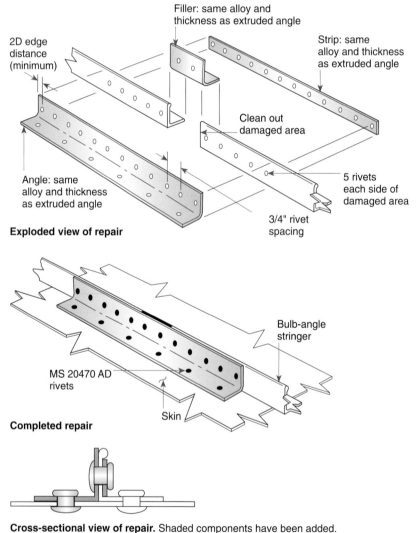

Figure 2-97. *A typical stringer repair*

Repairs to Pressure Vessels

When the skin of a pressurized aircraft is damaged, it must be repaired in such a way that the pressurizing air does not leak through the repair. Figure 2-98 shows a typical flush patch to a pressure vessel skin. The damage is cleaned out and all the corners are given an ample radius to prevent cracks.

Make the doubler and patch of the same alloy and thickness as the damaged skin, and observe the minimums for the rivet spacing and edge distances. Apply a coating of sealant to the doubler, and rivet it in place. Then rivet the patch to the doubler.

pressure vessel. The portion of a pressurized aircraft structure that is sealed and pressurized.

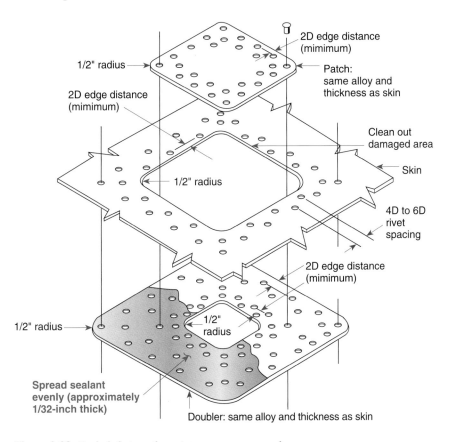

Figure 2-98. *Exploded view of repair to a pressure vessel*

Repairs to Floats and Seaplane Hulls

Floats and seaplane hulls are repaired in much the same way as pressure vessels. The patch is designed in the same way as one for any other structure exposed to similar loads, but before the patch is riveted in place, it is coated with a resilient sealant, and the rivets are dipped in the sealant before they are driven.

Replacement of a Section of the Aircraft Skin

It is sometimes advisable to replace an entire section of skin rather than patching it. When doing this, be sure to support the structure so the skin being replaced is not under any kind of load. Carefully drill out all the rivets holding the old skin, and cut the new skin of the same thickness and alloy as the one you are replacing. Mark the rivet holes with a transfer punch. Drill enough rivet holes to secure the new skin with Cleco fasteners and secure it in place. Locate the remaining holes with a hole finder. The manufacturer of the aircraft can often furnish replacement skins that have all of the rivet holes located with pilot holes. It is especially important to get a new skin from the manufacturer when replacing a skin with compound curves or corrugations, as these are very difficult to fabricate.

If you are not replacing an entire skin, but making a new seam, determine the number of rivets by duplicating the number of rivets in the nearest seam that is inboard or forward of this new seam.

Approval of the Repair

Before aircraft progressed to their present state of complexity, repairs and alterations were relatively simple. Information included in Advisory Circular 43.13-1B *Acceptable Methods, Techniques, and Practices — Aircraft Inspection and Repair* and Advisory Circular 43.13-2A *Acceptable Methods, Techniques, and Practices — Aircraft Alteration* was used as authority for the work. Now that aircraft fly so fast and carry such great loads, and the structure is so light, this generalized information is no longer adequate for use as authority.

To get a repaired or altered aircraft approved for return to service, you must complete an FAA Form 337 *Major Repair and Alteration (Airframe, Powerplant, Propeller, or Appliance)*. *This* form requires two types of approval: approval of the data, and approval of the work. The specific design of the repair or the data used for the repair must be approved by the FAA, then an authorized person or agency must examine the repair and sign a statement that the repair conforms in all respects to the data that has been approved.

Before performing a major repair or major alteration, carefully research the project and consult the aircraft manufacturer if necessary. Make a sketch or drawing of the work and identify all pertinent materials and components. Include or reference all approved data. Submit this outline of the work to be done to the local FAA Maintenance Inspector for his or her approval. If there is any reason that this repair might not be approved, it is far better to learn of it before the work is begun.

Answers begin on Page 167. **Page numbers refer to chapter text.**

100. The minimum recommended edge distance for a rivet in a repair is _____ times the rivet shank diameter. *Page 130*

101. If it is possible to slip a thin feeler gage under the head of a rivet that is beyond the area of visible damage, it is possible that the rivet has been _____ . *Page 128*

102. Aluminum alloy structure that has been allowed to rest on a bare concrete floor for some time is likely to be damaged by _____ . *Page 128*

103. A small crack in a piece of aircraft sheet metal can be stopped from growing by drilling a hole with a number _____ or _____ drill at its end. *Page 128*

104. The limits for the distance between the centers of adjacent rivets in a stressed skin patch are between _____D and _____D. *Page 130*

105. When patching an aircraft structural component, the material used for the patch should be of the same alloy and _____ as the damaged material. *Page 129*

106. When making a new seam in a piece of aircraft skin, you can duplicate the number of rivets in the nearest seam that is _____ or _____ of the seam. *Page 136*

107. Information included in Advisory Circular 43.13-1B _____ (may or may not) be used as approved data for making a major repair on an aircraft. *Page 136*

108. Two types of approval must be made for all major repairs and major alterations. These are approval of the
    a. _____
    b. _____
       Page 136

Aircraft Welding

A major technical breakthrough in the early days of aviation history was the replacement of the wood-and-wire-truss fuselage structure with a welded-steel tubing structure. The steel tubular structure is stronger, easier to build and maintain, and much safer in the event of a crash.

Most welding of early-day aircraft structure was done with oxyacetylene torches because the available electric arc equipment did not allow sufficient control for the thin-wall tubing used in aircraft structure.

World War II saw the development of the shielded arc process of welding, which used electronically controlled equipment making arc-welding of aircraft structure practical. This equipment has been developed and perfected to the extent that it is now an accepted method of constructing and repairing aircraft tubular steel structure.

The high-strength alloys used in modern aircraft construction are more difficult to weld than simple steel tubing, so much welding is done in specially equipped shops by technicians who specialize in welding. All technicians, however, should be well aware of the different types of welding and know their advantages and limitations.

Remember:
A certified aviation maintenance technician does not need to be able to weld, but must be capable of determining whether or not a weld is airworthy, and be able to return a welded part to service. Someone else can do the actual welding, but the A&P must certify it as airworthy and sign it off.

Types of Welding

Three basic types of welding are used in aircraft construction and maintenance, and each has applications for which it is best suited. Gas welding is generally best suited for welding thin sheets and tubes made of steel, aluminum, and magnesium. Electric arc welding is best suited for heavy sheets and castings. Electric resistance welding is mainly used for welding thin sheets of aluminum alloy and stainless steel for such applications as fuel tanks.

Gas Welding

Gas welding is a fusion process in which heat is supplied by burning a mixture of oxygen and a fuel gas such as acetylene or hydrogen. A welding torch is used to mix the gases in the proper proportions and to direct the flame against the parts to be welded. The molten edges of the parts then flow together, and after cooling form a single solid piece. Usually a welding rod is dipped into the molten pool to add additional material to the joint to increase its strength.

Acetylene is the most widely used fuel gas because of its high flame temperature when it is mixed with oxygen. The temperature of an oxyacetylene flame ranges from about 5,700°F to 6,300°F, which is far above the melting temperature of all commercially used metals.

Hydrogen is often used as a fuel gas for welding aluminum and magnesium because it produces a very clean flame. The temperature of an oxyhydrogen flame is slightly lower than that of an oxyacetylene flame, and it is hot enough for welding aluminum.

Gas Welding Equipment

Gas welding equipment may be either portable or stationary. Stationary equipment usually consists of an oxygen and an acetylene manifold that supplies several welding stations. Portable welding equipment is normally mounted on a hand truck so it can be moved to any location in the shop.

The typical equipment needed for gas welding consists of:

- Oxygen and acetylene cylinders
- Oxygen and acetylene regulators with pressure gages
- Welding hoses
- Welding torch with extra tips and connectors
- Welding goggles, torch lighter, special wrench, and fire extinguisher

Fuel Gases

Most gas welding for aircraft maintenance is oxyacetylene welding, and in this introduction, we will consider only the two gases oxygen and acetylene.

Oxygen

Oxygen is a colorless, odorless gas that does not burn by itself. It supports combustion and combines with other fuel gases to cause them to release a great amount of heat when they are burned.

Oxygen makes up about 21% of the volume of the earth's atmosphere, and is one of the major components of water. Commercial oxygen is produced by cooling air to such a low temperature that it changes into a liquid. Then, at a carefully controlled temperature, the liquid air is allowed to boil and release its oxygen. Another way of producing commercial oxygen is to break water into its two components, hydrogen and oxygen, electrolytically. Both gases are collected and compressed for use in welding. Welding oxygen is called "technical" oxygen, and differs from aviators' breathing oxygen because stringent controls are used to remove all traces of water from breathing oxygen. Aviators' breathing oxygen can be used for welding, but technical oxygen must never be used to charge the breathing oxygen system in an aircraft.

Acetylene

Acetylene is a colorless, flammable gas that has a distinctive unpleasant odor detectable even when it is greatly diluted with air. Acetylene is not a natural gas, but is produced by the reaction of calcium carbide with water.

Acetylene is stable when stored under a pressure of less than 15 psi, but at pressures above this, it becomes dangerously unstable. Because of this instability, it is stored in steel cylinders filled with a porous material such as a mixture of asbestos and charcoal. The mixture is then saturated with

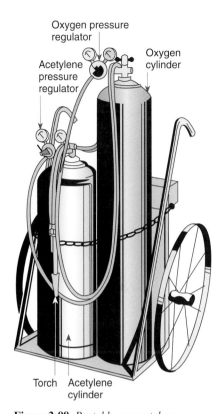

Figure 2-99. *Portable oxyacetylene welding equipment*

acetone. The acetone absorbs approximately 25 times its own volume of acetylene, and allows the cylinder to be charged to a pressure of 250 psi without the acetylene becoming unstable.

Gas Storage Cylinders

Oxygen is stored in seamless steel cylinders under a pressure of 2,200 psi at 70°F. The cylinders for technical oxygen are painted solid green, but those used for aviators' breathing oxygen are green with a white band around the top. Oxygen cylinders are fitted with a cylinder valve that has a safety disk that will burst and release the gas if the cylinder pressure builds up to a dangerous level. The valve has a handwheel and a stem seal that seals when the valve is fully open. For this reason, when a regulator is attached to the cylinder, the valve must be fully open to prevent loss of oxygen around the stem. The outlet nipple on an oxygen cylinder has male threads to prevent the possibility of installing an acetylene regulator.

A steel cap must be screwed onto an oxygen cylinder to cover the valve any time the regulator is not attached. This prevents damage if the cylinder is knocked over. If a valve is ever knocked off an oxygen cylinder, the escaping high-pressure gas will convert the cylinder into a jet-propelled missile that can do extensive damage to anyone or anything it hits.

Acetylene gas is stored in a seamless steel cylinder that has a recessed ring around both ends. The head ring protects the valve from damage, and the foot ring protects the cylinder from moisture and corrosion. The stem of the cylinder valve has a square shank on which a special wrench fits, and the regulator screws into female threads. Special safety fuse plugs screw into both the top and bottom of the cylinder. In case of a fire, a low-melting-point alloy in a small passage in these plugs melts and allows the gas to escape without building up its pressure to a dangerous level. The holes in these plugs are too small for the flame to burn back into the cylinder and cause an explosion.

Pressure Regulators

Pressure regulators attach to the cylinder valves of both the oxygen and acetylene cylinders. These are normally two-stage regulators. The first stage reduces the pressure to a constant intermediate value, and the second stage reduces this pressure to a much lower level that is appropriate for the torch being used.

Oxygen Regulator

Oxygen regulators have a sealing nipple and a nut to attach the regulator to the cylinder valve. The hose connection on the oxygen regulator has right-hand threads, while the hose connection on the acetylene regulator has left-hand threads. The cylinder-pressure gage shows the pressure inside the oxygen cylinder when the cylinder valve is turned on. It is graduated to a maximum pressure of 3,000 psi. The low, or torch, pressure gage has a top reading of 200 psi. The adjusting handle in the center of the regulator controls the pressure of the oxygen delivered to the torch. When the handle is screwed to the left until it turns freely with no opposition, the regulator is shut off and no oxygen can flow to the torch.

If the regulator should leak, a safety disk in the low-pressure side will rupture and release the oxygen out the back of the regulator before the pressure can build up enough to damage the regulator diaphragm.

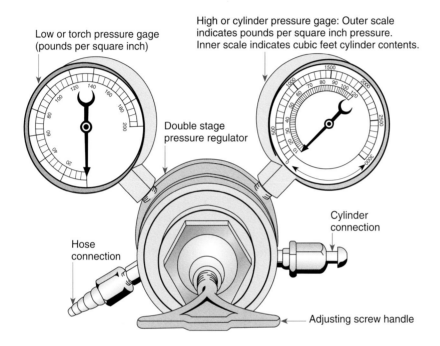

Low or torch pressure gage (pounds per square inch)

High or cylinder pressure gage: Outer scale indicates pounds per square inch pressure. Inner scale indicates cubic feet cylinder contents.

Double stage pressure regulator

Cylinder connection

Hose connection

Adjusting screw handle

Figure 2-100. *A typical two-stage oxygen regulator for welding*

Acetylene Regulator

The acetylene regulator has a sealing nipple and male threads that screw into the nut on the acetylene cylinder valve. The hose connection has left-hand threads. The high-pressure gage that reads the cylinder pressure when the cylinder valve is open has a range up to about 400 psi, and the torch gage has a range of up to about 30 or 40 psi. The regulator has a safety disk similar to that in the oxygen regulator that will rupture if the regulator should leak. The handle in the center of the regulator adjusts the acetylene pressure delivered to the torch, and when it is turned to the left until no opposition is felt, the valve is shut off and no acetylene can flow to the torch.

Hoses

The hoses used to connect the regulators to the torch are typically made of a high-quality rubber surrounded with two layers of rubber-impregnated fabric. An outer layer of tough rubber protects the hose from abrasion. The

Important safety reminder:
Open the valve on the acetylene bottle about a quarter of a turn so, in an emergency, it can be quickly closed. Turn the regulator adjusting screw handle until the pressure at the torch is between 5 and 7 psi. It is important to recognize that free acetylene gas becomes unstable at pressures above about 15 psi and can cause an explosion.

oxygen and acetylene hoses, called twin hoses, are joined side-by-side so they are less prone to tangle when in use. The acetylene hose is red, its fittings have left-hand threads, and the coupling nuts have a groove around the center of the hexes to indicate left-hand threads. The oxygen hose is green, its fittings have right-hand threads, and the coupling nuts do not have a groove, indicating right-hand threads.

Torches

Welding torches mix the gases in correct proportion and control the amount of gas delivered to the tip to regulate the size and type of flame. Almost all torches have two valves, one for the oxygen and one for the acetylene. Torches designed for welding heavy materials usually have the valves at the hose end of the mixing chamber, while those designed for welding lightweight metals have the valves at the tip end. There are two basic types of torches in use; balanced-pressure torches and injector torches. The choice of torch type depends upon the source of the acetylene.

Balanced-Pressure Torches

Use balanced-pressure torches when the acetylene is supplied from a cylinder and can be delivered to the torch under the required pressure. The pressures generally used are between one and five psi for both the oxygen and the acetylene, with the actual pressure depending upon the thickness of the metal being welded.

Oxygen and acetylene flow from the regulators into the torch handle, through oxygen and acetylene tubes to the needle valves. From the needle valves, the gases flow into the mixing head where they are mixed and then delivered to the tip.

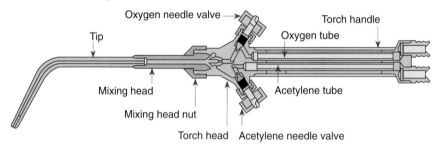

Figure 2-101. *A balanced-pressure welding torch for aircraft use*

Injector Torches

When the acetylene is supplied from an acetylene generator, its pressure is usually very low. To get the proper amount to the tip to produce the required heat, oxygen under a much higher pressure, usually 10 to 40 times as high as that of the acetylene, flows through a small orifice. The resulting high velocity produces a low pressure which draws the acetylene into the mixing chamber.

Torch Tips

Welding torch tips are generally made of hard copper, and the size of the orifice in the tip determines the velocity of the gases leaving the torch. The temperature of the welding flame is determined by the gases used, but the amount of heat delivered to the work is determined by the amount of gas burned.

The size tip to use is determined by not only the thickness of the material being welded, but also by the nature of the weld, the experience of the welder, and the position in which the weld is to be made. There is no uniform system for numbering the tips that relate to the amount of heat they will produce, but Figure 2-102 gives a starting point for determining the size orifice in the tip to use with various thicknesses of steel.

Keep the orifice in the tip clean and undistorted. When the tip is used it often becomes clogged with carbon and the flame is distorted. Any time the flame splits or becomes misshapen, shut the torch down and clean the tip with tip cleaners made for the purpose. Never use a drill or any other hard metal to clean a tip, as it will distort the hole.

Tip Orifice Drill Size	Approximate Steel Thickness (inch)
76-70	0.031 (1/32)
69-60	0.062 (1/16)
57-54	0.125 (1/8)
53-48	0.250 (1/4)

Figure 2-102. *Relationship between tip orifice size and the thickness of the metal to be welded*

Torch Lighters

Never light welding torches with a match or a cigarette lighter. They offer no protection for your hand when the gasses ignite. Use a flint-type lighter that has a flame cup for preventing the flame from reaching out.

Welding Goggles

Wear welding goggles that fit close to the face at all times when welding or cutting. The dark lenses protect your eyes from the ultraviolet and infrared rays that are produced, and clear glass lenses that are inexpensive to replace protect the colored glass from damage caused by molten metal splattering against them.

The color of the lens is determined by the type of welding: Green or brown lenses are typically used for welding steel, but blue lenses are often used for welding aluminum because it is easier to detect the condition of the surface of the metal. The shade of the lens is identified by a number, with the lower numbers indicating the lighter shades.

Filler Rod

When two pieces of metal are welded, their edges melt and they flow together to form a single piece. To strengthen the weld, filler metal is added to the molten pool so it becomes part of the weld. This filler metal comes in the form of welding rods. Standard welding rods are 36 inches long, copper plated to keep them from rusting, and available in diameters from $\frac{1}{16}$ to $\frac{1}{4}$ inch.

When selecting the rod for a particular job, follow the recommendations of the rod manufacturer to ensure that the alloy of the rod is correct for the type of metal you are welding.

Setting Up the Equipment

The gas welding equipment for most maintenance shops is mounted on a cart and ready for operation as soon as it is wheeled into position. There are some precautions and procedures that should be observed for maximum safety.

Compressed Gas Safety

The oxygen's high pressure makes special precautions necessary when the cylinders are replaced. As soon as you remove the regulator from the cylinder, screw a steel cap in place to protect the valve. When you've installed the new cylinder on the cart, secure it with the chain or clamp so it cannot accidentally fall over. Be sure that no greasy rags or tools are used around the oxygen cylinder. Oxygen does not burn, but it supports combustion so violently that an oily or greasy rag can catch fire.

It is permissible to store oxygen cylinders on their side, but acetylene cylinders should always be stored upright. If one has been stored on its side, place it in an upright position for at least 2 hours before connecting it into the welding rig. This allows the acetone to settle to the bottom of the cylinder so it will not be drawn out with the gas. Be sure the regulator reduces the pressure below 15 psi, because acetylene is unstable above this pressure.

Connecting the Equipment

It is important that oxyacetylene equipment be properly set up and adjusted. This is the procedure to follow:

• Before attaching the regulators to the cylinders, momentarily open the cylinder valves and allow any dirt or contamination that may be in the valve to be blown out.

• After installing the regulators, connect the hoses to the regulators and tighten the nuts with the correct-size open-end wrench.

• Screw the adjusting handles of the regulators all of the way to the left until you meet no resistance. This shuts the gas off to the hose fitting.

• Open the oxygen cylinder valve by turning the handwheel all the way to the left. This valve seats in its fully open position and prevents the oxygen leaking past the valve stem.

• Open the acetylene valve a quarter of a turn and leave the wrench on the valve stem. This allows the acetylene to be turned off in a hurry if a fire should ever start.

• Before connecting the torch to the hoses, screw in the adjusting screw handles enough to cause gas to flow and purge the lines of air and any contaminants that may have collected in the hose. After purging the hoses, screw the adjusting screw handles back out.

• After connecting the torch to the hoses, turn the torch valves off and screw in the adjusting screw handles until about 20 psi is indicated on the oxygen gage and 5 psi is shown on the acetylene gage.

• Screw the adjusting screw handles to the left to shut off all flow to the torch and watch the torch gages for any indication of leakage. If the hoses and torch do not hold the pressure, there is probably a leak. Cover the suspected area with a soap and water solution and watch for bubbles. Do not check for a leak with a flame or with any type of oil. If you find a leak, correct it before proceeding.

Lighting and Adjusting the Torch

With the torch connected and the correct size tip for the work being welded installed, the torch can be lit and adjusted.

Open the oxygen valve on the torch and turn the adjusting screw on the regulator in until the torch gage indicates the correct pressure for the size orifice in the tip. The correct pressures are shown in Figure 2-103. When the pressure is adjusted, turn off the oxygen valve on the torch.

Turn on the torch acetylene valve and adjust the acetylene pressure in the same way as you did the oxygen. Then shut off the torch valve for the acetylene until you are ready to light the torch.

When the torch is to be lit, slightly open the torch acetylene valve for about a quarter to half of a turn. Use the torch lighter to ignite the acetylene, and then open the acetylene valve until the flame leaves the tip for about $^1/_{16}$ inch. Open the torch oxygen valve until the flame returns to the face of the tip and changes to a bluish-white color, and an inner cone forms.

The relationship between the acetylene and oxygen is indicated by the type of flame. *See* Figure 2-104.

Generally a neutral flame is used, because it does not alter the composition of the base metal to any extent, and can be used for most metals. The temperature of a neutral flame is approximately 5,900°F. To get a neutral flame, control the torch oxygen valve until there is a definite white feather around the inner cone, and then increase the oxygen until the feather just disappears. The end of the inner cone should be rounded, and the outer flame should be blue with a tinge of purple around its outer edges and at the point.

A reducing flame, sometimes called a carburizing flame, is cooler and its temperature is about 5,700°F. A reducing flame should be used only for very special purposes, as the extra acetylene causes carbon to be deposited in the molten metal. A reducing flame is identified by a very distinctive white feather around the inner cone, and the outer flame will be whiter than it is around a neutral flame.

An oxidizing flame is one in which there is more oxygen than in a neutral flame. The inner cone is pointed rather than rounded, and the outer flame is smaller than that around a neutral flame. A hissing sound is often heard when the torch is adjusted to produce an oxidizing flame. The temperature of an oxidizing flame is around 6,300°F.

neutral flame. An oxyacetylene flame produced when the ratio of oxygen and acetylene is correct and there is no excess of oxygen or carbon. A neutral flame has a rounded inner cone and no feather around it.

Tip Orifice (Drill Size)	Torch Pressure (psi)	
	Oxygen	Acetylene
60 – 69	4	4
54 – 57	5	5
44 – 52	8	8
40 – 50	9	9

Figure 2-103. *Recommended torch pressures for various size tip orifices*

carburizing flame. An oxyacetylene flame produced by an excess of acetylene. This flame is identified by a feather around the inner cone. A carburizing flame is also called a reducing flame.

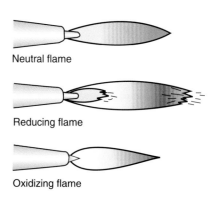

Neutral flame

Reducing flame

Oxidizing flame

Figure 2-104. *Oxyacetylene flames*

oxidizing flame. An oxyacetylene flame in which there is an excess of oxygen. The inner cone is pointed and often a hissing sound is heard.

Welding flames may be classified as soft or harsh. The temperature of the flame is a function of the welding gases, and the amount of heat put into a weld is a function of the amount of gas being burned. The softness or harshness of a flame is a function of the velocity of the gases flowing from the tip. A soft flame is one in which the velocity of the gases is low, and a harsh flame is one in which the velocity is high.

When a soft flame is required to put a lot of heat into the metal, use a tip with a larger orifice than usual.

Shutting Down the Equipment

After the welding is completed, the equipment must be properly shut down. Extinguish the flame by turning off the torch acetylene valve and then the torch oxygen valve. If the torch remains unlit for any period of time, both of the cylinder valves should be turned off. Open the torch acetylene valve to allow the gas in the line to escape. Close the acetylene valve and open the torch oxygen valve until the oxygen all bleeds out. Close the oxygen valve and then turn the adjustment screws in both regulators to the left until no opposition is felt and the gases are shut off to the torch. Coil the hoses up neatly to protect them from damage.

Gas Welding Techniques

Most gas welding by aviation maintenance technicians is to relatively thin-gage steel, and so the techniques involved in this type of welding are the ones discussed here.

Holding the Torch

For the best control when welding thin-gage material, hold the torch as is seen in Figure 2-105. The tip should be in line with the joint being welded, and inclined between 30° and 60° from the perpendicular, with the actual angle depending upon the amount of penetration needed. The thicker the material, the more nearly vertical the torch is held.

If the inner cone of the flame is held about $\frac{1}{8}$ inch from the surface of the metal, a puddle of molten metal will form. This puddle should be composed of equal parts of the two pieces of metal being joined. As soon as the puddle appears, begin moving the tip in a circular pattern around the outer edge of the puddle, moving it slightly in the direction you want the weld to progress, melting just a little bit of the forward edge on each circle. This pattern ensures an even distribution of heat between the two pieces of metal. *See* Figure 2-106.

For thin-gage tubing and sheet metal, point the torch in the direction the weld is progressing. Add the filler rod to the puddle as the edges of the joint melt before the flame. This is called forehand welding. *See* Figure 2-107.

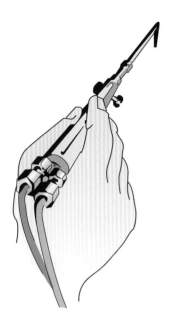

Figure 2-105. *Correct method of holding an oxyacetylene torch*

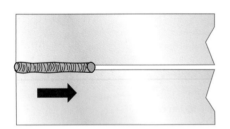

Figure 2-106. *The tip of the torch should form a series of circles, with each one moving slightly in the direction the weld is to progress.*

forehand welding. Welding in which the torch is pointed in the direction the weld is progressing.

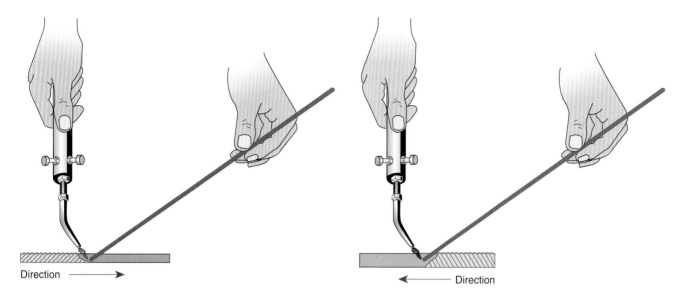

Figure 2-107. *Forehand welding is used for thin-gage tubing and sheet.*

Figure 2-108. *Backhand welding is used for heavy-gage sheet steel.*

The preferred method for welding heavy-gage metal is the backhand method, shown in Figure 2-108. Point the torch away from the direction the weld is progressing. Add the rod to the puddle between the flame and the finished weld. Backhand welding is not used on thin-gage metal because the greater amount of heat produced in the metal is likely to overheat and burn it.

backhand welding. Welding in which the torch is pointed away from the direction the weld is progressing.

Welding Positions

The ideal position for welding is the flat position, in which the material is flat and the welding is all done from the top with the torch pointed down on the work. But this is not always possible in the real world of aircraft repair. When welding on tubular structure, some of the weld is flat, some is horizontal, some is vertical, and some is overhead.

When welding in the overhead position point the torch upward toward the work and prevent the puddle from sagging by keeping it small and not allowing a drop to form. Use the rod to control the puddle and keep the volume of flame to the minimum needed to ensure good fusion of the base metal and the filler rod.

Horizontal welding is done by holding the torch in such a way that the flame is inclined upward at an angle between 45° and 60°. Dip the rod in the top of the puddle and do not allow the weld to get too hot.

Vertical welds are started at the bottom with the flame inclined upward between 45° and 60°. It is important that a vertical weld not be allowed to become overheated. To prevent overheating, you may have to periodically remove the flame from the weld for an instant and then return it to the puddle. Add the rod at the top of the puddle in front of the flame.

Welded Joints

Three types of welded joints find common use in aircraft construction and repair: the butt joint; lap joint; and T, or fillet, joint.

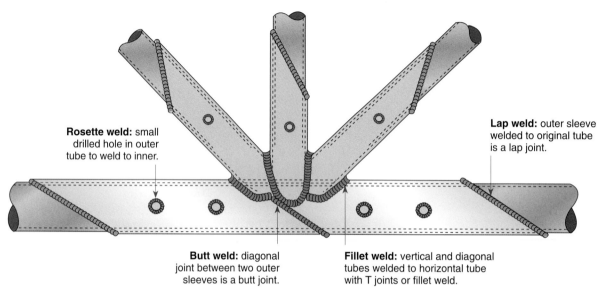

Rosette weld: small drilled hole in outer tube to weld to inner.

Lap weld: outer sleeve welded to original tube is a lap joint.

Butt weld: diagonal joint between two outer sleeves is a butt joint.

Fillet weld: vertical and diagonal tubes welded to horizontal tube with T joints or fillet weld.

Figure 2-109. *Types of welded joints*

rosette weld. A method of securing one metal tube inside another by welding. Small holes are drilled in the outer tube and the inner tube is welded to it around the circumference of the holes.

depth of penetration for welds:
Butt weld—100% thickness of the base metal
Fillet weld—25%-50% thickness of the base metal

A butt joint is made when two pieces of material are placed edge to edge so there is no overlapping. Use filler rod in a butt joint to give the metal the strength it needs.

Lap joints are the most common type of joint in tubular structure repair. When one tube is placed over another, the edges of the outside tube are welded to the inner tube with a lap joint.

T joints, or fillet welds, are often used in tubular structure to join one tube to another at an angle, or to attach lugs to the tubing. A single fillet is satisfactory for thin-gage metal, but heavier materials should be welded on both sides. A proper fillet weld should penetrate the base metal by 25% to 50% of its thickness.

Control of Expansion and Contraction

Metal heated for welding expands, and when it cools it contracts. These dimensional changes cause the metal to buckle. When the weld is completed, the contraction may cause the metal to crack.

An easy way to see the effect of expansion and contraction is to watch what happens when two pieces of steel sheet are butt-welded together. If the two sheets are placed side by side and welded, one sheet will overlap the other before the weld is completed. To prevent overlapping, separate the sheets by their thickness at one end, and by approximately $\frac{1}{8}$ to $\frac{1}{4}$ inch per foot of length at their other end. The actual separation depends upon the thickness and type of the metal. Begin the weld, and watch the sheets draw together. If they have been separated by the correct distance, they will draw together without overlapping by the time the weld is completed. *See* Figure 2-110.

Another way to prevent excessive warping when making a straight butt weld is to use the process of skip welding, as seen in Figure 2-111. Place the sheets beside each other with about the thickness of the metal separating them. Tack weld them together by forming small puddles at the ends and about every $1\frac{1}{4}$ to $1\frac{1}{2}$ inches along the length of the sheets. Begin the welding at point A and weld back to the edge of the sheet. Then start at point B and weld back to point A, next weld from C to B, and finally from the edge to point C.

You can prevent large welded structures from warping by first clamping all the parts in a heavy jig or fixture and then performing the welding. After the welding is completed the entire structure is normalized to relieve the strains caused by the concentrations of heat during the welding process. With the structure still clamped in the jig, it is heated uniformly to a red heat and allowed to cool slowly in still air.

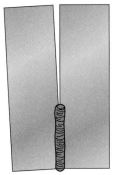

Sheets placed beside each other with more space at one end.

The gap closes as the weld progresses.

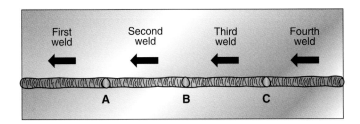

Figure 2-111. *Distortion can be minimized in a long butt weld by skip welding. Tack weld the pieces together and then complete the welds as is shown by the arrows.*

Figure 2-110. *Allowance for expansion in a straight butt weld*

Characteristics of a Good Weld

In a good weld:

- The seam should be smooth with the bead ripples evenly spaced and of a uniform thickness.
- The weld should be built up, providing extra thickness at the joint.
- The weld should taper off smoothly into the base metal.
- Oxides that form on the base metal beyond $\frac{1}{2}$-inch either side of a weld are unacceptable.
- The weld should show no signs of blow holes, porosity, projecting globules, or undercutting of the base metal.
- The base metal should show no signs of burns, pits, cracks, or distortion.

Never file welds to improve their appearance, and never fill them with solder, brazing material, or filler of any sort. If it is necessary to reweld a joint, remove all the old weld before rewelding.

tack weld. A method of holding parts together before they are permanently welded. The parts are assembled, and small spots of weld are placed at strategic locations to hold them in position.

normalizing. A process of strain-relieving steel that has been welded and left in a strained condition. The steel is heated to a specified temperature, usually red hot, and allowed to cool in still air to room temperature.

Oxyacetylene Cutting

Oxyacetylene cutting rapidly oxidizes the metal. Ferrous metals combine with oxygen in the air to form iron oxide, or rust. Heat accelerates the combining action, and if pure oxygen is substituted for the air, the combination is extremely rapid.

A cutting torch, such as the one in Figure 2-112, is typical of those used in aviation maintenance shops. The torch is attached to the same hoses used for welding and lit in the same way as a welding torch. Typical regulator pressures for cutting steel up to about $\frac{1}{4}$-inch thick are 4 psi for the acetylene and 15 psi for the oxygen. The oxygen needle valve is adjusted to get a neutral flame from the preheating orifices, and the cutting oxygen lever is depressed to produce a flow of high-velocity oxygen through the flame.

To cut the steel, mark the cut with soapstone or chalk, and begin at the edge of the material. Hold the tip perpendicular to the surface until a spot in the metal turns red hot, then gradually depress the oxygen control lever. As soon as the cutting starts and a stream of sparks appears on the bottom of the material, depress the oxygen lever fully. Continue to move the torch across the work at a speed just fast enough for the cut to continue to penetrate the material completely.

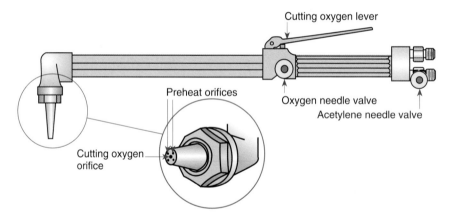

Cutting oxygen lever

Preheat orifices

Oxygen needle valve

Acetylene needle valve

Cutting oxygen orifice

Figure 2-112. *A typical oxyacetylene cutting torch*

Gas Welding of Aluminum

Aluminum welding presents a special problem in that aluminum does not change color as steel does before it melts. It is very easy to melt a hole through the metal rather than correctly fuse its edges. Thin aluminum sheet and tubing may be gas welded, but arc welding is preferred for thick aluminum sheet and castings.

Not all aluminum alloys are suitable for welding. Alloys 2014, 2017, 2024, and 7075 should not be welded, as the strength in the area of the weld is drastically reduced and the corrosion resistance is seriously impaired. Alloys 1100, 3003, 5052, 5056, 6061 and 6063 are suitable for welding.

When the welding torch is held vertically over a piece of sheet aluminum and the flame brought down until the tip of the inner cone nearly touches the metal, it will very suddenly, and without warning, melt and a hole will appear. But if the torch is held at an angle of about 30° to the plane of the surface, you will be able to melt the surface without forming a hole. As you slowly move the flame across the surface, a small puddle will form, and it will solidify as quickly as the flame is lifted.

Practice welding aluminum by forming a flange along the edges of two pieces that sticks up about the thickness of the metal. Place the two flanges next to each other, as shown in Figure 2-113, and practice welding them together without using any filler rod.

Figure 2-113. *Aluminum sheets flanged for practice welding*

Two alloys are used for aluminum welding rods. Alloy 1100 rods are used for welding 1100 and 3003 aluminum because they give good ductility and good corrosion resistance. Rods made of 4043 alloy are used for all other wrought alloys and for castings because of their superior strength.

Because oxides form rapidly on the surface of aluminum, the use of flux is very important. The oxides chemically combine with the flux and are kept away from the molten metal.

Most fluxes are available as a powder that is mixed with water to form a paste. Apply this flux generously to both the top and bottom of the material to be welded, and to the flange, if one is used. After completing the welding, it is extremely important to scrub away all traces of the flux with a stiff bristle brush and hot water, as flux is corrosive to metal.

When using a filler rod to weld aluminum, cover the area to be welded with flux, and hold the torch at a low angle over its surface. Move the torch with a small circular motion over the starting point until the flux melts, and then scrape the rod across the surface, lifting it after each pass to prevent it melting before the parent metal. As soon as the surface of the metal is sufficiently hot, the rod will penetrate the surface. When the rod penetrates, hold it in the flame just long enough to melt some of it to reinforce the weld.

Forehand welding is preferred, because the flame preheats the metal before it is welded and keeps the flame away from the completed weld. The amount of heat put into the weld is actually controlled by the angle between the torch and the surface of the metal.

Brazing and Soldering

In the process of thermally joining metals, there are three procedures: welding, brazing, and soldering. In welding, the edges of two pieces of metal are melted and allowed to flow together to form one piece. Filler rod is usually added to the molten metal to increase the strength of the joint.

Brazing and soldering are methods of joining metals by heating them enough to melt a relatively low-melting-point nonferrous alloy. When the alloy melts, it flows out and wets the parent metal. When it cools it holds the metal parts together. The difference between brazing and soldering is

brazing. A method of thermally joining metal parts by wetting the surface with a molten nonferrous alloy. When the molten material cools and solidifies, it holds the pieces together.

Brazing materials melt at a temperature higher than 800°F, but lower than the melting temperature of the metal on which they are used.

soldering. A method of thermally joining metal parts with a molten nonferrous alloy that melts at a temperature below 800°F. The molten alloy is pulled up between close-fitting parts by capillary action. When the alloy cools and hardens, it forms a strong, leak-proof connection.

parent metal. The metal being welded. This term is used to distinguish the metal being welded from the metal of the welding rod.

basically the temperature of the alloy. Brazing materials melt at temperatures higher than 800°F, but lower than the melting temperature of the metals being joined. Solder melts at a temperature lower than 800°F.

Brazing

Brazing is the process of joining metal parts by melting a brazing alloy on the surface. These alloys generally have a bronze base and they melt at about 1,600°F. (Steel melts at around 2,600°F.)

Thoroughly clean the surface to be brazed and heat it, in the case of steel, to a dull red. Heat the brazing rod and dip it in a flux made of borax and boric acid. The flux adheres to the rod so none need be applied to the metal. Move the torch with a neutral flame in a semicircular pattern over the seam to be brazed and hold the brazing rod in the flame near the tip. When the rod melts and flows over the base metal that is hotter than the melting point of the rod, the bronze alloy flows into the joint by capillary attraction. Continue to add rod until the joint is built up to the smooth seam you want. After the seam is completed, allow it to cool slowly.

A brazed joint is not strong enough for most aircraft structural applications, and it can be used as a repair procedure only in applications in which brazing was originally approved. A brazed joint should never be repaired by welding, as the brazing material gets into the structure of the metal and prevents a proper weld.

Silver Soldering

Silver soldering is a form of brazing used for attaching the fittings to high-pressure oxygen lines. Its chief characteristics are its ability to withstand vibration and high temperature.

Clean and assemble the end of the tube and the inside of the fitting. The fitting must fit tightly over the end of the tube as the solder is drawn into the joint by capillary attraction. Prepare borax and boric acid paste flux and wipe it on the tube to cover the area where the fitting is installed. Use a soft, neutral flame to heat the fitting and tube until the flux turns liquid. Shortly after the flux liquefies, touch the joint with the silver solder. It will melt and be drawn into the fitting around the tubing. Only an extremely small film of solder is needed to give the joint the integrity it needs.

Soft Soldering

Soft soldering is done with an alloy of tin and lead, and its melting temperature is determined by the ratio of these two components. An alloy of 50% tin and 50% lead is commonly used for general soldering. Its melting point is 414°F. Solder used for electronic components is usually 63% tin and 37% lead, and it melts at 361°F.

Metal parts that can be washed after soldering may be soldered using an acid flux to clean the metal, but electrical components must never be soldered with an acid flux. Most solder is available in the form of a hollow wire with the flux on the inside. The solder used for electrical components has its hollow core filled with a synthetic resin that melts and flows out ahead of the solder to exclude air from the hot metal and prevent the formation of oxides.

Soft solder should never be depended upon for strength. The joint must be designed to have all of the needed mechanical strength, and then solder is melted and flowed over the joint to make it air- and liquid-tight and to give it good electrical conductivity.

STUDY QUESTIONS: GAS WELDING, CUTTING, BRAZING AND SOLDERING

Answers begin on Page 167. Page numbers refer to chapter text.

109. The most widely used fuel gas for aircraft gas welding is _____ . *Page 138*

110. It _____ (is or is not) permissible to use technical oxygen for charging a breathing oxygen system in an aircraft. *Page 139*

111. Acetylene gas is produced when _____ reacts with water. *Page 139*

112. The acetylene in a storage cylinder is absorbed in _____ which makes it safe to store under pressure. *Page 140*

113. The hose connection on an oxygen regulator has _____ (right-hand or left-hand) threads. *Page 140*

114. The hose connection on an acetylene regulator has _____ (right-hand or left-hand) threads. *Page 141*

115. The temperature of the flame used for gas welding is determined by the _____ . *Page 143*

116. A twist drill _____ (is or is not) the correct tool to use to clean the orifice in a welding torch tip. *Page 143*

117. The valve on the oxygen cylinder should be opened _____ (all the way or part way). *Page 144*

118. The valve on the acetylene cylinder should be opened _____ (all the way or part way). *Page 144*

Continued

119. Welding hoses and connections should be checked for leaks with _____ .
     Page 145

120. The oxyacetylene flame that is the hottest is a/an _____ (reducing, neutral, or oxidizing) flame. *Page 145*

121. A flame that has a rounded inner cone and no feather around it is a/an _____ (reducing, neutral, or oxidizing) flame. *Page 145*

122. Thin steel tube and sheet is best welded by the _____ (backhand or forehand) method. *Page 147*

123. A flame that has a definite feather around its inner cone is a/an _____ (reducing, neutral, or oxidizing) flame. *Page 145*

124. Another name for a reducing flame is a /an _____ flame. *Page 145*

125. When making a vertical weld, the weld should be started at the _____ (top or bottom). *Page 147*

126. When welding aluminum, flux should be applied to _____ (both sides or top side only) of the metal. *Page 151*

127. After welding aluminum, all traces of the flux should be removed by scrubbing the area with a bristle brush and _____ . *Page 151*

128. The amount of heat put into the metal when gas welding aluminum is controlled by varying the _____ between the torch and the metal. *Page 151*

129. Brazing flux is applied to the heated brazing _____ . *Page 152*

130. The recommended oxyacetylene flame for brazing is _____ (neutral, oxidizing, or reducing). *Page 152*

Electric Welding

There are two basic types of electric welding: electric arc welding and electrical resistance welding. Electric arc welding is typically used for rather heavy material. The metal is melted in the extreme heat of an electric arc between the work and a hand-held electrode. Electrical resistance welding is used for thin sheets of metal. Thin sheets of metal are clamped between two electrodes or rollers and high-amperage, low-voltage current flows through the metal. The resistance of the metal to the flow of current causes enough heat to melt the metal and fuse the pieces together.

Electric Arc Welding

Electric arc welding has been used for many years as the primary method of joining heavy steel. Developments in the last few decades allow electric arc welding to be used in aircraft manufacture and maintenance for welding thin-wall tubing.

This section discusses several types of electric arc welding.

Shielded Metal Arc Welding (SMAW)

Electric arc welding that uses a flux-covered rod is called shielded metal arc welding. This type of welding has been used for many years for heavy steel construction, but it finds little use in aircraft maintenance except for building shop equipment. The welding machine that produces the low-voltage and high-current power for this welding may be either a motor-driven DC generator or an AC transformer-type machine. Each type of machine has advantages and disadvantages.

Gas Shielded Arc Welding

One of the problems encountered with welding is the contamination of the molten metal with oxides caused by oxygen in the air. This problem is often handled by using flux that dissolves the oxides that have formed and covers the molten metal to exclude the oxygen and prevent further oxide formation.

Aluminum and magnesium are difficult to weld by conventional methods, and in 1942 when the Northrop company received a contract from the U.S. Army Air Corps to build an all-magnesium, all-welded, tailless fighter, the XP-56, the welding process known as Heliarc® welding was developed. The welding arc is shielded by a flow of helium gas that excludes oxygen from the molten metal. The results are a neat, sound weld with a minimum of splatter and distortion.

Gas shielded arc welding has become extremely important in modern technology and there are two versions of it in use; one that uses a consumable wire rod as the electrode and the other that uses a nonconsumable tungsten electrode. The first was originally called metal inert gas, or MIG, welding, and the second was called tungsten inert gas, or TIG, welding. As the technologies

MIG welding. Metal inert gas welding is a form of electric arc welding in which the electrode is a consumable wire. MIG welding is now called GMA (Gas Metal Arc) welding.

TIG welding. Tungsten inert gas welding is a form of electric arc welding in which the electrode is a nonconsumable tungsten wire. TIG welding is now called GTA (Gas Tungsten Arc) Welding.

developed, other gases, some not inert, were used as shielding gases, and the names for these types of welding were changed to gas metal arc welding (GMAW) and gas tungsten arc welding (GTAW). In this introduction to gas shielded arc welding, we will discuss the more generally used GTAW.

Gas Tungsten Arc Welding (GTAW)

In GTA welding, the electrode is a fine nonconsumable tungsten wire used to create the arc, and filler rod is used to reinforce the weld as in oxyacetylene welding. Figure 2-114 shows the typical setup for GTA welding. The gas supply with a regulator and flowmeter provides a constant flow of shielding gas to the torch and the electrical current for welding is supplied by a power unit. A ground wire attached to the work from the power unit completes the setup.

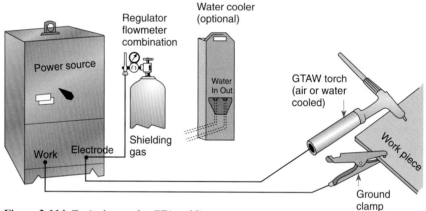

Figure 2-114. *Typical setup for GTA welding*

Shielding Gases

The gases used to shield the arc in GTA welding are either argon or helium. An arc shielded with helium is hotter than one shielded with argon and it produces a deeper penetration, but there is a greater tendency to splatter. Because of argon's greater density, it produces a cleaner weld and is used almost exclusively for welding very thin material. Helium and argon are stored in steel cylinders similar to those used for oxygen. Both helium and argon cylinders are painted gray, but helium cylinders have an orange band at the top and argon cylinders have a white band.

Regulator and Flowmeter

A regulator, similar to a single-stage oxygen regulator, is used on the shielding gas cylinder, and a flowmeter is installed between the regulator and the torch to give the technician an indication of the amount of shielding gas flowing over the weld. The amount of flow is controlled by the regulator, and should be kept at the value recommended for the particular type of welding being done.

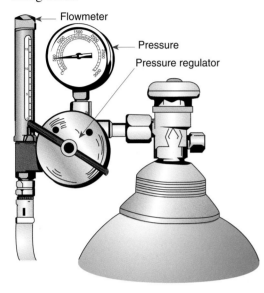

Figure 2-115. *A typical regulator and flowmeter for the shielding gas used in GTA welding*

Power Unit

The power unit used for GTA welding can supply DC-straight polarity (the electrode is negative), DC-reverse polarity, (the electrode is positive), and AC. DC-straight polarity produces the most heat and deepest penetration, but DC-reverse polarity has an advantage in welding aluminum and magnesium that, as the electrons flow from the work into the electrode, they blast off the surface oxides that have formed on the metal.

AC welding is similar to a combination of straight polarity and reverse polarity DC, but if the oxide coating on the surface of the metal is strong enough, it acts as a rectifier and no current flows during the half cycle when the electrode is positive, and the welding is similar to DC-straight polarity.

reverse polarity welding. DC-electric arc welding in which the electrode is positive with respect to the work.

straight polarity welding. DC-electric arc welding in which the electrode is negative with respect to the work.

rectification. A condition in AC-electric arc welding in which oxides on the surface of the metal act as a rectifier and prevent electrons flowing from the metal to the electrode during the half cycle when the electrode is positive.

To overcome this problem of rectification, a high-voltage, high-frequency, low-amperage AC signal is superimposed on the AC welding current. This high voltage penetrates the oxide film and allows the weld to have the good characteristics of both types of DC welding. This superimposed high-frequency AC gives these advantages:

- The arc can be started without touching the electrode to the work.
- The arc has better stability.
- A longer arc is possible.
- The tungsten electrodes have a longer life.
- A wider range of current can be used for a specific diameter of electrode.

Figure 2-116. *Welding equipment such as this Miller Electric TIG Synchrowave 250 DX allows a welder to make repairs to such thin metal as this exhaust sleeve without burning through. (Courtesy Miller Electric Manufacturing Co.)*

Hand-Held Torches

Torches for GTA welding are available in both air-cooled and water-cooled versions with air cooling used for the lower current welding applications. Both an air-cooled torch and a water-cooled torch are shown in Figure 2-117. Gas and cooling water are brought into the water-cooled torch through appropriate hoses, and after cooling the torch, the water drains back through the tube which encases the power cable.

The electrode is held in the torch with a split collet that allows it to be extended as it is consumed. The gas flows out around the electrode and is directed against the work by a ceramic gas shielding cup that screws onto the torch.

Electrodes

The electrodes for GTA welding are made of tungsten wire and are available in diameters from 0.010 inch to 0.250 inch and in lengths from 3 inches to 24 inches. Pure tungsten electrodes are used for most general welding of steel, but its current-carrying ability is limited. Tungsten alloyed with thorium emits electrons more readily than pure tungsten, it resists contamination better, and makes the arc easier to start and more stable. But, thorium alloyed rods are much more expensive than pure tungsten electrodes. Tungsten

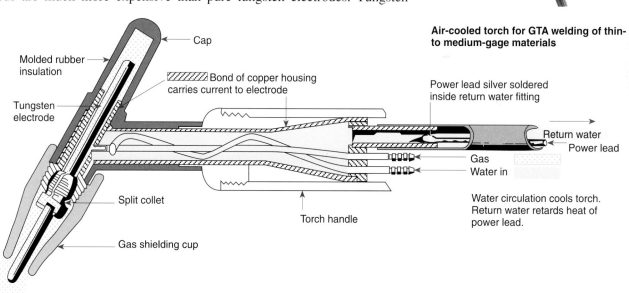

Air-cooled torch for GTA welding of thin- to medium-gage materials

Typical water-cooled GTA torch

Figure 2-117. *GTAW hand-held torches*

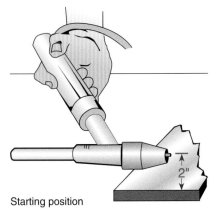

Starting position

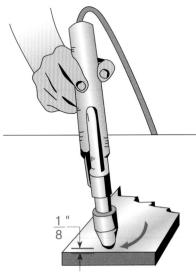

Striking the arc

Figure 2-118. *Starting the arc*

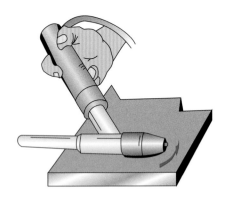

Figure 2-119. *Breaking the arc*

electrodes alloyed with zirconium fall between the characteristics of pure tungsten and tungsten alloyed with thorium, but they are superior in some instances when used for some types of AC welding.

Electrodes used for DC-straight polarity welding should have its end pointed and may be smaller than that used for DC-reverse polarity and AC welding. For the latter two types of welding, the end of the electrode is normally rounded.

Welding Techniques and Procedures

GTA welding is specially suited for aluminum and most of the aluminum alloys, as there is no need to use corrosive flux. Some alloys, specifically 2024 and 7075, should not be fusion-welded because of hot cracking and impairment of their corrosion resistance, but most others can be welded. The corrosion resistance and heat treatment of some alloys such as 2014 and 2017 are affected by welding, and when a heat-treatable alloy is welded, it should be re-heat-treated after the welding is completed.

The steps to follow in GTA welding are:

- Choose the correct electrode size and gas cup for the thickness of the material being welded and, after polishing the electrode with steel wool, install it in the torch so that it protrudes about $\frac{1}{8}$ to $\frac{1}{4}$ inch from the end of the gas cup for butt welding or $\frac{1}{4}$ to $\frac{3}{8}$ inch for fillet welding.
- Select the correct filler rod for the material being welded. Typically 1100 rod can be used for 1100 or 3003 alloys and 4043, 5154, 6356, or 5456 should be used for the other alloys. Clean the rod and the metal to be welded to remove all traces of oil or grease.

Almost all aluminum welding will be done using AC with superimposed high-frequency AC. With this type of current, the arc can be started without actually touching the metal with the electrode tip.

- Hold the torch horizontally about 2 inches above the work and swing the tip down until it is about $\frac{1}{8}$ inch from the work with a smooth wrist movement. This should start the arc.
- The downward motion of the torch should be rapid so there will be a maximum amount of gas protection in the weld zone.
- When making the first start while AC welding, the electrode will have to be moved closer to the work before the arc starts than it is when the electrode is hot.

To stop the arc, snap the electrode back to the horizontal position.

After starting the arc, preheat the work by moving the torch in a small circular motion until a molten puddle 3 to 5 times the thickness of the material is developed, then hold the torch at an angle of approximately 75° to the surface of the work with the end of the electrode about $\frac{1}{8}$ inch above the work.

When the puddle becomes bright and fluid, move the torch slowly and steadily along the joint at a speed which will produce a bead of uniform penetration or width. No oscillating or other movement of the torch except for a steady forward motion is required.

When filler rod is required, hold the rod at an angle of approximately 15° to the work, and just clear of the arc stream. Once the puddle has formed, move the torch to the rear of the puddle and add filler rod by quickly touching it in the leading edge of the puddle. Add only a small amount of rod, then remove the rod and bring the torch back up to the leading edge. When the puddle is again bright, repeat these steps.

The arc speed is governed by the amount of current and the thickness of the material. The speed should be adjusted to obtain a bead that has uniform height and width. Good penetration is indicated by a very small, smooth bead, and the penetration should be uniform on the underside of the work.

Some precautions to be observed when running a bead are:

- Do not insert filler rod until the puddle is well established.

- Do not insert the filler rod in the arc stream. This will cause considerable spatter and will melt an excessive amount of the rod.

- Do not attempt to hold the filler rod in the molten puddle. The amount of filler rod determines the buildup of the bead, and little or no buildup is necessary.

Inspection of the Weld

After completing a weld, inspect it carefully to determine that it is completely adequate for the purpose for which it was made. Some possible defects and their most probable causes are:

- Bead too narrow. This usually indicates that the weld was made at an excessive speed.

- Bead too wide. This usually indicates that the weld was made with too slow a speed.

- Weld is contaminated. This is indicated by a black deposit on the weld and is caused by the electrode coming in contact with the weld metal.

- Weld is oxidized. This is caused by an insufficient supply of shielding gas.

Electrical Resistance Welding

Electrical resistance welding is a special type of welding used for joining very thin sheets of metal, and it replaces riveting in many instances. There are two types of resistance welding, spot welding and seam welding. One of the widely used aviation applications for spot and seam welding is that of welding fuel tanks for aircraft.

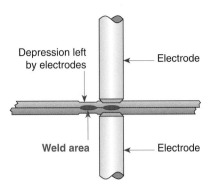

Figure 2-120. *The principle of spot welding*

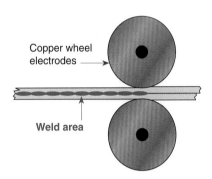

Figure 2-121. *The principle of seam welding*

Spot and Seam Welding

The heat required for spot welding is generated when current flows through the metal being welded, while considerable pressure is exerted on the electrodes that carry the current into and out of the metal.

Figure 2-120 shows the principle of spot welding. Two copper electrodes are forced together with the metal being welded between them. A pulse of high-current electricity flows through the metal and heats it to near its melting point. As it softens, the pressure on the electrodes forces the softened metal to form a spot between the sheets that joins them. The length of time the current flows is called the dwell time, and it is controlled by an electronic controller to ensure that all of the spots will be uniform.

Seam welding is similar to spot welding except that copper wheels replace the rod-type electrodes. The controller sends pulses of current between the wheels so that spot welds are made close enough together to overlap and form a solid seam.

STUDY QUESTIONS: ELECTRIC WELDING

Answers begin on Page 167. Page numbers refer to chapter text.

131. In straight polarity DC welding, the electrode is _____ (positive or negative). *Page 157*

132. The electrode used for DC reverse polarity GTA welding is _____ (larger or smaller) than that used for DC straight polarity. *Page 160*

133. The filler rod is dipped into the _____ front or back of the puddle when using GTA welding. *Page 161*

134. Too wide a bead indicates that the weld was made too _____ (fast or slow). *Page 161*

135. A black deposit on a weld bead is an indication that the weld is _____ . *Page 161*

136. Two methods of welding very thin aluminum alloy and stainless steel sheets are _____ and _____ . *Page 162*

Repair of Aircraft Structure by Welding

The welded steel tubular structure of low-performance aircraft is relatively easy to repair. Advisory Circular 43.13-1B *Acceptable Methods, Techniques, and Practices — Aircraft Inspection and Repair* illustrates many of the typical repairs that can be made. The repairs described in AC 43.13-1B are *acceptable*, not *approved*, data and therefore cannot be used as authorization for a major repair, but they can be submitted to the local FAA maintenance inspector for his or her approval for a specific repair *before* the repair is made.

Any welded structure that needs repair on modern sheet metal aircraft, especially those that are part of the engine mount or landing gear, should be studied with caution, and only the repairs made that are specifically approved by the aircraft manufacturer. Some welded structural members that are heat-treated must not be repaired by welding.

repair. A maintenance procedure in which a damaged component is restored to its original condition, or at least to a condition that allows it to fulfill its design function.

Specific Welded Repairs

The repairs described here are taken from AC 43.13-1B and illustrate good practices. Before making any repair on a certificated aircraft, make a sketch of the desired repair and have it approved by the FAA.

Welded Patch Repair

If the damage to a tube does not extend to more than $\frac{1}{4}$ of its circumference, repair it by welding a tapered patch over the damaged area. The area to be covered must be free from cracks, abrasions, and sharp corners, and it must be substantially re-formed without cracking. The patch material should be the same type of steel and one gage thicker than the damaged tube.

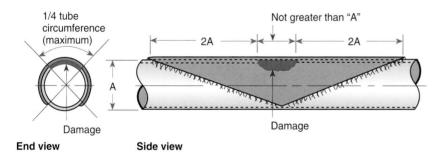

Figure 2-122. *A welded patch repair*

Longeron Dented at a Cluster

If a fuselage longeron is dented at a cluster, re-form the dent as much as possible and weld a finger patch over it similar to the one in Figure 2-123. Make a pattern of lightweight cardboard and cut the patch from the same material and thickness as the longeron. Remove all of the finish from the tubing to be covered and tack-weld the patch to the longeron and heat it and form it around the tubes so that there is no gap of more than $\frac{1}{16}$ inch between the tubing and the patch. After the patch is formed and tack-welded in place, complete the welding.

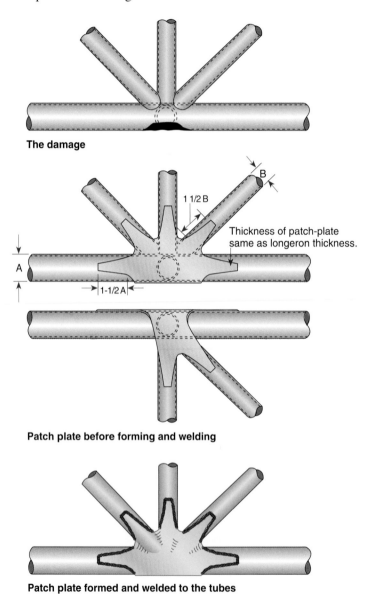

The damage

1 1/2 B

B

Thickness of patch-plate same as longeron thickness.

A

1-1/2 A

Patch plate before forming and welding

Patch plate formed and welded to the tubes

Figure 2-123. *Repair to a longeron dented at a cluster*

Tubing Spliced by the Inner-Sleeve Method

A new piece of tubing may be spliced into a structure by using an inner-sleeve splice, such as the one in Figure 2-124, by following these steps:

1. Remove the damaged section of tubing by making a 30° diagonal cut at each end.

2. Select the replacement tubing of the same material and wall thickness as the original and cut both of its ends with the same diagonal angle. This replacement tube should allow $\frac{1}{8}$ inch of space at each end so the outside tube can be welded to the inner sleeve.

3. Select tubing for the inner sleeve of the same material and wall thickness as the original, but with an outside diameter that just fits into the inside of the original tubing.

4. Drill holes in the outer tube for the rosette welds. These holes have a diameter of $\frac{1}{4}$ the outside diameter of the outer tube.

5. Put the inner sleeves inside the replacement tube and insert the replacement in the damaged area. Center the inner sleeves inside the diagonal cuts.

6. Weld the two outer tubes together, and to the inner sleeve at each end, and weld the inner sleeve to the outer tube through the rosette weld holes.

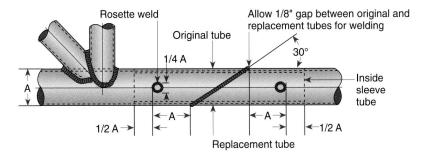

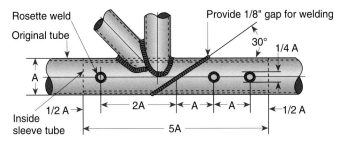

Figure 2-124. *Tube splicing by the inner-sleeve method*

Tubing Spliced by the Outer-Sleeve Method

If the repair is in a location that it does not cause a bulge in the outside fabric, splice the tubing by the much easier outer-sleeve method shown in Figure 2-125. Follow these steps:

1. Remove the damaged section of tubing by making straight cuts across its ends.

2. Select the replacement tubing of the same material and wall thickness as the original. The length of the replacement must be the same as that of the damaged section so that the total spacing between the end of the stub of the original tubing and the replacement does not exceed $^1/_{32}$ inch.

3. Select the outer-sleeve material that is the same material and at least the same wall thickness as the original tubes, and with an inside diameter that does not allow more than $^1/_{16}$ inch clearance between the outer sleeve and the original tubing.

4. Cut the outer tube with a fishmouth cut as is shown in Figure 2-125. Drill holes in the outer tube for the rosette welds. These holes should have a diameter of $^1/_4$ the outside diameter of the original tubing.

5. Center the outer sleeves over each end of the repair and weld them to the original and the replacement tubes, and weld the outer sleeve to the tubing through the holes for the rosette welds.

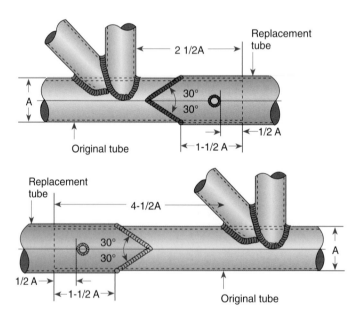

Figure 2-125. *Tube splicing by the outer-sleeve method*

Answers begin below. **Page numbers refer to chapter text.**

137. The welded structural repairs shown in Advisory Circular 43.13-1B _____
     (may or may not) be used by themselves as authorization for making a similar repair to the structure
     of a certificated aircraft. *Page 163*

138. Heat-treated landing gear components _____ (may or may not) be repaired by welding.
     Page 163

139. The material used for a patch over a damaged longeron should be of the same material and the same wall
     thickness as the _____ . *Page 164*

140. When making an inner-sleeve repair, there should be a gap of _____ inch between the
     ends of the replacement tube and the original tubing to allow the outer tubing to be welded to the
     inner sleeve. *Page 165*

141. The diameter of the holes for a rosette weld is _____ of the diameter of the original
     tubing. *Page 165*

Answers to Chapter 2 Study Questions

1. monocoque
2. semimonocoque
3. a. tension
   b. compression
   c. torsion
   d. bending
   e. shear
4. stress
5. strain
6. elastic limit
7. a. copper
   b. magnesium
   c. zinc
8. solution
9. intergranular
10. aging
11. precipitation
12. artificial aging
13. slowly
14. can

15. T3
16. T6
17. H14
18. O
19. is not
20. annealing
21. is not
22. clad
23. weaker
24. anodized
25. conversion
26. more
27. does
28. ferrous
29. carbon
30. chromium, nickel
31. ultimate
32. hardness
33. 186,000
34. does not

35. 70,000
36. shear
37. shear
38. 2117
39. 1100
40. 2017
41. 2024
42. 5056
43. AD, 2117, B, 5056
44. 2017, 2024
45. 5056
46. a. 100° countersunk,
       2117, $\frac{1}{8}$, $\frac{1}{4}$
    b. Universal, 2024, $\frac{3}{16}$, $\frac{1}{2}$
47. Monel
48. are not
49. are

Continued

50. locking collar
51. Rivnut
52. shear
53. Sharpie-type fine permanent marker
54. thickness
55. 2
56. 70
57. numbers, letters, fractions
58. larger
59. cornice
60. slip roll former
61. sand bag
62. few
63. greater
64. 3, 4
65. silver
66. $\frac{3}{32}$
67. inside
68. compressive
69. across
70. $\frac{1}{4}$
71. less
72. 0.4
73. 0.232
74. 0.112
75. less
76. inside bend tangent
77. bend radius
78. ends
79. center
80. stiffness
81. 5056
82. 3
83. pitch
84. $\frac{3}{8}$, $1\frac{1}{2}$
85. $\frac{3}{8}$
86. $\frac{3}{16}$
87. shear
88. Sharpie-type fine permanent marker
89. 30
90. 40
91. thickness
92. a. coin dimpling
    b. radius dimpling
93. coin
94. larger
95. $1\frac{1}{2}$
96. $1\frac{1}{2}$
97. $\frac{1}{2}$
98. microshaver
99. 2
100. 2
101. stretched
102. corrosion
103. 40, 30
104. 3, 12
105. thickness
106. inboard, forward
107. may not
108. a. data
     b. work
109. acetylene
110. is not
111. calcium carbide
112. acetone
113. right-hand
114. left-hand
115. gases used
116. is not
117. all of the way
118. part way
119. soap and water
120. oxidizing
121. neutral
122. forehand
123. reducing
124. carburizing
125. bottom
126. both sides
127. hot water
128. angle
129. rod
130. neutral
131. negative
132 larger
133 front
134 slow
135. contaminated
136. spot welding, seam welding
137. may not
138. may not
139. longeron
140. $\frac{1}{8}$
141. $\frac{1}{4}$

NONMETALLIC AIRCRAFT STRUCTURES

3

Continued

Aircraft Fabric Covering *(Continued)*

Continued

NONMETALLIC AIRCRAFT STRUCTURES

3

Aircraft Wood Structure

Wood is a highly desirable material for aircraft construction. It is lightweight, strong, and has long life when it is properly preserved. It was used extensively in the early days of aircraft construction, but is out of favor for modern commercial aircraft because it does not lend itself to automated high-volume production. This role has been filled by all-metal aircraft, which is currently being challenged by composite structures.

composite. Something made up of different materials combined in such a way that the characteristics of the resulting material are different from those of any one of the components.

Aircraft Wood

There are two basic classifications of wood, hardwood and softwood. These classifications are not based on the actual hardness of the wood, but on its cell structure.

Hardwoods come from deciduous trees whose leaves fall each year. The wood has visible pores and is usually (but not always) heavier and denser than softwoods. Softwoods come from evergreen trees that have needles and cones and are typified by their fiber-like cells.

The properties of the various woods that are used in aircraft construction are seen in Figure 3-1.

deciduous. A type of tree that sheds its foliage at the end of the growing season. Hardwoods come from deciduous trees.

hardwood. Wood from a broadleaf tree that sheds its leaves each year.

softwood. Wood from a tree that bears cones and has needles rather than leaves.

Species of wood	Strength compared with spruce	Remarks
Sitka spruce	100%	Reference wood
Douglas fir	Exceeds spruce	Difficult to work, more difficult than spruce, has some tendency to split.
Noble fir	Slightly exceeds spruce except in shear	Satisfactory for direct replacement for spruce.
Western hemlock	Slightly exceeds spruce	Less uniform than spruce.
Northern white pine	85% to 96% of spruce	Must use increased size to compensate for lower strength.
White cedar	Exceeds spruce	May be used as a substitute for spruce.
Yellow poplar	Slightly less than spruce	Must use increased size to compensate for lower strength.

Figure 3-1. *Properties of aircraft structural wood*

laminated wood. A type of wood made by gluing several pieces of thin wood together. The grain of all pieces runs in the same direction.

plywood. A wood product made by gluing several pieces of thin wood veneer together. The grain of the wood in each layer runs at 90° or 45° to the grain of the layer next to it.

veneer. Thin sheets of wood "peeled" from a log. A wide-blade knife held against the surface of the log peels away the veneer as the log is rotated in the cutter.

Veneer is used for making plywood. Several sheets of veneer are glued together, with the grain of each sheet placed at 45° or 90° to the grain of the sheets next to it.

annual rings. The rings that appear in the end of a log cut from a tree. The number of annual rings per inch gives an indication of the strength of the wood. The more rings there are and the closer they are together, the stronger the wood.

The pattern of alternating light and dark rings is caused by the season variations in the growth rate of the tree. A tree grows quickly in the spring and produces the light-colored, less dense rings. The slower growth during the summer, or latter part of the growing season, produces the dark colored, denser rings.

springwood. The portion of an annual ring in a piece of wood that is formed principally during the first part of the growing season, the spring of the year. Springwood is softer, more porous, and lighter than the summerwood.

summerwood. The less porous, usually harder portion of an annual ring that forms in the latter part of the growing season, the summer of the year.

Types of Wood

Solid wood is often used for aircraft wing spars, but the difficulty in getting a single piece of wood large enough for a spar that meets all of the specifications for aircraft structural wood often makes laminated spars less expensive and thus preferable to solid spars.

Laminated wood is made of strips of wood glued together in such a way that the grain of all strips run in the same direction. Wing spars made of strips of Sitka spruce glued together are acceptable as a direct replacement for solid spars, provided both spars are of the same high-quality material.

Wooden propellers are made of laminations of birch glued together so that the propeller has more uniformity and strength than it would have if it were made of a single piece of birch.

Plywood is made of sheets of wood veneer glued together with the grains of adjacent layers crossing each other at either 45° or 90°. Aircraft plywood with surface plies of mahogany, birch, or spruce often has a core of poplar or basswood to provide the strongest glue bond between the plies. Plywood up through $\frac{3}{16}$ inch in thickness normally has three plies, and $\frac{1}{4}$ inch or thicker plywood has five plies.

Evaluating Wood for Aircraft Use

When you look at the end of a piece of wood, you will notice that it has concentric rings that are alternately light and dark. These are called annual rings because each dark and light pair represents one growth cycle. The light ring is called springwood and it marks the rapid growth of the tree during the early spring of the year. The dark ring is called summerwood and shows the amount the tree grew during the summer when growth is slower. Summerwood is denser and heavier than springwood.

Wood fibers swell as they absorb moisture and shrink as they lose it. These dimensional changes are greatest along the annual rings and much less across the rings.

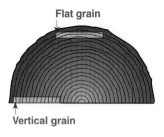

Figure 3-2. *Planks cut tangent to the annual rings (flat grain) distort, or warp, as their moisture content changes. Planks cut across the annual rings (vertical grain) change their dimensions very little as moisture content changes.*

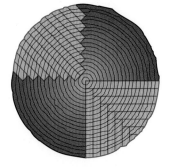

Figure 3-3. *A log is quartersawn to produce the maximum number of planks with vertical "C" grain. Two methods of quartersawing are illustrated.*

Aircraft structural wood is cut from the tree in such a way that most of the grain lies at 45° or more to the wide dimension of the wood plank. Wood cut in this way is said to have vertical grain.

Logs are quartersawn to produce planks with vertical grain.

Sitka spruce is the reference wood for aircraft structure, and it must meet certain requirements to be used for this purpose. Typical requirements for aircraft spruce, and for approved substitutes, are included in the FAA Advisory Circular 43.13-1B *Acceptable Methods , Techniques, and Practices—Aircraft Inspection and Repair*. These requirements are shown in Figure 3-4.

quartersawn wood. Wood sawed from a tree in such a way that the annual rings cross the plank at an angle greater than 45°.

Moisture content — 12%
Minimum annual rings per inch — 6
Maximum slope of the grain — 1 inch in 15 inches

Defects permitted:

Cross grain — Spiral grain, diagonal grain, or a combination of the two is acceptable providing the grain does not diverge from the longitudinal more than 1 in 15. A check of all four faces of the board is necessary to determine the amount of divergence. The direction of free-flowing ink will frequently assist in determining grain direction.
Wavy, curly and interlocked grain — Acceptable, if local irregularities do not exceed limitations specified for spiral and directional grain.
Knots — Sound hard knots up to ⅜ inch in maximum diameter are acceptable providing: (1) They are not in the projecting portions of I-beams, along the edges of rectangular or beveled unrouted beams, or along the edges of flanges of box beams (except in low-stressed portions) (2) They do not cause grain divergence at the edges of the board or in the flanges of a beam of more than 1:15. (3) They are not in the center third of the beam and are not closer than 20 inches to another knot or other defect (pertains to ⅜-inch knots—smaller knots may be proportionally closer). Knots greater than ¼ inch must be used with caution.
Pin knot clusters — Small clusters are acceptable providing they produce only a small effect on grain direction.
Pitch pockets — Acceptable, in center portion of a beam providing they are at least 14 inches apart when they lie in the same growth ring and do not exceed 1½ inch length by ⅛ inch width by ⅛ inch depth, and providing they are not along the projecting portions of I-beams, along the edges of rectangular or beveled unrouted beams, or along the edges of the flanges of box beams.
Mineral streaks — Acceptable, providing careful inspection fails to reveal any decay.

Defects not permitted:

Cross grain — Not acceptable, except as noted above.
Wavy, curly, and interlocked grain — Not acceptable, except as noted above.
Hard knots — Not acceptable, except as noted above.
Pin knot clusters — Not acceptable if they produce large effect on grain direction.
Spike knots — These are knots running completely through the depth of a beam, perpendicular to the annual rings and appear most frequently in quarter sawed lumber. Reject wood containing this defect.
Pitch pockets — Not acceptable, except as noted above.
Mineral streaks — Not acceptable if accompanied by decay.
Checks, shakes, and splits — Checks are longitudinal cracks extending, in general, across the annual rings. Shakes are longitudinal cracks usually between two annual rings. Splits are longitudinal cracks induced by artificially induced stress. Reject wood containing these defects.
Compression wood — This defect is very detrimental to strength and is difficult to recognize readily. It is characterized by high specific gravity; has the appearance of an excessive growth of summerwood; and in most species shows but little contrast in color between springwood and summerwood. In doubtful cases, reject the material, or subject samples to a toughness machine test to establish the quality of the wood. Reject all material containing compression wood.
Compression failures — This defect is caused from the wood being overstressed in compression due to natural forces during the growth of the tree, felling trees on rough or irregular ground, or rough handling of logs or lumber. Compression failures are characterized by a buckling of the fibers that appear as streaks on the surface of the piece substantially at right angles to the grain, and vary from pronounced failures to very fine hairlines that require close inspection to detect. Reject wood containing obvious failures. In doubtful cases reject the wood, or make a closer inspection in the form of microscopic examination or toughness test; the latter means being the more reliable.
Decay — Examine all stains and discolorations carefully to determine whether or not they are harmless, or in a stage of preliminary or advanced decay. All pieces must be free from rot, dote, red heart, purple heart, and all other forms of decay.

Figure 3-4. *Typical requirements for aircraft spruce*

Incorrect:
Joint has end grains of both pieces in contact.

Incorrect:
Joint has end grain of one piece in contact
with edge grain of the other.

Correct:
Both pieces are cut parallel to grain. This grain
orientation produces the strongest joint.

Figure 3-5. *Grain orientation for a
scarfed glue joint*

Glues and Gluing

Wood aircraft depend entirely on glued joints for their strength. Tiny nails are
often used in joints securing a plywood gusset to a wing rib cap strip and cross
member, but the nails do not supply any strength to the joint; they only provide
the clamping pressure needed to allow the glued joint to develop its maximum
strength.

Glued joints should carry the full strength of the wood across the joint
under all stress directions to which the wood is subjected. To accomplish
this, the glue must meet the specifications, gluing procedures and conditions
found in Chapter 1 of Advisory Circular 43.13-1B.

Types of Glue

Today there are a number of high-strength glues on the market. Plastic resin
and resorcinol are generally FAA-approved for use on certificated airplanes.
Other glues, such as epoxies, also produce extremely strong glued joints, but
they should be specifically approved by the local FAA inspector before they
are used on certificated aircraft.

Surface Preparation for Gluing

A good glued joint in a wood aircraft structure should be stronger than the
wood itself. When a glued joint is broken, the wood fibers should tear before
the glue separates.

The surfaces to be glued should be perfectly flat and smooth to provide
intimate contact. Apply the glue according to the recommendations of the
glue manufacturer, and clamp the parts together to provide the proper amount
of pressure. The glue penetrates into the surface of the parts and bonds them
together.

The design of a glued joint is important. The joint must be loaded in shear
only, and the grain of the two pieces must be parallel. Proper and improper
grain orientation is illustrated in Figure 3-5.

The moisture content of the wood is important. Twelve percent is ideal,
but it is very important that both pieces have the same content. Ensure this by
keeping both pieces in the same room at least overnight. Do not give the
surfaces the final preparation more than eight hours before the glue is applied.

Cut the wood with a fine-tooth saw and smooth it with a planer or jointer.
Since the strength of the glued joint is provided by the glue entering the fibers
of the wood of both pieces, the pieces should be in intimate contact. Tooth
planing or other means of roughening the surface are not recommended
because this prevents intimate contact.

Don't sand the surfaces, because sanding dust will get into the fibers and
prevent the entry of the glue. Scrape the surfaces with a piece of window glass
that has been scored with a glass cutter and broken so that it is perfectly
straight, if you want to ensure perfect contact.

Proper Gluing Procedures

Once the wood has been prepared for gluing, mix the glue according to the manufacturer's recommendations and apply it to either one surface or both surfaces. One technique that ensures excellent adhesion is to apply one coat of glue to each of the surfaces and force it into the pores of the wood with a putty knife, then brush on a second coat and assemble the parts.

When the parts have been assembled and properly aligned, apply the correct amount of pressure, using cabinetmaker's parallel clamps to ensure that the pressure is evenly applied. For softwoods used for wing spars and ribs, tighten the clamps firmly but not excessively tight (125 to 150 pounds per square inch). For hardwoods, tighten the clamps more to get between 150 and 200 pounds per square inch.

Truss-type wing ribs have a large number of end-grain joints that do not produce the full strength of the wood. To increase the strength of these joints, glue a gusset made of thin plywood over the joints as shown in Figure 3-6. The pressure needed when gluing a gusset to the rib is provided by brass-plated, cement-coated aircraft nails. The brass plating prevents the nails from rusting and the cement improves their holding power. There should be at least four nails per square inch, and in no instance should the nails be more than ¾ inch apart.

gusset. A small plate attached to two or more members of a truss structure. A gusset strengthens the truss.

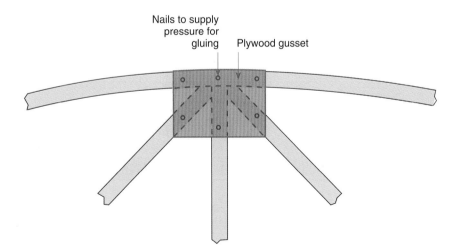

Nails to supply pressure for gluing

Plywood gusset

Figure 3-6. *A plywood gusset glued over the joints in a truss-type wing rib provides the strength needed for an end-grain joint. The pressure needed for the gluing is provided by aircraft nails.*

Construction and Repair of Wood Structures

Amateur-built aircraft are often made of wood because the materials are less expensive than those for metal aircraft, and less special tooling is required. Commercial aircraft manufacturers have just about completely phased out wood construction because of the high cost of the labor they require.

There are still quite a few smaller general aviation airplanes flying that have wooden wing spars and wooden ribs, and a few have some plywood covering. Some of the repairs these aircraft are most likely to need are described here.

Wing Spar Repair

The spars are the main stress-carrying members of a truss-type aircraft wing. They are typically made of aircraft-grade Sitka spruce and may be solid, laminated, or built up.

Most of the loads carried by a wing spar are carried in its upper and lower caps. The web, or center portion, of the spar carries a much smaller load than the caps, and it is possible to decrease the weight of the spar by removing some of the web thickness.

If part of the web is removed, there must be solid wood of full thickness at each point where the wing attaches to the fuselage and where the struts attach to the wing. These locations are typically reinforced with birch plywood to provide a good bearing surface for the attachment bolts.

Elongated bolt holes or cracks near the bolt holes in a wood spar usually require the replacement of the spar or the removal of the damaged area. A new section of spar can be spliced in. The splice or its reinforcing plates must not be under any fitting.

Figure 3-7 shows a typical method for splicing a solid or laminated spar. Before any actual spar splice is made, make a sketch of the repair including all the pertinent details and submit it to the FAA maintenance inspector for his or her approval.

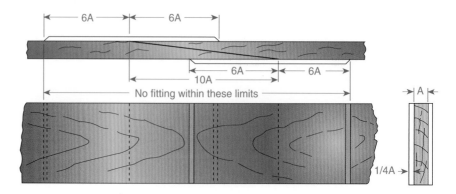

Figure 3-7. *Acceptable method for splicing a solid or laminated wood wing spar*

Remove the damaged area by cutting the spar at a 12-to-1 scarf angle (10:1 is the minimum allowable angle) and cutting a piece of new aircraft-grade wood of the same dimensions, and with the same scarf angle.

Spread the FAA-approved or accepted glue on the two prepared ends and place a pressure block on each side. Clamp the spar and pressure blocks together with cabinetmaker's parallel clamps. Check to be sure that the joint is perfectly straight, then tighten the clamps until a uniform bead of glue is squeezed from the joint. Wipe this glue off and allow the pressure to remain for at least the time specified for the particular glue at the existing ambient temperature.

Once you remove the clamps, cut the solid spruce or birch plywood reinforcing plates as wide as the spar, 12 times as long as the spar is thick, and one-fourth as thick as the spar. Taper the ends of these plates with a slope of about 5 to 1 to prevent an abrupt change in the cross-sectional area, and prepare the plates to be glued in place. The center of the reinforcing plates should be in line with the end of the cut in the spar, and they must overlap by twice the thickness of the spar. Scrape the surface of the spar and the reinforcing plates with the edge of a piece of glass to remove all surface contamination or roughness, and glue the reinforcing plates in position. *See* Figure 3-7.

Rib Repairs

The most common damage to a wing rib is a broken cap strip. This may be repaired by removing the damaged area by cutting the cap strip with a 12:1 taper (10:1 minimum). Cut the replacement material with the same taper and glue the pieces together. When cutting the taper in both pieces of wood, be sure that the cuts are parallel to the grain of the wood so there will be no end-grain glue joints. *See* Figure 3-5 on Page 178.

Glue the pieces together and when the glue is completely dry, cut reinforcing plates of aircraft-grade plywood as shown in Figure 3-8, and glue them in place using aircraft nails to supply the pressure. The face grain of the plywood must be parallel to the cap strip.

scarf joint. A joint in a wood structure in which the ends to be joined are cut in a long taper, normally about 12:1, and fastened together by gluing. A glued scarf joint makes a strong splice because the joint is made along the side of the wood fibers rather than along their ends.

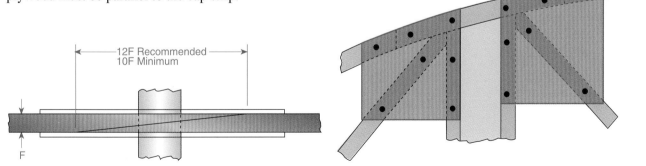

Figure 3-8. *Wing rib cap strip splice at a spar*

Repair to Damaged Plywood Structures

You can repair small holes in a plywood skin if they can be cleaned out to a diameter of less than one inch. Repair them by doping a fabric patch over them, unless the damage is in the leading edge of a wing. The fabric should extend at least one inch beyond the edges of the hole.

You can repair plywood skins $\frac{1}{8}$ inch thick or less that are damaged between or along framing members with surface, or overlay, patches. Bevel the edges of all these patches back for a distance of four thicknesses of the wood to prevent an abrupt change in cross-sectional area.

Repair small holes in plywood skins not more than $\frac{1}{10}$ inch thick whose largest dimensions are not over 15 times the skin thickness with a splayed patch.

Trim the damage to a circular hole with a maximum dimension of 15 times the skin thickness, and taper the edges of the hole back five times the skin thickness. Cut a patch that exactly fills the cleaned-out and tapered hole and orient the face ply in the same direction as that of the damaged skin.

Glue the patch in place, and when the glue is thoroughly dry, sand the surface and refinish it to match the rest of the skin.

A properly prepared and inserted scarf patch is the best repair for damaged plywood skins and is preferred for most skin repairs. Clean out the damaged area and taper back the edges of the hole at least 12 times the thickness of the skin. Cut the patch and taper its edges to match those of the prepared hole and glue it in place. Apply pressure with a nailing strip that is nailed in place over a piece of cellophane or vinyl sheeting to prevent the strip sticking to the skin. After the glue is completely dry, break away the nailing strip and remove the nails with a pair of diagonal cutters. Sand the surface and refinish it to match the rest of the skin.

Protection and Inspection of Wooden Aircraft Structures

Decay and dry rot (caused by a certain species of fungus) are major problems associated with wood aircraft. This fungus gets its nourishment from the cellulose of the wood and reproduces by forming microscopic spores, or seed. These spores are carried by the air currents and when they settle on an unprotected piece of wood in the presence of moisture, they multiply and cause the wood to disintegrate.

The low points of the aircraft must have an adequate number of drain holes, so moisture that accumulates inside the structure will drain out. These holes also ventilate the structure to prevent water from condensing inside it.

Decay first shows up as a discoloration of the wood, usually black, gray, or brown. Discoloration is not always caused by decay, but you should check any discolored area. Stick a sharp-pointed knife blade into the discolored area

---

splayed patch. A type of patch made in an aircraft plywood structure in which the edges of the patch are tapered for approximately five times the thickness of the ply-wood. A splayed patch is not recommended for use on plywood less than 1/10-inch thick.

nailing strip. A method of applying pressure to the glue in a scarf joint repair in a plywood skin. A strip of thin plywood is nailed over the glued scarf joint with the nails extending into a supporting structure beneath the skin. The strip is installed over vinyl sheeting to prevent it sticking to the skin. When the glue is thoroughly dry, the nailing strip is broken away and the nails removed.

decay. Decomposition. The breakdown of the structure of wood fibers. Wood that shows any indication of decay must be rejected for use in aircraft structure.

dry rot. Decomposition of wood fibers caused by fungi. Dry rot destroys all strength in the wood.

fungus (*plural* fungi). Any of several types of plant life that include yeasts, molds, and mildew.

and pry the wood up. If it comes up as a long splinter, the wood is good, and no decay is present. But if it comes up as a chunk about the size of the knife blade tip or crumbles when disturbed by the knife, the wood has decayed and must be replaced.

You can protect aircraft structure against decay by keeping air and moisture from the wood. Wood whose moisture content is kept below about 20% will not decay.

After you've completed all of the cutting, drilling, and gluing in an aircraft repair, saturate the wood with a wood preservative (typically a non-oil-base vehicle with copper naphthonate or pentachlorophenol). After the preservative is dry, give the structure several coats of varnish to seal the surface.

STUDY QUESTIONS: AIRCRAFT WOOD CONSTRUCTION

Answers begin on Page 263. **Page numbers refer to chapter text.**

1. Wood that comes from a cone-bearing tree is a _____ (softwood or hardwood). *Page 175*

2. Hardwoods _____ (are or are not) always more dense than softwoods. *Page 175*

3. The standard for comparing all aircraft structural wood is _____ . *Page 175*

4. A wood product made of strips of wood glued together in such a way that all of the grains run in the same direction is called _____ wood. *Page 176*

5. Wood propellers are made of laminations of _____ (what kind of wood). *Page 176*

6. The grains in the plies of a sheet of aircraft plywood cross each other at either _____ or _____ degrees. *Page 176*

7. Aircraft plywood with mahogany or birch faces often have cores made of _____ or _____ . *Page 176*

8. The light bands seen in the end of a piece of wood are called _____ (springwood or summerwood). *Page 176*

9. The desirable moisture content of aircraft spruce is _____ percent. *Page 177*

10. The maximum allowable grain divergence in aircraft spruce is 1:_____ . *Page 177*

Continued

11. A sound hard knot that is ⅜ inch in diameter in the web of a solid wood wing spar _____ (is or is not) an acceptable defect. *Page 177*

12. A pitch pocket 1 inch long, ⅛ inch wide and 3/32 inch deep in the center of a solid wood wing spar _____ (is or is not) an acceptable defect. *Page 177*

13. A wood wing spar blank containing some compression wood _____ (is or is not) acceptable for use. *Page 177*

14. Nails in a glued joint _____ (do or do not) increase the strength of the joint. *Page 178*

15. A properly designed glued joint should be loaded in _____ (shear or tension). *Page 178*

16. There should be a time lapse of no more than _____ hours between the final surfacing of the wood and the application of the glue. *Page 178*

17. When preparing solid wood for a glued joint, the surface _____ (should or should not) be roughened to help the glue adhere. *Page 178*

18. Final smoothing of the wood surfaces to be joined _____ (should or should not) be done with fine sandpaper. *Page 178*

19. When using aircraft nails to apply pressure for gluing gussets to a wing rib, the maximum distance between nails is _____ inch. *Page 179*

20. A laminated wood spar _____ (may or may not) be used to replace a solid wood spar if they are both made of the same quality wood. *Page 180*

21. The majority of the flight loads applied to a wing spar are carried in the _____ (caps or web) of the spar. *Page 180*

22. Locations where bolts pass through a wooden spar are reinforced with plywood made of _____ . *Page 180*

23. Elongated bolt holes in a wing spar _____ (should or should not) be repaired by drilling the hole oversize and using the next larger size bolt. *Page 180*

24. The minimum taper to use when splicing a solid or laminated wood wing spar is _____ to 1. *Page 181*

25. The reinforcing plate over a splice in a wing spar _____ (may or may not) be in a location through which the wing strut bolts pass. *Page 180*

26. A small hole in the leading edge of a plywood wing that cleans out to less than one inch in diameter _____ (can or cannot) be repaired with a fabric patch. *Page 182*

27. The choice repair for all types of plywood skin damage is a _____ (splayed or scarf) patch. *Page 182*

28. Aircraft wood with a moisture content of less than _____ % is not susceptible to decay or dry rot. *Page 183*

29. When a sharp knife point stuck into a piece of aircraft wood pries up a chunk of wood instead of a hard splinter, the wood _____ (is or is not) likely infected with decay. *Page 183*

Aircraft Fabric Covering

Fabric Covering Systems

Fabric-covered aircraft were at one time the most popular type, but today, all-metal construction is standard. Aviation maintenance technicians are likely to encounter fabric covering only on some of the special-purpose aircraft, such as those used for agricultural applications, or when restoring antique airplanes. Many amateur-built aircraft are fabric-covered, and the newly introduced light-sport aircraft (LSA) category will likely bring about new FAA-certificated fabric-covered aircraft.

In this *Aviation Maintenance Technician Series*, we are concerned with aircraft fabric covering as it applies to FAA-certificated aircraft. While these principles also apply to amateur-built aircraft, the freedom from restrictive Federal Aviation Regulations allows an amateur builder to use some materials and procedures that are not approved for certificated aircraft.

Organic Fabrics

Cotton and linen are two popular natural, or organic, covering fabrics. Cotton is still used, but linen is not readily available in the United States.

For many years, mercerized long-staple Grade-A cotton was the standard covering material for aircraft. This fabric weighs approximately 4.5 ounces per square yard, has between 80 and 84 threads per inch (tpi), and a minimum tensile strength of 80 pounds per inch in both the warp and fill

tensile strength. The customary determinant for the strength of aircraft fabric. It is expressed in pounds per inch, and is the amount of pull needed to break a strip of fabric one inch wide.

directions. Grade-A cotton fabric meets Aeronautical Material Specification AMS 3806 and Military Specifications MIL-C-5646, and it is manufactured under Technical Standard Order TSO-C15. Grade-A fabric is approved for use on aircraft that have wing loadings greater than 9 pounds per square foot (psf) and with never-exceed speeds (V_{NE}) in excess of 160 miles per hour.

Inorganic Fabrics

There are two inorganic fabrics used for covering FAA-certificated aircraft; fabric made from polyester fibers and fabric made of glass filaments.

Fabric made from polyester fibers is sold under such trade names as Ceconite®, Superflite®, and Poly-Fiber® and is the most widely used covering material today. Polyester fibers used in aircraft covering are heated and stretched during manufacturing. This hot stretching orients the molecules and increases the strength and toughness of the fibers. Once the fibers are made into threads and woven into the fabric, they will return to their original unstretched length when reheated. Polyester used for aircraft covering is applied in its greige condition. It has not been passed through shrinking rollers, and it still contains some sizing, which is the lubricant required on the warp threads when the fabric is woven in the high-speed dry looms.

Fiberglass cloth is a loose weave of glass filaments treated with tinted butyrate dope to hold the filaments together for ease of installation. Both polyester and glass fiber fabric must be installed and finished according to the instructions in the STC that is sold with the material.

Glass cloth has been used to cover some aircraft structures because it is impervious to moisture, mildew, chemicals, and acids. It is also fire resistant. However, it was not very popular because it added significantly more weight than cotton and linen.

Covering System Approvals

Appendix A of Federal Aviation Regulations Part 43, *Maintenance, Preventive Maintenance, Rebuilding, and Alteration,* classifies the re-covering of an aircraft as a major repair. As any major repair, it must meet specific criteria, and an FAA Form 337, *Major Repair and Alteration* must be completed and properly filed to accompany the repair.

Original Equipment Manufacturer

When an aircraft is designed and the prototype is built, the FAA approves all the materials and methods used for the covering. When the aircraft is re-covered, the same type of materials must be used and they must be installed in the same way as was approved by the FAA. Re-covering an aircraft in this way is considered to be a major repair.

Supplemental Type Certificates

Most fabric-covered aircraft were certificated before synthetic fabrics became popular, and their certification calls for cotton fabric covering. The lower cost, additional strength, weight saving, and increased service life make re-covering these aircraft with one of the polyester fabrics a very practical alteration.

Since changing the type of fabric on the aircraft is a major alteration and prevents the aircraft conforming to its Approved Type Certificate (ATC), it must be issued a Supplemental Type Certificate (STC).

The holder of the STC authorizes its use as approved data when all of the materials specified in the STC are used, and when all of its procedures are followed.

FAA Field Approval

If for some reason you do not want to use the same materials used by the original manufacturer, nor the materials specified in an STC, consider getting FAA field approval. A field approval is time-consuming and not typically cost-effective, but it does allow for use of new or different materials or procedures.

To get a field approval, submit an FAA Form 337 to the FAA Flight Standards District Office describing in detail the procedure you want to follow. The FAA maintenance inspector may approve the data, or he or she may require more data to prove that this new procedure will allow the aircraft to meet or exceed the requirements for its original certification. When this data is approved, you may make the alteration. Then an IA must inspect the work for conformity to the approved data. If it conforms, the aircraft is approved for return to service and the Form 337 is completed and returned to the FAA FSDO.

FAA FSDO. Federal Aviation Administration Flight Standards District Office. An FAA field office serving an assigned geographical area staffed with Flight Standards personnel who serve the aviation industry and the general public on matters relating to certification and operation of air carrier and general aviation aircraft.

Aircraft Re-Covering

Re-covering an aircraft is an expensive and time-consuming project. Do not undertake it until it is definitely necessary. The structure to be re-covered must be thoroughly inspected, and all measures must be taken to preserve the structure, since it will not be visible for another inspection for several years.

Is Re-Covering Necessary?

The fabric on an aircraft is allowed to deteriorate until its strength is 70% of that required for the original fabric. New Grade-A cotton fabric has a strength of 80 pounds per inch, and it is allowed to deteriorate until its strength is 56 pounds per inch.

Figure 3-9. *The Maule fabric tester indicates the strength of the fabric in pounds per inch without making a hole in the fabric.*

plasticizer. A constituent in dope or lacquer that gives its film flexibility and resilience.

rejuvenate. Restore the resilience to an aircraft finishing material. This is done by the use of a rejuvenator.

An airplane whose V_{NE} is less than 160 mph and whose wing loading is less than 9 psf may be covered with intermediate fabric whose new strength is 65 pounds per inch. Any fabric installed on this type of aircraft is allowed to deteriorate to 46 pounds per inch (70% of 65 pounds per inch) before it must be replaced.

Often the dope on aircraft fabric dries out and cracks, giving the appearance that the aircraft needs re-covering, when what has actually happened is that the plasticizers have dried out of the dope and it is brittle. If the fabric is still good, the finish can be rejuvenated. Rejuvenation does nothing to improve the strength of the fabric, however. When the fabric deteriorates to 70% of the strength required for new fabric, it must be replaced.

Fabric Testing

The technician is required on each 100-hour or annual inspection to determine that the fabric meets at least its minimum strength requirements. Two commonly used methods of determining the strength of the fabric are the Maule test and the Seyboth test.

The Maule tester, Figure 3-9, is a precision spring-loaded instrument with a blunt pin on its end and a scale calibrated in pounds per inch. Hold the tester squarely against the fabric and press until the scale indicates the minimum allowable strength of the fabric. If the tester penetrates the fabric, it indicates that the fabric strength is below the minimum allowable. If both the fabric and the finish are good, the tester will make a small depression that will return to its original smooth surface with no permanent damage.

The Seyboth tester has a specially shaped, spring-loaded sharp point and an indicator pin that is marked with green, yellow, and red-colored bands. To use this tester, hold it straight against the fabric and press it down until the point penetrates the fabric enough to allow the wide shoulder to rest on the surface of the fabric. The amount of force required to penetrate the fabric is indicated by the color of the band on the indicator pin that protrudes from the body of the tester. If the fabric is very weak, only a small amount of force is needed, and the red band will show. If the fabric is somewhat stronger, more force is needed and the yellow band will be exposed. If the fabric is airworthy, enough force will be needed to cause one of the green bands to show. When the test is completed, place a small circular patch over the hole left by the tester. *See* Figure 3-10.

The indications given by these two testers are adequate to identify good fabric, but since both of them test fabric that is covered by the dope film, they do not indicate the actual strength of the undoped fabric. If the fabric strength indicated by the tester is marginal, a further test should be performed. To determine the actual strength of the fabric by itself, remove a strip of fabric about 1¼ inch wide and 6 inches long from the upper surface of the wing or fuselage. Take it from an area that is finished with a dark color, because dark colors absorb heat and in these locations the fabric is most likely to be weakened. Soak the fabric strip in dope thinner to remove all the dope, then pull the threads from the edges until you have a strip that is exactly one inch wide. Clamp the strip in a fabric pull tester and pull it until the strip breaks. The indication on the tester when the strip breaks is the tensile strength of the fabric.

Preparation for Re-Covering

If the fabric is too weak to be airworthy, you should begin to prepare the aircraft for re-covering. In this portion of our text, we follow the procedure used for covering the popular Piper Super Cub, as this procedure is typical for most fabric-covered aircraft.

First remove the wings and tail surfaces and carefully store them in the proper type of cradle so they will not be damaged while the aircraft is disassembled.

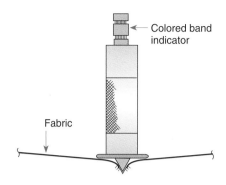

Figure 3-10. *The Seyboth fabric tester indicates the relative strength of the fabric with colored bands around the indicator pin. This pin protrudes from the top of the tester when it is pushed in until the wide face of the plunger rests on the fabric.*

Remove the Old Fabric

Carefully remove the fabric by cutting it along one of the fuselage longerons or the trailing edges of the wings and tail surfaces. Cut all the lacing cord used to hold the fabric to the structure. If the fabric is held to the wing with screws or clips, cut the surface tape and remove them.

Roll up the old covering and keep it until the re-covering job is complete, because you will probably need it to locate the positions for inspection rings and the holes through which control cables must pass. If the old finish is dope, and/or the fabric is oil soaked, take extra care to store the fabric away from possible sources of ignition.

Inspect the Structure

When the structure is completely uncovered, inspect the parts that are not visible when the covering is in place.

The lower longerons in the tail end of the fuselage are exposed to moisture and dirt and are likely to be rusted. Carefully sand off any rust and probe the entire tubing with a sharp-pointed awl to determine whether or not rust has weakened the metal.

Inspect the controls under the floorboards and replace any components that are worn or damaged, and lubricate those joints that will be difficult to reach when the covering is in place.

Inspect the tail surfaces for any indication of rust or damage. Check the hinges to be sure that they have not worn excessively and check for cracks. Carefully inspect the stabilizer adjustment mechanism or trim tabs if any are installed.

The wings demand the most attention. Check the spars for condition, especially at the root end and at the locations where the wing struts attach. Check wooden spars to be sure that none of the varnish has cracked. Revarnish any areas that show bare wood.

compression strut. A heavy structural member, often in the form of a steel tube, used to hold the spars of a Pratt truss airplane wing apart. A compression strut opposes the compressive loads between the spars arising from the tensile loads produced by the drag and antidrag wires.

drag wire. A structural wire inside a Pratt truss airplane wing between the spars. Drag wires run from the front spar inboard, to the rear spar at the next bay outboard. Drag wires oppose the forces that try to drag the wing backward.

antidrag wire. A structural wire inside a Pratt truss airplane wing between the spars. Antidrag wires run from the rear spar inboard, to the front spar at the next bay outboard. Antidrag wires oppose the forces that try to pull the wing forward.

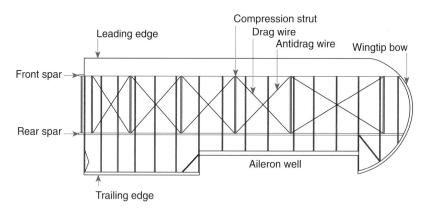

Figure 3-11. *Truss-type airplane wing*

Inspect the leading and trailing edges for corrosion or cracks. The leading edges of these wings are covered with thin aluminum alloy sheet back to the front spar, and this metal is easily dented. Repair any dents or replace sections of the metal that are dented beyond repair.

Check the control cables and pulleys. Replace any pulleys that are stuck or that show wear from the cables. Check the electrical wiring and replace any whose insulation is cracked. Secure the wire to the structure by the method used by the manufacturer. Check the pitot-static plumbing to be sure there are no leaks in the lines to be covered.

Check the wing truss for squareness. Use a wood or metal trammel bar and a pair of trammel points. Place a mark in the center of the top of both the front and rear spars aligned with the center of each of the compression struts. Set the trammel points to measure distance A, Figure 3-12, then measure distance B. If these distances are not exactly the same, adjust the drag and antidrag wires until they are.

After all the adjustments are made, look down each of the spars to determine that they are perfectly straight. If they are not, repeat the trammel process.

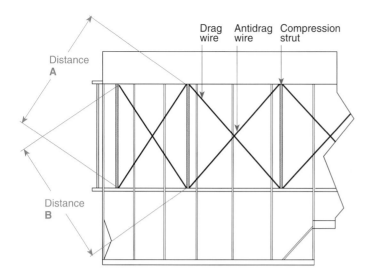

Figure 3-12. *A truss-type wing is squared up by measuring the diagonal distance across each of the bays with a trammel bar and trammel points. If distances A and B are not identical, adjust the drag and antidrag wires.*

trammel (*verb*). The procedure used to square up the Pratt truss in an airplane wing. Trammel points are set on the trammel bar so they measure the distance between the center of the front spar, at the inboard compression strut, and the center of the rear spar at the next compression strut outboard. The drag and antidrag wires are adjusted until the distance between the center of the rear spar at the inboard compression strut and the center of the front spar at the next outboard compression strut is exactly the same as that between the first points measured.

trammel bar. A wood or metal bar on which trammel points are mounted to compare distances.

trammel points. A set of sharp-pointed pins that protrude from the sides of a trammel bar.

Prepare the Structure

Once the structural inspection is complete and the repairs made, prepare the structure to receive the covering.

Remove all the dried dope that was used to attach the original fabric to the steel tubing, and prime the tubing with a good primer, such as one of the epoxies.

When preparing the wing, cover all the overlapping edges of the leading edge metal with cloth tape to protect the fabric.

Use reinforcing tape to brace all the ribs so they will remain in position until the fabric is stitched in place. This tape is applied across the middle of the ribs in the manner shown in Figure 3-13. Start at the root rib, work out to the tip, and loop the tape around the tip bow and back to the root rib. At the root rib, tie the ends together.

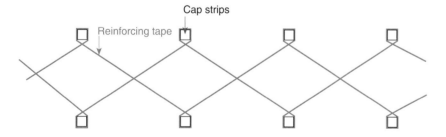

Figure 3-13. *Wing ribs are braced with reinforcing tape wrapped around the middle of the cap strips in this fashion.*

Cotton Fabric Covering

In this section we consider the procedure for covering an aircraft with Grade-A cotton, and then in the following section we will emphasize the differences when using polyester.

Textiles

Purchase the fabric from a legitimate supplier of aircraft materials. Grade-A fabric should be stamped TSO-C15 or AMS 3806 along the selvage edge. This fabric is usually available either by the yard in widths of 50 or 64 inches, or in pre-sewn envelopes tailored for specific aircraft.

Thread for sewing the fabric must meet VT-276 specifications, and the fabric is attached to the aircraft structure with waxed linen rib-lacing cord which meets MIL-T-6779 specifications.

Reinforcing tape is a narrow tape made of heavy cotton thread. It is placed over all of the ribs and any part of the structure to which the fabric is to be laced. It is normally available in widths from $\frac{1}{4}$ to $\frac{1}{2}$ inch, and wider for special applications. Reinforcing tape is also used to support the wing ribs before the fabric is installed, as shown in Figure 3-13 on Page 191.

Surface tape is made of Grade-A cotton and cut with pinked, or notched, edges to prevent its raveling. This tape is doped over all of the ribs after the rib lacing is completed, around the leading and trailing edges, and around the tips of all of the surfaces.

The length of most surface tape is parallel to the warp threads, but there is a bias-cut tape whose threads cross its length at a 45° angle. Bias-cut tape is used around the tips of some wings and tail surfaces where straight-cut tape will not lie down smoothly.

Chemicals

The finish for a fabric-covered aircraft involves use a number of highly specialized chemicals such as cements, dopes, thinners, solvents, retarders, and rejuvenators. It is extremely important when buying these chemicals that they are all fresh and compatible. The best way of assuring this is to use materials from the same manufacturer and purchase them from a reputable supplier of aircraft materials.

There are many places where the fabric is glued to the structure rather than sewn. The adhesive used to attach the fabric is similar to a heavy nitrate dope, but it contains different plasticizers. It can be thinned to the proper brushing consistency with nitrate thinner, but because of its different components, it should not be mixed with dope.

Aircraft dope consists of a film base, solvents, plasticizers, and thinners. The film base is made of cellulose fibers dissolved in an acid. It wets and encloses, or encapsulates, the fibers of the fabric, and when it dries it shrinks the fibers and pulls them tightly together. Solvents dissolve the film base material, and plasticizers are mixed with the dissolved film base to control its characteristics and give it resilience to prevent its cracking when it dries.

bias-cut surface tape. A fabric tape in which the threads run at an angle of 45° to the length of the tape. Bias-cut tape may be stretched around a compound curve such as a wing tip bow without wrinkling.

Safety note:
When using any of these materials, read and observe all chemical hazard warning notes on the containers as some of them may contain components that are known cancer risks.

Thinners adjust the viscosity of dope, giving it the correct consistency for brushing or spraying. Two basic types of dopes are used on fabric-covered aircraft: nitrate and butyrate.

Nitrate dope is the oldest type of aircraft fabric dope. It has excellent encapsulating properties, which make it the best material for attaching the fabric to the structure and for the initial coats of dope, but it has the serious drawback of being highly flammable.

Butyrate dope has better tautening characteristics than nitrate dope, and while it will burn, it does not ignite as easily as nitrate. Its main drawback is that it does not encapsulate the fibers as well as nitrate.

The solvents used in butyrate dope are more potent than those used in nitrate dope, and butyrate dope will soften the nitrate film base and may be applied over it. The solvents used in nitrate dope will not adequately soften the butyrate film, and nitrate dope should not be applied over butyrate dope.

Clear dope is an organic product and the fabrics to which it is applied are weakened by the ultraviolet rays of the sun. To prevent this damage, extremely tiny flakes of aluminum metal are mixed with clear dope and sprayed over the coats of clear dope. The aluminum flakes spread out and form a light-tight covering that prevents the ultraviolet rays reaching the clear dope and the fabric.

The aluminum flakes are available as a powder and also in the more convenient form of a ready-mixed paste. To prepare the dope, first mix about three and a half ounces of paste with dope thinner and then pour a gallon of unthinned butyrate dope into the thinned paste.

Colored dopes are used to give an aircraft an attractive finish and to protect it from the elements. For many years, aircraft were finished only with aluminum-pigmented dope. This provided the needed ultraviolet protection and added a minimum of weight. Modern aircraft are finished with many different colors, although lighter colors predominate because they absorb the least heat from the sun, so fabric finished with light-colored dope lasts longer.

Some pigments, especially some of the reds, are soluble in the solvents used in their application and they will bleed up through any of the finishing coats that are applied over them. Bleeding dopes must be applied after all the other coats have dried.

Aircraft dope is a complex mixture of film base, solvents, and plasticizers. Its viscosity must be adjusted by the addition of thinner before it is brushed or sprayed on the fabric. Because of its complex composition, only thinners that are made especially for the particular dope should be used.

The dope dries when the solvents and thinner evaporate and leave the resilient film attached to the fabric. If the solvents evaporate too rapidly, they will absorb enough heat to drop the temperature of the air, allowing moisture to condense and deposit on the surface of the wet dope. The moisture causes the cellulose to precipitate from the dope film and form a white porous deposit called blush. A blushed doped surface is weak, porous, and unattractive.

bleeding dope. Dope whose pigments are soluble in the solvents or thinners used in the finishing system. The color will bleed up through the finish coats.

blush. A defect in a lacquer or dope finish caused by moisture condensing on the surface before the finish dries.

If the humidity of the air is high, the evaporation of the solvents cools the air enough to cause the moisture to condense. The water condensed from the air mixes with the lacquer or dope and forms a dull, porous, chalky-looking finish called blush. A blushed finish is neither attractive nor protective.

If the humidity of the air in the paint room is high enough for the dope to blush, you can use retarder in place of some of the thinner. Retarder is a thinner that has certain additives that slow its rate of evaporation.

Cotton and linen fabrics are susceptible to destruction by mildew and fungus, which can weaken the fabric in a relatively short time unless you mix fungicidal paste, including a small amount of nonbleeding dye, with thinned clear dope for the first coat. This dope must thoroughly penetrate and encapsulate the fabric for the fungicidal agent to be effective.

Installing the Fabric

When the structure has been inspected and repaired as necessary, and the covering system has been chosen, you are ready for the most important steps in re-covering, installing the fabric.

The Envelope Method

If you are using a pre-sewn envelope, you are ready to install the fabric. Begin with the simplest structures first and then, as you gain experience, progress to the more complex components. Install in this order: flaps, ailerons, tail surfaces, landing gear legs, wings, and fuselage.

When covering small components, first brush a primer coat of full-bodied nitrate cement on the structure where the fabric will attach and allow it to dry. Then slip the envelope over the structure and straighten the seam so that it runs straight down the trailing edge. Don't pull the fabric tight, just smooth. Close the open end by cementing the fabric to the structure. Secure the fabric in place by flooding the area over the dried cement with a second coat, thinned to good brushing consistency to soften that which was applied to the structure. Work the fabric down into the wet cement with your fingers to get all of the air bubbles out of it.

When covering the wings, slip the envelope over the tip and straighten the seam around the center of the tip bow and along the trailing edge. Any chordwise seams should all be parallel to the line of flight and should not lie over a wing rib.

When the covering is in place with all the seams straight, begin cementing the fabric at the tip end of the aileron well. Give the metal a full-bodied coat of nitrate cement. When it is thoroughly dry, brush on a coat of thinned cement. Place the fabric in position, and pull it smooth. Press it down into the wet cement and work out the air bubbles. Some aircraft use a metal strip secured with screws or other fasteners to retain the fabric in the aileron well.

Turn the wing over and coat the fabric you have just cemented in the aileron well with a coat of thinned cement. Pull the fabric smooth and work its edges down into the wet dope.

full-bodied. Not thinned.

Close out the aileron well and then the root end of the wing. When doing this work it is very important to continually check that the seams are not pulled away from the center of the trailing edge.

Be sure that the tubing to which the fabric is to attach is absolutely clean and primed with epoxy primer, then coat it with full-bodied nitrate cement. When it is dry, slip the fuselage envelope over the structure from the tail. Apply a thinned coat of cement over the area to which the fabric is to attach and press the edges of the fabric into it, working out all of the air bubbles. Trim the fabric so it will wrap around the tubing but not lap up onto the fabric on the inside.

If the fuselage has an integral vertical fin, slip the fin cover in place with the seams straight along the leading edge, and cement the fabric from the fin to the fabric from the fuselage.

The Blanket Method

When pre-sewn envelopes are unavailable, use the blanket method. Choose the width of fabric that will let you sew up a blanket with at least one foot of fabric at the tip and at the root, and will not cause chordwise seams to lie over a wing rib.

Sew the blanket using an FAA-approved machine-sewing thread and any of the seams shown in Figure 3-14. Apply a full-bodied coat of cement to both sides of the trailing edge and the wingtip bow. When this is dry, cover it with a coat of thinned cement and press the fabric from one side of the wing down into it, working out all of the air bubbles. After the cement is dry, trim the fabric, and turn the wing over. Pull the fabric smooth but not tight, and brush a coat of thinned nitrate cement over the fabric that has just been cemented down. Press the fabric down into the wet cement and work out all the air bubbles. Continue all around the trailing edge and the wingtip bow.

When the cement is dry, trim the fabric with pinking shears to leave at least a one-inch overlap around the wing tip and the trailing edge. Cement the overlap and close out the aileron well as described in the envelope method section.

Removing the Wrinkles

You can remove wrinkles from installed fabric by wetting the fabric with distilled or demineralized water. Wet the fabric thoroughly but do not use so much water that it runs down the inside of the structure.

The wet fabric will pull up to a drumhead tightness and all of the wrinkles will pull out. It will lose some of its tightness when it dries, but the wrinkles will be gone.

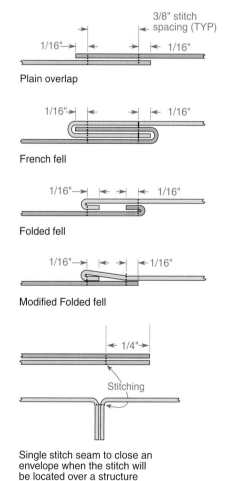

Plain overlap

French fell

Folded fell

Modified Folded fell

Single stitch seam to close an envelope when the stitch will be located over a structure

Figure 3-14. *Some of the machine-sewed seams used to join aircraft cotton fabric.*

It is important not to cut the fabric around any fittings while it is wet. It moves about considerably while it is shrinking, so the hole would end up too large and in the wrong location.

The First Coat of Dope

Allow the water to dry completely, but do not allow more than 48 hours to elapse between the time the fabric is installed and the fungicidal dope is applied. If the fabric is left untreated for longer than this, airborne fungus spores will settle on the fabric.

Pour unthinned nitrate dope into fungicidal paste at the ratio of one gallon of dope for four ounces of paste. Stir until the paste is mixed evenly throughout the dope and then thin the dope with equal parts of nitrate dope thinner.

Use a good quality animal-bristle brush and work the thinned fungicidal dope well into the fabric so that the threads in the fabric are completely surrounded, but none of the dope runs down inside the fabric. The dye in the fungicidal paste helps you see when the fabric is completely treated and gives an indication of the uniformity of the application.

When you apply the first coat of dope, the fabric becomes stiff and baggy, but it will shrink when you apply additional coats of dope.

Attaching the Fabric

The fabric must be attached to the wing ribs in such a way that the aerodynamic force caused by the low pressure above the wing is transmitted into the structure, lifting the entire aircraft.

Many aircraft have the fabric laced to the ribs with waxed linen rib-lacing cord. This is a time-consuming operation, and much time is saved by attaching the fabric with metal clips or sheet metal screws. The fabric must be attached by the method used by the manufacturer unless a Supplemental Type Certificate is used.

The rib-stitch spacing is based on the never-exceed speed (V_{NE}) of the aircraft. Be sure to copy the spacing used by the manufacturer, or use the chart in Figure 3-15, and submit this rib-stitch spacing to the FAA when having your data for the re-covering approved before starting the work.

If the aircraft has a V_{NE} of 250 mph or more, apply antitear strips (made of the same fabric used for the covering and wide enough that the rib stitching will pass through them) to the upper surface of the wing and also the bottom surface inside the slipstream. The antitear strips are doped over each rib cap strip so they will be between the fabric and the reinforcing tape.

antitear strip. Strips of aircraft fabric laid under the reinforcing tape before the fabric is stitched to an aircraft wing.

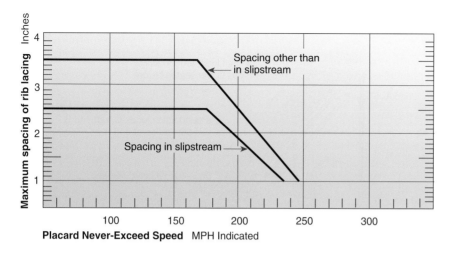

Figure 3-15. *Rib-stitch spacing chart*

Mark each rib with a lead pencil where the rib stitches will be placed. The spacing between the first and last stitches is one half of the spacing for all of the other stitches. Notice that the stitch spacing inside the slipstream is much closer than the spacing outside. For this purpose, the slipstream is considered to be the diameter of the propeller plus an additional rib on each side.

Soak strips of reinforcing tape in nitrate dope and squeeze the dope through the tape with your fingers to completely saturate it, with no air in the fibers. Place the tape over each rib with about a half-inch extending beyond the first and last stitches. Pull the tape smooth and press it down over the rib with your fingers.

Use a rib-stitch needle and punch holes on each side of each rib at the location marked for the stitches. Make the holes as close to the cap strips as you can get them. Place the knots on the side of the wing where they will be least visible. On a high-wing aircraft, place them on the top and on a low-wing aircraft, place them on the bottom.

For the typical wing, begin with lengths of rib-stitch cord about four times the length of the wing chord. Follow the procedure in Figure 3-16. Begin at the holes nearest the trailing edge and, using a long rib-stitch needle, make a double loop of the cord around the rib and tie a square knot in the center of the reinforcing tape on the side of the wing opposite that on which the regular stitches will be made.

Bring both ends of the cord back through the same holes and tie them with another square knot, this one placed on the side of the reinforcing tape. Lock this knot on both sides with half hitches around the loop, and cut off the excess cord on the short end. *See* Figure 3-16 on the next page.

reinforcing tape. A narrow strip of woven fabric material placed over the fabric as it is being attached to the aircraft structure with rib lacing cord. This tape carries a large amount of the load and prevents the fabric tearing at the stitches.

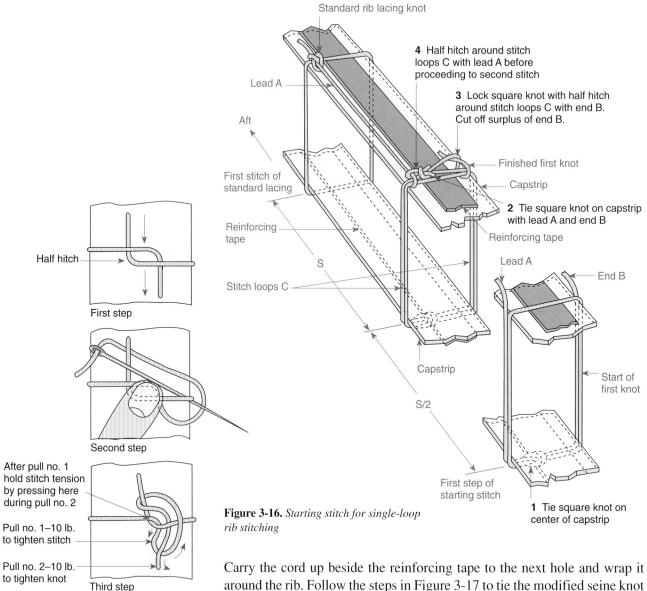

Standard rib lacing knot

4 Half hitch around stitch loops C with lead A before proceeding to second stitch

3 Lock square knot with half hitch around stitch loops C with end B. Cut off surplus of end B.

Lead A

Aft

First stitch of standard lacing

Finished first knot

Capstrip

2 Tie square knot on capstrip with lead A and end B

Reinforcing tape

Reinforcing tape

S

Stitch loops C

Lead A

End B

Capstrip

S/2

Start of first knot

First step of starting stitch

1 Tie square knot on center of capstrip

Figure 3-16. *Starting stitch for single-loop rib stitching*

Half hitch

First step

Second step

After pull no. 1 hold stitch tension by pressing here during pull no. 2

Pull no. 1–10 lb. to tighten stitch

Pull no. 2–10 lb. to tighten knot

Third step

Completed knot

Figure 3-17. *Modified seine knot used for rib stitching*

Carry the cord up beside the reinforcing tape to the next hole and wrap it around the rib. Follow the steps in Figure 3-17 to tie the modified seine knot that is most generally used for rib stitching.

Bring the end of the cord up through the fabric and over the cord from the preceding stitch. Pull the cord with about a 10-pound pull to tighten the stitch (pull 1). Hold your thumb over the stitch to hold the tension and bring the free end of the cord over the one going into the fabric and under the cord from the first stitch, then through the loop just formed. Now pull the cord tight with about a 10-pound pull to tighten the knot (pull 2). Position the knot beside the reinforcing tape at the edge of the hole in the fabric, but do not pull the knot down inside the fabric.

Make the final stitch at one-half the normal spacing, and use a double loop similar to that used for the first stitch. If the rib stitching cord is not long enough to completely lace a rib, it may be spliced using the splice knot shown in Figure 3-18. Do not use a square knot for splicing the cord because it will slip.

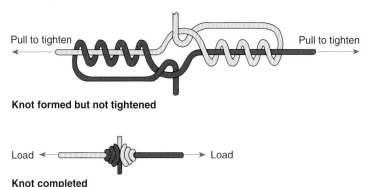

Knot formed but not tightened

Knot completed

Figure 3-18. *Use this splice knot to join lengths of waxed rib lacing cord.*

Because rib stitching is such a labor intensive operation, several manufacturers use metal wire clips to attach the fabric to metal wing ribs. Two types of clips commonly used are the Martin-type clip and the Cessna-type clip seen in Figure 3-19.

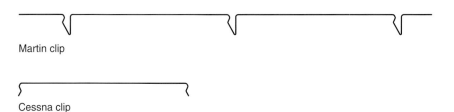

Martin clip

Cessna clip

Figure 3-19. *Fabric clips used to secure fabric to the wings of some aircraft*

Using a clip to attach the fabric to a wing that originally used rib stitching constitutes a major alteration to the airframe, and should be approved by the FAA before the work is started.

Another method of attaching the fabric to the wing ribs is by using very short sheet metal screws and a plastic or thin aluminum washer like that in Figure 3-20. Before drilling screw holes in a wing rib to which the fabric was originally stitched, have the alteration approved by the FAA.

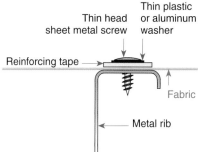

Figure 3-20. *Attachment of fabric to metal wing rib cap strips with sheet metal screws and a plastic or thin aluminum washer*

Drain Grommets and Inspection Rings

Drain grommets are attached to the fabric at all of the low points in the structure to ventilate the aircraft and prevent condensed moisture from rotting the fabric. These grommets are small doughnut-shaped pieces of acetate plastic with an outside diameter of about $\frac{3}{4}$ inch and with a $\frac{5}{16}$-inch hole in the center. Seaplane grommets are made with a small scoop formed in the plastic. They are installed with the opening to the rear to prevent water from spraying into the structure when the aircraft operates on the water. After completing the re-covering job, open the drain grommets by cutting the fabric from the inside of the grommet with a sharp-pointed knife blade.

Inspection rings are also made of acetate plastic and have an outside diameter of $4\frac{5}{8}$ inches and an inside diameter of $3\frac{1}{2}$ inches. They are installed at the locations chosen by the aircraft manufacturer to allow access to the inside of the structure for inspection and servicing. After re-covering the aircraft, cut the center from those inspection rings where access is required to the structure for the assembly. Do not open any inspection holes until they are needed. When the holes are cut, an inspection plate can be slipped into place to make a neat cover for the inspection hole.

Application of Surface Tape

After the fabric has been attached to the wings, brush on a coat of full-bodied butyrate dope.

Allow this coat of dope to dry completely and then lightly dry-sand it with 320-grit sandpaper. Sand it just enough to remove the rough nap of the fabric raised by the dope. Be extremely careful when sanding. It is terribly easy for the sharp sandpaper to cut completely through the doped fabric.

Before beginning to dry-sand any fabric-covered aircraft structure, ground it electrically by connecting some metal part of the structure to a cold water pipe or to some metal part of the shop building. Rubbing the dry fabric with sandpaper will generate enough static electricity to, unless the structure is adequately grounded, produce a spark that could cause the nitrate dope fumes to explode.

Cut lengths of 2-inch pinked-edge surface tape long enough to go from the trailing edge around the leading edge, and then back to the trailing edge. Saturate this tape with dope, and brush a coat of full-bodied dope over the rib. Place the tape in the dope, centered over the rib, and work it down into the dope with two fingers straddling the reinforcing tape. Press out all the air bubbles.

By this time the fabric has some stiffness, and will not move around any more, so you can cut it around all of the fittings that are to protrude. Use a very sharp knife to cut around the fittings, and then apply surface tape or a pinked-edge patch to reinforce the fabric at these points.

surface tape. Strips of aircraft fabric that are doped over all seams and places where the fabric is stitched to the aircraft structure. Surface tape is also doped over the wing leading edges where abrasive wear occurs.

The edges of surface tape are pinked, or notched, to keep them from raveling before the dope is applied.

nap of the fabric. The ends of the fibers in a fabric. The first coat of dope on cotton or linen fabric raises the nap, and the fiber ends stick up. These ends must be carefully removed by sanding to get a smooth finish.

pinked-edge tape. Cloth tape whose edges have small V-shaped notches cut along their length. The pinked edges prevent the tape from raveling.

Install all the drain grommets and inspection rings by soaking them in dope to soften them and then placing them in a heavy bed of dope. Work them down to the fabric with your fingers.

Cover all of the glued-down edges of the fabric in the aileron wells with 2-inch surface tape worked down into a coat of dope.

Cut a piece of 4-inch-wide surface tape long enough to go from the root of the wing along the leading edge and around the tip to the aileron well. Brush a coat of full-bodied dope along the leading edge and press the fabric down into it, working the air bubbles out of it with your fingers. Brush a coat of dope around the wing tip bow, and pull the tape tight. Center it around the tip, and clamp it at the aileron well with a spring clamp. Pulling the tape tight around the tip causes the edges to lie down on both sides of the tip. Lift the edges of the tape and work a small brush, wet with thinned dope, up underneath the tape to completely saturate it. Work the tape down on one side of the tip, and then on the other side rather than working down both sides at the same time.

Cover the trailing edge with 3-inch surface tape that has been notched along both edges at intervals not exceeding 6 inches. If the tape should separate from the trailing edge, it will tear at one of the notches rather than loosening the entire strip, which could seriously affect the controllability of the aircraft.

Application of the Finish System

The finishing system of a fabric-covered aircraft consists of the fill coats, the ultraviolet-blocking coat, and the finish coats. These are all discussed in the portion of this chapter dealing with "Fabric Finishing," beginning on Page 219.

ultraviolet-blocking dope. Dope that contains aluminum powder or some other pigment that blocks the passage of ultraviolet rays of the sun. This coat of dope protects the organic fabrics and clear dope from deterioration by these rays.

Inorganic Fabric Covering

Organic fabrics are thought of as the "standard system" for fabric-covered aircraft, but inorganic fabrics have gained so much popularity that the vast majority of aircraft today are covered with some form of inorganic material, with polyester fabrics being the most important.

Polyester fabric approved for aircraft covering is stronger than Grade-A cotton, and has an exceptionally long life. Because it is so widely used, its price has decreased to well below that of Grade-A cotton.

In this portion of the text we will consider the major differences between the application of polyester and cotton.

Covering an aircraft with polyester fabric that was originally covered with cotton constitutes a major alteration and usually requires the use of a Supplemental Type Certificate (STC), obtained by the manufacturer or distributor of the materials.

The STC requires that the person installing the fabric follow the instructions in the procedures manual furnished with the materials. There must be no substitution of materials and no deviation from the procedures described in the manual. When the aircraft is ready to be approved for return to service, an FAA Form 337 must be completed, listing the STC as approved data. A technician holding an Inspection Authorization must inspect the work for conformity to the instructions in the STC manual, and if it conforms, he or she can then approve the aircraft for return to service.

The Poly-Fiber System

One system for covering aircraft with polyester fabrics is that perfected by Poly-Fiber Aircraft Coatings of Riverside, California. Pertinent differences between the procedures for using cotton and Poly-Fiber have been condensed from the *Poly-Fiber Covering and Painting Manual,* and are included here with their permission.

Materials Used

Three weights of Poly-Fiber fabric are available, all three are lighter than Grade-A cotton, and two of them are considerably stronger. All three of the fabrics approved for use with this STC are identified with a stamp similar to the one in Figure 3-21 stamped along one edge at three-foot intervals.

Both machine sewing and hand sewing require polyester thread, and there are two types of polyester rib-lacing cord used with this system. One is a round cord, and the other is a flat braided cord used where the minimum protrusion is desired.

A woven twill-type polyester reinforcing tape with an adhesive coating applied to one side is used over the wing ribs and is available in several widths. A tape made of the same material without the adhesive coating is available for inter-rib bracing.

Pinked-edge finishing tape is available in the various weights of fabric and widths. Linear tape is used for most of the required taping, and bias tape, with the threads oriented at 45° to the length, is available for use around wingtip bows and other severe compound curves.

The fabric is attached to the structure with a high-strength cement called Poly-Tak. When Poly-Tak is used with the recommended overlaps, there are no wing loading or V_{NE} restrictions.

The fabric is heat-shrunk on the structure, and Poly-Brush, which is a high-solids-content one-part air-drying adhesive coating, is used to seal the weave of the fabric.

Almost the only natural enemy of polyester fabric is the sun. The fill coats of Poly-Spray are aluminum pigmented to prevent the ultraviolet rays from reaching the fabric, and to provide a sanding base for a smooth finish.

For the finish coats, use Poly-Tone material. For a more chemical resistant finish, use Aero-Thane enamel, a flexible, two-part polyurethane enamel.

Poly-Fiber Acft.
P-103
F.A.A. P.M.A.
68 x 68 threads
2.7 oz./sq. yd.
Over 116 lbs./in.

Figure 3-21. *Markings such as this are used to identify fabric used when re-covering an aircraft by the Poly-Fiber system.*

enamel. A type of finishing material that flows out to form a smooth surface. Enamel is usually made of a pigment suspended in some form of resin. When the resin cures, it leaves a smooth, glossy protective surface.

Installing and Shrinking the Fabric

The fabric in the Poly-Fiber system is installed in basically the same way as cotton fabric, except that it is fixed to the structure with Poly-Tak cement.

Shrink the fabric by using a steam or dry iron calibrated according to the Poly-Fiber manual. A hand-held infrared thermometer can also be used. Move it lightly touching the fabric at a speed of about 4 to 7 inches per second. Go over the entire surface, and then go back and repeat the process, using several 250° passes. After the fabric has shrunk as much as it will at 250°F, increase the temperature to 350° and make several passes to give the fabric its final tautening and stabilizing.

When the fabric has reached its final tautness, scrub it with Poly-Fiber reducer or MEK on a clean rag to remove as much sizing as possible. When it dries, go over it with a tack rag to remove any lint or dust. Brush on the first coat of Poly-Brush to thoroughly saturate the fabric, but be careful that none of the liquid runs down on the inside of the fabric. This first coat of Poly-Brush should close the porosity of the fabric.

tack rag. A clean, lintless rag, slightly damp with thinner. A tack rag is used to wipe a surface to prepare it to receive a coat of finishing material.

Attaching the Fabric

Attach the fabric to the structure with sheet metal screws (or with clips if they were originally used by the aircraft manufacturer). Any change in the method of securing the fabric must be approved on a FAA Form 337 before the change is made. This includes changing from screws to rib-lacing. Rib lacing as described for the cotton covering system may be used with Poly-Fiber, but the STC procedure manual describes a rib lacing method for this system that produces a much cleaner (aerodynamically and esthetically) attachment.

Application of Surface Tape and Hole Reinforcements

Attach plastic inspection rings and drainage grommets to the fabric with Poly-Tak cement, and for longevity, cover them with fabric patches.

Apply surface tape by brushing thinned Poly-Brush on the structure where the tape is to go and then press the tape down into it with your fingers. Allow the Poly-Brush to dry, and then apply a second coat. When this coat dries, use a 225°F iron to smooth down the tape edges and form the tape around the corners.

The Finish

After completing the fabric installation and placing all of the tapes and hole reinforcements, apply the second coat of Poly-Brush.

When the Poly-Brush coats are dry, spray on three coats of Poly-Spray, wet-sanding after the second coat. When the third coat is applied , completely cover all the surface to block the ultraviolet rays of the sun from the fabric.

Light from a 60-watt bulb held near the surface of the fabric should not be visible from inside the structure.

Finish Poly-Fiber with either Poly-Tone or Aero-Thane.

The Superflite System

Superflite is the registered trade name for a series of inorganic fabric covering and finishing materials produced by Superflite of Elk Grove Village, Illinois. Superflite fabrics are woven of polyester fibers on a loom that uses water rather than ethylene glycol as its lubricant. This is especially important for aircraft fabric, because of the tenacity with which dope adheres to fabric that has been woven on water-lubricated looms.

The following information has been excerpted from the Superflite Systems manuals and is used with their permission. When re-covering an aircraft with any material that requires a Supplemental Type Certificate, it is extremely important, and a legal requirement, that only the materials specified in the STC be used and all of the procedures described in the manual be followed in detail.

Superflite System I

Superflite System I uses Superflite 102 fabric that is attached to the structure with SuperBond cement. After the fabric is in place and all of the edges cemented to the structure, shrink it by ironing it with an accurately calibrated iron adjusted to 250°F. After shrinking the surface evenly at this temperature, increase the temperature to 350°F and further shrink it. This temperature should produce a fully tightened, wrinkle-free surface.

Once the fabric is uniformly tight, brush a full wet coat of reduced Dac-Proofer over the entire surface. When the first coat is dry, use a brush or a short-nap, bonnet-type paint roller to apply the second coat. This one is applied at right angles to the first coat. This second coat should be thinned with enough retarding thinner to allow it to dry slowly and not rope.

The Dac-Proofer acts as a foundation for the fill and topcoats. It penetrates the fabric and encapsulates the fibers, bonding to itself on the back side of the fabric. Since it is not used as a filler, use only enough to give the fabric an even blue appearance.

Attach the dried, Dac-Proofer coated fabric to the structure with screws, clips, or rib lacing, as it was originally attached by the manufacturer. You can follow the procedure for rib lacing described earlier in the organic fabrics section, but the applications manual also describes a hidden-knot method of lacing you can use with this system.

Apply the surface tapes, using either nitrate or butyrate dope. Use a roller and apply a swath of full-bodied dope slightly wider than the tape where the tape is to go. Lay the tape into the dope and smooth it in place with your fingers. Then roll on a second coat of dope, applying enough pressure to squeeze out all of the air bubbles. Extra passes of the roller will pick up the dope that has been squeezed out and will result in a smooth surface.

dope roping. Brushing aircraft dope onto a surface in such a way that it forms a stringy, uneven surface rather than flowing out smoothly.

Install the inspection rings and drainage grommets with SuperBond cement. When the dope and cement are dry, spray on three full-bodied cross coats of SpraFil. SpraFil is a high-solid, nonshrinking butyrate dope that contains aluminum pigment. It serves as the fill coats and also provides the ultraviolet protection for the fabric. After the SpraFil has dried overnight, sand the taped areas smooth and sand any spots that may have been caused by dust that settled on the surface while the SpraFil was wet. Remove all of the sanding dust with a damp cloth.

Do the final finish with three or more cross coats of Superflite pigmented gloss dope, waiting at least three hours between coats. An especially fine finish can be provided by spraying on a topcoat which consists of clear butyrate dope to which 10% colored dope has been added, and the combination thinned with an equal part of retarder.

Superflite System II

Superflite System II uses the same fabric and the same installation procedure as System I, but it uses special chemicals to allow a polyurethane enamel to be used for its famous wet look.

Attach the fabric to the structure using SuperFlite U-500 urethane adhesive. Use a mixture of primer base, catalyst, flexative, and reducer as both the primer and fill coats. Spray three coats of the mixture on the entire surface, waiting only until the surface is dry to touch between coats.

The final finish is provided by two coats of Superthane pigmented polyurethane, to which has been added the catalyst, a flexative, and the required reducer. Spray this on in a light tack coat and allow it to set for a few minutes, and then follow it with a full wet coat.

The Ceconite 7600 System

The Ceconite 7600 system is approved by the use of an STC for covering FAA-certificated aircraft. This system differs from other systems in the chemicals used and their unique method of application. The information given here has been condensed from the procedures manual furnished with the STC by the Blue River Aircraft Supply of Harvard, Nebraska, and used with their permission. When covering an aircraft with this system, follow the procedures manual in detail.

Materials Used

The Ceconite 7600 system uses a 3.8-, 2.8-, or 1.9-ounce-per-square-yard polyester fabric that has been precoated under controlled temperature and pressure with a thermoset water-borne epoxy-ester resin. This precoating makes the fabric easy to work with and ensures the proper bonding of its chemicals.

cross coat. A double coat of aircraft finishing material in which the second coat is sprayed at right angles to the first coat, before the solvents have evaporated from the first coat.

Surface tapes are available in the 2.8- and 1.9-ounce material, and with both plain and pinked edges and with linear and bias cuts. The reinforcing tape, rib-stitching cord, and both machine- and hand-sewing threads are also made of polyester fibers.

Installing the Fabric

When installing the fabric, pull it snug over the surface, and cut the holes for all protruding fittings so that the fabric will fit smoothly.

Attach the fabric to the structure with 7602 Cement and 7603 Cement Activator. Do not mix these two chemicals, but first apply a full brush coat of the cement and allow it to dry thoroughly in locations where the fabric is to be attached to the structure, then apply a second coat and allow it to dry. When the cement is completely dry, brush a coat of activator over it and press the fabric down into the activated cement. Apply a coat of activator over the fabric, and while it is still wet, wipe it off with a soft cloth or paper towel. This smooths the cemented surface and ensures complete penetration of the fabric. All cemented seams should lie over some structural member, and should have a 3-inch overlap. A correctly made cemented seam has a uniform dark green appearance with no visible voids.

Shrinking the Fabric

Use an electric iron that is accurately calibrated to 400°F to tauten the fabric. Begin over the ribs and cemented areas with a close-quarter iron set below the 400°F limit. When these areas have been shrunk initially, reduce the large iron's temperature to below 400°F and move it slowly over all of the open areas of the fabric, working out all the wrinkles. Don't try to do this with one pass, but use patience and several passes of the iron. When the wrinkles are out and the fabric is smooth, increase the temperature of the iron to a maximum of 400°F. Iron the entire surface at this temperature one time and allow the fabric to cool, then iron it a second time to give the fabric its final tautening and stabilizing.

Attaching the Fabric

The reinforcing tape used over the wing ribs and the other places where the fabric is stitched to the structure is a woven polyester tape with adhesive on one side. Press the tape down over each rib, allowing it to extend slightly beyond each rib stitch.

Attach the fabric to the structure in the same way it was when the aircraft was originally built. If it was attached by rib stitching, use the procedures described for the application of organic fabrics.

Apply the surface tape and hole reinforcements by applying a coat of 7602 cement to the areas where they should go and allow it to dry. Apply a coat of cement to one side of the tape and allow it to dry. When the cement is dry, apply

close-quarter iron. A small hand-held iron with an accurately calibrated thermostat. This iron is used for heat-shrinking polyester fabrics in areas that would be difficult to work with a large iron.

a coat of cement activator to the cement on the surface and press precut lengths of cement-covered surface tape into the activated cement.

Apply a second coat of activator to the top of the tape and wipe it off with a soft cloth, working it into the tape to remove any air bubbles or voids.

As soon as the activated cement becomes tacky, after about 10 to 15 minutes, press the tape down against the reinforcing tape and rib stitches with a very short bristle brush, working the tape down to eliminate all air bubbles.

Put cement around the leading edge, wing tip, and trailing edges of the surface. Activate it, and pull the surface tape tight so it will lie down around the curves. Severe curves should be taped with bias-cut tape. Heat the edges of the tape with the close-quarter iron to shrink the fabric so it will lie perfectly flat, then work cement activator under the tape, and finish it with more activator on top of the tape.

Attach inspection rings to the fabric by applying two coats of cement in a circular area slightly larger than the ring. When the cement is dry, apply activator and work the ring down into the activated cement with a twisting motion. Cover the ring with a circular patch of fabric worked down into more activated cement. Be sure the fabric is pressed down tightly against the edges of the ring.

Apply drain grommets in the same way, and when the fabric patches are in place and pressed down tight and the activated cement has dried, melt the holes through the fabric with a $\frac{1}{4}$-inch soldering iron tip whose end has been filed round rather than pointed.

The Finish

The 7601 Filler Coat used with this system contains many solids to provide a surface that blocks the ultraviolet rays of the sun and also fills the weave of the fabric. This material must be mixed thoroughly to completely suspend all the solids, and then strained to remove any clumps of pigment.

Clean the fabric area to remove all dust, then wipe it down with a cloth dampened in Flexi-Gloss Cleaner to remove all fingerprints and all traces of oil that may have gotten onto the fabric. Dampen the fabric thoroughly with distilled or demineralized water applied with a sponge, and while the fabric is still wet, apply the filler with a foam brush, paying special attention to get even coverage.

Apply subsequent coats of the filler with a spray gun. Use the material unthinned and with only enough air pressure on the gun to get thin, even coats. After enough filler has been sprayed on the surface to fill the weave, wet- or dry-sand the surface with 320 or 400 sandpaper, taking care not to cut through the fabric.

With the Ceconite 7600 system, use finish coats either of catalyzed polyurethanes or several coats of pigmented butyrate dope (applied by the methods described in the section on aircraft painting and finishing).

Repair of Aircraft Fabric

14 CFR Part 43, Appendix A gives examples of airframe major repairs as "Repair of fabric covering involving an area greater than that required to repair two adjacent ribs," and "Replacement of fabric on fabric-covered parts such as wings, fuselages, stabilizers, and control surfaces."

Advisory Circular 43.13-1B *Acceptable Methods, Techniques, and Practices—Aircraft Inspection and Repair* gives some examples of repairs to fabric. It is important to understand that this is *acceptable* data, not *approved* data, and any major repair to an aircraft must be based on approved data. Before beginning any major repair, describe exactly what you plan to do, and list the materials that will be used. Submit this data to the FAA FSDO. The procedure to follow is described in the *General* textbook of this *Aviation Maintenance Technician Series*. When the data is approved, follow it in detail, and have the work inspected for conformity to the data by a technician holding an Inspection Authorization.

The repairs described here are adequate to return the fabric covering to an airworthy condition and are used with utility-finished aircraft. Repairs to show-type finishes are much more complex, but they result in repairs that can hardly be detected.

Tear in the Fabric

Figure 3-22 shows a typical L-shaped tear in the fabric covering of an aircraft. Use a curved needle and well-waxed thread. Start at the apex of the tear and work back to the end of the tear. Use a baseball stitch and lock it every 8 to 10 stitches with a half hitch, and at each end with a modified seine knot like the one in Figure 3-17 on Page 198.

After sewing the edges of the tear together, soften the old dope with fresh dope, and using a putty knife, scrape away all of the finish down to the clear dope coats. Cut a patch of the same type of fabric as the kind you are repairing. Make it large enough to extend 1½ inches beyond the damage in all directions, and cut the edges with pinking shears to assist it in sticking down. Place the patch in a bed of full-bodied dope and press it down into the dope with your fingers to remove all of the air bubbles. Finish the repaired area to match the rest of the structure.

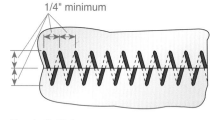

1/4" minimum

Baseball stitch

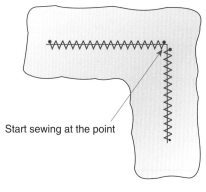

Start sewing at the point

Lock stitching every 8 or 10 stitches, and at ends with modified seine knot

Figure 3-22. *Repair to tears in aircraft fabric*

Doped-on Patch

You can make doped-on, or unsewed, repairs to all fabric-covered aircraft surfaces provided the never-exceed speed is not greater than 150 miles per hour and the damage does not exceed 16 inches in any direction.

Cut out the damaged fabric, making a round or oval-shaped opening. Clean the edges of the fabric to be covered, and remove the old dope down to the clear coats by sanding or using dope thinner.

For holes up to 8 inches in size, make the fabric patch of sufficient size to overlap the edges of the hole by at least 2 inches in all directions. On holes larger than 8 inches, size the patch so it will overlap the fabric around the hole by at least one quarter of the hole diameter with a maximum overlap of 4 inches. If the hole extends over a rib or closer than the required overlap to a rib or other laced member, extend the patch at least 3 inches beyond the rib. In this case, after the edges of the patch have been doped in place and the dope has dried, lace the patch to the rib over a new section of reinforcing tape in the usual manner. Do not remove the old rib lacing and reinforcing tape. All patches should have pinked edges, or if smooth, should be finished with pinked-edge surface tape.

STUDY QUESTIONS: AIRCRAFT FABRIC COVERING

Answers begin on Page 263. Page numbers refer to chapter text.

30. Grade-A cotton fabric is manufactured under Technical Standard Order TSO C-_____ .
    Page 186

31. New Grade-A cotton fabric has a minimum strength of _____ pounds per inch in both warp and fill directions. *Page 185*

32. Three types of fabric that may be used to cover an aircraft structure are: _____ , _____ , and _____ . *Pages 185 and 186*

33. Re-covering an aircraft with the same materials and the same methods used by the original manufacturer is classified as a _____ . *Page 186*

34. Re-covering an aircraft with different materials from those used by the original manufacturer is classified as a _____ . *Page 187*

35. When an aircraft is re-covered, the work must be inspected by an aviation maintenance technician who holds an Inspection Authorization, and an FAA Form _____ must be completed and filed with the FAA FSDO. *Page 187*

Continued

36. Aircraft fabric must be replaced when its strength has deteriorated to _____ % of the strength of the fabric required for the aircraft. *Page 187*

37. A fabric whose strength has deteriorated to 65% of that required for new fabric _____ (can or cannot) have some of its strength restored by rejuvenation. *Page 188*

38. Cracks in the finish of a fabric-covered structure _____ (are or are not) an indication that the fabric should be replaced. *Page 188*

39. When making a fabric test, check the fabric in an area that is finished with a _____ (dark or light) color. *Page 188*

40. The squareness of a wing truss is checked by making comparative diagonal distance checks across each bay with a _____ bar and points. *Page 190*

41. Grade-A cotton must have the identification marks _____ or _____ stamped along its selvage edge. *Page 192*

42. Pinked-edge surface tape has a series of V-shaped notches cut along its edges to prevent it _____ . *Page 192*

43. Surface tape that lies down most smoothly around wing tips and the tips of control surfaces is _____ (bias or straight) cut. *Page 192*

44. The two types of dopes are _____ and _____ . *Page 193*

45. The type of dope that is best for the initial attachment of the fabric to the structure is _____ (butyrate or nitrate). *Page 193*

46. It _____ (is or is not) proper to apply nitrate dope over butyrate dope. *Page 193*

47. Aircraft dope and fabric are protected from damage by ultraviolet rays of the sun by a layer of _____ -pigmented dope applied over the clear dope. *Page 193*

48. When mixing aluminum paste with clear dope you should pour the _____ (dope into the paste or paste into the dope). *Page 193*

49. If a bleeding dope is to be used for one of the colors on an aircraft, it should be applied _____ (first or last). *Page 193*

50. The two methods of applying fabric to an aircraft structure are the _____ and _____ methods. *Pages 194 and 195*

51. The openings for strut fittings _____ (should or should not) be cut while Grade-A cotton fabric is wet with water to remove the wrinkles. *Page 196*

52. When mixing fungicidal paste with clear dope you should pour the _____ (dope into the paste or paste into the dope). *Page 196*

53. Wrinkles are pulled out of cotton fabric by wetting the fabric with _____ (dope or water). *Page 195*

54. The first coat of dope applied to cotton fabric is typically _____ (nitrate or butyrate). *Page 196*

55. The first coat of dope applied to cotton fabric should be _____ (full bodied or thinned). *Page 196*

56. The rib stitch spacing for the end stitches is _____ that of the rest of the stitches. *Page 197*

57. Replacing rib stitching with metal clips constitutes a major _____ (repair or alteration). *Page 199*

58. The second coat of dope that is applied to cotton fabric should be _____ (nitrate or butyrate). *Page 200*

59. Before dry-sanding any doped surface, the aircraft structure should be _____ to prevent a spark caused by static electricity. *Page 200*

60. Surface tape, drain grommets, and inspection rings are applied with the _____ (first or second) coat of dope. *Page 200*

61. The description of a repair in AC 43.13-1B _____ (does or does not) constitute approved data for making a major repair to a fabric-covered aircraft. *Page 208*

62. When sewing an L-shaped tear in aircraft fabric covering, start sewing at the _____ (ends or apex) of the tear. *Page 208*

63. A doped-on patch repair may be made to a fabric-covered aircraft provided the V_{NE} is not greater than _____ mph and the damage does not exceed _____ inches in any direction. *Page 209*

64. When baseball stitching a patch into an aircraft structure, the stitches should be spaced approximately _____-inch apart and locked with a half hitch ever _____ or _____ stitches. *Page 208*

Aircraft Painting and Finishing

Painting and finishing is a highly specialized field. Just a glance at the beautiful finishes that are evident at air meets like Oshkosh show that aircraft finishing is a true art form. In this section we introduce the basic finishing systems for both metal and fabric aircraft.

Metal Finishing

An aircraft's finish is important for more than just cosmetic reasons. It preserves the metal, and its smoothness reduces air resistance, making the aircraft fly more efficiently.

The many hours transport aircraft fly today have brought about some serious problems, known as problems of the "aging fleet." These aircraft often have hidden corrosion that must be found and properly treated, then the aircraft refinished.

In this section of the *AMTS* we consider the preparation of the structure for receiving the finish and review the finishing systems.

Paint Removal

Begin preparing the metal to receive the finish by removing any old finish.

For years the only way to remove old finish was to use chemical stripper that loosened it and allowed it to be washed away. But today with the emphasis on environmental protection, the residue from chemical stripping is considered hazardous waste, and the cost of its disposal has made dry-stripping a viable alternative.

Before beginning any paint removal, prepare the aircraft by very carefully masking off all areas that should not be stripped. Protect windshields and windows with aluminum foil taped down tightly so no stripper can get under it, and cover all of the other parts with a good grade of polyethylene sheeting.

Caution: It is very important that any time you work with potent chemicals you have adequate physical protection. Follow the recommendations of the manufacturer of the chemicals for the type of respiratory and eye protection you will need.

Chemical Stripping

There are two basic types of finish on metal aircraft, enamels and lacquers, and each requires different procedures for its removal.

Enamel cures to a hard, impervious finish that bonds tightly to the primer on the surface of the metal. To remove it, apply a heavy coat of stripper with a bristle brush or a nonatomizing spray, and cover it with polyethylene sheeting to prevent it evaporating before it does its work. The potent solvents, principally methylene chloride, in the stripper enter the enamel film and swell it enough that it buckles, or wrinkles up, and pulls away from the primer.

Most strippers of this type contain wax that gets between the wrinkled-up film and the metal to prevent it resticking. Leave the stripper on the surface until all of the finish has swelled up and pulled away from the primer. If some areas dry out too soon, apply more stripper. After the entire surface has wrinkled up, remove the old finish with a soft plastic or wooden scraper. Wash the remaining residue off with hot water or steam and dispose of it in a way that is compatible with environmental regulations.

There will be some residue left around the rivets and other fasteners as well as along the seams in the skin. Scrub these areas with a 3m Scotch Brite pad, a brass wire brush or aluminum wool. Do not use steel wool, as particles of the steel will become embedded in the softer aluminum and will cause severe corrosion.

Any wax left from the stripper will prevent subsequent coats of finish from adhering to the surface, so it must be completely removed. After removing all traces of the paint residue, scrub the entire surface with a solvent such as acetone or methyl-ethyl-ketone (MEK), toluol, or xylol, which will absorb the wax. Lacquer thinner will not absorb the wax but it will just move it around and leave the surface contaminated.

Polyurethane enamels are gaining wide acceptance because of their chemical resistance and their shiny wet look. Polyurethanes are more difficult to remove than other enamels because their impervious film is not easily attacked by the solvents in the strippers. But, if you apply the stripper and cover it with polyethylene sheeting to slow its evaporation, the active agent in the stripper will wrinkle the finish and loosen its bond to the primer.

Acrylic lacquer does not expand and wrinkle up when it is attacked by the solvents in the stripper, instead it simply softens. Apply the stripper the same way you would for enamel, and cover it with polyethylene sheeting. When it has been on the surface for a sufficient length of time, roll the sheeting back to expose a small section of the softened finish. Remove the finish from the surface with a Plexiglas or hard rubber scraper and scrub the cleaned off area with a rag wet with MEK or acetone, being very careful to get all traces of the wax from around the rivets and out of the seams in the skin. Roll back the sheeting and remove the finish from more of the surface.

Do not use chemical paint strippers on aircraft fabric or on fiberglass parts such as radomes or wheel speed fairings. The solvents in the stripper may attack the resins in these parts and weaken or distort them. Remove the finish by sanding or by plastic media blasting.

Plexiglas. The registered trademark of the Rhom & Haas Company.

plexiglass. A generic term for acrylic sheet plastic.

Dry Stripping

Aircraft refinishing shops that work on large aircraft have an expensive problem of disposing of the hazardous waste products left when paint is chemically stripped. These shops have done quite a bit of research into dry stripping or plastic media blasting (PMB), and this has proven to be an effective method of removing paint from heavy-skinned aircraft, especially

plastic media blasting (PMB). A method of removing paint from an aircraft surface by dry-blasting it with tiny plastic beads.

military aircraft. The finish is blasted from the surface with tiny sharp-edged plastic beads. The size, shape, and hardness of these beads and the air pressure used to propel them determine the amount of finish that will be removed.

PMB requires a high degree of skill, but it gives the operator far better control when removing the finish than chemical stripping. With proper choice of beads and air pressure, the finish can be removed without causing any damage to the underlying metal, even to the primer. The beads can be reused, and the residue from the old finish is much easier to dispose of than that left from chemical stripping. One of the limitations of the present PMB paint removal is that it can damage thin-skinned general aviation aircraft, but continued research may eliminate this problem.

Preparation for Painting

When the finish is removed from a metal aircraft, you have an opportunity to carefully inspect it for any indication of corrosion, to remove all traces you may find, and to protect it from further corrosion. Finally you have the opportunity to prepare it to receive the new finishing system.

Corrosion Detection

Review the section on Cleaning and Corrosion Control in the *General* textbook of the *Aviation Maintenance Technician Series* to get a good understanding of the appearance and causes of corrosion. Any traces of corrosion you find must be removed and the surface treated to prevent the formation of subsequent corrosion.

The form of corrosion that is most likely to be found under a paint film is filiform corrosion. This is a thread-like corrosion primarily caused by improperly cured wash primer that left some of the phosphoric acid trapped beneath the paint film. If there are any tracks left from the corrosion or gray powdery residue on the surface of the metal, scrub it all away with a nylon scrubber such as a Scotch-Brite pad.

Carefully examine the area around all fasteners for any indication of galvanic corrosion. Any blisters in the metal that could indicate intergranular corrosion should be probed with a sharp tool to determine whether or not they are actually pockets of corrosion deposits. If you find traces of intergranular corrosion, use an eddy current or ultrasonic tester to determine its extent. Intergranular corrosion is usually difficult to remove and often requires the replacement of the affected metal.

Conversion Coating

Three conditions must be met for a metal to corrode: there must be an electrode potential difference, there must be a conductive path between the areas of potential difference, and an electrolyte must cover these areas. A surface may be protected from corrosion by the elimination of any one or more of the three.

Important note about painting preparation:

It is important when preparing any surface for painting that after it has been cleaned, you do not touch it with your bare hands. There is enough oil on your skin that it can contaminate the surface enough that the finish will not adhere, and cause any number of other paint surface defects. It is critical to keep this possibility in mind as you follow the described procedures in this section.

After removing all traces of corrosion from the metal and repairing any damages, you can treat the surface with a conversion coating, which is a chemical that forms an airtight film on the surface that prevents any electrolyte reaching the metal. Phosphoric acid can be used to form a phosphate film on the metal surface.

Another well-known treatment is the proprietary product Alodine. To apply Alodine, follow these steps:

1. Brush on a coat of aluminum cleaner such as Alumiprep or Metal Prep. This cleans and etches the metal and prepares it for further treatment.

2. Rinse the surface with water and check to be sure that it supports an unbroken film of water, indicating that there are no contaminants on the surface.

3. Brush or spray a liberal coat of Alodine on the surface. Allow it to remain on the surface for two to five minutes and then rinse it off. The film will be soft while it is wet, but as soon as it dries, it will become hard and protective.

Caution: Rags used to apply the Alodine coating must be kept wet until they can be thoroughly washed before discarding. Rags with dry Alodine chemical in them can constitute a fire hazard.

Primers

A primer provides a good bond between the surface being finished and the material used for the topcoats. There are several types of primers available, but the three discussed here are zinc chromate, wash primer, and epoxy primer.

primer. A component in a finishing system that provides a good bond between the surface and the material used for the topcoats.

Zinc Chromate

For decades zinc chromate has been the standard primer for use on aircraft. It is an inhibitive primer, meaning that its base of alkyd resin is somewhat porous and when water enters it, some of the chromate ions are released and held on the surface of the metal. This ionized surface prevents the electrolytic action necessary for corrosion to form.

epoxy. A polyether resin that has wide application, as a matrix for composite materials, and as an adhesive that bonds many different types of materials.

Zinc chromate can be used on both ferrous and nonferrous metals and is compatible with most finishing materials, but there are some necessary precautions. It should not be applied over a wash primer unless the phosphoric acid has been completely converted into the phosphate film. The zinc chromate will tend to trap water and allow filiform corrosion to form. Also zinc chromate is not recommended for use under acrylic lacquers because the solvents used with acrylics tend to lift the zinc chromate.

Zinc chromate primer conforms to MIL-P-8585A and is available in both yellow and dark green colors. It is thinned with toluene or proprietary thinners to get it to the proper consistency for spraying. To increase the usefulness of this primer, it is also available in aerosol spray cans.

Caution: There have been some studies that indicate there may be a possible link between an excessive inhalation of zinc chromate dust and lung cancer.

Wash Primer

High-volume production of aircraft requires a primer that cures quickly and allows the topcoat to be sprayed on relatively soon after its application. A three-part wash primer that meets specification MIL-P-15328 satisfies this requirement and is widely used in aircraft factories.

Wash primer is prepared by mixing 4 parts of the primer with 1 part of its activator, a phosphoric acid diluent, and adjusting its viscosity with between 4 and 8 parts of thinner. Allow it to stand for 20 minutes to begin its cure, stir it, and spray it on the surface. It should be sprayed on in a very thin coat, only about 0.000 3 inch (0.3 mil). A coat of this thickness does not hide the surface of the metal, but gives it a slightly greenish-amber tint.

The acid in the primer requires about 30 minutes to convert into the phosphate film, and you must not apply the topcoats until this has taken place. But you must apply them within 8 hours or the primer will harden to the extent that the topcoats will not adhere as they should. If the topcoat is not applied within this time limit, spray on another coat of the primer, this time without the activator. When the primer is dry to the touch it is ready for the topcoats.

It is important that there is enough moisture in the air to convert the acid in the primer into the phosphate film. Specific information is given with the primer, but, basically, if the relative humidity is less than 55% with a paint room temperature of 75°F, you should add about an ounce of distilled water to one gallon of the thinner to provide the needed water.

Epoxy Primer

Epoxy primer gives the best corrosion protection of any of the modern primers. This two-component primer produces a tough dope-proof finish, and it can be used over all metals as well as composite materials. When you need maximum corrosion protection, you can apply epoxy primer over wash primer.

To use epoxy primer, first wash the surface with a clean rag wet with MEK, toluol, or acrylic lacquer thinner. Then mix the epoxy primer with the amount of mixing liquid specified by the primer manufacturer. Stir these components separately and then stir them together. Add the required amount of thinner to adjust the viscosity for spraying and allow the mixture to sit for 30 minutes to begin its cure. Spray on a single, light, even coat of primer, just enough to slightly color the metal.

Epoxy primer must be allowed at least five hours, and preferably overnight, to develop enough hardness to prevent acrylic lacquer or synthetic enamel topcoats from sinking into it and losing their gloss. Polyurethanes are ideally suited for application over epoxy primer and can be applied after a wait of only one hour.

Important note about wash primer:
If wash primer is not allowed to cure properly before the application of the top coats, filiform corrosion will be rampant under the paint and cause extreme damage to the sheet metal skin.

MEK. Methyl-ethyl-ketone, an organic chemical solvent that is soluble in water and is used as a solvent for vinyl and nitrocellulose films. MEK is an efficient cleaner for preparing surfaces for priming or painting.

If epoxy primer has been applied for more than 24 hours before the application of the topcoat, its surface must be scuffed with a Scotch-Brite pad or 600-grit sandpaper to break the glaze enough for the topcoats to bond.

Finishing Systems

Three popular finishing systems are used for all-metal aircraft. Most of the high-volume general aviation aircraft were finished at the factory with acrylic lacquer because of the speed with which the entire finishing system could be applied. Synthetic enamels have been used for many years because of the good finish they produce and their ease of application. But the most popular finishing system today is the polyurethane system because of its chemical resistance, durability, and high-gloss "wet look."

Acrylic Lacquer

Apply acrylic lacquers over a wash primer or over an epoxy primer. After the primer has completely cured, rub it down with a handful of wadded-up kraft paper to provide enough surface roughness so the topcoats will bond properly.

The low solids content of acrylic lacquer requires careful attention to its application. The finished color is best applied over a white base coat, and it should be applied in several thin coats rather than fewer heavy coats. Thin 4 parts of lacquer with 5 parts of thinner, and spray on a very light tack coat. As soon as the solvents have evaporated, spray on at least three cross coats, allowing about a half-hour between the coats. The gloss of the final coat may be improved by adding about one-fourth as much retarder as there is thinner. When retarder is used, the finish should dry overnight before doing any taping or masking.

Synthetic Enamel

Synthetic enamels are made of pigments suspended in resins that cure by oxidization. These enamels have been used for years to finish automobiles and have been used to some extent for metal aircraft. They produce a glossy finish that does not require rubbing but their chemical and abrasive resistance is not nearly so good as that of polyurethanes.

Synthetic enamel can be applied over a zinc chromate primer and is thinned to the proper viscosity for spraying. Spray a light mist coat on the surface and as soon as the thinner evaporates out, in about 10 or 15 minutes, spray on a wet cross coat. After drying for about 48 hours the surface will be ready to tape and mask for trim coats.

lacquer. A finishing material made of a film base, solvents, plasticizers, and thinners. The film base forms a tough film over the surface when it dries. The solvents dissolve the film base so it can be applied as a liquid. The plasticizers give the film base the needed resilience, and the thinners dilute the lacquer so it can be applied with a spray gun. Lacquer is sprayed on the surface as a liquid and when the solvents and thinners evaporate, the film base remains as a tough decorative and protective coating.

kraft paper. A tough brown wrapping paper like that used for paper bags.

Polyurethane

Polyurethane is the most popular finish for modern metal aircraft because of its chemical and abrasive resistance and its high gloss. It is a two-part, chemically cured finish that contains approximately twice the solids used in acrylic lacquer. Its exceptionally good finish is due to its slow-flowing resins which continue to flow after the thinners evaporate until they form a perfectly flat surface, and cure uniformly throughout. Light reflecting from this flat surface gives the finish its shiny appearance.

Polyurethane finishes resist most of the chemicals used in agricultural application as well as the acid and alkali fumes in the battery box areas. Solvents such as acetone have a minimal effect on it, and paint strippers must be held in contact with the finish for a considerable length of time before they penetrate the film and loosen it from the primer.

The primer used with polyurethanes is an important part of the complete system. For maximum corrosion protection, cover a well-cured wash primer with an epoxy primer and then apply the polyurethane finish.

Mix the polyurethane and its catalyst in the proportions specified on the can, and allow it to sit for an induction time of 20 to 30 minutes as directed by the manufacturer. Thin the mixed material by adding the proper reducer until its viscosity, as determined by a viscosity cup, is correct for spraying. Dip the cup into the thinned material and measure the time in seconds from the instant the cup is lifted from the liquid until the first break in the flow through the hole in the bottom of the cup. There is a definite pot life for the mixed material. This time is noted on the can, and if the material is not used within this time period, it must be discarded and a new batch mixed.

Spray a very light tack coat of the material on the surface, and when the thinner evaporates, spray on a full wet cross coat. Polyurethane is not as flexible as some of the other finishes, and it is important that the cross coat not be too thick. If the material builds up at the skin lap joints it could crack when it dries.

The low surface tension and slow drying time allow the material to flow out perfectly flat, and it takes several days before the finish attains its final hardness and smoothness. Its surface is usually dry enough to tape in about 5 hours, but if possible, delay taping until the finish has cured for at least 24 hours.

Polyurethanes are catalyzed materials whose catalysts are highly reactive to moisture. Cans of the materials should not be left open longer than is necessary, as moisture could enter and, when the can is closed, react with the material, causing it to expand and burst the can.

It is extremely important that the spray equipment be thoroughly cleaned before the polyurethane material hardens. If it cures in the spray guns and hoses, it is almost impossible to remove.

viscosity. The resistance of a fluid to flow. Viscosity refers to the "stiffness" of the fluid, or its internal friction.

viscosity cup. A specially shaped cup with an accurately sized hole in its bottom. The cup is submerged in the liquid to completely fill it. It is then lifted from the liquid and the time in seconds is measured from the beginning of the flow through the hole until the first break in this flow. The viscosity of the liquid relates to this time.

pot life. The length of time a resin will remain workable after the catalyst has been added. If a catalyzed material is not used within its usable pot life, it must be discarded and a new batch mixed.

tack coat. A coat of finishing material sprayed on the surface and allowed to dry until the solvents evaporate. As soon as the solvents evaporate, a wet full-bodied coat of material is sprayed over it.

Fabric Finishing

The finishes for fabric-covered aircraft are different from those used on metal or composite aircraft because of the amount of flexing that the fabric does. There are several new types of finishes used on amateur-built aircraft, but only the materials and systems approved for use on FAA-certificated aircraft are discussed here.

Organic Fabric Finishes

In the section of this text on Aircraft Fabric Covering, we discussed the way an aircraft structure is covered with Grade-A cotton. That discussion carried the process from the installation of the fabric through the initial shrinking. In this section we will discuss the finishing of the fabric and in a later section the application of the registration numbers and trim.

The Fill Coats

After the fabric has been shrunk initially, the rib stitching done, and the surface tape in place, apply the fill coats of dope. The number of coats of dope applied depends upon the type of finish you want. A utility finish uses the minimum number of coats needed to give satisfactory shrinkage and coverage. It usually consists of two coats of full-bodied clear butyrate dope brushed on, and two full, wet, cross coats of clear dope sprayed on. Wet-sand the surface with 400-grit sandpaper after the dope has fully dried. By this time, the weave of the fabric should be completely filled and the fabric ready to receive the ultraviolet-blocking coats.

Show-type finishes, with their deep, glass-like appearance, are achieved with fill provided by the clear dope and not by the aluminum dope. Spray on a wet cross coat of clear dope and wet-sand it with 400-grit and then 600-grit sandpaper. Wash all of the sanding residue off and dry the surface, then apply another cross coat of clear dope. Continue sanding and applying coats until the finish is as smooth as you desire.

The Ultraviolet-Blocking Coats

Use clear dope in which tiny flakes of aluminum metal are suspended to protect the clear dope fill coats and the fabrics by blocking the ultraviolet rays of the sun.

To properly prepare aluminum-pigmented dope, mix 1 pound of aluminum paste with 5 gallons clear dope. This is the same as $3\frac{1}{2}$ ounces of paste per gallon of dope. When mixing it, mix some thinner into the paste and then pour the dope into the thinned paste. When the aluminum paste and dope are thoroughly mixed, prepare the dope for spraying by thinning it with equal parts of thinner and pouring it through a paint strainer to remove any clumps of the aluminum powder.

utility finish. The finish of an aircraft that gives the necessary tautness and fill to the fabric and the necessary protection to the metal, but does not have the glossy appearance of a show-type finish.

show-type finish. The type of finish put on aircraft intended for show. This finish is usually made up of many coats of dope with much sanding and rubbing of the surface between coats. A show-type finish can also be obtained using a polyurethane enamel.

Too much aluminum powder in the dope or too many coats applied to the surface will cause the dope to delaminate. The finish coats will adhere to one layer of aluminum flakes, and the fill coats will adhere to another layer. The fill coats should provide the needed smoothness and the aluminum pigment should be used only to block the sun.

The Finish Coats

When rebuilding an aircraft, it is often the procedure to finish all of the components up through the aluminum-pigmented dope and apply the finish coats to all of the surfaces at the same time. This ensures that the final finish will be uniform. However, the finish on some of the surfaces that were the first re-covered must be "opened up" so they will accept the finish coats. Spray a mixture of half thinner and half retarder over the old dope. The retarder prevents the thinner evaporating before it softens the dope surface. If the dope has been applied for a long time, it may be necessary to open it up by spraying on a mixture of equal parts of thinner and rejuvenator. Allow the doped surface to dry only until it is no longer tacky and immediately spray on the colored dope.

All colored dope is slightly transparent, and to get the truest color from the dope and to ensure uniformity, all of the surfaces should be given a first coat of white dope. The richest color is produced when the maximum amount of light reflects from the smooth coat of white dope and shines through the semitransparent colored dope.

The white dope should dry for at least 24 hours before the colored coats are sprayed on. The best finish with butyrate dope is obtained by using extra thinner and some retarder to give the dope a longer time to flow out and smooth itself. The final coat may be made more glossy by mixing about 20% clear dope with the colored dope and replacing some of the thinner with retarder. Be sure when applying any dope to follow the instructions of the dope manufacturer in detail.

Inorganic Fabric Finishes

Some aircraft covered with polyester fabrics are finished with pigmented nontautening butyrate dope. These finishing systems are similar to those described for organic fabrics.

Other inorganic fabric systems use proprietary finishes and these are described in the section "Inorganic Fabric Covering," beginning on Page 201.

Finishing Problems

The function of a finishing system on an aircraft is to provide a surface that is both protective and decorative, and anything that prevents either of these qualities can be considered to be a finishing problem. The problems considered here are common with cellulose dope finishes.

Poor Adhesion

A topcoat of dope can actually peel off of the fill coats. This indicates the use of improper topcoat materials or too much aluminum powder in the fill coats.

The solvents in nitrate dope are not potent enough to open up a dried butyrate dope film, and if nitrate is sprayed over butyrate, it will not sink in to form the needed bond. When it dries, it can be peeled off.

If there is too much aluminum pigment in the fill coats of dope, the dope in the fill coats will bond to one layer of aluminum powder and the finish coats will bond to another layer. There is not a sufficient bond between the layers of aluminum powder to prevent the topcoat peeling away.

Blushing

Blushing is the most common problem with dope finishes. When the humidity is high, the drop in temperature that occurs when the solvents in the dope evaporate cause water to condense from the air. When this water mixes with the wet dope film, it causes the cellulose to precipitate out. This gives the film a chalky appearance which is neither strong nor attractive.

Prevent blushing by heating the air in the spray booth. Warm air can hold more water in its vapor state, and the temperature drop caused by the thinners evaporating will not cause water to condense out.

If the humidity is not too high, some retarder can be mixed with the dope in place of some of the thinner. The slower evaporation of the solvents in the retarder does not drop the temperature enough for water to condense from the air.

retarder. Dope thinner that has certain additives that slow its rate of evaporation to prevent the dope blushing.

If the dope you have just sprayed blushes, spray over it a very light mist coat consisting of a mixture of one part retarder and two parts thinner. Allow it to dry and then spray on another coat. The blushed surface should melt down and re-form as a smooth glossy surface. If this does not remove the blush, sand the surface to remove the blushed area and reapply the finish when the humidity is lower.

Pinholes

Aircraft dope is composed of solids and solvents. The solids remain on the surface of the fabric and the solvents evaporate. If the dope film is exposed to too much heat or to a draft of air, the surface will harden enough to prevent the vapors escaping as the solvents evaporate. Tiny bubbles of vapors will unite beneath this hardened surface until they form a large bubble with enough pressure to force its way through the surface. Rather than the surface re-forming smoothly, pits or pinholes will remain where each bubble burst.

Excessive atomizing air on the spray gun will force enough air into the dope film that will also cause pinholes to form.

Orange Peel

Dope should dry from the fabric outward, with the surface drying last. Dope shrinks as it dries, and if the surface dries first, the shrinkage of the body of the dope will cause the surface to wrinkle and resemble the skin, or peel, of an orange.

Improper spray techniques, a draft or air over the surface, or the use of thinners that evaporate too fast will give the surface an orange-peel appearance.

Fisheyes

Fisheyes are localized spots in the finish that do not dry. They are typically caused by surface contaminations such as wax, oil, or some of the silicone products. The contaminants change the surface tension of the immediate area causing the finish to crawl away, creating a crater in the finish. The ability of the finish to dry or harden will also be impaired.

Fisheyes can be prevented by keeping the surface clean and free of the contaminants. Before spraying the dope on the surface, scrub it with a rag damp with acetone toluol or MEK.

Runs and Sags

Runs and sags in a doped finish indicate too much finish. You can apply too much finish by moving the spray gun too slowly, holding the gun too close to the surface, or improperly thinning the dope.

It is always better to apply several thin coats of dope rather than a single heavy coat. The thin coats are far less likely to run or sag.

Dope Roping

Dope roping is the rough trail of dope that is left behind the brush when the dope is too heavy for properly application. This means you are not using enough thinner, or that the dope is too cold for proper brushing.

Ringworms and Rejuvenation

Plasticizers are used in cellulose dopes to give resilience to their film. In time these plasticizers migrate from the film and leave it brittle. When a blunt object is pressed against the brittle film, the film cracks in a series of concentric circles that resemble a ringworm. If these ringworms are not properly treated, they will allow sunlight and moisture to reach the fabric and cause it to deteriorate in a very short time. When the film dries and ringworms form, the fabric should be rejuvenated.

Rejuvenation is the process in which a dried dope film is softened with strong solvents and held in its softened state until new plasticizers in the rejuvenator combine with the film base.

Before rejuvenating a fabric surface, determine the condition of the fabric. Rejuvenation does nothing to restore the strength of the fabric, and if

rejuvenate. Restore the resilience to an aircraft finishing material. This is done by the use of a rejuvenator.

rejuvenator. A finishing material used to restore resilience to an old dope film. Rejuvenator contains strong solvents to open the dried-out film and plasticizers to restore resilience to the old dope.

its strength has deteriorated to its allowed minimum, the fabric should be replaced rather than the finish rejuvenated. If the fabric is good, scrub it with clear water and a nylon scrubber such as a Scotch-Brite pad. If the surface has been waxed, scrub it with a rag damp with toluol or MEK. Spray the surface with a mixture of one part rejuvenator and one part butyrate thinner. Allow the rejuvenator to soften the dope film and reflow the dope into the cracks.

Paint and Dope Application

The application of dope was at one time a very common function of an aircraft mechanic, but today, aircraft finishing has pretty much been relegated to specialty shops, and few aviation maintenance technicians are seriously involved with it. But, as with other aspects of this profession, we should be familiar with its fundamentals.

Finishing Equipment

In this section, we consider the basic equipment necessary for setting up a paint shop in a facility that could do an occasional paint job. Fixed base operators that specialize in aircraft finishing have special buildings used solely for aircraft painting. These buildings have provisions for filtering the air and removing all paint fumes. Stringent OSHA (Occupational Safety and Health Act) requirements must be met in regard to paint storage, electrical outlets, personal protection, and fire safety, as well as the collection and disposition of the materials removed from the aircraft when the finish is stripped.

Spray Area

When aircraft finishing is occasional, the area in which it is done may be isolated from the rest of the shop in a temporary spray booth. Build it with a framework that can be covered with polyethylene sheeting to contain the fumes and paint overspray. An exhaust fan driven by a non-sparking motor located near the floor should be able to move enough air that there is never more than just a slight odor of the finishing material. There should be no electrical extension cords or unprotected electrical outlets in the spray booth that could cause an electrical spark, and there should be adequate fire extinguishers inside the spray booth.

An ample supply of running water should be available to flush your eyes if you should get any finishing material in them. There should also be provisions for flushing the floor with water when sweeping up dried overspray from dope and lacquer. This overspray is highly flammable when it is dry, but can safely be swept when it has been wet with water.

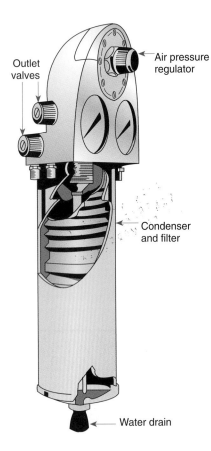

Figure 3-23. *The air transformer contains a water drain trap, a filter element, a pressure regulator, and the necessary gages and connections for spray guns.*

Outlet valves

Air pressure regulator

Condenser and filter

Water drain

Air Supply

There should be an air compressor available that can supply enough clean air to supply all of the spray guns you are likely to need at one time.

The air storage tank should have a water drain trap that can be drained daily, and there should an air transformer conveniently located in the booth. The air transformer, Figure 3-23, contains an air pressure regulator and pressure gages showing the inlet air pressure and the pressure being delivered to the spray gun. It also has an air filter and a container in which moisture which collects from the compressed air can be trapped and held until it can be drained out, at least daily.

Spray Equipment

Most of the smaller paint shops use air-atomized spray equipment exclusively. This equipment uses compressed air to atomize the material and propel it to the surface being finished. This is the only type of equipment that will be discussed beyond an introduction here.

Airless spray equipment atomizes the material and propels it by forcing it through a small atomizing nozzle at a pressure often above 1,000 psi. Airless spraying is usually used only where large volumes of material must be deposited in a minimum amount of time.

Electrostatic spray equipment is another specialized system seldom used in small repair shops. This system places a high electrostatic potential on the atomized material leaving the spray gun. An opposite potential is placed on the object being painted, and it attracts the spray, even causing it to wrap around and coat the side of the object away from the spray gun.

Electrostatic spraying causes very little overspray, and produces a much more uniform coating than either air or airless spraying alone.

Air-Atomized Spray Equipment

The air-atomizing spray gun like the one in Figure 3-24 is typical of the gun used in aircraft maintenance shops. This gun can be used as either a suction cup gun or a pressure pot gun by changing the fluid tip.

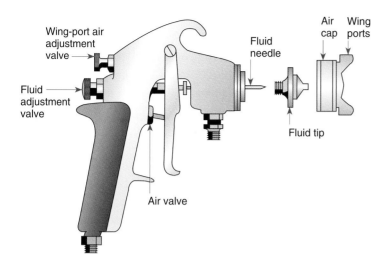

Figure 3-24. *An air-atomizing spray gun can be used as either a suction cup gun or a pressure pot gun by changing the fluid tip.*

This spray gun has three valves to give the operator control of the material that is being applied.

When the trigger is first pulled, it opens the air valve which sends atomizing air into the wing-port holes. Continued pulling of the trigger opens the fluid valve and allows the material to spray from the gun.

The wing-port air valve is adjusted by the upper knob, and it determines the shape of the spray pattern. When the valve is screwed in, very little air flows through the wing-port holes and the pattern is circular. Opening the valve flattens the spray pattern. The wide part of the spray pattern is always perpendicular to the wing ports.

The fluid adjustment valve, the lower knob, controls the amount of fluid that is allowed to flow from the gun. Screwing the knob out increases the amount of fluid that can be discharged.

The spray gun in Figure 3-24 can be used as either a suction cup gun or a pressure pot gun by changing the fluid tip. When it is used as a suction cup gun with a one-quart cup attached, the proper fluid tip extends beyond the air cap. When a pressure pot is connected to the gun, a fluid tip is used that is flush with the air cap. *See* Figure 3-25.

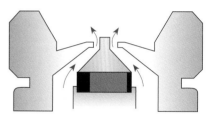

Suction-feed gun

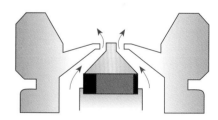

Pressure-feed gun

Figure 3-25. *The fluid tip determines whether the spray gun is set up for a suction cup or a pressure pot.*

A tip that protrudes from the air cap produces enough suction to draw material from a cup attached to the gun.

A tip that is flush with the air cap is used when the material is forced by air pressure from the pressure pot to the gun.

Cartridge-type mask

Hood-type respirator

Figure 3-26. *Respiratory protection devices for paint spray safety*

Safety Equipment

Painting aircraft is a maintenance operation that requires unique safety precautions. Painting involves the application of combustible materials in an atomized form that can be easily ignited. Some chemicals are prone to spontaneous combustion, and many of them are toxic or at least irritating to the skin.

Fire Safety

All large aircraft paint shops are equipped with sprinkler systems that will deluge the entire shop with water if a fire should develop. Small shops should be protected by a sufficient number of carbon dioxide fire extinguishers of adequate size strategically located within the shop.

All solvents in the paint shop should be stored in safety cans of a type that is approved by the insurance company that carries the policy for the shop.

Rags that have been used for the application of conversion coating materials should be kept wet until they can be thoroughly washed out, and then they should be kept in closed containers until they are disposed of.

Dried dope and lacquer overspray should never be dry-swept from the paint shop. Flood the floor with water and sweep the overspray while it is wet.

Respiratory Safety

The exhaust fan should remove most of the vapors from the paint booth, but there are usually enough contaminants left in the air that they could cause respiratory problems.

Two types of protective devices that can be used when painting aircraft are: cartridge-type masks, and hoods that cover the entire head. Some cartridge masks filter out only solid particles, while others remove certain fumes. The hoods are slightly pressurized with compressed air, and they prevent any fumes reaching the wearer.

Always wear the type of mask that is recommended by the manufacturer of the finishing material, and on cartridge-type masks, change the cartridges at the recommended intervals.

Toxicity Safety

Some finishing materials are toxic and irritating to certain people. When using any toxic material, protect yourself with gloves, long polyethylene sleeves, and a face mask. If any toxic material gets on your skin, flush it off immediately. If any gets in your eyes, flush it out with plenty of fresh water and get medical aid without delay.

Application of the Finish

A finish that is both attractive and protective depends upon two very basic factors, the proper preparation of the surface and the proper application of the finish. We have discussed the preparation of the surface, and in this section we will discuss the proper application of the finish.

Spraying on the Finish

Finish for an entire aircraft is applied with a pressure pot similar to that in Figure 3-27. Suction cups like that in Figure 3-28 are used for applying trim and any time a small amount of finishing material is to be sprayed.

When using a pressure pot, mix the finishing material as recommended by the paint manufacturer and add the proper amount of thinner to give the finish the correct viscosity.

Dip a viscosity cup into the material to fill it. Lift the cup, and measure the time from the instant the bottom of the cup is raised above the fluid until the first break occurs in the flow from the hole in the bottom of the cup. Adjust the viscosity until this time is the same as that for a batch of the finish that you know had the proper viscosity.

Adjust the air pressure on the pot to the value that will deliver the correct amount of material. Do this by adjusting the air pressure on the gun to about 35 to 40 psi measured at the gun as shown in Figure 3-29, and then bring up the pressure on the pot until the correct amount of material is being sprayed. The pot pressure is normally around 6 to 8 psi, and never above 10 psi.

Figure 3-27. *A pressure pot is used for painting an entire aircraft.*

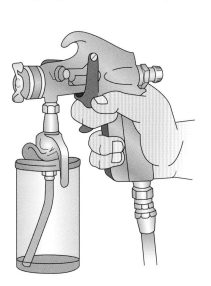

Figure 3-28. *A suction cup gun is used for applying the trim and for small paint jobs.*

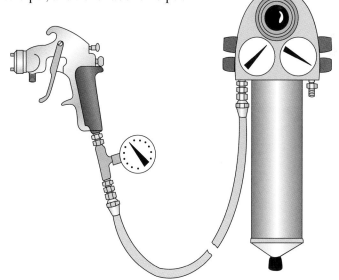

Figure 3-29. *Measure the correct air pressure for spraying at the gun, not at the compressor. The difference between the two pressures arises from the pressure loss in the hose.*

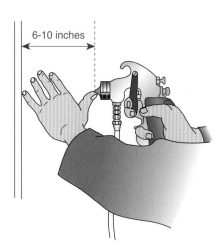

Figure 3-30. *Hold the nozzle of the spray gun between 6 and 10 inches from the surface being sprayed.*

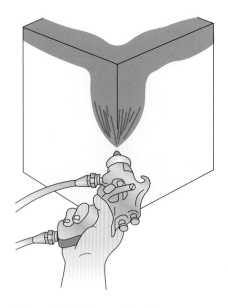

Figure 3-31. *When painting the corners of a surface, spray parallel to the corner first and then blend this in with the rest of the surface by spraying perpendicular to the corner.*

Adjusting the Spray Pattern

With the air pressure on the gun and on the pressure pot correctly adjusted, adjust the valves on the spray gun to get the best spray pattern. Open the wing-port air valve completely and the fluid valve about 1½ turns for a starter. *See* Figure 3-24 on Page 225.

Turn the air cap until the wing ports are perpendicular to the direction you want the spray pattern and pull the trigger all the way. This opens both the air valve and the fluid valve, and the fluid will spray out of the gun. Adjust the wing-port air valve to get a properly flat pattern and the fluid valve to get the correct amount of material.

Hold the spray gun perpendicular to the surface and between 6 and 10 inches from the surface being sprayed. This distance should produce a good wet coat and yet not deliver enough material to cause runs or sags. Move the gun parallel to the surface. Begin the stroke and pull the trigger. Release the trigger before completing the stroke.

Do not move the spray gun in an arc, as this will make an uneven film, thick when the gun is near the surface and thin when the spray is arced away.

Sequence of Painting

When the spray gun is properly adjusted, you may begin to apply the material. Before spraying the flat portions of the aircraft, spray the edges and corners. By spraying along the corner, the thickest film will be along the edges, and it will blend out in the flat portion.

Each time you make a pass with a spray gun, you deposit a single layer of finishing material about 10 to 12 inches wide. This coat is slightly thicker in the center and tapers off at the edges. To get an even buildup of finish, spray the first pass across the surface, then come back and spray the second pass, overlapping all but about two or three inches of the finish left by the first pass. Continue overlapping most of the previous stroke with each new stroke until you have an even film of the correct thickness with no runs or sags.

When painting a complete aircraft, first paint the ends and leading edges of the ailerons and flaps, then the flap and aileron wells. Then paint the wing tips and the wing leading and trailing edges. Paint all the landing gear and wheel wells and all of the control horns and hinges. After all of these difficult areas have been sprayed, spray the flat surfaces.

Spray the tack coats crosswise on the fuselage and spanwise along the wing and tail surfaces. Spray the primer and finish coats lengthwise on the fuselage and chordwise on the wing and tail surfaces.

Paint Gun Problems

Professional paint spray guns are precision tools and when they are properly cared for they will produce a good finish, but they can have problems. Knowing the cause of the most common problems will help produce a smooth, even finish.

Distorted Spray Pattern

The correct and incorrect spray patterns are illustrated in Figure 3-32. A correct spray pattern is an ellipse, and a pattern that is more round than elliptical indicates an insufficient amount of atomizing air pressure. Excessive atomizing air pressure will cause the pattern to be dumbbell shaped. A pattern that is somewhat pear shaped is caused by a material buildup around one side of the fluid nozzle, cutting off the atomizing air to one side of the pattern. A banana-shaped pattern indicates that one of the wing-port holes is plugged and the pattern is being blown to one side by air through the opposite wing-port hole.

Spray Gun Spitting

Suction cup spray guns spit when air gets into the fluid as it is being sprayed. This can indicate too little material in the cup, or air leaking into the fluid line between the cup and the fluid nozzle.

Cleaning the Spray Equipment

Clean paint spray equipment immediately after you finish spraying. If you used a suction cup, dump all of the finishing material from it and put some thinner in it. Spray this thinner through the gun, triggering the gun repeatedly to flush out all of the passageways, and clean the tip of the needle. Continue this until there is no trace of the material leaving the gun with the thinner.

If you have been spraying with a pressure pot, empty the gun and hoses back into the pot. Loosen the lid on the pot and the air cap on the gun. Hold a rag over the air cap and pull the trigger. This will force air back through the gun and hose and push all of the material back into the pot. Empty and clean the pot and put thinner in it. Replace the lid and spray the thinner through the hose and gun until no trace of the material comes out with the thinner.

Soak the nozzle of the spray gun in a container of thinner, but do not soak the entire gun, as it will ruin the packings.

Application of Trim and Registration Numbers

Federal Aviation Regulations Part 45 gives the requirements for the color and placement of the registration numbers on FAA-certificated aircraft.

The registration numbers must be of a color that contrasts with that of the rest of the aircraft. Silver may be considered to be a contrasting color, but because of its reflective characteristics, its use should be approved by the local FAA maintenance inspector before it is used.

14 CFR Part 45 gives some exceptions to this rule, but generally the registration marks must consist of the Roman capital letter N followed by the registration number assigned to the particular aircraft. For a fixed-wing aircraft, these characters should be placed on the side of the fuselage so they are between the trailing edge of the wing and the leading edge of the horizontal stabilizer.

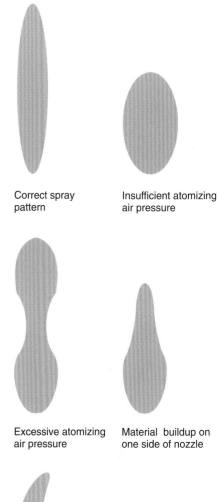

Correct spray pattern

Insufficient atomizing air pressure

Excessive atomizing air pressure

Material buildup on one side of nozzle

One wing-port hole is plugged up

Figure 3-32. *Paint spray patterns*

For rotorcraft, they must be displayed on both sides of the cabin, fuselage, boom, or tail.

The characters should be of equal height and at least 12 inches tall and two-thirds as wide as they are tall. The width of the letters M and W may be the same as their height. The stroke of the characters should be one-sixth as thick as the character is high, and the spacing between them should be at least one-fourth of the character width.

Figure 3-33 gives an example of all of the numerals and letters that are used in the registration numbers.

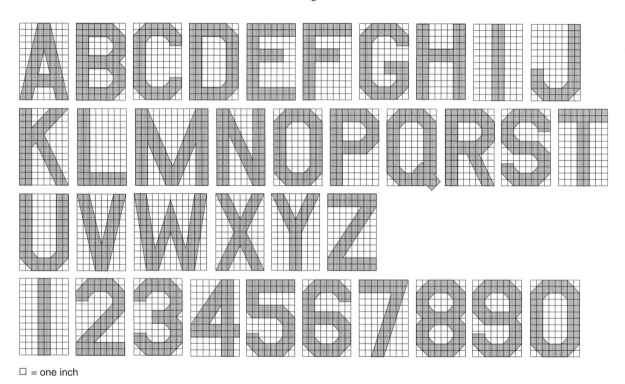

□ = one inch

Figure 3-33. *Letters and numerals used for aircraft registration numbers*

Ready-made masks, or stencils, are available that have the characters die-cut into an adhesive paper. You may apply the body color and stick the stencil in place. Remove the letter portion of the mask and spray on the color for the numbers. Or, you may spray on the color for the numbers and stick the stencil in place and remove all but the letter portion, then spray on the body color.

There is a typical universal template that will allow you to lay out the registration numbers. This template is shown in Figure 3-34, and it may be made from thin aluminum sheet.

After applying the base color to the fuselage and allowing it to dry for at least 24 hours, you may lay out and apply the registration numbers. It is very important when laying out the numbers that you use only the very best quality professional masking tape you can get. Poor quality tape does not seal the edges tight, and it causes rough edges of the letters.

Lay down two strips of half-inch tape, 12 inches apart, to form the top and bottom of the letters. Block out the letters as is seen in Figure 3-35 and then, using the template, outline the letter on the fabric, making very light marks with a soft lead pencil. Do not use a ball-point pen, as the ink will bleed up through the finish.

Mask the characters with fine-line type masking tape made for this purpose. Press down firmly and smoothly along the edges of the tape with a thumbnail, being careful not to apply so much pressure that the tape is stretched out of shape. This action will help prevent the trim paint from bleeding under the edge of the tape onto the base color. Do not cut the tape as there is a danger of cutting the fabric; rather tear it back against the edge of a knife blade or piece of thin aluminum sheet held flat against the surface. Fill in all parts of the characters that you do not want to paint, and mask beyond the top and bottom of the numbers with a good quality masking paper or aluminum foil. Do not use newspapers as they will allow some of the finishing material to bleed through. Ordinary kraft paper or polyethylene sheeting may be used to mask any portion of the structure where the overspray will be dry.

Spray a coat of the body color over the masked-off area first. If any paint bleeds under the masking tape it will be the body color and it will not produce ragged edges. When this is no longer tacky, spray on the color used for the numbers. The edges of the registration numbers will be smooth if the masking tape is removed as soon as the paint is no longer tacky to the touch. If the tape is allowed to remain until the paint is completely dry, the edges of the characters will likely be sharp and rough.

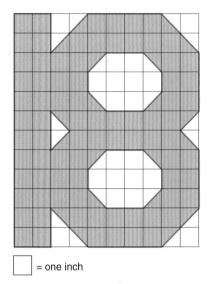

= one inch

Figure 3-34. *Universal template for laying out registration numbers*

Important note about masking tape:
Masking tape should be removed from a surface as soon as the finish has dried to the extent that it is no longer tacky. If the tape is left on the surface too long, it will cure to the finish and will be extremely difficult to remove. Pull the tape sharply in the direction of removal so it rolls off the surface, cutting the paint smartly at the edge, with minimal tendency to lift the trim paint off of the base color. Do not allow the tape to be exposed to the elements or to sit on the base paint for days.

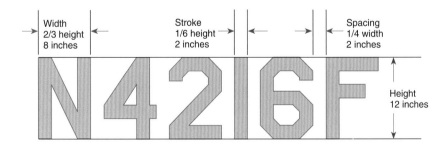

Figure 3-35. *Layout of registration numbers*

Answers begin on Page 263. Page numbers refer to chapter text.

65. Paint strippers remove _____ (enamel or lacquer) by swelling the film and causing it to pull away from the primer. *Page 212*

66. Paint strippers remove acrylic lacquer by _____ (softening or swelling) the film. *Page 213*

67. The wax left on a surface after paint stripper has been used _____ (can or cannot) be removed with lacquer thinner. *Page 213*

68. The finish may be dry-stripped from an aircraft surface by blasting it with _____ . *Page 214*

69. Corrosion that occurs in the form of thread-like deposits under a paint film is called _____ corrosion. *Page 214*

70. If intergranular corrosion is suspected, the area should be inspected with a/an _____ or _____ instrument. *Page 214*

71. Acrylic lacquers should be applied in _____ (one heavy coat or several light coats). *Page 217*

72. Synthetic enamels _____ (may or may not) be applied over zinc chromate primer. *Page 217*

73. Synthetic enamel should dry for at least _____ hours before it is taped for the trim coats. *Page 217*

74. Polyurethane enamels should be applied over a/an _____ primer. *Page 218*

75. It is best if polyurethane enamel is allowed to dry for _____ hours before it is taped for the trim coats. *Page 218*

76. The fill coats of dope _____ (should or should not) completely fill the weave of cotton fabric. *Page 219*

77. The aluminum-pigmented dope _____ (is or is not) used primarily to provide a smooth surface for the finish coats of dope. *Page 220*

78. For the richest colors in a doped finish, all of the surfaces should be undercoated with _____ dope. *Page 220*

79. A doped surface is more likely to blush when the relative humidity is _____ (high or low). *Page 221*

80. A draft of air across the surface of freshly applied dope will cause _____ (pinholes or fisheyes). *Page 221*

81. A surface resembling the peel of an orange may be caused by the thinner in the dope evaporating too _____ (fast or slow). *Page 222*

82. Fisheyes can be prevented by scrubbing the surface to be sprayed with a rag damp with _____ or _____ . *Page 222*

83. A topcoat of nitrate dope _____ (will or will not) bond to butyrate fill coats. *Page 221*

84. Rejuvenation _____ (does or does not) restore strength to weakened fabric. *Page 222*

85. The shape of the spray pattern produced by a paint spray gun is determined by the amount of air flowing through the _____ holes. *Page 228*

86. The exhaust fan in a spray booth should be _____ (near the floor or high up on the wall). *Page 223*

87. To get the proper thickness of paint film, the spray gun should be held between _____ and _____ inches from the surface being sprayed. *Page 228*

88. Each pass of the spray gun should overlap all but about _____ or _____ inches of the previous pass. *Page 228*

89. The correct shape for the spray pattern of a paint gun is a/an _____ . *Page 229*

90. A dumbbell-shaped spray pattern is caused by too _____ (much or little) atomizing air pressure. *Page 229*

91. A paint spray gun _____ (should or should not) be cleaned by soaking the entire gun in a container of thinner. *Page 229*

92. The registration numbers of an aircraft certificated in the United States must be preceded by the letter _____ . *Page 229*

93. The minimum height of a registration number on a fixed-wing aircraft must be _____ inches. *Page 230*

Continued

94. A ball-point pen _____ (is or is not) a good instrument to use when laying out registration numbers on a doped fuselage. *Page 231*

95. The masking tape used to lay out the registration numbers _____ (should or should not) be removed as soon as the finish is no longer tacky to the touch. *Page 231*

Composite Structures

Aircraft structures have evolved fully as much as have their powerplants. The very first airframes were made of open trusses of either wood strips or bamboo. The aerodynamic surfaces were made of lightweight wood covered with cotton or linen fabric, shrunk and made air tight with a syrup-like collodion product that dried to a hard film.

The next major development came with the welded steel tube fuselage structure that replaced the wooden truss. This structure is strong, but it has the disadvantage that to give it a streamlined shape, a superstructure must be built around the load-bearing truss. This adds weight but is needed for aerodynamic smoothness and esthetics.

In the late 1920s, the Lockheed Company developed a streamlined wooden monocoque structure that carried virtually all of the stresses in its outer skin. This lightweight streamlined structure was used on some of the most efficient aircraft of the time. It, however, had the disadvantage of being extremely labor intensive in its construction.

The next logical step in the evolution of aircraft structure was to replace the wooden monocoque with a thin aluminum alloy monocoque. This decreased the dependence upon skilled craftsmen for its construction and made mass production of interchangeable parts practical and cost effective.

Metal stressed-skin aircraft structure has been the standard since the 1930s, but a new era is dawning, that of composites. Composite structure can be made stronger, lighter in weight, more rigid, and less costly than metal.

We have experienced what may be termed a plastics revolution. Early plastic materials such as celluloid and Beetleware gave promise of a low-cost, easy-to-manufacture material, but they did not have the strength needed for structural applications. One of the first plastic materials used in aviation was a thermosetting phenol-formaldehyde resin that was reinforced with paper or linen cloth. This phenolic material, called Micarta, pioneered in the early 1930s, is still used for control cable pulleys and fairleads and for electrical insulators.

collodion. Cellulose nitrate used as a film base for certain aircraft dopes.

monocoque. A single-shell type of aircraft structure in which all of the flight loads are carried in the outside skin of the structure.

plastics. The generic name for any of the organic materials produced by polymerization. Plastics can be shaped by molding or drawing.

Glass fibers, both woven into cloth and packed into loose mat and roving, have been reinforced with polyester resins and used for radomes, wing tips, and wheel pants since the early 1950s. This material is truly a composite, and may be thought of as being the ancestor of modern composite structural materials.

Modern composite materials use fibers of graphite and Kevlar® as well as glass for most applications, with boron and ceramic used in some special applications. These fibers are primarily bonded into an epoxy resin matrix.

Composite structural components have the advantage over metal of being lighter in weight, stronger, more rigid, and better able to withstand the sonic vibrations that are commonly encountered in aircraft structure.

The military forces have been responsible for much of the development in advanced composite structure because performance and the successful accomplishment of military goals have always been more important than cost. The airlines have also contributed to its development because every pound of weight saved by replacing metal with composite materials adds a pound of payload capability for each flight and reduces the fuel burn.

Builders of amateur-built aircraft have made extensive use of some of the simpler composites because they can be used to produce beautiful, stream-lined, lightweight, and strong aircraft structure without requiring elaborate tooling. Construction is quite labor intensive, but, since homebuilt aircraft are usually labors of love, the long hours required for their construction are not a deterrent.

General aviation, held back by economic constraints, has made few uses of advanced composites, but aircraft such as the Beech *Starship* show that

Figure 3-36. *The Beech Starship is one of the first commercially produced general aviation aircraft to make extensive use of composite construction. Photo courtesy Robert Scherer (www.rps3.com).*

there are applications in this area. A new generation of general aviation aircraft such as the type-certificated Lancair ES and Cirrus aircraft are now being produced. Their structural requirements will continue to increase in the years to come. Repairs to modern composite structure are complex. It requires special training and experience to produce a repair that restores the structure to its original strength, stiffness, rigidity, vibration characteristics, and aerodynamic smoothness.

In this text, we introduce the technology of composites to an extent that will allow you to profit from the specialized training offered by the aircraft manufacturers and by specialized composite repair training facilities. Most of the materials and procedures described are those used in the construction and repair of FAA-certificated aircraft rather than homebuilt or military aircraft.

Composite Materials

Modern composite structure consists of high-strength fibers oriented in the proper direction to withstand the stresses imposed upon them. These fibers are encapsulated in a matrix that bonds them together and carries the aero-dynamic and structural loads into the fibers.

By their very nature, composite materials are divided into two basic categories: the reinforcing materials and the matrix.

Reinforcing Materials

Reinforcing materials consist of fibers that may be made into tapes, woven into a fabric, grouped together into a loosely compacted mat, or lightly twisted into a roll, or strand, called roving.

roving. A lightly twisted roll or strand of fibers.

Fiberglass

Thin fibers are drawn from molten glass and spun together into threads and woven into a shiny, white cloth. There are two types of glass used for fibers, E-glass (electrical glass) and S-glass (structural glass). E-glass has high electrical strength and is used for most nonaviation and some aviation applications. S-glass is stronger, tougher, and stiffer than E-glass and is used in applications where its superior qualities outweigh its higher cost.

Kevlar

Kevlar is the DuPont Company's registered trade name for its aramid fiber. It has a yellow color and is lightweight, strong, and extremely flexible and has excellent resistance to the chemicals normally associated with aircraft operations.

Kevlar is used to replace fiberglass in many applications. A properly designed Kevlar part has the strength of a similar metal part, but is much lighter in weight.

Kevlar®. A patented synthetic aramid fiber noted for its flexibility and light weight. It is to a great extent replacing fiberglass as a reinforcing fabric for composite construction.

One of the major advantages of Kevlar is its flexibility under load and its ability to withstand impact, shock, and vibration. It is often used for helicopter rotor blades where twisting and vibration cause metal blades to fatigue and develop cracks. Blades made of Kevlar can absorb these stresses without damage.

Graphite

Graphite, or carbon, fibers are woven into a black fabric that is extremely strong for its weight and is very stiff. It is used for primary structure where high strength and rigidity are the prime considerations. The stiffness of graphite fibers has made it possible to explore the potential of the efficient forward-swept wing in the research airplane, the Grumman X-29.

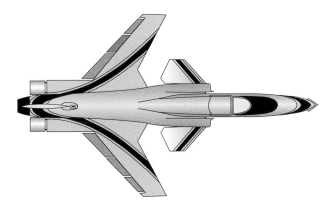

Figure 3-37. *The aerodynamic advantages of a forward-swept wing were not able to be exploited until graphite fibers were developed. The extreme stiffness of graphite made it possible to build a wing that does not twist under aerodynamic loads.*

Graphite may be bonded to aluminum alloy components, but take special care, because contact with the graphite is likely to cause the aluminum alloy to corrode.

Fiber Orientation

Wood is weak across its grain, but strong parallel to it, and when it is necessary for wood to have multidirectional strength, it is made into plywood whose thin veneers are glued together with their grains oriented at 45° or 90° to each other.

The same thing is true about composite materials whose major strength and stiffness is parallel to its fibers. Strength and stiffness can be tailored to the aerodynamic loads it must carry by the proper choice of the fabric weave and by the orientation of the fibers in the adjacent plies in the fabric layup.

Unidirectional Fabrics

Fabric made with all of the major fibers running in the same direction is called a unidirectional fabric. Unidirectional fabric is not woven, but the major fibers are laid in the warp direction and are held together with small cross threads.

unidirectional fabric. Fabric in which all of the threads run in the same direction. These threads are often bound with a few fibers run at right angles, just enough to hold the yarns together and prevent their bunching.

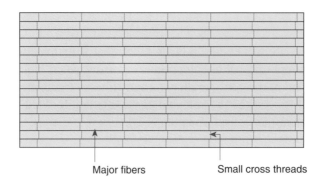

Major fibers   Small cross threads

Figure 3-38. *All of the major fibers in a piece of unidirectional fabric run in the same direction.*

When the maximum amount of strength and rigidity are needed in a structure, several layers of unidirectional fabric can be laid up with the fibers of each of the layers running in the direction required to furnish the required strength. The stiffness required in the Grumman X-29 forward-swept wing is furnished by a wing box whose covers are made up of crisscrossed tapes of unidirectional graphite, crossing each other at 45° angles to oppose the aerodynamic stresses. There are 156 layers of material at the point of maximum thickness. This type of design in which the characteristics of the material are matched to the aerodynamic loads is called aeroelastic tailoring.

aeroelastic tailoring. The design of an aerodynamic surface whose strength and stiffness are matched to the aerodynamic loads that will be imposed upon it.

Bidirectional Fabrics

Woven fabrics are made by interlacing fill threads with the warp threads as the fabric is being woven on the looms. The particular weave is chosen to give the fabric the desired characteristics. Some of the most generally used weaves are the plain weave and various types of satin weaves.

warp threads. Threads that run the length of the roll of fabric, parallel to the selvage edge. Warp threads are often stronger than fill threads.

In the plain-weave fabric, Figure 3-39, each warp thread passes over one fill thread and under the next. Plain-weave fabrics are the most stable for lay-ups because the threads slip less than other weaves.

Satin weaves are those in which one warp thread passes over several fill threads and under just one. Satin weaves are used when the fabric must be draped into complex shapes with a high degree of smoothness.

plain-weave fabric. Fabric in which each warp thread passes over one fill thread and under the next. Plain-weave fabric typically has the same strength in both warp and fill directions.

satin-weave fabric. Fabric in which the warp threads pass under one fill thread and over several more. Satin-weave fabrics are used when the lay-up must be made over complex shapes.

In crowfoot satin, each warp thread passes under one fill thread and over three. In five-harness satin weave, each warp thread passes under one fill thread and over four. In eight-harness satin-weave, each warp thread passes over one fill thread and under seven.

fill threads. Threads in a piece of fabric that run across the width of the fabric, interweaving with the warp threads. Fill threads are often called woof, or weft, threads.

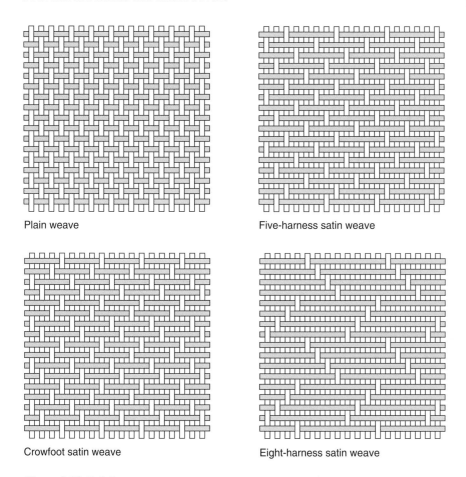

Plain weave

Five-harness satin weave

Crowfoot satin weave

Eight-harness satin weave

Figure 3-39. *Fabric weaves*

Hybrids

A hybrid fabric is composed of different types of fibers woven together to obtain special characteristics. One of the more popular hybrid composites is Kevlar and graphite. Fibers of each material are woven together to produce a fabric that has some of the better characteristics of both of the fibers.

Matrix Materials

matrix. The material used in composite construction to bond the fibers together and to transmit the forces into the fibers. Resins are the most widely used matrix materials.

The two components of a composite material are the reinforcing materials and the matrix that binds these materials together and transfers stresses into them. The matrix materials used for most composite materials are in the form of resins, but some of the ceramic composites use a metallic matrix.

Two basic types of resins are used in aircraft construction: thermoplastic and thermosetting. A thermoplastic resin is one that may be softened with heat. The transparent acrylic plastic material that is used for windshields and side windows of most of the small general aviation aircraft is a familiar type of thermoplastic material. When a piece of acrylic plastic is heated to a specified temperature, it may be formed into almost any shape that is needed. When it cools, it retains its shape. It may be reshaped by again heating it.

thermoplastic resin. A type of plastic material that becomes soft when heated and hardens when cooled.

Thermosetting resins are used to reinforce glass, Kevlar, and graphite fibers. These resins are cured by heat and once cured, they do not change their shape, even when they are reheated. The two basic thermosetting resins used in aircraft construction are polyester and epoxy.

thermosetting resin. A type of plastic material that, when once hardened by heat, cannot be softened by being heated again.

Polyester Resins

Polyester resins were the first developed, and have been used primarily with fiberglass. Polyesters do not provide the strength needed for most of the modern applications, but because of their low cost and relative ease of use, they are used for some nonstructural applications such as fairings.

polyester resin. A thermosetting resin used as a matrix for much of the fiberglass used in composite construction.

Polyester resins are two-part materials: a resin and a catalyst. Typically about one ounce of catalyst is used with one gallon of resin.

Epoxy Resins

A number of epoxy resins are used as a matrix material. Each of them have different characteristics. Some are liquids as thin as water, and others are thick syrups. Some have good high-temperature characteristics, others are better suited for low-temperature applications. Some are very rigid, while others are quite flexible. Some cure quickly, and others allow for a longer working time before they cure.

Almost all aircraft structural epoxy is a two-part material, resin and catalyst, that is quite different from polyester resins. Rather than using a small amount of catalyst to initiate the resin's cure as is done with polyester, epoxy resins use a different type of catalyst, or hardener, and use much more of it.

It is extremely important to follow the approved instructions when mixing epoxy resins. The material must be fresh; that is, it must be used within its allowable shelf life which is stamped on the container. You must use the correct resin and the correct hardener, and the two materials must be accurately weighed and mixed for the recommended length of time. After mixing the materials, you must use them within the usable pot life, which is given in terms of minutes, and which is stamped on the container.

Preimpregnated Materials

It is critical to ensure that all of the fibers are uniformly wet with the matrix material. In order to properly transfer stresses into the reinforcing material, all of the fibers must be completely encapsulated. Some of the epoxy resins are rather viscous and it is difficult to thoroughly saturate the material.

When absolute uniformity is required for volume production of composite structure, manufacturers often use preimpregnated materials called prepregs. Prepregs are made by immersing graphite, fiberglass, or Kevlar fabric in a resin solution that contains the correct amount of catalyst. The excess resin is removed and the material is dried. A sheet of parting film is placed on one side of the material and it is rolled up and placed in a refrigerator to prevent its curing until it is used.

prepreg. Preimpregnated fabric. A type of composite material in which the reinforcing fibers are encapsulated in an uncured resin. Prepreg materials must be kept refrigerated to prevent them from curing before they are used.

Adhesives

An adhesive is a resin that is used to bond parts together. Some adhesives are available as two-part liquids that are mixed when they are needed. Another form of adhesive that is extremely handy for certain types of construction and repair is film-type adhesive. This adhesive is made up of catalyzed resin that is formed into a thin film. A plastic backing sheet is put on one side and stored in a refrigerator. To use it, cut a piece of the film to the proper size and put it into place between the prepared surface and a prepreg patch. Heat and pressure cure the adhesive and securely bond the patch in place.

Foaming adhesives are used to bond sections of honeycomb core. This adhesive is in the form of a thick tape or sheet which is wrapped around the replacement core plug. When heat is applied, the adhesive foams up and expands to fill all of the crevices and hardens to ensure a good joint.

Core Materials

Aluminum alloy has a high enough tensile strength that a very thin sheet may be strong enough for a given application, but this thin sheet does not have enough stiffness to make it a totally adequate structural material. One of the early incursions into the field of composite materials was done by bonding end-grain balsa wood between two thin sheets of aluminum alloy. The metal provided the strength, and the balsa wood provided the thickness and thus the stiffness without adding too much weight. This type of composite is called sandwich construction.

Sandwich construction in which a lightweight core material is bonded between face plies of metal or resin-reinforced fabric is used today for all types of aircraft from homebuilt machines to high-speed, state-of-the-art military aircraft.

sandwich material. A type of composite structural material in which a core material is bonded between face sheets of metal or resin-impregnated fabric.

Foam

Many of the composite-construction homebuilt aircraft are made by laying resin-impregnated fiberglass or Kevlar fabric over a foam form. There are two basic types of foam used for this purpose, polystyrene (commonly called styrofoam) and urethane foam.

The Styrofoam used for aircraft construction is not the same material used for coffee cups and picnic ice chests. It is closed-cell foam whose cell size and density are carefully controlled. Styrofoam is cut with a hot wire, and it must be used with epoxy resin, as polyester resin will dissolve it.

Urethane foam has an advantage over Styrofoam in that, unlike Styrofoam, it is fuel proof. It must not be cut with a hot wire as it gives off noxious fumes, but it can be cut and shaped with a sharp knife. Either epoxy or polyester resins can be used with urethane foam.

Honeycomb

While foam finds most of its applications in lightweight aircraft construction, honeycomb is used as the sandwich core for most of the high-performance applications.

Honeycomb for aircraft structural applications is made of aluminum, paper, fiberglass, stainless steel, and Nomex®, which is gaining a high degree of popularity. Honeycomb is made by forming the core material into a ribbon which contains a series of crimps, then joining them together as seen in Figure 3-40. Honeycomb core material is normally loaded in such a way that compressive stresses are imposed perpendicular to the cells, in the thickness direction. The core has little strength in its width direction, and it is important when replacing a piece of honeycomb core to be sure that the cells are properly oriented so that the length, or the ribbon, of the new piece runs in the same direction as the length of the core in the damaged area.

hot-wire cutter. A cutter used to shape blocks of Styrofoam. The wire is stretched tight between the arms of a frame and heated by electrical current. The hot wire melts its way through the foam.

Nomex®. A patented nylon material used to make the honeycomb core for certain types of sandwich materials.

ribbon direction. The direction in a piece of honeycomb material that is parallel to the length of the strips of material that make up the core.

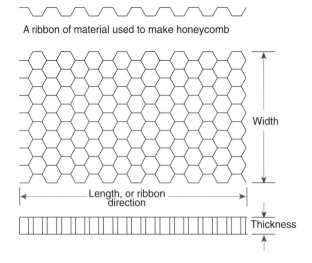

Figure 3-40. *Honeycomb core material is made of strips, or ribbons, of material formed into crimps and joined into the familiar hexagonal pattern. It is best suited for compressive loads along its thickness. It has strength along its length, but little along its width.*

Fillers

Often the resins used in composite construction do not have the consistency needed for the application. When this is the case, fillers can be added to change the thin liquid into a syrup or a paste. The most widely used filler is microballoons, or microspheres. This product is made up of tiny hollow glass spheres that are mixed with the resin. The spheres displace four to six times their weight in most resins, and the cured resin forms a low-density product that can be sanded or filed.

The consistency of the finished product is determined by the amount of filler mixed with the resin. The resin is mixed with the correct amount of hardener and then the microballoons are folded into it. Approximately equal volumes of resin and microballoons produce a wet slurry mix. Two to four times as much filler as resin produces a syrupy mixture and a greater amount of microballoons results in a dry paste.

Manufacturing Methods

The manufacturing of a composite structure requires entirely different procedures from those used with sheet metal. The basic principle of much composite construction involves the process of laying up the reinforcing material in such a way that the maximum strength of each ply is oriented in the correct direction. The engineers who designed the part have computed all of the stresses to which the part will be subjected and have specified the orientation of the fibers. As was mentioned earlier, the top and bottom skins of the wing box of the forward-swept wing of the Grumman X-29 are made up of unidirectional graphite tapes. The plies of these tapes are oriented at 45° increments to give the wing its unique ability to withstand the twisting loads without the divergence that has prevented the use of the efficient forward-swept configuration in the past.

After the correct number of plies of material have been laid up with the proper orientation, the complete assembly must be cured. This is typically done with pressure and heat. There are three ways to apply heat and pressure: by matched dies, by a vacuum bag, and in an autoclave.

Matched Dies

When a large number of identical parts are to be made, manufacturers use a set of heated matched dies similar to the ones in Figure 3-41. Prepreg material is placed over the female die, or unimpregnated fibers are laid in a bed of resin in the female die. The male die is then forced down into the female die to give the finished product the desired shape and to ensure that all of the fibers are completely encapsulated with the resin. Pressure and heat are applied for a specific length of time to cure the resin.

microballoons. Tiny, hollow spheres of glass or phenolic material used to add body to a resin.

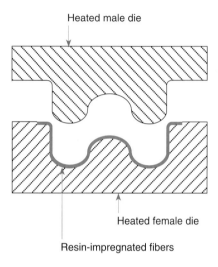

Heated male die

Heated female die

Resin-impregnated fibers

Figure 3-41. *Heated matched dies are used for making a large number of identical parts.*

autoclave. A pressure vessel inside of which air can be heated to a high temperature and pressure raised to a high value.

Autoclaves are used in the composite manufacturing industry to apply heat and pressure for curing the resins.

Vacuum Bag

You can use a female mold, if not enough identical parts are being manufactured to justify the expense of a set of matched dies. Lay out the resin-impregnated fabric according to the specifications of the engineers, and place a vacuum bag over the lay-up, as shown in Figure 3-42. Connect the bag to a vacuum pump and evacuate it to the specified low pressure. The pressure of the atmosphere forces the plies tightly together and ensures complete encapsulation of all of the fibers. If the mold is not heated, you can place a heating pad inside the vacuum bag, or place the mold, lay-up, and vacuum bag in an oven with accurate temperature control and held at the specified temperature for the length of time specified for the particular component.

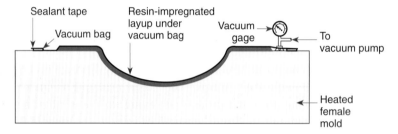

Figure 3-42. *A vacuum bag may be used to apply the pressure to a composite lay-up to ensure that it takes the shape of the female die and to ensure that all of the individual fibers are completely encapsulated.*

Autoclaves

An autoclave is a pressure vessel in which air can be heated to a high temperature and pressure raised to a high value. Many manufacturers of composite structures use autoclaves to apply the heat and pressure needed to cure resins.

Filament Winding

When a component such as a helicopter rotor blade or a propeller blade must have the most strength possible, it may be filament-wound as illustrated in Figure 3-43. A mandrel in the shape of the component is mounted in a fixture that rotates it. Preimpregnated filaments are fed off spools and wrapped around the mandrel. The head through which the filaments pass is computer-controlled so the different layers of the filaments can be oriented at the angle specified by the engineers. When the wrapping is completed, the component is placed in an autoclave and heated and held under the required pressure for the specified length of time.

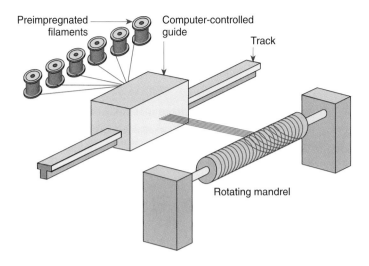

Figure 3-43. *When the maximum strength is required, the part may be filament-wound and cured in an autoclave.*

Composite Structure Inspection and Repair

Composite construction of aircraft is a new technology, and its inspection and repair have not yet been standardized. Each damaged area must be individually assessed and the repair designed so that it will meet the requirements specified by the manufacturer's engineering department and described in the structural repair manual (SRM). No general text can describe all types of repairs, but some fundamental considerations are common to most repairs, and these are described here.

SRM. Structural Repair Manual. An SRM, issued by the aircraft manufacturer, details various typical repairs applicable to a specific aircraft.

Inspection

Before any repair is considered, you must determine the extent of the damage and choose a method of repair.

Delamination is one of the most common types of damage found in composite structure. If the face plies separate from the core material, or if some of the plies separate from each other, the material loses its strength and must be repaired. One of the simplest methods of inspecting a structure for delaminations is to tap the suspected area with the edge of a coin. If there is no delamination, the coin will produce a clear ringing sound, but if there is delamination, the sound will be a dull thud. The coin tap procedure is not a quantitative test, but it may give an indication when further investigation is needed.

delamination. The separation of the layers of a laminated material.

Cracks in the surface may be indications of serious damage, or they may be superficial and require no repair other than touching up the paint. It is important to be able to determine which is the case. Ultrasonic inspection may be used to determine if a part is actually damaged. Pulses of high-frequency vibrations are fed into the part and reflected back into a pickup. The results are displayed on the screen of a cathode-ray tube or computer-driven display.

Radiograpic inspection, such as X-ray and gamma-ray, can be used to examine the inside of a piece of composite structure. This method is about the only way water inside a honeycomb core can be detected.

Repair

Assume that a careful inspection has found damage in a piece of honeycomb-core composite material that has three plies of fabric on each side. The damage extends through the surface skin into the core material. Two typical repairs are described in this section to show the room-temperature cure and the hot curing method.

Room-Temperature Cure

First, outline the damaged area. In this example, no part of the damage extends beyond a two-inch circle. The edges of the cleaned-out hole will taper back so that one inch of each ply is exposed on each side of the damage. For this repair in a three-ply face sheet, an area 10 inches in diameter must be cleaned up and prepared.

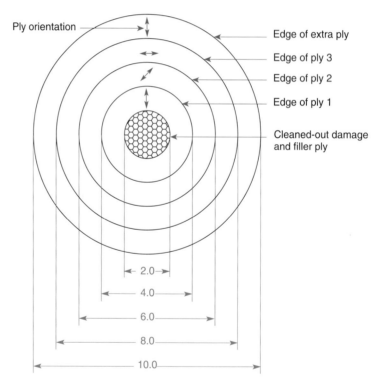

Figure 3-44. *Typical dimensions for a room-temperature repair to the face plies of a honeycomb core composite panel*

Draw a circle with a diameter of 11 inches, centered on the damage. Carefully mask the area to be repaired so the adjacent finish will not be damaged. Remove all the finish from this area by sanding carefully with 80- to 150-grit sandpaper. During this sanding, be careful that you do not allow heat to build up that could cause delamination. Never use any type of paint stripper on composite structure, because some of the fibers may absorb the chemicals from the stripper, which would prevent proper bonding of the patch. Do not sand into the fibers in this top layer of fabric.

Remove the damage with a high-speed router. First cut through the top skin and remove it. Then, using a flush cutter, remove the honeycomb down to within about $\frac{1}{16}$ inch from the bottom skin. This last bit of core material can be removed by careful hand sanding.

Draw a circle with an eight-inch diameter, centered on the damage. This will be the outer edge of the original material. Use a small right-angle pneumatic sander, and carefully sand through the first ply of material. Taper the sanding so you get through this ply in one inch. You can tell when you are through a layer by watching the direction of the threads, as each layer of fabric is oriented in a different direction. Sand through the next ply in such a way that you are through it in another inch. Continue through the third ply, and be extremely careful as you approach the edge of the hole that you do not expose the core.

After removing the damage and scarfing back the area to receive the repair, remove all the sanding residue with a vacuum cleaner. Don't use compressed air, because you might delaminate the plies that are now exposed. Clean the surface with a rag damp with a solvent such as methyl-ethyl-ketone (MEK) or acetone to remove any of the oils that may have been left by your fingers as you were feeling to determine the progress in the sanding. Oils from a fingerprint will prevent the patches from bonding properly.

Cut a plug of honeycomb of the same material and density as that removed from the damaged area. When inserting it into the hole, be sure to orient it so that the ribbon direction is the same as that in the structure being repaired. Secure the plug with the type of adhesive that is specified in the structural repair manual. Plugs are often installed by wrapping them with foaming adhesive. When the repair is cured, the adhesive foams and bonds the core to the surrounding honeycomb.

Lay out the repair ply inserts by tracing circles the actual size of each insert onto pieces of clear plastic. Mark an arrow on each circle to show the orientation of the warp threads.

Place the fabric for the replacement plies on a sheet of clean plastic. Be sure that the fabric is the type of material, weight, and weave specified in the structural repair manual (SRM). When handling the material, use clean lint-free or latex gloves to prevent getting oils from your hand on the material.

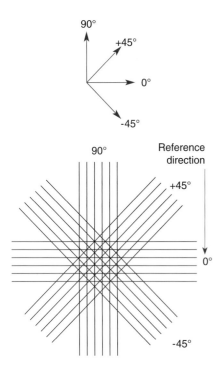

Figure 3-45. *A warp clock is included in a structural repair manual to show the correct orientation of the warp threads in each ply of the material.*

warp clock. An alignment indicator included in a structural repair manual to show the orientation of the plies of a composite material. The ply direction is shown in relation to a reference direction.

parting film. A layer of thin plastic material placed between a composite lay-up and the heating blanket. It prevents the blanket from sticking to the fabric.

bleeder. A material such as glass cloth or mat that is placed over a composite lay-up to absorb the excess resin forced out of the ply fibers when pressure is applied.

Mix the resin as directed in the SRM. Be sure that the resin is the one specified for the repair and that it is within its usable shelf life. Mix it according to the instructions furnished by the resin manufacturer. Pour enough of the mixed resin over the fabric to provide between a 50-to-55%-by-weight fabric-to-resin combination, and very carefully work it into the weave. Each thread must be thoroughly encapsulated, but the weave must not be distorted.

Place the plastic patterns for each of the ply inserts over the resin-impregnated material, observing the direction of the warp threads. Cut the inserts from the material, following the outline you have made.

The structural repair manual shows the orientation of the plies of the fabric by the use of a warp clock such as the one in Figure 3-45. The 0° (or reference direction) is shown and the orientation of each ply is noted in degrees positive or negative from the reference direction.

Be sure that the structure is ready to receive the patch. Spread a thin layer of resin on the repair area before laying any of the plies in place. Remove the plastic from the filler ply which is the same diameter as the exposed core, and carefully lay it in place, observing the direction of the warp threads. Remove the plastic from the first repair ply insert and lay it in place. Follow this with the second ply and the third ply, and finally put the extra ply in place. Put a thin sanding ply over the extra ply. This ply is to give aerodynamic smoothness to the repair.

Lay a piece of perforated parting film over the repair, and place a sheet of bleeder material over it. This bleeder is a porous material that holds the resin that is squeezed from the material as the pressure is put on it.

Lay down four strips of sealing tape around the repair area and place the vacuum bagging material that has the fitting for the vacuum pump over the tape. Press it down into the tape to produce a seal. Connect the vacuum pump and check for the presence of leaks, which will be indicated by a hissing sound. Hold the vacuum on the repair for the time specified by the structural repair manual. *See* Figure 3-46.

Hot-Bond Repair

You can make a stronger repair using the hot-bond process, in which the laid-up repair is cured with both heat and pressure. For the two-inch damage, the repair is smaller, because each ply is cut back less than is necessary for the room-temperature cure.

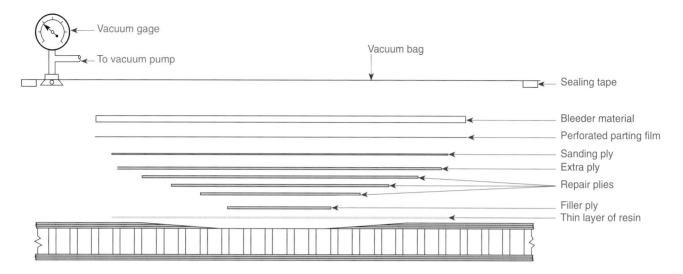

Figure 3-46. *Typical lay-up for vacuum-bagging of a room-temperature cured repair*

Prepare the area as described above, using the dimensions shown in Figure 3-47. In a hot-bond repair, cut back each layer half an inch on each side.

Remove the damaged material and draw a circle with a five-inch diameter, centered on the damage. This will be the outer edge of the original material. Carefully sand through each ply of material, tapering the sanding so you expose half an inch of each ply, but do not expose the core. Clean the surface with a rag damp with methyl-ethyl-ketone (MEK) or acetone.

Cut a plug of honeycomb as described in the room-temperature-cured repair section, and wrap it with a foaming adhesive. When the repair is cured, the heat causes the adhesive to foam and bond the core to the surrounding honeycomb.

Lay out the repair ply inserts by tracing the actual size of each insert onto pieces of clear plastic. Mark an arrow on each circle to show the orientation of the warp threads.

Use prepreg and the adhesive specified in the SRM to make this repair. Lay the plastic patterns for each of the ply inserts over the prepreg, orienting the arrow on the plastic with the warp threads, and cut the inserts, following the pattern.

Be sure that the structure is ready to receive the patch. Lay a piece of film adhesive in place, and remove the plastic from the filler ply that is the same size as the exposed core. Carefully put it in place, observing the direction of the warp threads as specified in the SRM. Then remove the plastic from each of the repair plies and the extra ply, and lay them in place, again paying attention to the ply orientation.

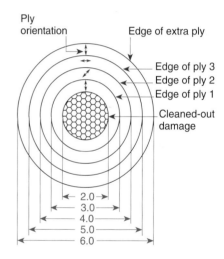

Figure 3-47. *Typical dimensions for a hot-bond repair to the face plies and core of a honeycomb composite panel*

Place a thin sanding ply and then a piece of perforated parting film over the repair, and you are ready to vacuum bag the repair to apply heat and pressure. *See* Figure 3-48.

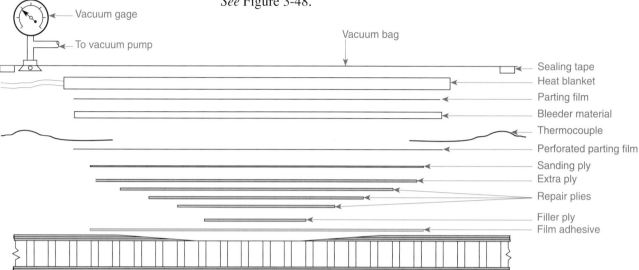

Figure 3-48. *Typical lay-up for a hot bond repair*

Place the thermocouples from the heater on top of the parting film and lay a sheet of bleeder material over the film. This bleeder is a porous material that holds the resin squeezed from the material as it is placed under pressure to cure the repair. Place a piece of nonperforated parting film over the bleeder and the heat blanket on top of it.

Lay the sealing tape around the repair area, and then carefully seal around the wires for the heat blanket and the thermocouple. Place the vacuum bagging material that has the fitting for the vacuum pump over the tape. Press it down into the tape to produce a seal. Connect the vacuum pump and check for leaks.

Curing the Repair

Some of the lower-strength resins cure at room temperature, but almost all of the stronger matrix systems require heat, and the structural repair manuals specify the rate of heat rise, curing temperature and time, and the rate of cooling. You can only maintain this curing program by using some type of programmed controller.

The controller in Figure 3-49 is ideally suited for curing a patch like the one in our example. The vacuum line, the thermocouples, and the heat blanket are connected, and the controller is programmed to apply the vacuum and to increase the temperature at the rate specified in the SRM to the required cure temperature.

When this temperature is reached, it will hold it for the required length of time and then will decrease the temperature at the recommended rate to allow the resin to achieve its maximum strength without becoming brittle.

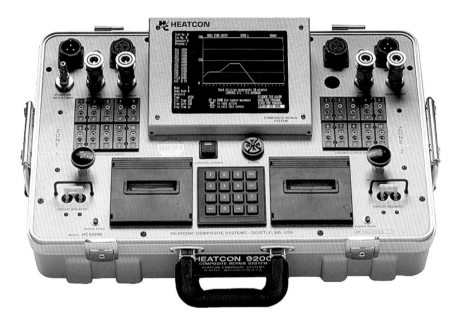

Figure 3-49. *Computerized controller for applying the heat and pressure to the repair at a carefully programmed rate. (Courtesy Heatcon® Composite Systems.)*

Cutting and Sanding Composite Materials

You can cut uncured reinforcing materials with conventional heavy-duty industrial fabric shears, but there are special ceramic-blade shears with serrated edges that are better for cutting Kevlar. The serrations hold the fibers, allowing the cut to be made with a minimum of pulling and fraying.

Cured composite materials may be cut, drilled, and otherwise machined. Some of the tools used for working with composites are different from those used with metal.

Kevlar generates special problems during drilling because of the fibers' tendency to pull and stretch. This leaves the fuzzy ends of the fabric inside the hole. Special drills are available for Kevlar, including the brad-point drill in Figure 3-50. When drilling, use a high speed and little pressure, especially as the drill cuts through the back of the material. *See* Figure 3-50.

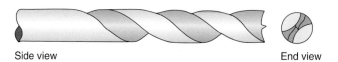

Side view   End view

Figure 3-50. *Brad-point drills are used to drill Kevlar without leaving fuzz inside the hole.*

Side view   End view

Figure 3-51. *Spade drill for drilling graphite material*

Hole cutters designed to cut fuzz-free holes in Kevlar are available. They have carbide cutting edges and diameters from $7/16$ inch up to 3 inches.

Drill graphite with a spade drill like the one in Figure 3-51. This drill has ample space for the drill dust to leave the hole, so it will not enlarge the hole. Graphite, like Kevlar, should be drilled at a high speed with only a little pressure on the drill.

Glass and graphite fibers will dull ordinary steel saw blades, so be sure to use carbide-tipped saws or saws with diamond dust for their cutting edges when you are cutting cured composite materials.

The best way to scarf laminated materials is to sand with a small, high-speed, right-angle sander. These sanders can be fitted with one-inch, two-inch, or three-inch-diameter disks, and they turn at about 20,000 rpm. Aluminum oxide disks are suitable for sanding glass or Kevlar, but you should use silicon carbide for sanding graphite.

You *must* wear a dust respirator when sanding composite materials because the tiny airborne particles can be extremely hazardous to your lungs.

Safety Around Composites

Certain chemicals used with composite construction cause allergic reactions for some people, so take precautions when working with them. Take special care when handling chemicals classified as hazardous materials, and be sure to dispose of their residue in a manner that complies with local environmental requirements.

The Material Safety Data Sheets (MSDS) that come with the chemicals contain information about their flammability, ventilation requirements, and health precautions. Learn and heed this information. Keep a copy of the MSDS to give to medical personnel in the event of a chemical medical emergency, so they can take the appropriate action.

Skin Care

Take special care to keep the chemicals used in composite construction and repair from direct contact with the skin. If any of them do, wash them off immediately. Wear latex or butyl gloves when working with these chemicals, and wear a shop coat to prevent the chemicals from contaminating your clothing and holding the vapors in contact with your skin.

There are protective hand gels that can be used on your hands before working with the resins. These gels leave a thin, invisible, flexible film on your hands that prevent the chemicals getting to your skin. The gel is easy to wash off when the work is finished. Typically this protective gel must not be used when wearing gloves.

Eye Care

Take all precautions to protect your eyes. It is extremely important to wear goggles that provide complete eye protection when working with composite materials. Be sure that the goggles you wear protect your eyes from splashed chemicals as well as from sanding dust and particles that fly when you cut or drill the cured materials.

If you should get any chemicals in your eyes, rinse them immediately with plenty of fresh water and get medical assistance at once.

Respiratory Care

Particles of glass and graphite produced by sanding can be extremely hazardous to your lungs, and you should not sand without wearing a respirator that protects against these particles.

When working with resins such as epoxies in a poorly ventilated area, you should wear a respirator mask designed to protect against these vapors.

MSDS. Material Safety Data Sheets. MSDS are required by the Federal Government to be available in workplaces to inform workers of the dangers that may exist from contact with certain materials.

Answers begin on Page 263. Page numbers refer to chapter text.

96. An aircraft structure that carries most of the aerodynamic stresses in its outer skin is called a/an _____ structure. *Page 234*

97. The glass fibers that produce the stronger structure are made of _____ (E or S)-glass. *Page 236*

98. Kevlar fabric is noted for being _____ (flexible or stiff). *Page 236*

99. Graphite fabric is noted for being _____ (flexible or stiff). *Page 237*

100. Corrosion can be a problem with aluminum alloys when they are bonded to _____ (fiberglass or graphite). *Page 237*

101. The type of plastic material that is softened by heat and that regains its hardness when it is cooled is a _____ (thermoplastic or thermosetting) material. *Page 240*

102. Polyester resins _____ (are or are not) used as a matrix material for modern high-strength composite structures. *Page 240*

103. There _____ (is or is not) more than one type of epoxy resin. *Page 240*

104. Prepregs are prevented from curing before they are used by storage in a/an _____ . *Page 241*

105. Film-type adhesives _____ (do or do not) need to be stored in a refrigerator to extend their shelf life. *Page 241*

106. The adhesive recommended to bond a plug of honeycomb material into a honeycomb panel is a/an _____ adhesive. *Page 241*

107. A block of Styrofoam to be used as the form for an aircraft component _____ (can or cannot) be cut with a hot-wire cutter. *Page 242*

108. Urethane foam _____ (can or cannot) be used with a polyester resin. *Page 242*

109. Three ways heat and pressure can be applied to composite component are:
    a. _____
    b. _____
    c. _____
    Page 243

Continued

110. The simplest method to check a piece of composite structure for possible delamination damage is to tap the suspected area with the edge of a/an _____ . *Page 245*

111. A method of nondestructive inspection used to check a piece of composite structure for crack damage is a/an _____ inspection. *Page 245*

112. Water inside a honeycomb core can be detected by using _____ inspection. *Page 246*

113. The finish on a piece of composite structure to be repaired may be properly removed with _____ (paint stripper or sandpaper). *Page 247*

114. After the damage has been removed from a piece of honeycomb-core composite material, all of the sanding dust should be removed with _____ (vacuum or compressed air). *Page 247*

115. When installing the replacement plug in a piece of honeycomb core, it is important that the length or _____ direction of the plug be the same as that of the structure. *Page 247*

116. When drilling cured composite materials, the drill should be turned _____ (fast or slow). *Page 252*

Transparent Plastics

Acrylic plastics have been used for windshields and side windows of the smaller general aviation aircraft for many years. Acrylics are of the thermoplastic family of resins, which means that they can be softened by heat, and when they are cooled they will regain their original hardness and rigidity. They are not damaged by repeated heating and cooling, so long as they are not overheated. Acrylic plastics are known by their trade names of Plexiglas and Lucite in the United States, and in the United Kingdom as Perspex.

It is possible that acetate plastics may be encountered in some older aircraft. These are also thermoplastic, but since they yellow and become brittle with age, they have almost all been replaced with the superior acrylic. Determine whether the material is acetate or acrylic by rubbing its surface with a cotton rag or swab saturated with acetone. If it softens, it is probably acetate, but if the surface turns white and does not soften, it is acrylic.

Storing and Handling Transparent Plastic Materials

Transparent acrylics are strong, but their surface is soft and easily damaged if they are mishandled or improperly stored. Sheets of the material from the manufacturer are covered with sheets of paper. Leave this paper on the surface while storing the material, and as much as possible when the material is being worked. Formed components such as windshields are usually covered with a plastic protector sprayed on the finished component. It forms a tough film you can easily strip off when the windshield is installed.

If at all possible, store flat sheets in a bin in which they are tilted approximately 10° from the vertical. If they must be stored horizontally, be sure there are no chips or dirt between the sheets, and do not make the stacks more than 18 inches high. Put the smaller sheets on top so no sheets will overhang.

Working with Transparent Plastic Materials

Acrylic plastics are soft and can be sawed and drilled in much the same way as aluminum alloys. The basic difference between working with metal and acrylic is acrylic's poor heat conduction. It tends to get hot and melt if proper provisions are not made for cooling.

Cutting

A band saw is the favored tool for cutting acrylics. Mark the outline of the part on the protecting paper and cut to within about $\frac{1}{16}$ inch of the line. Do the final trimming with a disk or belt sander.

Use a circular saw for straight cuts if the blades are hollow ground, or have enough set to the teeth to prevent binding. When cutting thick material, take care not to feed it into the saw too fast. This will cause overheating and the material will begin to melt at the edges of the cut. If the material smokes, or starts to soften, slow the cutting.

Drilling

The poor heat conductivity of acrylics requires the use of a coolant when drilling deep holes. Use a water-soluble cutting oil, which will provide adequate cooling and not attack the plastic.

The drill used for acrylic should have smooth flutes and a 0° rake angle, and the included angle should be greater than that used for drilling aluminum. Turn the drill at a high speed and use a light to moderate pressure. Back up thin material with a piece of wood so the drill will not break or chip the edges of the hole when it comes through the back side.

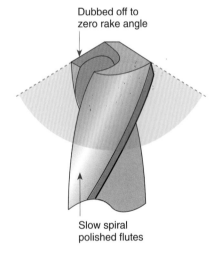

Dubbed off to zero rake angle

Slow spiral polished flutes

Figure 3-52. *Drill for acrylic plastics*

Forming Acrylic Plastics

Acrylic plastics can be heated until they are soft, and then formed either by draping them or stretching them over a male die or by pulling them into a female die with vacuum. Acrylics should not be cold formed except for very large-radius simple curves, neither should they be pulled into shape in a curved frame without heating. Either of these two forming methods places the plastic under a severe strain and can cause crazing.

Soften small pieces of acrylic by placing them in an oil bath and heating them. Hold them at a specified temperature for the recommended time and then allow them to cool slowly. You can't use water because it boils at a temperature below that required for softening the acrylic.

For example, you can form a landing light cover from 0.125-inch acrylic by following these steps:

1. Make a wooden form with the exact curvature of the wing leading edge, and cover it with outing flannel.

2. Make a paper pattern of the cover and transfer it to the acrylic. Trim the acrylic to a size slightly larger than the finished dimensions and polish the edges so there will be no stress risers. Remove the protective paper.

3. Heat the acrylic in an oil bath to approximately 230°F and hold it for two hours. Remove it from the oil and drape it over the form. Use cotton gloves to smooth it down over the form, and allow it to cool slowly. Remove it from the form and trim it to the final dimensions with a file. Polish the edges and drill the holes for attachment.

Form complex compound-curved parts like bubble canopies by using a female mold and a vacuum pump. Heat the sheet of plastic and place it over the female mold. Clamp the edges tightly enough so it will not buckle, but loose enough to allow slippage. Apply the suction to the mold and the plastic will pull down to form the part. Allow the molded component to cool slowly, and then remove it from the mold and trim the edges.

Cementing Transparent Plastic Materials

A properly made joint in a piece of acrylic plastic is almost as strong as the material itself. The joint is made by actually melting the edges of the part and forcing them to flow together as seen in Figure 3-53 on the following page.

crazing. A form of stress-caused damage that occurs in a transparent thermoplastic material. Crazing appears as a series of tiny, hair-like cracks just below the surface of the plastic.

Commercial plastic forming operators use large specialized ovens to heat the acrylic sheet. The sheets are clamped in racks and hung vertically while being heated.

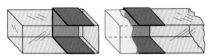

Edge of one piece is soaked in solvent.

Solvent forms a cushion
on edge of the plastic.

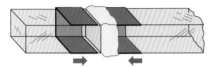

Press two pieces together and hold
pressure until solvents evaporate.

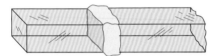

When solvents evaporate, joint is
almost as strong as rest of material.

Figure 3-53. *Cementing acrylic plastics by the soak method*

The cements used with acrylics are usually clear thin liquids such as methylene chloride or ethylene dichloride. To make a good joint with the soak method, follow these steps:

1. Mask off the parts of the plastic that are not to be affected by the solvent.

2. Soak the edge of one of the pieces in the solvent until a soft cushion forms.

3. Press the pieces together so the cushion will diffuse into the other piece and form a cushion on it.

4. Allow the pressure to remain until the solvent has evaporated from the cushions and they become hard. Remove the excess material and dress the repair to conform to the original material.

You can also cement plastics with the glue method. Dissolve some acrylic shavings in the liquid solvent to make it into a viscous syrup. Apply the syrup to either one or both of the parts and allow the cushion to form. Assemble the parts and apply pressure. Allow the pressure to remain until the solvents evaporate and the cushions harden.

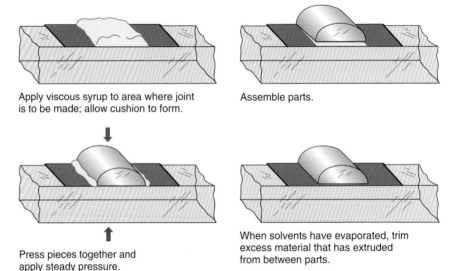

Apply viscous syrup to area where joint
is to be made; allow cushion to form.

Assemble parts.

Press pieces together and
apply steady pressure.

When solvents have evaporated, trim
excess material that has extruded
from between parts.

Figure 3-54. *Cementing acrylic plastics by the glue method*

Methods of Applying Pressure

Pressure must be applied to the plastic in some way that will maintain a constant force as the plastic shrinks when the solvents evaporate. The best way of applying pressure to small areas is with spring clamps. Weights can also be used effectively. (C-clamps or parallel clamps are not usable.)

Curing Transparent Plastic Materials

The solvents in a cemented joint never completely evaporate, and since the cushion has expanded, the joint is slightly weaker than the original material. These joints can be strengthened by forcing the solvents to diffuse into more of the material. Figure 3-55 shows the way the solvents concentrate in the joint. If the plastic is heated to about 120°F and held at this temperature for about 48 hours, the cushions will expand and the solvents in them will diffuse into a larger volume. The solvent content and the strength of the cured material is nearly the same as that of the original material.

Cleaning Transparent Plastic Materials

Acrylic plastics are soft and their surfaces are easily scratched. When cleaning a plastic windshield or window, flush it with plenty of fresh water and use your bare hand to dislodge any dirt particles. Do not use a rag, because particles remain in cloth and will scratch the plastic. For particularly stubborn areas, or areas that have oil or grease on them, use a mild soap and water solution to clean the area.

Polishing and Protection

There are several good commercial polishes on the market that clean and polish plastic windshields. These cleaners typically contain an antistatic material that prevents the windshield from attracting dust, and wax that fills the minute surface scratches. When applying these waxes, use only a clean, soft cloth or a lint-free wiper. Do not use ordinary shop rags, because they collect tiny particles of metal and abrasives that are not removed in their normal laundering. Specialized synthetic wipes, such as DuPont Sontara®, are available for polishing plastic.

A good grade of paste wax will protect the plastic and cause rain to bead up and blow off rather than spreading out and distorting vision.

Installing Plastic Windshields and Windows

Replacing a windshield in an airplane requires patience and attention to detail. You can obtain new windshields from the aircraft manufacturer or from component manufacturers whose products are made under a Parts Manufacturer Approval (FAA-PMA). New windshields are formed to fit generally, but there is usually an excess of material that you must trim away for a perfect fit.

Remove the old windshield and clean out all the old sealant from the channels. Using the old windshield as a pattern, file or grind away the excess plastic from the edges of the new one. To prevent cracks from occurring later, be certain to sand and then polish the edges according to the manufacturer's recommendations.Install the type of sealer specified in the aircraft structural repair manual and put the new windshield in place.

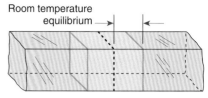

Solvent in a cemented joint is concentrated in the cushions.

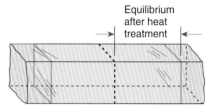

By heating repaired area and holding it at elevated temperature, solvents disburse and joint becomes stronger.

Figure 3-55. *Curing of an acrylic plastic cemented joint*

The new windshield should fit into the retainer for the full depth specified by the manufacturer, and there should be at least ⅛-inch clearance between the edges of the plastic and the structure to allow for dimensional changes as the temperature changes. Replace all the screws in the retainers.

Some windshields are held in place with machine screws and self-locking nuts. When the screws pass through holes in the plastic, special care must be taken. The holes in the plastic should be ⅛-inch oversize to allow the plastic to shift with temperature changes. Some installations use spacers to prevent the screws being overtightened, but in the absence of spacers, tighten each nut to a firm fit, then back it off for one full turn.

Repairing Transparent Plastic Materials

Inspection and repair of windshields and side windows in pressurized aircraft are important jobs for the aviation maintenance technician. These transparencies are part of the pressure vessel and you must take special care when inspecting and maintaining them to find and repair all damage.

Crazing

The most common types of damage are crazing and cuts. Crazing, or tiny, hair-like cracks that may or may not extend all of the way to the surface, may be caused by stresses or by chemical fumes. These tiny cracks cannot be felt, but must be removed with abrasives. It is extremely important, after removing all of the damage, to ensure that the window still has the required thickness, and that the removal has not caused visual distortion. Because of the high cost of the windows and the disastrous consequences if they were to blow out, any damage to windows of pressurized aircraft should be assessed and repaired by specialists. Repair stations who specialize in window repair can measure thickness of the repaired window accurately with ultrasonic thickness measuring instruments, and use grid patterns to check for optical distortion.

An AMT can usually repair minor damage to windshields and side windows for small unpressurized general aviation aircraft by using progressively finer sandpapers and finishing the repair by polishing it with Micro-Mesh®, the registered trademark of Micro Surface Finishing Products of Wilton, Iowa.

Remove a scratch in a window by beginning the sanding with 320 wet-or-dry sandpaper wrapped around a foam sanding block, sanding with straight strokes, and using firm, but not hard pressure. Do not use circular strokes, and periodically change the direction of the strokes by 90°. Remove the damage with the 320-grit paper, then remove the pattern it left with 400-grit paper. Next remove the pattern of this paper with 600-grit.

After you remove the damage, the surface retains the pattern left by the 600-grit paper. Restore the full transparency by polishing it with Micro-Mesh. Micro-Mesh comes with a graduated series of cloth-backed cushioned sheets,

Micro-Mesh®. A patented graduated series of cloth-backed cushioned sheets that contain abrasive crystals. Micro-Mesh is used for polishing and restoring transparency to acrylic plastic windows and windshields.

containing abrasive crystals. As you rub the Micro-Mesh across the surface, the soft cushion lets the crystals seek a common level with their broader facets oriented along the surfaces. This produces a planing action which cuts the surface smooth and level, rather than gouging it the way the sharp edges of sandpaper grit do.

First apply a mist spray of water on the window. Use the coarsest abrasive (the lowest number in the kit) wrapped around a foam block to remove all of the pattern left by the 600-grit sandpaper. When this pattern is removed, clean the surface thoroughly and use the sheet with the next finer abrasive. Remove the scratches left by the preceding sheet and clean the surface and go to the next finer sheet. Continue through to the sheet with the finest abrasive in the kit, and then clean the surface and apply a very thin film of antistatic cream/wax with a flannel cloth. Rinse out the Micro-Mesh sheets, dry them, and store them in their plastic envelopes for future use.

Micro-Mesh is also available in disc form for use with a random orbital sander. Orbital sanders, however, should be used on transparent plastics only by technicians with skill and training in this application.

Holes

Holes and cracks in transparent plastic materials can be repaired if they are not in the line of the pilot's vision. If they are in the line of vision, the entire windshield or window should be replaced.

Clean out the damage and round all of the edges to prevent stress concentrations. Cut a patch of the same type and thickness of material as the original that is large enough to extend at least ¾ inch beyond the edges of the cleaned-out damage. Bevel the edges of the patch, and if the original material is curved, form the patch to match. Soften it by placing it in a pan of oil that is heated to between 250°F and 300°F. When it is soft, form it to match the damaged area. Thoroughly clean the patch and soften the side that is to contact the original part with a viscous cement. Put it in place and apply pressure for at least three hours. Allow the patch to cure for at least 24 hours before doing any further polishing.

Cracks

Vibration causes cracks to develop along the edges of plastic material. These cracks usually begin at nicks or scratches on the edge of the material and progress across the sheet.

All the stresses that caused the original crack are concentrated at the point, and the stresses acting on this extremely small area can cause the crack to continue. To stop it, drill a hole about ⅛ inch in diameter at the end of the crack. Now the stresses have a much larger area to act on and the crack cannot continue.

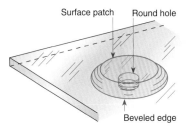

Surface patch for a round hole

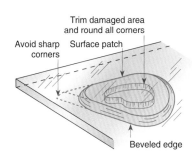

Surface patch for irregularly-shaped damage

Figure 3-56. *Repair of a hole in a piece of transparent acrylic plastic*

After stop-drilling the crack, cut a patch of the same type and thickness of material as the original that is large enough to extend at least ¾ inch beyond the edges of the cleaned-out damage. Form the patch and cement it in place in the same way as described for repairing a hole.

All stresses concentrate at end of crack.

Stop-drilling end of crack spreads stresses around entire circumference and stops crack.

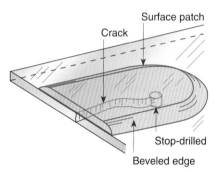
Finished repair has piece of acrylic cemented over damage.

Figure 3-57. *Repair of a crack in a piece of transparent acrylic plastic*

STUDY QUESTIONS: TRANSPARENT PLASTICS

Answers begin on the next page. Page numbers refer to chapter text.

117. One of the biggest differences in working aluminum and acrylic plastics lies in the _____ (better or poorer) heat conduction of the acrylic. *Page 256*

118. Acetone _____ (does or does not) soften acrylic plastic. *Page 255*

119. The preferable way to store flat sheets of acrylic plastic is _____ (horizontal or vertical). *Page 256*

120. When a piece of acrylic plastic is cut on a band saw to the approximate outline of the part, the final trim can be made with a/an _____ . *Page 256*

121. When drilling acrylic plastics, the drill should be turned _____ (fast or slow). *Page 256*

122. Small pieces of acrylic plastic can be heated for forming in a/an _____ (oil or water) bath. *Page 257*

123. Two chemicals that can be used as a solvent for acrylic plastic are:
    a. _____
    b. _____
    Page 258

124. A C-clamp _____ (is or is not) recommended for holding pressure on an acrylic plastic material while it is being cemented. *Page 258*

125. The best type of clamp to use to apply pressure when cementing two pieces of acrylic plastic together is a/an _____ clamp. *Page 258*

126. The best method of removing dirt from a plastic windshield is by flushing it with _____ . *Page 259*

127. Oil and grease can be removed from acrylic plastic with a _____ solution. *Page 259*

128. After cleaning a windshield, it should be coated with a good grade of _____ . *Page 259*

129. The window of a pressurized aircraft can be checked for thickness with a/an _____ thickness measuring instrument. *Page 260*

130. Crazing can be removed from an acrylic windshield with _____ . *Page 260*

131. When removing scratches from a windshield with sandpaper, the paper should be moved in a _____ (straight or circular) motion. *Page 260*

132. A patch cemented over a hole or crack should extend for _____ inch beyond the damage. *Page 262*

Answers to Chapter 3 Study Questions

1. softwood	10. 15	19. ¾
2. are not	11. is	20. may
3. Sitka spruce	12. is	21. caps
4. laminated	13. is not	22. birch
5. birch	14. is not	23. should not
6. 45, 90	15. shear	24. 10
7. poplar, basswood	16. 8	25. should not
8. springwood	17. should not	26. cannot
9. 12	18. should not	27. scarf

Continued

28. 20
29. is
30. 15
31. 80
32. cotton, polyester, fiberglass
33. major repair
34. major alteration
35. 337
36. 70
37. cannot
38. are not
39. dark
40. trammel
41. TSO-C-15, AMS 3806
42. raveling
43. bias
44. nitrate, butyrate
45. nitrate
46. is not
47. aluminum
48. dope into the paste
49. last
50. envelope, blanket
51. should not
52. dope into the paste
53. water
54. nitrate
55. thinned
56. ½
57. alteration
58. butyrate
59. grounded
60. second
61. does not
62. apex
63. 150, 16

64. ¼, 8, 10
65. enamel
66. softening
67. cannot
68. plastic beads
69. filiform
70. eddy currents
71. several light coats
72. may
73. 48
74. epoxy
75. 24
76. should
77. is not
78. white
79. high
80. pinholes
81. fast
82. toluol, MEK
83. will not
84. does not
85. wing port
86. near the floor
87. 6, 10
88. 2, 3
89. ellipse
90. much
91. should not
92. N
93. 12
94. is not
95. should
96. monocoque
97. S
98. flexible
99. stiff

100. graphite
101. thermoplastic
102. are not
103. is
104. refrigerator
105. do
106. foaming
107. can
108. can
109. a. matched dies
     b. vacuum bag
     c. autoclave
110. coin
111. ultrasonic
112. radiographic
113. sandpaper
114. vacuum
115. ribbon
116. fast
117. poorer
118. does not
119. vertical
120. sander
121. fast
122. oil
123. a. methylene chloride
     b. ethylene dichloride
124. is not
125. spring
126. fresh water
127. soap and water
128. wax
129. ultrasonic
130. abrasives
131. straight
132. ¾

ASSEMBLY AND RIGGING

4

Continued

ASSEMBLY AND RIGGING

4

Airplane Controls

This chapter considers the hardware used to control aircraft, and the way aircraft are assembled and rigged for the most efficient flight.

Airplane Primary Flight Controls

An airplane is controlled by rotating it about one or more of its three axes. The ailerons rotate it about its longitudinal axis to produce roll, elevators or their equivalent rotate it about its lateral axis to produce pitch, and the rudder rotates the airplane about its vertical axis to produce yaw.

Controls for Roll

Ailerons and spoilers are used to roll, or rotate an aircraft about its longitudinal axis by varying the amount of lift produced by the two wings. Ailerons increase the lift on one wing while decreasing lift on the opposite wing. Spoilers are used on some airplanes to aid the ailerons by spoiling the lift on one wing to make it move downward.

Ailerons

Ailerons are the primary roll control. To roll an airplane to the left, turn the control wheel to the left. The aileron on the left wing moves up, decreasing the camber, or curvature, of the left wing and decreasing the lift it produces. A carry-through, or balance, cable pulls the right aileron down, increasing its camber and lift. The airplane rolls to the left about its longitudinal axis. *See* Figure 4-1 on the next page.

An airplane is turned to the left by banking, or rolling, it to the left. When the right aileron moves down to increase the lift on the right wing and start the roll, it also increases the induced drag, which pulls the nose to the *right*. As soon as the wing rises, the lift tilts and its horizontal component pulls the nose around to the left as it should.

The movement of the nose in the wrong direction at the beginning of a turn is called adverse yaw, and is minimized by using differential aileron travel. The aileron moving upward travels a greater distance than the aileron

roll. Rotation of an aircraft about its longitudinal axis.

spoilers. Flight controls that are raised up from the upper surface of a wing to destroy, or spoil, lift. Flight spoilers are used in conjunction with the ailerons to decrease lift and increase drag on the descending wing. Ground spoilers are used to produce a great amount of drag to slow the airplane on its landing roll.

longitudinal axis. An imaginary line, passing through the center of gravity of an airplane, and extending lengthwise through it from nose to tail.

balance cable. When the control wheel is rotated, a cable from the cockpit pulls one aileron down and relaxes the cable going to the other aileron. The balance cable pulls the other aileron up.

banking. The act of rotating an aircraft about its longitudinal axis.

differential aileron travel. Aileron movement in which the upward-moving aileron deflects a greater distance than the one moving downward. The up aileron produces parasite drag to counteract the induced drag caused by the down aileron.

Differential aileron travel is used to counteract adverse yaw.

Frise aileron. An aileron with its hinge line set back from the leading edge so that when it is deflected upward, part of the leading edge projects below the wing and produces parasite drag to help overcome adverse yaw.

vertical axis. An imaginary line, passing vertically through the center of gravity of an airplane.

yaw. Rotation of an aircraft about its vertical axis.

speed brakes. A secondary control of an airplane that produces drag without causing a change in the pitch attitude of the airplane. Speed brakes allow an airplane to make a steep descent without building up excessive forward airspeed.

balance panel. A flat panel that is hinged to the leading edge of some ailerons that produces a force which assists the pilot in holding them deflected. The balance panel divides a chamber ahead of the aileron in such a way that when the aileron is deflected downward, for example, air flowing over its top surface produces a low pressure that acts on the balance panel and causes it to apply an upward force to the leading edge as long as it is deflected.

servo tab. A small movable tab built into the trailing edge of a primary control surface of an airplane. The cockpit controls move the tab in such a direction that it produces an aerodynamic force that moves the surface on which it is mounted.

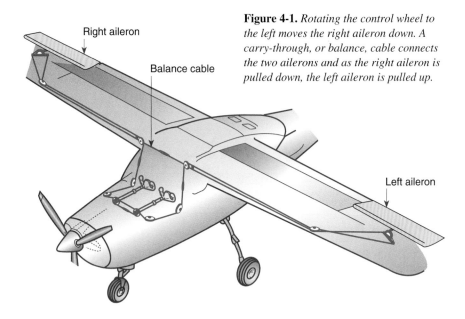

Right aileron

Balance cable

Left aileron

Figure 4-1. *Rotating the control wheel to the left moves the right aileron down. A carry-through, or balance, cable connects the two ailerons and as the right aileron is pulled down, the left aileron is pulled up.*

moving downward. The extra upward travel creates just about enough parasite drag to counteract the induced drag caused by the lowered aileron. The aileron shown in Figure 4-2 is a Frise aileron. Part of its nose extends below the bottom wing surface as an additional aid in preventing adverse yaw.

At the beginning of a turn, the pilot uses the rudder to overcome adverse yaw by rotating the airplane about its vertical, or yaw, axis. This starts the nose moving in the correct direction. As soon as the bank is established, the adverse yaw force disappears and the rudder is neutralized. The rudder controls of some airplanes, such as the one in Figure 4-3, are interconnected with the aileron controls through a spring in such a way that rotating the control wheel pulls the rudder cable.

Many large jet transport airplanes have two ailerons on each wing and flight spoilers to assist in roll control. The flight spoiler deflects on the wing with the upward moving aileron. *See* Figure 4-34 on Page 286. The outboard ailerons are locked in their faired, or streamline, position when the trailing edge flaps are up. The inboard ailerons and the flight spoilers provide enough roll control for high-speed flight, but when the flaps are lowered, the inboard and outboard ailerons work together to provide the additional roll control needed for low-speed flight. All the flight spoilers can be raised together to act as speed brakes.

The ailerons are hydraulically powered, but they have internal balance panels and servo tabs to help move them in case of hydraulic system failure.

Elevons

Delta airplanes, and airplanes with highly swept wings that do not have a conventional empennage to provide pitch control, use elevons. These are movable control surfaces on the wings' trailing edge. The elevons operate together for pitch control, and differentially for aileron control.

Controls for Pitch

When an airplane is trimmed for straight and level flight at a fixed airspeed, the downward force on the horizontal stabilizer balances the nose-down tendency caused by the center of gravity's position ahead of the center of lift. All of the aerodynamic forces are balanced and no control forces are needed. But the airplane can be rotated about its lateral axis by increasing or decreasing the downward tail load.

Elevator

The most generally used pitch control for an airplane is the fixed horizontal stabilizer with a movable elevator hinged to its trailing edge, as is illustrated in Figure 4-4 on the next page. When the pilot pulls back the control yoke, the trailing edge of the elevator moves up and increases the down load caused by the horizontal tail surface. The tail moves down and rotates the airplane nose-up about its lateral axis.

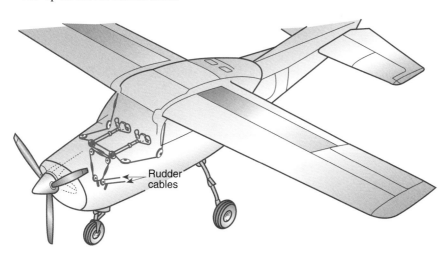

Figure 4-3. *The rudder of this airplane is connected to the aileron controls through springs. This starts the nose moving in the correct direction without the pilot having to use the rudder pedals.*

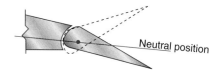

Neutral position

Figure 4-2. *Differential aileron movement is used to minimize adverse yaw when a turn is begun. The aileron moving upward travels a greater distance than the one moving downward. This produces additional parasite drag to oppose the induced drag on the opposite wing caused by the downward deflected aileron.*

delta airplane. An airplane with a triangular-shaped wing. This wing has an extreme amount of sweepback on its leading edge and a trailing edge that is almost perpendicular to the longitudinal axis of the airplane.

elevons. Movable control surfaces on the trailing edge of a delta wing or a flying wing airplane. These surfaces operate together to serve as elevators, and differentially to act as ailerons.

pitch. Rotation of an aircraft about its lateral axis.

lateral axis. An imaginary line, passing through the center of gravity of an airplane, and extending across it from wing tip to wing tip.

control yoke. The movable column on which an airplane control wheel is mounted. The yoke may be moved in or out to actuate the elevators, and the control wheel may be rotated to actuate the ailerons.

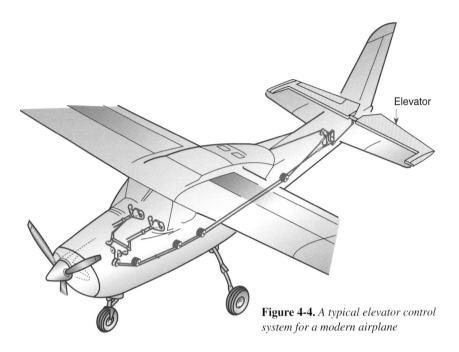

Figure 4-4. *A typical elevator control system for a modern airplane*

Stabilator

stabilator. A single-piece horizontal tail surface that serves the functions of both the horizontal stabilizer and the elevators. The stabilator pivots about its front spar.

Some airplanes use a stabilator for pitch control. This is a single-piece horizontal surface that pivots about a point approximately one third of the way back from the leading edge. When the control wheel is pulled back, the leading edge of the stabilator moves down and increases the downward force produced by the tail. This rotates the nose up. When the wheel is pushed in, the nose of the stabilator moves up, decreasing the tail load, and the airplane rotates nose down.

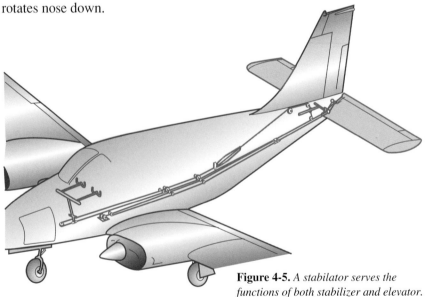

Figure 4-5. *A stabilator serves the functions of both stabilizer and elevator.*

Ruddervators

Some airplanes, most notably V-tail Beech Bonanzas, have two fixed stabilizers and two movable ruddervators arranged in a V. *See* Figure 1-33 on Page 29. The control system is such that moving the control wheel in and out actuates the movable surfaces together so they act as elevators and rotate the airplane about its lateral axis. When the rudder pedals are depressed, the surfaces move differentially, acting as a rudder to rotate the airplane about its vertical axis.

Canard

Conventional aircraft achieve longitudinal stability and control through horizontal stabilizers on the tail that produce a downward aerodynamic force. This downward force acts as part of the flight load, and the wing must produce lift to overcome it.

A canard is a horizontal stabilizing surface located ahead of the main wing that makes the airplane inherently stall-proof. The center of gravity is located ahead of the main wing, and the angle of incidence of the canard is greater than that of the main wing, so it will stall first. *See* Figure 4-6. When the canard stalls, the nose drops and the smooth airflow over the canard is restored, and its lift is increased to bring the airplane back to straight and level flight.

Some canards have movable surfaces on their trailing edge for pitch control and others pivot the entire surface for control. The angle of sweep of canards mounted on some high-performance airplanes may be varied in flight to optimize the flight characteristics.

Figure 4-6. *The angle of incidence of the canard is greater than that of the main wing and it will stall first. When it stalls, the nose of the airplane drops and flying speed is restored.*

Controls for Yaw

An airplane is turned by tilting the lift vector with the ailerons. The rudder is used only at the beginning of the turn to overcome adverse yaw and for such flight conditions as crosswind takeoffs and landings.

Figure 4-7 on the next page shows a typical rudder control system. When the pilot presses the left rudder pedal, the trailing edge of the rudder moves to the left and produces an aerodynamic load on the vertical tail which moves the tail to the right and the nose to the left.

Some airplanes have eliminated the movable rudder entirely, and others have connected it to the aileron controls through springs so that when a turn is started, the rudder moves in the correct direction automatically.

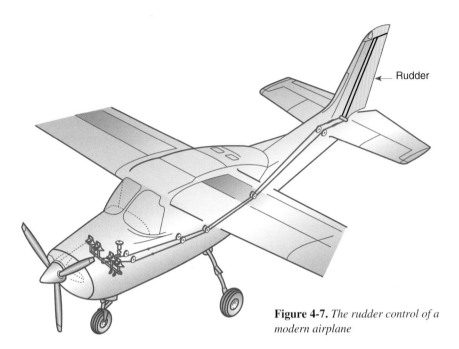

Figure 4-7. *The rudder control of a modern airplane*

Airplane Secondary Flight Controls

Primary flight controls rotate the airplane about its three axes, but secondary controls are used to assist or to modify the effect of the primary controls. There are two basic types of secondary flight controls: those that modify the amount of lift the primary controls produce, and those that change the amount of force needed to operate the primary controls.

Surfaces That Modify the Lift

Aerodynamic lift is determined by the shape and size of the airfoil section, and can be changed by modifying either or both of these factors. A more recent approach to modifying lift is by controlling the flow of air over the surface.

Flaps

Flaps are the most widely used method for modifying lift. Most flaps are on the trailing edge of the wing inboard of the ailerons, but some are located on the wings' leading edges.

Plain Flaps

The simplest type of flap is the plain flap, illustrated in Figure 4-8. This flap is simply a hinged portion of the trailing edge of the wing inboard of the ailerons. It can be lowered to increase the camber. Lowering plain flaps increases the maximum coefficient of lift and produces a great deal of drag.

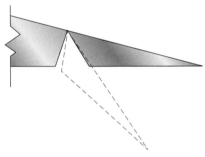

Figure 4-8. *Plain flaps are a hinged portion of the trailing edge of a wing inboard of the ailerons.*

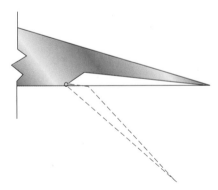

Figure 4-9. *A split flap is a plate that extends below the wing's lower surface. It increases both the lift and the drag.*

Split Flaps

A split flap, such as the one in Figure 4-9, consists of a plate that is deflected from the lower surface of the wing. Lowering a split flap increases the maximum coefficient of lift slightly more than a plain flap, but it produces a turbulent wake and therefore increases the drag much more than a plain flap. Some airplanes use a narrow-chord split flap mounted on the rear wing spar that does not extend to the wing trailing edge.

Slotted Flaps

A slotted flap, similar to the one in Figure 4-10, acts like a simple flap, except that there is a slot between the leading edge of the flap and the inner surface of the flap well. High-energy air from below the wing flows through the slot and speeds up the air over the upper surface of the flap. This delays airflow separation to a higher coefficient of lift. Slotted flaps produce a much greater increase in the coefficient of lift than either the plain or split flap.

Fowler Flaps

Fowler flaps are similar to slotted flaps, except that they move aft along a set of tracks to increase the chord of the wing (and thus its area) when they are lowered. A Fowler flap produces a greater increase in lift with the least change in drag than any other type of flap. *See* Figure 4-11.

Triple-Slotted Flaps

Many large jet transport airplanes use triple-slotted flaps like the one in Figure 4-12. As this flap is lowered, it slides out of the wing on tracks and increases the camber and wing area in the same way as a Fowler flap, but it separates and forms slots between its segments. The air flowing through these slots is forced down against the flap upper surface, which delays airflow separation and produces additional lift.

Leading Edge Flaps

Some high-performance airplanes have flaps on the leading edges as well as on the trailing edges. Figure 4-13 on the next page shows a drooped leading edge that is lowered at the same time as the trailing edge flaps to increase the camber of the wing and allow it to attain a higher angle of attack before the airflow breaks away over the upper surface.

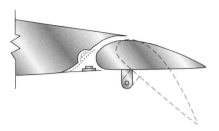

Figure 4-10. *A slotted flap forms a slot between the flap and the flap well that ducts high-energy air back over the top of the flap to delay airflow separation.*

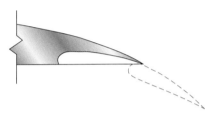

Figure 4-11. *Fowler flaps move aft along a set of tracks to increase the wing chord when they are lowered. They produce a large increase in lift and a minimum increase in drag.*

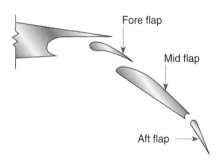

Fore flap

Mid flap

Aft flap

Figure 4-12. *A triple-slotted flap forms slots between the flap segments when it is lowered. Air flowing through these slots energizes the air above the flap surface and delays airflow separation while increasing the lift the flap produces.*

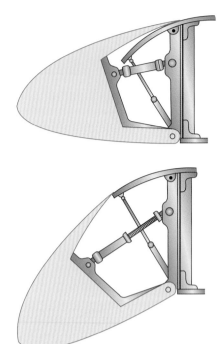

Figure 4-13. *A drooped leading edge that folds down when the trailing edge flaps are lowered allows the wing to reach a higher angle of attack before the airflow breaks away from its upper surface.*

A Kruger flap, as seen in Figure 4-14, is a special type of leading edge flap that effectively increases the camber of the wing when it is lowered. The leading edge flaps shown on the wing of the Boeing 727 airliner in Figure 4-34 on Page 286 are Kruger flaps. These flaps are controlled by movement of the trailing edge flaps.

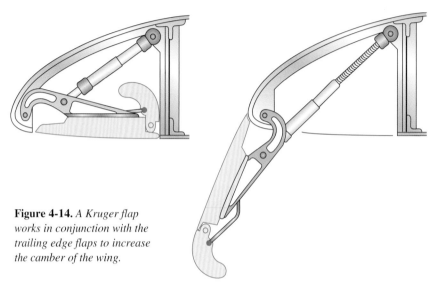

Figure 4-14. *A Kruger flap works in conjunction with the trailing edge flaps to increase the camber of the wing.*

Slats

A slat forms the leading edge of the wing when it is retracted, and when it is extended it forms a duct that forces high-energy air across the surface of the wing to delay airflow separation. *See* Figure 4-15. The Boeing 727 wing shown in Figure 4-34 on Page 286 has four slats and three leading edge flaps. When the outboard trailing edge flaps are extended 2°, two slats on each side extend, and when they are lowered more than 5°, all the slats and leading edge flaps are extended.

Many high-performance military fighter airplanes have retractable leading edge slats fitted into the wing with curved support rails that ride between bearings. When the wing has a low angle of attack, the air forces the slat tightly against the leading edge of the wing where it produces a minimum of interference. At a high angle of attack, aerodynamic forces pull the slat out from the leading edge, and it forms a duct that forces high-energy air down over the upper surface of the wing and delays airflow separation to a higher angle of attack.

Spoilers

Flight spoilers are hinged surfaces located ahead of the flaps. They are used in conjunction with the ailerons to assist in roll control. When the ailerons are deflected, the flight spoilers on the wing with the up aileron automatically

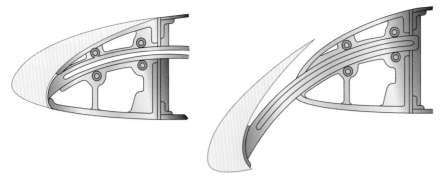

When slat is retracted, it forms leading edge of wing.

When slat is extended, it increases camber of wing and forms duct that directs high-energy air back over upper surface of wing.

Figure 4-15. *Automatic slat used on high-performance fighter aircraft*

deploy to a maximum of 30° to decrease the lift on the wing that is moving down. They also produce additional parasite drag to overcome adverse yaw. When a large amount of aileron is used, the spoilers account for about 80% of the roll rate.

Flight spoilers move differentially when they are used for roll control, but they may be deployed symmetrically and used as speed brakes by actuating the speed brake control. When used as speed brakes they may be extended between 0° and 45° depending on the position of the speed brake control. Ground spoilers deploy to their full 45° opening when the airplane is on the ground with weight on the landing gear and the speed brake lever is moved through its 10° position.

Some high-performance general aviation airplanes have spoilers, or speed brakes, installed on the front wing spar in such a way that they may be raised above the upper wing surface in flight to allow the airplane to make a steep descent without gaining an excess of speed, and without having to decrease the engine power to the extent that the cylinders will be damaged by too rapid cooling.

Devices That Change the Operating Forces

Stability is an important function of an airplane, but controllability is equally important. As airplanes have become larger and faster and have higher performance, the control system loads have become extremely high and the pilot must have some kind of assistance to move them. The controls on most large airplanes are moved by electrical or hydraulic servos. This section, however, discusses only the devices that change the forces aerodynamically.

stability. The characteristic of an aircraft that causes it to return to its original flight condition after it has been disturbed.

controllability. The characteristic of an aircraft that allows it to change its flight attitude in response to the pilot's movement of the cockpit controls.

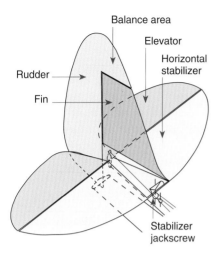

Balance area
Elevator
Horizontal stabilizer
Rudder
Fin
Stabilizer jackscrew

Figure 4-16. *This empennage has an aerodynamically balanced rudder. The top portion of the rudder extends ahead of the hinge line to provide an aerodynamic assist in deflecting it.*

trim tab. A small control tab mounted on the trailing edge of a movable control surface. The tab may be adjusted to provide an aerodynamic force to hold the surface on which it is mounted deflected to trim the airplane for hands-off flight at a specified airspeed.

balance tab. An adjustable tab mounted on the trailing edge of a control surface to produce a force that aids the pilot in moving the surface. The tab is automatically actuated in such a way it moves in the direction opposite to the direction the control surface on which it is mounted moves.

Balance Surfaces

Some controls have a portion of the surface extending out ahead of the hinge line, like the rudder in Figure 4-16. When the rudder is deflected, air strikes the portion ahead of the hinge line and assists in deflecting it and holding it deflected. Some aerodynamic balance surfaces are also weighted to give them static balance.

Tabs

Small auxiliary devices on the trailing edges of the various primary control surfaces are used to produce aerodynamic forces to trim the aircraft or to aid the pilot in moving the controls. Some tabs are fixed to the surface and are adjustable only on the ground. These tabs are used to produce a fixed air load on the control surface to trim the airplane against a permanent out-of-balance condition. The tabs discussed in this section are adjustable to compensate for varying flight conditions.

Trim Tabs

Trim tabs such as those in Figure 4-17 may be installed on the rudder, aileron, and elevator. They are controllable from the cockpit and allow the pilot to deflect them in such a direction that they produce an aerodynamic force on the control surface that holds it deflected to correct for an out-of-balance condition. This allows the airplane to be adjusted to fly straight and level with hands and feet off of the controls. Once a trim tab is adjusted, it maintains a fixed relationship with the control surface as it is moved.

Balance Tabs

A balance tab, like that in Figure 4-18, works automatically to produce an air load on the control surface that assists the pilot in moving the surface. When the cockpit control is moved to raise the trailing edge of the control surface, the linkage pulls the balance tab so that it moves in the opposite direction. This opposite deflection produces an aerodynamic force that assists the pilot in moving the surface. The linkage for many balance tabs is adjustable to allow the position of the tab to be changed in flight so the tab can serve as a trim tab as well as a balance tab.

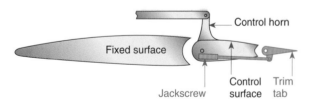

Control horn
Fixed surface
Jackscrew
Control surface
Trim tab

Figure 4-17. *A trim tab is adjustable from the cockpit to allow the pilot to trim the airplane so it will fly straight and level with hands and feet off of the controls.*

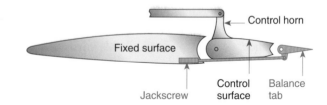

Control horn
Fixed surface
Jackscrew
Control surface
Balance tab

Figure 4-18. *A balance tab moves in the direction opposite to that of the control surface on which it is mounted. This opposite deflection produces an aerodynamic force that aids the pilot in moving the surface. This balance tab may be adjusted in flight so that it also acts as a trim tab.*

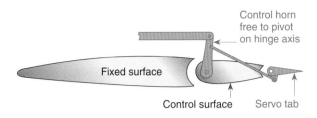

Figure 4-19. *A servo tab is controlled from the cockpit to produce an aerodynamic force which moves the primary control surface.*

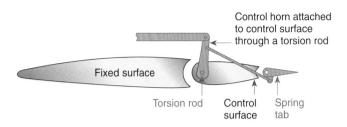

Figure 4-20. *A spring tab deflects only when control forces become so high that the pilot needs assistance in moving the primary control surface.*

Servo Tabs

A servo tab, also called a control tab, is installed on the control surfaces of airplanes requiring such high control forces that it is impractical to move the primary surface itself. The cockpit control is attached to the servo tab so that it moves in the direction opposite that desired for the primary surface. Deflection of the servo tab produces an aerodynamic force that deflects the primary surface, which in turn rotates the airplane about the desired axis. *See* Figure 4-19.

Spring Tabs

A spring tab is used on high-performance airplanes that, under high-speed conditions, develop aerodynamic forces so great that assistance is needed to help the pilot move the controls. Figure 4-20 shows that the control horn is attached to the control surface through a torsion rod. For normal flight the horn moves the control surface and the spring tab does not deflect. But at high speeds when the control force becomes excessive, the torsion rod twists and allows the horn to move relative to the surface. The linkage deflects the spring tab in such a direction that it produces an aerodynamic force that aids the pilot in moving the primary surface.

Antiservo Tabs

An antiservo tab is installed on the trailing edge of a stabilator to decrease its sensitivity. The tab is attached to the aircraft structure through a linkage rod and a jackscrew to allow it to be used as a trim tab.

When the stabilator is deflected, air strikes the portion ahead of the pivot point and tries to increase its deflection. This makes the stabilator too sensitive. To decrease this sensitivity, the antiservo tab on its trailing edge moves in the same direction as the stabilator. When the trailing edge of the stabilator moves up, the antiservo tab moves up and produces a downward load that tries to move the stabilator back to its streamline position. When the trailing edge of the stabilator moves down, the antiservo tab moves down, producing an upward force that tries to streamline the stabilator. *See* Figure 4-21.

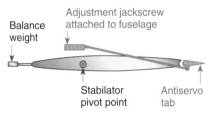

Antiservo tab is connected to adjustable jackscrew to allow pilot to position it to produce correct tail-down load for hands-off straight and level flight.

When control wheel is pulled back, stabilator nose moves down, increasing down load on tail and rotating airplane nose up about its lateral axis. Antiservo tab moves up to produce stabilizing force on stabilator.

When control wheel is moved forward, stabilator nose moves up, decreasing downward tail load and allowing airplane to rotate nose down about its lateral axis. Antiservo tab moves down.

Figure 4-21. *Antiservo tab*

torsion rod. A device in a spring tab to which the control horn is attached. For normal operation, the torsion rod acts as a fixed attachment point, but when the control surface loads are high, the torsion rod twists and allows the control horn to deflect the spring tab.

antiservo tab. A tab installed on the trailing edge of a stabilator to make it less sensitive. The tab automatically moves in the same direction as the stabilator to produce an aerodynamic force that tries to bring the surface back to a streamline position. This tab is also called an antibalance tab.

jackscrew. A hardened steel rod with strong threads cut into it. A jackscrew is rotated by hand or with a motor to apply a force or to lift an object.

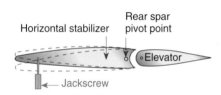

Figure 4-22. *Some airplanes provide longitudinal trim by pivoting the horizontal stabilizer about its rear spar and raising or lowering the leading edge by means of a jackscrew.*

Adjustable Stabilizer

Rather than using tabs on the trailing edge of the primary control surface, some airplanes are trimmed longitudinally by adjusting the position of the leading edge of the horizontal stabilizer. These stabilizers pivot about the rear spar, and a jackscrew controlled from the cockpit raises or lowers the leading edge. Raising the leading edge gives the airplane nose-down trim, and lowering the leading edge trims the airplane in a nose-up direction. *See* Figure 4-22.

Balance Panel

A balance panel, such as the one in Figure 4-23, is used on some large airplanes to assist the pilot in moving the ailerons. The hinged balance panel forms a movable partition for the sealed space ahead of the aileron. When the aileron is deflected upward, as seen here, the air over its bottom surface speeds up and produces a low pressure below the balance panel. This low pressure pulls the balance panel down and puts a force on the leading edge of the aileron in such a direction that it assists the pilot in holding the aileron deflected upward.

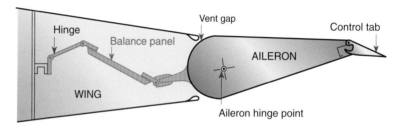

Figure 4-23. *A balance panel uses the low pressure caused by the deflected aileron to create a force that helps hold the aileron deflected.*

Bungee Spring

Some airplanes have a spring whose tension may be controlled by the pilot. The spring holds a mechanical force on the control system to trim the airplane for hands-off flight at the desired airspeed. Such a bungee system is shown in Figure 4-24.

Figure 4-24. *The force provided by the bungee spring may be adjusted in flight by the pilot to provide the correct force on the control wheel to trim the airplane for hands-off flight at any desired airspeed.*

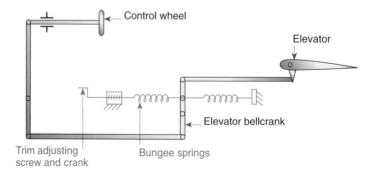

Elevator Downspring

To increase the aft CG limit, the manufacturers of some airplanes install elevator downsprings like the one in Figure 4-25.

When an airplane is operating with its CG at its aft limit, the elevator trim tab is adjusted to move the elevator so it will decrease the aerodynamic down load produced by the tail. Under some loading conditions, the elevator will actually be deflected downward to produce an upward tail load. If the airplane in this unstable condition encounters turbulence when it is slowed for its landing approach, the elevator will momentarily streamline, and at this slow speed the trim tab does not have enough power to force it back down to lower the nose. The airplane is likely to stall, which at this low altitude can be fatal.

The elevator downspring produces a mechanical force that tries to move the elevator down and lower the nose. In normal flight conditions, this force is overcome by the elevator trim tab which adjusts the stabilizing down load. But under the conditions just noted, when the trim tab loses its effectiveness and is unable to move the elevator down, the downspring exerts its force and moves the elevator down, lowering the nose and preventing a stall.

elevator downspring. A spring in the elevator control system that produces a mechanical force that tries to lower the elevator. In normal flight this spring force is overcome by the aerodynamic force from the elevator trim tab. But in slow flight with an aft CG position, the trim tab loses its effectiveness and the downspring lowers the nose to prevent a stall.

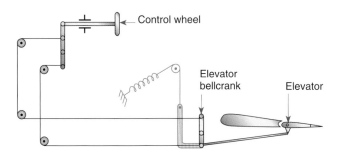

Figure 4-25. *The elevator downspring produces a mechanical force on the elevator that lowers the nose and prevents a stall when an aft CG location causes the tail load to be ineffective at low airspeed.*

Control System Operating Methods

There are a number of methods of actuating the control surfaces from the cockpit. The time-honored method is to connect the surface to the cockpit control with a steel cable, but there are other mechanical methods discussed here, as well as electrically and hydraulically operated controls.

Cable Operated Systems

In the cable-operated control system, the cockpit controls are connected to the control surfaces with high-strength steel cable. In this section, we will examine the types of cables and the components used in this popular system.

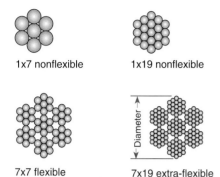

1x7 nonflexible   1x19 nonflexible

7x7 flexible   7x19 extra-flexible

Figure 4-26. *Steel control cables used in aircraft control systems*

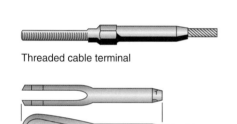

Threaded cable terminal

Fork-end cable terminal

Eye-end cable terminal

Figure 4-28. *Swaged control cable terminals*

Figure 4-29. *Nicopress thimble-eye cable terminals have 100% of the strength of the cable on which they are installed.*

Control Cables

Steel cables used in aircraft control systems may be of any of the four types shown in Figure 4-26. These cables are available in sizes from $\frac{1}{32}$-inch through $\frac{1}{4}$-inch diameter and may be made of either corrosion-resistant steel or galvanized steel.

Nonflexible cable is used for straight runs where the cable does not pass over any pulley. Flexible cable can be used where it passes over a pulley, but should not be used where the flexing requirements are extreme, as they are in most primary flight control systems. The extra-flexible, or 7 x 19, cable is the one most widely used for primary control systems.

The strengths of 7 x 7 and 7 x 19 cable are shown in Figure 4-27. These strengths are for straight runs of cable and do not include the effect of wrapped ends.

The smallest cable that can be used in the primary control system of an aircraft is $\frac{1}{8}$ inch, but smaller cables may be used to actuate trim tabs if the manufacturer has approved it.

Cable Diameter (inch)	Breaking Strength (pounds)	
	Carbon Steel	Corrosion Resistant Steel
1/16	480	480
1/8	2,000	1,760
3/16	4,200	3,700
1/4	7,000	6,400

Figure 4-27. *Breaking strength of 7 x 7 and 7 x 19 aircraft steel control cable*

Most modern cable installations use swaged terminals such as those in Figure 4-28. When properly swaged, these terminals have 100% of the strength of the cable itself.

Some of the older and smaller aircraft use a Nicopress thimble-eye terminal shown in Figure 4-29. In this type of terminal the end of the cable is passed through a heavy copper sleeve, wrapped around a steel thimble and passed back into the sleeve. The sleeve is then crimped with a special crimping tool. This type of terminal has 100% of the strength of the cable on which it is installed.

There is more information on cable terminals in the *General* textbook of this *Aviation Maintenance Technician Series.*

Fairleads and Pulleys

Anytime a cable passes through a bulkhead or near one, a fairlead should be used to protect both the cable and the structure. A fairlead should never be used to change the direction of a control cable, and it should never deflect a control cable more than 3°. *See* Figure 4-30.

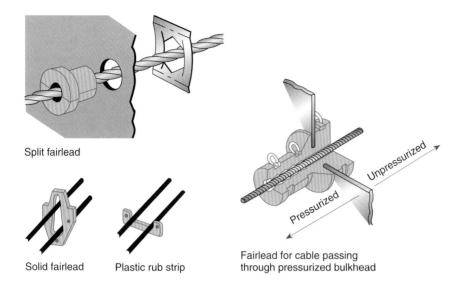

Split fairlead

Solid fairlead   Plastic rub strip

Fairlead for cable passing
through pressurized bulkhead

Pressurized

Unpressurized

Figure 4-30. *Fairleads are used to guide control cables where they pass through a structural member.*

fairlead. A plastic or wooden guide used to prevent a steel control cable rubbing against an aircraft structure.

Pulleys are used where a control cable must make a change in direction. Most pulleys are made of a phenolic plastic-reinforced fabric or aluminum, and they may have either a sealed ball bearing or a bronze bushing. Each pulley installed in the aircraft must have a cable guard installed to prevent the cable from slipping out of the pulley groove when it is slacked off. *See* Figure 4-31.

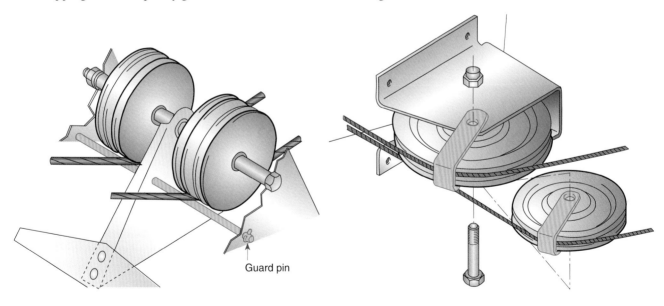

Guard pin

Figure 4-31. *Two types of guards used with a pulley to prevent the cable from slipping out of the groove*

Push-Pull Rod Systems

Another popular type of control actuation system is the push-pull rod system, which is used extensively in helicopter controls. In this system the cockpit control is connected to the device to be operated with a hollow aluminum tube whose ends are fitted with threaded inserts and a clevis, or more frequently, a rod-end bearing. Figure 4-32 shows such a push-pull rod.

Both the cockpit control and the device to be actuated are locked in the correct rigging position, and the rod ends are screwed in or out on the threaded end of the inserts to get the rod to the correct length and the rod end in correct alignment, then the check nuts are screwed tightly against the rod-end fittings to lock them in place.

Figure 4-32. *A typical push-pull control rod*

Rod-End Fittings

The rod-end bearing shown in Figure 4-33 is typical of the terminal used on a push-pull rod. When installing this type of fitting be sure that the threaded portion of the rod end extends into the fitting far enough that the inspection hole is covered. This ensures that there are enough threads engaged to give full strength to the joint. On an inspection, try to insert a piece of safety wire into the inspection hole. The threaded end of the rod should prevent the wire from going through the hole.

The antifriction bearing installed in a rod-end fitting is covered with a disc of thin sheet metal held in place by the edges of the fitting peened over the disc. When you install the bearing, you must be sure that the closed side of the fitting is next to the device to which the rod is attached, as illustrated in Figure 4-33. The rod will still remain attached to the device even if the bearing should fail.

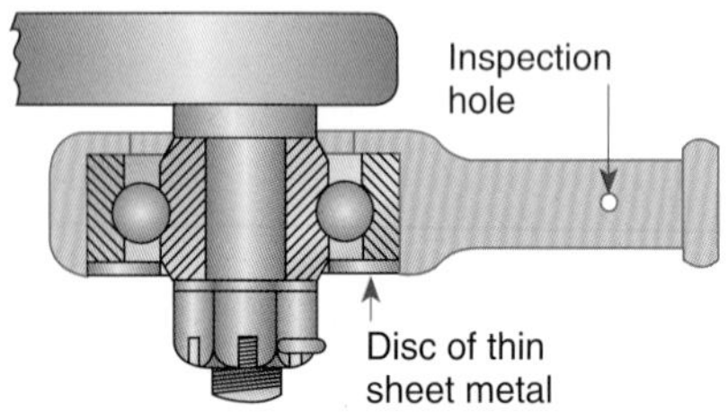

Figure 4-33. *The correct installation of an antifriction rod-end bearing*

torque tube. A tube in an aircraft control system that transmits a torsional force from the operating control to the control surface.

Torque Tube Systems

A torque tube is a hollow metal tube used to transmit a torsional, or twisting, force between the actuating control and the device being controlled. The flaps and ailerons of small airplanes are often actuated from the cockpit by means of torque tubes.

Large airplane control systems often use torque tubes between an electric or hydraulic motor and a jackscrew to actuate flaps, slats, and other control surfaces.

Fly-By-Wire Systems

Some state-of-the-art modern airplane designs use fly-by-wire systems to connect the flight control surfaces to the cockpit controls with electrical wires, rather than with steel cables, push-pull tubes, torque tubes, or other mechanical methods. The cockpit controls are devices that convert the movements or pressures exerted by the pilot into electrical signals which are sent into a computer programmed with all of the flight characteristics of the airplane.

The computer output is directed through more wires to electrohydraulic valves that convert the electrical signal into hydraulic fluid flow. This flow changes the position of a main control valve, which directs hydraulic fluid to the appropriate control actuators. Within the actuators, linear variable displacement transducers complete the loop and send feedback signals to the computer, informing it of the amount and speed of actuator movement.

Rather than using a control wheel or stick that actually moves, some fly-by-wire-equipped airplanes have sidestick controllers to fly the airplane. Pressures exerted on the controller mounted on the cockpit side console are converted into electrical signals, just as are movements of conventional controls. The General Dynamics F-16 uses a sidestick controller.

Fly-By-Light Systems

While fly-by-wire systems offer the significant benefits of reduced aircraft weight, simplified control routing, and improved control consistency, they do have one significant drawback—they are susceptible to electromagnetic interference (EMI). Fly-by-light systems use fiber optic cables rather than wires to transmit the control signals. Digital electrical signals from the computer are converted into light signals and sent through the aircraft via fiber optic cables to electro-optic converters. Here the light signals are changed back to electrical signals for the actuation of the hydraulic control valves.

The weight saving, freedom from EMI, and capability of high-speed data transmission ensure that fly-by-light systems will be found on an increasing number of aircraft in the future.

Control Actuation Systems for Large Airplanes

The control forces required by large transport airplanes are too great for a pilot to fly them manually, so the control surfaces are actually moved by hydraulic servos, or actuators. Figure 4-34 on the next page identifies the flight control surfaces on a Boeing 727 airplane. We will consider each of these surfaces and the way they are actuated.

The primary flight controls of this airplane consist of inboard and outboard ailerons, elevators, and upper and lower rudders. These controls are operated hydraulically from two independent hydraulic systems, the A system and the B system.

fly-by-wire. A method of control used by some modern aircraft in which control movement or pressures exerted by the pilot are directed into a digital computer where they are input into a program tailored to the flight characteristics of the aircraft. The computer output signal is sent to actuators at the control surfaces to move them the optimum amount for the desired maneuver.

sidestick controller. A cockpit flight control used on some of the fly-by-wire equipped airplanes. The stick is mounted rigidly on the side console of the cockpit, and pressures exerted on the stick by the pilot produce electrical signals that are sent to the computer that flies the airplane.

The ailerons and elevators typically are powered from both A and B systems, but either system can operate the controls, which also can be operated manually.

The upper rudder is operated by B system. The lower rudder is operated by A system, and also can be operated by the standby hydraulic system.

There are five flight spoilers on each wing to assist the ailerons in roll control. The three inboard spoilers are operated by B system and the two outboard spoilers are operated by A system. All the flight spoilers plus two ground spoilers on each wing may be operated when the airplane is on the ground and weight is on the landing gear.

The leading edge of the horizontal stabilizer may be raised or lowered with an electrically operated jackscrew. If the electrical actuator should fail, the stabilizer may be positioned manually with a trim wheel.

Hydraulic actuators supplied from A system actuate the leading edge flaps and slats, but if A system should fail, these devices may be extended by the standby hydraulic system.

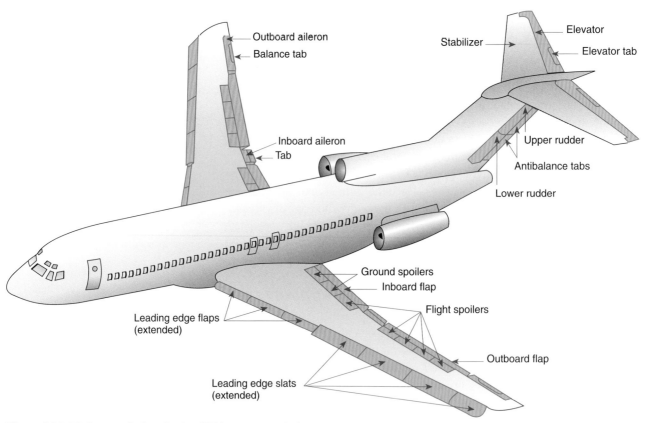

Figure 4-34. *Flight controls for a Boeing 727 jet transport airplane*

Roll Control

Each wing has two ailerons that are powered by a dual power unit supplied from both A and B systems. Either system can give full actuation of the ailerons. Movement of the ailerons is assisted by internal balance panels and balance tabs.

When the flaps are up, the outboard ailerons are locked in their faired position, but as the flaps extend, the outboard ailerons become progressively effective, and by the time the outboard flaps have extended 5°, 80% of the outboard aileron travel is available.

If all hydraulic pressure is lost, the tab on the inboard aileron is mechanically linked to the control wheel. This allows the pilot to move the tab to produce aerodynamic forces on the aileron, which deflects it to provide roll control.

The aileron trim control allows the pilots to center the hydraulic power units, which can provide aileron trim when the hydraulic systems are functioning.

The flight spoilers actuate with the ailerons in normal flight to provide roll control by deflecting to a maximum of 30°. They can also be actuated by movement of the speed brake control for deflections between 0° and 45°, depending upon the position of the speed brake handle. When the airplane is on the ground, the ground spoilers extend to their full 45° when the speed brake lever is moved through 10°.

The hydraulic pressure that actuates the flight spoilers will be relieved if the air loads on the spoilers become great enough to stall the actuator. This allows the spoilers to blow down until the airspeed is decreased.

Pitch Control

The elevators are controlled by two dual hydraulic power units that are supplied by both A and B systems and controlled by fore-and-aft movement of the control column. The elevator tabs act as balance tabs for normal flight when hydraulic pressure is available, but if hydraulic pressure should fail, the tabs can be moved from the cockpit so that they act as control tabs to produce aerodynamic forces that move the elevators.

A feel computer is incorporated in the elevator system. It senses airspeed, which gives the pilot a progressive restraint on the control column, and indicates the amount of control forces being used.

Pitch trim is provided by varying the angle of incidence of the horizontal stabilizer with a jackscrew that can be actuated electrically or manually.

Yaw Control

The Boeing 727 has two separate, independent rudders. The upper rudder power unit is supplied from B system and the lower rudder is operated from A system, or from the standby system. Both rudders have antibalance tabs.

The rudder system is protected against structural damage in high-speed flight by automatically limiting the hydraulic pressure to the rudder power systems when the trailing edge flaps are retracted.

The rudder pedals, in addition to controlling the rudder, also steer the nose wheel through 8° of travel, but this control may be overridden by the nose wheel steering wheel.

A yaw damper controls the rudder power systems all the time pressure is available from the main hydraulic systems. Yaw is sensed by the rate gyros in the two turn and slip indicators, and they provide rudder displacement proportional to, but opposite in direction to, the amount of yaw. One rate gyro controls the yaw damper for the upper rudder, and the other controls the yaw damper for the lower rudder. There is no yaw damper action for the lower rudder when it is being operated by the standby system.

yaw damper. An automatic control of an airplane that senses yaw with a rate gyro and moves the rudder an amount proportional to the rate of yaw, but in the opposite direction.

Wing Flaps

The two triple-slotted Fowler flaps on each wing's trailing edge are operated by torque tubes and jackscrews which are powered by separate hydraulic motors for the inboard and outboard flaps. The hydraulic motors are supplied by A system. When the outboard flaps extend 2° the leading edge flaps and slats extend.

In the event of loss of all hydraulic pressure, the flaps may be operated by electric motors which drive the torque tubes, while the hydraulic fluid circulates in the hydraulic motors without causing opposition.

STUDY QUESTIONS: AIRPLANE CONTROLS

Answers are on Page 317. Page numbers refer to chapter text.

1. The aileron that moves upward travels a _____ (greater or lesser) distance than the aileron that moves downward. *Page 269*

2. Large transport aircraft have two ailerons on each wing. For high-speed flight the _____ (inner or outer) aileron is locked in place and does not move. *Page 270*

3. When the ailerons of a large transport airplane are deflected, the flight spoilers on the wing with the _____ (up or down) aileron extend automatically. *Page 270*

4. Flight spoilers may be extended the same amount on each wing to act as _____ . *Page 270*

5. Delta-wing airplanes have movable control surfaces on the trailing edge of the wings that act as both elevators and ailerons. These surfaces are called _____ . *Page 271*

6. The movable control surfaces on a V-tail airplane act as both elevators and rudders. These surfaces are called _____ . *Page 273*

7. In a conventional airplane using a horizontal stabilator and elevators mounted on the tail, the normal aerodynamic force acts _____ (upward or downward). *Page 271*

8. A canard surface has an angle of incidence that causes it to stall _____ (before or after) the main wing stalls. *Page 273*

9. The type of wing flap that produces the greatest amount of increase in lift with the minimum change in drag is the _____ flap. *Page 275*

10. A leading edge flap _____ (increases or decreases) the camber of a wing. *Page 275*

11. Slats extend from the leading edge of the wing to _____ (increase or decrease) the wing camber. *Page 277*

12. A trim tab _____ (does or does not) move relative to the control surface on which it is installed as the surface is moved in flight. *Page 278*

13. A balance tab moves in the _____ (same or opposite) direction as the control surface on which it is mounted. *Page 278*

14. The type of tab that is controlled from the cockpit to produce an aerodynamic force that moves the primary control surface is called a/an _____ tab. *Page 279*

15. A servo tab moves in the _____ (same or opposite) direction as the control surface on which it is mounted. *Page 279*

16. A spring tab automatically deflects when the control forces are _____ (high or low). *Page 279*

17. An antiservo tab moves in the _____ (same or opposite) direction as the control surface on which it is mounted. *Page 279*

18. Adjusting the leading edge of a movable stabilizer upward gives the airplane a nose-_____ (up or down) trim. *Page 280*

19. An elevator downspring is effective in slow flight when the CG position is at or beyond its _____ (forward or aft) limit. *Page 281*

Continued

20. The strength of a swaged cable terminal is _____ percent of the cable strength. *Page 282*

21. The smallest size cable that can be used in a primary control system is _____ inch diameter. *Page 282*

22. The strength of a Nicopress thimble-eye cable terminal is _____ percent of the cable strength. *Page 282*

23. A fairlead should not deflect a control cable more than _____ degrees. *Page 282*

24. To determine that a rod-end bearing is properly installed on a push-pull rod, the threads of the rod end _____ (should or should not) cover the inspection hole. *Page 284*

25. When installing an antifriction rod-end bearing, the _____ (open or closed) side of the bearing should be against the device being actuated. *Page 284*

26. A tube that is used to apply a torsional force to a control surface is called a _____ tube. *Page 284*

27. The Boeing 727 airplane uses _____ (electrical or hydraulic) actuators to move the primary flight control surfaces. *Page 285*

Airplane Assembly and Rigging

Airplanes must be assembled and rigged in strict accordance with the airplane manufacturer's instructions. Improper assembly procedures can damage the aircraft, and if it is not rigged properly, it cannot fly as the manufacturer designed it to do.

Manufacturer's maintenance manuals provide information on the assembly of the aircraft and the Type Certificate Data Sheets issued by the FAA list pertinent rigging information that must be adhered to.

Airplane Assembly

Airplane assembly, like almost all other aspects of aviation maintenance, has grown in complexity as airplanes become more efficient and complex. No step-by-step assembly procedure can be described that would apply to all airplanes or all situations, but several pointers do apply in most instances.

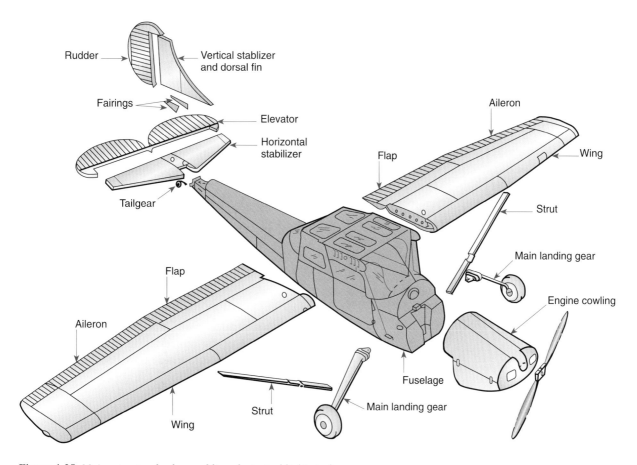

Figure 4-35. *Major structural subassemblies of a typical light airplane*

Installing the Wings and Landing Gear

Before installing the landing gear, support the fuselage by the method recommended by the manufacturer. This sometimes involves constructing a heavy wooden cradle with supports cut to conform to the fuselage frame that the manufacturer recommends. These supports should be well padded to prevent damage to the aircraft skin. The landing gear of most low-wing airplanes is in the wing, so the wing must be installed first. The wing assembly is usually quite heavy and either it must be raised in place to meet the fuselage, or the fuselage must be lowered into the wing. With either method, proper equipment must be used to support the wing or fuselage so they can be slowly and carefully mated. Be sure that all the needed new attachment hardware is available and all the needed alignment punches and drifts are within easy reach. When assembling high-wing airplanes, the landing gear is usually installed first and then the wing.

spirit level. A curved glass tube partially filled with a liquid, but with a bubble in it. When the device in which the tube is mounted is level, the bubble will be in the center of the tube.

surveyor's transit. An instrument consisting of a telescope mounted on a flat, graduated, circular plate on a tripod. The plate can be adjusted so it is level, and its graduations oriented to magnetic north. When an object is viewed through the telescope, its azimuth and elevation may be determined.

dihedral. The positive angle formed between the lateral axis of an airplane and a line which passes through the center of the wing or the horizontal stabilizer.

cantilever wing. A wing that is supported by its internal structure and requires no external supports.

Leveling the Airplane

With the wings and landing gear installed, the next step is to level the airplane so there will be the proper reference from which all alignment can be done. The Type Certificate Data Sheets for the particular airplane specifies the method the manufacturer used for leveling the airplane, and you should use this same method. Some manufacturers require you to drop a plumb bob from some point on the structure, which must align with another point below it. Other manufacturers call for the use of a spirit level placed at a specified location. Many of the large airplanes are leveled by using a surveyor's transit to align marks at the front and rear of the fuselage for longitudinal leveling, and objects on the wings for lateral leveling.

Aligning the Wings

Two very important alignments must be made for the wings of an airplane: the dihedral and the angle of incidence must be correct.

Dihedral

Cantilever wings are constructed in such a way that the dihedral cannot be changed. The main wing spar is generally bolted to the center section with special high-strength bolts or high-strength dowel pins held in place with bolts. Figure 4-36 shows the way the front spar of both a low-wing and a high-wing cantilever airplane are attached to the center section.

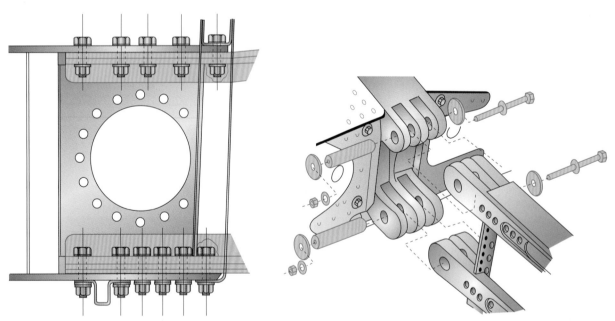

A low-wing airplane uses several bolts on both sides of top and bottom flanges of the front spar.

A high-wing airplane attaches the front-wing spar to the center section with high-strength dowel pins held in place by bolts and nuts.

Figure 4-36. *Front spar attachment for cantilever-wing airplanes*

The dihedral of strut-braced airplanes can be adjusted by changing the length of the strut that attaches to the front wing spar. The amount of dihedral is measured using a dihedral board, which is a tapered board made with the angle specified in the airplane service manual. It is held against the lower surface of the wing under the front spar. When the dihedral angle is correctly adjusted, a spirit level held against the bottom of the board will be level.

Angle of Incidence

The angle of incidence of some cantilever wings may be adjusted at the rear spar. One popular way of doing this is by the use of eccentric bushings. This is illustrated in Figure 4-38. The hole in the wing rear spar fitting is larger than that in the fuselage rear spar carry-through fitting. An eccentric bushing is installed in both sides of the wing spar fitting and the bolt and nut are installed but not tightened. The angle of incidence is checked at the point specified by the manufacturer using a protractor or an incidence board and a spirit level. The bushings on both sides of the wing spar are turned to raise or lower the rear spar until the incidence angle is correct, then the nut is torqued to the recommended value.

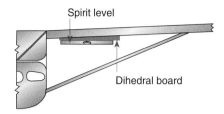

Figure 4-37. *The dihedral angle is checked with a dihedral board and a spirit level.*

eccentric bushing. A special bushing used between the rear spar of certain cantilever airplane wings and the wing attachment fitting on the fuselage. The portion of the bushing that fits through the hole in the spar is slightly offset from that which passes through the holes in the fitting. By rotating the bushing, the rear spar may be moved up or down to adjust the root incidence of the wing.

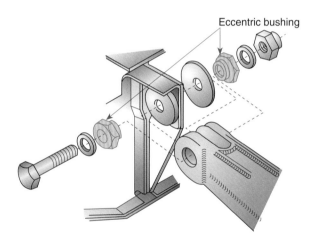

Figure 4-38. *The angle of incidence of some cantilever airplanes is adjusted by rotating eccentric bushings in the rear wing spar fitting.*

Wash In and Wash Out

Wing-heavy flight conditions are often corrected on strut-braced airplanes by adjusting the length of the rear struts. A wing may be washed in by shortening the rear strut. This twists the wing and increases the angle of incidence, increasing the lift and the induced drag on that wing. This typically decreases the airspeed slightly. Lengthening the rear strut decreases the angle of incidence and washes the wing out. If very much correction is needed, one wing is washed in and the opposite wing is washed out.

wash in. A twist in an airplane wing that increases its angle of incidence near the tip.

wash out. A twist in an airplane wing that decreases its angle of incidence near the tip.

wing heavy. An out-of-trim flight condition in which an airplane flies hands off, with one wing low.

Installing and Aligning the Empennage

The fixed horizontal and vertical tail surfaces are installed according to the manufacturer's recommendations, and a symmetry check is performed to ensure that the wings and tail are all symmetrical with the fuselage.

Symmetry Check

The manufacturer's maintenance manual lists the points to be measured on a symmetry check. These usually include measuring from a point near the tip of the vertical fin to a point near the tip of both sides of the horizontal stabilizer, and from the point on the vertical fin to points on each wing near the tip. Another measurement is made from the point near each wing tip to a point on the nose of the fuselage. All of the measurements on the right and left sides should be the same within the tolerances allowed by the manufacturer. Any difference in these measurements is an indication of structural deformation. A careful investigation must be made to find the reason for the difference and appropriate action taken to correct the problem.

Control Surface Installation and Rigging

When the airplane has been assembled and its alignment checked, all of the attachment bolts are tightened to the manufacturer's recommendations and marked with a spot of paint to signify that they have been properly torqued. Then the control surfaces should be installed and rigged.

Control Surface Balancing

Most modern airplanes are so aerodynamically clean and they fly at such high speeds that it is extremely important that all movable control surfaces be statically balanced. If the balance is improper, it is very likely that the surfaces will flutter in some condition of high-speed flight. When flutter develops, the surface can be damaged or destroyed, and this can cause loss of the aircraft.

The manufacturer recommends the method of checking the surfaces for static balance and gives the tolerances in the maintenance manual for the aircraft. Figure 4-39 shows a typical control surface balancing fixture.

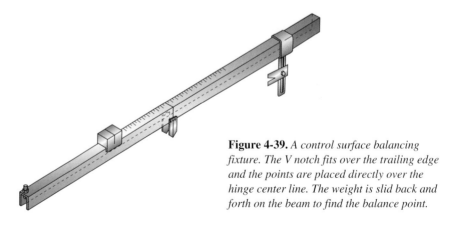

Figure 4-39. *A control surface balancing fixture. The V notch fits over the trailing edge and the points are placed directly over the hinge center line. The weight is slid back and forth on the beam to find the balance point.*

Check an aileron for static balance by mounting it upside down with a bolt through its hinge bearings resting on the knife edges of two balancing mandrels. Place the balancing fixture on the aileron, as directed in the manufacturer's maintenance manual, with the points over the hinge line. Move the weight until the assembly balances, and note the location at which the balance is attained. This gives the inch-pounds of overbalance or underbalance. If the surface does not balance within the tolerance specified by the manufacturer, change the balance weight in the leading edge of the surface as indicated in the maintenance manual.

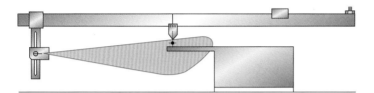

Figure 4-40. *Checking aileron balance*

When all the surfaces are balanced within the tolerances allowed by the manufacturer, they are ready for installation and rigging. Install the surface according to the directions in the appropriate maintenance manual and use only the hardware specified in the illustrated parts list.

Rigging the Ailerons

Lock the control yoke in position. One way to do this is to use a special rigging pin that fits in holes the manufacturer has provided in the control column and the support where it passes through the instrument panel. Such a device is shown in Figure 4-41.

Put a control lock between the aileron and the flap to hold the aileron in its neutral position and then connect the control cables. Adjust the cable tension to the value specified in the maintenance manual.

Adjusting Cable Tension

If cable tension is too light, the cables might slip out of the pulley grooves, and if it is too heavy, the controls will be difficult to move and there will be excessive wear in the control system. To complicate this problem, an all-metal airplane changes its dimensions considerably as its temperature changes, and the cable tension varies a great deal because of these changes. If the cables are rigged with the correct tension when the airplane is sitting on a hot ramp, the airplane will contract when it gets cold at high altitude and the cables will become extremely loose. Large airplanes typically have automatic cable tension regulators that compensate for dimensional changes in the airframe and maintain a relatively constant cable tension.

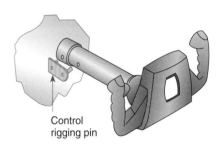

Control rigging pin

Figure 4-41. *The control yoke of some airplanes may be held in position for rigging by using a special rigging pin that fits in holes the manufacturer has provided in the control yoke and its support.*

A control cable rigging chart typical of those furnished for a specific airplane is shown in Figure 4-42. For example, to find the tension that is required for an $\frac{1}{8}$-inch 7 x 19 cable when the airplane temperature is 100°F, follow the vertical line for 100°F upward until it intersects the curve for $\frac{1}{8}$ inch, 7 x 19 cable. From this point, draw a line horizontally to the right to the rigging load index. This cable at this temperature should be rigged to a tension of 79 pounds.

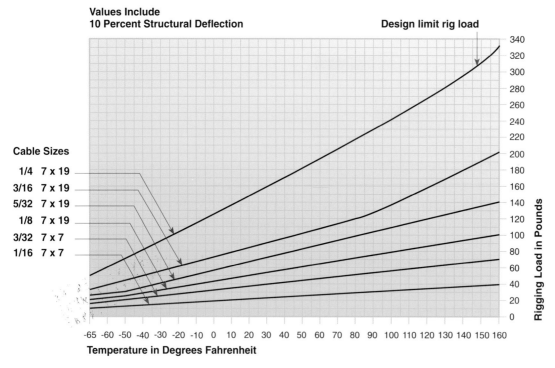

Figure 4-42. *A typical rigging load chart for aircraft steel control cables*

Check the cable tension with a tensiometer like the one in Figure 4-43. Release the trigger of the tensiometer and pass the cable between the anvils and the riser. Then clamp the trigger against the housing, to cause the riser to press against the cable. Push the pointer lock in to lock the pointer, and then remove the tensiometer and read the indication. Use the chart furnished with the tensiometer to convert the dial indication to the cable tension. The chart in Figure 4-44 is similar to the chart furnished with the tensiometer.

To find the tensiometer indication that shows the cable is adjusted to 79 pounds, use the chart in Figure 4-44 and interpolate. Seventy-nine pounds is 90% of the way between 70 and 80, so the tensiometer indication will be 90% of the way between 50 and 57, or 56.

Install riser No. 1 in the tensiometer, and adjust the turnbuckles until the tensiometer reads 56. The cable tension will then be 79 pounds, which is correct for 100°F.

Checking Control Travel

The Type Certificate Data Sheets for the airplane specifies the travel for each of the primary controls. Once you've adjusted the cable tension, you are ready to check for the correct travel.

One type of tool you can use for this is the protractor shown in Figure 4-45. Attach it to the upper surface of the aileron with its rubber suction cup, and with the aileron locked in its streamline position, rotate the circular dial until zero is below the tip of the weighted pointer. Remove the rigging tool from the control column and unlock the aileron. Move it to its full up position and read the protractor to find the number of degrees the aileron has traveled. Without changing the protractor, move the aileron to its full down position and read the degrees of downward deflection. If the travel is not correct, follow the instructions in the maintenance manual to adjust it so that it is within the tolerance allowed by the manufacturer.

A precision measuring instrument you can use for measuring control surface deflection is the universal propeller protractor in Figure 4-46. This instrument can measure deflection to a tenth of a degree and is primarily used for measuring propeller pitch. Flight control travel is not usually measured to the fraction of a degree. This instrument has a movable ring and a movable disk with a spirit level in the center of the disk. To use it, follow these steps:

1. Align the zeroes on the ring and the disk scales.

2. Place the bottom of the protractor on top of the aileron.

3. Unlock the ring from the frame and rotate the ring until the bubble centers in the spirit level.

4. Lock the ring to the frame and deflect the aileron fully up. Unlock the disk from the ring and turn the disk adjuster until the bubble centers in the spirit level.

5. Read the up deflection on the disk scale against the zero mark on the ring. *See* Figure 4-46 on the next page.

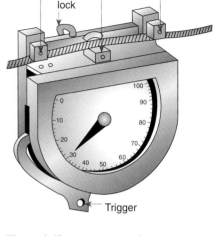

Figure 4-43. *A tensiometer determines control cable tension by measuring the force required to deflect the cable a specific amount.*

Figure 4-45. *This type of control surface protractor is held on the surface with its rubber suction cup when measuring control surface travel.*

Use Riser No. 1 with 1/16, 3/32, and 1/8 inch cable Use Riser No. 2 with 5/32 and 3/16 inch cable					
Tensiometer Indication Cable Diameter (inch)					**Cable Tension (pounds)**
1/16	3/32	1/8	5/32	3/16	
12	16	21	12	20	30
19	23	29	17	26	40
25	30	36	22	32	50
31	36	43	26	37	60
36	42	50	30	42	70
41	48	57	34	47	80
46	54	63	38	52	90
51	60	69	42	56	100
			46	60	110
			50	64	120

Figure 4-44. *Typical chart relating control cable tension to a given tensiometer reading*

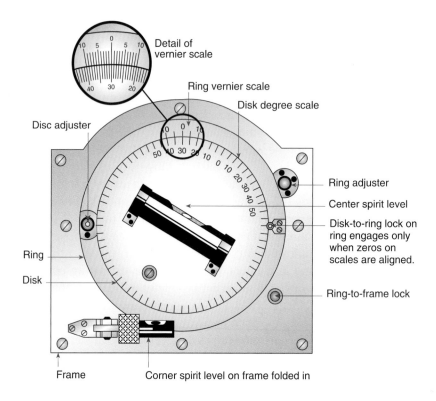

Figure 4-46. *A universal propeller protractor can be used to measure control surface deflection*

Checking and Safetying the System

After adjusting the cable tension and checking to be sure the controls have their proper up and down travel, check and safety the entire system.

Since many of the bolts in the control system are subject to rotation, they should not have self-locking nuts unless the manufacturer has used them and they are specified in the illustrated parts list. The bolts should all be installed in the direction that is shown in the illustrated parts list.

Be sure that every pulley has the proper cable guard installed and that with full travel of the controls no cable fitting comes within 2 inches of any fairlead or pulley, and check to see than no fairlead deflects the cable more than 3°. If a turnbuckle should come closer than is allowed to any pulley, readjust the cable to prevent it, and if it cannot be kept from coming this close, replace the cable assembly.

Safety the turnbuckles using one of the methods shown in Figure 4-47 or with a special clip such as that in Figure 4-49 on the next page. Be sure that no more than 3 threads are exposed on either side of the turnbuckle barrel, and that both ends of all safety wires are ended with at least 4 full turns around the turnbuckle fitting. *See* Figure 4-47.

turnbuckle. A component in an aircraft control system used to adjust cable tension. A turnbuckle consists of a brass tubular barrel with right-hand threads in one end and left-hand in the other end. Control cable terminals screw into the two ends of the barrel and turning the barrel pulls the terminals together, shortening the cable.

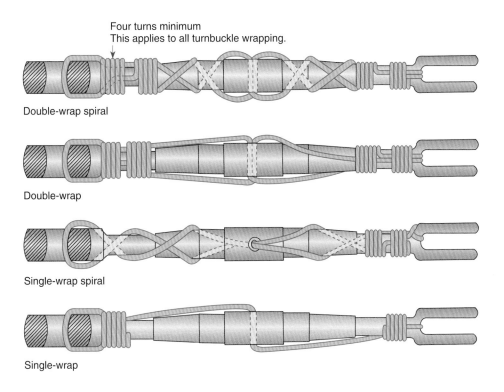

Four turns minimum
This applies to all turnbuckle wrapping.

Double-wrap spiral

Double-wrap

Single-wrap spiral

Single-wrap

Figure 4-47. *Methods of safety wiring turnbuckles*

The size and type of safety wire for each cable size is shown in Figure 4-48.

Cable Diameter	Type of Wrap	Diameter of Wire	Material of Wire
1/16	Single	0.040	Brass
3/32	Single	0.040	Brass
1/8	Single	0.040	Stainless Steel
1/8	Double	0.040	Brass
1/8	Single	0.057 (min)	Brass

Figure 4-48. *Turnbuckle safetying guide*

Figure 4-49. *MS Clip-type locking device for turnbuckles.*

Rigging the Elevator

The elevators are rigged in essentially the same way as the ailerons. The control yoke is locked in the same way, and the elevators are streamlined with the horizontal stabilizer with a control surface lock. The cable tension is adjusted in the same way, the travel is measured in the same way, and the system is inspected and safetied in the same way.

Rigging the Rudder

Before adjusting the control cable tension, lock the controls in their neutral position using the method specified in the airplane manufacturer's service manual. A common method for holding the rudder pedals in place is to clamp a piece of wood across the pedals with C-clamps, as shown in Figure 4-50.

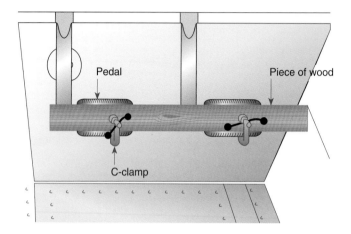

Figure 4-50. *Rudder pedals may be held in place for rigging by clamping a piece of wood across the pedals with C-clamps.*

Hold the rudder centered by clamping straightedges on both sides, and centering the rudder midway between them as shown in Figure 4-51. Adjust the turnbuckles to get the recommended cable tension.

After adjusting the cable tension, remove the straightedges and the lock from the rudder pedals, and check for full travel in both directions. Two common ways of checking this travel are illustrated in Figure 4-52. You can make a wire pointer of a welding rod taped to the aft end of the fuselage and bending it until it touches the trailing edge of the rudder. Deflect the rudder each way, and measure the distance between the pointer and the rudder trailing edge. The manufacturer's service manual specifies the distance tolerance for this type of measurement.

When the cable tension and the rudder travel are correct, check the entire system for freedom of operation, and safety all of the nuts and turnbuckles.

Control Movement Check

It seems almost unnecessary to mention this, but controls have been known to be rigged backward. The final check in any rigging procedure is to be sure all the control surfaces move in the correct direction when the cockpit control is moved.

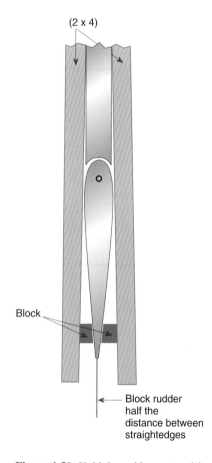

Figure 4-51. *Hold the rudder centered for adjusting cable tension by clamping straightedges on either side and centering the rudder trailing edge between them.*

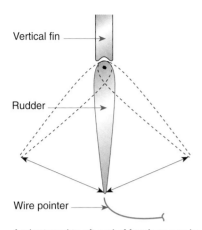

Vertical fin

Rudder

Wire pointer

A wire taped to aft end of fuselage can be bent until it touches rudder trailing edge when rudder is locked in place. Deflect rudder and measure distance between end of wire and rudder trailing edge.

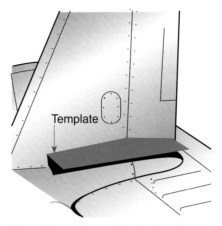

Template

A template made according to plans in aircraft maintenance manual can be held against vertical fin to measure amount of rudder deflection.

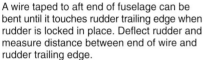

Figure 4-52. *Methods of measuring rudder deflection*

When the control wheel is pushed in to rotate the airplane nose down about its lateral axis, the trailing edge of the elevators should move down. When it is pulled back to rotate the airplane nose up, the elevator trailing edge should move up.

When the control wheel is rotated to the right to rotate the airplane to the right about its longitudinal axis, the trailing edge of the right aileron should move upward and the trailing edge of the left aileron should move down. Rotating the wheel to the left moves the controls in the opposite direction.

Moving the right rudder pedal forward deflects the trailing edge of the rudder to the right, and moving the left pedal forward moves the rudder trailing edge to the left.

Rotating the elevator trim tab to trim the airplane for nose-down flight raises the trailing edge of the tab. This creates an aerodynamic load on the elevator that moves it down and deflects the airplane nose down.

STUDY QUESTIONS: AIRPLANE ASSEMBLY AND RIGGING

Answers are on Page 317. **Page numbers refer to chapter text.**

28. The method that should be used for leveling an aircraft for proper assembly and rigging may be found in the _____ for the aircraft. *Page 292*

29. The dihedral on a strut-braced airplane is adjusted by changing the length of the _____ (front or rear) strut. *Page 293*

Continued

30. Twisting a wing in such a way that its angle of incidence at the tip is increased is called washing the wing _____ (in or out). *Page 293*

31. A check to determine that the major components of an airplane are in their proper basic alignment is called a/an _____ check. *Page 294*

32. If a bolt in the control system is subject to rotation, a self-locking nut _____ (should or should not) be used. *Page 298*

33. Use the rigging load chart in Figure 4-42 and find the proper rigging load for a ⅛-inch 7 x 19 extra flexible cable when the temperature is 85°F. The cable should be rigged to a tension of _____ pounds. *Page 296*

34. Use the tensiometer chart of Figure 4-44. For a ⅛-inch 7 x 19 cable to have a tension of 73 pounds, the tensiometer should read _____ . *Page 297*

35. A turnbuckle in a control system must not come closer to a pulley or fairlead than _____ inch/es. *Page 298*

36. To ensure that the turnbuckle ends have sufficient threads inside the barrel to develop their full strength, no more than _____ threads are allowed to be outside of a turnbuckle barrel. *Page 298*

37. When safetying a turnbuckle with safety wire, the safetying must terminate with at least _____ turns of wire around the turnbuckle end. *Page 299*

38. When the control wheel is pulled back, the trailing edge of the elevators should move _____ (up or down). *Page 301*

39. When the control wheel is moved forward, the trailing edge of the elevators should move _____ (up or down). *Page 301*

40. When the control wheel is rotated to the right, the trailing edge of the right aileron should move _____ (up or down). *Page 301*

41. When the control wheel is rotated to the left, the trailing edge of the left aileron should move _____ (up or down). *Page 301*

42. When the right rudder pedal is pushed in, the trailing edge of the rudder should move to the _____ (right or left). *Page 301*

43. When the elevator trim tab is adjusted for a nose-down condition, the trailing edge of the tab should move _____ (up or down). *Page 301*

Helicopter Assembly and Rigging

Helicopter Controls

Successful rotor-wing development started with the autogiro, which uses aerodynamic forces rather than an engine to turn the rotor. The more simple autogiros were controlled by tilting the rotor mast to tilt the plane of the rotor. But the success of rotor-wing flight has been made possible by the development of the control systems that compensate for torque of the main rotor, and systems that rotate the helicopter about its three axes while overcoming the problems of dissymmetry of lift.

The pilot of a helicopter has three basic controls; the collective pitch control, the cyclic pitch control, and the antitorque pedals.

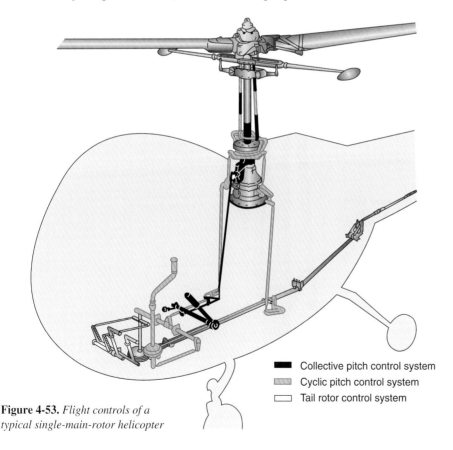

■ Collective pitch control system
▨ Cyclic pitch control system
□ Tail rotor control system

Figure 4-53. *Flight controls of a typical single-main-rotor helicopter*

swashplate. The component in a helicopter control system that consists basically of two bearing races with ball bearings between them.

The lower, or nonrotating, race is tilted by the cyclic control, and the upper, or rotating, race has arms which connect to the control horns on the rotor blades.

Movement of the cyclic pitch control is transmitted to the rotating blades through the swashplate. Movement of the collective pitch control raises or lowers the entire swashplate assembly to change the pitch of all of the blades at the same time.

Figure 4-54. *A typical swashplate assembly that mounts around the base of the rotor mast.*

The Swashplate

The heart of the typical helicopter control system is the swashplate assembly shown in Figure 4-54. This unit mounts around the rotor mast near its base, and it contains a nonrotating bearing race and a rotating race. The non-rotating race has two control arms 90° apart that are connected to the cyclic control so the swashplate can be tilted fore and aft or sideways. Running through the center of the swashplate assembly and rotating with the rotor shaft is a collective pitch sleeve that can be raised or lowered by the collective pitch control.

The Collective Pitch Control

The collective pitch control adjusts the pitch of all of the blades at the same time. This changes the lift of the entire rotor disc and allows the helicopter to go up or down. The engine throttle is coordinated with the collective pitch control in such a way that when the collective control is pulled up to increase the rotor blade pitch, the engine is automatically given more fuel so that the additional drag produced by the increased pitch does not slow the rotor. A motorcycle-type twist-grip throttle control is mounted on the collective pitch control. If the engine speed does not remain constant when the collective pitch is increased, the throttle grip can be rotated to get the correct RPM.

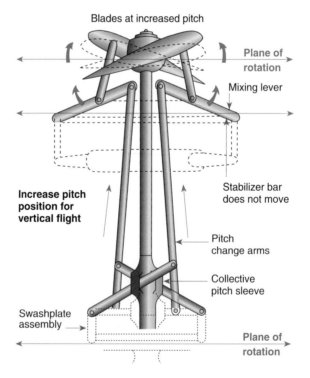

Figure 4-55. *Raising the collective pitch control raises the collective pitch sleeve which causes the pitch of all of the rotor blades to increase at the same time.*

The operation of the collective pitch control is illustrated in Figure 4-55. When the pilot raises the collective pitch control, the collective pitch sleeve is raised, forcing the pitch change arms upward. This raises the inner end of the mixing lever, which causes the pitch control links to increase the pitch of all of the rotor blades at the same time.

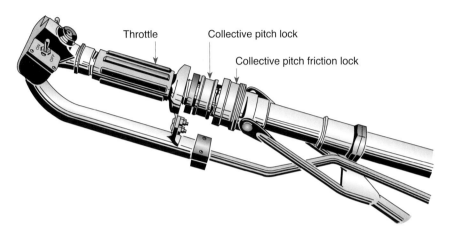

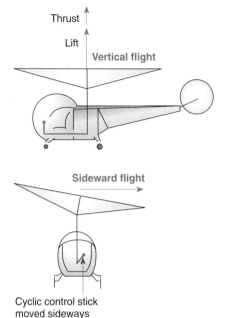

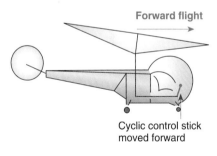

Figure 4-56. *The collective pitch control lever has a twist-grip throttle control to allow the pilot to trim the RPM to the exact value needed.*

The Cyclic Pitch Control

The cyclic pitch control operated by the pilot's right hand tilts the swash plate to change the pitch of the rotor blades at a particular point in their rotation. This pitch change tilts the plane of rotation of the rotor disk. The lift always acts along the bisector of the coning angle, and when the rotor disc is tilted the lift develops a horizontal vector that moves the helicopter in the direction the disc is tilted.

The cyclic control operates the two pitch arms on the swash plate. When the pilot moves the cyclic control forward, the swash plate tilts forward. *See* Figure 4-58 on the next page. When the swash plate tilts forward, the pitch of the advancing blade is decreased and the pitch of the retreating blade is increased. Because of gyroscopic precession, the effect of the pitch change will be felt 90° after the point the pitch change is made, and the rotor disc will tilt forward.

Figure 4-57. *The lift produced by a helicopter rotor always acts along the bisector of the coning angle of the rotor blades. This produces a horizontal vector that moves the helicopter in the direction the rotor is tilted.*

coning angle. The angle formed between the plane of rotation of a helicopter rotor blade when it is producing lift and a line perpendicular to the rotor shaft.

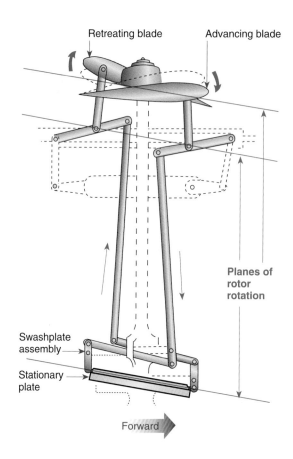

Retreating blade   Advancing blade

Planes of
rotor
rotation

Swashplate
assembly

Stationary
plate

Forward

Figure 4-58. *When the cyclic control is moved forward, the swashplate tilts forward. This decreases the pitch of advancing blade and increases the pitch of the retreating blade. Because of gyroscopic precession, the rotor disc will tilt forward.*

Horizontal Stabilizers

The rotor disc must be tilted forward in order for a helicopter to fly forwards. This results in a nose-low attitude for the fuselage, which is an inefficient flight attitude. To allow the fuselage to achieve a more level attitude in forward flight, most helicopters have some form of horizontal stabilizer mounted near the rear of the fuselage. Some of these stabilizers are synchronized with the cyclic control, so their downward force increases as the pilot moves the cyclic stick forward to increase the forward airspeed. Other helicopters have fixed stabilizers with a deeply cambered airfoil that produces a large aerodynamic download.

Torque Compensation

When the engine mounted in the fuselage of a helicopter turns the rotor, a force is produced that tries to rotate the fuselage in the opposite direction. This force, called torque, must be compensated for in order to allow the fuselage to remain pointed in the direction of desired flight. A number of methods have been tried, many unsuccessful, but three have been most successful: dual rotors mounted on coaxial shafts, dual rotors with one ahead of the other or one on either side of the fuselage, and a single main rotor with a torque-compensating tail rotor spinning in a vertical plane. The latter approach is by far the most common.

One of the latest approaches to torque compensation is NOTAR, or No Tail Rotor, developed by McDonnell-Douglas Helicopters. *See* Figure 4-59. This system does away with the dangers, complexities and noise of a tail rotor. A controllable-pitch fan, driven by the transmission, blows air down the hollow tail boom to a nozzle at the end of the shaft that is fitted with a set of 90° turning vanes. Both the pitch of the fan and the size of the nozzle openings are varied by the pilot's pedals to control the antitorque force the jet of air produces.

Two slots in the bottom of the tail boom direct air out in a tangential fashion, blowing to the left side. This air mixes with the downwash from the main rotor and accelerates it on the right side and deflects it to the left. The resulting low pressure on the right side and deflection of air to the left provide most of the antitorque force in a hover. In forward flight, when the down-washed air does not strike the tail boom, the antitorque force is provided by the tail jet and by a vertical stabilizer.

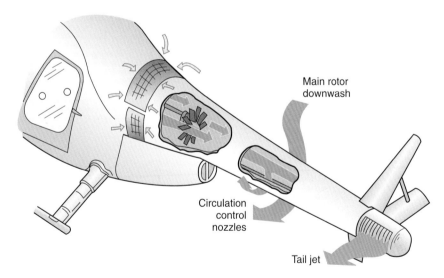

Figure 4-59. *The NOTAR or No Tail Rotor system developed by McDonnell-Douglas Helicopters controls the circulation of the main rotor downwash to compensate for torque in a hover. The thrust from the air leaving the tail boom compensates for torque in forward flight.*

The single main rotor with a vertical auxiliary tail rotor is by far the most popular configuration. The engine drives the main rotor through a transmission that reduces the engine RPM to a speed proper for the rotor. A takeoff from the transmission drives a long shaft to a tail rotor gear box on whose output shaft the tail rotor mounts.

Figure 4-61 illustrates a typical tail rotor control system. The main rotor of most helicopters rotates to the left, as viewed from above, and the torque tries to rotate the fuselage to the right. When the antitorque pedals are even, the tail rotor produces enough thrust to the right to counter the torque rotational force to the left. When the pilot moves the left pedal forward, the pitch of the tail rotor blades increases, and the thrust increases enough to overcome the torque effect and rotate the fuselage to the left. When the pilot moves the right pedal forward, the tail rotor pitch is decreased. This decreases the thrust and allows the torque to pull the nose to the right.

The side thrust caused by the tail rotor causes a helicopter to drift to the right, and to compensate for this, the main rotor mast is often rigged so that it is offset to the left a few degrees to produce a thrust component to the left.

Figure 4-60. *The tail rotor supplies sideways thrust to prevent torque from the engine rotating the fuselage. The pitch of the tail rotor is controlled by the pilot's antitorque pedals.*

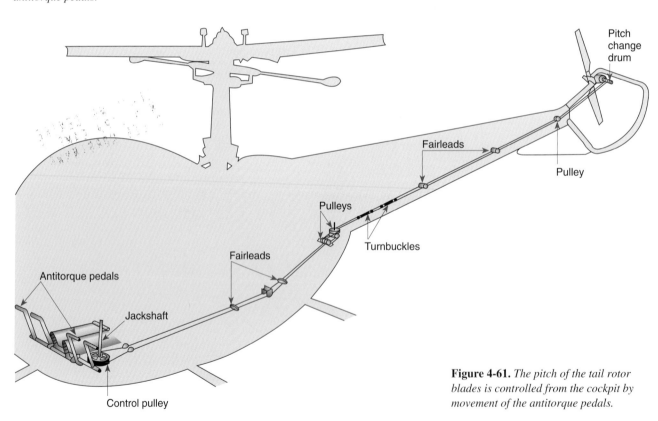

Figure 4-61. *The pitch of the tail rotor blades is controlled from the cockpit by movement of the antitorque pedals.*

Stabilizer Systems

A helicopter is statically stable but dynamically unstable, and because of this, requires some form of stabilization. One system that has been used very successfully is the stabilizer bar system, illustrated in Figure 4-62.

The bar with weighted ends is mounted on the rotor mast so that it turns with the rotor and is free to pivot about the mast. The stabilizer bar acts as a gyroscope and possesses the characteristic of rigidity in space. It will try to remain in the same plane as the helicopter pitches and rolls.

Look at Figure 4-62 and follow this explanation. The drawing is made with the helicopter in level flight. Now, suppose the nose of the helicopter drops. The mast tilts forward, but the stabilizer bar continues to rotate in the same plane. The pitch control links increase the pitch of the advancing blade (the one toward you in the illustration), and decrease the pitch of the retreating blade. Gyroscopic precession causes the pitch change to be effective 90° of rotation ahead of the point of application. This will cause the nose to rise back to level flight attitude.

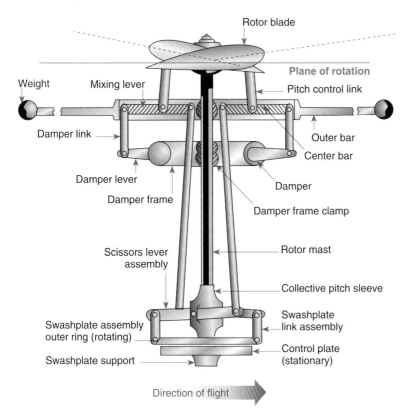

Figure 4-62. *A stabilizer bar and flight control linkage*

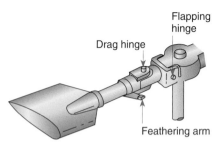

Fully articulated rotor blades are free to flap, drag, and feather.

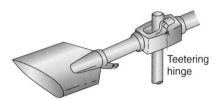

Blades of semirigid rotor are free to feather, and blades flap as rotor rocks back and forth as a unit.

Blades of rigid rotor are free to feather, but are not hinged to flap or drag.

Figure 4-63. *Helicopter rotor systems*

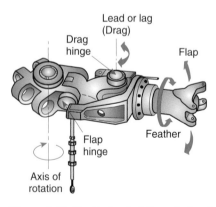

Figure 4-64. *The blade of a fully articulated rotor is free to flap, drag, and feather.*

Rotor Systems

Three basic types of rotor systems are used in modern helicopters: fully articulated, semirigid, and rigid. Each system has advantages and disadvantages. *See* Figure 4-63.

Fully Articulated Rotors

Rotors with more than two blades are typically of the fully articulated type. The blades of a fully articulated rotor are free to move up and down (flap), move back and forth in their plane of rotation (drag), and rotate about their longitudinal axis (feather). *See* Figure 4-64.

As the helicopter moves horizontally, the increased speed of the advancing blade gives it more lift, and since this blade is mounted to the hub through a flapping hinge, it is free to rise. As it flaps upward, its angle of attack decreases and the lift is decreased. Flapping reduces the asymmetrical lift caused by horizontal movement of the helicopter.

The coriolis effect causes a rotor blade to try to move back and forth in its plane of rotation as it flaps up and down. To prevent the vibration and the strain on the blades this would cause, the blade is hinged to the hub through the drag, or lead-lag, hinge.

The pitch of the rotor blades is controlled by pitch change arms rotating the blade about its feather axis. The collective pitch control changes the blade angle of all blades at the same time, and the cyclic control changes the blade angle of each blade at a certain location in its rotation.

Semirigid Rotor

Most two-blade rotors are of the semirigid type. These have the blades attached to the hub through a feathering bearing that allows their pitch to be changed, but there are no flapping or drag hinges. The hub of a semirigid rotor is mounted on the mast with a seesaw, or teetering, hinge that allows the entire rotor to rock as a unit. The advancing blade rises and the retreating blade descends to compensate for dissymmetry of lift.

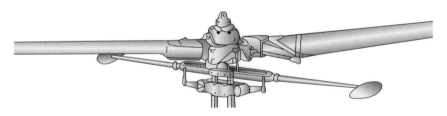

Figure 4-65. *A semirigid rotor attaches to the mast with a teetering hinge that allows it to flap as a unit. Pitch change arms control each blade about its feather axis.*

Rigid Rotor

A relatively recent type of rotor is the rigid rotor, which is attached to the mast in such a way that its only freedom of motion is around its feather axis. The blades are made of a material that allows them to flex enough to provide the necessary flapping and dragging.

Helicopter Powerplants

The lack of suitable powerplants slowed the development of the helicopter. Some helicopters use reciprocating engines similar to those used in airplanes, but the ideal powerplant is a turbine engine, and almost all modern helicopters except the small trainers are turbine powered.

Reciprocating Engines

Some reciprocating engines are mounted with their crankshaft vertical, and these engines must have dry sump lubrication systems which carry their oil supply in tanks outside of the engine. The engines in some of the smaller helicopters are mounted horizontally and drive the transmission through a series of V belts.

A helicopter has two engine problems that are not shared with airplanes. Helicopters have no propeller to act as a flywheel and to supply cooling air to the cylinders. The engine is coupled through the transmission to the rotor, and so must be operated with a higher idling speed than a comparable airplane engine. The engine is cooled by belt-driven blowers that force air through the engine cooling fins.

The engine of a helicopter is controlled differently from the engine of an airplane. The power output is controlled by a linkage to the collective pitch control that supplies the fuel needed to maintain the desired engine and rotor RPM. When the collective pitch is increased, the rotor loads the engine, and additional fuel is supplied to bring the engine speed back up to the desired RPM. The relationship between the indications of the tachometer and mani-fold pressure gage gives the pilot an indication of the power the engine is supplying to the rotor.

Turbine Engines

The requirement for relatively constant engine speed, small size, and light weight makes the turbine engine ideal for helicopters. For this reason, almost all helicopters except the small trainers are powered by turboshaft engines.

Turboshaft engines used in helicopters may be of either the direct-shaft or the free-turbine type. Direct-shaft engines have a single rotating element and are similar to turbojet engines except that they have additional turbine stages. These extra turbine stages extract additional energy from the expand-ing gases and use it to drive the rotor through the transmission. A free-turbine engine has one or more turbine stages that drive an output shaft that is entirely independent of the rotating element in the gas-generator portion of the engine. Free-turbine engines may be designed so that the output shaft extends from either the hot end or the cold end.

Transmission

The engine drives the rotor through a transmission that reduces the engine output shaft speed to the much lower speed needed to drive the rotor. Some transmissions are mounted directly on the engine and others are driven by a splined shaft. The transmission on some of the smaller helicopters is driven from the engine with a series of rubber V belts.

The tail rotor is usually driven from the transmission, so its speed is directly proportional to the speed of the main rotor.

Clutch

Reciprocating engines and direct-shaft turbine engines must have some form of clutch between the engine and the transmission to remove the load of the rotor from the engine when the engine is being started. These clutches are often automatic, so that they are disengaged when the engine is being started, but as soon as the engine reaches a predetermined speed, they automatically engage and couple the engine to the rotor. Helicopters normally have a dual tachometer with one needle indicating the engine speed and the other the rotor speed. When the clutch is only partially engaged, the needles are split, but when it is fully engaged, the needles are superimposed and are said to be "married."

Free-turbine engines do not need a clutch, as the engine is not connected to the gas-generator portion of the engine and therefore does not place any load on the starter.

Some of the smaller helicopters that drive the transmission through V belts use a manual belt tightener as a clutch. The belts are loosened for starting the engine, and when the rotors are to be engaged, the belt tightener is engaged by the pilot and the transmission is gradually connected to the engine.

Freewheeling Unit

All helicopters must have some means of disconnecting the engine from the rotor in case of engine failure. These units are always automatically operated and are often of the sprag type seen in Figure 4-66.

When the engine is driving the rotor, the rollers bind between the sprocket and the cam, and the sprocket drives the cam. Any time the engine slows and the drive sprocket speed drops below that of the output shaft, the cam allows the rollers to move back away from the sprocket and disengage the rotor from the engine. As part of the pretakeoff check, the throttle is rolled back enough for the engine speed to drop below the rotor speed. This allows the pilot to determine that the rotor disengages. When the throttle is opened, the engine speed increases and the freewheeling unit re-engages.

Rollers bind between sprocket and cam. Sprocket drives cam and stub shaft.

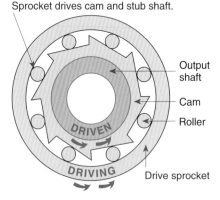

Output shaft

Cam

Roller

Drive sprocket

Freewheeling unit engaged, with engine driving rotor

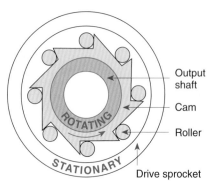

Output shaft

Cam

Roller

Drive sprocket

Freewheeling unit disengaged, in autorotation position

Figure 4-66. *Sprag-type freewheeling unit*

Helicopter Vibrations

Any device with the rotating mass a helicopter has is bound to have vibrations, and to complicate these vibrations, aerodynamic forces produce additional vibrations. As a result, vibration is a major problem with helicopters.

Before you can correct abnormal vibrations, you should understand them. There are two basic types of vibration, lateral and vertical, and two basic frequency ranges: low frequency and high frequency.

Low-frequency vibrations are those that are related to the main rotor and are usually classified as 1:1 or 2:1. This means that the vibration frequency is the same as the rotor RPM (1:1) or twice the rotor speed (2:1).

Low-frequency vertical vibration is usually caused by one rotor blade producing more lift than the other. This is usually caused by the blades having the wrong pitch angle or not being adjusted for proper track. Low-frequency lateral vibration is caused by the main rotor blades being out of static balance.

High-frequency vibrations are felt as a buzz rather than a beat and are usually associated with the engine, cooling fan, or the tail rotor.

The first step in minimizing the vibration is to be sure that the rotors are in static balance, both spanwise and chordwise. Chordwise balance of a semirigid rotor is obtained by changing the length of the drag braces at the root of the rotor blade. Articulated rotors are balanced by balancing the hub without any blades installed, and balancing each of the blades against a master blade. The final balancing is done in flight.

When the main rotor has been statically balanced and installed on the helicopter, you must check it for track.

An early method of blade tracking was to have the blade tips leave colored marks on the cloth curtain of a tracking flag. The blade tips were marked with colored wax crayons, a different color on each tip. The engine was started and the helicopter lifted, almost to a hover, and a tracking flag, like the one in Figure 4-67, was very carefully tilted in toward the rotor until the tips just touched the flag curtain.

When the tips touched the curtain, they left marks on the cloth. The colors of these marks showed which blade was flying high and which was flying low. Pitch adjustments were made so the blades followed in the same track.

A much better way to track a rotor is by using strobe lights, as shown in Figure 4-68 on the next page. The advantage of strobe tracking is that it can be done in flight, and much more can be determined about the true track of the rotor than can be done with the older flag method.

For this method, distinctive reflectors are installed on the tips of each of the rotor blades, and the helicopter is flown. Shine a strobe light on the rotor blade tips and observe the reflections. If the blades are in track, the reflections will form a straight line, and if they do not, you will be able to determine which blade is riding high or low by the identity of its reflection.

The state-of-the-art method of checking helicopter vibration involves using an electronic balancer/analyzer such as the Chadwick-Helmuth Model 8500C shown in Figure 4-69. This instrument eliminates the need for sepa-

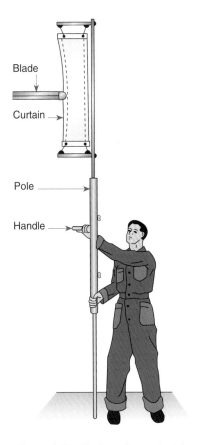

Figure 4-67. *Checking the track of the blades of a helicopter rotor using a cloth tracking flag*

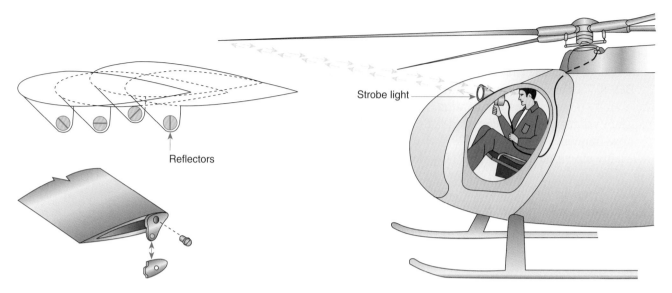

Figure 4-68. *Checking helicopter rotor blade track with a strobe light*

rate track and balance calculations, and it eliminates the need for costly flight tests to determine whether or not the adjustments were correct.

Complete vibration information on the specific helicopter or airplane is stored in a personal computer (PC), and when a vibration check is to be made, this information is downloaded to a disc which is inserted into the balancer/analyzer and is taken to the aircraft. Here it shows where to install sensors, connect cables, and the correct location for the balancing weights.

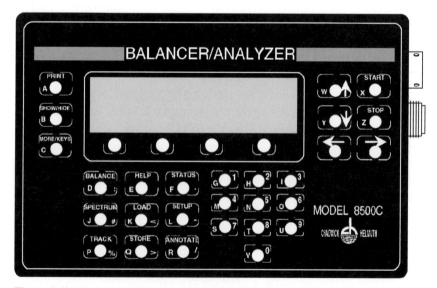

Figure 4-69. *The Chadwick-Helmuth Model 8500C is a state-of-the-art balancer/analyzer that allows you to take the correct action to minimize vibrations in a helicopter.*

A typical track and balancing test flight consists of a hover, then a forward flight at 130 knots, and the return to land. During this flight, the balancer/analyzer gathers data, determines corrective action, and displays the solution. Changes to weight, sweep, pitch link, and tab are made as indicated, and a second flight is made to verify the results. The vibration was measured in two flight regimes, but the corrections that were chosen by the balancer/analyzer minimize vibration for all speeds from hover to the never-exceed speed V_{NE}.

blade track. The condition of a helicopter rotor in which each blade follows in exactly the same path as the blade ahead of it.

STUDY QUESTIONS: HELICOPTER ASSEMBLY AND RIGGING

Answers are on Page 317. **Page numbers refer to chapter text.**

44. The throttle of a helicopter is automatically controlled by movement of the _____ (collective or cyclic) pitch control. *Page 304*

45. The twist-grip throttle control is mounted on the _____ (collective or cyclic) pitch control. *Page 305*

46. When the cyclic control is moved backward, the pitch of the advancing blade is _____ (increased or decreased). *Page 305*

47. The direction a helicopter moves in flight is determined by the direction the _____ is tilted. *Page 305*

48. The main rotor of most single-rotor helicopters rotates to the _____ (right or left) as viewed from above. *Page 308*

49. Torque on a single-rotor helicopter is compensated by varying the _____ (pitch or speed) of the tail rotor. *Page 308*

50. To compensate for drift caused by thrust of the tail rotor, the main rotor mast is offset a few degrees to the _____ (right or left). *Page 308*

51. The horizontal stabilizer on a helicopter is designed to hold the fuselage relatively level in _____ (high or low) speed flight. *Page 306*

52. When the pitch of the advancing blade is increased, the helicopter will rotate nose _____ (up or down). *Page 305*

53. Another name for the drag hinge in a helicopter rotor is the _____ hinge. *Page 310*

Continued

54. The blades of a rigid rotor are allowed to rotate about their _____ (flap, drag, or feather) axis. *Page 311*

55. Fully articulated rotor blades typically have _____ (two or more than two) blades. *Page 310*

56. Cooling air for a helicopter reciprocating engine is normally provided by an engine-driven _____ . *Page 311*

57. A helicopter with a free-turbine engine _____ (does or does not) require a clutch between the engine and the transmission. *Page 312*

58. A helicopter with a free-turbine engine _____ (does or does not) require a freewheeling system between the rotor and the transmission. *Page 312*

59. Low frequency vibrations in a helicopter are normally related to the _____ . *Page 313*

60. A 1:1 vertical vibration is usually caused by a main rotor blade being out of _____ (balance or track). *Page 313*

61. A 1:1 lateral vibration is usually caused by a main rotor blade being out of _____ (balance or track). *Page 313*

62. A strobe light check of blade track _____ (can or cannot) be made in flight. *Page 313*

Answers to Chapter 4 Study Questions

1. greater	22. 100	43. up
2. outer	23. 3	44. collective
3. up	24. should	45. collective
4. speed brakes	25. closed	46. increased
5. elevons	26. torque	47. rotor disc
6. ruddervators	27. hydraulic	48. left
7. downward	28. Type Certificate Data Sheets	49. pitch
8. before	29. front	50. left
9. Fowler	30. in	51. high
10. increases	31. symmetry	52. up
11. increase	32. should not	53. lead-lag
12. does not	33. 73	54. feather
13. opposite	34. 52	55. more than two
14. servo	35. 2	56. blower
15. opposite	36. 3	57. does not
16. high	37. 4	58. does
17. same	38. up	59. main rotor
18. down	39. down	60. track
19. aft	40. up	61. balance
20. 100	41. up	62. can
21. $\frac{1}{8}$	42. right	

HYDRAULIC AND PNEUMATIC POWER SYSTEMS

5

Continued

Hydraulic System Components   *343*

Continued

HYDRAULIC AND PNEUMATIC POWER SYSTEMS

5

An Introduction to Fluid Power Systems

Fluid power systems are mechanical systems in which a moving fluid performs work. This fluid may be either a compressible gas or an incompressible liquid. Systems that use compressible fluids are called pneumatic systems, and those that use incompressible fluids are called hydraulic systems.

Historical Overview

With the free and almost unlimited power available in flowing water, much early human industry was located along rivers. People used water for transportation, and diverted water to flow over large wooden waterwheels that turned shafts inside factory buildings. Pulleys and belts drove the lathes and drill presses from these water-driven shafts.

As civilization moved westward and farming and cattle raising became important industries, the all-essential water was taken from wells by pumps driven by windmills, a pneumatic device.

Today we still use waterwheels and windmills, although the form has changed. Instead of using slow-turning waterwheels to drive the machine tools, we use high-speed turbines, driven by water collected behind huge dams, to generate the electricity that drives our industrial tools. Modern windmills also use the inexhaustible power in moving air to drive electrical generators.

Modern aircraft would not be nearly as efficient as they are if it were not for fluid power systems. Hydraulic brakes allow the pilot to control the aircraft on the ground without using complex mechanical linkage. Hydraulic retraction systems pull the heavy landing gear up into the wheel wells to reduce wind resistance, and hydraulically boosted controls make it possible for human and automatic pilots to fly heavy, high-speed jet transport aircraft. High-pressure pneumatic systems are used as backups for hydraulic systems, and low-pressure pneumatic systems drive many of the gyro-operated flight instruments. Pneumatic deicer systems break off ice that has formed on the leading edges of the flight surfaces.

fluid power. The transmission of force by the movement of a fluid.

The most familiar examples of fluid power systems are hydraulic and pneumatic systems.

fluid. A substance, either a liquid or a gas, that flows and tends to conform to the shape of its container.

turbine. A rotary device actuated by impulse or reaction of a fluid flowing through vanes or blades that are arranged around a central shaft.

hydraulics. The system of fluid power which transmits force through an incompressible fluid.

pneumatics. The system of fluid power which transmits force by the use of a compressible fluid.

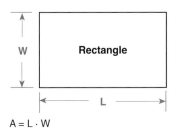

A = L · W

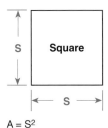

A = S²

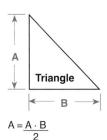

$A = \dfrac{A \cdot B}{2}$

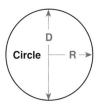

A = π · R² or 0.7854 · D²

Figure 5-1. *Formulas for finding area*

Basic Laws of Physics

Fluid power systems are essentially systems for gaining a mechanical advantage. The law of conservation of energy does not allow us to create nor destroy energy, but we have a wide latitude of things we can do with the energy we have. Most of the energy we use is involved in doing work for us.

Review of Terms and Relationships

Here, we will review some of the terms and the principles of basic physics used in this study. There is a comprehensive discussion of Basic Physics in the *Aviation Maintenance Technician Series, General* textbook.

Area

Area is measured in square inches or square feet in the English system, and in square centimeters and square meters in the metric system.

To find the area of a plane rectangular surface, multiply the surface's length by its width.

Area = Length · Width

Find the area of a square by squaring the length of one of its sides.

Area = Side²

The area of a plane triangular figure is exactly one half of the area of a rectangle whose sides are the same length as the base and the altitude of the triangle.

Area = (Base · Altitude) ÷ 2

In most hydraulic and pneumatic actuators, the fluid acts on a piston that has a circular head. To find the area of a circle, use the formula:

Area = π · R²
π = 3.1416
R = radius of the piston head

A simpler formula uses the diameter of the piston rather than its radius:

Area = 0.7854 x D²
0.7854 = a constant (or, π ÷ 4)
D = diameter of the piston head

The constant 0.7854 is near enough to ¾ (75%) to allow you to quickly estimate the area of a circle by squaring its diameter and taking three-quarters of this value. To find the approximate area of a circle with a 10-inch diameter, square its diameter (10² = 100) and multiply this by 0.75. The approximate area is 75 square inches. The actual area is 78.54 square inches.

Distance

Practical mechanics is concerned with movement. The distance an object is moved enters into many computations.

Distance is measured in inches or feet in the English system, and in centimeters or meters in the metric system.

Volume

Many fluid power computations find or use the amount of fluid available or the amount of fluid moved.

Fluid volume is measured in cubic units. The English system uses cubic inches or cubic feet; the metric system uses cubic centimeters or cubic meters.

Find the volume of a square or rectangular container by multiplying the length, width, and height of the container.

Volume = Length · Width · Height

Find the volume of a cylinder by multiplying the area of its end by its height.

Volume = $0.7854 \cdot \text{Diameter}^2 \cdot \text{Height}$

Find the volume of a spherical container (such as an accumulator), with this formula:

Volume = $(\pi \div 6) \cdot D^3$

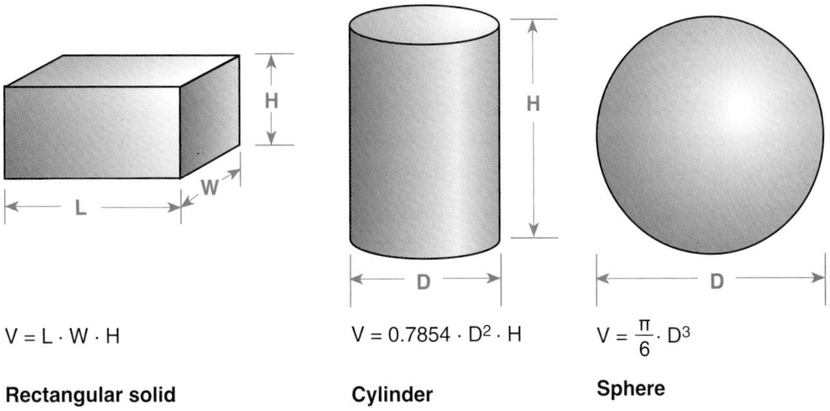

$V = L \cdot W \cdot H$

Rectangular solid

$V = 0.7854 \cdot D^2 \cdot H$

Cylinder

$V = \dfrac{\pi}{6} \cdot D^3$

Sphere

Figure 5-2. *Formulas for finding volume*

circle. A closed plane figure with every point an equal distance from the center. A circle has the greatest area for its circumference of any enclosed shape.

rectangle. A plane surface with four sides whose opposite sides are parallel and whose angles are all right angles.

square. A four-sided plane figure whose sides are all the same length, whose opposite sides are parallel, and whose angles are all right angles.

triangle. A three-sided, closed plane figure. The sum of the three angles in a triangle is always equal to 180°.

constant. A value used in a mathematical computation that is the same every time it is used.

For example, the relationship between the length of the circumference of a circle and the length of its diameter is a constant, 3.1416. This constant is called by the Greek name of pi (π).

work. The product of force times distance.

force. Energy brought to bear on an object that tends to cause motion or to change motion.

foot-pound. A measure of work accomplished when a force of 1 pound moves an object a distance of 1 foot.

inch-pound. A measure of work accomplished when a force of 1 pound moves an object a distance of 1 inch.

gram. The basic unit of weight or mass in the metric system. One gram equals about 0.035 ounce.

kilogram. One thousand grams.

horsepower. A unit of mechanical power that is equal to 33,000 foot-pounds of work done in 1 minute, or 550 foot-pounds of work done in 1 second.

Figure 5-3. *Relationship between force, pressure, and area*
F=P·A

Work

Work is the product of a force multiplied by the distance over which the force acts.

When you lift a 10-pound weight 4 feet, you are doing 40 foot-pounds of work. And, if a 10-pound force pushes a 200-pound handcart across the hangar floor for a distance of 4 feet, it is doing 40 foot-pounds of work.

It requires the same amount of work to carry a case of oil up a flight of stairs in one trip with all of the cans in a box as to carry the same amount of oil up the same stairs in many trips, carrying one can at a time. Work is simply force times distance, and does not consider time.

In the English system of measurement, work is expressed in such units as foot-pounds, inch-pounds, or inch-ounces. In the metric system, work is measured in meter-kilograms or centimeter-grams.

Power

Power is a measure of the amount of work done in a given period of time. If you lift a 10-pound weight 4 feet in 1 second, you use 40 foot-pounds per second. Find power by dividing the amount of work by the amount of time used to do it.

Power = (Force · Distance) ÷ Time

The horsepower is the standard unit of mechanical power. One horsepower is 33,000 foot-pounds of work done in 1 minute, or 550 foot-pounds of work done in 1 second. One horsepower is also equal to 746 watts of electrical power.

In the metric system, 1 metric horsepower is 4,500 meter-kilograms of work done in 1 minute, or 75 meter-kilograms of work done in 1 second. One metric horsepower is equal to 0.986 horsepower.

Compute power in a hydraulic system by multiplying the flow rate in gallons per minute by the pressure of the fluid in pounds per square inch. This gives the force-distance-time relationship. One gallon is equal to 231 cubic inches, and a flow of 1 gallon per minute (gpm) under a pressure of 1 pound per square inch (psi) will produce 0.000 583 horsepower.

Horsepower = gpm · psi · 0.000 583

Relationship Between Force, Pressure and Area

In the English system of measurement, force is measured in pounds, area in square inches, and pressure in pounds per square inch.

The amount of force a fluid power system can produce is determined by the amount of pressure used and the area on which the pressure is acting. The relationship between pressure, force, and area is illustrated in the circle in Figure 5-3. The value of the upper half of the circle is equal to the product of the two lower quarters of the circle.

Some examples of this relationship are:

A 1,000-psi hydraulic system, acting on a piston with an area of 0.5 square inch, will produce a force of 500 pounds.

$$F = P \cdot A$$
$$= 1,000 \cdot 0.5$$
$$= 500 \text{ pounds}$$

The area needed for a 1,000-psi hydraulic system to produce a force of 5,000 pounds is 5 square inches.

$$A = F \div P$$
$$= 5,000 \div 1,000$$
$$= 5 \text{ square inches}$$

A pressure of 2,500 psi is needed to act on a piston with an area of 2 square inches to produce 5,000 pounds of force.

$$P = F \div A$$
$$= 5,000 \div 2$$
$$= 2,500 \text{ psi}$$

Relationship Between Volume, Area and Distance

Find the amount of fluid needed to move an actuator using the relationship illustrated in Figure 5-4. With this relationship, you can find the amount of fluid needed to move a piston of a given size a given distance. Or, find the distance a given amount of fluid will move the piston, or the size piston needed for a given distance of movement when you know the volume of the fluid.

When a piston with an area of 20 square inches is moved into a cylinder for a distance of 5 inches, 100 cubic inches of fluid will be displaced.

$$V = A \cdot D$$
$$= 20 \cdot 5$$
$$= 100 \text{ cubic inches}$$

To move 100 cubic inches of fluid from a cylinder with a piston movement of 5 inches, the piston must have an area of 20 square inches.

$$A = V \div D$$
$$= 100 \div 5$$
$$= 20 \text{ square inches}$$

A piston with an area of 20 square inches will displace 100 cubic inches of fluid when it is moved 5 inches into a cylinder.

$$D = V \div A$$
$$= 100 \div 20$$
$$= 5 \text{ inches}$$

power. The time rate of doing work. Power is force multiplied by distance (work), divided by time.

pressure. Force per unit area. Hydraulic and pneumatic pressure are normally given in units of pounds per square inch (psi).

watt. The basic unit of electrical power. One watt is equal to 1/746 horsepower.

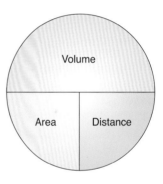

Figure 5-4. *Relationship between volume, area, and distance*
$V = A \cdot D$

potential energy. Energy that is possessed
by an object because of its position,
configuration, or by the chemical arrangement of its constituents.

kinetic energy. Energy that is possessed
by an object because of its motion.

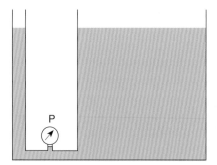

Figure 5-5. *The pressure exerted by a
column of fluid is determined by the
density of the fluid and by the height of the
top of the fluid above the bottom of the
container.*

Liquid	Density (pounds per cubic inch)
Gasoline	0.02602
JP-4	0.02857
Methyl alcohol	0.02926
Kerosine	0.02961
Oil (petroleum)	0.03178
Oil (synthetic)	0.03359
Water (fresh)	0.03615

Figure 5-6. *Density of various liquids*

The Law of Conservation of Energy

We can neither create nor destroy energy, but we can change the form of the
energy in order to use it. When the form is changed, we have exactly the same
amount of energy we started with.

Most mechanical devices produce less useful work than is put into them.
This is because of friction or inefficiency, but the total energy output is the
same as the total energy input.

Energy in a fluid power system may be in one of two forms: potential or
kinetic. Potential energy in a fluid power system is expressed in the pressure
of the fluid, and kinetic energy is expressed in the velocity of the moving fluid.

Relationship Between Height and Pressure

The pressure a static fluid exerts is determined by the height of the fluid, and
has nothing to do with its volume. If the height of the liquid in a piece of half-
inch tubing is exactly the same as the height of the liquid in a 100-gallon tank,
the pressure at the bottom of the tube will be exactly the same as the pressure
at the bottom of the tank. *See* Figure 5-5.

One gallon of pure water weighs 8.35 pounds and contains 231 cubic
inches. Therefore a one-square inch column of water 231 inches high exerts
a force on the bottom of the container of 8.35 pounds and produces a pressure of 8.35 pounds per square inch. If the water level in a 100 gallon tank is
231 inches above the bottom, every square inch of bottom area is acted on
by 8.35 pounds of force, and the pressure is 8.35 psi. Neither the shape of the
container nor the amount of water has any effect on the pressure. Pressure is
determined only by the density of the fluid and by the height of the top of the
fluid above the bottom of the container.

The densities of common liquids you as an aviation maintenance technician are likely to encounter are listed in Figure 5-6.

To find the pressure exerted by a column of fluid, use this formula:

Pressure $=$ Density $\cdot$ Height

Find the pressure at the bottom of a tank of kerosine whose height is 60 inches.
Use the formula:

$$
\begin{aligned}
\text{Pressure} &= \text{Density} \cdot \text{Height} \\
&= 0.02961 \cdot 60 \\
&= 1.78 \text{ psi}
\end{aligned}
$$

Pascal's Law

Pascal's law explains the way power is transmitted in a closed hydraulic or pneumatic system. Stated in simple terms, Pascal's law says that pressure in an enclosed container is transmitted equally and undiminished to all parts of the container, and it acts at right angles to the walls that enclose it.

Figure 5-7 shows an open container that is filled with a liquid. Pressure gages show that the pressure is determined by the difference between the height of the gage and the top of the liquid.

In Figure 5-8, a piston is placed on the top of the liquid and the weight (W) presses down on it. This creates a pressure inside the container of liquid, and the pressure on each of the gages increases by the same amount.

Find the amount of pressure increase by multiplying the area of the piston by the force caused by the weight. It is the same on every one of the gages regardless of their position in the system, or of the shape of the container.

Pascal's law explains why automobile hydraulic brakes have equal braking action, for example. When the brake pedal is depressed, the pressure is transmitted equally to each of the wheels regardless of the distance between the brake master cylinder and the wheel cylinder.

static. Still, not moving

Pascal's law. A basic law of fluid power which states that the pressure in an enclosed container is transmitted equally and undiminished to all points of the container, and the force acts at right angles to the enclosing walls.

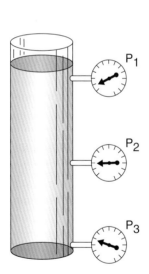

Figure 5-7. *The pressure produced by liquid in an open container is caused by the height of the liquid above the point at which the pressure is measured. The higher the liquid above the gage, the greater the pressure.*

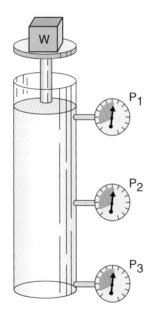

Figure 5-8. *When pressure is applied to a liquid in a closed container, the pressure rises to the same amount in all parts of the container.*

Mechanical Advantage

An application of Pascal's law shows the mechanical advantage in a hydraulic system. To briefly review the principle of mechanical advantage, look at the balance in Figure 5-9.

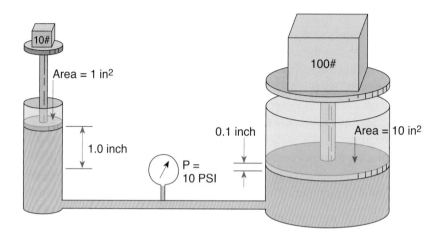

Figure 5-9. *Hydraulic cylinders produce a mechanical advantage. The work done by the small piston is exactly the same as that done by the large piston. A small force on the small piston will produce a large force on the large piston, but the small piston must travel farther than the large one.*

Figure 5-9 is a simple hydraulic jack. The small piston has an area of 1 square inch, and the large piston has an area of 10 square inches. When a force of 10 pounds is applied to the small piston, a pressure of 10 psi is built up in the fluid. According to Pascal's law, this pressure is the same throughout the system, and 10 pounds of force acts on each square inch of the large piston. This pressure produces a force of 100 pounds on the large piston that lifts the weight.

When the small piston moves down 1 inch, 1 cubic inch of fluid is forced out of the small cylinder into the large cylinder. This fluid spreads out over the entire large piston and it raises it only 0.1 inch. The small piston must move down 10 inches to raise the large piston 1 inch.

The work done by the small piston is 10 inches times 10 pounds, or 100 inch-pounds. The work done by the large piston is also 100 inch-pounds (1 inch x 100 pounds).

Hydraulic systems are quite efficient, and we do not usually consider system losses in the study of practical hydraulic systems.

Bernoulli's Principle

Pascal's law deals with the static, or still, condition of the fluid. When fluid is in motion, other things happen, and these are best explained by Bernoulli's principle.

When considering fluid in motion, start with the premise that the total amount of energy in the fluid remains constant. No energy is added to the fluid, nor is any lost from it.

Bernoulli's principle explains the relationship between pressure and velocity in a stream of moving fluid. The total energy in the fluid is made up of potential energy and kinetic energy. The potential energy relates to the pressure of the fluid, and the kinetic energy relates to its velocity. *See* Figure 5-10.

An incompressible fluid flowing through a tube with a constant cross-sectional area has a specific velocity. This fluid exerts a given amount of pressure on the wall of the tube. When the fluid flows through the restriction, it speeds up and its kinetic energy increases. Since the total energy remains constant, the increase in kinetic energy results in an accompanying decrease in potential energy, its pressure.

When the fluid leaves the restricted area and returns to the original size tube, its velocity decreases to its original value and its pressure rises back to its original value.

Bernoulli's principle tells us that as long as the total energy in a flow of fluid remains constant, any increase in the velocity of the fluid will result in a decrease in the pressure that is exerted by the fluid.

Bernoulli's principle. The basic principle that explains the relation between kinetic energy and potential energy in fluids that are in motion.

When the total energy in a column of moving fluid remains constant, any increase in the kinetic energy of the fluid (its velocity) results in a decrease in its potential energy (its pressure).

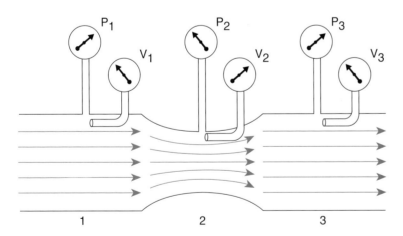

Figure 5-10. *The total energy in the fluid flowing through this venturi tube remains constant at all points.*

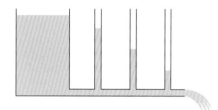

Figure 5-11. *The friction encountered as fluid flows through a tube causes a pressure drop.*

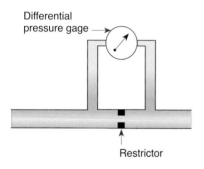

Figure 5-12. *When fluid flows through a restrictor, pressure is dropped across it that is proportional to the rate of flow.*

restrictor. A fluid power system component that controls the rate of actuator movement by restricting the flow of fluid into or out of the actuator.

hydraulic fuse. A type of flow control valve that allows a normal flow of fluid in the system but, if the flow rate is excessive, or if too much fluid flows for normal operation, the fuse will shut off all further flow.

Pressure Drop in Moving Fluid

There are many similarities between the flow of electrons in an electrical system and the flow of fluid in a fluid power system. One of these similarities is the drop in pressure as the flow of fluid encounters an opposition. This is the same as the drop in voltage caused by current flowing through a resistance.

Figure 5-11 shows the way the pressure drops along a tube through which fluid is flowing. The pressure in the reservoir is shown by the height of the liquid. The pressure decreases along the line leaving the reservoir as is indicated by the height of the fluid in each of the vertical tubes. The friction encountered by the fluid causes the pressure drop in the same way resistance in an electrical system causes a pressure drop.

The pressure drop in a moving fluid can be used in fluid control devices like hydraulic fuses. When fluid flowing through a tube encounters a restrictor, pressure is dropped across it. The amount of this pressure drop is proportional to the rate of flow of the fluid. In a hydraulic fuse, an excessive rate of flow will cause enough pressure drop to shut off all flow.

Advantages and Disadvantages of Fluid Power Systems

There are three primary systems for actuating landing gear, flaps, control surfaces, airstair doors, and other devices on an aircraft; these are hydraulic, pneumatic, and electrical. Each of these systems has advantages and disadvantages.

A number of aircraft use electric motors to raise and lower the landing gear and to operate the wing flaps. Some aircraft use high-pressure compressed air to actuate these devices as well as the brakes. In a majority of aircraft, however, these devices are actuated by hydraulic power.

Some of the simplest airplanes use hydraulic brakes, and many use hydraulic actuators to raise and lower the landing gear. Large airplanes also use hydraulic power to operate the primary flight controls.

Hydraulic systems are highly efficient, and experience very little loss due to fluid friction. They are lightweight and easy to maintain and can produce almost any force needed. Hydraulic systems can operate with a stalled actuator without causing any fire danger. Backup systems are simple, with electrically operated pumps or hand pumps to take over in the event of failure of an engine-driven pump, and in case of the loss of all hydraulic fluid, emergency backup pneumatic systems can use stored high-pressure compressed air to lower the landing gear and actuate the brakes.

Pneumatic systems have an additional advantage in that they use air as their operating fluid, and since there is an unlimited supply of air, no return system is needed. The air is compressed, directed to the actuator, and used, and then it is exhausted overboard.

Fluid power systems do have disadvantages. All of the actuators must be connected to the system with tubing that carries high-pressure fluid. These lines and fittings have considerably more weight than wires used in electrical systems, and fluid is prone to leak, especially when it is required to pass through fittings that allow movement. The high-pressure air that is used in pneumatic systems requires special care in its operation, as it can be quite dangerous if improperly handled. Charged high-pressure gas resevoirs are considered Class C explosives by the Department of Transportation.

STUDY QUESTIONS: AN INTRODUCTION TO FLUID POWER SYSTEMS

*Answers begin on Page 416. **Page numbers refer to chapter text.***

1. A fluid power system that uses a noncompressible fluid is called a _____ (hydraulic or pneumatic) system. *Page 323*

2. A fluid power system that uses a compressible fluid is called a _____ (hydraulic or pneumatic) system. *Page 323*

3. A hydraulic piston that has a diameter of 3.0 inches has an area of _____ square inches. *Page 324*

4. A cylindrical hydraulic reservoir that has a diameter of 6.0 inches and a height of 8.0 inches has a volume of _____ cubic inches. *Page 325*

5. A spherical container whose diameter is 12 inches has a volume of _____ cubic inches. *Page 325*

6. A 395-pound drum of oil is rolled 40 feet across the hangar floor. It requires a force of 15 pounds to roll the drum. The work done in rolling this drum is _____ foot-pounds. *Page 326*

7. The amount of power needed to raise a weight is increased when the time used to raise it is _____ (increased or decreased). *Page 326*

8. One horsepower is the equivalent of _____ foot-pounds of work done in one minute. *Page 326*

9. One horsepower is the equivalent of _____ foot-pounds of work done in one second. *Page 326*

Continued

10. One horsepower is equivalent to _____ watts of electrical power. *Page 326*

11. A 700-pound engine is raised with a hoist for a distance of 5 feet in 30 seconds. This requires _____ horsepower. *Page 326*

12. One U.S. gallon is equal to _____ cubic inches. *Page 326*

13. A flow of 3 gallons per minute of hydraulic fluid under a pressure of 1,000 psi produces _____ horsepower. *Page 326*

14. A 3,000-psi hydraulic system acts on a piston having an area of 2 square inches. The piston produces _____ pounds of force. *Page 327*

15. A force of 4,000 pounds is required by a 1,000-psi hydraulic system. This force will require a piston having an area of _____ square inches. *Page 327*

16. For a piston with an area of 2.0 square inch to produce a force of 500 pounds, a hydraulic hand pump must furnish _____ psi of pressure. *Page 327*

17. When a piston with an area of 3.0 square inches is moved 6.0 inches, _____ cubic inches of fluid will be moved. *Page 327*

18. For a piston with an area of 6.0 square inches to move 36 cubic inches of fluid, it must be moved _____ inches. *Page 327*

19. A piston must move 100 cubic inches of fluid when it is moved 5.0 inches. In order to do this, the piston must have an area of _____ square inches. *Page 327*

20. Kinetic energy in a fluid power system is in the form of the _____ (pressure or velocity) of the fluid. *Page 331*

21. Potential energy in a fluid power system is in the form of the _____ (pressure or velocity) of the fluid. *Page 331*

22. The pressure on the bottom of a reservoir caused by kerosine that has a level of 18 inches above the bottom is _____ psi. *Page 328*

23. A hydraulic jack requires a force on the handle of 30 pounds to exert a force of 600 pounds on the object being raised. The jack has a mechanical advantage of _____. *Page 330*

24. According to Bernoulli's principle, when the total energy in a column of moving fluid remains constant, an increase in the velocity of the fluid results in a corresponding _____ (increase or decrease) in the pressure. *Page 331*

25. The pressure drop caused by an obstruction in a line carrying a flow of fluid is directly proportional to the _____ (rate or volume) of flow. *Page 332*

Basic Aircraft Hydraulic Systems

All hydraulic systems must have several basic components, a fluid to transmit the force, a reservoir to hold the fluid, a pump to move the fluid, an actuator to change the flow of fluid into mechanical work, lines to carry the fluid, and valves to control the flow and pressure of the fluid. Other components increase the efficiency of the systems.

The hydraulic systems in a modern airplane can be quite complex, but they become less difficult to understand when we look at the way the systems have evolved from the most simple to the complete modern system.

When flying was less complex than it is today, there was little need for hydraulic systems. Airplanes flew so slowly that drag was no great concern, so the landing gear did not need to be retracted. Landing speeds were so slow that there was no need for wing flaps, and once the airplane was on the ground, the tail skid served as a very effective brake. Paved runways, however brought about the need for brakes, and the first simple hydraulic system came into being.

Sealed Brake System

A diaphragm-type master cylinder and an expander tube brake such as the one in Figure 5-13 is a complete hydraulic system in its simplest form.

The entire system is sealed, and when the brake pedal is depressed, it moves a diaphragm which forces fluid into a synthetic rubber expander tube mounted around a frame on the wheel. When fluid expands the tube, it pushes against asbestos-type brake blocks, and they produce friction with the brake drum that rotates with the wheel. When the brake pedal is released, the return spring moves the diaphragm back and releases the brake. This type of system is so small that expansion of the fluid caused by heat is taken up by the flexibility of the diaphragm in the master cylinders.

actuator. A fluid power device that changes fluid pressure into mechanical movement.

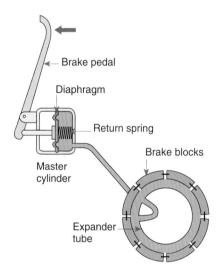

Figure 5-13. *The expander-tube brake and diaphragm-type master cylinder is the simplest type of hydraulic system.*

Reservoir-Type Brake System

Heavier and faster airplanes require more pressure and a greater volume of fluid to operate the brakes. This requirement brought about the vented brake system similar to the one used in automobiles.

The master cylinder is a single-acting pump. The piston is moved inward by the pilot's foot, and it is returned by a spring when foot pressure is released.

Figure 5-14 illustrates this system. The first movement of the piston closes the compensator port in the master cylinder, and the piston forces fluid into the wheel cylinder. This moves the wheel pistons outward, which forces the brake linings against the inside of the rotating brake drum to create the friction that slows the airplane. When the pedal is released, a spring forces the master cylinder piston back beyond the compensator port, and the entire system is vented to the atmosphere through the reservoir. When heat expands the fluid, it backs up into the reservoir and does not create any pressure in the system that could cause the brakes to drag. When there is a small leak in the brake lines or wheel cylinders, the master cylinder replaces the fluid lost each time the piston is moved back beyond the compensator port.

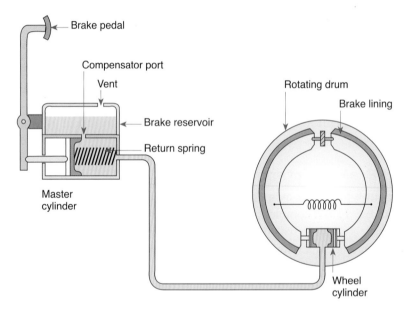

Figure 5-14. *A reservoir-type master cylinder vents the lines and wheel cylinders to the atmosphere through the compensator port to prevent heat expansion of the fluid from causing the brakes to drag. It also replenishes fluid lost in the system.*

Single-Acting Actuator System

As airplane weight and speed increased, flaps were installed that allowed the pilot to slow the airplane for landing. Many of the flaps on the small airplanes were mechanically operated, but some used single-acting hydraulic cylinders. The selector valve was rotated to the FLAPS-DOWN position and the hand pump was pumped. Fluid forced the piston in the flap actuator to move the flaps down. When the pilot rotated the selector valve to the FLAPS-UP position, a spring inside the flap actuator moved the piston back, raising the flaps and returning the fluid to the reservoir. Two check valves inside the pump allow as much fluid to be pumped as is needed to lower the flaps.

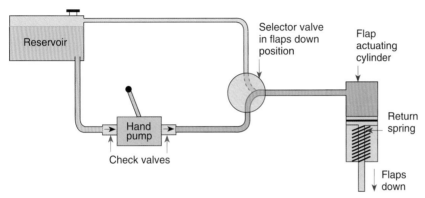

Figure 5-15. *A selector valve allows fluid from the hand pump to go to the actuator cylinder, or to return from the actuator to the reservoir.*

Double-Acting Actuator System

A single-acting actuator is satisfactory for hydraulic brakes and for very simple wing flaps, but when airplanes began to fly fast enough that parasite drag became a major problem, retractable landing gear was installed that required double-acting actuators. These actuators use hydraulic pressure to move the actuator piston in both directions.

Figure 5-16 on the next page illustrates a very simple system using a reservoir, a hand pump, a selector valve, and a double-acting actuator. To lower the landing gear, turn the selector valve to the GEAR-DOWN position and actuate the hand pump. Fluid under pressure enters the top of the cylinder and moves the piston down, forcing the landing gear down. The fluid that had been on the bottom of the piston returns to the reservoir through the selector valve. To raise the landing gear, turn the selector valve to the GEAR-UP position and actuate the hand pump. Fluid under pressure now enters the bottom of the actuator and moves the piston up. The fluid that had been in the top of the actuator returns to the reservoir through the selector valve.

single-acting actuator. A linear hydraulic or pneumatic actuator that uses fluid power for movement in one direction and a spring force for its return.

selector valve. A flow control valve used in hydraulic systems that directs pressurized fluid into one side of an actuator, and at the same time directs return fluid from the other side of the actuator back to the reservoir.

There are two basic types of selector valves: open-center valves and closed-center valves. The four-port closed-center valve is the most frequently used type.

check valve. A hydraulic component that allows full flow of fluid in one direction but blocks all flow in the opposite direction.

double-acting actuator. A linear actuator moved in both directions by fluid power.

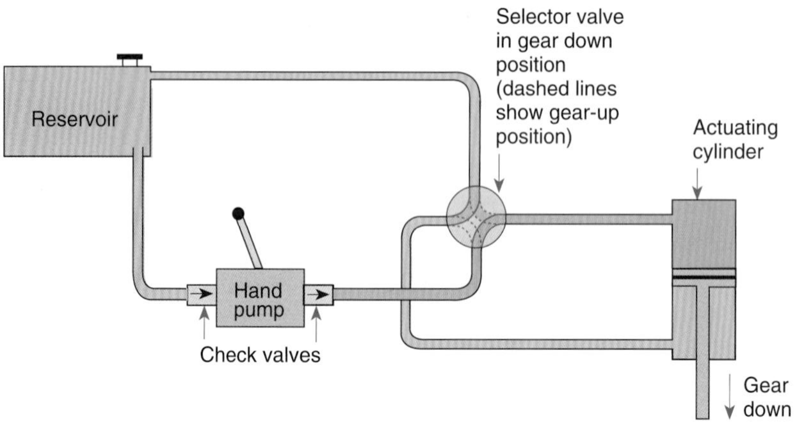

Figure 5-16. *The selector valve allows fluid from the hand pump to go to one side of the actuator cylinder to lower the landing gear. Fluid on the other side of the actuator piston returns through the selector valve to the reservoir.*

constant-displacement pump. A pump which displaces, or moves, a constant amount of fluid each time it turns.

The faster a constant-displacement pump turns, the more fluid it moves.

pump control valve. A control valve in a hydraulic system that allows the pilot to manually direct the output of the hydraulic pump back to the reservoir when no unit is being actuated.

relief valve. A pressure-control valve that relieves any pressure over the amount for which it is set. They are damage-preventing units used in both hydraulic and pneumatic systems.

Pressure relief valves prevent damaging high pressures that could be caused by a malfunctioning pressure regulator, or by thermal expansion of fluid trapped in portions of the system.

power control valve. A hand-operated hydraulic pump unloading valve.

When the valve is open, fluid flows from the pump to the reservoir with little opposition. To actuate the unit, turn the selector valve, and manually close the power control valve. Pressurized fluid flows to the unit, and when it is completely actuated, the power control valve automatically opens.

Power Pump Systems

As airplanes continued to evolve into heavier and faster machines with greater demands for their hydraulic systems, an engine-driven pump became the prime fluid mover. A hand pump was used as an emergency backup source of pressure and to actuate the system when the engine was not running.

Most engine-driven pumps are constant-displacement pumps that move a specific volume of fluid each time they rotate. This type of pump requires some means of relieving the pump of its load when system actuation is not needed, and some means must be provided to relieve any pressure in excess of a safe level.

Manual Pump Control Valve System

In this basic system, an engine-driven pump receives its fluid from the reservoir and moves it continually. When no unit is actuated, the fluid flows through the pump control valve back to the reservoir through the filter. The fluid circulates continually, but since it encounters very little restriction, almost no power is taken from the engine to drive the pump.

To lower the landing gear, the pilot places the selector valve in the GEAR-DOWN position and then closes the pump control valve (turns it ON). This shuts off the return of fluid to the reservoir, and the pump forces fluid into the landing gear actuating cylinders and lowers the landing gear.

When the landing gear is down and locked, the pressure builds up, but it cannot damage the system because it is relieved by the pressure relief valve until the pilot opens the pump control valve and unloads the pump. Some pump control valves are automatic and open when the pressure builds up after the actuation is completed. *See* Figure 5-17.

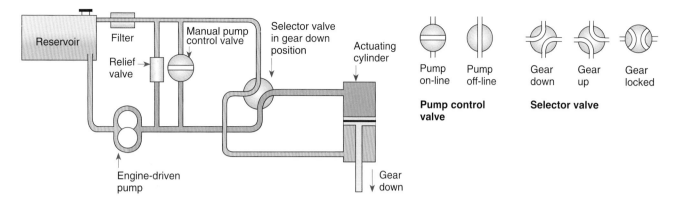

Figure 5-17. *A manual pump control valve keeps the pump unloaded when no unit is actuated.*

Power Control Valve System

A power control valve is similar in its function to a pump control valve. It is closed manually, but opens automatically. When no unit is actuated, the valve remains in its OPEN position and fluid circulates freely between the pump and the reservoir.

To actuate a unit, move the selector valve to the correct position and push the power control valve in to its CLOSED position. As soon as actuation is complete and the pressure builds up, the power control valve will automatically open and relieve the pump.

Because the power control valve opens automatically, pressure never rises high enough to operate the system pressure relief valve. To check its operation, push the power control valve in to its CLOSED position and hold it there until the pressure builds up high enough for the relief valve to function.

Automatic Unloading Valve System

The final stage in the evolution of the basic hydraulic system includes an automatic pump control valve called an unloading valve, or system pressure regulator, and an accumulator to maintain system pressure when the pump is unloaded. *See* Figure 5-18 on the next page.

The engine-driven pump receives its fluid from the reservoir, and moves it through the unloading valve into the system pressure manifold, where the accumulator holds it under pressure. When the system pressure rises to a specified value, called the kick-out pressure, the unloading valve shifts and directs the pump outlet into the return manifold. A check valve inside the unloading valve traps the fluid in the pressure manifold, where it is kept pressurized by the accumulator. The pump circulates the fluid through the unloading valve and the system filter back into the reservoir all the time the system pressure is above the unloading valve kick-in pressure. This circulation has almost no opposition, and very little engine power is used to drive the pump.

unloading valve. This is another name for system pressure regulator. *See* system pressure regulator.

system-pressure regulator. An automatic hydraulic-system pressure control valve. When the system pressure is low, the output of the constant-delivery pump is directed into the system. When the pressure builds up to a specified kick-out pressure, the regulator shifts and unloads the pump so its output is directed back into the reservoir with very little opposition. The pump remains unloaded until the system pressure drops to the regulator kick-in pressure.

accumulator. A hydraulic component that consists of two compartments separated by a movable component such as a piston, diaphragm, or bladder. One compartment is filled with compressed air or nitrogen, and the other is filled with hydraulic fluid and is connected into the system pressure manifold.

pressure manifold. The portion of a fluid power system from which the selector valves receive their pressurized fluid.

kick-in pressure. The pressure at which an unloading valve causes a hydraulic pump to direct its fluid into the system manifold.

return manifold. The portion of a fluid power system through which the fluid is returned to the reservoir.

kick-out pressure. The pressure at which an unloading valve shuts off the flow of fluid into the system pressure manifold and directs it back to the reservoir under a much reduced pressure.

standpipe. A pipe sticking up in a tank or reservoir that allows part of the tank to be used as a reserve, or standby, source of fluid.

hydraulic power pack. A small, self-contained hydraulic system that consists of a reservoir, pump, selector valves, and relief valves. The power pack is removable from the aircraft as a unit to facilitate maintenance and service.

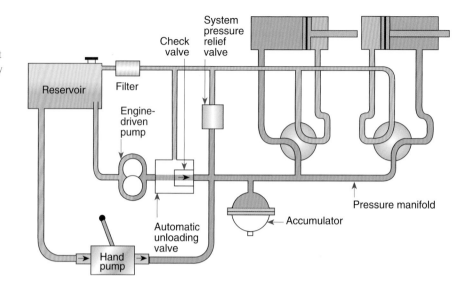

Figure 5-18. *The accumulator holds pressure on the system, and the automatic unloading valve keeps the pump unloaded as long as the operating range of pressure is maintained.*

When some component in the system is actuated, the system pressure drops to the unloading valve kick-in pressure, and the unloading valve shifts to shut off the flow to the reservoir and direct the pump output into the system pressure manifold. The pump supplies all of the fluid needed for the actuation.

A hand pump draws its fluid from the bottom of the reservoir, and may be used to produce pressure or actuate the system when the engine is not operating. If a leak in the system should allow all the fluid available to the engine-driven pump to be pumped overboard, the hand pump still has access to enough fluid below the standpipe in the reservoir to lower the landing gear and actuate the brakes. The system pressure relief valve in this system serves the same function as that in the simpler system.

Open-Center System

To minimize the complexity of hydraulic systems, some small and medium-sized aircraft use an open-center hydraulic system.

An open-center system such as the one in Figure 5-19 does not use a system pressure regulator, but rather uses special open-center selector valves installed in series with each other. When no unit is being actuated, the fluid flows from the reservoir through the open center of all of the valves, back into the reservoir. When either the landing gear or flaps is actuated, the selector valve for that system is shifted so that fluid flows into one side of the actuator. Fluid from the opposite side of the actuator returns to the reservoir through the other selector valves.

When the actuation is complete, the pressure builds up and automatically shifts the valve back into its open-center position. This allows the fluid to circulate through the system with almost no load on the pump.

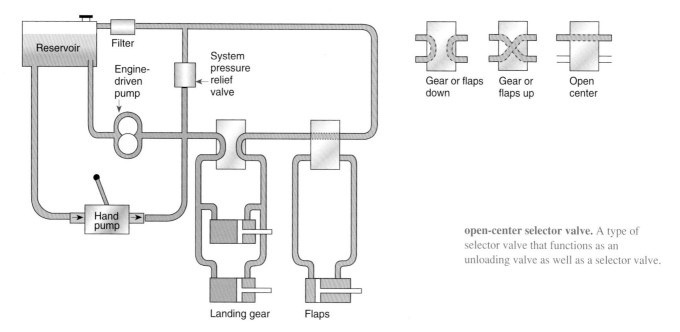

open-center selector valve. A type of selector valve that functions as an unloading valve as well as a selector valve.

Figure 5-19. *An open-center system requires no separate unloading valve, but returns fluid to the reservoir through the open center of the selector valves when no unit is actuated.*

Power Pack System

The hydraulic power pack was developed to make hydraulic systems easy to service and lightweight. The system shown in Figures 6-18 and 6-19 of Chapter 6 uses a power pack that contains the reservoir, pump, high-pressure relief valve, low-pressure control valve, and a shuttle valve all in one unit. *See* Figures 6-18 and 6-19 on Pages 436 and 437.

STUDY QUESTIONS: BASIC AIRCRAFT HYDRAULIC SYSTEMS

Answers begin on Page 416. Page numbers refer to chapter text.

26. The master cylinder in a simple brake system is a _____ (single or double)-action pump. *Page 336*

27. In a reservoir-type brake system, the brake line and wheel cylinders are vented to the atmosphere through the _____ port in the master cylinder. *Page 336*

Continued

---

28. Fluid is returned from a single-acting actuator by the action of a _____ pushing on the piston. *Page 336*

29. Hydraulic fluid from the return side of a double-acting actuator returns to the reservoir through the _____ . *Page 337*

30. An engine-driven hydraulic pump that moves a specific amount of fluid each time it rotates is called a _____ -displacement pump. *Page 338*

31. An engine-driven constant-displacement pump _____ (does or does not) require some type of valve to unload the pump when no component in the system is actuated. *Page 338*

32. When lowering the landing gear in an airplane equipped with a hydraulic system using a manual pump control valve, the gear selector valve is placed in the DOWN position _____ (before or after) the pump control valve is closed. *Page 338*

33. The hydraulic pump is unloaded when the manual pump control valve is _____ (opened or closed). *Page 338*

34. A power control valve is similar to a pump control valve. Both are turned ON manually, but the power control valve opens, or turns OFF, _____ (automatically or manually). *Page 339*

35. A valve that prevents pressure rising to a dangerous level in a hydraulic system is called a/an _____ valve. *Page 338*

36. Another name for an automatic unloading valve is a/an _____ . *Page 339*

37. When an automatic unloading valve is used in a hydraulic system, the pressure is held on the system when the pump is unloaded by a/an _____ . *Page 339*

38. The selector valves in an open-center hydraulic system are arranged in _____ (series or parallel). *Page 340*

39. An open-center hydraulic system _____ (does or does not) need a pump unloading valve. *Page 340*

Hydraulic System Components

This section describes the purpose and operation of a number of hydraulic system components.

Hydraulic Fluids

Aircraft reciprocating engines use hydraulic valve lifters to open the intake and exhaust valves, and these lifters use engine lubricating oil as their fluid. Turbine engines are often equipped with variable inlet guide vanes and compressor bleed valves that are moved by hydraulic actuators that use fuel as the fluid. A pneumatic system uses air as its fluid. Almost any fluid, either liquid or gaseous, can be used to transmit a force, but in an aircraft hydraulic system, more requirements must be met than just those of transmitting a force.

Fluid that is used in an aircraft hydraulic system must be as incompressible as practical, and it must have a low viscosity so it will flow through the lines with a minimum of friction. It must be chemically stable, have good lubricating properties so the pump and system components will not wear excessively, and it must not foam in operation. It must be compatible with the metal in the components and with the elastic materials of which the seals are made, and it must have a high flash point and a high fire point.

The technical bulletins furnished by the fluid manufacturer provides information about the compatibility of the hydraulic fluids with the various aircraft materials.

Types of Hydraulic Fluids

Four basic types of hydraulic fluids are used in aircraft hydraulic systems: vegetable base, mineral base, synthetic hydrocarbon base, and phosphate ester base. Except as noted, these fluids are not compatible with each other, and you must be able to identify each of them and understand their advantages and limitations. If a system is inadvertently serviced with the wrong type of fluid, all the fluid must be drained, the system flushed with the proper solvent, and all of the seals in the system changed.

Vegetable-Base Hydraulic Fluid

MIL-H-7644, vegetable-base fluid, was used in the past when aircraft hydraulic system requirements were not nearly so severe as they are today. Vegetable-base hydraulic fluid is essentially castor oil and alcohol, and it is dyed blue for identification. Natural rubber seals can be used with vegetable-base fluid, and a system using this fluid can be flushed with alcohol.

You are unlikely to find vegetable-base hydraulic fluid when servicing modern aircraft, but you may encounter it in some of the independent brake systems of older aircraft.

Mineral-Base Hydraulic Fluid

MIL-H-5606 mineral-base hydraulic fluid is still widely used for aircraft hydraulic systems. A kerosine-type petroleum product that has good lubricating characteristics, it contains additives that inhibit foaming and keep it from reacting with metal to form corrosion. MIL-H-5606 fluid is chemically stable, and it has a very small change in its viscosity as its temperature changes. Its main disadvantage is that it is flammable.

Mineral-base hydraulic fluid is dyed red for identification, and systems that use this fluid may be flushed with naphtha, varsol, or Stoddard solvent. Nitrile, fluorosilicone seals and hoses may be used with mineral-base hydraulic fluid. If you spill mineral-base hydraulic fluid on an aircraft tire, remove it by washing the tire with soap and water.

Synthetic Hydrocarbon-Base Hydraulic Fluid

The familiar "red oil," as MIL-H-5606 is commonly known, is being replaced in some military aircraft with MIL-H-83282 fluid. This is also dyed red, but it has a synthetic hydrocarbon base. It is compatible with all of the materials used with 5606 fluid. The main advantage of 83282 fluid is that it is fire resistant.

Another fluid that is compatible with MIL-H-5606 fluid is MIL-H-81019 fluid, which is used in extremely low temperatures. It is operational at a temperature as low as -90°F. This fluid is also dyed red to prevent it being inadvertently used with systems that should use fluids that have other than a mineral base.

Phosphate Ester Hydraulic Fluid

Mil-H-5606 hydraulic fluid can create a fire hazard if a line breaks and sprays the fluid out under high pressure into an area near a hot engine.

As jet aircraft became the standard for the transportation industry and hydraulic systems became more demanding, a new type of nonflammable hydraulic fluid was developed. This is a phosphate ester fluid available as Skydrol LD-4 and 500B-4 from Solutia Inc., and HyJet V and HyJet IV-A[plus] from Exxon.

Phosphate ester base fluids are only slightly heavier than water with specific gravities of 1.009 and 1.057. When new, these fluids are light purple in color, but this color may change toward yellow as it ages. For this reason, color is not a reliable indicator of the fluid's condition. You must determine its condition with the physical property test recommended by the manufacturer.

One of the main advantages of phosphate ester fluid is its wide range of operating temperatures. It can function properly with temperature as low as -65°F to temperature greater than 225°F.

For all of its advantages, phosphate ester fluid is not without its limitations. Human tissues, especially the delicate tissues like the eyes are especially susceptible and if any fluid gets into the eyes, it must be flushed out immediately and medical attention obtained as quickly as possible.

naphtha. A volatile and flammable hydrocarbon liquid used chiefly as a solvent or as a cleaning fluid.

varsol. A petroleum product similar to naphtha used as a solvent and a cleaning fluid.

Stoddard solvent. A petroleum product, similar to naphtha, that is used as a solvent and a cleaning fluid.

Skydrol hydraulic fluid. The registered trade name for a synthetic, non-flammable, phosphate ester-base hydraulic fluid used in modern high-temperature hydraulic systems.

LD. Low Density

Phosphate ester fluids are quite susceptible to contamination by water from the atmosphere, so containers of the fluid must be kept tightly sealed. Phosphate ester fluid will attack polyvinyl chlorides, and must not be allowed to drip onto electrical wiring, as it will damage the insulation. It will also act as a paint remover and lift most types of finishing materials other than epoxy or polyurethane from an aircraft. If you spill phosphate ester fluid on aircraft tires, remove it with soap and water.

Phosphate ester fluid will not damage the metals commonly used in aircraft construction, and is compatible with natural fibers and with such synthetics as nylon and some polyesters. Ethylene propylene, or Teflon seals may be used with phosphate ester fluid. When servicing a system that uses phosphate ester fluid, be very careful to use only seals that have the part numbers specified by the aircraft manufacturer, because seals that may be compatible with other types of hydraulic fluid will be ruined if they are installed in a system that uses phosphate ester fluid.

Contaminated phosphate ester systems should be flushed with clean phosphate ester fluid. Components used in these systems may be cleaned with Stoddard solvent, methyl-ethyl-ketone (MEK), isopropyl alcohol, or the proprietary fluid SkyKleen made by Solutia Inc.

Contamination and Protection of Hydraulic Fluids

Hydraulic systems operate with high pressures, and the components used in these systems have such close fitting parts that any contamination in the fluid will cause the components to fail.

When servicing a hydraulic system, be sure to use only the correct fluid. The service manual for the aircraft specifies the type of fluid, and the reservoir should have the required type of fluid plainly marked with a placard near the filler opening.

Use the patch test to determine whether or not hydraulic fluid is contaminated. Pass a measured volume of fluid through a special patch-type filter in a test kit available through the fluid manufacturer. After all of the fluid has passed through, analyze the filter and observe the type and amount of contaminants. The instructions that accompany the test kit explain the procedures used to evaluate the test patch.

To give an idea of the importance of using perfectly clean and uncontaminated fluid, Figure 5-20 on the next page shows a comparison of contaminant size. One micron is one millionth of a meter, or approximately 0.000039 inch. (One inch is equal to 25,400 microns.) The unaided human eye can see contaminants as small as 40 microns, and modern hydraulic filters can filter out contaminants larger than 3 microns. This high degree of filtration is important because some of the clearances in new hydraulic components are as small as 2 microns (0.000 080 inch). From this, it is obvious that you cannot see the contaminants that are harmful, so you must follow the contamination control procedures recommended by the fluid manufacturer.

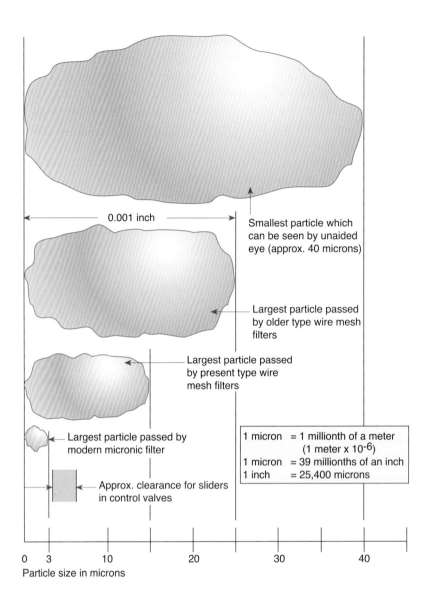

0.001 inch

Smallest particle which can be seen by unaided eye (approx. 40 microns)

Largest particle passed by older type wire mesh filters

Largest particle passed by present type wire mesh filters

Largest particle passed by modern micronic filter

Approx. clearance for sliders in control valves

1 micron	= 1 millionth of a meter (1 meter x 10^{-6})
1 micron	= 39 millionths of an inch
1 inch	= 25,400 microns

0   3   10   20   30   40

Particle size in microns

Figure 5-20. *Relative sizes of hydraulic system contaminants*

STUDY QUESTIONS: HYDRAULIC FLUIDS

Answers begin on Page 416. **Page numbers refer to chapter text.**

40. Vegetable-base hydraulic fluid is dyed _____ for identification. *Page 343*

41. Hydraulic systems using vegetable-base fluid can be flushed out with _____ . *Page 343*

42. Hydraulic systems using vegetable-base fluid have seals made of _____ rubber. *Page 343*

43. Mineral-base hydraulic fluid is dyed _____ for identification. *Page 344*

44. Hydraulic systems using mineral-base fluid can be flushed out with _____ . *Page 344*

45. Hydraulic systems using mineral-base fluid have seals made of _____ . *Page 344*

46. Mineral-base hydraulic fluid can be removed from an aircraft tire by washing the tire with _____ . *Page 344*

47. The names for two brands of phosphate ester hydraulic fluids are _____ and _____. *Page 344*

48. The color of a phosphate ester hydraulic fluid _____ (is or is not) a good indication of the condition of the fluid. *Page 344*

49. Hydraulic systems using phosphate ester-base fluid can be flushed out with _____ . *Page 345*

50. Hydraulic systems using phosphate ester-base fluid have seals made of _____ . *Page 345*

51. Phosphate ester hydraulic fluid that has been spilled on aircraft tires can be removed with _____ . *Page 345*

Hydraulic Reservoirs

The reservoir is the component that stores the fluid and serves as an expansion chamber to provide a space for the fluid when its volume increases because of temperature. The reservoir also serves as a point at which the fluid can purge itself of any air it accumulates in its operational cycle.

Reservoirs must have enough capacity to hold all of the fluid that can be returned to the system with any configuration of the landing gear, flaps, and all other hydraulically actuated units. It is important when servicing a reservoir to decrease the system pressure to zero, as this will return the maximum amount of fluid to the reservoir. If the reservoir is filled when the accumulator is charged with fluid, it will be overfull when the accumulator is discharged.

Nonpressurized Reservoirs

Airplanes that fly at relatively low altitudes are usually equipped with nonpressurized reservoirs such as the one in Figure 5-21 on the next page. The fluid-return fitting in the reservoir is usually directed in such a way as to minimize foaming, and any air that is in the fluid will be swirled out, or extracted. Some reservoirs have filters built into their return line to filter all of the fluid that is returned from the system.

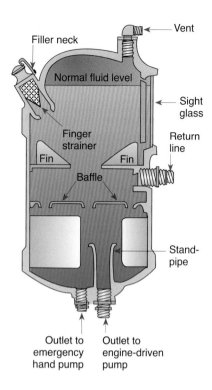

Figure 5-21. *A typical nonpressurized hydraulic reservoir*

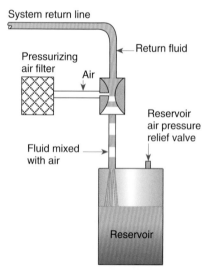

Figure 5-22. *A venturi tee fitting in the fluid return line to the reservoir pulls outside air into the hydraulic fluid to produce an air pressure above the fluid in the reservoir.*

The reservoirs for all but the simplest hydraulic systems have two outlets. One outlet is located either partially up the side of the reservoir or is connected to a standpipe inside the reservoir. This outlet supplies fluid to the engine-driven hydraulic pump. The other outlet is located at the bottom of the reservoir, and connects to the emergency hand pump. If a leak develops in the system that causes a loss of all of the fluid that can be moved by the engine-driven pump, there will still be enough fluid left in the bottom of the reservoir for emergency extension of the landing gear and for emergency application of the brakes.

There is a trend in many of the smaller aircraft with limited hydraulic systems to incorporate all of the hydraulic power system into a power pack which contains the reservoir, valves, and electric pump all in one easy-to-service unit. Such a system is illustrated in Figures 6-18 and 6-19 on Pages 434 and 435.

Pressurized Reservoirs

When airplanes fly at high altitudes, where the outside air pressure is low, there is not enough air pressure to force the hydraulic fluid from the reservoir into the inlet of the pump, so the pump tends to cavitate, or chatter. Also, the hydraulic fluid that is returned to the reservoir develops a tendency to foam at high altitudes. To prevent pump cavitation and foaming of the return fluid, reservoirs in high-flying aircraft are pressurized. It is important to relieve the pressure in the reservoir before opening it for servicing.

One method of pressurizing a reservoir is to inject air into the returning fluid through an aspirator, or venturi tee fitting as shown in Figure 5-22. The fluid flowing back into the reservoir passes through the venturi, where it creates a low pressure and draws air from outside the reservoir into the venturi throat. The hydraulic fluid with air in it is swirled as it enters the top of the reservoir, and the air is expelled from the fluid. A relief valve in the reservoir maintains an air pressure of about 12 psi on the fluid.

Some turbine-engine-powered aircraft use a small amount of filtered compressor bleed air to pressurize the reservoir. These systems have an air pressure regulator between the engine and the reservoir to reduce the pressure to the proper value.

Another way to pressurize the hydraulic reservoirs in turbine-engine-powered airplanes is to use the hydraulic system pressure acting on a small piston inside the reservoir. This small piston applies a force to a much larger piston that pressurizes the fluid. *See* Figure 5-23.

The fluid in this reservoir is pressurized to approximately 30 psi when the 3,000-psi system hydraulic pressure acts on a small piston inside the reservoir. This small piston moves a larger piston that has 100 times its area. The larger piston applies a force to the fluid inside the reservoir and builds up its pressure to 30 psi.

cavitation. A condition that exists in a hydraulic pump when there is not enough pressure in the reservoir to force fluid to the inlet of the pump. The pump picks up air instead of fluid.

chatter. A type of rapid vibration of a hydraulic pump caused by the pump taking in some air along with the hydraulic fluid.

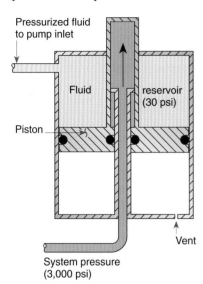

Pressurized fluid to pump inlet

Fluid   reservoir (30 psi)

Piston

System pressure (3,000 psi)

Vent

Figure 5-23. *The principle of a pressurized hydraulic reservoir, using hydraulic system pressure*

STUDY QUESTIONS: HYDRAULIC RESERVOIRS

*Answers begin on Page 416. **Page numbers refer to chapter text.***

52. Fluid taken from the standpipe in a hydraulic reservoir goes to the _____ (engine-driven pump or emergency hand pump). *Page 348*

53. A hydraulic unit that contains the reservoir, pump, and all of the valves is called a/an _____ . *Page 348*

54. Some hydraulic reservoirs are pressurized to prevent the pump _____ . *Page 348*

55. Three methods of pressurizing a hydraulic reservoir are:
    a. _____
    b. _____
    c. _____
    Pages 348 and 349

Hydraulic Pumps

Fluid power is produced when fluid is moved under pressure. The pumps used in a hydraulic system are simply fluid movers rather than pressure generators. Pressure is produced only when the flow of fluid from the pump is restricted.

The two basic types of hydraulic pumps are those operated by hand, and those driven by some source of mechanical power (such as an electric motor, or an aircraft engine).

Hand Pumps

single-acting hand pump. A hand-operated fluid pump that moves fluid only during one stroke of the pump handle. One stroke pulls the fluid into the pump and the other forces the fluid out.

double-acting hand pump. A hand-operated fluid pump that moves fluid during both strokes of the pump handle.

Single-acting hand pumps move fluid only on one stroke of the piston, while double-acting pumps move fluid with both strokes. Double-acting pumps are commonly used in aircraft hydraulic systems because of their greater efficiency. Figure 5-24 shows a diagram of a piston-rod displacement, double-acting hydraulic hand pump.

On the stroke of the handle that pulls the piston outward, fluid is drawn into the pump through the inlet check valve. The outlet check valve inside the piston is seated, and the fluid on the back side of the piston is forced out of the pump outlet.

On the return stroke of the pump handle, the piston is forced into the cylinder. The pump inlet check valve seats, and the outlet check valve opens, allowing fluid to flow into the chamber that has the piston rod. The piston rod causes the volume of this side of the pump to be less than the volume of the fluid that was taken in, and approximately one half of the fluid that has just been taken into the pump is forced out the pump outlet.

To better understand the way this pump works, assume some values. The large end of the piston has an area of two square inches. The area of the piston rod is one square inch. The piston moves one inch each time the handle is moved through its full travel.

When the piston moves all the way to the left, two cubic inches of fluid are pulled into the cylinder through the inlet check valve, and the check valve closes. Now, when the piston is moved all of the way to the right, this two cubic inches of fluid passes through the outlet check valve. The volume of the chamber on the left side of the piston is only one cubic inch because the piston rod takes up the other cubic inch. Therefore one cubic inch of fluid leaves the pump through the outlet port, and the other cubic inch of fluid remains in the chamber on the left side of the piston. Each time the piston moves to the right, one cubic inch of fluid leaves the pump and no fluid is taken in. Each time the piston moves to the left, two cubic inches of fluid is taken into the pump and one cubic inch of fluid leaves the pump.

Hand pumps are simple devices and give little trouble, but their simplicity does not prevent some problems. For example, if the handle of a rebuilt hand pump cannot be moved in the normal pumping direction, there is a good probability that the outlet check valve is stuck closed or incorrectly installed. If the outlet check valve is stuck in the open position, the handle will kick back during the normal intake stroke. Pressure from the accumulator will push back on the piston.

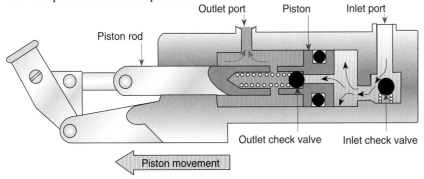

Piston is moved to the left, pulling 2 cubic inches of fluid into inlet port and forcing 1 cubic inch of fluid out the outlet port.

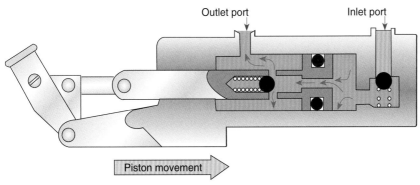

Piston is moved to the right, taking in no fluid and forcing 1 cubic inch of fluid out the outlet port.

Figure 5-24. *A double-acting, piston-rod displacement hydraulic hand pump*

Power Pumps

Power pumps are classified as either constant-displacement or variable-displacement. A constant-displacement pump moves a specific amount of fluid each time it rotates. A pump of this type must have some sort of relief valve or unloading device to prevent its building up so much pressure that it will rupture a line or perhaps damage itself. The drive shaft of almost all power pumps has a necked-down portion called a shear section that will shear or break if the pressure relief device fails, or if the pump should seize. See the necked-down section of the coupling shaft in the pump in Figure 5-28 on Page 355. When this breaks, the pump will no longer operate, but the system will not be damaged.

shear section. A necked-down section of the drive shaft of a constant-displacement hydraulic pump: If the pump should seize, the shear section will break and prevent the pump being destroyed.

Some pumps use a shear pin rather than a shear section.

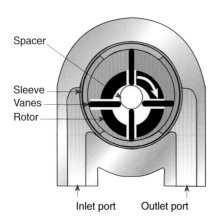

Figure 5-25. *A vane-type pump moves a relatively large volume of fluid under a low pressure.*

Variable-displacement pumps move a volume of fluid that is determined by the demands of the system. Variable-displacement pumps are often of the piston type, and the volume of their output is varied by changing either the actual or the effective stroke of the pistons.

Constant-Displacement Pumps

Constant-displacement pumps that produce a high volume of flow with a low pressure, a medium volume with medium pressure, and low volume with high pressure are available. In this section we will look at each of these.

Vane-Type Pumps

The vane pump is one of the simpler types of constant-displacement pumps used to move a large volume of fluid with a pressure of up to about 300 psi. *See* Figure 5-25.

The four steel vanes are free-floating in slots cut in the rotor. They are held against the wall of the steel sleeve by a steel pin spacer. As the rotor turns in the direction shown by the arrow, the volume between the vanes on the inlet side of the pump increases, and the volume between the vanes on the discharge side of the pump decreases. This change of volume pulls fluid into the pump through the inlet port and forces it out through the discharge port.

Vane-type pumps are used in some aircraft hydraulic systems, but they are more often used as fuel pumps and as air pumps to supply air for gyroscopic instruments and pneumatic deicer boots.

Gear-Type Pumps

Gear-type pumps move a medium volume of fluid under a pressure of between 300 and 1,500 psi. Two types of gear pumps are used in aircraft hydraulic systems, the simple spur-gear pump and the gerotor pump.

The spur-gear pump illustrated in Figure 5-26 uses two meshing external-tooth gears that fit closely into a figure-eight-shaped housing. One of the gears is driven by an engine accessory drive, and this gear drives the other one. As the gears rotate in the direction shown by the arrows, the space between the teeth on the inlet side of the pump becomes larger. Fluid is pulled into this space, trapped between the teeth and the housing, and carried around to the discharge side of the pump. Here the teeth of the two gears come into mesh and decrease the volume. As the volume is decreased, fluid is forced from the pump outlet.

A small amount of fluid leaks past the gears and around the shaft to help lubricate, cool, and seal the pump. This fluid drains back into the hollow shafts of the gears, where it is picked up by the low pressure at the inlet side of the pump. A case-pressure relief valve holds the fluid inside the hollow shafts of the gears, until it builds up a pressure of about 15 psi. This pressure is maintained to prevent air being taken into the pump in the event the shaft or the shaft seal becomes damaged. Fluid will be forced out of the pump rather than allowing air to be drawn into it. If air leaked into the pump, it would take the place of the fluid needed for lubrication and the pump would be damaged.

An overboard drain line connects to the base of the pump, and any hydraulic fluid dripping from this line indicates a damaged pump shaft seal. Engine oil dripping from this line indicates a damaged engine accessory drive oil seal.

As the output pressure of a gear-type pump builds up, there is a tendency for the case to distort which would allow fluid to leak past the ends of the gears. To prevent this leakage, some pumps direct high-pressure fluid from the discharge side of the pump back through a check valve into a cavity behind the bushing flanges. This high-pressure fluid forces the bushings tightly against the sides of the gears to decrease the side clearance of the gears and minimize leakage. It also compensates for wear of the bushings.

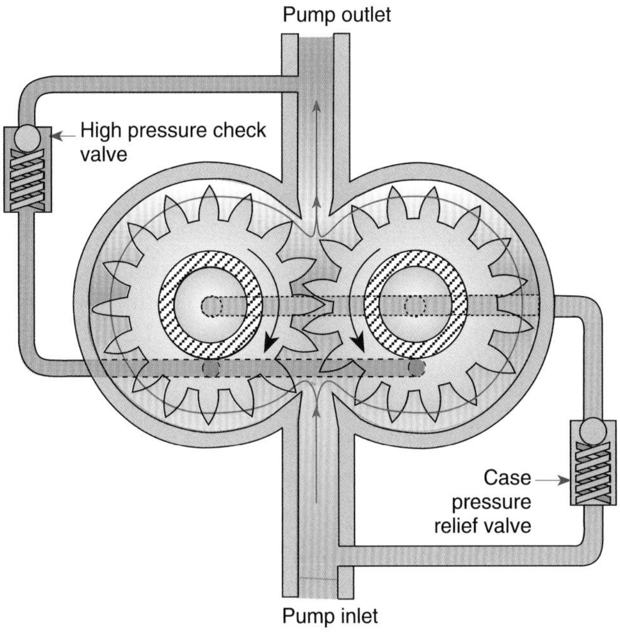

case pressure. A low pressure that is maintained inside the case of a hydraulic pump.

If a seal becomes damaged, hydraulic fluid will be forced out of the pump rather than allowing air to be drawn into the pump.

Figure 5-26. *A spur-gear-type pump moves a medium amount of fluid under a medium pressure.*

gerotor pump. A form of constant-displacement gear pump. A gerotor pump uses an external-tooth spur gear that rides inside of and drives an internal-tooth rotor gear. There is one more tooth space inside the rotor than there are teeth on the drive gear.

As the gears rotate, the volume of the space between two of the teeth on the inlet side of the pump increases, while the volume of the space between two teeth on the opposite side of the pump decreases.

If the reservoir should become emptied, or if for any reason air gets into the pump inlet line, the pump intermittently picks up air and fluid, which causes the pump to chatter or cavitate. The lack of continuous lubrication causes the pump to overheat, which will cause its damage or destruction.

Gerotor Pumps

A gerotor pump, illustrated in Figure 5-27, is a combination internal and external gear pump.

The four-tooth external spur gear is driven by an engine accessory drive, and as it turns, it rotates an internal five-tooth rotor. As the gear and the rotor turn in the direction shown by the arrows, the volume of the space between the teeth below the inlet opening becomes larger. As this volume increases, the pressure drops and pulls fluid into the pump. The volume of the space between the teeth below the outlet opening becomes smaller and forces the fluid out of the pump.

Piston Pumps

Aircraft hydraulic systems that require a relatively small volume of fluid under a pressure of 2,500 psi or more often use fixed-angle, multiple-piston pumps, such as the one in Figure 5-28.

There are usually seven or nine axially-drilled holes in the rotating cylinder block of this type of pump, and each hole contains a close-fitting piston attached to a drive plate by a ball-jointed rod. The cylinder block and the pistons are rotated as a unit by a shaft that is driven from an engine accessory drive.

The housing is angled so that the pistons on one side of the cylinder block are at the bottom of their stroke while the pistons on the other side of the block are at the top of their stroke. As the pump rotates, half of the pistons move from the top of their stroke to the bottom, increasing the volume of the cylinders, lowering the pressure, and pulling fluid into the pump. The pistons on the opposite side of the block move from the bottom of their stroke to the top, decreasing the volume and forcing fluid out of the pump.

A valve plate that has two crescent-shaped openings covers the ends of the cylinders. The pump outlet port is above the pistons that are moving up, and the inlet port is above the pistons that are moving down.

Variable-Displacement Pumps

An unloading valve of some sort must be used with a constant-displacement pump, but the same force used to control the unloading valve may be used to control the output of a variable-displacement pump, so there is no need for a separate control.

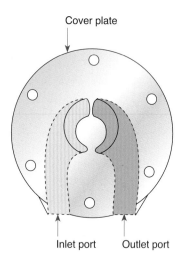

Cover plate

Inlet port   Outlet port

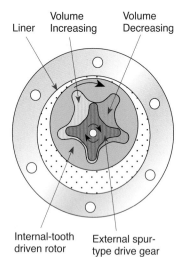

Liner   Volume Increasing   Volume Decreasing

Internal-tooth driven rotor   External spur-type drive gear

Figure 5-27. *A gerotor pump uses an external spur-type drive gear inside an internal-tooth driven gear.*

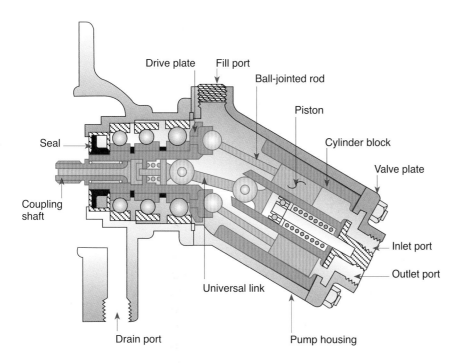

Seal

Coupling
shaft

Drive plate   Fill port

Ball-jointed rod

Piston

Cylinder block

Valve plate

Inlet port

Outlet port

Universal link

Drain port

Pump housing

Figure 5-28. *Fixed-angle, multiple-piston pump*

One of the more popular types of variable-displacement pumps is the Strato-power demand-type pump, shown in Figure 5-29 on the next page. This pump uses nine axially oriented cylinders and pistons. The pistons are driven up and down inside the cylinders by a wedge-shaped drive cam, and the pistons press against the cam with ball joint slippers.

When the slipper is against the thick part of the cam, the piston is at the top of its stroke, and, as the cam rotates, the piston moves down in the cylinder until the slipper is riding on the thin part of the cam. When the slipper is in this position, the piston is at the bottom of its stroke.

The physical stroke of the piston is the same regardless of the amount of fluid demanded by the system, but the effective length of the stroke controls the amount of fluid moved by this pump.

A balance between the fixed compensator spring force and the variable force caused by pump output pressure acting on an enlarged portion of the compensator stem moves the sleeves up or down over the outside of the pistons. This varies the position of the piston when the pressure is relieved, and thus varies the effective stroke of the piston.

Notice in the simplified diagram of the control system in Figure 5-30 that a passage from the discharge side of the pump directs output fluid pressure around the compensator stem. This stem is cut with a shoulder which serves as a piston. As the system pressure rises, this stem is pushed to the right,

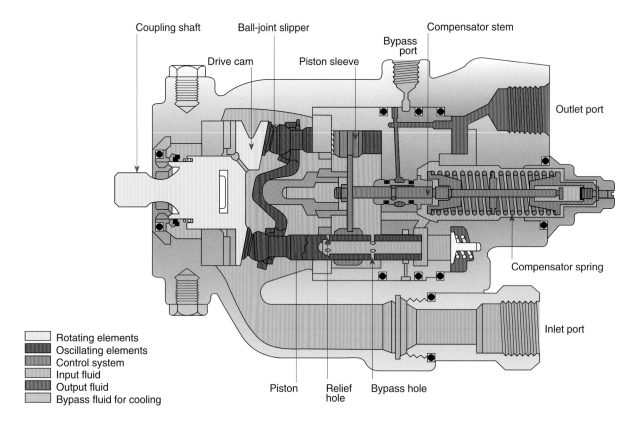

Coupling shaft
Drive cam
Ball-joint slipper
Piston sleeve
Bypass port
Compensator stem
Outlet port
Compensator spring
Inlet port
Piston
Relief hole
Bypass hole

Rotating elements
Oscillating elements
Control system
Input fluid
Output fluid
Bypass fluid for cooling

Figure 5-29. *Cutaway view of the Stratopower variable-displacement hydraulic pump*

compressing the compensator spring. The spider that moves the sleeves over the outside of the pistons is attached to the stem to vary the effective length of the piston stroke.

When the system pressure is low, as it is in Figure 5-30, the compensator spring forces the spider to move the sleeves to the left, or down on the pistons. The sleeves keep the relief holes covered for the full stroke of the piston, and the pistons move fluid out through the check valves into the pump discharge line during their entire stroke.

When the system pressure is high, as it is in Figure 5-31, it acts on the compensator-stem piston and compresses the compensator spring. This pulls the sleeves to the right, or up on the pistons so the relief holes are uncovered during most of their stroke. The pistons move through their full stroke, but since the fluid passes out the relief holes, no fluid is forced from the pump.

Any time the system pressure is at an intermediate value, the sleeves close the relief holes at some point along the stroke of the piston. In this way, just enough fluid is pumped to maintain the system pressure at the level for which the compensator spring is set.

When the pistons are at the extreme top of their stroke, the bypass hole in the piston aligns with a passage in the housing that connects to the outside bypass port. *See* Figure 5-29. A small amount of fluid flows though the bypass port back to the reservoir on each pressure stroke. This fluid picks up heat from the pump, and after it leaves the pump it passes through a case drain filter and a check valve and into a finned tubing heat exchanger inside one of the fuel tanks. *See* Figure 5-32 on the next page. From the heat exchanger it flows back into the reservoir. This flow of bypass fluid cools the pump by keeping fresh fluid flowing through it during the time in which there is no flow from the output port.

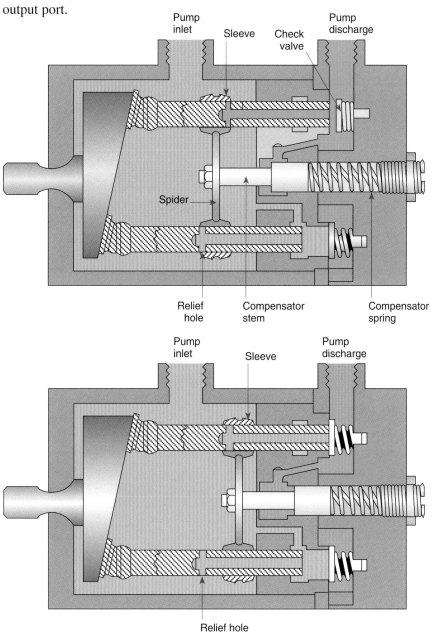

Figure 5-30. *The system pressure is low, the compensator spring has moved the spider and the sleeves to the left so that the relief holes are covered for most of the piston stroke, and fluid is moved out of the pump through the check valve.*

Figure 5-31. *The system pressure is high. Fluid pressing on the step cut in the compensator stem has compressed the compensator spring and moved the sleeves to the right so the relief holes are uncovered for almost all of the piston stroke. No fluid is moved out of the pump.*

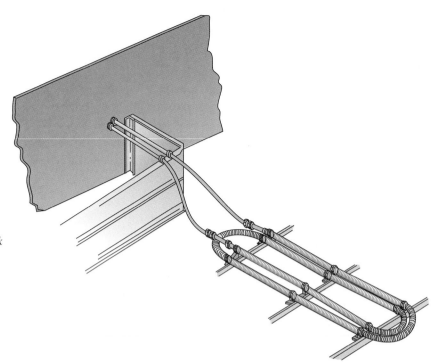

Figure 5-32. *Bypass fluid from the hydraulic pump flows through finned tubing submerged in fuel inside a fuel tank to remove heat from the fluid.*

STUDY QUESTIONS: HYDRAULIC PUMPS

*Answers begin on Page 416. **Page numbers refer to chapter text.***

56. A hydraulic hand pump that moves some fluid every time the pump handle is moved is called a _____ -acting pump. *Page 350*

57. A piston-rod displacement hand pump is a _____ (single or double)-acting pump. *Page 350*

58. If the handle of a rebuilt hydraulic hand pump cannot be moved in the direction of normal pumping, the probable cause is an improperly installed _____ (inlet or outlet) check valve. *Page 350*

59. A pressure regulator, or unloading valve, must be used with a _____ (constant or variable)-displacement hydraulic pump. *Page 351*

60. An engine-driven hydraulic pump is prevented from building up damagingly high pressure if the pressure regulator and relief valve fail by a/an _____ in the drive shaft. *Page 351*

61. A vane-type engine-driven fluid pump is usually used for applications that must move a _____ (large or small) volume of fluid. *Page 352*

62. Hydraulic fluid flowing through a spur-gear-type pump moves _____ (between or around) the gears. *Page 352*

63. Hydraulic fluid dripping from the overboard drain line connected to an engine-driven pump base indicates a damaged pump shaft _____ . *Page 353*

64. An air leak in the inlet line to an engine-driven hydraulic pump will cause the pump to _____ or _____, which will cause the pump to _____. *Page 354*

65. A piston-type engine-driven fluid pump is usually used for applications that require a _____ (high or low) pressure. *Page 354*

66. A variable-displacement hydraulic pump _____ (does or does not) require a pressure regulator or unloading valve. *Page 354*

67. A Stratopower variable-displacement hydraulic pump varies the discharge flow by altering the _____ (actual or effective) stroke of the pistons. *Page 355*

68. The hydraulic fluid that flows through the heat exchanger in the fuel tank is fluid that flows from the _____ port of the Stratopower variable-displacement pump. *Page 357*

Hydraulic Valves

Fluid power systems are much like electrical systems in that the object of the system is to control a flow so it can perform work. In hydraulic systems there are two types of valves, those that control flow and those that control pressure.

Flow Control Valves

Flow control valves are much like switches in an electrical system. Some allow fluid to flow or prevent it from flowing. Others direct flow from one device to another, and still others regulate the rate of flow.

Check Valves

Aircraft hydraulic systems include many situations where the fluid must flow in one direction and not flow in the opposite direction. Reverse flow can be prevented by the use of check valves.

The most common check valves are the ball-type, the cone-type, and the flapper, or swing-type, check valve.

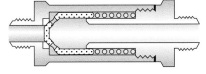

Ball-type check valve

Cone-type check valve

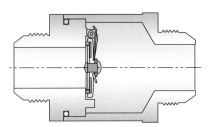

Flapper-type check valve

Figure 5-33. *Typical check valves. All of these valves allow a full flow from the left to right, but prevent any flow from right to left.*

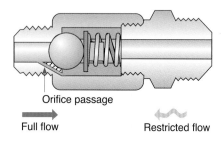

Orifice passage

Full flow   Restricted flow

Figure 5-34. *An orifice check valve allows full flow of fluid in one direction but a restricted flow in the opposite direction.*

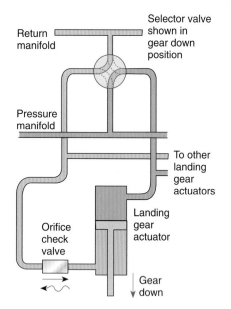

Return manifold

Selector valve shown in gear down position

Pressure manifold

To other landing gear actuators

Orifice check valve

Landing gear actuator

Gear down

Figure 5-35. *Installation of an orifice check valve in a landing gear actuating cylinder to slow the fluid flow during lowering the gear but allowing full flow for raising it.*

Fluid enters the ball-type check valve from the left side, forces the ball off of its seat, and flows through the valve. Fluid cannot flow through the valve in the opposite direction because the ball is held tightly against its seat by the spring force and by the fluid.

A cone-type check valve works in the same way as the ball-type valve, except the ball is replaced with a hollow cone. Fluid flows through the valve from left to right, forcing the cone off of its seat and passing through the holes in the surface of the cone. Reverse flow is prevented by the fluid and the spring holding the cone tight in its seat.

Large volumes of low-pressure fluid are often controlled by a flapper, or swing-type, check valve. Fluid flows through this valve from left to right, forcing the flapper off of its seat. Fluid flow in the reverse direction is prevented by the spring and the fluid hold the flapper tight against its seat.

Orifice Check Valve

Certain applications require full flow of fluid in one direction, but rather than blocking all of the fluid flowing in the opposite direction, these allow fluid to flow through the valve at a restricted rate. For these applications, an orifice check valve is used. *See* Figure 5-34.

An orifice check valve may be used in a landing gear system to slow the extension of the gear and yet allow it to retract as quickly as possible. When used for this application, it is installed in the landing gear actuator gear-up line illustrated in Figure 5-35. When the landing gear selector valve is placed in the GEAR-DOWN position, the up locks release the landing gear and it falls out of the wheel well. The weight of the gear and the force of air blowing against the wheel as it drops down try to speed up the extension. The check valve restricts the flow of the fluid coming out of the actuator and prevents the landing gear from dropping too quickly. When the selector valve is placed in the GEAR-UP position, the fluid flows into the actuator gear-up line through the check valve in its unrestricted direction, and full flow raises the landing gear.

Selector Valves

One common type of flow control valve is the selector valve, which controls the direction of flow of the fluid used to actuate some hydraulic component.

Two types of selector valves are open-center valves and closed-center valves. An open-center valve directs fluid through the center of the valve back to the reservoir when no units are being actuated. A closed-center valve stops the flow of fluid when it is in its neutral position.

Both types of selector valves direct fluid under pressure to one side of the actuator, and vent the opposite side of the actuator to the reservoir.

Plug-Type Closed-Center Selector Valve

Systems that use a relatively low pressure for actuation may use a simple plug-type selector valve such as the one in Figure 5-36. In one position of the selector handle, the pressure port and the side of the actuator that extends the piston are connected. The side of the actuator that retracts the piston is connected to the return line. When the selector handle is rotated 90°, the actuator ports are reversed; the retract port is connected to the pressure line, and the extend port is connected to the return line. Some selector valves have a neutral position in which the actuator is isolated from both the pressure and return manifolds.

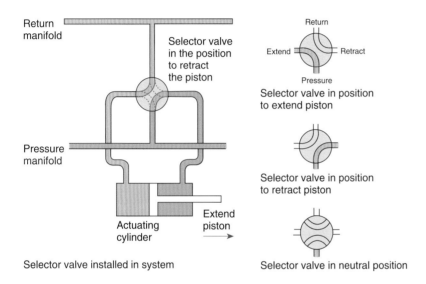

Figure 5-36. *Simplified diagram of a plug-type, closed-center, four-port selector valve*

Poppet-Type Closed-Center Selector Valve

Selector valves used in high-pressure hydraulic systems must have a much more positive shutoff of the fluid than provided by a plug-type valve, and often use poppet-type selector valves.

In the valve in Figure 5-37A on the next page, the selector valve control handle has been turned so that the cam lobes have lifted poppets 2 and 4 off of their seats, and fluid flows from the pressure manifold through the open valve 2 to the actuator extend line that moves the piston rod out of the cylinder. Return fluid from the right side of the actuating cylinder flows through the actuator retract line and through valve 4, back to the return manifold.

When the selector valve handle is rotated 90°, the cam allows valves 2 and 4 to close and opens valves 1 and 3. This is shown in Figure 5-37B. Fluid flows from the pressure manifold through valve 3 to the actuator retract line, and the piston rod moves into the cylinder. Fluid forced from the actuator flows through valve 1 to the return manifold. Another 90° of the selector valve handle closes all of the valves, as shown in Figure 5-37C. This shuts off all of the flow to and from the actuator.

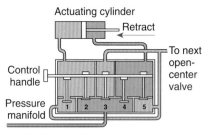

A Flow through valve to extend piston rod from cylinder

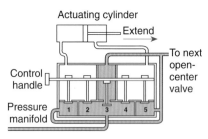

B Valve position to retract piston rod into cylinder.

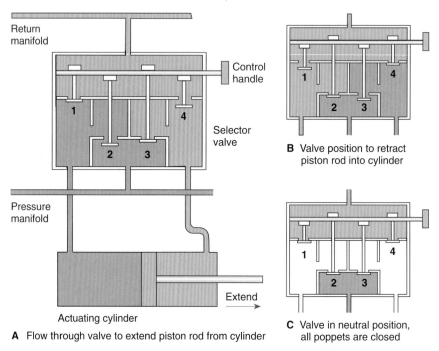

A Flow through valve to extend piston rod from cylinder

B Valve position to retract piston rod into cylinder

C Valve in neutral position, all poppets are closed

Figure 5-37. *Poppet-type closed-center selector valve*

C Valve in neutral position. All poppets are closed except poppet 3, which allows fluid to flow directly from pressure manifold to the next open-center valve.

Figure 5-38. *Poppet-type open-center selector valve*

Poppet-Type Open-Center Selector Valve

The open-center selector valve in Figure 5-38 is much like the closed-center valve, except for poppet number 3, which allows fluid to flow straight through the valve when nothing is actuated. Open-center selector valves are connected in series, rather than in parallel, as are closed-center valves.

Figure 5-38A shows the valve in the position to extend the actuator rod. Poppets 2 and 5 are off their seats, and fluid flows from the pressure manifold around poppet 2 to the actuator. The return fluid flows from the actuator around poppet 5 to the next open-center selector valve and then to the reservoir. *See* Figure 5-38A.

To retract the actuator rod, Figure 5-38B shows poppets 1 and 4 are off their seats. Fluid flows from the pressure manifold around poppet 4 to the actuator, and from the actuator around poppet 1 the next selector valve.

When nothing is being actuated, the selector valve is turned to its neutral position shown in Figure 5-38C. Poppet 3 is off its seat and all of the others are seated. Fluid flows from the pressure manifold around poppet 3, through the next selector valve, and then back to the reservoir.

Spool-Type Closed-Center Selector Valve

Some applications have only a small amount of force to actuate a control valve that directs fluid into and out of an actuator. These applications often use a spool-type selector valve.

Figure 5-39A shows the way the spool-type selector valve is installed in the system. View B shows the position of the spool that directs fluid into the actuator extending the piston. View C shows the position of the spool that retracts the piston, and view D shows the spool in the neutral position with all flow to the actuator cutoff.

Sequence Valves

Some modern aircraft with retractable landing gear have doors that close in-flight to cover the wheel-wells and make the airplane more streamlined.

Sequence valves are often used to ensure that the landing gear does not extend or retract while the doors are closed. Sequence valves are check valves that allow fluid to flow in one direction but prevent it from flowing in the opposite direction until the valve is opened manually, so the fluid can flow in either direction.

Figure 5-40 shows the location of the sequence valves in a landing gear retraction system. When the landing gear selector handle is placed in the GEAR-DOWN position, fluid flows to the wheel-well door actuator, but cannot flow to the landing gear actuator because it is blocked by the sequence valve. When the wheel-well doors are fully open, a part of the door depresses the plunger in the sequence valve, and fluid flows into the landing gear actuator cylinder to lower the landing gear.

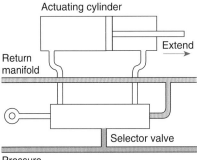

A Installation of valve in system

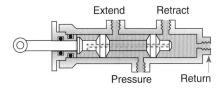

B Position of spool to extend piston

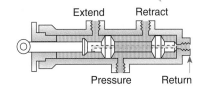

C Position of spool to retract piston

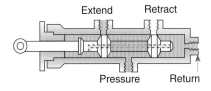

D Neutral position of spool

Figure 5-39. *Spool-type closed-center selector valve*

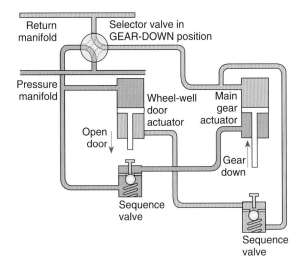

Figure 5-40. *A landing gear retraction system using a sequence valve to ensure that the wheel well doors are fully open before the landing gear extends.*

sequence valve. A valve in a hydraulic system that requires a certain action to be completed before another action can begin.

Sequence valves are used to ensure that the hydraulically actuated wheel-well doors are completely open before pressure can be directed to the landing gear to lower it.

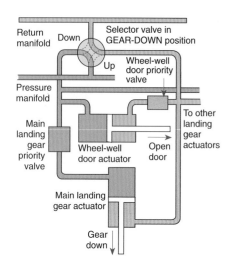

Figure 5-41. *Installation of priority valves in a landing gear actuating system to ensure that the wheel well doors are fully open before the main landing gear is extended, and that the wheels are fully retracted before the wheel well doors close.*

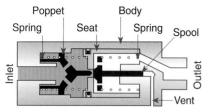

A Insufficient pressure, wheel-well doors are being actuated.

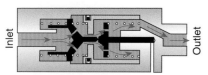

B Full pressure, landing gear is being lowered.

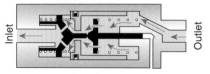

C Return fluid flow when gear is being retracted.

Figure 5-42. *Principle of operation of a priority valve*

When the landing gear selector valve is placed in the GEAR-UP position, fluid flows into the landing gear actuator to raise the landing gear, but the sequence valve prevents it flowing into the wheel-well door actuator. As soon as the landing gear is fully retracted, a part of the landing gear depresses the plunger in the wheel-well door sequence valve and opens it so fluid can flow into the wheel-well door actuator and close the wheel-well doors.

Priority Valve

A priority valve is similar to a sequence valve except that it is opened by hydraulic pressure rather than by mechanical contact.

Priority valves get their name from the fact that they control the sequence of operation of landing gear retraction and wheel-well door actuation by allowing the units that require the least pressure to have priority, or to actuate first.

Figure 5-41 shows the landing gear selector valve in the GEAR-DOWN position. Fluid flows to the wheel-well door actuator to open the doors, but it cannot flow to the main landing gear actuator, because it is shut off by the main landing gear priority valve.

Figure 5-42 shows the principle on which the priority valve operates. Figure 5-42A shows the valve in the position it is in before the wheel-well doors are fully open.

As soon as the doors are fully open, pressure builds up in the gear-down line and moves the poppet inside the priority valve to the right, as seen in Figure 5-42B. A pin on the poppet forces the spool valve off its seat and allows fluid to flow to the main landing gear actuator.

When the landing gear selector valve is placed in the GEAR-UP position, return fluid from the main landing gear actuator flows through the priority valve in the reverse direction as seen in Figure 5-42C. The fluid moves the seat to the left so that it opens the spool valve and allows fluid to flow through the selector valve to the reservoir.

Figure 5-41 shows a wheel-well door priority valve in the close-door line to the wheel-well door actuator. When the landing gear selector is placed in the GEAR-UP position, fluid flows into the main landing gear actuator to raise the gear. When the gear is up, the pressure builds up high enough to shift the poppet inside the wheel-well door priority valve. The poppet opens the spool valve and fluid flows into the wheel-well door cylinder to close it.

Flap Overload Valve

It is very important that wing flaps not be lowered when the airspeed is too high, and if the airspeed becomes too high when they are lowered, they must be raised. An excessive airload on the flaps can cause structural damage or unwanted pitching forces.

A flap overload valve can be installed in the wing flap hydraulic system to prevent the flaps from being lowered at too high an airspeed. If they are down when the airspeed increases, the valve allows them to raise automatically until the air load is within safe limits. *See* Figure 5-43.

When the flap selector valve is placed in the FLAPS-DOWN position, fluid flows through the overload valve from ports P to F and into the flaps-down side of the actuator. If they are being lowered when the airspeed is too high, the air loads on the flaps will require more pressure than the overload valve will allow. The valve shifts, returning the fluid from the overload valve back into the reservoir through port R, the check valve, and the selector valve. As soon as the air load decreases to an allowable level the overload valve allows fluid to flow into the actuator to continue lowering the flaps.

flap overload valve. A valve in the flap system of an airplane that prevents the flaps being lowered at an airspeed which could cause structural damage. If the pilot tries to extend the flaps when the airspeed is too high, the opposition caused by the airflow will open the overload valve and return the fluid to the reservoir.

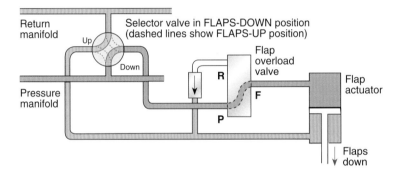

Figure 5-43. *The flap overload valve prevents the flaps from being lowered at too high an airspeed. If the flaps are down and the airspeed increases to too high a value, the flaps will raise automatically.*

If the airspeed increases to such an extent that the air load on the flaps becomes dangerously high when the flaps are down with the selector valve in the NEUTRAL position, the pressure on the down side of the actuator will increase and shift the overload valve so fluid flows through it from ports F to R and through the check valve to the up side of the actuator, allowing the flaps to retract until the air load is no longer excessive.

Flow Equalizer Valve

Some airplanes use a flow equalizer between the main landing gear actuating cylinders to cause the two landing gears to extend and retract evenly. *See* Figure 5-44 on the next page.

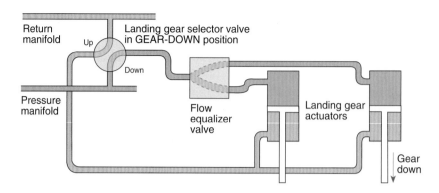

Figure 5-44. *A flow equalizer in the gear-down lines of a landing gear retraction system causes the two landing gears to move at the same speed as they retract and extend.*

crossflow valve. An automatic flow-control valve installed between the gear-up and gear-down lines of the landing gear of some large airplanes.

When the landing gear is released from its uplocks, its weight causes it to fall faster than the hydraulic system can supply fluid to the gear-down side of the actuation cylinder. The crossflow valve opens and directs fluid from the gear-up side into the gear-down side. This allows the gear to move down with a smooth motion.

When the landing gear handle is placed in the GEAR-DOWN position, fluid flows through the selector valve and the flow equalizer valve on its way to the gear-down side of the two main-gear actuator cylinders. The fluid divides inside the flow equalizer and flows through two internal passages that are connected by a free-floatig metering piston. If the right gear binds slightly, more fluid flows into the left actuator than to the right, and the metering piston moves over and restricts the flow to the left cylinder, forcing more fluid to flow into the right cylinder, keeping the flow to the two cylinders the same.

When the selector valve is moved to the GEAR-UP position, return fluid from the two actuators flows through the flow equalizer. The metering piston moves to whichever side is necessary to restrict the flow from the actuator that is moving fastest, and forces them to retract at the same speed.

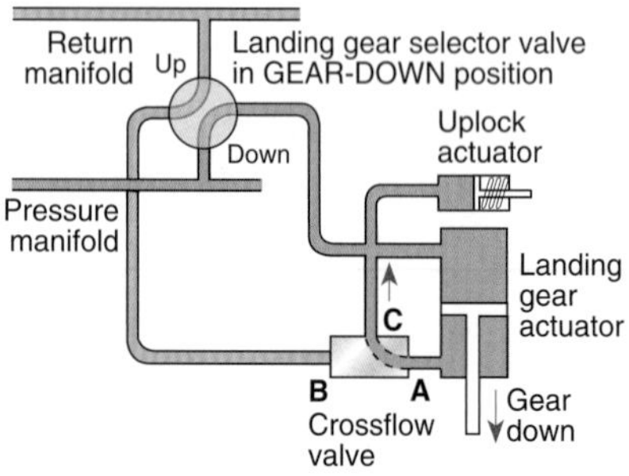

Landing Gear Crossflow Valve

When a heavy landing gear is released from its uplocks, it pulls the actuator piston out faster than fluid from the selector valve can fill the down-side of the cylinder. A crossflow valve allows fluid to flow directly from the up-side of the actuator to the down-side until the system fluid can catch up with the demands of the actuator. *See* Figure 5-45.

When the landing gear selector is placed in the GEAR-DOWN position, fluid releases the uplock and the landing gear drops down. The weight of the gear pulls the piston out of the cylinder, and fluid from the up-side of the actuator flows through the crossflow valve from port A, out through port C directly to the down-side of the actuator. This allows the gear to fall smoothly

Figure 5-45. *When a heavy landing gear is released from its uplocks, its weight causes the piston to move faster than fluid from the selector valve can fill the gear-down side of the cylinder. Fluid flows through the crossflow valve and allows the gear to fall with a smooth and even motion.*

and evenly. As soon as the pump catches up with the demands for fluid in the down-side of the actuator, the crossflow valve shuts off port C and fluid returns to the reservoir through port B and the selector valve.

When the gear selector is placed in the GEAR-UP position, fluid flows through the crossflow valve from port B to A with no appreciable restriction.

Hydraulic Fuses

Hydraulic systems on modern jet aircraft are extremely important, not only for raising and lowering the landing gear, but also for operating boosted control systems, thrust reversers, flaps, brakes, and many of the auxiliary systems. Most aircraft have more than one independent hydraulic system, and hydraulic fuses are used in these systems to block a line and shut off the flow of fluid if a serious leak should develop.

There are two types of hydraulic fuses; one shuts off the flow after a specific amount of fluid has flowed through it, and the other shuts off the flow if the pressure drop across the fuse indicates a broken line.

Figure 5-46 shows a pressure-drop-type fuse. Fluid flows through the fuse from left to right. When the flow rate is within the normal operating range, there is not enough pressure drop across the fuse to move the piston over against the force of the spring, and fluid flows through the fuse to the actuator. But if a line should break, the pressure at the break will be so low that the piston will be forced to the right and will shut off the flow of fluid to the actuator.

The fuse has no effect on the return flow of fluid from the actuator in normal action. The return fluid flowing through the fuse forces the piston to the left and uncovers the ports so fluid can flow through the fuse with no restriction.

The second type of fuse is shown in Figure 5-47 on the next page. This fuse shuts off the flow of fluid any time a specific amount of fluid flows through it, and prevents a loss of fluid even though the leak is not severe enough to cause the large pressure drop required to operate the other type of fuse.

In normal operation, (view A), fluid has forced the sleeve valve over to the right and fluid flows through the valve with a minimum of opposition. As the fluid flows through the fuse, some of it flows through the metering orifice and pushes the piston to the right.

By the time a specified amount of fluid passes through the fuse, the piston is forced all the way to the right, where it covers the ports and shuts off the flow of fluid through the fuse (view B).

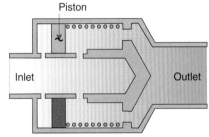
Flow of fluid though fuse for normal operation

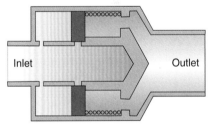
An excessive pressure drop has occurred and piston has been forced to the right, shutting off flow of fluid.

Figure 5-46. *Hydraulic fuse that operates on the principle of an excessive pressure drop.*

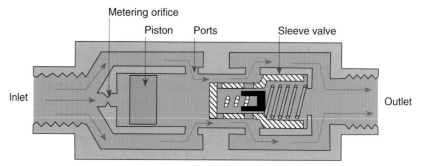

A Normal flow through fuse. The piston is moving over an amount proportional to amount of fluid that has passed through fuse.

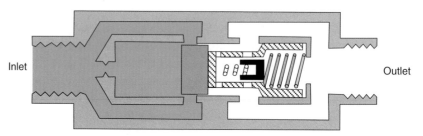

B The piston has moved over to block the ports, and no more fluid can flow through the fuse.

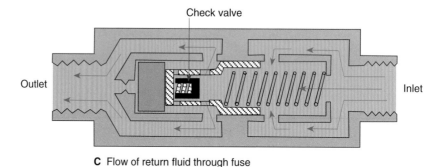

C Flow of return fluid through fuse

Figure 5-47. *Hydraulic fuse that shuts off the flow of fluid after a specific amount of fluid flows through*

When fluid flows through the fuse in the reverse direction, the sleeve valve and the piston are both moved to the left and fluid can flow through the fuse unrestricted (view C). *See* Figure 5-47.

Pressure Control Valves

There are two basic types of pressure control valves used in fluid power systems: pressure regulators and pressure relief valves. Pressure regulators relieve the fluid pump of its load while circulating fluid back to the reservoir. Relief valves do not relieve the pump of its load, but return just enough fluid to the reservoir to prevent pressure from becoming excessive.

Relief Valves

The simplest type of pressure control valve is the relief valve. In practical systems, however, a relief valve is used primarily as a backup device to prevent high pressure from damaging the system rather than as a pressure control device. When a relief valve relieves pressure, heat is generated and power is lost.

The system pressure relief valve opens and relieves any pressure above that which is maintained by the system pressure regulator. Only in the event of a malfunction of the regulator will the relief valve be required to function.

There are typically a number of pressure control valves in a hydraulic system with a wide range of relief pressures. To adjust any of the relief valves, you must temporarily adjust the pressure regulator to a pressure above that of the highest relief valve. Adjust the relief valve with the highest setting first, and then adjust the other valves in descending order of their relief pressure. When you have adjusted all of the relief valves, adjust the system pressure regulator to its correct pressure.

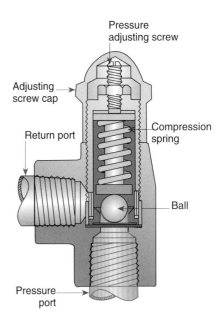

Figure 5-48. *Typical two-port pressure relief valve*

Thermal Relief Valves

Pressure can build up in parts of a hydraulic system where fluid is trapped in a line between the actuator and its selector valve. The trapped fluid gets hot and expands, and if there is no way to relieve the pressure, it can rupture a line or damage some of the components.

A thermal relief valve is a pressure relief valve that is installed between the portion of the system in which the pressure is trapped and the system return manifold. Thermal relief valves relieve pressure above the setting of the normal system pressure relief valve before it builds up high enough to do any damage. They do not interfere with normal system operation.

thermal relief valve. A relief valve in a hydraulic system that relieves pressure that builds up in an isolated part of the system because of heat. Thermal relief valves are set at a higher pressure than the system pressure relief valve.

closed-center hydraulic system. A
hydraulic system in which the selector
valves are installed in parallel with each
other. When no unit is actuated, fluid
circulates from the pump back to the
reservoir without flowing through any of
the selector valves.

Automatic Pressure Regulators or Unloading Valves

Closed-center hydraulic systems require an automatic regulator to maintain
the pressure within a specified range and to keep the pump unloaded when no
unit in the system is actuated. There are two basic types of automatic pressure
regulators, the spool type and the balanced type. Both regulators accomplish
the same purpose, and the principle of operation of the simpler balanced type
regulator is illustrated in Figure 5-49.

Starting with a discharged system in which there is no fluid pressure in
the accumulator, the pump pushes fluid through the check valve into the
system and into the accumulator. The accumulator fills with fluid, and when
no fluid is needed for actuation, the pressure builds up. This pressure enters
both the top and bottom of the regulator. It pushes up on the piston and down
on the ball.

The upward and downward forces reach a balance. The fluid pressure on
the ball and the spring force on the piston are both downward forces, and the
hydraulic pressure on the piston is an upward force. When the hydraulic
pressure is 1,500 psi, these forces are balanced.

To understand the operation of this regulator, assume that the piston has
an area of 1 square inch and the ball seat has an area of $\frac{1}{3}$ square inch. When
the system pressure is 1,500 psi, there is a force of 1,500 pounds pushing up
on the piston. To balance this upward force, there is a downward force of
1,000 pounds applied by the spring, and 500 pounds of force applied when
the 1,500-psi hydraulic pressure pushes down on the $\frac{1}{3}$-square inch ball
seat area.

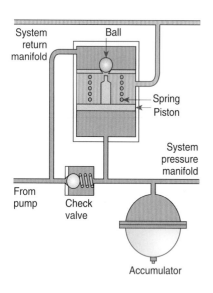

Upward force
    Piston area = 1 square inch
    Pressure = 1,500 psi
    Total upward force = 1,500 · 1 = 1,500 pounds

Downward force
    Spring = 1,000 pounds
    Ball area = 0.333 square inch
    Force on ball = 1,500 · 0.333 = 500 pounds
    Total downward force = 1,000 + 500 = 1,500 pounds

Figure 5-49. *Balanced-type system
pressure regulator installed in a hydraulic
system*

When the pressure produced by the hydraulic pump rises above 1,500 psi,
the force pushing up on the piston and the force pushing down on the ball
both increase, but the spring force remains constant. The increased pressure
pushing up on the large area of the piston moves the piston upward until the
pin forces the ball off its seat and pump output flows through the valve to the
return manifold.

As soon as the ball moves off its seat, the pressure on the pump side of the
check valve drops to almost zero and the check valve seats, trapping pressure
in the system where it is held by the accumulator. The pump is unloaded, and
it circulates fluid through the system with very little opposition.

The system will continue to operate with the pump unloaded until the pressure held by the accumulator drops to slightly below 1,000 psi. As soon as the pressure below the piston drops to a value that produces an upward force is less than the downward force of the spring (1,000 pounds), the spring pushes the piston down and the ball seats. When the ball is seated, flow to the reservoir is shut off and the pressure builds back up to 1,500 psi. The pressure at which the pump unloads, 1,500 psi, is called the kick-out pressure and the pressure at which the ball seats to load the pump, 1,000 psi, is called the kick-in pressure.

Pressure Reducer

Some automatic pilots require less than system pressure for their actuation. These may use a simple pressure reducer like the one in Figure 5-50. This valve operates on the principle of a balance between hydraulic and spring forces.

Assume that the piston has an area of 1 square inch, and it is held against its seat by a spring that pushes down with a force of 100 pounds. The piston has a shoulder area of 0.5 square inch, and this area is acted on by the full system pressure, 1,500 psi. The cone-shaped seat of this valve has an area of 0.5 square inch, and it is acted on by the reduced pressure of 200 psi.

A tiny hole in the piston bleeds fluid into the chamber inside the piston, and a relief valve maintains the pressure of this fluid at 750 psi.

When the automatic pilot uses some of the fluid, the reduced pressure drops. The relief valve unseats, and the pressure above the piston decreases. System pressure raises the valve off of its seat and the reduced pressure rises back to its desired 200 psi value. As soon as the pressure rises to this value, the relief valve again seats, the pressure behind the piston builds back up to 750 psi, and the piston moves down to hold the reduced pressure constant.

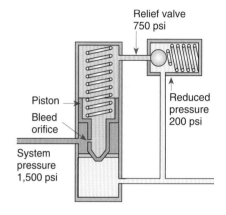

Figure 5-50. *Pressure reducer valve*

STUDY QUESTIONS: HYDRAULIC VALVES

Answers begin on Page 416. Page numbers refer to chapter text.

69. A flow control valve that allows full flow in one direction but no flow in the opposite direction is called a/an _____ valve. *Page 359*

70. A flow control valve that allows a full flow in one direction but a restricted flow in the opposite direction is called a/an _____ . *Page 360*

71. A mechanically operated flow control valve that prevents fluid flowing to one unit before some other unit has actuated completely is called a/an _____ valve. *Page 363*

Continued

72. A pressure-operated flow control valve that prevents fluid flowing to one unit until another unit has actuated and hydraulic pressure has built up to a value high enough to shift the valve is called a/an _____ valve. *Page 364*

73. A flap overload valve is placed in the _____ (flaps-up or flaps-down) line. *Page 365*

74. Heavy landing gears are assisted in falling smoothly and evenly from the wheel wells by allowing fluid to flow from the up-side of the actuator to the down side through a _____ valve. *Page 366*

75. Two types of selector valves are _____ and _____ . *Page 360*

76. Plug-type selector valves are used in _____ (high or low)-pressure fluid power systems. *Page 361*

77. One characteristic of a spool-type selector valve is that it requires a _____ (large or small) force to operate the control. *Page 363*

78. A flow equalizer valve installed in the landing gear gear-down line _____ (does or does not) equalize the flow for both extension and retraction of the landing gear. *Page 366*

79. A component that shuts off the flow of hydraulic fluid if a line should rupture is called a hydraulic _____ . *Page 367*

80. A pressure relief valve is usually used as a _____ (primary or backup) pressure regulating valve. *Page 369*

81. A thermal relief valve is adjusted to relieve at a pressure _____ (lower or higher) than that for which the main system pressure relief valve is adjusted. *Page 369*

82. Another name for a system pressure regulator is a/an _____ valve. *Page 370*

83. When one subsystem requires a lower pressure than the normal system operating pressure, a/an _____ valve is used. *Page 371*

Hydraulic Accumulators

Hydraulic fluid is not compressible, and in order to keep it under pressure, it must be stored against something compressible, such as the air or nitrogen in an accumulator.

Three basic types of accumulators are: the bladder-type, the diaphragm-type and the piston-type. The bladder and diaphragm accumulators are both steel spheres, and the piston-type is in the form of a cylinder.

Bladder-type accumulators have a heavy bladder, or bag, inside the steel sphere. This bladder is made of neoprene or ethylene propylene rubber, depending upon the type of fluid used. The bladder is filled with a compressed gas such as air or nitrogen, and the hydraulic fluid is pumped into the sphere on the outside of the bladder. As the hydraulic fluid is pumped into the accumulator, it takes up some of the space the bladder had originally taken up, and the gas inside the bladder is further compressed.

The bladder presses against the hydraulic fluid inside the accumulator with a force that causes the pressure of the liquid on the outside of the bladder to be the same as the pressure of the gas inside the bladder. A metal plate is fitted into the bladder to cover the fluid entry port so that the bladder will not be extruded out into this opening. *See* Figure 5-51.

The diaphragm-type accumulator is made of two steel hemispheres fastened together with a folded neoprene or ethylene propylene rubber diaphragm between the two halves. One side of the diaphragm is the air chamber and the other side is the fluid chamber.

When the hydraulic pump is not operating, the compressed gas forces the diaphragm over until the air chamber fills the entire sphere. As hydraulic fluid is pumped into the accumulator, the diaphragm is moved down, further compressing the gas and storing the hydraulic fluid under pressure. *See* Figure 5-52.

The piston-type accumulator is made of a steel or aluminum alloy cylinder divided into two compartments by a floating piston. Compressed air or nitrogen is put into one end of the cylinder and the hydraulic fluid is put into the other end. As more fluid is forced into the accumulator, the piston is moved over, further compressing the gas and storing the hydraulic fluid under pressure. *See* Figure 5-53 on the next page.

Accumulators are charged with compressed air or nitrogen to a pressure of approximately one third of the hydraulic system pressure. As the pump forces hydraulic fluid into the accumulator, the gas is further compressed, and it exerts a force on the hydraulic fluid, holding it under pressure after the system pressure regulator has unloaded the pump.

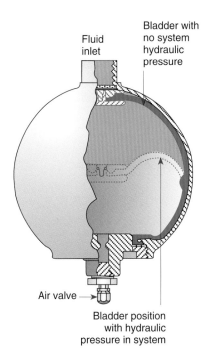

Figure 5-51. *Bladder-type accumulator*

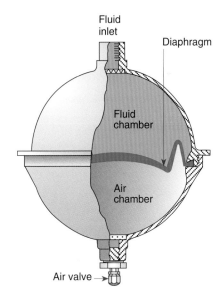

Figure 5-52. *Diaphragm-type accumulator*

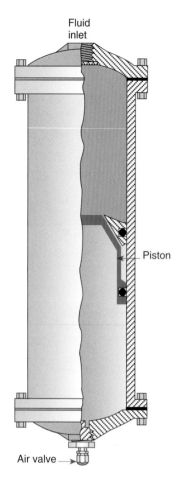

Figure 5-53. *Piston-type accumulator*

Air valves used in accumulators may be one of three types. The most simple is the AN812 valve in Figure 5-54. This valve seals the air inside the accumulator with a high-pressure core that is similar in appearance, but different in construction from the valve core that is used in tires. The valve core used in an accumulator air valve is identified by the letter H embossed on the end of the stem.

To deflate an accumulator equipped with an AN812 valve, do not depress the valve stem, but loosen the valve body in the accumulator. The bleed hole in the side of the valve allows the air to leak past the loosened threads.

Both AN6287-1 and MS28889 valves seal the air inside the accumulator with a steel-against-steel seal. The AN6287-1 valve has a valve core similar to the one used in the AN812 valve, but it has a swivel nut around the stem. To charge an accumulator equipped with an AN6287-1 valve, remove the protective cap from the valve, attach the charging hose to the valve, and loosen the swivel nut for one turn. Loosening the swivel nut backs the valve body off enough to allow air to pass into the accumulator. To deflate an accumulator fitted with this valve, remove the protective cap, loosen the swivel nut one turn, and depress the stem of the valve core. *See* Figure 5-55.

The MS28889 valve does not use a valve core. It depends entirely on the metal-to-metal seal to hold air in the accumulator. To charge an accumulator equipped with this valve, remove the protective cap, install the charging hose on the valve, loosen the swivel nut, and allow air to flow into the accumulator. To discharge the accumulator, remove the protective cap and loosen the swivel nut. *See* Figure 5-56.

The MS28889 and AN6287-1 valves are similar in appearance, except that there is no valve core in the MS28889 valve, and its swivel nut is the same size as the body of the valve. (The swivel nut on the AN6287-1 valve is smaller than the valve body). Another difference is that the MS28889 valve has a roll pin in its body that prevents the stem of the valve being screwed too far into the body.

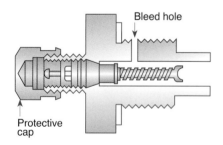

Figure 5-54. *AN812 high-pressure air valve*

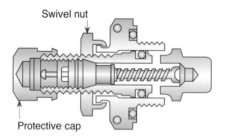

Figure 5-55. *AN6287-1 high-pressure air valve*

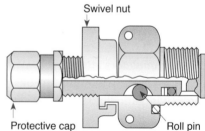

Figure 5-56. *MS28889 high-pressure air valve*

When an accumulator is installed in an aircraft it must be given an air preload charge. The amount of this charge is specified in the aircraft maintenance manual, and it is usually about one third of the normal system operating pressure. Some accumulators have an air pressure gage and an air filler valve that is accessible for line servicing. Other accumulators do not have any way of directly measuring the air preload pressure. If the accumulator does not have an air pressure gage, you may determine the preload pressure by following these steps:

1. Build up hydraulic system pressure with the hand pump until the system pressure gage indicates the rated pressure.

2. Very slowly bleed the pressure off by operating some component such as the flaps. Watch the pressure gage carefully while the pressure is bleeding down. The indication will decrease slowly until the preload pressure is reached, and then it will drop instantly to zero. The pressure indicated on the gage just before its sudden drop is the accumulator preload air pressure.

The system pressure gage in some hydraulic systems actually measures the air pressure in the accumulator rather than hydraulic fluid pressure. When there is no fluid pressure in the system, this type of gage will read the accumulator air preload charge, and as soon as fluid is pumped into the accumulator the fluid and air pressure will be the same and the gage will indicate the pressure on the hydraulic fluid. If the air preload pressure is 1,000 psi, and fluid is pumped into the accumulator until the gage reads 2,000 psi, the air and fluid pressure are both 2,000 psi. If the gage ever reads 0 psi, there is no accumulator preload air.

Before removing any component from the pressure manifold on which an accumulator is holding pressure, all of the system pressure must be bled off. Do this by actuating any unit whose movement will not cause any damage. Actuate the unit until the system pressure drops to zero, then it is safe to remove components from the pressure manifold.

accumulator air preload. Compressed air or nitrogen in one side of an accumulator. The air preload is usually about one third of the system hydraulic pressure. When fluid is pumped into the oil side of the accumulator the air is further compressed, and the air pressure and the fluid pressure will be the same.

STUDY QUESTIONS: HYDRAULIC ACCUMULATORS

Answers begin on Page 416. Page numbers refer to chapter text.

84. In order to store an incompressible fluid under pressure in a hydraulic system, a/an
_____ must be used. *Page 373*

85. The initial pressure of compressed air or nitrogen used to preload in an accumulator is approximately
_____ of the system pressure. *Page 373*

Continued

86. The air valve core used in an accumulator is identified as a high-pressure core by the letter _____ embossed on the stem. *Page 374*

87. An accumulator fitted with an AN812 air valve _____ (should or should not) be deflated by depressing the valve stem. *Page 374*

88. When hydraulic fluid is pumped into an accumulator, the preload air pressure will _____ (increase, decrease, or remain the same). *Page 375*

sintered metal. A porous material made by fusing powdered metal under heat and pressure.

epoxy. A flexible thermosetting (does not soften when heated) resin made by the polymerization of an epoxide.

Epoxy is noted for its durability and chemical resistance.

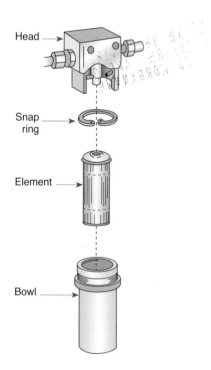

Head

Snap
ring

Element

Bowl

Figure 5-57. *External view of a hydraulic filter assembly*

Hydraulic Filters

Hydraulic fluid must be kept clean. As many of the solid contaminants as possible must be removed from the fluid. These contaminants can damage the pumps, valves, and actuators in a hydraulic system.

The filtering capability of a hydraulic filter is measured in microns. One micron is one millionth of a meter, or 39 millionths of an inch (0.000 039 inch). The unaided human eye can see contaminants as small as 40 microns, and an effective filter should be able to remove contaminants larger than 5 microns. *See* Figure 5-20 on Page 346.

Two basic types of filters are used in aircraft hydraulic systems: surface filters and edge filters.

Surface filters trap the contaminants on the surface of the element, which may be made of sintered metal or a specially treated cellulose material. These filters usually have a bypass valve built into them that opens to allow the fluid to bypass the element if it should become clogged. Wire mesh and some sintered metal filter elements may be cleaned and reused, but others are noncleanable and are discarded on a regular scheduled basis.

Some of the latest filter elements are known as 5-micron noncleanable elements. These elements are made of a combination of organic and inorganic fibers integrally bonded with epoxy resin and faced with metallic mesh on both sides for protection and added mechanical strength. These elements should never be cleaned, but are replaced on a regular maintenance schedule.

Another new type of 5-micron filtering element is made of layers of very fine stainless steel fibers drawn into a random but controlled matrix. The matrix is then processed by compressing it and bonding all of the wires at their crossing points into a very thin layer. This type of filtering element is made in both cleanable and noncleanable forms.

The filter assembly in Figure 5-57 is typical of modern system filters. The filter head is installed in the hydraulic system either in the pressure side of the pump or in the return line to the reservoir. The filter bowl can be unscrewed from the head to remove the filter element. When the bowl is removed, the shut-off diaphragm closes to prevent the loss of any fluid that is in the system downstream of the filter.

A bypass poppet valve is installed in this filter assembly to allow fluid to flow through the system in the event the filter element clogs. If the element clogs, there will be a large pressure drop across it, and the inlet fluid will force the valve off its seat. Unfiltered fluid will flow through the system. When enough pressure builds up across the filter to unseat the bypass valve, the red differential-pressure indicator button pops up to inform the maintenance technician that the filter element is clogged and has bypassed fluid. This indicator may also be connected to a switch to give an electrical signal to the maintenance computer that the filter is clogged. *See* Figure 5-58.

Edge filters, often called Cuno filters, are made up of stacks of thin metal disks with scrapers between them. All of the fluid flows between the disks, and contaminants are stopped on the edges of the disks. The degree of filtration is determined by the thickness of the separators between the disks.

Cuno filters are cleaned by turning the shaft that rotates the disks and scrapes the contaminants from between them into the outer housing, where they can be removed by draining the filter bowl.

Cuno filter. The registered trade name for a particular style of edge-type fluid filter.

Cuno filters are made up of a stack of thin metal disks that are separated by thin scraper blades. Contaminants collect on the edge of the disks, and they are periodically scraped out and allowed to collect in the bottom of the filter case for future removal.

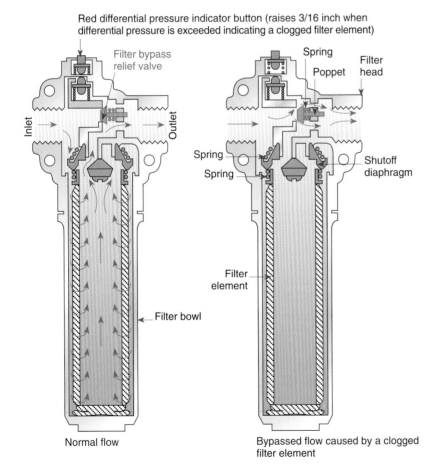

Red differential pressure indicator button (raises 3/16 inch when differential pressure is exceeded indicating a clogged filter element)

Filter bypass relief valve

Inlet

Outlet

Spring

Poppet

Filter head

Spring

Spring

Shutoff diaphragm

Filter element

Filter bowl

Normal flow

Bypassed flow caused by a clogged filter element

Figure 5-58. *Hydraulic filter assembly incorporating a differential pressure indicator*

Answers begin on Page 416. Page numbers refer to chapter text.

89. An efficient hydraulic filter should be able to remove contaminants larger than _____ microns. *Page 376*

90. A red indicator button sticking up on the top of a hydraulic filter is an indication that the filter element is _____ . *Page 377*

91. If a hydraulic filter clogs, unfiltered fluid flows to the system through a _____ valve in the filter. *Page 377*

92. The degree of filtration of a Cuno filter is determined by the thickness of the _____ (disks or separators). *Page 377*

hydraulic actuator. The component in a hydraulic system that converts hydraulic pressure into mechanical force. The two main types of hydraulic actuators are linear actuators (cylinders and pistons) and rotary actuators (hydraulic motors).

linear actuator. A fluid power actuator that uses a piston moving inside a cylinder to change pressure into linear, or straight-line, motion.

Hydraulic Actuators

The ultimate function of a hydraulic or pneumatic system is to convert the pressure in the fluid into work. In order to do this, there must be some form of movement, and this movement takes place in the actuator. Linear and rotary actuators are the most widely used. This section of the text discusses both types.

Linear Actuators

Linear actuators are made up of a cylinder and a piston. The cylinder is usually attached to the aircraft structure, and the piston is connected to the component that is being moved.

If two linear actuating cylinders with pistons having the same cross-sectional area but different lengths of stroke are connected to the same source of hydraulic pressure, they will exert equal amounts of force, and move at the same rate of speed. But it will take them a different length of time to reach the end of their stroke. If the cylinders have different areas, but are connected to the same source of pressure, they will produce different amounts of force.

The rate of movement of the piston in a linear actuator can be controlled by restricting the fluid flowing into or out of the cylinder.

Figure 5-59 shows three basic types of linear actuators. A single-acting actuator has a piston that is moved in one direction by hydraulic fluid, and is returned by a spring. A double-acting actuator uses hydraulic fluid to move the piston in both directions. An unbalanced, double-acting actuator has a piston rod extending from only one side of the piston, and a double-acting balanced actuator has piston rods extending from both sides of the piston.

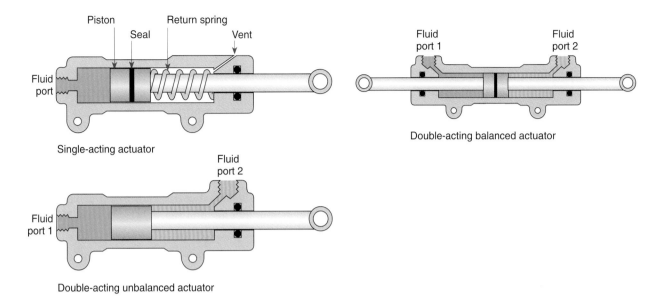

Figure 5-59. *Linear hydraulic actuators*

Unbalanced actuators have more area on one side of the piston than on the other because of the area that is taken up by the piston rod. As much force as possible is needed to raise the landing gear, so the fluid pushes against the full area of the piston. Not as much force is needed to lower the landing gear because of the weight of the struts and wheels, so the fluid is directed into the end of the actuator that has the piston rod. The fluid pushes on only the portion of the piston that is not taken up by the rod.

A balanced actuator has a shaft on both sides of the piston, so the area is the same on each side, and the same amount of force is developed in each direction. Balanced actuators are commonly used for hydraulic servos used with automatic pilots.

Linear actuators may have features that adapt them to special jobs. Figure 5-60 (Page 380) illustrates a landing gear actuator that has internal locks to hold the landing gear down. The actuator is locked with the piston retracted all the way into the cylinder until hydraulic pressure releases it. In Figure 5-60A, the piston is retracted, and the landing gear is down and locked by the locking balls that are forced into the groove in the end of the piston by the locking pin.

balanced actuator. A hydraulic or pneumatic actuator that has the same area on both sides of the piston.

unbalanced actuator. A hydraulic or pneumatic actuator that has a greater area on one side of the piston than on the other.

When the landing gear selector is placed in the GEAR-UP position, fluid flows into the cylinder and forces the locking pin to the right, which allows the balls to drop down and release the piston. The spring forces the collar to the left to hold the balls against the locking pin. Movement of the locking pin pulls the check valve back and allows fluid to flow into the cylinder, extending the piston and raising the gear. *See* Figure 5-60B.

When the landing gear selector is placed in the GEAR-DOWN position, fluid moves the actuator piston into the cylinder, and the fluid on the gear-up side of the piston forces the check valve back. The fluid leaves the actuator. As the piston reaches its fully retracted position, it forces the collar back, and the spring behind the locking pin pushes it to the left and forces the balls into the groove at the end of the piston, locking it in place.

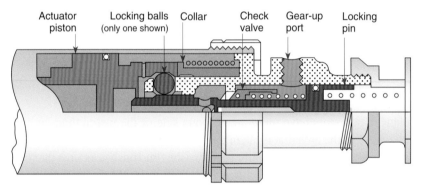

A Landing gear is down and locked with actuator piston fully retracted into cylinder and locked in place.

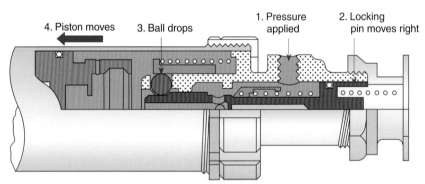

B Fluid has pushed locking pin back to release locking balls and allow fluid to force piston to extend, raising landing gear.

Figure 5-60. *Landing gear actuating cylinder with internal down lock*

Rotary Actuators

The efficient rack-and-pinion actuator is used on the single-engine Cessna airplanes to retract their landing gear. A piston with rack teeth cut onto its shaft rotates the pinion as the piston moves in or out of the cylinder. Rotation of the pinion gear raises or lowers the landing gear. *See* Figure 5-61.

rotary actuator. A fluid power actuator whose output is rotational. A hydraulic motor is a rotary actuator.

rack-and-pinion actuator. A form of rotary actuator where the fluid acts on a piston on which a rack of gear teeth is cut. As the piston moves, it rotates a pinion gear which is mated with the teeth cut in the rack.

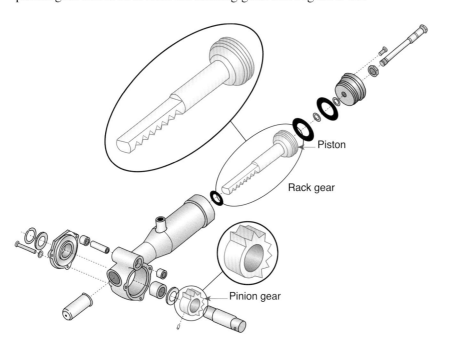

Piston

Rack gear

Pinion gear

Figure 5-61. *Rack-and-pinion linear hydraulic actuator with a rotary output.*

Hydraulic motors are used to maintain continued rotation. Hydraulic motors are similar to hydraulic pumps except for certain design detail differences. Piston motors have many applications on larger aircraft where a considerable amount of power with good control is needed. The advantages of hydraulic motors over electric motors are its ability to instantaneously reverse the direction of rotation and its lack of fire hazard in the event of a stalled rotor.

Vane-type hydraulic motors that have provisions for balancing the load on the shaft are also used. Some of the pressure is directed to both sides of the motor, as is seen in the balanced-vane-type motor in Figure 5-62.

hydraulic motor. A hydraulic actuator that converts fluid pressure into rotary motion.

Hydraulic motors have an advantage in aircraft installations over electric motors, because they can operate in a stalled condition without the danger of a fire.

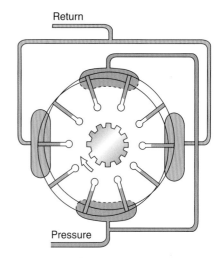

Return

Pressure

Figure 5-62. *Balanced-vane-type hydraulic motor*

Servo Actuators

Heavy, high-performance airplanes require so much force to move the control surfaces that the pilot is assisted by hydraulically boosted controls. Rather than moving the control surface itself, the cockpit controls move flow control valves connected to servo actuators that move the surfaces.

Movement of the pilot's control causes the flow control valve to direct hydraulic fluid to the proper side of the actuating piston to move the flight control surface in the correct direction. As the actuator piston moves to the position called for by the pilot's control, the internal linkage moves the flow control valve back to a neutral position and stops the flow of hydraulic fluid, and thus the movement of the piston.

Many modern high-performance aircraft incorporate a fly-by-wire system in which there is no mechanical connection between the cockpit control and the control surfaces. Electrical input signals are generated by the position and force applied to the cockpit control, the position of the control surface, the air load on the surface and other parameters chosen by the aircraft manufac-

---

STUDY QUESTIONS: HYDRAULIC SYSTEM ACTUATORS

Answers begin on Page 416. Page numbers refer to chapter text.

93. Two types of hydraulic actuators are _____ and _____ actuators. *Page 378*

94. A linear hydraulic actuator that has the same area on both sides of its piston is called a/an _____ actuator. *Page 379*

95. If two linear actuators with pistons having the same cross sectional area but different piston strokes are connected to the same source of hydraulic pressure, the pistons will move at _____ (the same or different) rates of speed. *Page 378*

96. If two linear actuators with pistons of different cross sectional area are connected to the same source of hydraulic pressure, the pistons will produce _____ (the same or different) forces. *Page 378*

97. The rate of movement of the piston in a linear actuator may be controlled by installing a/an _____ in the inlet or outlet port of the actuator. *Page 378*

98. A hydraulic actuator whose piston is moved in both directions by hydraulic fluid under pressure is called a/an _____ actuator. *Page 378*

99. A rack-and-pinion linear hydraulic actuator has an output that is _____ (linear or rotary). *Page 381*

100. On an aircraft having boosted controls, the pilot actually moves a _____ valve which directs fluid to the proper side of an actuator that moves the control surface. *Page 382*

turer. These signals are fed into a computer that controls electrohydraulic servo actuators that move the surface the correct direction to produce the desired flight attitude change. Feedback transducers signal the computer when the desired change has been made to stop the action.

High-Pressure Seals

Seals are used throughout hydraulic and pneumatic systems to minimize leakage and the loss of system pressure. There are two types of seals in use, gaskets and packings. Gaskets are used when there is no relative motion between the parts that are being sealed, and packings are used where relative motion does exist between the parts.

Chevron Seals

There are many different kinds of seals used in aircraft applications. These seals range all of the way from flat paper gaskets up through complex, multicomponent packings.

V-ring packings, or chevron seals, like the ones in Figure 5-63, are found in many high-pressure actuators. Chevron seals are single-direction seals with the pressure applied to their open sides. They are usually installed either in pairs, or in larger stacks with metal backup rings and spreaders used to force the lip of the seal tightly against the surfaces being sealed. The amount the chevron seal spreads is determined by the tightness of the adjusting nut that holds the seal on the shaft.

gasket. A seal between two parts where there is no relative motion.

packing. A seal between two parts where there is relative motion.

chevron seal. A form of one-way seal used on the piston of some fluid-power actuators. A chevron seal is made of a resilient material in the shape of the letter V. The pressure being sealed must be applied to the open side of the V.

Cross section of a chevron seal

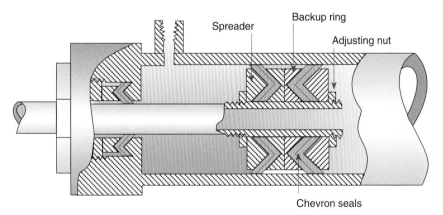

Proper installation of chevron seals

Figure 5-63. *Chevron seals, or V-ring packings*

O-ring. A widely used type of seal made in the form of a rubber ring with a round cross section. An O-ring seals in both directions, and it can be used as a packing or a gasket.

O-ring Seals

Many modern hydraulic and pneumatic systems use O-rings for both packings and gaskets. O-rings are fitted into grooves that are usually about 10% wider than the width of the O-ring, and deep enough that the distance between the bottom of the groove and the other mating surface is a little less than the cross-sectional diameter of the O-ring. This provides the squeeze needed for the O-ring to seal under conditions of zero pressure. If the O-ring is not squeezed, fluid will leak past it.

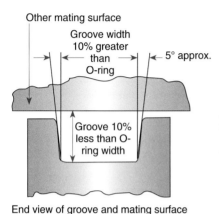

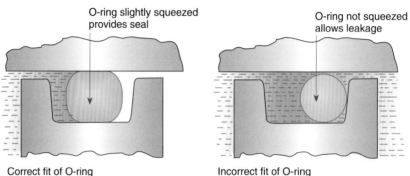

Figure 5-64. *O-ring seals*

An O-ring seal of the correct size can withstand pressures of up to about 1,500 psi without distortion, but beyond this, there is a tendency for the ring to extrude into the groove between the two mating surfaces. Figure 5-65 shows that as the pressure of the fluid increases, the O-ring begins to wedge in tight between the wall of the groove and the inside of the cylinder. To prevent this, an anti-extrusion, or backup, ring is used.

Spiraled Teflon backup rings are used for pressures higher than 1,500 psi. The ends of the Teflon ring are scarfed, and it is possible for the ring to spiral in such a direction that the scarfs will be on the wrong side, and the ring will be damaged. Figure 5-66A shows the improper spiral of the ring. Figure 5-66B shows the proper spiral, and Figure 5-66C shows the way the ring looks after pressure has been applied and the ring has taken its set.

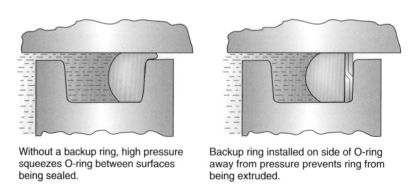

Figure 5-65. *The use of a backup ring to prevent extrusion of the O-ring*

T-Seals

Another type of two-way seal is the T-seal shown in Figure 5-67. This seal can fit in the standard O-ring grooves, and is backed up with two Teflon backup rings. These backup rings often have an inner radius to match the fillet radius of the T-seal. When installing these backup rings be careful to align the radius of the backup ring with that of the seal. T-seals are most often installed in high-pressure (3,000 psi) systems.

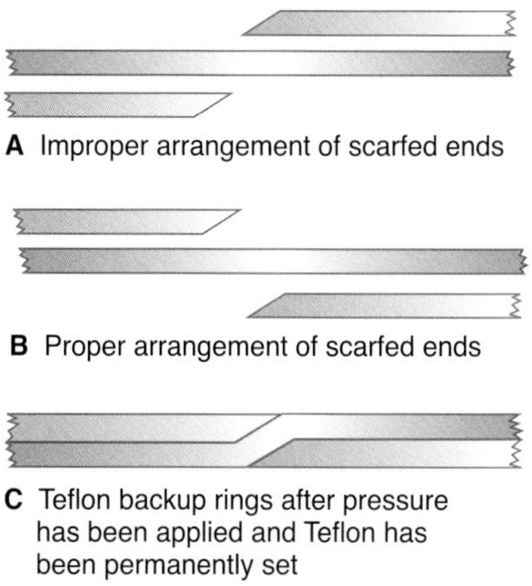

Seal Identification

The material of which a seal is made is dictated by the fluid used in the system. Seals are identified by colored marks. *See* Figure 5-68.

There is perhaps no other component as small as a hydraulic seal upon which so much importance is placed. The correct seal and a wrong seal may look alike, and it is highly probable that if the wrong seal is installed, it may appear to work. The material of which the seal is made, its age, and its hardness are all important when making the proper replacement.

When replacing seals in a hydraulic system, use only the specific part number of the seal specified by the aircraft manufacturer. Purchase seals from the equipment manufacturer or a reputable aircraft parts supplier, and they should be sealed in individual packages marked with the part number, the composition of the seal, the name of the manufacturer, and the cure date.

The cure date is the date the seal was manufactured, and it is given in quarters. For example, 2Q05 indicates that the seal was manufactured in the second quarter, during the months of April, May, or June, of 2005.

Hydraulic seals must be bought only from a reputable supplier, because out-of-date seals can be repackaged and stamped with a fresh date by an unethical distributor. The old seal could be installed in good faith by an aviation maintenance technician and fail because of deterioration due to excessive age. The technician is the one liable for the failure because installing an improper part in an aircraft is a violation of Federal Aviation Regulations.

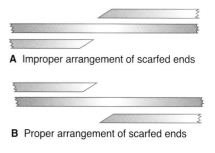

A Improper arrangement of scarfed ends

B Proper arrangement of scarfed ends

C Teflon backup rings after pressure has been applied and Teflon has been permanently set

Figure 5-66. *The proper installation of a Teflon backup ring*

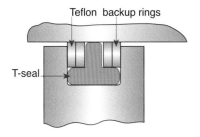

Figure 5-67. *The T-seal fits in an O-ring groove and is installed with Teflon backup rings on both sides.*

Color	Use
Blue dot or stripe	Air or MIL-H-5606 fluid
Red dot or stripe	Fuel
Yellow Dot	Synthetic engine oil
White Stripe	Petroleum-base engine oil
Green dash	Phosphate ester hydraulic fluid

Figure 5-68. *The colored marks on an O-ring seal show the fluid type with which the seal should be used.*

Seal Installation

When installing O-rings, take extreme care that the ring is not twisted, nicked, or damaged by either sharp edges of the machine threads over which the ring is installed, or by the installation tool. Figure 5-69 shows some of the special O-ring installation and removal tools that can be used. These tools are usually made of brass and are polished so that there are no sharp edges that could nick the seal.

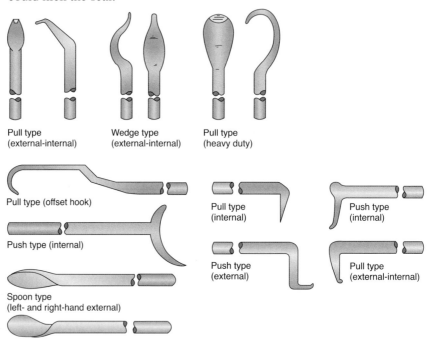

Pull type
(external-internal)

Wedge type
(external-internal)

Pull type
(heavy duty)

Pull type (offset hook)

Push type (internal)

Spoon type
(left- and right-hand external)

Pull type
(internal)

Push type
(external)

Push type
(internal)

Pull type
(external-internal)

Figure 5-69. *Typical tools for installation and removal of O-ring seals*

Figure 5-70 shows how to use these O-ring installation tools, and the proper method of installing and removing O-rings in both internal and external grooves.

When installing an O-ring over a sharp edge, cover the edge with paper, aluminum foil, brass shim stock, or a piece of plastic, as in Figure 5-71. *See* Figure 5-71 on Page 388.

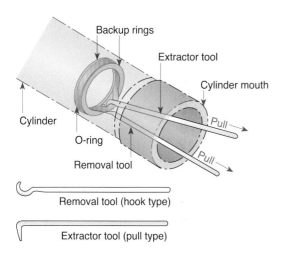

Internal O-ring removal using pull-type extractor
and hook type removal tools

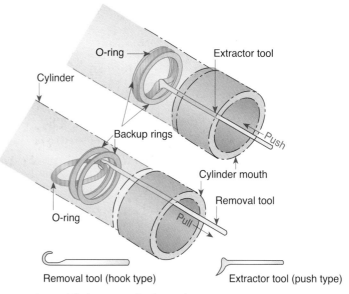

Internal O-ring removal using push type extractor
and hook type removal tools

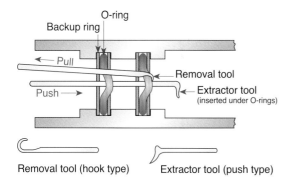

Dual internal O-ring removal using push type extractor
and hook type removal tools

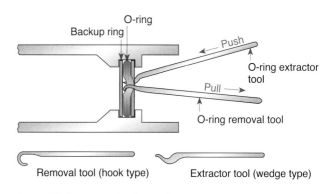

Internal O-ring removal using wedge type extractor
and hook type removal tools

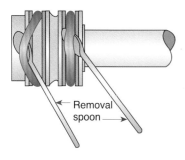

External O-ring removal using spoon type
extractor and removal tools

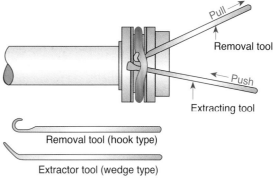

External O-ring removal using wedge type extractor
and hook type removal tools

Figure 5-70. *Proper procedure for removing O-ring seals*

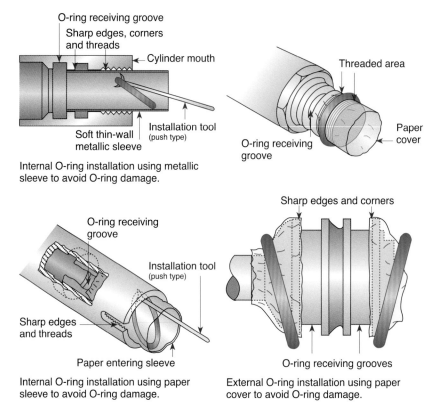

O-ring receiving groove
Sharp edges, corners and threads
Cylinder mouth
Installation tool (push type)
Soft thin-wall metallic sleeve

Internal O-ring installation using metallic sleeve to avoid O-ring damage.

Threaded area
Paper cover
O-ring receiving groove

O-ring receiving groove
Installation tool (push type)
Sharp edges and threads
Paper entering sleeve

Internal O-ring installation using paper sleeve to avoid O-ring damage.

Sharp edges and corners
O-ring receiving grooves

External O-ring installation using paper cover to avoid O-ring damage.

Figure 5-71. *Proper methods of protecting O-ring seals from damage when installing them over threads and sharp edges*

Wipers

O-rings and chevron seals do not seal around the shaft completely. Enough fluid is allowed to leak to lubricate the shaft, and this lubricant attracts dust. A Teflon wiper, or scraper ring is usually installed in a counterbore around the shaft to keep the seals from being damaged when the shaft is retracted into the cylinder. This wiper removes any dirt or dust without restricting the movement of the shaft.

STUDY QUESTIONS: HIGH-PRESSURE SEALS

*Answers begin on Page 416. **Page numbers refer to chapter text.***

101. A high-pressure seal used to seal between two fixed surfaces is called a _____ (gasket or packing). *Page 383*

102. A high-pressure seal used to seal between a fixed and a movable surface is called a _____ (gasket or packing). *Page 383*

103. A chevron seal is a _____ (one-way or two-way) seal. *Page 383*

---

104. A chevron seal must be installed in such a way that the pressure is on the side of the _____ (apex or open end). *Page 383*

105. An O-ring seal is a _____ (one-way or two-way) seal. *Page 384*

106. An O-ring of the correct size can withstand pressures of up to about _____ psi without distortion. *Page 384*

107. When installing a spiraled Teflon backup ring behind an O-ring, the points of the scarfed ends of the ring should be _____ (next to or away from) the outsides of the ring. *Page 385*

108. A backup ring is installed on the side of an O-ring _____ (toward or away from) the pressure. *Page 384*

109. An O-ring seal used with MIL-H-5606 hydraulic fluid will be identified with a _____ (what color) mark. *Page 385*

110. Four important bits of information that should be on the sealed envelope containing an O-ring seal are:
    a. _____
    b. _____
    c. _____
    d. _____
    Page 385

111. A Teflon ring is usually installed around an actuator shaft to prevent dust and dirt entering the actuator and damaging the seals. This is called a/an _____ or _____ ring. *Page 388*

Fluid Power System Lines and Fittings

Any fluid power system, either a hydraulic or a pneumatic system, requires a source of fluid under pressure, actuators to change the pressure into force, valves to control the flow, and fluid lines to carry the fluid to and from the actuators. This section discusses fluid lines and their fittings. *See* Chapter 9 of the *General* textbook of this *Aviation Maintenance Technician Series* for a more in-depth discussion of these components.

Fluid Lines

There are two kinds of fluid lines used in aircraft systems, rigid and flexible. Rigid tubing is used where there is no relative movement within the system, and flexible hoses are used when a piece of rigid tubing connects to an actuator or other device with relative movement between the two.

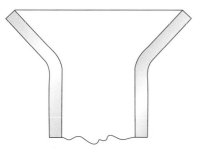

Single flare

Double flare

Figure 5-72. *Flared fittings used on aircraft rigid tubing*

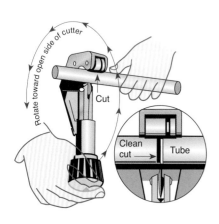

Figure 5-73. *Rigid tubing should be cut with a wheel-type tubing cutter to ensure a clean, square cut.*

Rigid Tubing

Most rigid fluid lines used in low-pressure hydraulic or pneumatic systems are made of 5052-O aluminum alloy. This metal is easy to form, and it has enough strength for most of the hydraulic systems used in smaller aircraft. High-pressure (3,000 psi) hydraulic systems often use 2024-T aluminum alloy, or annealed stainless steel tubing. High-pressure oxygen systems are required to use stainless steel tubing.

Rigid tubing must not have any dents in the heel of a bend, but dents are allowed in the straight part of the tubing if they are less than 20% of the outside diameter of the tube. Scratches or nicks that are less than 10% of the tubing wall thickness are allowed in aluminum alloy tubing provided they are not in the heel of a bend, and can be burnished so they will have no sharp edges.

There are two methods of attaching fittings to rigid tubing, flaring the tubing or using flareless fittings.

Preparation for Flared-Tube Fittings

Aircraft flared-tube fittings have a 37°-flare cone angle to distinguish them from the flatter 45°-flare cone angle used on automotive fittings. Thirty seven degree flaring tools may be obtained from aviation supply sources and must be used rather than the 45° tools purchased from automotive supply houses. A double flare is recommended for use on soft aluminum alloy tubing of ⅜-inch diameter or smaller, and a single flare may be used on tubing of all sizes.

It is extremely important to use the correct procedure when making a flare in a piece of tubing.

Cut the end of the tube perfectly square, using either a tubing cutter or a fine-tooth hacksaw. If you use a tubing cutter such as the one in Figure 5-73, feed the cutting blade into the tube by turning the cutter knob in small increments as the cutter is rotated around the tube, as shown in Figure 5-73. After you cut the end of the tube, deburr the inside edge with a special deburring tool or with a sharp scraper. Smooth the ends and the outside edge of the tube with a fine file or with abrasive cloth, working around rather than across the end.

A number of flaring tools are available. The one shown in Figure 5-74 will single-flare tubing from 3/16-inch through 3/4-inch outside diameter. To flare a tube using this tool, first prepare the end of the tube by polishing out all nicks and scratches to prevent the flare splitting, then slide the nut and sleeve over the end of the tube. Rotate the dies to get the correct size for the tubing beneath the flare cone, and insert the end of the tube between the dies and adjust it so its end rests against the built-in stop. Then clamp the dies tightly against the tube.

Lubricate the flaring cone with hydraulic fluid and screw it into the tube until the flare is the correct size. The outside edge of the flare should stick up above the top of the sleeve, but its outside diameter must not be larger than that of the sleeve. *See* Figures 5-74 and 5-75.

Preparation for Flareless Fittings

Install flareless fittings for rigid tubing, such as those in Figure 5-76, by first cutting and polishing the end of the tube (as described for the flaring process). Slip a nut and a sleeve over the end of the tube and insert the end into a presetting tool like the one in Figure 5-77. Be sure that the end of the tube bottoms out on the shoulder of the tool.

Lubricate the sleeve and the threads, and screw the nut down finger-tight. Hold the tube against the shoulder of the tool and screw the nut down 1¾ turn. This presets, or crimps, the sleeve onto the tube. There should be a uniform ridge of metal raised above the surface of the tube that is 50% as high as the thickness of the front edge of the sleeve, and the sleeve should be slightly bowed. The sleeve may be rotated on the tube, but there must be no back and forth movement along the tube.

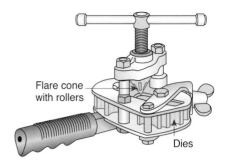

Figure 5-74. *Roller-type flaring tool*

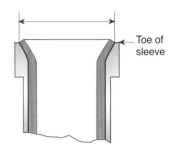

Minimum diameter of flare

Maximum diameter of flare

Figure 5-75. *Proper flare dimensions*

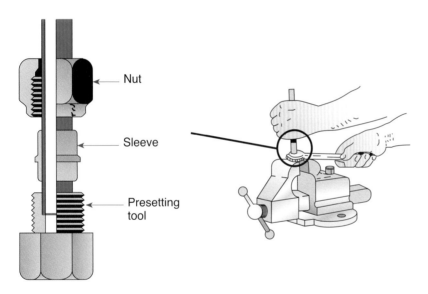

Figure 5-77. *Presetting a flareless fitting on a rigid fluid line*

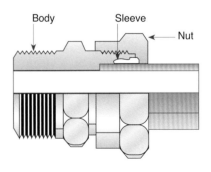

Figure 5-76. *MS Flareless fitting for rigid fluid lines*

Tubing OD inches	Minimum Bend Radius (inches)	
	Aluminum Alloy	Steel
1/8	3/8	
3/16	7/16	21/32
1/4	9/16	7/8
5/16	3/4	1 1/8
3/8	15/16	1 5/16
1/2	1 1/4	1 3/4
5/8	1 1/2	2 3/16
3/4	1 3/4	2 5/8
1	3	3 1/2

Figure 5-78. *Minimum bend radius for aluminum alloy tubing*

Bending Rigid Tubing

Almost all tubing used for aircraft hydraulic systems has thin walls, and you must take special care when bending it. Observe the minimum bend radius shown in Figure 5-78.

Figure 5-79 illustrates both good and bad bends in a piece of thin-wall tubing. Good operating practices do not allow the outside diameter of a piece of tubing to be decreased in the flattest part of the bend to less than 75% of its original diameter.

Because it is so difficult to keep the tubing from flattening or wrinkling, you must almost always bend it using some form of tubing bender, such as the hand bender, shown in Figure 5-80.

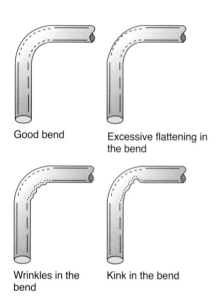

Good bend

Excessive flattening in the bend

Wrinkles in the bend

Kink in the bend

Figure 5-79. *Correct and incorrect tubing bends*

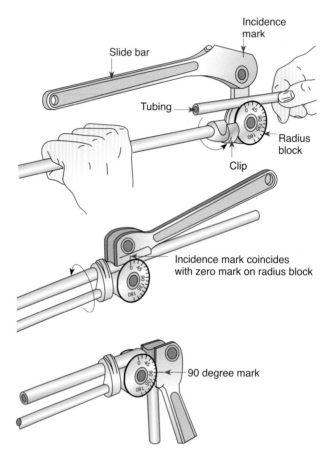

Figure 5-80. *Hand-operated tubing benders can bend thin-wall tubing up to 3/4-inch diameter without the walls collapsing.*

Flexible Fluid Lines

Any time there is relative movement between the aircraft and the fluid power component, flexible fluid lines must be used to connect the device into the system. These fluid lines are available in three basic types: low-pressure hose, medium-pressure hose, and high-pressure hose.

The size of a rigid fluid line is its outside diameter measured in $\frac{1}{16}$-inch increments, but the size of a flexible line is approximately its inside diameter, also given in $\frac{1}{16}$-inch increments.

Low-Pressure Hose

Low-pressure flexible fluid lines are seldom used for hydraulic systems, but they are used in low-pressure pneumatic systems and in aircraft instrument installations. The maximum pressure allowed for low-pressure hose is typically less than 250 psi.

Low-pressure hose, MIL-H-5593, has a seamless synthetic rubber inner liner covered with a single cotton braid reinforcement. All low-pressure hose is covered with either a layer of smooth or ribbed synthetic rubber.

Figure 5-81. *Low-pressure hose has an inner liner and one layer of fabric-braid reinforcement.*

Medium-Pressure Hose

MIL-H-8794 hose has a smooth synthetic rubber inner liner covered with a cotton braid, and this braid is in turn covered with a single layer of steel wire braid. Over all of this is a rough, oil-resistant outer layer of cotton braid.

The operating pressure allowed for medium-pressure hose varies with its size. The smaller the diameter of the hose, the higher the allowable operating pressure. Generally MIL-H-8794 hose is used in hydraulic systems that operate with pressures of about 1,500 psi.

All of the flexible hose used in aircraft fluid power systems have a lay-line, a yellow-painted stripe that runs along the length of the hose. This stripe allows you to tell at a glance whether or not the hose is twisted. When installing flexible hose, be sure that the lay-line does not spiral around the hose. *See* Figure 5-82 on the next page.

Figure 5-82. *Medium-pressure hose has an inner liner and one layer of cotton braid and one layer of steel wire braid. It has a rough outer cover.*

High-Pressure Hose

MIL-H-8788 hose has a smooth synthetic inner liner, two high-tensile carbon steel braid reinforcements, a fabric braid, and a smooth black synthetic rubber outer cover.

Another high-pressure flexible hose is similar to MIL-H-8788, but it has a butyl inner liner and a smooth synthetic rubber outer cover that is colored green instead of black. The lay-line and the markings on this hose are white instead of yellow.

This green hose is to be used only with phosphate ester hydraulic fluid, and it is suitable for pressures of up to 3,000 psi, the same as MIL-H-8788 hose.

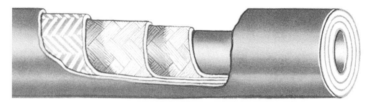

Figure 5-83. *High-pressure hose has an inner liner and two or three layers of steel wire braid. It has a smooth outer cover.*

Teflon Hose

The liner of Teflon hose is made of tetrafluorethylene, or Teflon, resin and covered with a stainless steel braid. Medium-pressure Teflon hose is covered with one stainless steel braid, and high-pressure hose has two layers of stainless steel braid.

Teflon hose has some very desirable operating characteristics and it may be used in fuel, lubricating oil, hydraulic, and pneumatic systems in aircraft. It has one characteristic, however, that you must be aware of in order to get the best service from it. The inner liner of Teflon hose is extruded, and it will take a set, or will become somewhat rigid, after it has been used with high-temperature or high-pressure fluids. After Teflon hose has been used, it should not be bent or have any of its bends straightened out. When Teflon hose is removed from an aircraft, it should be supported in the shape it had when it was installed.

Medium-pressure Teflon hose is covered with one layer of stainless steel braid.

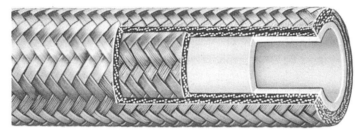

High-pressure Teflon hose is covered with two layers of stainless steel braid.

Figure 5-84

Fluid Line Fittings

It is important when installing or servicing a fluid power system in an aircraft to install only the correct fittings and to use correct installation procedures.

Pipe Fittings

Some components in aircraft hydraulic systems use National Pipe Taper (NPT) fittings to attach fluid lines to castings. Figure 5-85 shows a typical fitting.

The end of these fittings that screws into the casting is tapered about $\frac{1}{16}$ inch to the inch, and when it is installed in a casting, the first thread should be inserted into the hole and an approved thread lubricant applied sparingly to the second thread. When the fitting is screwed into the casting, the lubricant will squeeze out between the threads and prevent the threads from galling, and yet none of the lubricant will squeeze out and contaminate the system.

The way a tapered pipe fitting is measured is somewhat confusing. For example, the commonly used $\frac{1}{8}$-inch pipe fitting to which a $\frac{1}{4}$-inch rigid tube attaches does not measure $\frac{1}{8}$ inch either inside or outside. Its outside diameter and its threads are the same as those of a piece of standard iron pipe that has an inside diameter of $\frac{1}{8}$ inch. The hole into which a $\frac{1}{8}$-inch NPT fitting screws has a diameter of about $\frac{3}{8}$ inch.

galling. Fretting or pulling out chunks of a surface by sliding contact with another surface or body.

Figure 5-85. *An AN816 nipple has tapered pipe threads on one end and fittings for an AN flare fitting on the other end.*

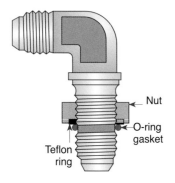

Screw nut onto upper threads and slip a Teflon ring and an O-ring gasket over lower threads into groove.

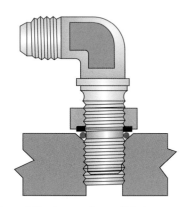

Screw fitting into casting until O-ring contacts housing.

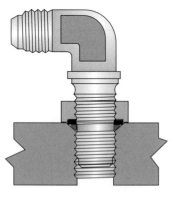

Align fitting with connecting lines and screw nut down until it contacts housing. The compressed O-ring forms fluid-tight seal.

Figure 5-87. *Proper installation of a bulkhead fitting*

AN and AC Flare Fittings

Flare fittings do not depend on any type of sealant to effect a good seal. They depend, rather, on a good fit between the flare cone and the flare in the end of the tube.

One word of caution regarding flare fittings: There are two types of flared tube fittings that look much alike, but they are definitely not interchangeable.

Figure 5-86 illustrates an AN fitting and an AC fitting. At first glance, these two fittings are similar, but a close inspection shows the differences. The AN fitting has a short shoulder between the first thread and the base of the flare cone, while the threads on the AC fitting start right at the flare cone. The threads on the AC fitting are generally finer (this is not the case with the smaller size fittings), and the aluminum alloy AN fittings are dyed blue, while the aluminum alloy AC fittings are dyed gray or yellow.

The dash number of these fittings designates the outside diameter of the rigid tube they fit. For example, an AN815-6D union is used to connect two $\frac{3}{8}$-inch ($\frac{6}{16}$-inch) outside diameter tubes.

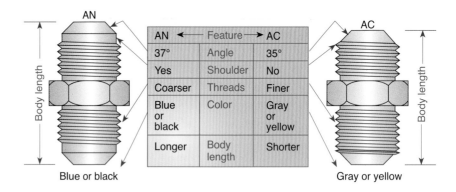

AN	Feature	AC
37°	Angle	35°
Yes	Shoulder	No
Coarser	Threads	Finer
Blue or black	Color	Gray or yellow
Longer	Body length	Shorter

Figure 5-86. *Comparison between AN and AC fittings*

Universal or Bulkhead Fittings

Fittings such as the AN833 elbow are used to screw into castings or to carry fluid lines through a bulkhead. Figure 5-87 shows the correct way to install this fitting in a casting. Screw an AN6289 nut onto the top threads with the counterbored side of the nut toward the end of the fitting. Work a Teflon ring up into the counterbore of the nut, and then carefully slip the proper O-ring over the threads and up into the groove between the two sets of threads. Screw the nut down until the Teflon ring touches the O-ring and the O-ring rests against the inner end of the lower set of threads. Screw the fitting into the casting until the O-ring contacts the chamfered edges of the hole. Hold the nut with a wrench and screw the fitting into the hole for 1 to $1\frac{1}{2}$ turns to position the fitting so that it points in the proper direction. Hold the fitting in proper alignment and torque the nut to the value that is specified in the aircraft service manual.

MS Flareless Fittings

There is a full line of flareless-type tube fittings available for use with the crimped-on sleeve and nut. The inside of the fitting has a smooth counterbore into which the end of the tube fits. The taper at the mouth of the fitting provides the seal between the fitting and the sleeve, and the seal between the sleeve and the tube is provided by the bite of the sleeve into the tube.

You must not overtorque flareless-type fittings. When assembling a fitting of this type, be sure that the sleeve is properly preset on the tube, and the tube inserted straight into the fitting. Screw the nut down finger-tight and then tighten it with a wrench for one sixth of a turn, one hex, or at the very most, one third of a turn, two hexes.

If the fitting leaks, rather than attempting to fix it by applying more torque, disassemble the fitting and find out what the trouble is. It is usually a damaged fitting or contamination between the sleeve and the fitting.

Quick-Disconnect Fittings

It is often necessary to actuate a hydraulic system without running the aircraft engine. This is usually done with pressure supplied by a ground-power unit also called a GPU, or hydraulic "mule." The inlet and outlet lines are disconnected from the engine-driven pump and connected to the pump in the mule. To prevent loss of fluid when making this change, the lines to the pump are fitted with quick-disconnect fittings such as the ones shown in Figure 5-88.

When the lines are disconnected the springs inside both halves of the fitting pull the poppet valves tightly into their seats and seal off the lines. When the lines are connected, plungers in each fitting meet and force the poppets off of their seats allowing fluid to flow freely through the fittings.

quick-disconnect fitting. A hydraulic line fitting that seals the line when the fitting is disconnected. Quick-disconnect fittings are used on the lines connected to the engine-driven hydraulic pump. They allow the pump to be disconnected and an auxiliary hydraulic power system connected to perform checks requiring hydraulic power while the aircraft is in the hangar.

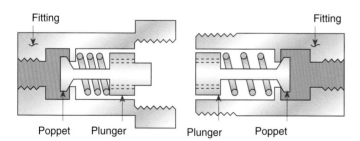

When fittings are disconnected, the springs hold poppet valves tightly on their seats.

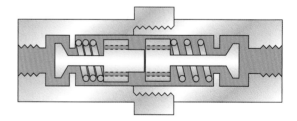

When fittings are connected, the plungers force poppets off their seats and fluid flows freely through the fittings.

Figure 5-88. *Quick-disconnect fittings*

Fluid Line Installation

Not only must the correct fluid lines be installed in an aircraft, but they must be installed properly. Here are a few basic rules regarding their installation:

Rigid Lines

When manufacturing a replacement rigid fluid line, be sure that all of the angles are correct, and inspect all of the bends to be sure that none of them are collapsed, kinked, or wrinkled. Fit the line in place to ensure that the tube aligns with the fittings at each end. The line should be straight with the fitting and should apply a slight pressure against it.

1. No tube, regardless of how short, should be installed unless there is at least one bend in it. This bend allows for vibration, and for the inevitable expansion and contraction that are caused by temperature changes and by the line being pressurized.

2. Never attempt to pull a tube up to the fitting with the nut. This will place a strain on the flare or the preset bite, and vibration can easily cause the tube to fail.

3. Where a fluid line is brought through a bulkhead, if it is not carried through with a bulkhead fitting, it must be supported with bonded cushion clamps and centered in the hole in such a way that there is protection against chafing.

4. All fluid lines should be run below electrical wire bundles so that there is no possibility of fluid dripping onto the wire.

5. All fluid lines should be identified at each end, and at least once in each compartment with color-coded tape to identify the type of fluid it carries.

6. Support clamps should be placed no farther apart than:

    $\frac{1}{8}$" tubing every 9 inches
    $\frac{1}{4}$" tubing every 12 inches
    $\frac{3}{8}$" tubing every 16 inches

    These clamps should be placed as near the bend as possible so the tubing will have a minimum amount of overhang.

Flexible Lines

Any time there is relative movement between the two ends of a fluid line, there should be a section of flexible hose installed.

1. The lay line along a flexible hose should never spiral. This would indicate the hose has twisted and had a built-in strain. Pressure surges in a twisted line can cause failure.

2. Always use a fitting that allows the hose to approach it without any bends near its end. Elbows are available in both 90° and 45° angles.

3. Never attempt to pull a hose up to its fitting with the nut. When pressure is applied to a hose, it will tend to expand its diameter and shorten its length. Allow the line to have slack of about 5 to 8 percent of its length.

4. Use the proper size cushion clamp to support the hose any time it goes through a bulkhead, or any place where vibration may place a twisting force on the fitting.

5. The liner of Teflon hose is extruded, and it has ample strength for applications in which there is no twist, but it is susceptible to failure if it is twisted or if it is bent with too small a bend radius.

6. Be sure to observe the minimum bend radius for all flexible hose. For MIL-H-8788 hose, the following are the minimum acceptable bend radii:

   -4 hose   3.0 inch minimum bend radius
   -6 hose   5.0 inch minimum bend radius
   -8 hose   5.75 inch minimum bend radius
   -10 hose   6.5 inch minimum bend radius

   If the hose is subjected to flexing, this radius must be increased.

7. It is possible to make up high-pressure hose if your shop is equipped with the proper tools. But, because of the extremely critical nature of high-pressure fluid lines, it is generally advisable to buy the replacement high-pressure fluid lines from the aircraft manufacturer, or from an approved supplier that makes them according to the manufacturer's specifications. By installing only fluid lines that carry the correct manufacturer's part number, you will be ensured that the line is constructed of the proper material, and that it has been tested according to the procedure required by the manufacturer.

8. Before installing any fluid line, be sure to blow it out with compressed air to remove any obstructions or particles that may have been left in the process of manufacture, or which may have been allowed to enter the hose while it was in storage. Before a line is stored, cap both ends to prevent the entry of any contaminants.

Answers begin on Page 416. Page numbers refer to chapter text.

112. Rigid tubing used in low-pressure hydraulic systems is usually made of _____ aluminum alloy. *Page 390*

113. Rigid tubing used for high-pressure hydraulic systems is usually made of _____ aluminum alloy or annealed _____ . *Page 390*

114. A dent that is 10% of the diameter of a piece of aluminum alloy tubing _____ (is or is not) permissible if it is in the heel of a bend. *Page 390*

115. A scratch in a piece of aluminum alloy tubing is permissible if its depth is less than _____ percent of the tubing wall thickness, and it is not in the heel of a bend. *Page 390*

116. The flare cone angle used for aircraft flared tubing fittings has an angle of _____ degrees. *Page 390*

117. Soft aluminum alloy tubing should be double flared if its diameter is _____ inch or less. *Page 390*

118. A properly preset MS flareless fitting _____ (is or is not) allowed to rotate on the tube. *Page 391*

119. The minimum bend radius for a piece of ³⁄₈-inch aluminum alloy tubing is _____ inch/es. *Page 392*

120. The maximum flattening allowed in the bend in a piece of rigid fluid line reduces the outside diameter of the tube in the bend to _____ percent of the original tube diameter. *Page 392*

121. A piece of flexible hose that has a ribbed outer covering is a _____ (low, medium, or high)-pressure hose. *Page 393*

122. A piece of flexible hose that has a rough outer covering is a _____ (low, medium, or high)-pressure hose. *Page 393*

123. A piece of flexible hose that has a smooth green outer covering is a _____ (low, medium, or high)-pressure hose. *Page 394*

124. A piece of flexible hose that has a smooth green outer covering is designed to carry _____ (mineral or phosphate ester)-base fluid. *Page 394*

125. The highest pressure that can be carried in a low-pressure flexible hose is normally considered to be _____ psi. *Page 393*

126. Medium-pressure flexible hose is used in hydraulic systems with pressures up to _____ psi. *Page 393*

127. High-pressure flexible hose is used in hydraulic systems with pressures up to _____ psi. *Page 394*

128. A flexible hose with a stainless steel braid outer covering has a liner made of _____ . *Page 394*

129. When installing a tapered pipe thread in a casting, thread lubricant should be applied to the _____ (first or second) thread. *Page 395*

130. The nut of an MS flareless fitting should be screwed down finger tight on the fitting and then it should be tightened with a wrench for _____ or at the most _____ of a turn. *Page 397*

131. When a fluid line is routed through a section of an aircraft structure parallel with an electrical wire bundle, the fluid line should be _____ (above or below) the wire bundle. *Page 398*

132. A run of $\frac{3}{8}$-inch rigid fluid line should be supported with a cushioned clamp at least every _____ inches. *Page 398*

133. The colored line that extends the length of a piece of flexible hose that is used to tell whether or not the hose was twisted during installation is called a/an _____ line. *Page 399*

134. Flexible hose changes its dimensions when it is pressurized. A piece of flexible hose should be between _____ and _____ percent longer than the distance between the fittings to which it attaches. *Page 399*

135. The minimum recommended bend radius for a piece of MIL-H-8788 hose is _____ inches. *Page 399*

Pneumatic Systems

Pneumatic systems are fluid power systems that use a compressible fluid, air. These systems are dependable and lightweight, and because the fluid is air, there is no need for a return system.

Some aircraft have only a low-pressure pneumatic system to operate the gyro instruments; others use compressed air as an emergency backup for lowering the landing gear and operating the brakes in the event of a hydraulic system failure. Still others have a complete pneumatic system that actuates the landing gear retraction, nose wheel steering, passenger doors, and propeller brakes. Each of these types of systems is discussed in this section.

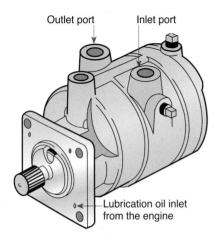

Figure 5-89. *This wet-type air pump is lubricated by engine oil taken into the pump through holes in the mounting flange.*

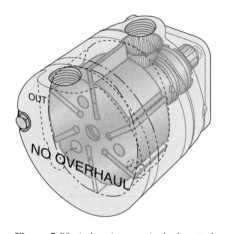

Figure 5-90. *A dry air pump is the heart of the low-pressure pneumatic system installed in most modern aircraft.*

deicer system. A system that removes ice after it has formed.

Low-Pressure Pneumatic Systems

The need for modern aircraft to fly anywhere any time has increased the importance of low-pressure pneumatic systems. These systems provide air for gyroscopic attitude and direction indicators and air to inflate the pneumatic deicer boots. This compressed air is usually provided by a vane-type engine-driven air pump.

This section of text covers a basic introduction to low-pressure pneumatic systems. A more comprehensive discussion is included in the sections on ice control and flight instruments.

Engine-Driven Air Pumps

For many years, engine-driven air pumps were used primarily to evacuate the case of air-driven gyroscopic instruments, so they were commonly called vacuum pumps. Later, the discharge air from these pumps was used to inflate deicer boots, and these pumps are now more correctly called air pumps. There are two types of air pumps that may be used: "wet" pumps and "dry" pumps.

Wet pumps have steel vanes that are lubricated and sealed with engine oil drawn in through the pump mounting pad and exhausted with the discharge air. This oil must be removed with an air-oil separator before the air can be used to inflate the deicer boots and drive the instrument gyros.

Dry pumps, such as the one in Figure 5-90, were developed so there would be no oil in the pump discharge air. The vanes in these pumps are made of carbon, and they need no lubrication. The basic problem with dry pumps is that the carbon vanes are breakable, and can easily be damaged by any contaminants entering the pump. It is extremely important that all air taken into these pumps be filtered, and when servicing the system that no contaminants be allowed to enter.

Pneumatic Deicer Systems

The compressed air system used for inflating deicer boots with a wet vacuum pump is shown in Figure 5-91. The oily air leaves the pump and passes through baffles in the oil separator. The oil collects on the baffles and drains down and is collected in the lower part of the separator and returned to the engine oil sump. Clean air leaves the separator and flows through the deicer on-off valve to an air pressure refrigerator that drops the pressure to the value needed for the boots. It then flows to the timer and distributor valve that distributes the air to the proper boots in the proper sequence. When the system is turned off, the air is directed overboard by the deicer on-off valve.

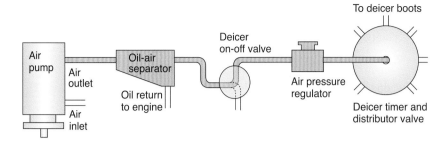

Figure 5-91. *Compressed air source for a pneumatic deicer system*

Pneumatic Gyro Power Systems

The gyroscope in pneumatic gyro instruments is driven by air impinging on buckets cut in the periphery of the wheel. There are two ways of obtaining this air. In some systems, like the one in Figure 5-92, the air pump evacuates the instrument case and air is drawn into the case through an air filter. The clean air is directed through a nozzle and it strikes the buckets and drives the gyro. A suction relief valve regulates the suction to the correct value for the instruments, and a suction gage reads the pressure drop across the instruments.

Since many modern airplanes fly at such high altitude that there is not enough atmospheric air pressure to drive the instruments when the case is evacuated, another method must be used. The pneumatic gyros installed in these airplanes are driven by the air from the pressure side of a dry air pump using a system such as that in Figure 5-93.

The air is filtered before it is taken into the air pump, and after it leaves, its pressure is regulated by an air pressure regulator. The air then flows through an in-line filter and into the instruments where it drives the gyros, and is then evacuated overboard.

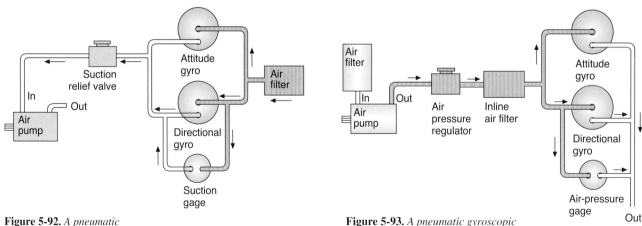

Figure 5-92. *A pneumatic gyroscopic instrument system using the suction side of the air pump*

Figure 5-93. *A pneumatic gyroscopic instrument system using the pressure side of a dry air pump*

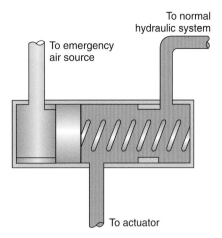

To emergency air source

To normal hydraulic system

To actuator

Figure 5-94. *A shuttle valve is used to direct either normal system hydraulic pressure or emergency compressed air into an actuator cylinder.*

shuttle valve. An automatic selector valve mounted on critical components such as landing gear actuation cylinders and brake cylinders.

For normal operation, system fluid flows into the actuator through the shuttle valve, but if normal system pressure is lost, emergency system pressure forces the shuttle over and emergency fluid flows into the actuator.

Backup High-Pressure Pneumatic Systems

In case the hydraulic systems in an aircraft fail, there must be provision for emergency extension of the landing gear and the application of the brakes.

The pneumatic backup system is simple and effective. A steel bottle, or cylinder, that contains approximately 3,000 psi of compressed air or nitrogen is installed in the aircraft, and a shuttle valve in the line to the actuator directs hydraulic fluid into the actuator for normal actuation, or compressed air for emergency actuation. If there is a failure in the hydraulic system and the landing gear must be lowered with the emergency air system, the landing gear selector is put in the GEAR-DOWN position to provide a return path for the hydraulic fluid in the actuators, and the emergency air valve is opened. High-pressure air shifts the shuttle valve and this air is directed into the actuator to lower the landing gear. This system is discussed in more detail in the chapter on landing gears.

Full Pneumatic Systems

The majority of airplanes built in the United States use hydraulic or electric power for such heavy-duty applications as landing gear retraction, but compressed air can also be used for these systems.

Some advantages of compressed air over other heavy-duty power systems are:

1. Air is universally available in an unlimited supply.

2. Pneumatic system components are reasonably simple and lightweight.

3. Weight is saved because compressed air is lightweight and no return system is needed.

4. There is no fire hazard, and the danger of explosion is slight.

5. Contamination is minimized by the use of proper filters.

Figure 5-95 shows a closed-center, high-pressure pneumatic system that uses two air compressors driven from the accessory gear boxes of the turboprop engines. Air is taken into the first stage of the compressor through an inlet air duct, and compressed. This compressed air then passes on successively to three other stages within the pumps. The discharge air from the fourth stage is routed through an intercooler and a bleed valve to the unloading valve. The bleed valve is held closed by oil pressure. In the event of oil pressure failure, the valve will open and relieve the pump of its load.

The unloading valve maintains air pressure in the system between 2,900 and 3,300 psi. When the pressure rises to 3,300 psi, a check valve traps it and unloads the pump by dumping its output overboard. When the system pressure drops to 2,900 psi, the pump is loaded and its output is directed back into the system.

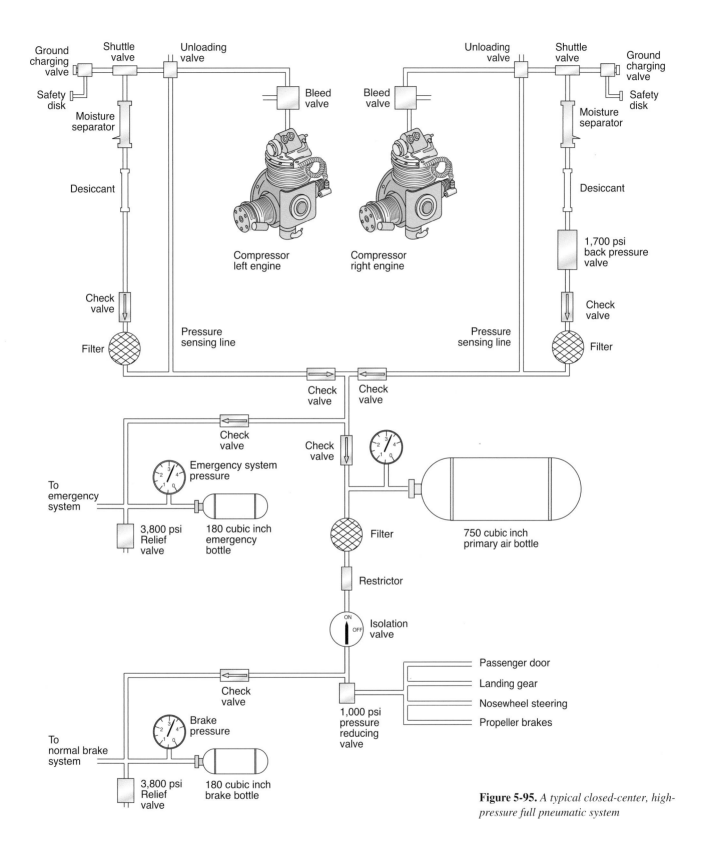

Figure 5-95. *A typical closed-center, high-pressure full pneumatic system*

A shuttle valve in the line between the compressor and the main system makes it possible to charge the system from a ground source. When the engine is not running and air pressure is supplied from the external source, the shuttle slides over and isolates the compressor.

Moisture in a compressed air system will freeze as the air pressure drops when a component is actuated. For this reason, every bit of water must be removed from the air. A separator collects moisture from the air and holds it on a baffle until the system is shut down. When the inlet pressure to the moisture separator drops below 450 psi, a drain valve opens and all of the accumulated moisture is discharged overboard. An electric heater prevents water that is trapped in the separator from freezing.

After the air leaves the moisture separator with about 98% of its moisture removed, it passes through a desiccant, or chemical dryer, to remove the last traces of moisture. Before the air enters the operating portion of the pneumatic system, it is filtered as it passes through a 10-micron, sintered-metal filter. (The smallest object we can usually see with our naked eye is about 40 microns.)

The system in the right engine nacelle has a back-pressure valve. This is essentially a pressure relief valve in the supply line. The back-pressure valve does not open until the pressure from the compressor or from the ground charging system is above 1,700 psi. This ensures that the moisture separator will operate most efficiently. If it is necessary to operate the system from an external source whose pressure is less than 1,700 psi, the source can be connected into the left side of the system where there is no back-pressure valve.

There are three air storage bottles in this airplane, a 750-cubic-inch bottle for the main system, a 180-cubic-inch bottle for normal brake operation, and a second 180-cubic-inch bottle for emergency system operation.

A manually operated isolation valve allows the technician to close off the air supply so the system can be serviced and components changed without having to discharge the storage bottles.

The majority of the components in this system operate with a pressure of 1,000 psi, so a pressure-reducing valve is installed between the isolation valve and the supply manifold. This reduces the air pressure for normal operation of the landing gear, the passenger door, the propeller brake, and the nose wheel steering. This pressure-reducing valve not only lowers the pressure to 1,000 psi, but it also serves as a backup pressure relief valve.

An emergency system stores compressed air under the full system pressure of 3,300 psi and supplies it for the emergency extension of the landing gear and for emergency brake application.

moisture separator. A component in a high-pressure pneumatic system that removes most of the water vapor from the compressed air.

When the compressed air is used, its pressure drops, and this pressure drop causes a drop in temperature. If any moisture were allowed to remain in the air it would freeze and block the system.

desiccant. A chemical that absorbs moisture to remove it from the air.

Answers begin on Page 416. Page numbers refer to chapter text.

136. Oil from the discharge of a wet-type air pump is collected by a/an _____ and returned to the engine. *Page 402*

137. The vanes of a dry-type air pump are made of _____ . *Page 402*

138. The air pressure in a full pneumatic system is maintained in the correct range by the action of the _____ valve. *Page 404*

139. If the lubrication system for the high-pressure compressor fails, the _____ valve will relieve the pump of all of its load. *Page 404*

140. Water is removed from the compressed air in a full pneumatic system by the _____ . *Page 406*

141. The actuating components in a full pneumatic system may be serviced without discharging the air storage bottles by closing the _____ valve. *Page 406*

Large Aircraft Fluid Power Systems

Hydraulic power is so important for large aircraft that more than one main hydraulic system is installed, and in addition to these main systems, there are backup and emergency systems to supply power in case of main system failure.

Sources of Hydraulic Power

The main hydraulic power for large aircraft typically comes from engine-driven pumps, but there are also pumps driven by electric motors. These electric pumps, commonly driven by three-phase AC motors supply pressurized fluid to the system when the engines are not operating. Another source of hydraulic power is from pumps driven by compressed air from an auxiliary power unit (APU), a ground power unit (GPU), a ram air turbine (RAT) or from engine bleed air.

ram air turbine (RAT). An emergency source for hydraulic pressure used on some large transport aircraft. If hydraulic pressure is lost, the turbine can be extended into the air stream to drive a hydraulic pump and provide pressure for one of the hydraulic systems.

Power transfer units (PTUs) are used on some aircraft to pressurize one hydraulic system from another system without transferring any fluid between the systems. The PTU consists of a hydraulic motor driving a hydraulic pump. If, for example, pressure is needed in a system that is usually pressurized by an engine-driven pump without running the engine, pressure from another system that is powered by an electric pump can be used to drive the PTU. The pump in the PTU pressurizes the system.

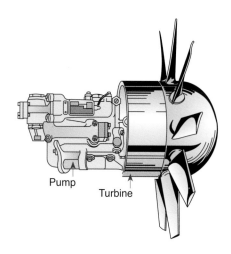

Figure 5-96. *A ram air turbine can be lowered into the air flowing around the aircraft to supply hydraulic pressure for emergency actuation of systems needed to get the aircraft safely on the ground.*

In the event that all hydraulic power is lost, some airplanes can extend a ram air turbine (RAT) into the airstream outside the aircraft and the air flowing through the turbine blades drives a hydraulic pump to produce enough hydraulic power to actuate the systems needed to get the aircraft safely on the ground.

Jet Transport Airplane Hydraulic System

Large jet transport airplanes such as the Boeing 777 have complex hydraulic systems that supply power to actuate the landing gear, brakes and steering, primary flight controls, flaperons, spoilers, trailing edge flaps and leading edge slats. Figure 5-97 is a simplified block diagram of such a system.

Hydraulic Systems

The Boeing 777 has three independent 3,000-psi hydraulic systems; the left, right, and center systems. Each system has its own reservoir, pumps and filters.

The left system has one engine-driven pump (EDP) and one AC motor-driven pump (ACMP). It supplies hydraulic power to the flight controls and to the left engine thrust reverser. The right system also has one EDP and one ACMP that supplies power to the flight controls, the normal main gear brakes and the right engine thrust reverser.

The center system has two ACMPs, two air driven pumps (ADPs) and one ram air turbine (RAT) pump. Pneumatic power from the two engines or the auxiliary power unit (APU) operates the ADPs. The center system supplies power to:

• Flight controls

• Leading edge slats

• Trailing edge flaps

• Alternate and reserve main gear brakes

• Normal and reserve nose gear steering

…and nose gear extension-retraction:

• Main gear extension-retraction

• Main gear steering.

The ram air turbine deploys automatically during flight and supplies emergency hydraulic power to the primary flight controls if any of these conditions occur:

• Both engines are shut down

• Both AC buses are not powered

• All three hydraulic system pressures are low.

Only the flight controls use hydraulic power from the RAT.

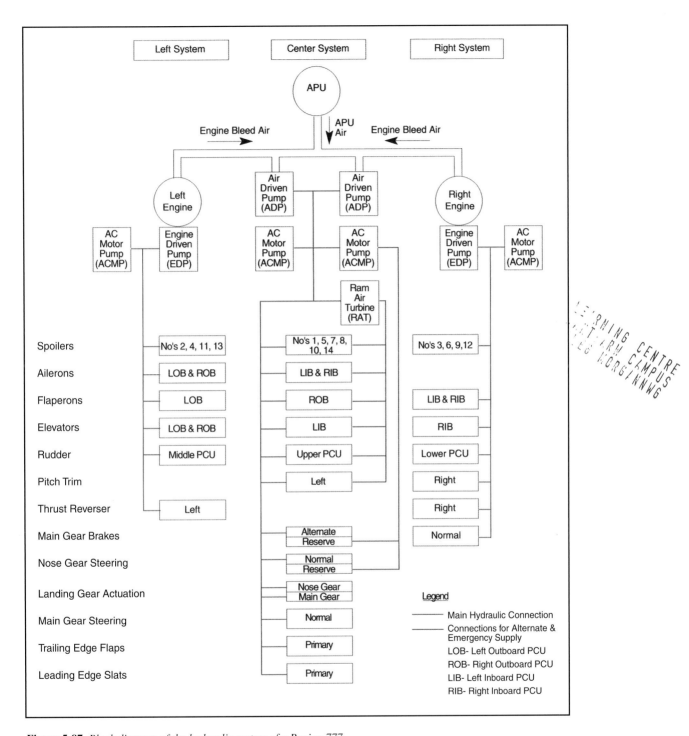

Figure 5-97. *Block diagram of the hydraulic system of a Boeing 777.*

The EDPs in the left and right systems and the ACMPs in the center system are the primary pumps. They operate continuously. The ACMPs in the left and right systems, and the ADPs in the center system are the demand pumps. They operate automatically when there are heavy demands on the systems. This part-time operation increases pump life, system efficiency and reliability.

Hydraulic fuses are installed in some of the fluid lines to protect against a loss of fluid in these systems:

• Main gear steering

• Brakes

• Main gear actuation

• Flight controls

All of the electric pumps as well as all of the air driven pumps and engine driven pumps are interchangeable. The hydraulic reservoirs and filters are all near the pumps they supply, and all of the reservoirs may be filled from a single-point reservoir servicing station.

Hydraulic System Indications

Each pump has an amber fault light that illuminates when a pump overheats or is producing low pressure, and there is a green light that shows high RAT output pressure and an amber light illuminates when the RAT is unlocked.

The Engine Indicating and Crew Alerting System (EICAS) displays a number of hydraulic system alerts and their levels, these are:

• RAT unlocked

• Low system pressure

• Low pump pressure

• Pump overheat

• Reservoir low quantity

• Reserve brake and steering failure

• HYDIM (Hydraulic Interface Module) failure

The status display shows the reservoir quantity and system pressure for each system. The hydraulic synoptic display shows a real-time diagram of the operational status of the entire hydraulic system, and the hydraulic maintenance page displays all of the pertinent hydraulic data needed by the maintenance personnel.

Automatic Control

The Hydraulic Interface Module (HYDIM) cards are the computer components that control the automatic operation and indication of the hydraulic system. There is one card for the left system, two for the center system, and one for the right system. These cards receive data from the various sensors and send it to the Airplane Information Management System (AIMS). They control these functions:

- Demand pump AUTO operation
- RAT deployment
- Landing gear Auto-Off operation
- Center hydraulic system isolation

These cards also control these hydraulic system indications:

- System pressure
- Pump pressure
- Pump temperature
- Reservoir quantity
- Reservoir temperature
- Reservoir pressure

STUDY QUESTIONS: LARGE AIRCRAFT FLUID POWER SYSTEMS

Answers begin on Page 416. Page numbers refer to chapter text.

142. Hydraulic pumps supplying pressure for large aircraft may be driven by four methods. These are:
    a. _____
    b. _____
    c. _____
    d. _____
    Page 408

143. The nominal system pressure for the Boeing 777 hydraulic systems is _____ psi.
    Page 408

144. The air driven pumps in the center system operate _____ (all the time, or when system demand is heavy). *Page 410*

145. The operational status of the entire hydraulic system is shown on the hydraulic synoptic display of the _____. *Page 410*

146. All three hydraulic systems have hydraulic _____ in some of the fluid lines to prevent the loss of all the fluid if a line should burst. *Page 410*

147. Pump overheating or low pump pressure is indicated by a/an _____. *Page 410*

Continued

148. The quantity of fluid in each of the reservoirs is shown on the _____ of the EICAS. *Page 410*

149. The computer components that control the automatic operations and indications in the hydraulic systems are the _____ . *Page 410*

150. If the system pressure of all three hydraulic systems becomes low in flight, emergency pressure is automatically supplied by the _____ . *Page 408*

Hydraulic System Maintenance and Troubleshooting

Hydraulic system maintenance consists of keeping the system filled with the proper fluid, maintaining all lines and fittings so there are no leaks, and cleaning or replacing system filters on the schedule recommended by the aircraft manufacturer.

If any system has been serviced with the wrong fluid, all of the fluid must be drained and the system flushed with the recommended solvent. The filter elements must be cleaned or replaced, and any seal that was touched by the wrong fluid must be replaced with a new seal bearing the correct part number, and a current cure date.

If any system component has failed, contaminants have probably gotten into the system, and the fluid must be drained and the filters replaced. Any components that operated with contaminated fluid should be carefully checked to be sure that there are no contaminants in the unit.

Hydraulic System Troubleshooting

Regardless of the system, the basic principle of troubleshooting is the same. Isolate the problem, and then eliminate everything in that area that is operating properly. Whatever is left is bound to contain the trouble.

You cannot isolate a problem unless you know the system thoroughly. Modern hydraulic systems are complex, and no troubleshooting can be done systematically without having the schematic diagram of the system before you.

Hydraulic systems are logically divided into power and actuation sections. The power section can be further divided into the main, the backup, and the emergency subsystems.

If some part of an actuation system does not work when running off the main power system, but does when running off the hand pump, the trouble could be a low supply of fluid in the reservoir (the fluid could be below the engine-driven pump supply port). Or, the pump itself could be at fault.

Always check the more simple possibility first and eliminate it before moving on to the more difficult possibility.

If the system does not work properly with either the main power system or the backup system (the engine-driven pump or the hand pump), but it can be actuated by the emergency system, the actuation system is working but neither main nor the backup power systems are working. The systems could be out of fluid, or an unloading or a relief valve could be stuck in the open position.

If only one system fails to work, and there is pressure in the system, the trouble is in the actuation system. If, for instance, you cannot lower the landing gear, but the flaps actuate normally, the trouble is probably in the landing gear selector valve or between the gear selector valve and the gear actuators.

Troubleshooting Tips and Procedures

1. If no pressure is indicated on the system pressure gage, yet there is a return flow into the reservoir, the trouble probably does not lie with the pump, but in the pressure control valves for the system. Pumps are fluid movers, not pressure generators. A pressure regulator or a relief valve is probably stuck open.

2. If there is a restriction in the pump outlet or between the pump outlet and the system pressure regulator, the system pressure will drop when some unit is actuated. The pump is unable to provide the volume of fluid the system requires.

3. System pressure that is higher than normal could mean that the unloading valve is failing to unload the pump and a relief valve is maintaining the pressure. Knowing the setting of each relief valve will help determine which valve is doing the work. When a relief valve holds the system pressure, it usually makes a buzzing noise, and gets quite warm.

4. A loud hammering noise in a system that has an accumulator indicates an insufficient air preload in the accumulator. The pump goes on the line, or kicks in, and since there is no compressible fluid in the accumulator, the system pressure immediately builds up to the kick-out pressure and the pump goes off the line. This kicking in and out without any air to compress and cushion the shock causes the heavy hammering. Few hydraulic systems have air gages on the accumulators to show the amount of air preload, so, to find the amount of air pressure in the accumulator, pump the hand pump slowly, and watch the hydraulic pressure gage. The pressure will not rise at first, but when it does, it will jump up suddenly, and as you continue to pump, it will continue to rise, but slowly. The pressure jumped at the point fluid was first forced into the accumulator where it was opposed by the air. The amount of pressure shown on the gage after the first jump is the amount of air preload in the accumulator.

(Continued)

5. Pump chattering and subsequent overheating indicates air in the line. The most logical place for the air to enter is from a low reservoir. Another possibility is a leak in the suction line between the reservoir and the inlet to the pump.

6. Slow actuation of a unit is often caused by internal leakage in a valve or an actuator. This leakage also causes the pump to kick on and off the system more often than it should. If the system uses an electric pump, you will notice that the ammeter shows the pump to be operating quite often when nothing is actuated. The leaking component may be heated by the fluid leaking, and it can be identified by feeling all of the suspected units and checking the one that is unnaturally warm.

7. Spongy actuation is usually a sign of air in the system. Most double-acting systems are self-bleeding, so after a component has been replaced, it should be cycled a number of times to purge it of all of the air in the actuator and the lines back to the reservoir. If the actuating time decreases each time the system is cycled, the air is being worked out of the fluid.

   Some systems do not purge normally, and the manufacturer usually has special instructions in the service manual to explain the method that should be used to remove all of the trapped air.

8. Many hydraulic systems have several relief valves that are set to relieve at different pressures. To check these valves, screw the adjustment on all of the valves down so they will relieve at a pressure higher than the highest setting of any of the valves.

   Adjust the valve that requires the highest pressure first, and then adjust the rest of the valves, beginning at the valve that has the next highest setting and continue to the valve that has the lowest setting.

9. Sometimes a hydraulic pressure gage fluctuates rapidly, with the pointer forming a blur. This is an indication that a there is air in the gage line or that the gage is not adequately snubbed.

   Hold a shop rag around the back of the instrument and crack the fitting just enough to purge any air from the line, and then retighten it. If this does not cure the fluctuation, the gage snubber must be replaced.

10. Knowing which lines have pressure and which do not can be an aid in troubleshooting. For flexible lines this can usually be determined by grasping the line. A hose that is pressurized is usually firm while one that has no pressure will be limp and flexible.

Troubleshooting hydraulic and pneumatic systems is usually a logical application of basic principles, and, as with all types of aircraft maintenance, the aircraft must be maintained in such a way that it continues to meet the conditions of its original airworthiness certification.

All of the work must be done according to the recommendations of the aircraft manufacturer. Whenever you have a particularly difficult problem, do

snubber. A device in a hydraulic or pneumatic component that absorbs shock and/or vibration. A snubber is installed in the line to a hydraulic pressure gage to prevent the pointer fluctuating.

not hesitate to contact the manufacturer's service representative for help. He or she has probably encountered the problem before and can save time and money in getting the aircraft back into productive service.

STUDY QUESTIONS: HYDRAULIC SYSTEM TROUBLESHOOTING

Answers begin on the next page. Page numbers refer to chapter text.

151. No systematic troubleshooting can be done without the use of a/an _____ diagram of the system. *Page 412*

152. The two basic sections of a hydraulic system are the _____ and the _____ sections. *Page 412*

153. There are three subdivisions of the power section of a hydraulic system. These are _____ , _____ , and _____ . *Page 412*

154. If only one system fails to operate as it should, and there is pressure in the system, the trouble is in the _____ (actuation or power) system. *Page 413*

155. If there is no pressure indicated on the system pressure gage, yet there is fluid flowing back into the reservoir, the problem is probably in the _____ (pump or pressure control valves). *Page 413*

156. If the system pressure drops when some unit is actuated, a probable cause could be a restriction in the line between the _____ (pump and the pressure regulator or selector valve and actuator). *Page 413*

157. A higher than normal system pressure is most likely to be caused by a malfunctioning _____ (unloading valve or relief valve). *Page 413*

158. A heavy chattering or banging in a hydraulic system is often caused by an insufficient air preload in the _____ . *Page 413*

159. Hydraulic pump chattering and overheating is usually caused by air in the pump _____ (inlet or discharge) line. *Page 414*

160. Spongy actuation of a hydraulic system is usually caused by _____ in the system. *Page 414*

161. When there are several relief valves in a hydraulic or pneumatic system, always begin adjusting with the valve that should be set to the _____ (highest or lowest) pressure first. *Page 414*

162. Rapid fluctuation of the pointer on a hydraulic pressure gage is usually an indication of _____ in the pressure gage line. *Page 414*

Answers to Chapter 5 Study Questions

1. hydraulic
2. pneumatic
3. 7.07
4. 226.2
5. 904.8
6. 600
7. decreased
8. 33,000
9. 550
10. 746
11. 0.212
12. 231
13. 1.75
14. 6,000
15. 4
16. 250
17. 18
18. 6
19. 20.0
20. velocity
21. pressure
22. 0.53
23. 20
24. decrease
25. rate
26. single
27. compensator
28. spring
29. selector valve
30. constant
31. does
32. before
33. opened
34. automatically
35. pressure relief
36. system pressure regulator
37. accumulator
38. series
39. does not
40. blue
41. alcohol
42. natural
43. red

44. varsol
45. nitrile, fluorosilicone
46. soap and water
47. Skydrol and HyJet
48. is not
49. clean phosphate ester fluid
50. Ethylene, propylene, or Teflon
51. soap and water
52. engine-driven pump
53. power pack
54. cavitating
55. a. aspirator
    b. engine compressor bleed air
    c. system hydraulic pressure
56. double
57. double
58. outlet
59. constant
60. shear section
61. large
62. around
63. seal
64. chatter, cavitate, overheat
65. high
66. does not
67. effective
68. bypass
69. check
70. orifice check valve
71. sequence
72. priority
73. flaps-down
74. crossflow
75. open-center, closed-center
76. low
77. small
78. does
79. fuse
80. backup
81. higher
82. unloading

83. pressure reducing
84. accumulator
85. one third
86. H
87. should not
88. increase
89. 5
90. clogged
91. bypass
92. separators
93. linear, rotary
94. balanced
95. the same
96. different
97. restrictor
98. double-acting
99. rotary
100. flow control
101. gasket
102. packing
103. one way
104. open end
105. two way
106. 1,500
107. next to
108. away from
109. blue
110. a. part number
    b. composition of the seal
    c. name of the manufacturer
    d. cure date
111. wiper, scraper
112. 5052-O
113. 2024-T, stainless steel
114. is not
115. 10
116. 37
117. $\frac{3}{8}$
118. is
119. $\frac{15}{16}$
120. 75
121. low
122. medium

123. high
124. phosphate ester
125. 250
126. 1,500
127. 3,000
128. Teflon
129. second
130. $\frac{1}{6}$, $\frac{1}{3}$
131. below
132. 16
133. lay
134. 5, 8
135. 5.75
136. air/oil separator
137. carbon

138. unloading
139. bleed
140. moisture separator
141. isolation
142. a. engines
    b. AC electric motors
    c. engine bleed air
    d. ram air turbine
143. 3,000
144. when system demand is heavy
145. EICAS
146. fuses
147. amber fault light
148. status display

149. HYDIM cards
150. ram air turbine
151. schematic
152. power, actuation
153. main, backup, emergency
154. actuation
155. pressure control valves
156. pump and pressure regulator
157. unloading valve
158. accumulator
159. inlet
160. air
161. highest
162. air

AIRCRAFT LANDING GEAR SYSTEMS

6

Continued

Continued

Aircraft Landing Gear Systems

6

No other single part of an aircraft structure takes the beating the landing gear is subjected to. A single hard landing can apply forces that are many times the weight of the aircraft to the tires, wheels, shock-absorbing system, and the entire structure. For this reason the landing gear system must be carefully inspected and maintained. This chapter examines the different types of landing gear, shock absorbers, retraction systems, wheels, brakes, antiskid systems, tires, and tubes.

Landing Gear Types

There are three basic types of landing surfaces: water, snow or ice, and hard or earthen surfaces. Each type of landing surface requires a different type of landing gear.

Operation from Water

Before the worldwide network of large airports was built, huge flying boats such as the 42-ton, four-engine Boeing 314A Clippers were used for carrying passengers and mail across both the Atlantic and Pacific oceans. But during World War II, large airports were built throughout the world, and the more efficient landplane took over for long distance flying, and large flying boats were no longer manufactured.

Small general aviation amphibians have been built with a flying boat hull and a retractable landing gear, but the large fuselage required by this basic design is aerodynamically inefficient. Almost all water operations today employ conventional land airplanes fitted with twin floats such as those in Figure 6-1. When aircraft must operate from land as well as water, amphibious floats with wheels are installed. The wheels retract into wells inside the float or fold over the top of the float, so they will not interfere with water operation.

amphibian. An aircraft with a landing gear that allows it to operate from both water and land surfaces.

Figure 6-1. *A conventional land airplane may be fitted with twin amphibious floats that allow operation from either land or water.*

Operation from Snow and Ice

An aircraft may safely operate from ice or snow when skis are installed. Some airplanes use wheel-replacement skis like the one in Figure 6-2. The wheel is removed and the ski is installed on the landing gear axle. A rubber shock cord keeps the nose of the ski pulled up in flight and steel cables limit the nose-up or nose-down movement of the ski.

Some airplanes use retractable skis. These skis fit around the wheels of the normal landing gear and are equipped with hydraulic cylinders that allow them to be moved up or down relative to the wheel. *See* Figure 6-3. For landing on a dry runway, the skis are pulled up so that the wheel protrudes below the ski, and for landing on ice or snow, the ski is lowered so that it is below the wheel.

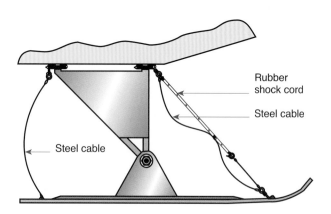

Rubber shock cord

Steel cable

Steel cable

Figure 6-2. *A wheel-replacement ski*

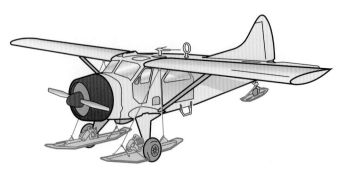

Figure 6-3. *Retractable skis allow the airplane to be operated from either dry runways or ice and snow without changing the landing gear.*

Operation from Hard Surfaces

Most flying is done from hard surfaces by landplanes equipped with wheels and tires. The landing gear for these airplanes has undergone quite an evolution.

Before hard-surfaced runways became abundant, most airplanes used a landing gear that allowed them to touch down on landing with a high angle of attack at the slowest possible landing speed. This landing gear had two main wheels located ahead of the airplane's center of gravity and a tail skid located at the very aft end of the fuselage. Early airplanes operated from grass fields and did not have any brakes. The tail skid acted as a brake to slow the airplane after landing. When wheel brakes were added to the main landing gear, the tail skid was replaced by a tail wheel.

The advent of hard-surfaced runways and the further development of airplanes replaced the tail wheel with a nose wheel. This so-called tricycle landing gear became the most popular configuration because it made airplanes easier to control during takeoff and landing as well as maneuvering on the ground.

When airplanes cruised at a slow airspeed, parasite drag was not a major consideration and light weight and ruggedness were the prime requirements for the landing gear. But when airplanes began to fly faster, streamlined covers were installed over the wheels to reduce the drag. These speed fairings, or wheel pants as they were originally called, added a small amount of weight, but appreciably reduced the drag. Finally, when speed became of major importance, retractable landing gear was developed.

The tail wheel landing gear is used for airplanes that primarily operate from unpaved areas.

Retractable landing gear minimizes parasite drag and is used on airplanes where speed is a primary consideration.

Tricycle landing gear is popular because of its good ground handling characteristics.

Figure 6-4. *Modern landing gear configurations*

Shock Absorbers

To absorb shock, the mechanical energy of the landing impact must be converted into some other form of energy. This is accomplished on most modern aircraft by using air-oil, or oleo, shock absorbers. Mechanical energy is converted into heat energy in the fluid. Taxi shocks are cushioned by air inside the strut. Some smaller aircraft use spring-oil shock absorbers that cushion the taxi shocks with a heavy steel coil spring.

Figure 6-5 shows a typical oleo shock absorber in the nose gear of a modern airplane. The wheel is attached to the piston of the oleo strut, and the piston is held in the cylinder by torque links, or scissors. The torque links allow the piston to move in and out of the cylinder, but they prevent its turning. The cylinder is attached to the structure of the aircraft through the trunnion that allows it to swing upward to retract.

Figure 6-6 shows the inside of an oleo shock absorber. The strut is made of two chambers that are separated by an orifice and a tapered metering pin which moves in and out of the orifice. The outer cylinder is attached to the aircraft structure, and the wheel assembly attaches to the piston.

When the aircraft takes off, the combined weight of the wheel and the air pressure inside the strut force the piston out to the limit allowed by the piston extension stop. Almost all the oil in the strut flows down into the hollow piston.

When the aircraft touches down on landing, the oil is forced into the upper chamber through the orifice, into the snubber tube, and out into the inner cylinder through the flapper valve, which is a one-way check valve. The small end of the metering pin is in the orifice at the beginning of the strut compression, and its tapered shape steadily decreases the area of the orifice as the strut collapses. The energy in the landing impact is absorbed by the oil as it is forced through the decreasing size orifice and by the air which compresses as the oil is forced into the upper chamber.

The momentum of the aircraft at touchdown compresses the strut to more than is required to support the aircraft weight, and when maximum compression is reached, the aircraft tries to rebound, or bounce. Fluid tries to flow back into the piston, but the flapper valve closes and the fluid must flow through the small holes in the snubber tube. This restriction of fluid flow prevents the rapid extension of the strut that would cause the airplane to bounce.

After the initial landing impact has been absorbed by the transfer of oil between the compartments, the taxi shocks are absorbed by the cushion supplied by the compressed air.

The combination of the snubber tube and the snubber knob on the top of the metering pin controls the rate of strut extension after takeoff. The combined forces of the compressed air in the top of the strut and the weight of the wheel, tire, and brake would cause the piston to extend very rapidly, and if the rate of extension were not controlled, damage would most likely result. The small holes in the snubber tube slow the extension by controlling

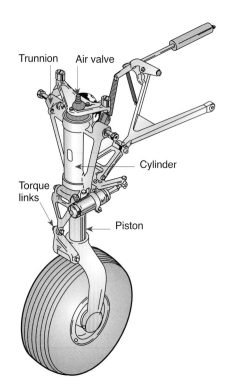

Figure 6-5. *Nose landing gear assembly*

the rate at which the oil in the cylinder is allowed to flow into the piston. Metering the oil through the snubber tube holes is effective until the strut is almost fully extended. Just before the piston reaches its full extension, the snubber knob on the end of the metering pin enters the orifice and greatly restricts the flow of oil through the orifice into the piston and almost completely stops the extension just before the piston extension stop reaches the extension stop sleeve.

scissors. A name commonly used for torque links. *See* torque links.

trunnion. Projections from the cylinder of a retractable landing gear strut about which the strut pivots to retract.

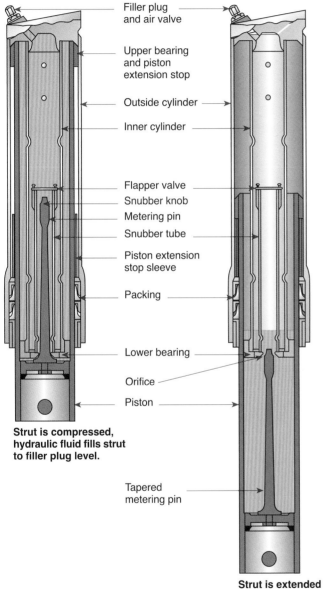

Filler plug and air valve

Upper bearing and piston extension stop

Outside cylinder

Inner cylinder

Flapper valve
Snubber knob
Metering pin
Snubber tube

Piston extension stop sleeve

Packing

Lower bearing

Orifice

Piston

Strut is compressed, hydraulic fluid fills strut to filler plug level.

Tapered metering pin

Strut is extended to limit allowed by the piston extension stop.

Figure 6-6. *Diagram of an oleo shock absorber*

Servicing Oleo Shock Struts

To service an oleo shock strut, jack the aircraft so there is no weight on the wheels. Deflate the strut through the high-pressure air valve, and then remove the filler plug. The strut can be moved in and out by hand on small aircraft, but an exerciser jack like that in Figure 6-7 is needed for large aircraft. Completely collapse the strut, and fill it with the proper fluid to the level of the filler plug. The proper fluid is specified in the aircraft maintenance manual and should also be noted on a placard attached to the shock strut. Remove the valve core from an AN812 high-pressure air valve (*see* Figure 5-56 on Page 374), and attach a bleeder hose; then screw the valve into the filler plug opening. Put the other end of the hose in a container of clean hydraulic fluid and work the piston up and down inside the cylinder until no air bubbles appear in the fluid. Completely collapse the strut and install the proper high-pressure air valve. Remove the aircraft from the jacks, and with the weight of the aircraft on the strut, put compressed air or nitrogen into the strut until it extends to the height specified in the aircraft maintenance manual.

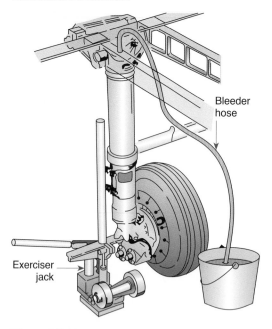

Figure 6-7. *Use an exerciser jack to move the piston in and out of the shock strut when servicing it with fluid.*

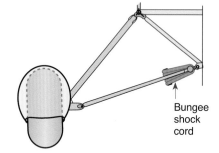

Figure 6-8. *This landing gear, typical of that used on many early Piper airplanes, softened the landing impact and taxi shocks with rings of rubber bands encased in a loose-weave cotton braid.*

Nonshock-Absorbing Landing Gears

Not all airplanes use shock absorbers. The popular single-engine series of Cessna airplanes uses a steel leaf or a tubular steel spring to accept the energy of the landing impact and return it to the aircraft. In a properly conducted landing, energy is returned in such a way that it does not cause any rebound. *See* Figure 6-4 on Page 425.

Another type of landing gear that does not use a shock absorber was used on many of the early light airplanes. Elastic shock cord, called bungee cord, that is made up of many small strands of rubber encased in a loose-weave cotton braid, stretches with the landing impact and returns the energy to the airframe.

Wheel Alignment

It is important for the wheels of an airplane to be in proper alignment with the airframe. Two alignment checks are important: toe-in or toe-out and camber.

Toe-In or Toe-Out

A wheel is toed in when lines perpendicular to the axles of a main landing gear cross ahead of the aircraft. The front of the tires are closer together than the rear, and when the aircraft is rolled forward, the wheels try to move together.

Toe-out is the opposite condition; the front of the tires are farther apart than the rear, and when the aircraft rolls forward, the wheels try to move farther apart.

To check for wheel alignment, put two aluminum plates, about 18 inches square, with grease between them under each main wheel and rock the aircraft to relax the landing gear. Place a straightedge against the tires as seen in Figure 6-9, and hold a carpenter's square against the straightedge so it touches the tire just below the axle nut. Measure the distance between the square and the front and rear of the wheel rim. The wheel alignment should be within the tolerance specified in the aircraft maintenance manual.

bungee shock cord. A cushioning material used with the non-shock absorbing landing gears installed on older aircraft.

Bungee cord is made up of many small rubber bands encased in a loose-woven cotton braid.

camber (wheel alignment). The amount the wheels of an aircraft are tilted, or inclined, from the vertical. If the top of the wheel tilts outward, the camber is positive. If the top of the wheel tilts inward, the camber is negative.

toe-in. A condition of landing gear alignment in which the front of the tires are closer together than the rear. When the aircraft rolls forward, the wheels try to move closer together.

toe-out. A condition of landing gear alignment in which the front of the tires are farther apart than the rear. When the aircraft rolls forward, the wheels try to move farther apart.

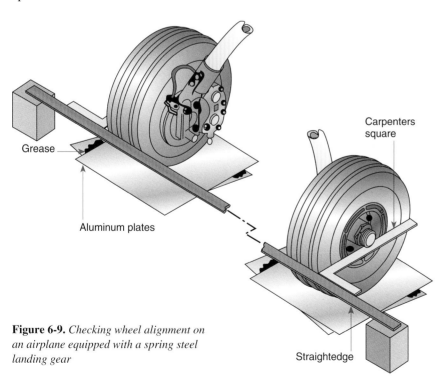

Figure 6-9. *Checking wheel alignment on an airplane equipped with a spring steel landing gear*

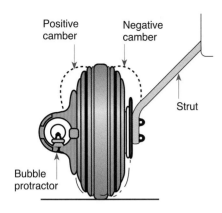

Figure 6-10. *Landing gear camber is measured with a bubble protractor.*

Camber

Camber is the amount the wheels of an aircraft are tilted, or inclined, from the vertical. If the top of the wheel tilts outward, the camber is positive, and if the top tilts inward, the camber is negative.

Wheel Alignment for Spring Steel Landing Gears

Align wheels of airplanes that use spring steel landing gears by adding or removing shims between the axle and the landing gear strut. The thickness of the shims necessary is determined by trial and measurement. The maximum thickness allowable is specified in the manufacturer's maintenance manual.

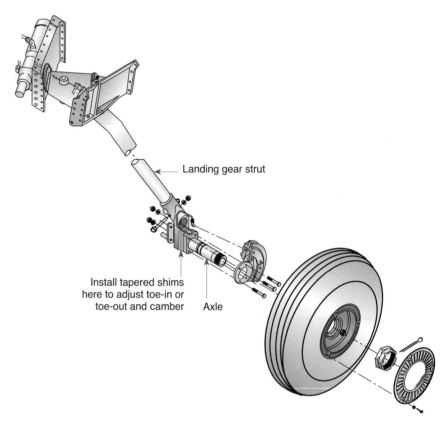

Figure 6-11. *Wheel alignment on spring-steel landing gears is adjusted by adding or removing shims between the axle and the fitting on the end of the landing gear strut.*

Wheel Alignment for Landing Gears with Oleo Struts

Check the wheel alignment of aircraft that use oleo shock struts with a straight-edge and a carpenter's square. Place the straightedge so that it touches the front or back of the two main gear tires and hold the square against the straightedge and the rim of the wheel as in Figure 6-12. Determine the amount of toe-in or toe-out by measuring between the square and the wheel rim. Correct any misalignment by inserting or removing shims between the arms of the torque links as in Figure 6-13.

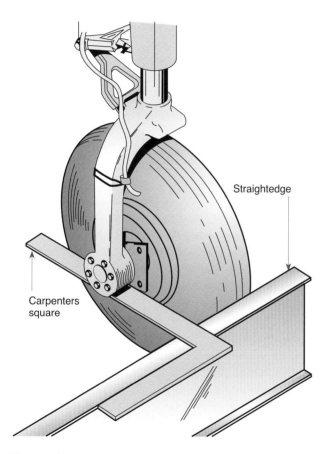

Straightedge

Carpenters square

Figure 6-12. *Checking alignment of wheels on an oleo landing gear*

Ground Steering with a Tail Wheel

Most of the smaller tail wheel airplanes are steered on the ground with a steerable tail wheel that is connected to the rudder control horn through a spring and chain. This allows the pilot to steer the airplane when the tail is on the ground. The tail wheel automatically breaks into a full swiveling action when the wheel is forced more than about 45° from its trailing position for maneuvering in close quarters. When the airplane is moved straight ahead, the tail wheel returns to its steerable condition.

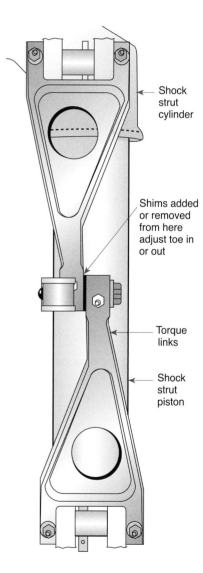

Shock strut cylinder

Shims added or removed from here adjust toe in or out

Torque links

Shock strut piston

Figure 6-13. *Wheel alignment of an oleo landing gear is adjusted by adding or removing shims between the arms of the torque links.*

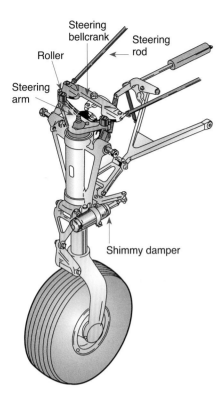

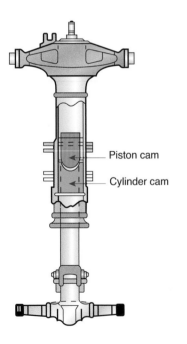

Figure 6-14. *Nose wheel steering for a retractable landing gear*

Figure 6-15. *Nose wheel centering cam*

The tail wheels of most of the larger airplanes are full-swiveling, but can be locked in alignment with the airplane's longitudinal axis. The wheel is locked for takeoff and landing to help hold the airplane straight down the runway when there is not enough airspeed for the rudder to be effective. When the airplane slows down, the tail wheel can be unlocked, allowing it to swivel freely. The airplane is then steered with differential use of the brakes.

Ground Steering with a Nose Wheel

The nose wheels of small airplanes may be either steerable or castering. A castering nose wheel is used on only the smallest airplanes, and steering is done by independent use of the brakes.

On some small airplanes, the nose wheels are steered by direct linkage to the rudder pedals. This results in a rather large turning radius, and to overcome this limitation other small airplanes have a cam arrangement that allows the nose wheel to be steered through a rather limited angular range, after which it breaks out and is free to caster until it reaches its built-in travel limits. When the airplane rolls straight ahead, its steering ability is restored.

One way of providing steering for the nose wheel of a retractable landing gear is seen in Figure 6-14. When the landing gear is down and locked, the steering bell crank presses against rollers on the steering arm which is a part of the oleo strut. When the landing gear is retracted, the wheel moves backward and the steering arm moves away from the steering bell crank.

It is very important when a nose wheel is being retracted that the wheel is centered so that it will fit into the wheel well. To accomplish this, a centering cam is installed inside the oleo strut in such a way that, as the strut extends, the cam forces the wheel straight ahead.

Large airplanes are steered by hydraulic pressure in the steering cylinders. These cylinders, shown in Figure 6-17 on the next page, act as shimmy dampers for takeoff and landing but as steering cylinders for taxiing. Fluid is directed into and out of these cylinders by a steering control valve moved by the rudder pedals or a nose wheel steering wheel.

Shimmy Dampers

Nose wheels may shimmy at certain speeds. Shimmy dampers like the one in Figure 6-16 may be installed between the piston and the cylinder of the nose wheel oleo strut to prevent this.

The simple shimmy damper in Figure 6-16 has two compartments joined through a small bleed hole, or orifice. As the nose wheel fork rotates, hydraulic fluid is forced from one compartment into the other through the orifice. This restricted flow of fluid has no effect on normal nose wheel steering but opposes rapid movement of the piston and prevents shimmying.

Large aircraft typically combine shimmy damping and nose wheel steering. Hydraulic fluid under pressure is directed into one or the other of two steering cylinders mounted on the nose wheel strut as shown in Figure 6-17.

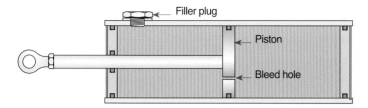

Figure 6-16. *A shimmy damper installed between the nose wheel cylinder and piston absorbs the shimmying vibrations by the transfer of hydraulic fluid from one side of the piston to the other through the bleed hole.*

A control wheel operated by the pilot directs pressure to one side of the nose wheel steering pistons, and fluid from the opposite side of the pistons is vented back into the reservoir through a pressure relief valve that holds a constant pressure on the system to snub shimmying. An accumulator in the line to the relief valve holds pressure on the system when the steering control valve is in its neutral position.

shimmy damper. A small hydraulic shock absorber installed between the nosewheel fork and the nosewheel cylinder attached to the aircraft structure.

shimmy. Abnormal, and often violent, vibration of the nose wheel of an airplane. Shimmying is usually caused by looseness of the nose wheel support mechanism, but may also be caused by tire imbalance.

centering cam. A cam in the nose-gear shock strut that causes the piston to center when the strut fully extends.

When the aircraft takes off and the strut extends, the wheel is straightened in its fore-and-aft position so it can be retracted into the wheel well.

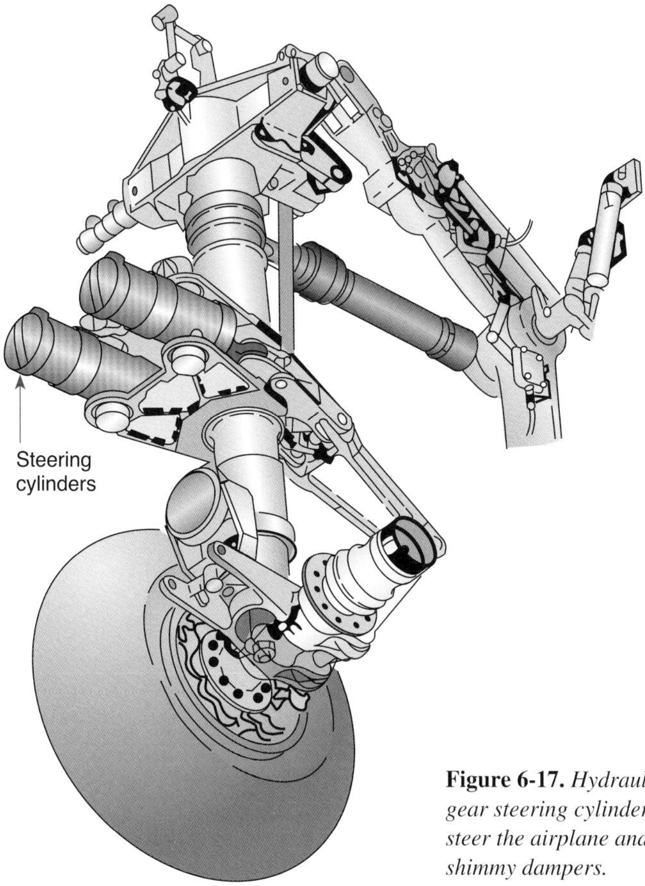

Figure 6-17. *Hydraulically operated nose gear steering cylinders allow the pilot to steer the airplane and also serve as shimmy dampers.*

Answers are on Page 490. Page numbers refer to chapter text.

1. A spring steel landing gear _____ (does or does not) absorb shock. *Page 428*

2. An air-oil oleo shock strut absorbs the energy from the initial landing impact with the _____ (air or oil). *Page 426*

3. The opposition to the landing impact is gradually increased in an oleo shock strut by a tapered _____ decreasing the size of the orifice. *Page 426*

4. An air-oil oleo shock strut absorbs taxi shocks with the _____ (air or oil). *Page 426*

5. A spring-oil shock strut absorbs taxi shocks with the _____ (spring or oil). *Page 426*

6. Rebound is minimized with an oleo shock strut by restricting the flow of oil by the closing of the _____ valve. *Page 426*

7. Two places in which you can find the specification number for the proper fluid to use to service an oleo shock strut are:
   a. _____
   b. _____
      Page 428

8. An oleo shock strut can be charged with high-pressure compressed air or with _____ . *Page 428*

9. The correct amount of air in an oleo shock strut is measured by the _____ of the strut. *Page 428*

10. If the main wheels of an airplane are closer together at the front than at the rear, the landing gear is toed _____ (in or out). *Page 429*

11. If the top of the main wheel of an airplane tilts outward, the wheel has a _____ (positive or negative) camber. *Page 430*

12. The wheels of an airplane equipped with a spring steel landing gear are aligned by adding shims between the _____ and the _____ . *Page 430*

13. The wheels of an airplane equipped with an oleo shock absorber are aligned by adding shims between the _____ . *Page 431*

14. When a large transport category airplane is not being steered on the ground, the nose gear steering cylinders act as _____ . *Page 433*

15. An airplane with a castering nose wheel is steered by differential use of the _____ . *Page 432*

16. A retractable nose wheel is prevented from being retracted when it is not straight ahead by a/an _____ in the nose gear oleo strut. *Page 432*

Landing Gear Retraction Systems

As the speed of aircraft becomes high enough that the parasite drag of the landing gear is greater than the induced drag caused by the added weight of a retracting system, it becomes economically practical to retract the landing gear into the aircraft structure.

Small aircraft use simple mechanical retraction systems. Some use a hand crank to drive the retracting mechanism through a roller chain, and the most simple system of all uses a direct hand lever mechanism to raise and lower the wheels.

Many aircraft use electric motors to drive the gear-retracting mechanism, and some European-built aircraft use pneumatic systems. Most American-built aircraft use hydraulically retracted landing gears.

Power Pack System

The hydraulic power pack was developed to make hydraulic systems easy to service and lightweight. The system in Figure 6-18 (Page 436) uses a power pack that contains the reservoir, pump, thermal relief valve, high-pressure control valve, low-pressure control valve, and a shuttle valve all in one unit.

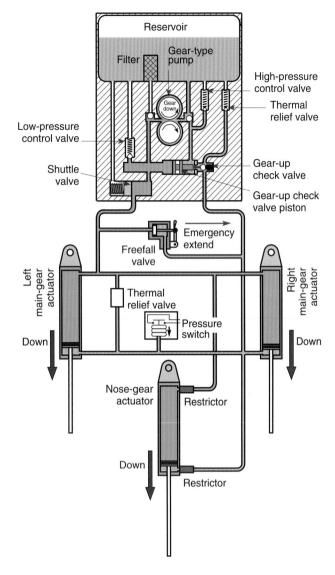

Figure 6-18. *Hydraulic power pack system while the landing gear is being lowered*

Lowering the Landing Gear

To lower the landing gear, the pilot moves the landing gear handle to the GEAR-DOWN position, and these events take place:

1. The landing gear handle actuates a switch that turns on the hydraulic pump motor in the power pack so that it turns in the direction shown by the arrows in Figure 6-18.

2. Fluid flows through the passage and check valve on the right side of the pump and around the outside of the gears.

3. The output from the pump moves the gear-up check valve piston to the right and unseats the gear-up check valve.

4. The pump output then flows down to the shuttle valve and forces it to the left, opening the passage to the gear-down side of the actuating cylinders.

5. Fluid flows into the down side of the three actuating cylinders and forces the pistons out. The nose gear is much easier to move than the main gears, so the fluid flows into and out of the nose-gear actuating cylinder through restrictors.

6. Return fluid from the up side of the actuators flows through the opened gear-up check valve back to the inlet side of the pump.

7. As each gear reaches its down-and-locked position, the pressure in the gear-down line builds up and fluid is bypassed back into the reservoir through the low-pressure control valve. When all three gears are down and locked, limit switches turn the pump motor off.

Raising the Landing Gear

When the airplane is in the air, the pilot can retract the landing gear by moving the landing gear handle to the GEAR-UP position. These events take place:

1. The landing gear handle actuates a switch that turns on the hydraulic pump motor in the power pack so that it turns in the direction shown in Figure 6-19.

2. Fluid flows through the filter and the check valve on the left side of the pump, around the gears, and out the right side, down to the gear-up check valve.

3. The fluid from the pump moves the gear-up check valve piston to the left, and the fluid unseats the ball and flows to the gear-up side of each of the gear actuating cylinders. The first movement of the piston releases the mechanical down locks and allows the gear to retract.

4. Fluid returns from the gear-down side of the actuators past the shuttle valve, which the spring has forced to the right, back into the reservoir.

5. This landing gear system does not have any mechanical up locks, but the gear is held retracted by hydraulic pressure. When all three gears are fully retracted, the pressure continues to build up until it reaches a value that opens the pressure switch and shuts the hydraulic pump motor off. If the pressure in the system leaks down to a specified value, the pressure switch will close and start the pump so it will restore the pressure to the cutout value.

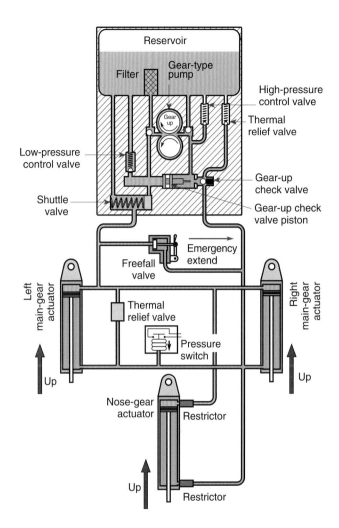

Figure 6-19. *Hydraulic power pack system while the landing gear is being raised*

Typical Landing Gear Retraction System

The landing gear retraction system shown in Figure 6-20 is for a tricycle landing gear airplane that has wheel-well doors that close when the landing gear is retracted. The schematic shows the system with the landing gear down and locked and the gear selector in the GEAR-UP position. Fluid flows to the three landing gear downlocks and releases them by moving their locking pins inward against the spring force so the landing gears can be retracted. Fluid flows into the up side of the three landing gear actuators and forces the pistons out. The oil flowing into the main-gear actuator passes through orifice check valves in the full-flow direction to retract the gears as soon as possible.

Both of the gear-door sequence valves are closed, and no fluid can flow through them until the main gears fully retract and the sequence valve plungers are depressed.

Return fluid from the main-gear actuators flows through the main-gear sequence valves which are held open by the gear-door actuators.

Emergency Extension of the Landing Gear

All aircraft with retractable landing gear are required to have some acceptable method of lowering the gear in flight if the normal actuating systems fail.

The landing gear shown in Figures 6-18 and 6-19 (Pages 436 and 437) has a free-fall valve between the gear-up and the gear-down lines of the power pack. If the power pack fails, the pilot can move the free-fall handle to the EMERGENCY EXTEND position, which opens the free-fall valve and allows fluid from the gear-up side of the actuating cylinders to flow directly to the gear-down side. The gear will then fall from the wheel wells with little opposition, and its weight combined with the air moving past it will force it to mechanically lock in place.

More complex landing gear systems use compressed air or nitrogen to provide the pressure for emergency extension of the gear. In such systems, a shuttle valve like the one shown in Figure 5-94 on Page 404 is installed at the actuator where the main hydraulic pressure and the emergency air pressure meet. During normal operation, fluid enters the actuator through one side of the shuttle valve. In the event of failure of the hydraulic system, the pilot can place the gear handle in the GEAR-DOWN position, which releases the emergency air supply into the system. The piston in the shuttle valve moves over to seal off the normal hydraulic system and direct compressed air into the actuator.

shuttle valve. A type of hydraulic valve mounted on the landing gear and brake actuator cylinders. A shuttle valve allows normal system fluid to flow into the actuators when the system pressure is in the correct operating range.

If normal system pressure is lost and the emergency system is actuated, the shuttle valve will automatically shift and allow emergency fluid to actuate the landing gear and apply the brakes.

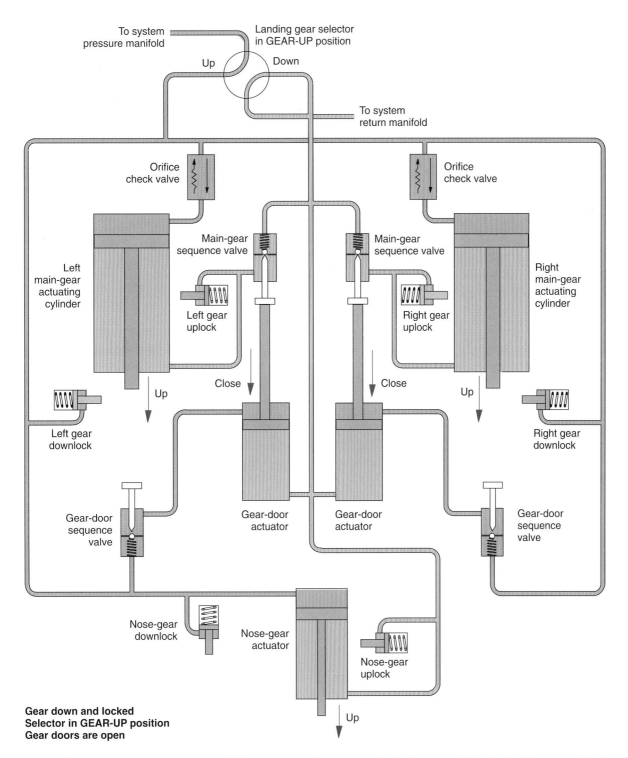

Figure 6-20. *Schematic diagram of a typical hydraulic system for a retractable landing gear with hydraulically actuated wheel-well doors*

Answers are on Page 490. Page numbers refer to chapter text.

17. Four methods of actuating a retractable landing gear are:
    a. _____
    b. _____
    c. _____
    d. _____
    Page 435

18. A hydraulic system that has the reservoir, pump, and valves in a single easy-to-service unit is called a/an _____ system. *Page 435*

19. The mechanically operated valve that prevents the landing gear actuator from lowering the main gear before the wheel well doors are open is called a/an _____ valve. *Page 438*

20. Emergency actuation of the landing gear of some small airplanes consists of opening the free-fall valve between the landing gear _____ and the _____ and allowing the gear to free fall from the wheel wells. *Page 438*

21. Two gases that may be used for the emergency backup system for a hydraulically actuated landing gear are compressed _____ and _____ . *Page 438*

22. When a landing gear is extended by the emergency system, compressed air or nitrogen is directed into the actuating cylinder through a/an _____ valve. *Page 438*

Aircraft Brakes

In the study of aircraft brakes we first consider different types of brake actuating units and then the various methods of providing hydraulic pressure to them.

Brake Actuating Units

Aircraft brake systems slow the airplane down by changing kinetic energy from the motion of the aircraft into heat energy generated by the friction between the linings and the brake drum or disk.

Two basic types of brakes are in use, energizing and nonenergizing. Energizing brakes use the friction developed between the rotating and stationary parts to produce a wedging action that increases the braking force and reduces the pilot effort needed to obtain the desired braking action. Nonenergizing brakes do not use this wedging action.

Energizing Brakes

Drum-type brakes, similar to those used on automobiles, are a form of dual-servo brake. Movement of the aircraft either forward or backward causes the brake linings to wedge against the rotating drum when the brakes are applied.

Energizing brakes used on some of the smaller aircraft have a single-servo action. Only forward motion of the aircraft helps apply the brakes.

Energizing brakes have their shoes and linings mounted on a torque plate in such a way that they are free to move out against the rotating drum. When the brakes are applied, two pistons in the brake cylinder move out and push the linings against a cylindrical cast-iron drum that rotates with the wheel. Friction attempts to rotate the linings, but they are held in place by the cylinder assembly. Rotation of the brake drum wedges the linings tightly against it. When the hydraulic pressure is released, the retracting spring pulls the linings back from the drum and releases the brakes.

One of the limitations of this type of brake is fading. When the brake is used, the friction heats the drum and causes the open end to expand in a bell-mouthed fashion. The drum expands away from the linings and the friction area decreases.

Nonenergizing Brakes

Nonenergizing brakes are the most common type of brake on modern aircraft. These brakes are actuated by hydraulic pressure, and the amount of braking action depends upon the amount of pressure applied. Expander tube, single-disk, and multiple-disk brakes are all nonenergizing brakes.

---

energizing brake. A brake that uses the momentum of the aircraft to increase its effectiveness by wedging the shoe against the brake drum.

Energizing brakes are also called servo brakes. A single-servo brake is energizing only when moving in the forward direction, and a duo-servo brake is energizing when the aircraft is moving either forward or backward.

single-servo brake. A brake that uses the momentum of the aircraft rolling forward to help apply the brakes by wedging the brake shoe against the brake drum.

fading of brakes. The decrease in the amount of braking action that occurs with some types of brakes that are applied for a long period of time.

True fading occurs with overheated drum-type brakes. As the drum is heated, it expands in a bell-mouthed fashion. This decreases the amount of drum in contact with the brake shoes and decreases the braking action.

A condition similar to brake fading occurs when there is an internal leak in the brake master cylinder. The brakes are applied, but as the pedal is held down, fluid leaks past the piston, and the brakes slowly release.

nonenergizing brake. A brake that does not use the momentum of the aircraft to increase the friction.

expander tube brake. A brake that uses hydraulic fluid inside a synthetic rubber tube around the brake hub to force rectangular blocks of brake-lining material against the rotating brake drum. Friction between the brake drum and the lining material slows the aircraft.

Expander Tube Brakes

Expander tube brakes use a heavy neoprene tube, such as the one in Figure 6-21, and have been used on airplanes as small as the Piper Cub, with a gross weight of 1,200 pounds, to the Boeing B-29 Superfortress bomber with a gross weight of 133,500 pounds.

In an expander tube brake, hydraulic fluid from the master cylinder is directed into the expander tube around the torque flange. When this tube is expanded by hydraulic fluid, it pushes the brake blocks out against the drum, and the friction between the blocks and the drum slows the aircraft. The heat generated in the lining is kept from damaging the expander tube by thin stainless steel heat shields placed between each of the lining blocks. As soon as the brake pedal is released, the return springs between the brake blocks collapse the expander tube and force the fluid back into the brake reservoir.

Some larger expander tube brakes have adjuster valves in the fluid line to the brake. This valve is a simple two-way relief valve that holds a given amount of pressure in the expander tube and keeps it from collapsing completely when the pedal is released. Brakes without adjuster valves cannot have their clearance adjusted. When the brake blocks have worn to the extent that the clearance between the block and the brake drum is greater than the aircraft service manual allows, the blocks must be replaced.

It is extremely important to avoid depressing the brake pedal when the brake drum is removed. Expanding the tube without the drum in place damages the brake blocks.

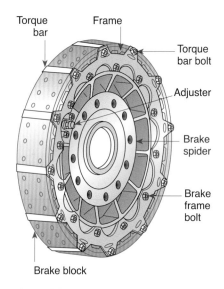

Assembled expander tube brake

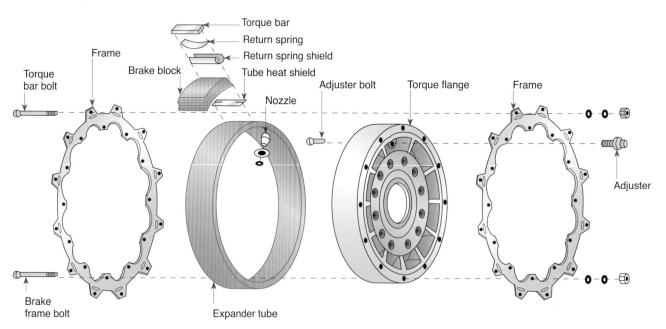

Exploded view of expander tube brake

Figure 6-21. *Expander tube brake*

Single-Disk Brakes

The most popular brake for modern light aircraft is the single-disk brake. This brake is actuated by hydraulic pressure from a master cylinder, and friction is produced when the rotating disk is squeezed between two brake linings in the caliper.

There are two types of single-disk brakes; one has the disk keyed into the wheel and it is free to move in and out as the brake is applied. This type of brake is called a floating-disk/fixed-caliper brake. The disk of the other type of brake is rigidly attached to the wheel, and the caliper moves in and out on two anchor bolts. This is called a fixed-disk/floating-caliper brake.

Figure 6-22 shows a typical Goodyear floating-disk/fixed-caliper single-disk brake. The disk is driven by hardened steel drive keys in the wheel so that it rotates with the wheel, but it is free to move in and out of the wheel on the keys. The disk is held centered in the wheel and kept from rattling by thin spring steel antirattle clips. The housing of the brake is bolted to the landing gear axle, and brake-lining pucks fit into cavities in the housing. One lining puck, the pressure-plate lining, fits into a recess against the piston in the caliper. The other puck, the backing-plate lining, fits into a recess in the backing plate. The disk rotates between the two linings and is clamped by them when hydraulic fluid under pressure forces the pressure-plate lining against the disk.

single-disk brakes. Aircraft brakes in which a single steel disk rotates with the wheel between two brake-lining blocks. When the brake is applied, the disk is clamped tightly between the lining blocks, and the friction slows the aircraft.

multiple-disk brakes. Aircraft brakes in which one set of disks is keyed to the axle and remains stationary. Between each stationary disk there is a rotating disk that is keyed to the inside of the wheel. When the brakes are applied, the stationary disks are forced together, clamping the rotating disks between them. The friction between the disks slows the aircraft.

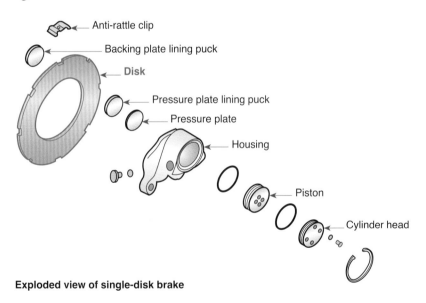

Exploded view of single-disk brake

Complete brake assembly for a light airplane

Figure 6-22. *Single-disk brake*

automatic adjuster. A subsystem in an aircraft disk brake that compensates for disk or lining wear. Each time the brakes are applied, the automatic adjuster is reset for zero clearance, and when the brakes are released, the clearance between the disks or the disk and lining is returned to a preset value.

backplate. A floating plate on which the wheel cylinder and the brake shoes attach on an energizing-type brake.

Some Goodyear single-disk brakes have automatic adjusters like the one in Figure 6-23. This feature automatically changes the amount the piston can return when the brakes are released, which compensates for the wear of the lining.

When the brake is applied, hydraulic fluid under pressure forces the piston over to the right and squeezes the disk between the two linings. The automatic adjusting pin is pulled through the grip so that when the brake is released, the piston and the lining move back only the amount allowed by the return spring.

As the lining wears, the adjusting pin is pulled into the grip and indicates the lining's wear. The aircraft service manual specifies the minimum amount the adjusting pin may protrude from the nut before the brake must be disassembled and the linings replaced.

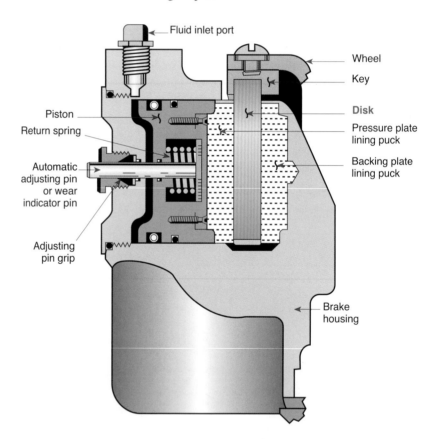

Figure 6-23. *Goodyear single-disk brake automatic adjuster*

To replace these linings, remove the antirattle clips and remove the wheel from the axle. The disk will remain between the linings. Carefully remove the disk, and lift out the lining pucks. Inspect the entire brake and install new lining pucks. Slip the disk between the pucks and re-install the wheel on the axle. Center the disk in the wheel with the antirattle clips, then adjust the axle nut and safety it with a cotter pin.

If the brake is not equipped with an automatic adjuster, measure lining wear by applying the brake and measuring the space between the disk and the inboard edge of the housing as shown in Figure 6-24. The aircraft service manual specifies the maximum distance before the brake must be disassembled and the linings replaced.

The Cleveland fixed-disk/floating-caliper brake uses a disk that is solidly bolted to the inner wheel half as shown in Figure 6-25. The brake assembly, Figure 6-26, is mounted on the aircraft by a torque plate that is bolted to the axle. One set of brake linings is riveted to the pressure plate and the other set is riveted to the backplate. The brake assembly, which consists of the brake cylinder, the pressure plate and its lining, and the backplate and its lining, attaches to the torque plate with two anchor bolts that slide back and forth through bushings in the torque plate. The disk that is bolted to the wheel rides between the two sets of linings. When the brakes are applied, hydraulic fluid under pressure forces the pistons out and squeezes the disk between the linings.

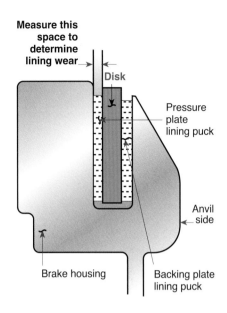

Figure 6-24. *Lining wear may be determined by measuring the space between the disk and the inboard side of the brake housing with the brakes applied.*

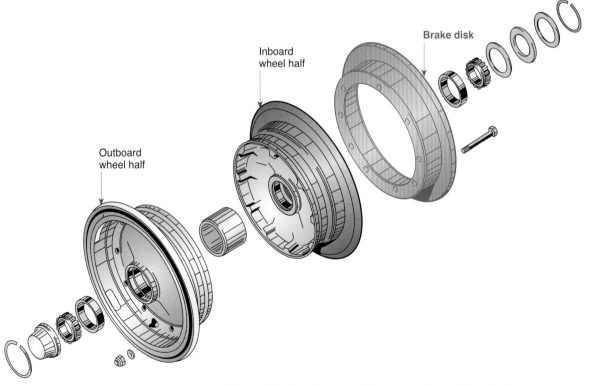

Figure 6-25. *Cleveland wheel showing the brake disk that bolts to the inner wheel half*

pressure plate. A strong, heavy plate used in a multiple-disk brake. The pressure plate receives the force from the brake cylinders and transmits this force to the disks.

You can replace the linings on Cleveland brakes without removing the wheel from the axle. Unbolt the cylinder assembly from the backplate, which will drop down and allow you to pull the entire assembly away from the torque plate, and then and slide the pressure plate off of the anchor bolts. One of the linings is riveted to the pressure plate and the other to the backplate. Replacement of the brake linings is made easy by using the brake relining kit available from the brake manufacturer. Remove the old rivets from the linings with the knockout punch. Inspect the entire brake and rivet new linings in place, using the rivet clinching tool and the rivets that are included in the kit.

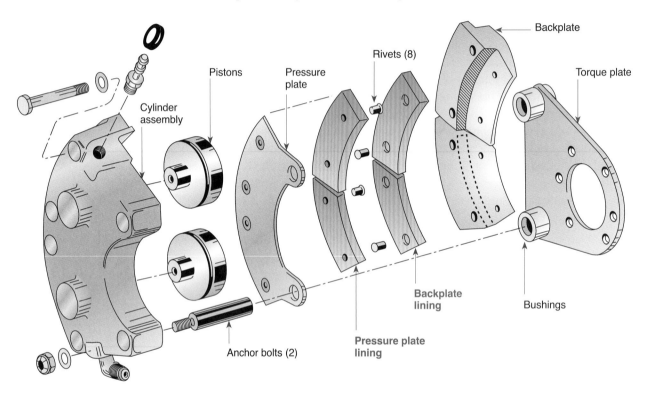

Figure 6-26. *Cleveland brake assembly. The disk that bolts to the wheel turns between the two sets of linings that are riveted to the pressure plate and the backplate. The entire brake assembly rides on the two anchor bolts which slide back and forth in bushings in the torque plate.*

Dual-Disk Brakes

Aircraft that need more braking action than a single-disk brake can supply, but not enough to justify the weight of a multiple-disk system, use the dual-disk brake.

The dual-disk brake is similar to a single-disk except that two disks rotate with the wheel, and there is a center carrier with brake lining pucks on both sides between these disks. The brake shown in Figure 6-27 has four cylinders, each with automatic adjusters. The housing assembly, center carrier, and backplate are all attached to the wheel axle with high-strength bolts. The disks mount inside the wheel and are driven by hardened steel keys that ride in the grooves around the periphery of the disks. When the brakes are applied, hydraulic fluid under pressure forces the pistons over and clamps the rotating disks between the linings which are backed up by the housing backplate.

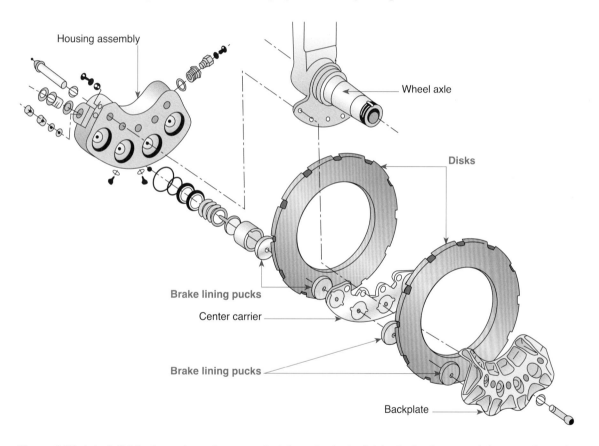

Figure 6-27. *A dual-disk brake works on the same principle as the single-disk brake, but has more disk area and more lining area.*

segmented-rotor brake. A heavy-duty, multiple-disk brake used on large, high-speed aircraft.

Stators that are surfaced with a material that retains its friction characteristics at high temperatures are keyed to the axle. Rotors which are keyed into the wheels mesh with the stators.

The rotors are made in segments to allow for cooling and for their large amounts of expansion.

Multiple-Disk Brakes

Simple physics determines the brake size for any given aircraft. The gross weight of the aircraft and the speed at the time of brake application determine the amount of heat generated when the brakes are applied. As the aircraft size, weight, and landing speed increase, the need for greater braking surface area and heat-dissipation capability also increases.

Thin-Disk Multiple-Disk Brake

The thin-disk multiple-disk brake was popular for heavy aircraft up through World War II. This brake provided maximum friction for minimum size and weight, and its action did not fade when the brake got hot. Two main disadvantages of this brake were the tendency of the disks to warp, causing the brakes to drag, and the need for manual adjustments as the disks wore.

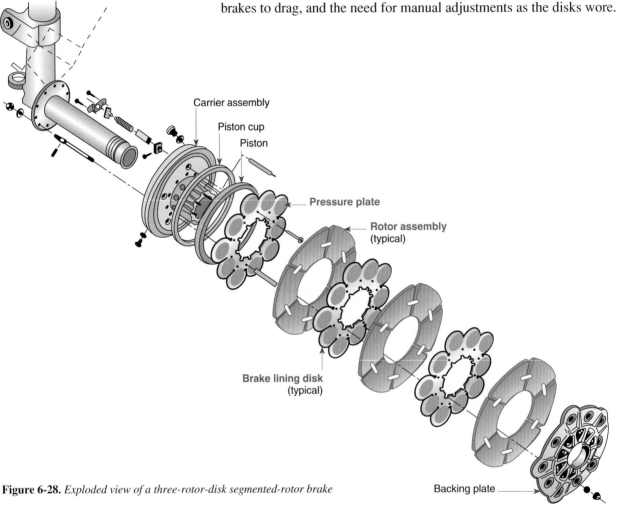

Figure 6-28. *Exploded view of a three-rotor-disk segmented-rotor brake*

This brake has a series of steel disks, called stators, keyed to the axle. A rotor, or rotating disk, made of copper- or bronze-plated steel, rotates between each of them. These disks are approximately ⅛ inch thick, and they get very hot when the brake is used. The disks form such a solid mass of material that the heat has difficulty escaping. If the pilot sets the parking brake after using these brakes, the entrapped heat will warp the disks.

Segmented-Rotor Multiple-Disk Brake

Segmented-rotor multiple-disk brakes, which can dissipate the tremendous amount of heat produced by aborted takeoffs or emergency landings, are standard on most high-performance aircraft.

The segmented-rotor multiple-disk brake in Figure 6-28 has three rotating disks, or rotors, that are keyed into the wheel. Between each rotor is a stator plate, or brake lining disk, keyed to the axle. Riveted to each side of each stator plate are linings or wear pads that are made of a material that retains its friction characteristics under conditions of extremely high temperature. A pressure plate and a backing plate complete the brake.

The brake shown in Figures 6-28, 6-29, and 6-30 uses an annular cup-type actuator to apply the force to the pressure plate to squeeze the disks together.

Automatic adjusters attach to the pressure plate and push it back when the hydraulic pressure to the brakes is released. When pressure is applied to the brakes, the pressure plate compresses the return spring on the indicator pin, and as the lining wears, the pin is pulled through its friction collar. This is a pressed fit, so that as the brake is released, the grip of the friction collar pulls the pressure plate back as much as the adjuster housing will allow. Each time the brakes are applied, they automatically adjust for the wear of the linings. The amount the automatic adjuster pin sticks out of the retainer housing is an indication of the condition of the brake linings.

The brakes used on most of the large jet transport airplanes use a number of round brake cylinders rather than a single annular cylinder. Figure 6-31 on the next page shows the brake cylinder assembly of the multi-disk segmented-rotor brake used on a McDonnell-Douglas DC-9. This brake has 14 cylinders whose pistons press against the pressure plate. Seven of these cylinders are supplied with hydraulic fluid under pressure from System A.

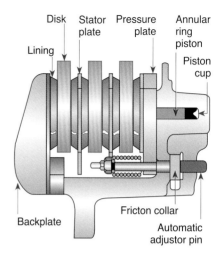

Figure 6-29. *Cutaway view of a three-rotor-disk segmented-rotor brake*

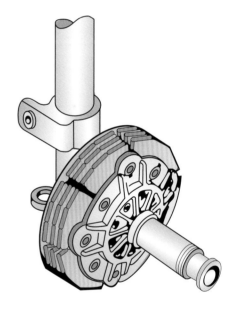

Figure 6-30. *View of an installed three-rotor-disk segmented-rotor brake*

Seven other cylinders between those shown are supplied by fluid from System B. In this drawing, only the cylinders served by System A are shown. System B is identical to System A. System A fluid enters through the pressure port and is distributed to all of the cylinders through passages drilled in the brake housing. There are two bleeder valves at the highest point of the wheel in both systems.

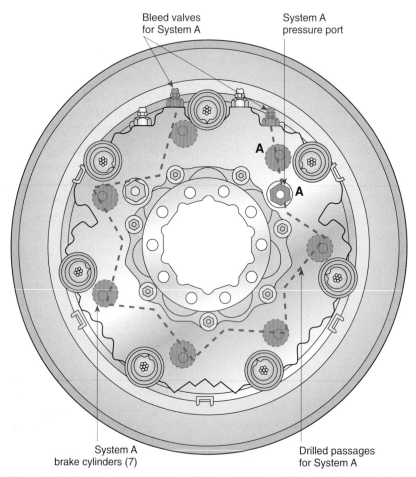

Figure 6-31. *Housing of the brake installed on a McDonnell-Douglas DC-9 showing the hydraulic ports and passages in System A. Identical cylinders, ports, and passages for System B are not shown.*

Carbon Disk Brakes

The latest development in aircraft brakes are multiple-disk brakes made of carbon composite material. These brakes, which have thick disks made of molded carbon fibers, are lighter in weight than a conventional brake with the same stopping power, and they can function at higher temperatures. Because of the greater cost of carbon brakes, they are currently used only on high-performance military aircraft and on certain transport airplanes where the weight they save makes them cost effective.

Figure 6-32. *Carbon disk brake assembly used on a Fokker 100 twin jet transport.*

Brake Actuation Systems

An aircraft brake system is composed of two subsystems: the friction producers and the actuating systems. The components in the wheels produce the friction that converts some of the aircraft's kinetic energy into heat energy. The hydraulic components in the aircraft allow the pilot to control the amount of friction the wheel units produce.

Independent Brake Master Cylinders

For years, independent master cylinders have been the most common pressure-generating systems for light aircraft brakes. The diaphragm-type master cylinder in Figure 6-33 on the next page is used for the simplest type of brakes.

The master cylinder and expander tube in the wheel are connected with the appropriate tubing, and the entire system is filled with hydraulic fluid from which all of the air has been purged. When the pilot pushes on the brake pedal, fluid is moved into the expander tube to apply the brake. This type of system is useful only on very small aircraft, and was used with success on the Piper Cub and Super Cub series of airplanes, which used one heel-operated master cylinder for each wheel. A single master cylinder of this type is turned around and operated by a cable from a pull handle under the instrument panel on Piper Tri-Pacers. This airplane has direct nosewheel steering, so independent braking is not needed, and one master cylinder supplies both brakes. For the parking brake, a shutoff valve is located between the master cylinder and the wheel unit. The brakes are applied and the shutoff valve traps pressure in the line.

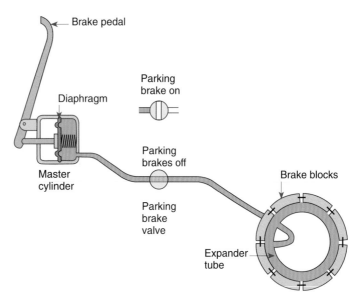

Figure 6-33. *The diaphragm-type master cylinder may be used to supply hydraulic fluid under pressure to the expander tube brakes of small aircraft.*

dragging brakes. Brakes that do not fully release when the brake pedal is released. The brakes are partially applied all the time, which causes excessive lining wear and heat.

compensator port. A small hole between a hydraulic brake master cylinder and the reservoir. When the brakes are released, this port is uncovered and the pressure on the fluid in the line to the brake master cylinder is the same as the atmospheric pressure.

When the brake is applied, the master-cylinder piston covers the compensator port and allows pressure in the line to the brake to build up and apply the brakes. When the brake is released, the piston uncovers the compensator port. If any fluid has been lost from the brake, the reservoir will refill the master cylinder.

Larger aircraft require more fluid for their brakes. This fluid must be vented to the atmosphere when the brakes are not applied. The vent for the brake system allows the fluid to expand when it is heated without causing the brakes to drag.

The many types of vented master cylinders all have the same basic components. The master cylinder in Figure 6-35 is typical of those used in modern light aircraft.

Each wheel cylinder is served by its own master cylinder, which is mounted on a pivot below the rudder pedals as in Figure 6-34. The pilot moves the entire rudder pedal forward for normal rudder actuation, but to actuate the brakes, the pilot applies pressure with his or her toes to lower the plunger into the cylinder.

The body of the master cylinder in Figure 6-35 serves as the reservoir for the fluid, and it is vented to the atmosphere. When the pedal is not depressed, the return spring forces the piston up so that the compensator sleeve holds the compensator port open to vent the fluid in the brake line and the wheel cylinder to the atmosphere.

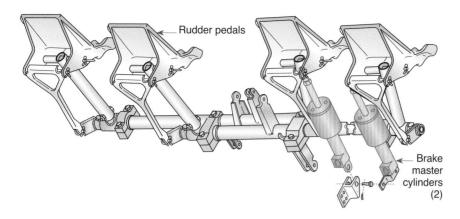

Rudder pedals

Brake
master
cylinders
(2)

Figure 6-34. *Individual brake master cylinders are installed below the rudder pedals. The brakes are applied by depressing the top of the pedal with the toe.*

Depressing the top of the rudder pedal pushes the piston away from the compensator sleeve, and a special O-ring and washer seals fluid in the line to the brake. The amount of pressure applied to the brakes is proportional to the amount of force the pilot applies to the brake pedal. When the pedal is released, the compensator sleeve contacts the piston and opens the compensator port. This vents the brake line into the reservoir.

The parking brake for this type of master cylinder is a simple spring-released ratchet mechanism that holds the piston down in the cylinder. To apply the parking brake, depress the brake pedal and pull the parking brake handle. This locks the piston down. To release the brake, depress the brake pedal more than was done for the initial application and the ratchet will release.

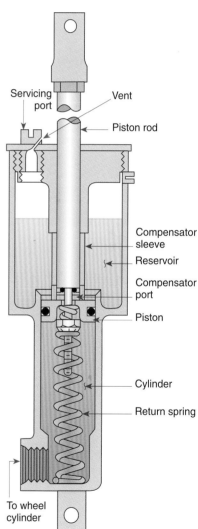

Servicing port

Vent

Piston rod

Compensator sleeve

Reservoir

Compensator port

Piston

Cylinder

Return spring

To wheel cylinder

Complete master cylinder assembly

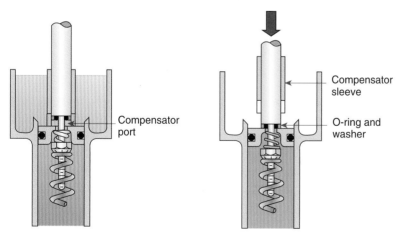

Compensator port

Compensator sleeve

O-ring and washer

Brake pedal is released and return spring has pushed piston rod to the top. Compensator sleeve holds the piston away from the seal and wheel cylinder is vented to the reservoir.

Brake pedal is depressed, piston rod pushes piston away from the compensator sleeve, and the O-ring seals piston to the piston rod.

Figure 6-35. *Individual vented brake master cylinder*

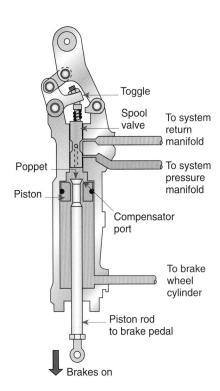

Toggle

Spool valve

To system return manifold

Poppet

To system pressure manifold

Piston

Compensator port

To brake wheel cylinder

Piston rod to brake pedal

Brakes on

Figure 6-36. *Boosted brake master cylinder. Brakes are off.*

Boosted Brakes

Some airplanes require more braking force than a manually applied independent master cylinder can produce, yet do not need the complexity of a power brake system. The boosted brake system is used for these airplanes.

In this system, the pilot applies pressure to the brake pedal as with any independent master cylinder. If more pressure is needed than the pilot can apply, continued pushing on the pedal allows some of the hydraulic system pressure to flow into the chamber behind the piston, and this pressure increases the force applied to the brakes.

The brake valve in Figure 6-36 attaches to the brake pedal in such a way that application of the brake pulls on the piston rod. The initial movement of the pedal closes the compensator port, the space between the poppet and the piston, and as the piston is pulled down, fluid is forced into the wheel cylinder to apply the brakes. If more pressure is needed at the wheel, the pilot pushes harder on the pedal. This additional movement causes the toggle to depress the spool valve which allows hydraulic system pressure to flow through the center of the spool valve and get behind the piston and help apply the brakes. The spring between the spool valve and the toggle acts as a regulator, preventing the pressure from continuing to build up when the brake pedal is held partially depressed.

As soon as the pilot releases the pedal, the spool valve moves back, shutting off the hydraulic system pressure. Fluid in the brake line is allowed to return to the reservoir through the system return manifold.

Power Brakes

Large aircraft brakes require more fluid and higher pressures than can be supplied by independent master cylinders, and brakes for these aircraft are actuated by pressure supplied from the main hydraulic power system of the aircraft. Power brake control valves operated by the pilot meter this pressure to give the pilot control of the braking action.

System Operation

To operate power brakes, the pilot depresses the brake pedal, which actuates the power brake control valve. Hydraulic fluid under pressure from the main hydraulic system is metered to the brake wheel cylinders proportionate to the amount of force the pilot applies to the brake pedal. The brake control valve is more of a regulator than a selector valve, because it must allow the pilot to hold the brakes partially applied without the pressure building up in the brake lines.

The brakes of these aircraft require a large volume of fluid, and its pressure must be considerably lower than that supplied by the main hydraulic system. The pressure supplied to the brake assembly by the brake control valve is lowered, and the volume increased, by deboosters installed near the wheels.

Since the brakes are in an area where damage can easily occur, hydraulic fuses are installed to prevent the loss of fluid in the event a hydraulic line is broken. There must also be an emergency brake system that can supply air or hydraulic pressure to the brake assemblies if the main hydraulic system should fail.

Figure 6-37 is a simplified schematic of a typical power brake system used in large jet aircraft. The brakes get their fluid from the main hydraulic system, and a check valve and an accumulator hold the pressure for the brakes in the event of a failure in the hydraulic system. The pilot and the copilot operate the power brake control valves through the appropriate linkages.

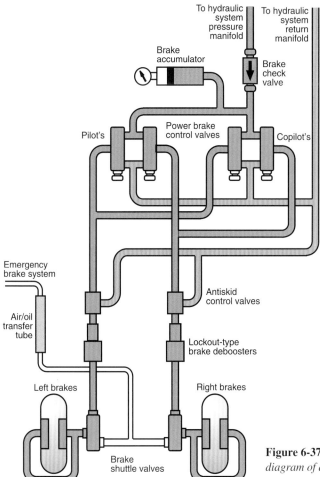

Figure 6-37. *A simplified schematic diagram of a power brake system for a large jet aircraft*

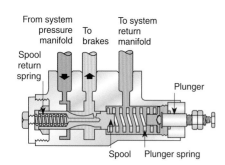

From system
pressure   To   To system
manifold brakes   return
                    manifold

Spool
return
spring
                            Plunger

        Spool   Plunger spring

Brake pedal is depressed and fluid is flowing
from system pressure manifold to brakes.

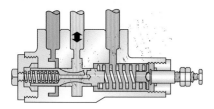

Brake pedal is held steady. Constant
pressure is maintained in brake line.

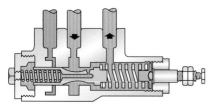

Brake pedal has been released and fluid is
returned to system return manifold. Brake
line is vented to the reservoir through brake
control valve.

Figure 6-38. *Sliding-spool-type power
brake control valve*

In large aircraft, the pilot has no feel for an impending skid of any of the tires, so an antiskid system is installed to sense the rate of deceleration of each wheel. This rate is compared with the maximum allowable deceleration rate, and if any wheel attempts to slow down too fast, as it does at the onset of a skid, the antiskid valve will direct fluid from the line to the affected brake assembly back into the system return manifold.

The pressure applied by the brake control valve is too high for proper brake application, so a debooster is installed in the line between the antiskid valve and the brake. This debooster lowers the pressure and increases the volume of fluid supplied to the wheel units.

In case of failure of the main hydraulic system, the pilot can actuate the emergency brake control valve that directs compressed nitrogen into an air/oil transfer tube. The resulting pressurized fluid shifts the shuttle valve on the brake assembly. This shuts off the main brake system and allows the brakes to be actuated by the emergency system.

Power Brake Control Valves

The diagrams in Figure 6-38 show the principle of the power brake control valve. Two types of these valves do the same thing, but they have a different physical appearance. One of the valves has its control spring mounted outside of the valve, and the other valve has the control spring inside, as shown in the figure.

In the top illustration, the pilot has applied the brake. The brake pedal acts on the plunger spring, which gives the pilot a feel of the amount of force he or she is applying to the brakes. This moves the spool to the left, shutting off the passage to the return manifold and connecting the pressure port to the brake line. Fluid under pressure goes to the brake and to the left end of the spool to move it back when the pressure called for by the pilot has been reached. This keeps the pressure supplied to the brake from increasing regardless of the length of time the brake pedal is depressed. If more pressure is needed at the brake, the pilot presses harder on the brake pedal. This further compresses the plunger spring and allows more fluid to flow to the brake.

When the brake pedal is held steady, the combined force of the spool-return spring and the fluid pressure on the spool moves the spool to the right just enough to shut off the passage to the pressure manifold, and fluid is trapped in the line to the brake actuating cylinders.

When the pilot releases the brakes, the force on the plunger spring is relaxed. The spool moves to the right, opening the passage between the brake line and the system return manifold. This allows fluid to flow from the brakes to the return line, releasing the brakes.

Antiskid System

Maximum braking is obtained when the wheel and tire rotate at about 80% of the speed of the aircraft. This rotational speed will produce the shortest stopping distance regardless of the runway surface conditions. Any increase or decrease in tire speed, including locking the brakes and sliding the tires on the runway, will increase the landing distance.

It is difficult to get effective braking on modern jet aircraft because of their small tires inflated to a high pressure and their high speed at touchdown. This problem is made increasingly difficult when the runway is covered with water. The surface friction is so low on a wet runway that the brakes tend to lock up, causing the tires to hydroplane on the surface of the water. When this happens, all braking action is lost for that wheel and directional control is difficult to maintain.

Airplanes that are so large that the pilot does not have a feel for each of the wheels must use an antiskid system to hold all of the tires in the slipping region without allowing a skid to develop. There are several methods of doing this, but the basics of the system described here illustrate the principle on which most antiskid systems operate.

When the pilot wants to stop the aircraft in the shortest distance, he or she depresses the brake pedals to produce maximum braking. Full braking pressure is sent to all of the brakes, but when any wheel begins to slow down fast enough to indicate that a tire is beginning to skid, the pressure in the brake of that wheel is dumped into the hydraulic system return manifold. The antiskid computer measures the amount of time needed for the wheel to spin back up, and then it shuts off the line to the return manifold. This allows a slightly lower pressure to build up in the brake, and if this lower pressure causes the tire to try to skid, the process is repeated, and a still lower pressure is held in the brake. As long as the brake pedals are held down, enough pressure is maintained in the brake cylinders to cause the tires to slip, but not skid. By continually sampling the deceleration rate of the wheel, just enough pressure is allowed into the brakes for maximum braking effectiveness.

If for any reason a wheel should lock up completely while another wheel is rotating, all of the pressure to that wheel is released. This feature of the anti-skid system is deactivated when the airplane speed is less than about 15 or 20 miles per hour. This allows normal braking for slow-speed turning and parking.

Antiskid System Components

There are two basic types of antiskid systems, those that use DC generators in the wheel-speed sensors and those that use AC generators. The typical antiskid system discussed here uses DC wheel-speed sensors.

antiskid system. An electrohydraulic system in an airplane's power brake system that senses the deceleration rate of every main landing gear wheel. If any wheel decelerates too rapidly, indicating an impending skid, pressure to that brake is released and the wheel stops decelerating. Pressure is then reapplied at a slightly lower value.

hydroplaning. A condition that exists when a high-speed airplane is landed on a water-covered runway. When the brakes are applied, the wheels lock up and the tires skid on the surface of the water in much the same way a water ski rides on the surface. Hydroplaning develops enough heat in a tire to ruin it.

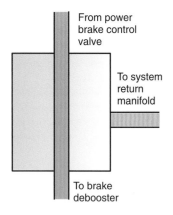

For normal operation, the valve serves only as passage between brake control valve and debooster.

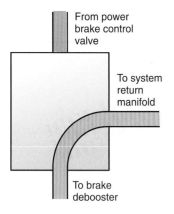

When wheel-speed sensor determines a skid is imminent, it directs antiskid control valve to shut off flow to debooster and vent debooster to system return manifold.

Figure 6-39. *Antiskid control valve*

Wheel-Speed Sensors

Wheel-speed sensors, or skid detectors, are small DC generators mounted in the axles of each of the main wheels. The armature of the detector generator is rotated by the wheel-hub dust cover so that it turns with the wheel and produces a voltage that is proportional to the speed of the wheel.

The voltage from the wheel-speed sensor is applied across a capacitor in an electronic control circuit in such a way that the faster the wheel turns, the greater the charge on the capacitor. As long as the wheel turns at a constant rate, or its speed is increasing or decreasing only slightly, the capacitor does not discharge appreciably. But if the wheel speed should decrease rapidly enough to exceed the limits programmed into the antiskid computer, there will be enough difference between the output voltage of the wheel-speed sensor and the voltage of the charge in the capacitor to signal an impending skid and actuate the antiskid control valve.

Antiskid Control Valves

The three-port electrohydraulic antiskid valve is installed in the pressure line between the brake control valve and the brake debooster. The third line connects the antiskid valve to the hydraulic system return manifold. *See* Figure 6-39.

For normal brake operation, the valve serves only as a passage and allows free flow of fluid to and from the debooster. When the wheel-speed sensor determines that one of the wheels is beginning to decelerate fast enough to cause a skid, the computer sends a signal to an electrical coil inside the antiskid valve that shuts off the pressure to the brake and opens the passage to the system return manifold.

Antiskid Control Box

The antiskid control box contains a computer and the electrical circuitry to interpret the signal from the wheel-speed sensors, compare them with a program tailored to the particular airplane, and send the appropriate signals to the antiskid control valves to hold the tires in a slip without allowing a skid to develop.

Figure 6-40 shows a block diagram of the antiskid system when the airplane is in the air before touchdown. The locked-wheel arming circuit is grounded through the airborne side of the landing-gear squat switch, and it causes the locked-wheel detector circuit to send a signal through the amplifier to the antiskid control valves to open the passages to the return manifold. This makes it impossible to land with the brakes applied.

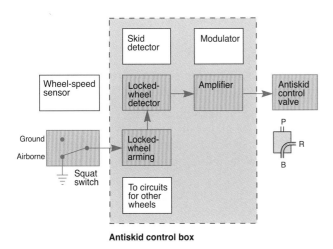

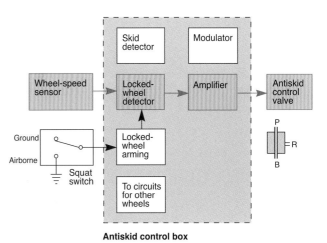

Figure 6-40. *Antiskid control box with the airplane in the air. The antiskid valve is held open so no pressure can be applied to the brake regardless of the position of the brake pedals.*

Figure 6-41. *Antiskid control box with the airplane on the ground. The wheels have built up a speed of 20 mph or more and the antiskid valve is open, allowing full pressure to be applied to the brakes.*

As soon as weight is on the landing gear, the squat switch changes position and opens the ground to the locked-wheel arming circuit. When the wheel speed builds up to about 20 miles per hour, the wheel-speed sensors produce enough voltage to cause the locked-wheel detector to send a signal to the antiskid valve allowing full pressure to go to the brake.

When the airplane is on the ground with all wheels turning at more than 20 mph, skid control is provided by the skid detectors and the modulator circuits. Any time a wheel decelerates at a rate higher than the programmed maximum, a signal is sent to the amplifier and then to the control valve to dump the brake pressure. At the same time, the skid detector sends a signal to the modulator which, by measuring the width of the skid detector signal, automatically establishes the amount of current that will continue to flow through the valve after the wheel has recovered from the skid. When the amplifier receives its signal from the modulator, it maintains this current, which is just enough to prevent the control valve from dumping all the pressure, but maintains a pressure slightly less than that which caused the skid.

squat switch. An electrical switch actuated by the landing gear scissors on the oleo strut. When no weight is on the landing gear, the oleo piston is extended and the switch is in one position, but when weight is on the gear, the oleo strut compresses and the switch changes its position.

Squat switches are used in antiskid brake systems, landing gear safety circuits, and cabin pressurization systems.

A timer circuit in the modulator then allows the pressure to increase slowly until another skid starts to occur and the cycle repeats itself. *See* Figure 6-42.

The antiskid system holds the tires in the slip area when the aircraft is operating on a wet or icy runway. If one tire begins to hydroplane or hits a patch of ice and slows down to less than 10 mph while its mated reference wheel is still rolling at more than 20 mph, the locked-wheel detector measures the width of the skid detector signal. If it is more than about $\frac{1}{10}$ second, it sends a FULL-DUMP signal to the control valve, which allows all of the fluid in the brakes to flow to the return manifold until the wheel spins back up to more than 10 mph.

When all of the wheels are turning at less than 20 mph, the locked-wheel arming circuit is inoperative. This gives the pilot full control of the brakes for low-speed taxiing and parking.

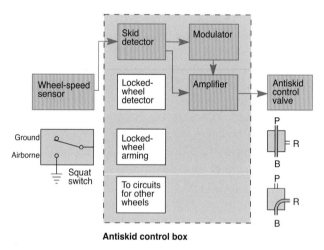

Antiskid control box

Figure 6-42. *Antiskid control box with the airplane on the ground. All wheels are turning at more than 20 mph. The skid detector is sensing the rate of change of wheel speed and sending the appropriate signal to the modulator. The signal from the modulator is amplified and sent to the antiskid control valve, which applies or releases the brakes to keep the tire in the slip area but prevents a skid from developing.*

System Tests

Antiskid braking systems include methods of checking system integrity before the brakes are needed. If the antiskid system does not function as it should, the pilot can disable it without affecting normal braking action.

Preflight Test

On a preflight inspection, the pilot can check the continuity of all of the wiring and the operation of the locked-wheel circuits, amplifiers, and control valves by depressing both brake pedals. Both brake indicator lights should illuminate. Since the wheel speed is zero and the locked-wheel arming circuit is not grounded through the squat switch, the locked-wheel detector cannot operate, and there is no signal to the control valve through the amplifier. The antiskid valve is fully open, directing all of the pressure from the brake valve to the brake.

With the brakes applied, pressing the antiskid test switch sends a signal through the speed sensors to the control boxes to simulate a wheel speed of more than 20 mph. This signal voltage is high enough to arm the locked-wheel detectors and high enough the keep them from sending a signal to the amplifier. Since there is no signal from the amplifier, the control valves are not energized and the brake indicator lights stay on. While the test switch is held down, the capacitor in the arming circuit is being charged.

When the test switch is released, the two brake indicator lights should go out, stay out for a few seconds, and then come back on. Releasing the switch drops the signal voltage to zero, which indicates a complete lockup of the wheels. The capacitor holds the voltage on the arming circuit, allowing the locked-wheel detectors to work. They detect the zero speed of the wheels and energize the amplifiers. Current is sent to the antiskid valves, causing them to dump all of the pressure into the return manifold and turn the brake indicator lights out.

The capacitor in the arming circuit soon discharges and prevents the locked-wheel detectors from working. This removes the signal from the amplifier and the control valve returns to its normal condition. The brakes are re-applied, and the brake indicator lights come back on.

Prelanding Check

With the airplane configured for landing and the landing gear down and locked, the pilot can determine that the antiskid system is operating properly by depressing the brake pedals. The brake indicator lights should remain off. The squat switch keeps the locked-wheel arming circuit energized, and the signal from the locked-wheel detectors causes the amplifier to send sufficient current into the control valves to hold the brakes fully released.

Depressing the brake test switch with the pedals depressed should cause the brake lights to turn on. This sends a signal through the wheel-speed sensors simulating a wheel speed of greater than 20 mph. If the system is operating properly, this voltage will override the signal from the squat switch and disable the locked-wheel arming circuit. This allows the locked-wheel detector to remove the signal from the amplifier so the control valve can restore normal action to the brakes. The brake indicator light should remain on as long as the test switch is held depressed.

When the test switch is released, the two brake lights should go out, indicating that the antiskid system is holding all of the pressure off of the brakes.

Disabling the System

If the antiskid system fails either the preflight or prelanding test, the system can be disabled without affecting normal braking in any way. Opening the antiskid switch removes all of the current from the control valve, allowing the valve to remain in the position for full flow of fluid between the brake valve and the brake.

Maintenance Checks

If an antiskid system has failed any of its tests, the source of the trouble is relatively simple to isolate. It is generally in one of three components: the wheel-speed sensor, the control box, or the control valve. Before blaming the antiskid system, however, be sure that the brakes are operating normally. There should be no warped disks or broken return springs, and there should be no air in the brake lines or cylinders.

The components of the antiskid system itself are quite complex and most of them must be repaired only by the manufacturer or an FAA-certificated repair station approved for the particular components.

Wheel-Speed Sensors

As in all systematic troubleshooting, first check the items that are easiest to reach or are most likely to fail. Remove the wheel hubcap and, with the brakes applied, flip the blade of the wheel-speed sensor to cause it to rotate in a clockwise direction. This blade will turn about 180° or less when it is flipped, but it is the rate, not the amount of movement, that is important. Watch the brake disk stack as the blade is flipped; the stack should relax and then retighten.

If the brakes do not release, remove the connector from the back of the sensor and check the resistance of the coil as the blade is rotated through a full revolution. The resistance should be that specified in the maintenance manual, and it should be smooth throughout the rotation of the blade. If the resistance is within the acceptable limits, place the multimeter on its lowest DC voltage scale and attach the leads to the pins, as indicated in the maintenance manual. Flip the blade in the clockwise direction and the voltmeter should indicate an upscale deflection. If a digital voltmeter is used, the voltage indication should be positive. If the wheel-speed sensor checks out electrically, check to be sure it is properly installed.

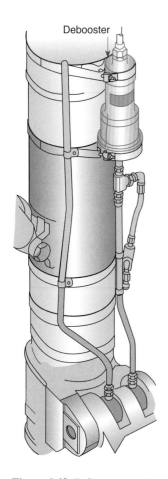

Figure 6-43. *Deboosters are installed between the power brake control valve and the brake cylinders to decrease the pressure and increase the volume of fluid going to the brakes.*

Control Box

The control boxes for many antiskid installations have two identical channels. If the antiskid system on the right side of the aircraft is malfunctioning but the system on the other side is functioning properly, check the control box by temporarily swapping the electrical leads going into the control box. If the malfunctioning system moves to the left side and the right side clears up, the control box is at fault, but if the trouble does not change, the fault lies elsewhere. It is extremely important to re-install the electrical connectors on their correct plug before the aircraft is returned to service.

Antiskid Control Valve

The control valve is an electrohydraulic device, and if systematic troubleshooting identifies it as defective, return it to an appropriate facility to be repaired.

Deboosters

Hydraulic system pressure is normally too high for effective brake action, so deboosters are installed between the antiskid valve and the wheel cylinders to reduce the pressure and increase the volume of fluid going to the brakes. Deboosters used in some of the larger aircraft have a lockout feature that allows them to double as hydraulic fuses. *See* Figure 6-43.

The principle of deboosters is illustrated in Figure 6-44, where 1,500 psi pressure is applied to a piston that has an area of one square inch. This pressure produces 1,500 pounds of force. The other end of this piston has an area of five square inches, and the 1,500 pounds of force is spread out over the entire five square inches, so the pressure it produces in the fluid is only 300 psi.

The other function of the debooster is to increase the volume of the fluid that is sent to the brakes. One cubic inch of fluid at the system pressure moves the small piston down one inch. The larger piston also moves down one inch, but because of its larger area, it moves five cubic inches of fluid out to the brakes.

The debooster shown in Figure 6-44 has a pin-operated ball valve that allows fluid in the large end of the cylinder to be replenished if there should be a leak in the line to the brakes. If the debooster piston moves down enough to allow the pin to force the ball off its seat, fluid under system pressure will enter the lower chamber and replenish the lost fluid. As soon as enough fluid enters the chamber, it raises the piston so that the ball will reseat.

Lockout deboosters act as hydraulic fuses. They have a spring-loaded valve that prevents fluid from flowing into the large end of the cylinder to replace any that has leaked out. The piston can travel all the way to the bottom of the cylinder where the pin pushes the ball off its seat, but the spring-loaded valve keeps the fluid from entering the lower chamber. When the maintenance technician fixes the cause of the leak, the reset handle can be lifted, allowing fluid to flow into the large end, refilling the brakes.

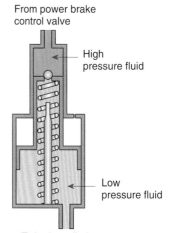

From power brake control valve

High pressure fluid

Low pressure fluid

To brake cylinders

High-pressure fluid from power brake control valve presses down on small end of piston. Large end of piston forces fluid out to brake wheel cylinder.

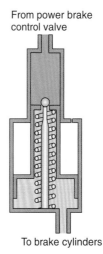

From power brake control valve

To brake cylinders

If leakage in brake line should cause loss of fluid, pin will force the ball off its seat, and large end of debooster cylinder will be replenished with fluid.

Figure 6-44. *Brake debooster valve*

Emergency Brake System

In case of a total failure of the hydraulic system, the pilot can operate a pneumatic valve on the instrument panel and direct compressed nitrogen into the brake system to apply the brakes.

Rather than allowing compressed nitrogen to enter the wheel cylinders, which would require that the entire system be bled to remove it, the emergency nitrogen is directed into the air/oil transfer tube where it pressurizes hydraulic fluid. If the pressure of this fluid from the emergency system is greater than the pressure from the brake debooster, the brake shuttle valves will move over and fluid from the emergency system will actuate the brakes. To release the brakes, the pilot rotates the emergency brake handle to the left and the nitrogen pressure is vented overboard. This in turn relieves the pressure in the brake cylinders.

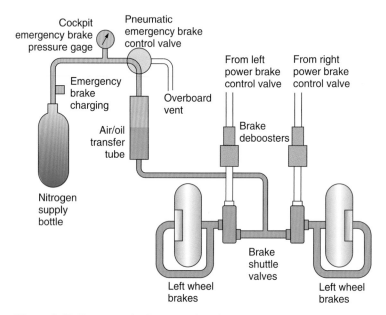

Figure 6-45. *Emergency brake system for a large jet transport airplane*

Dual Power Brake Actuating System

Many of the jet transport aircraft have dual power brakes that are operated by two independent hydraulic power systems. When the pilot or copilot depresses a brake pedal, the dual brake control valve directs fluid from each system into the brake actuating unit. Figure 6-31 on Page 450 shows the housing for one of the brakes installed on a McDonnell-Douglas DC-9. Seven of the brake-actuating cylinders are supplied with pressure from one hydraulic system through pressure port A, and the other seven cylinders are supplied with pressure from the other hydraulic system through pressure port B.

If either hydraulic system supplying pressure to the brakes should fail, the other system will supply enough pressure for adequate braking.

Auto Brake System

Some highly automated jet transport aircraft, such as the Boeing 757, have auto brake systems. A selector switch on the instrument panel allows the pilot to select a deceleration rate that will be controlled automatically after touchdown.

When the aircraft touches down with the auto brake system armed and the thrust levers at idle, the system will direct the correct amount of pressure to the brakes to achieve the desired rate of deceleration. The brake pressure will be decreased automatically to compensate for the deceleration caused by the thrust reversers and speed brakes.

The auto brake system will disengage if any of these things happen:

• The pilot moves the selector switch to the DISARM or OFF position.

• The pilot uses manual braking.

• The thrust levers are advanced.

• The speed brake lever is moved to the DOWN detent.

Brake Maintenance

The brakes of a modern aircraft take more abuse than almost any other component. The tremendous amount of kinetic energy caused by the weight and rolling speed of the aircraft must be transferred into the relatively small mass of the brake in order to stop the aircraft. Jet aircraft, for this reason, very often use thrust reversers to slow the aircraft after landing before the brakes are applied. An aborted takeoff is an emergency procedure that transfers far more heat into the brakes than they are designed to absorb, and the brakes, wheels, and tires are usually ruined.

aborted takeoff. A takeoff that is terminated prematurely when it is determined that some condition exists that makes takeoff or further flight dangerous.

If a brake shows any indication of overheating, or if it has been involved in an aborted takeoff, it should be removed from the aircraft, disassembled, and carefully inspected.

Carefully examine the housing for cracks or warping, and give it a hardness test at the points specified in the brake maintenance manual. Housings that have been overheated may have been softened and weakened to the extent that they are no longer airworthy. Seals that have been exposed to excessive heat must be replaced, as the heat destroys their ability to seal.

Disks in multiple-disk brakes often warp when they are overheated. Check all of the disks for warpage using the method specified in the brake maintenance manual.

Brakes that have sintered-metal friction material on the rotating disk often transfer some of this material to the stationary disk. Some transfer is allowed, but the disks must be carefully examined to ensure that the amount of allowable transfer has not been exceeded.

Glazed or warped disks cause the brake to apply and release many times a minute, which produces chattering or squealing. This is not only annoying, but the vibration it causes can damage the brake or the landing gear.

Warped disks can also cause the brakes to drag. They do not completely release when the pressure is relieved. This causes the brake to overheat and the disks to be further warped and damaged.

After thoroughly inspecting and reassembling the brake, you must pressure-test it according to the instructions in the maintenance manual. This test usually includes checking for proper application and release of the brakes and for any indication of leaks.

Installation of the Brake on the Aircraft

Brakes must be installed in exactly the way the manufacturer recommends in the aircraft maintenance manual. Use only the parts specified in the aircraft parts lists, and torque all of the bolts to the values specified in the maintenance manuals. Most bolt torque is specified for clean and dry threads, but some bolts on the brakes must be lubricated before they are torqued. Use only the lubricant specified by the manufacturer, and apply it only in the specified manner.

Bleeding the Brakes

Aircraft brakes are single-acting systems, and any air trapped in the fluid will give the brakes a spongy feel. They must be bled to remove all of the air from the fluid when they are first installed and any time the system is opened. There are two methods of removing air from brake systems: gravity bleeding and pressure bleeding.

Gravity Bleeding

Gravity bleeding, sometimes called top-down bleeding, is done by running the fluid from the master cylinder down through the brake cylinders. Power brakes can be bled only by this method.

Attach a clear plastic tube to the bleeder plug at the wheel cylinder, and immerse the end of the tube in a container of clean hydraulic fluid. Fill the reservoir, and slowly depress the brake pedal with the bleeder valve open. Watch the plastic tube as you continue to slowly pump the master cylinder. Continue to pump the brakes until fluid runs through the tube with no bubbles.

You may have to fill the reservoir a time or two in this process, as a large amount of fluid will have to be pumped through the system before all of the air is removed.

When the fluid runs clear of all traces of air, close the bleeder plug and remove the tube. Fill and cap the reservoir, making sure that the reservoir vent is open.

bleeding of brakes. The maintenance procedure of removing air entrapped in hydraulic fluid in the brakes. Fluid is bled from the brake system until fluid with no bubbles flows out.

spongy brakes. Hydraulic brakes whose pedal has a spongy feel because of air trapped in the fluid.

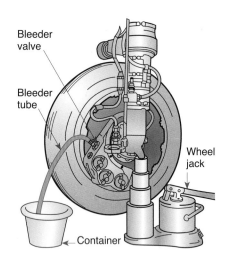

Figure 6-46. *Gravity bleeding of brakes*

Pressure Bleeding

Pressure bleeding is usually superior to gravity bleeding since it begins at a low point and drives the air out the top of the system, taking advantage of the natural tendency of air bubbles to rise in a liquid.

Connect a hose to the bleeder plug at the wheel cylinder, and attach a bleeder pot or hydraulic hand pump to the hose. Attach a clear plastic hose to a fitting in the top of the reservoir and immerse its free end in a container of clean hydraulic fluid. Open the bleeder plug and slowly force fluid through the brake, up through the reservoir, and out into the container of fluid. When the fluid flows out of the reservoir with no trace of air, close the bleeder plug and remove the hoses.

Some reservoirs may be overfilled in this process and fluid must be removed down to the "full" mark before replacing the reservoir cap. Do not reuse this removed fluid, but dispose of it in a manner approved by your local environmental laws. Be sure that the reservoir vent is open when the reservoir is capped.

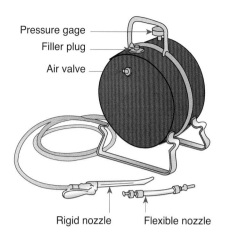

Figure 6-47. *Hydraulic brake pressure bleeder pot for pressure bleeding brakes*

STUDY QUESTIONS: AIRCRAFT BRAKES

Answers are on Page 490. Page numbers refer to chapter text.

23. A brake that uses friction to help apply the brakes is called a/an _____ brake. *Page 441*

24. An expander tube brake is a/an _____ (energizing or nonenergizing) brake. *Page 441*

25. Clearance between the drum and the blocks of an expander tube brake is maintained constant by an automatic adjuster which traps a certain amount of hydraulic fluid in the _____ . *Page 442*

26. Fading of a drum-type brake is caused by uneven _____ of the drum caused by heat. *Page 441*

27. A single-disk brake _____ (is or is not) an energizing brake. *Page 441*

28. An automatic adjuster in a single-disk brake determines the amount the piston moves when the brakes are _____ (applied or released). *Page 444*

29. The amount of lining wear is indicated on a single-disk brake with automatic adjusters by the amount the adjusting pin protrudes from the nut. The more the linings are worn, the _____ (more or less) the pin protrudes. *Page 444*

30. Brake lining wear is measured on a single-disk brake without automatic adjusters by measuring the distance between the disk and the _____ (piston or anvil) side of the brake housing. *Page 445*

Continued

31. A dual-disk brake is similar to a single-disk except for the additional braking area furnished by the additional disk and _____ area. *Page 447*

32. One of the main limitations of a thin-disk multiple-disk brake is the tendency of the disks to _____ . *Page 448*

33. The brake linings in a segmented-rotor brake are part of the _____ (rotor or stator). *Page 449*

34. In a segmented-rotor brake, the disks are squeezed between the _____ and the _____ . *Page 449*

35. Carbon-disk brakes are _____ (heavier or lighter) than a metal-disk brake that has the same stopping capability. *Page 450*

36. The fluid in the brake wheel cylinder is vented to the atmosphere through the _____ port in the master cylinder. *Page 452*

37. If the compensator port were plugged, expansion of the fluid in the brake lines caused by heat would cause the brakes to _____ . *Page 452*

38. The brake system that uses the aircraft hydraulic system pressure to assist the pilot in applying force to the piston in the brake master cylinder is called a/an _____ brake. *Page 454*

39. A power brake control valve is a form of pressure _____ . *Page 454*

40. For maximum braking effectiveness, the wheels of an airplane should be allowed to _____ but not allowed to _____ . *Page 457*

41. When an airplane wheel locks up on a wet runway and the tire skids across the surface of the water, the tire is said to be _____ . *Page 457*

42. The three major components in an antiskid brake system are:
    a. _____
    b. _____
    c. _____
    Page 458

43. When the antiskid system is operating normally, it _____ (is or is not) possible to land with the brakes applied. *Page 458*

44. Pressure in the brake cylinders is maintained at a value just below that which would cause the tires to skid by the _____ circuit in the antiskid control box. *Page 459*

45. The wheel-speed sensor in an antiskid system is a small _____ . *Page 458*

46. A brake debooster valve _____ (increases or decreases) the volume of fluid flowing to the brake. *Page 462*

47. A lockout debooster acts as a hydraulic _____ . *Page 463*

48. The emergency brake system of a jet transport airplane uses _____ to actuate the brakes. *Page 464*

49. Two causes of disk brakes chattering or squealing are the disks being _____ or _____ . *Page 466*

50. Brake cylinder seals that have been overheated should be _____ . *Page 465*

51. Warped brake disks will cause a brake to drag. This will cause the brakes to _____ . *Page 466*

52. A brake housing can be checked for hidden damage from overheating by giving it a _____ test. *Page 465*

53. Two methods of bleeding aircraft brakes are:
    a. _____
    b. _____
       Page 466

54. Power brakes are bled by the _____ method. *Page 466*

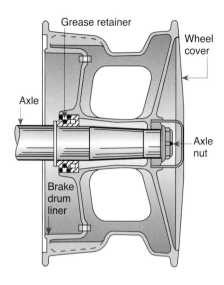

Figure 6-48. *Fixed-flange, drop-center wheel*

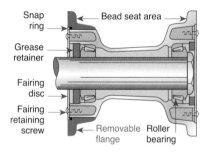

Figure 6-49. *Drop-center wheel with a removable outer flange*

Aircraft Wheels

Aircraft wheels have undergone as much evolutionary development as any aircraft part. Most aircraft up through the 1920s did not have any brakes, and the wheels were spoked, similar to those used on bicycles and motorcycles. The tires were relatively soft and could easily be pried over the rims. These wheels were streamlined with fabric or thin sheet metal to cover the spokes.

The next step in wheel development was the small diameter, fixed-flange, drop-center wheel which was intended to be used with a doughnut-type tire.

When stiffer tires were developed, wheels were designed that had one removable rim. The rim was removed and the tire and tube were assembled onto the wheel, and the rim was re-installed and held in place by a steel snap ring. Inflation of the tire locked the rim securely in place.

Tubeless tires prompted the development of the two-piece wheel, split in the center and sealed between the two halves with an O-ring. This is the most popular configuration of wheel in use today, and it is found on all types of aircraft from small trainers to large jet transport airplanes.

Wheel Nomenclature

Figure 6-50 is an exploded view of a typical two-piece aircraft wheel. These wheels are made of either aluminum or magnesium alloy, and depending upon their strength requirements, they may be either cast or forged.

Inboard Wheel Half

The inboard wheel half is fitted with steel-reinforced keys that fit into slots in the periphery of the brake disk to rotate the disk with the wheel. In the center of the wheel, there is a wheel-bearing boss into which is shrunk a polished steel bearing cup, or outer bearing race. A tapered roller bearing rides between this cup and a bearing race on the axle. A grease retainer covers the bearing and prevents dirt or water reaching the bearing surfaces.

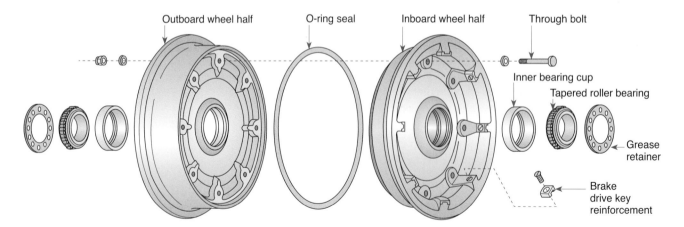

Figure 6-50. *Exploded view of a typical two-piece wheel for a light aircraft*

High-performance aircraft have one or more fusible plugs in the inboard wheel half. These plugs have a hole drilled through their center filled with a low-melting-point alloy. In the event of an aborted takeoff or other emergency braking, so much heat is produced in the brake that the air in the tire tries to expand, resulting in a pressure rise so high the wheel could explode. To prevent this, the center of the fusible plug melts and deflates the tire in a few seconds when the wheel reaches a dangerous temperature.

Some larger wheels also have an overinflation safety valve. When tires on these large wheels are inflated from a high-pressure air or nitrogen bottle, they can be overinflated to the extent that the tire could explode. If this happens, the overinflation safety valve will rupture and deflate the tire.

Outboard Wheel Half

The outboard wheel half also contains a shrunk-in outer race for a tapered roller bearing and a grease retainer similar to that used in the inner half of the wheel. A thin steel cap, held in place with a retaining ring, covers the end of the axle and the bearing. When the aircraft is equipped with an antiskid system, this cap has a built-in bracket that drives the blade of the wheel-speed sensor mounted in the landing gear axle.

If the wheel mounts a tubeless tire, there is an inflation valve in the outboard wheel half, and if a tube-type tire is used, there is a hole through which the tube valve stem protrudes.

Bead Seat Area

The bead seat area is the most critical part of an aircraft wheel. The metal in this area is under a high tensile load caused by the air pressure in the tire and intensified by hard landings. The bead seat area is rolled to prestress the surface with a compressive stress.

Wheel Maintenance

The abuse suffered by an aircraft wheel is directly related to the care given to the tire mounted on it. Tire care is discussed later in this chapter.

Wheel Removal

Aircraft wheels are lightweight and subjected to extremely heavy loads in hard landings. Some of the through bolts that hold the wheel halves together may have been weakened, and may break in the process of wheel disassembly. To preclude this possibility, always deflate the tire after the aircraft is on the jack and before loosening the axle nut. High-pressure tires should be deflated by screwing a deflator cap on the valve and allowing the air to escape through the hole in the cap. The high-pressure air in these tires can eject the valve core at a velocity high enough to cause personal injury. After all the air is out of the tire, remove the valve core.

fusible plugs. Plugs in the wheels of high-performance airplanes that use tubeless tires. The centers of the plugs are filled with a metal that melts at a relatively low temperature.

If a takeoff is aborted and the pilot uses the brakes excessively, the heat transferred into the wheel will melt the center of the fusible plugs and allow the air to escape from the tire before it builds up enough pressure to cause an explosion.

bead seat area. The flat surface on the inside of the rim of an aircraft wheel on which the bead of the tire seats.

deflator cap. A cap for a tire, strut, or accumulator air valve that, when screwed onto the valve, depresses the valve stem and allows the air to escape safely through a hole in the side of the cap.

Tire Removal

With the tire completely deflated, break the bead of the tire away from the wheel. Apply an even force as a straight push as near the rim as possible. Large wheels require a special tire-demounting tool, but you can break the smaller tires away from the wheel using an arbor press and a piece of wood to force the bead of the tire away from the wheel. Never use any kind of tire tool to pry the bead from the wheel, as the soft metal of which the wheel is made can easily be nicked or scratched. This will cause stress concentrations, or stress risers, that may ultimately cause the wheel to fail. When the bead is broken from both wheel halves, remove the nuts from the through bolts and remove the wheel halves and the O-ring seal from the tire.

Wheel Inspection

Clean the wheel with varsol or naphtha and scrub away all of the loosened deposits with a soft bristle brush. Dry the wheel with a flow of compressed air.

Inspect the entire wheel for indication of corrosion where moisture was trapped and held in contact with the metal. If you find any corrosion, you must dress it out by removing as little metal as is possible. After cleaning out all of the corrosion, treat the surface to prevent new corrosion from forming.

The rotor drive keys in the wheel are subjected to a great deal of stress, and absolutely no looseness is allowed between the drive keys and the slots in the rotor disks. Inspect the area around the slots with dye penetrant.

You can't inspect the bead seat area of the wheel with dye penetrant, because when the tire is removed, any cracks in this area will close up so tightly no penetrant can seep into them. When the tire is installed and inflated, the stresses will enlarge the cracks. Inspect these areas with eddy current equipment according to the instructions furnished by the wheel manufacturer.

Examine the fusible plugs carefully for any indication of softening of the core material that would indicate the wheel had been overheated. If there is any indication of deformation, replace all the plugs.

When aircraft wheels are manufactured, they are statically balanced. Balance weights are attached which must never be removed. The final balancing is done with the tire installed, and the weights used for final balancing are installed around the outside of the wheel rim or around the wheel bolt circle.

Bearing Maintenance

Remove the bearings from the wheel and soak them in a clean solvent such as varsol or naphtha to soften the dried grease. Remove all the residue with a soft bristle brush, and dry the bearing with a flow of low-pressure compressed air. Never spin the bearings with the air when drying them because the high-speed rotation of the dry metal-to-metal contact will overheat and damage the extremely smooth surfaces.

Carefully inspect the bearing races and rollers for any of the types of damage described in Figure 6-51. Any of these types of damage are cause for rejection of the bearing. Inspect the thin bearing cages that hold the rollers aligned on the races. Any damage or distortion to the cage is cause for replacing the bearing.

Galling	Damage caused by the rubbing of mating surfaces. When localized high spots rub against each other they become heated by friction enough to weld together. As they continue to move, the welded areas pull apart and destroy some of the surface.
Spalling	Damage in which chips are broken from the surface of a case-hardened material such as a bearing race. Spalling occurs when the bearing race is placed under a load great enough to distort the softer inner part of the metal and cause the hard, brittle surface to crack. Once a crack forms in the surface, chips break out.
Brinelling	Damage to the hardened surface of a bearing roller or race caused by excessive radial loads. When the bearing is overloaded, the rollers are forced into the race, and they leave small dips, or indentations, in the race on the surface of the roller.
Water stain	Black discolorations on bearing races and rollers where the surfaces were in contact in the presence of water. This discoloration is an indication of intergranular corrosion within the material.
Discoloration from overheating	Blue marks of the bearing rollers indicate that the bearing has been operated dry, or has been subjected to too high a rotational speed.
Rust	Rough red deposits on any of the rolling surfaces indicate that the bearing has been left unprotected from moisture in the air. Rust leaves pits that ruin the bearing surfaces.

Figure 6-51. *Types of damage that are cause for rejection of a wheel bearing*

Inspect the bearing cup that is shrunk into the wheel for any of the damages mentioned in Figure 6-51. If it is damaged, it must be replaced. Put the wheel half in an oven whose temperature can be carefully controlled. Heat it at the temperature specified in the wheel maintenance manual, generally no higher than 225°F for approximately 30 minutes. Remove the wheel from the oven and then tap the cup from its hole with a fiber drift.

To install a new cup, coat its outside surface with zinc chromate primer. Heat the wheel and chill the cup with dry ice, and then tap the cup into its hole with a plastic mallet or a fiber drift.

Pack the bearing with grease that meets the specification in the aircraft maintenance manual. Use a pressure packing tool if one is available. If you must pack them by hand, be sure to completely cover every roller and the inner cone. Wrap the greased bearing in clean waxed paper to protect it from dust and dirt until the wheel is ready to be reassembled and reinstalled.

Tire Installation

The installation of the tire on the wheel, final balancing, and installation of the wheel on the aircraft are discussed in the section, "Aircraft Tires and Tubes," beginning on Page 475.

Wheel Installation

Prepare the axle for receiving the wheel by removing any dirt or dried grease, inspecting it for any obvious damage, and checking the axle threads for their condition. Place the cleaned and greased bearings in the wheel and install the grease retainers. Slide the wheel on the axle and install the brake, following the instructions in the aircraft maintenance manual in detail.

One of the most critical items in the installation of a wheel is the torque on the axle nut. Some smaller aircraft only require that the axle nut be installed and tightened until a slight bearing drag is obvious when the wheel is rotated. Then back the nut off to the nearest castellation and install the cotter pin. The manufacturers of some of the larger aircraft specify two torque values, one to seat the bearing and the other for operational torque. First, while rotating the wheel, tighten the axle nut to the higher value to seat the bearing, then back the nut off and retighten it to the lower torque, then safety it.

STUDY QUESTIONS: AIRCRAFT WHEELS

Answers are on Page 490. **Page numbers refer to chapter text.**

55. Most of the wheels used on modern aircraft are of the _____ (single-piece or two-piece) type.
    Page 470

56. Wheels on modern high-performance airplanes are prevented from exploding from heat generated in the brakes by _____ installed in the inboard wheel half. *Page 471*

57. The most highly stressed part of an aircraft wheel is the _____ . *Page 471*

58. The bead seat area of a wheel is strengthened against tensile loads by prestressing the surface with a _____ stress. *Page 471*

59. A wheel should be cleaned with _____ or _____ and dried with compressed air. *Page 472*

60. The dye penetrant method of inspection _____ (is or is not) an effective method of inspection for the bead seat area of a wheel. *Page 472*

61. The bead seat area of a wheel should be inspected by the _____ method. *Page 472*

Aircraft Tires and Tubes

Aircraft tires are different from any other type of tire because of their unique requirements. The total mileage an aircraft tire experiences over its lifetime is extremely low compared to tires on an automobile or truck. But the aircraft tire withstands far more beating from the landing impact than an automotive tire will ever experience. Therefore aircraft tires are allowed to deflect more than twice as much as automotive tires.

The abrasive surface of the runway causes extreme tread-wear on touch-down, because the tire accelerates from zero to more than one hundred miles per hour in only a few feet.

Evolution of Aircraft Tires

The first flying machines did not use any wheels or tires. The *Wright Flyer* had skids and was launched from a rail. The first wheeled landing gear used bicycle or motorcycle wheels and tires. It was not until around 1909 that the first tires were made specifically for the unusual requirements of an airplane.

As flight speeds increased and parasite drag became an important consideration, streamlined tires were made to reduce the drag caused by the exposed fixed landing gear. Most aircraft up to this time had no brakes; so tread pattern was of no concern.

Almost all aircraft were operated from grass surfaces, and the Airwheel, which was a low-pressure, high-flotation tire that looked much like a fat doughnut, was popular for many smaller airplanes. These tires had no tread pattern, but many airplanes that used them had brakes in the small wheels on which they were mounted. These brakes were effective only for maneuvering during low-speed taxiing and were not used for slowing the airplane on landing.

Tires with a patterned tread became important when airplanes got effective brakes that could be used to slow the landing roll. At first this tread was simply a diamond pattern that provided good braking on wet grass, but the rib tread proved be superior for operation on hard-surfaced runways. Today, almost all aircraft tires have a rib tread that consists of straight grooves molded into the tread material.

An interesting development in the tires for large aircraft was the change in their size. When developmental study was done on the first truly large aircraft in the late 1930s, the machines such as the Douglas XB-19 and the Boeing XB-15 had only a few wheels with very large, relatively low-pressure tires. As aircraft developed, so did their tires. Modern large aircraft use many wheels with much smaller high-pressure tires.

Tire Construction

Figure 6-52 is a cross-sectional drawing of a typical aircraft tire showing its major components. This section of the text discusses each of these components.

The Bead

bead (tire component). The high-strength carbon-steel wire bundles that give an aircraft tire its strength and stiffness where it mounts on the wheel.

The bead gives the tire the needed strength and stiffness to ensure a firm mounting on the wheel. The bead is made of bundles of high-strength carbon-steel wire with two or three bead bundles on each side of the tire. Rubber apex strips streamline the round bead bundles to allow the fabric to fit smoothly around them without any voids. The bead bundles are enclosed in layers of rubberized fabric, called flippers, to insulate the carcass plies from the heat absorbed in the bead wires.

The Carcass

carcass (tire component). The layers of rubberized fabric that make up the body of an aircraft tire.

The carcass, or cord body, is the body of the tire that is made up of layers of rubberized fabric cut in strips with the threads running at an angle of about 45° to the length of the strip. These strips extend completely across the tire, around the bead, and partially up the side. Each ply is put on in such a way that the threads cross at an angle of about 90° to that of the adjacent plies. This type of construction is known as a bias ply tire. Radial tires, as used on most automobiles, have the threads in each layer of rubberized fabric running straight across the tire from one bead to the other.

The cords of the ply fabric were originally all cotton, then nylon became the most popular material. And now aramid fibers, which are stronger than nylon, polyester, or fiberglass, and even stronger, pound for pound, than steel, are used in some premium-quality tires.

The ply rating of a tire is not the actual number of plies of fabric used in the tire construction, but it indicates the number of plies of cotton fabric needed to produce the same strength as the actual plies.

Chafing strips, or chafers, are strips of rubberized fabric that wrap around the edges of the carcass plies and enclose the entire bead area. The chafing strips provide a smooth chafe-resisting surface between the tire and the bead seat area of the wheel.

The undertread is a layer of specially compounded rubber between the plies and the tread rubber that provides good adhesion between the tread and the carcass. Directly on top of the undertread are one or more plies of strong fabric that strengthen the tread and oppose centrifugal forces that try to pull the tread from the carcass during high-speed rotation. This tread reinforcement is not part of the ply rating, but it is used as a guide for retreaders to show when all of the tread rubber has been removed.

The inner liner of the carcass is a thin coating of rubber over the inside plies. For tubeless tires, this inner liner is made of a special rubber compound that is less permeable than the other rubber used in the tire. It seals the tire and minimizes the amount of air that can seep out, so the tire can act as an air container. For tube-type tires, the inner liner is specially smooth to prevent the tube from chafing against the inside of the tire.

ply rating. The rating of an aircraft tire that indicates its relative strength. The ply rating does not indicate the actual number of plies of fabric in the tire; rather it indicates the number of plies of cotton fabric needed to produce the same strength as the actual plies.

The Tread

The tread is the thick rubber around the periphery of the tire that serves as its wearing surface. The tread is made of specially compounded rubber and has a series of grooves molded into its surface to give the optimum traction with the runway surface.

A number of tread designs have been used on aircraft tires, but since the vast majority of aircraft operate from paved runways, the most popular tread is the rib tread, in which a series of straight grooves encircle the periphery of the tire as shown in Figure 6-52.

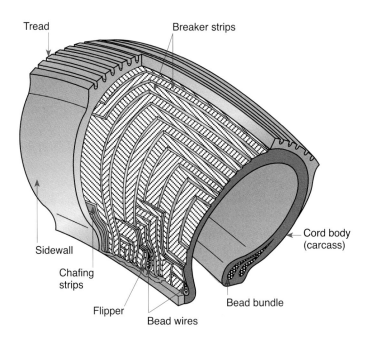

Figure 6-52. *The construction of an aircraft tire*

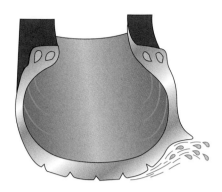

Figure 6-53. *Chines, or deflectors, are molded into the outer sidewall of nose wheel tires mounted on jet airplanes with engines mounted on the aft fuselage. These chines deflect water from the runway away from the engine inlets.*

The Sidewall

The side of a tire, from the tread to the bead, is covered with a special rubber compound that protects the ply fabric from cuts, bruises, and exposure to moisture and ozone.

The inner liner of tubeless tires is intended to hold air, but some will leak through. To prevent this air from expanding and causing the plies to separate when the tire gets hot, there are small vent holes in the sidewall near the bead. These vent holes are marked with paint and must be kept open at all times. The sidewalls of tube-type tires are vented to allow air trapped between the tube and the inner liner of the tire to escape.

Jet airplanes that have the engines mounted in pods on the rear of the fuselage ingest water that has been thrown up by the nose wheel tire when operating on wet runways. To prevent this problem, nose wheel tires for these airplanes have a chine, or deflector, molded into their outer sidewall that deflects the water outward so that it misses the rear engines.

The Inner Liner

The main difference between a tube-type tire and a tubeless tire is the inner liner. For tubeless tires, the inner liner is made of an impervious rubber compound, and no effort is made to keep it smooth. If a tube is used in a tubeless tire, it will be damaged by the rough surface. A tube-type tire has a smooth inner liner that will not chafe the tube in normal operation.

Tire Inspection

Modern aircraft tires so seldom give problems that they do not get the attention that they deserve. Tire inspection is simple, but it is extremely important.

Inflation

Heat is the greatest enemy of aircraft tires. Aircraft tires are designed to flex more than automobile tires, and the heat generated as the sidewalls flex can cause damage that is not likely to be detected until it causes the tire to fail.

The weight of the aircraft is supported by the air in the tires, and when the air pressure is correct, the tire flexes only within its design limits. But if the tire is operated with too low an inflation pressure, the sidewalls will flex enough to generate excessive heat.

If the tire is operated in an overinflated condition, the tread will not contact the runway as it should and the tire will have less resistance to skidding.

The proper inflation pressure for a tire is specified in the airframe service manual, and is the pressure of the tire when it is supporting the weight of the aircraft. Use this pressure rather than the inflation pressure specified in the tire manufacturer's manual. The same tire used on different airplanes will have different specified inflation pressures.

When a tire is loaded with the weight of the aircraft, it will deflect and its volume will decrease enough to increase the inflation pressure by approximately 4%. If the aircraft service manual specifies an inflation pressure of 190 psi, the tire should be inflated to 4% less than this or approximately 182 psi if it is inflated while the aircraft is on jacks or before the wheel and tire assembly is installed on the aircraft.

Inflation pressure should always be measured when the tire is cold, at least two to three hours after the last flight. Use a dial-type pressure gage that is periodically checked for accuracy.

The pressure of the air inside a tire varies with its temperature at the rate of about 1% for every 5°F. For example, a tire has an inflation pressure of 160 psi after it has stabilized at the hangar temperature of 60°F. If the airplane is moved outdoors where the temperature drops to 0°F, the pressure in the tire will drop by 12% to about 141 psi, and the tire is definitely underinflated.

Nylon tires stretch when they are first installed and inflated, and the pressure will drop by about 5 to 10% of the initial inflation pressure in the first 24 hours. Check newly mounted tires and adjust their pressure 24 hours after they are mounted.

Tread Condition

Notice the touchdown area of the runway of any modern airport and you will see that it is practically black. This is rubber left by the tires as they speed up from zero to the touchdown speed. The tread is worn away long before the carcass plies are dead of old age, and it is common practice to retread aircraft tires.

The tires should be operated with proper inflation pressure and removed for retreading while there is at least $\frac{1}{32}$ inch of tread at its shallowest point. If the tire is allowed to wear beyond this, there will not be enough tread for safe operation on a wet runway. A normally worn tread is shown in Figure 6-54A on Page 481. When it is removed at this time it can safely be retreaded.

When a tire has been worn until the tread is completely gone over the carcass plies, scrap the tire. It is no longer safe to operate, and it is worn too much to be retreaded.

When the tire has been operated in an overinflated condition, the center of the tread will wear more than the tread on the shoulders of the tire. You can retread a tread worn to the extent of the one shown in Figure 6-54C.

Underinflation will cause the tread to wear away from the shoulders before it wears in the center. This is shown in Figure 6-54D. If the carcass of this tire has not been damaged, you can retread it.

Uneven tread wear is normally caused by the landing gear being out of alignment. At the first indication of this type of wear, check the alignment and correct it according to the instructions in the aircraft maintenance manual.

Any time a cut extends more than halfway across a rib, or if any of the carcass plies are exposed, take the tire out of service.

Hydroplaning causes a wheel to lock up and there will normally be an oval-shaped burned area on the tire. Remove any tire showing this type of damage from service.

Operation on grooved runways will often produce a series of chevron-shaped cuts across the tread. Any time these cuts extend across more than half of the rib, remove the tire.

Sidewall Condition

The sidewall rubber protects the carcass plies from damage, either from mechanical abrasion or from the action of chemicals or the sun. Weather checking or small snags or cuts in the sidewall rubber that do not expose the cords do not require removal of the tire, but if the ply cords are exposed, the cords have probably been weakened, and tire must be replaced.

The liner of a tubeless tire contains the air, but some of it seeps through the body plies, and so the sidewalls of these tires are vented to allow this air to escape. As much as 5% of the inflation pressure of the tire is allowed to diffuse through these vents in a 24-hour period. Sometimes these vents, which are located near the wheel rim, become clogged and do not adequately relieve this air. When they are obstructed, the pressure can build up between the plies, causing ply separation which will ruin the tire.

Tire Maintenance

The most important preventive maintenance for aircraft tires is keeping them properly inflated and free of grease and oil. If the aircraft is to remain out of service for an extended period of time, take the weight off the tires if possible, and if not, move the aircraft enough to rotate the tires periodically to minimize nylon flat-spotting that develops in all nylon tires.

Inspection

When the tire is off the wheel, you can carefully evaluate it to determine if it can be retreaded, or if it must be scrapped.

Replace any tire that has been involved in an aborted takeoff or excessive braking, or has been exposed to enough heat to melt the center of a fusible plug in the wheel. Even if the damage may not be obvious, the heat has probably caused enough damage to make the tire unsafe for further flight.

Replace any tire that has been used in a dual installation where its mating tire has failed, even if there is no obvious damage. The extra load placed on the tire that did not fail can cause enough stresses to weaken it and make it susceptible to future failure.

Spread the beads apart to examine the inside of the tire. Use an even force to spread them to avoid kinking the bead bundles, as a kinked bead is cause for rejecting the tire. Examine the inside of the tire for any indication of

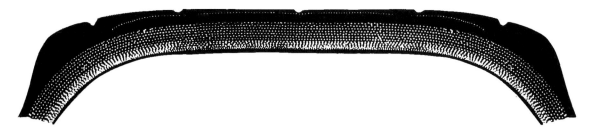

A Normally worn tread. Tire should be removed and retreaded.

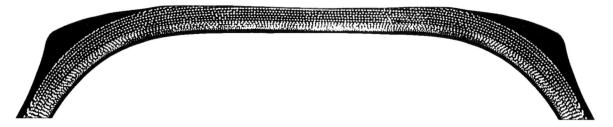

B Excessively worn tread. Worn down to the plies and too far gone for safe operation or retreading.

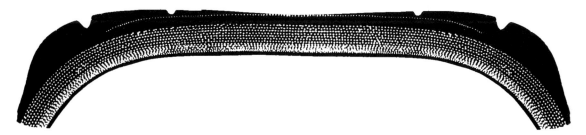

C Tire operated while overinflated. Center of tread worn more than on shoulders.

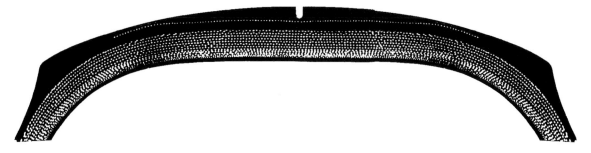

D Tire operated while underinflated. Shoulders of tread are worn more than in center.

Figure 6-54. *Tire tread wear patterns*

breakdown of the inner liner. Bulges or breaks in the inner liner may or may not be cause for rejection of the tire and should be evaluated by an approved facility which does aircraft tire retreading.

Inspect any bulges in the tread area that were marked when the tire was inflated. If the bulge indicates a separation of the plies, scrap the tire, but if it is a tread separation, you may be able to safely retread the tire.

Any cords that are exposed through cracks or other damage to the sidewall rubber are cause for rejecting the tire. These cords have probably been damaged, and the tire is weakened to the point that it cannot be safely retreaded.

Damage to the bead area is serious, and if the beads themselves have been damaged, scrap the tire. If the damage is restricted to the chafing strips, you can repair it when the tire is retreaded.

Retreading

retread. The replacement of the tread rubber on an aircraft tire.

Repairing aircraft tires is a special operation that requires a high degree of skill, experience, and equipment and should only be undertaken by an FAA-certificated repair station approved for this special work.

Advisory Circular 43.13-1B, *Acceptable Methods, Techniques, and Practices—Aircraft Inspection and Repair* lists a number of items that definitely render a tire unfit for retreading, and much time and expense can be saved by carefully inspecting the tire before sending it to a repair station for retreading. These damages render a tire irreparable:

- Breaks caused by flexing. Flexing damage is often the visible evidence of other damage that may not be visible.

- Any injury to the bead of a tubeless tire that would prevent the tire from sealing to the wheel

- Evidence of separation of the plies or around the bead wires

- Kinked or broken beads

- Weather cracks or radial cracks in the sidewall that extend into the cord body

- Evidence of blisters or heat damage

- Cracked, deteriorated, or damaged inner liner of tubeless tires

If there is no obvious damage that would prevent a tire from being retreaded, take it to a repair station for the work to be done.

When a tire is received, it is given a thorough inspection of its tread, sidewalls, and beads. The ply cords are checked for evidence of separation or fabric fatigue, and for any cords that have been damaged. If the tire passes this inspection, the old tread rubber is contour-buffed away to produce a smooth shoulder-to-shoulder surface. New tread rubber and reinforcement are applied to the buffed carcass, and the entire assembly is placed in a mold and is cured with heat. After the tire has cured and is removed from the mold, balance patches are bonded to the inside of the tire to give it the proper static balance. After this, the tire is given a final inspection and is approved for returned service.

A retreaded tire is identified by the letter "R" followed by a number showing the number of times it has been retreaded. The month and year the retread was applied and the name and location of the agency retreading the tire must also be marked on the tire.

The FAA does not specify the number of times a tire can be retreaded; this is determined by the condition of the carcass and by the policy of the user of the tire.

Storage

Aircraft tires and tubes are susceptible to damage from heat, sunlight, and ozone. They should be stored in an area that is not in the direct sunlight nor in the vicinity of fluorescent lights or such electric machinery as motors, generators, and battery chargers. All these devices convert oxygen into ozone, which is extremely harmful to rubber. The temperature in the storage area should be maintained between 32°F and 80°F (0°C and 27°C).

The storage area should be free from chemical fumes, and petroleum products such as oil, grease, and hydraulic fluid must not be allowed to come in contact with stored rubber products.

The tires should be stored vertically when possible in tire racks, with the tires supported on a flat surface which is at least three or four inches wide. If it is necessary to store them horizontally, do not stack them more than three to five tires high, depending on their size. When tubeless tires are stacked horizontally, the tires on the bottom of the stack may be distorted so much that a special bead-seating tool is needed to force the beads to seat on the wheel.

Mounting

The wheels installed on most modern airplanes are of the two-piece, split type which makes tire mounting and demounting far easier than it is with a single-piece drop-center wheel. Wheels are highly stressed components and, like all critical maintenance, mounting tires requires that all of the aircraft manufacturer's instructions be followed in detail, especially those regarding lubrication, bolt torque, and balancing.

ozone. An unstable form of oxygen produced when an electric spark passes through the air. Ozone is harmful to rubber products.

Tubeless Tires

Before mounting the tire on the wheel, carefully inspect the wheel for any indication of nicks, scratches, or other damage in the bead seat area and in the groove in which the O-ring seal between the halves is to fit. Examine the entire wheel for any indication of corrosion and be sure that all of the scratches and chips in the paint are touched up. Be sure that the wheel balance weights are properly and securely installed and check the condition of the fusible plugs. Carefully examine the O-ring seal for condition. There should be no nicks or breaks that could allow air to leak past. Clean the bead seat area of the wheel and the O-ring seating area with a cloth dampened with isopropyl alcohol, and place the inboard wheel half on a clean, flat surface where the wheel can be assembled.

Check the tire to ensure that it is approved for the particular aircraft and that it is marked with the word TUBELESS on the sidewall. Check the inside of the tire for any foreign matter, and after checking the bead area, wipe it clean with a rag damp with isopropyl alcohol.

Lubricate the O-ring with the same kind of grease that is used on the wheel bearings. If the old O-ring is in good condition and is re-used, place it in as nearly the same position it was in when it was removed as is possible.

Carefully place the tire over the inboard wheel half with the red dot on the tire, which represents the light point of the tire, adjacent to the inflation valve, or adjacent to whatever mark is used to identify the heavy point of the wheel. Now the outboard wheel half can be slipped into the tire so that its bolt holes align with those in the inboard half.

Check with the service manual regarding the use of lubricant on the bolt threads. Some wheel manufacturers recommend that the threads, both sides of the washers, and the bearing side of the nuts be lightly lubricated with an antiseize compound. Install all the bolts, washers, and nuts and tighten all of the nuts in crisscross fashion to one half of the recommended torque. Now, go back and torque all of the nuts to their final value, again tightening them in a crisscross fashion across the wheel. It is important to use an accurately calibrated torque wrench. Impact wrenches are not recommended for use on aircraft wheels, because their torque is applied in a series of blows which applies more stress to the bolt than it is designed to take.

All large tires should be put into some type of safety cage for their initial inflation because of the danger of personal injury if the through bolts should fail. Regardless of the size tire, position the wheel in such a way that if the bolts should fail, none of the flying parts will hit any one. Use a clip-on air chuck and inflate the tire gradually, being sure that the bead seats firmly against the bead seat area of the wheel.

All nylon tires stretch, and the inflation pressure will decrease by between 5% and 10% within the first 12 to 24 hours the tire sits with no load applied. After the tire has stretched, adjust the air pressure, and the wheel is ready to install on the aircraft.

Tube-Type Tires

The preparation of the tire and the wheel for a tube-type tire are essentially the same as that for a tubeless tire. Wipe the inside of the tire to remove all traces of dirt or other foreign matter, and dust the inside with an approved tire talcum. Dust the deflated tube with talcum and insert it inside the tire with the valve sticking out on the side of the tire that has the serial number. Align the yellow mark on the tube, that identifies its heavy point, with the red dot on the tire that identifies its light point. If there is no yellow mark on the tube, the valve is considered to be the heavy point.

Inflate the tube just enough to round it out, but not enough to stretch the rubber, and install the tire and tube on the outboard wheel half with the valve centered in the hole in the wheel. Put the inboard wheel half in place, being careful that the tube is not pinched between the halves. Install the through bolts and torque them as was described for the tubeless tire installation.

Inflate the tire to its recommended pressure to seat the beads, and then deflate it completely. Finally, reinflate the tire to the recommended pressure.

This inflation, deflation, and reinflation sequence allows the tube to relax itself inside the tire and straighten out all of the wrinkles.

The inflation pressure of a tube-type tire will drop within the first 12- to 24-hour period after inflation because of the stretching of the tire and because any air that is trapped between the tube and the tire will escape and increase the volume of the tube slightly.

After installing a tube-type tire on the wheel, paint a slippage mark 1 inch wide and 2 inches long across the tire sidewall and wheel rim. This mark should be permanent and of a contrasting color such as white, red, or orange. If this mark is broken, it indicates that the tire has slipped on the wheel, and there is good reason to believe that the tube has been damaged.

slippage mark. A paint mark that extends across the edge of an aircraft wheel onto a tube-type tire. When this mark is broken, it indicates that the tire has slipped on the wheel, and there is good reason to believe that the tube has been damaged.

Balancing

Aircraft wheels are balanced when they are manufactured, and tires are marked with a red dot to identify their light point. The tire is assembled on the wheel with its light point opposite the valve or other mark identifying the heavy point of the wheel. This approximately balances the wheel and tire, but a balancing stand is needed to get the degree of balance that will prevent the wheel from vibrating.

Place the wheel on a balancing stand and identify its light point. Then mark two spots 45° from this light point and place balance weights on these points that will bring the wheel into balance.

Three types of weights are used on aircraft wheels; one type is installed on brackets held under the head of the wheel through bolts, another type mounts on steel straps and is held onto the wheel rim with cotter pins, and the other is in the form of a lead strip attached to the inside of the wheel rim with its adhesive backing. Be sure that only the type of weight that is approved for the wheel is used.

Aircraft Tubes

Aircraft tubes are made of a special compound of rubber, and when they are properly installed and maintained, they are virtually maintenance-free. There are only two reasons for the tube leaking air; one is a hole, and the other is a leaking valve.

The brakes of a modern airplane absorb a tremendous amount of kinetic energy converted into heat. This heat can damage aircraft tubes by causing the inner circumference of the tube to take a set, or develop square corners. Any tube that shows any indication of this type of deformation should be rejected.

Store tubes in their original boxes whenever possible, but if the box is not available, they should be dusted with tire talcum and wrapped in heavy paper. They may also be stored inflated by dusting the inside of the proper size tire and putting them in the tire and inflating them just enough to round them out. Store the tube and tire in a cool dry area away from any electrical equipment or chemical fumes.

A Summary of Aircraft Tires

Aircraft tires are designed to absorb a tremendous amount of energy on landing, but they are not designed to tolerate the heat that is generated by taxiing long distances. Aircraft tires flex much more than automobile tires and thus generate much more heat. This heat is increased if the tire is allowed to operate with inflation pressure lower than is recommended.

Improper piloting technique can shorten the life of a tire. If the pilot makes taxiing turns by locking one brake and pivoting the airplane about one wheel, the tread can be twisted so severely that it may separate from the carcass.

Hard landings can burst a tire or wrinkle the sidewall enough that the tire will have to be scrapped. After any exceptionally hard landing, the tires should be removed and carefully examined for broken cords, liners, or cuts in the tread. The wheels should also be inspected for indications of damage.

Proper inflation is one of the best ways of extending the life of a tire. Be sure to use an accurate pressure gage and check the pressure regularly. Compensate for temperature changes. Remember that the pressure inside a tire changes by approximately 1% for every 5°F temperature change.

If a tire is inflated when it is off the aircraft, allow for the change in pressure when the weight of the aircraft is on the wheels. The pressure will increase approximately 4% when the weight is placed on the wheels.

When tires are installed in a dual installation, they should be of the same size, manufacture, and tread pattern. If there is a difference of more than 5 psi between the pressure of the two tires it should be noted in the aircraft maintenance record, and this pressure difference should be checked daily to determine if it is changing. If the pressure varies on successive pressure checks, the cause should be determined.

Any time a retreaded tire is installed on an airplane having a retractable landing gear, a retraction check should be performed to be sure that the tire does not bind in the wheel well.

STUDY QUESTIONS: AIRCRAFT TIRES AND TUBES

Answers are on Page 490. Page numbers refer to chapter text.

62. An aircraft tire is designed to flex, or deflect, _____ (more or less) than an automobile or truck tire. *Page 475*

63. The body of an aircraft tire is called the _____ . *Page 476*

64. A four-ply rating tire _____ (does or does not) necessarily have four plies of fabric. *Page 477*

65. The bundles of high-strength steel wires that are molded into a tire are called the _____ . *Page 476*

66. The threads in the plies of a tire cross the threads in adjacent plies at an angle of approximately _____ degrees. *Page 476*

67. The inner liner of a tubeless tire is _____ (smoother or rougher) than that used in a tube-type tire. *Page 478*

68. The tread design used on most modern aircraft tires is the _____ tread. *Page 477*

69. Nose wheel tires used on jet airplanes with engines mounted on the aft fuselage have a _____ or _____ molded into their outer sidewall. *Page 478*

70. Small holes in the sidewall of a tubeless tire are called _____ holes. *Page 478*

71. The correct tire inflation pressure to use is that which is recommended in the _____ (aircraft or tire) manufacturer's service manual. *Page 478*

72. The tire inflation pressure specified by the aircraft manufacturer is the pressure in the tire when the tire _____ (is or is not) supporting the weight of the aircraft. *Page 478*

73. The inflation pressure of a tire should not be measured until the tire has been able to cool down for _____ to _____ hours after flight. *Page 479*

Continued

74. The most accurate type of pressure gage to use for measuring tire inflation pressure is a _____ -type gage. *Page 479*

75. The air pressure inside a tire changes with the temperature. The pressure will increase approximately 1% for each _____ °F rise in temperature. *Page 479*

76. Inflation pressure will increase by approximately _____ -% when the weight of the aircraft is on the tire. *Page 479*

77. The inflation pressure of newly mounted nylon tires will decrease within the first day or so in service. This decrease is caused by the tire _____ . *Page 479*

78. Tires should be removed for retreading when the tread groove wears to a depth of _____ inch at the shallowest point. *Page 479*

79. A tire with the tread worn more in the middle than on the shoulders has been operated _____ (underinflated or overinflated). *Page 479*

80. A tire with the tread worn more on the shoulders than in the middle has been operated _____ (underinflated or overinflated). *Page 479*

81. Some air is allowed to seep through the inner lining of a tubeless tire and escape through vents in the sidewall rubber. As much as _____ % of the inflation pressure is allowed to seep out in a 24-hour period. *Page 480*

82. A burned area on a tire tread that indicates the tire has been hydroplaning _____ (is or is not) cause for removing the tire. *Page 480*

83. A tire should be removed from service if a cut extends across more than _____ of the width of a tread rib. *Page 480*

84. A shop tool that may be used to break a tire bead away from the wheel is a/an _____ . *Page 480*

85. A tire that has been involved in an aborted takeoff _____ (is or is not) safe for continued use. *Page 480*

86. A tire in a dual installation whose mate has failed should be _____ . *Page 480*

87. A kinked bead in a tire _____ (is or is not) a cause for rejecting the tire. *Page 482*

88. Exposed ply cords in the sidewall of an aircraft tire _____ (is or is not) cause for rejection of the tire. *Page 482*

89. The FAA _____ (does or does not) specify the number of times an aircraft tire can be retreaded. *Page 483*

90. Aircraft tires should be stored _____ (horizontally or vertically) whenever possible. *Page 483*

91. The red dot on an aircraft tire identifies the _____ (light or heavy) point of the tire. *Page 485*

92. The yellow mark on an aircraft tube identifies the _____ (light or heavy) point of the tube. *Page 485*

93. The valve of an aircraft tube should stick out on the side of the tire that _____ (does or does not) have the serial number. *Page 485*

94. The only lubricant approved for use between a tube and a tire is _____ . *Page 485*

95. When a retreaded tire is installed on an airplane with a retractable landing gear, a _____ test should be performed on the airplane. *Page 487*

Answers to Chapter 6 Study Questions

1. does not
2. oil
3. metering pin
4. air
5. spring
6. flapper
7. a. aircraft maintenance manual
   b. placard attached to shock strut
8. nitrogen
9. extension
10. in
11. positive
12. landing gear strut, axle
13. torque link arms
14. shimmy dampers
15. brakes
16. centering cam
17. a. mechanical
    b. electric motors
    c. hydraulic actuators
    d. pneumatic actuators
18. power pack
19. sequence
20. up line, down line
21. air, nitrogen
22. shuttle
23. energizing
24. nonenergizing
25. expander tube
26. expansion
27. is not
28. released
29. less
30. piston
31. lining
32. warp
33. stator
34. pressure plate, backing plate
35. lighter
36. compensating
37. drag
38. boosted
39. regulator
40. slip, skid
41. hydroplaning
42. a. wheel-speed sensors
    b. control boxes
    c. antiskid control valves
43. is not
44. modulator
45. DC generator
46. increases
47. fuse
48. nitrogen
49. warped, glazed
50. replaced
51. overheat
52. hardness
53. a. gravity
    b. pressure
54. gravity
55. two-piece
56. fusible plugs
57. bead seat area
58. compressive
59. varsol, naphtha
60. is not
61. eddy current
62. more
63. carcass
64. does not
65. beads
66. 90
67. rougher
68. rib
69. deflector, chine
70. vent
71. aircraft
72. is
73. 2, 3
74. dial
75. 5
76. 4
77. stretching
78. $1/32$
79. overinflated
80. underinflated
81. 5
82. is
83. $1/2$
84. arbor press
85. is not
86. replaced
87. is
88. is
89. does not
90. vertically
91. light
92. heavy
93. does
94. tire talcum
95. retraction

GLOSSARY

aborted takeoff. A takeoff that is terminated prematurely when it is determined that some condition exists that makes takeoff or further flight dangerous.

absolute pressure regulator. A valve used in a pneumatic system at the pump inlet to regulate the compressor inlet air pressure to prevent excessive speed variation and/or overspeeding of the compressor.

accumulator. A hydraulic component that consists of two compartments separated by a movable component such as a piston, diaphragm, or bladder. One compartment is filled with compressed air or nitrogen, and the other is filled with hydraulic fluid and is connected into the system pressure manifold.

An accumulator allows an incompressible fluid to be stored under pressure by the force produced by a compressible fluid. Its primary purposes are to act as a shock absorber in the system, and to provide a source of additional hydraulic power when heavy demands are placed on the system.

accumulator air preload. Compressed air or nitrogen in one side of an accumulator. The air preload is usually about one third of the system hydraulic pressure. When fluid is pumped into the oil side of the accumulator, the air is further compressed, and the air pressure and the fluid pressure become the same.

If an air preload pressure is too low, there will be almost no time between the regulator reaching its kick-in and kick-out pressures, and the system will cycle far more frequently than it should.

The amount of air preload is found by reducing the hydraulic pressure to zero and observing the reading on the accumulator air gage. If there is no air gage, slowly bleed the hydraulic pressure off the system while watching the hydraulic pressure gage. The pressure will drop slowly, until a point is reached at which it drops suddenly. This point is the air preload pressure.

advancing blade. The blade on a helicopter rotor whose tip is moving in the same direction the helicopter is moving.

adverse yaw. A condition of flight at the beginning of a turn in which the nose of an airplane momentarily yaws in the opposite direction from the direction in which the turn is to be made.

aeroelastic tailoring. The design of an aerodynamic surface whose strength and stiffness are matched to the aerodynamic loads that will be imposed upon it.

aging. A change in the characteristics of a material with time. Certain aluminum alloys do not have their full strength when they are first removed from the quench bath after they have been heat-treated, but they gain this strength after a few days by the natural process of aging.

airfoil. Any surface designed to obtain a useful reaction, or lift, from air passing over it.

Alclad. A registered trade name for clad aluminum alloy.

Alodine. The registered trade name for a popular conversion coating chemical used to produce a hard, airtight, oxide film on aluminum alloy for corrosion protection.

amphibian. An airplane with landing gear that allows it to operate from both water and land surfaces.

angle of attack (α). The acute angle formed between the chord line of an airfoil and the direction of the air that strikes the airfoil.

angle of incidence. The acute angle formed between the chord line of an airfoil and the longitudinal axis of the aircraft on which it is mounted.

annual rings. The rings that appear in the end of a log cut from a tree. The number of annual rings per inch gives an indication of the strength of the wood. The more rings there are and the closer they are together, the stronger the wood.

The pattern of alternating light and dark rings is caused by the seasonal variations in the growth rate of the tree. A tree grows quickly in the spring and produces the light-colored, less dense rings. The slower growth during the summer, or latter part of the growing season, produces the dark-colored, denser rings.

anodizing. The electrolytic process in which a hard, airtight, oxide film is deposited on aluminum alloy for corrosion protection.

antidrag wire. A structural wire inside a Pratt truss airplane wing between the spars. Antidrag wires run from the rear spar inboard, to the front spar at the next bay outboard. Antidrag wires oppose the forces that try to pull the wing forward.

anti-icer system. A system that prevents the formation of ice on an aircraft structure.

antiservo tab. A tab installed on the trailing edge of a stabilator to make it less sensitive. The tab automatically moves in the same direction as the stabilator to produce an aerodynamic force that tries to bring the surface back to a streamline position. This tab is also called an anti-balance tab.

antiskid brake system. An electrohydraulic system in an airplane's power brake system that senses the deceleration rate of every main landing gear wheel. If any wheel decelerates too rapidly, indicating an impending skid, pressure to that brake is released and the wheel stops decelerating. Pressure is then reapplied at a slightly lower value.

antitear strip. Strips of aircraft fabric laid under the reinforcing tape before the fabric is stitched to an aircraft wing.

arbor press. A press with either a mechanically or hydraulically operated ram used in a maintenance shop for a variety of pressing functions.

area. The number of square units in a surface.

aspect ratio. The ratio of the length, or span, of an airplane wing to its width, or chord. For a nonrectangular wing, the aspect ratio is found by dividing the square of the span of the wing by its area. Aspect Ratio = span^2 ÷ area

asymmetrical airfoil. An airfoil section that is not the same on both sides of the chord line.

asymmetrical lift. A condition of uneven lift produced by the rotor when a helicopter is in forward flight. Asymmetrical lift is caused by the difference between the airspeed of the advancing blade and that of the retreating blade.

autoclave. A pressure vessel inside of which air can be heated to a high temperature and pressure raised to a high value.
  Autoclaves are used in the composite manufacturing industry to apply heat and pressure for curing resins.

autogiro. A heavier-than-air rotor-wing aircraft sustained in the air by rotors turned by aerodynamic forces rather than by engine power. When the name Autogiro is spelled with a capital A, it refers to a specific series of machines built by Juan de la Cierva or his successors.

automatic adjuster. A subsystem in an aircraft disk brake that compensates for disk or lining wear. Each time the brakes are applied, the automatic adjuster is reset for zero clearance, and when the brakes are released, the clearance between the disks or the disk and lining is returned to a preset value.
  A malfunctioning automatic adjuster in a multiple-disk brake can cause sluggish and jerky operation.

autorotation. Descent of a helicopter without the use of engine power. An aerodynamic force causes the rotors to rotate.

aviation snips. Compound-action hand shears used for cutting sheet metal. Aviation snips come in sets of three. One pair cuts to the left, one pair cuts to the right, and the third pair of snips cuts straight.

backhand welding. Welding in which the torch is pointed away from the direction the weld is progressing.

backplate (brake component). A floating plate on which the wheel cylinder and the brake shoes attach on an energizing-type brake.

backup ring. A flat leather or Teflon ring installed in the groove in which an O-ring or T-seal is placed. The backup ring is on the side of the seal away from the pressure, and it prevents the pressure extruding the seal between the piston and the cylinder wall.

balance cable. A cable in the aileron system of an airplane that connects to one side of each aileron. When the control wheel is rotated, a cable from the cockpit pulls one aileron down and relaxes the cable going to the other aileron. The balance cable pulls the other aileron up.

balance panel. A flat panel hinged to the leading edge of some ailerons that produces a force which assists the pilot in holding the ailerons deflected. The balance panel divides a chamber ahead of the aileron in such a way that when the aileron is deflected downward, for example, air flowing over its top surface produces a low pressure that acts on the balance panel and causes it to apply an upward force to the aileron leading edge.

balance tab. An adjustable tab mounted on the trailing edge of a control surface to produce a force that aids the pilot in moving the surface. The tab is automatically actuated in such a way it moves in the direction opposite to the direction the control surface on which it is mounted moves.

balanced actuator. A linear hydraulic or pneumatic actuator that has the same area on each side of the piston.

banana oil. Nitrocellulose dissolved in amyl acetate, so named because it smells like bananas.

bank (*verb*). The act of rotating an aircraft about its longitudinal axis.

bead (tire component). The high-strength carbon-steel wire bundles that give an aircraft tire its strength and stiffness where it mounts on the wheel.

bead seat area. The flat surface on the inside of the rim of an aircraft wheel on which the bead of the tire seats.

bearing strength (sheet metal characteristic). The amount of pull needed to cause a piece of sheet metal to tear at the points at which it is held together with rivets. The bearing strength of a material is affected by both its thickness and the diameter of the rivet.

beehive spring. A hardened-steel, coil-spring retainer used to hold a rivet set in a pneumatic rivet gun.

   This spring gets its name from its shape. It screws onto the end of the rivet gun and allows the set to move back and forth, but prevents it being driven from the gun.

bend allowance. The amount of material actually used to make a bend in a piece of sheet metal. Bend allowance depends upon the thickness of the metal and the radius of the bend, and is normally found in a bend allowance chart.

bend radius. The radius of the inside of a bend.

bend tangent line. A line made in a sheet metal layout that indicates the point at which the bend starts.

Bernoulli's principle. The basic principle that explains the relation between kinetic energy and potential energy in fluids that are in motion.

   When the total energy in a column of moving fluid remains constant, any increase in the kinetic energy of the fluid (its velocity) results in a corresponding decrease in its potential energy (its pressure).

bias-cut surface tape. A fabric tape in which the threads run at an angle of 45° to the length of the tape. Bias-cut tape may be stretched around a compound curve such as a wing tip bow without wrinkling.

blade track. The condition of a helicopter rotor in which each blade follows in exactly the same path as the blade ahead of it.

bleeder. A material such as glass cloth or mat that is placed over a composite lay-up to absorb the excess resin forced out of the ply fibers when pressure is applied.

bleeding dope. Dope whose pigments are soluble in the solvents or thinners used in the finishing system. The color will bleed up through the finish coats.

bleeding of brakes. The maintenance procedure of removing air entrapped in hydraulic fluid in the brakes. Fluid is bled from the brake system until fluid with no bubbles flows out.

blimp. A cigar-shaped, nonrigid lighter-than-air flying machine.

blush. A defect in a lacquer or dope finish caused by moisture condensing on the surface before the finish dries. If the humidity of the air is high, the evaporation of the solvents cools the air enough to cause the moisture to condense. The water condensed from the air mixes with the lacquer or dope and forms a dull, porous, chalky-looking finish called blush. A blushed finish is neither attractive nor protective.

boundary layer. The layer of air that flows next to an aerodynamic surface. Because of the design of the surface and local surface roughness, the boundary layer often has a random flow pattern, sometimes even flowing in a direction opposite to the direction of flight. A turbulent boundary layer causes a great deal of aerodynamic drag.

brazing. A method of thermally joining metal parts by wetting the surface with a molten nonferrous alloy. When the molten material cools and solidifies, it holds the pieces together.

   Brazing materials melt at a temperature higher than 800°F, but lower than the melting temperature of the metal on which they are used.

bucking bar. A heavy steel bar with smooth, hardened surfaces, or faces. The bucking bar is held against the end of the rivet shank when it is driven with a pneumatic rivet gun, and the shop head is formed against the bucking bar.

buffeting. Turbulent movement of the air over an aerodynamic surface.

bulb angle. An L-shaped metal extrusion having an enlarged, rounded edge that resembles a bulb on one of its legs.

bulkhead. A structural partition that divides the fuselage of an aircraft into compartments, or bays.

bungee shock cord. A cushioning material used with the non-shock absorbing landing gears installed on older aircraft. Bungee cord is made up of many small rubber bands encased in a loose-woven cotton braid.

burnish (*verb*). To smooth the surface of metal that has been damaged by a deep scratch or gouge. The metal piled up at the edge of the damage is pushed back into the damage with a smooth, hard steel burnishing tool.

burr. A sharp rough edge of a piece of metal left when the metal was sheared, punched, or drilled.

buttock line. A line used to locate a position to the right or left of the center line of an aircraft structure.

Butyl. The trade name for a synthetic rubber product made by the polymerization of isobutylene.

Butyl withstands such potent chemicals as phosphate ester-base (Skydrol) hydraulic fluids.

calender (fabric treatment). To pass fabric through a series of heated rollers to give it a smooth shiny surface.

camber (wheel alignment). The amount the wheels of an aircraft are tilted, or inclined, from the vertical. If the top of the wheel tilts outward, the camber is positive. If the top of the wheel tilts inward, the camber is negative.

canard. A horizontal control surface mounted ahead of the wing to provide longitudinal stability and control.

cantilever wing. A wing that is supported by its internal structure and requires no external supports. The wing spars are built in such a way that they carry all the bending and torsional loads.

cap strip. The main top and bottom members of a wing rib. The cap strips give the rib its aerodynamic shape.

carburizing flame. An oxyacetylene flame produced by an excess of acetylene. This flame is identified by a feather around the inner cone. A carburizing flame is also called a reducing flame.

carcass (tire component). The layers of rubberized fabric that make up the body of an aircraft tire.

case pressure. A low pressure that is maintained inside the case of a hydraulic pump. If a seal becomes damaged, hydraulic fluid will be forced out of the pump rather than allowing air to be drawn into the pump.

cavitation. A condition that exists in a hydraulic pump when there is not enough pressure in the reservoir to force fluid to the inlet of the pump. The pump picks up air instead of fluid.

center of gravity. The location on an aircraft about which the force of gravity is concentrated.

center of lift. The location on the chord line of an airfoil at which all the lift forces produced by the airfoil are considered to be concentrated.

center of pressure. The point on the chord line of an airfoil where all of the aerodynamic forces are considered to be concentrated.

chatter. A type of rapid vibration of a hydraulic pump caused by the pump taking in some air along with the hydraulic fluid.

check (wood defect). Longitudinal cracks that extend, in general, across a log's annual rings.

check valve. A hydraulic or pneumatic system component that allows full flow of fluid in one direction but blocks all flow in the opposite direction.

chevron seal. A form of one-way seal used in some fluid-power actuators. A chevron seal is made of a resilient material whose cross section is in the shape of the letter V. The pressure being sealed must be applied to the open side of the V.

circle. A closed plane figure with every point an equal distance from the center. A circle has the greatest area for its circumference of any enclosed shape.

clad aluminum. A sheet of aluminum alloy that has a coating of pure aluminum rolled on one or both of its surfaces for corrosion protection.

Cleco fastener. A patented spring-type fastener used to hold metal sheets in position until they can be permanently riveted together.

close-quarter iron. A small hand-held iron with an accurately calibrated thermostat. This iron is used for heat-shrinking polyester fabrics in areas that would be difficult to work with a large iron.

closed angle. An angle formed in sheet metal that has been bent through more than 90°.

closed assembly time. The time elapsing between the assembly of glued joints and the application of pressure.

closed-center hydraulic system. A hydraulic system in which the selector valves are installed in parallel with each other. When no unit is actuated, fluid circulates from the pump back to the reservoir without flowing through any of the selector valves.

closed-center selector valve. A type of flow-control valve used to direct pressurized fluid into one side of an actuator, and at the same time, direct the return fluid from the other side of the actuator to the fluid reservoir.

Closed-center selector valves are connected in parallel between the pressure manifold and the return manifold.

coaxial. Rotating about the same axis. Coaxial rotors of a helicopter are mounted on concentric shafts in such a way that they turn in opposite directions to cancel torque.

coefficient of drag. A dimensionless number used in the formula for determining induced drag as it relates to the angle of attack.

coefficient of lift. A dimensionless number relating to the angle of attack used in the formula for aerodynamic lift.

coin dimpling. A process of preparing a hole in sheet metal for flush riveting. A coining die is pressed into the rivet hole to form a sharp-edged depression into which the rivet head fits.

collodion. Cellulose nitrate used as a film base for certain aircraft dopes.

compensator port (brake system component). A small hole between a hydraulic brake master cylinder and the reservoir. When the brakes are released, this port is uncovered and the fluid in the master cylinder is vented to the reservoir.

When the brake is applied, the master-cylinder piston covers the compensator port and allows pressure in the line to the brake to build up and apply the brakes. When the brake is released, the piston uncovers the compensator port. If any fluid has been lost from the brake, the reservoir will refill the master cylinder.

A restricted compensator port will cause the brakes to drag or cause them to be slow to release.

composite. Something made up of different materials combined in such a way that the characteristics of the resulting material are different from those of any of the components.

compound curve. A curve formed in more than one plane. The surface of a sphere is a compound curve.

compressibility effect. The sudden increase in the total drag of an airfoil in transonic flight caused by formation of shock waves on the surface.

compression failure. A type of structural failure in wood caused by the application of too great a compressive load. A compression failure shows up as a faint line running at right angles to the grain of the wood.

compression strut. A heavy structural member, often in the form of a steel tube, used to hold the spars of a Pratt truss airplane wing apart. A compression strut opposes the compressive loads between the spars arising from the tensile loads produced by the drag and antidrag wires.

compression wood. A defect in wood that causes it to have a high specific gravity and the appearance of an excessive growth of summerwood. In most species, there is little difference between the color of the springwood and summerwood.

Any material containing compression wood is unsuited for aircraft structural use and must be rejected.

concave surface. A surface that is curved inward. The outer edges are higher than the center.

coning angle. The angle formed between the plane of rotation of a helicopter rotor blade when it is producing lift and a line perpendicular to the rotor shaft.

The degree of the coning angle is determined by the relationship between the centrifugal force acting on the blades and the aerodynamic lift produced by the blades.

constant (mathematical). A value used in a mathematical computation that is the same every time it is used.

For example, the relationship between the length of the circumference of a circle and the length of its diameter is a constant, 3.1416. This constant is called by the Greek name of pi (π).

constant-displacement pump. A fluid pump that moves a specific volume of fluid each time it rotates; the faster the pump turns, the more fluid it moves.

Some form of pressure regulator or relief valve must be used with a constant-displacement pump when it is driven by an aircraft engine.

controllability. The characteristic of an aircraft that allows it to change its flight attitude in response to the pilot's movement of the cockpit controls.

control stick. The type of control device used in some airplanes. A vertical stick in the cockpit controls the ailerons by side-to-side movement and the elevators by fore-and-aft movement.

control yoke. The movable column on which an airplane control wheel is mounted. The yoke may be moved in or out to actuate the elevators, and the control wheel may be rotated to actuate the ailerons.

converging duct. A duct, or passage, whose cross-sectional area decreases in the direction of fluid flow.

convex surface. A surface that is curved outward. The outer edges are lower than the center.

Coriolis effect. The change in rotor blade velocity to compensate for a change in the distance between the center of mass of the rotor blade and the axis rotation of the blade as the blades flap in flight.

cornice brake. A large shop tool used to make straight bends across a sheet of metal. Cornice brakes are often called leaf brakes.

corrugated metal. Sheets of metal that have been made more rigid by forming a series of parallel ridges or waves in its surface.

cotter pin. A split metal pin used to safety a castellated or slotted nut on a bolt. The pin is passed through the hole in the shank of the bolt and the slots in the nut, and the ends of the pin are spread to prevent it backing out of the hole.

countersinking. Preparation of a rivet hole for a flush rivet by beveling the edges of the holes with a cutter of the correct angle.

Coverite surface thermometer. A small surface-type bimetallic thermometer that calibrates the temperature of an iron used to heat-shrink polyester fabrics.

crazing. A form of stress-caused damage that occurs in a transparent thermoplastic material. Crazing appears as a series of tiny, hair-like cracks just below the surface of the plastic.

critical Mach number. The flight Mach number at which there is the first indication of supersonic airflow over any part of the aircraft structure.

cross coat. A double coat of aircraft finishing material in which the second coat is sprayed at right angles to the first coat, before the solvents have evaporated from the first coat.

cross-flow valve. An automatic flow-control valve installed between the gear-up and gear-down lines of the landing gear of some large airplanes.

When the landing gear is released from its uplocks, its weight causes it to fall faster than the hydraulic system can supply fluid to the gear-down side of the actuation cylinder. The cross-flow valve opens and directs fluid from the gear-up side into the gear-down side. This allows the gear to move down with a smooth motion.

Cuno filter. The registered trade name for a particular style of edge-type fluid filter.

Cuno filters are made up of a stack of thin metal disks that are separated by thin scraper blades. Contaminants collect on the edge of the disks, and they are periodically scraped out and allowed to collect in the bottom of the filter case for future removal.

cusp. A pointed end.

Dacron. The registered trade name for a cloth woven from polyester fibers.

damped oscillation. Oscillation whose amplitude decreases with time.

debooster valve. A valve in a power brake system between the power brake control valve and the wheel cylinder. This valve lowers the pressure of the fluid going to the brake and increases its volume.

A debooster valve increases the smoothness of brake application and aids in rapid release of the brakes.

decay. Decomposition. The breakdown of the structure of wood fibers. Wood that shows any indication of decay must be rejected for use in aircraft structure.

deciduous. A type of tree that sheds its foliage at the end of the growing season. Hardwoods come from deciduous trees.

deflator cap. A cap for a tire, strut, or accumulator air valve that, when screwed onto the valve, depresses the valve stem and allows the air to escape safely through a hole in the side of the cap.

deicer system. A system that removes ice after it has formed on an aircraft.

delamination. The separation of the layers of a laminated material.

delta airplane. An airplane with a triangular-shaped wing. This wing has an extreme amount of sweepback on its leading edge, and a trailing edge that is almost perpendicular to the longitudinal axis of the airplane.

denier. A measure of the fineness of the yarns in a fabric.

density altitude. The altitude in standard air at which the density is the same as that of the existing air.

density ratio (σ). The ratio of the density of the air at a given altitude to the density of the air at sea level under standard conditions.

desiccant (air conditioning component). A drying agent used in an air conditioning system to remove water from the refrigerant. A desiccant is made of silica-gel or some similar material.

differential aileron travel. Aileron movement in which the upward-moving aileron deflects a greater distance than the one moving downward. The up aileron produces parasite drag to counteract the induced drag caused by the down aileron.

Differential aileron travel is used to counteract adverse yaw.

dihedral. The positive angle formed between the lateral axis of an airplane and a line that passes through the center of the wing or horizontal stabilizer. Dihedral increases the lateral stability of an airplane.

dirigible. A large, cigar-shaped, rigid, lighter-than-air flying machine. Dirigibles are made of a rigid truss structure covered with fabric. Gas bags inside the structure contain the lifting gas, which is either helium or hydrogen.

disc area (helicopter specification). The total area swept by the blades of a helicopter main rotor.

divergent oscillation. Oscillation whose amplitude increases with time.

diverging duct. A duct, or passage, whose cross-sectional area increases in the direction of fluid flow.

dope proofing. The treatment of a structure to be covered with fabric to keep the solvents in the dope from softening the protective coating on the structure.

dope roping. A condition of aircraft dope brushed onto a surface in such a way that it forms a stringy, uneven surface rather than flowing out smoothly.

double-acting actuator (hydraulic system component). A linear actuator moved in both directions by fluid power.

double-acting hand pump (hydraulic system component). A hand-operated fluid pump that moves fluid during both strokes of the pump handle.

doubler. A piece of sheet metal used to strengthen and stiffen a repair in a sheet metal structure.

drag (helicopter rotor blade movement). Fore-and-aft movement of the tip of a helicopter rotor blade in its plane of rotation.

dragging brakes. Brakes that do not fully release when the brake pedal is released. The brakes are partially applied all the time, which causes excessive lining wear and heat.

drag wire. A structural wire inside a Pratt truss airplane wing between the spars. Drag wires run from the front spar inboard, to the rear spar at the next bay outboard. Drag wires oppose the forces that try to drag the wing backward.

drill motor. An electric or pneumatic motor that drives a chuck that holds a twist drill. The best drill motors produce high torque, and their speed can be controlled.

dry rot. Decomposition of wood fibers caused by fungi. Dry rot destroys all strength in the wood.

ductility. The property of a material that allows it to be drawn into a thin section without breaking.

Duralumin. The name for the original alloy of aluminum, magnesium, manganese, and copper. Duralumin is the same as the modern 2017 aluminum alloy.

Dutch roll. An undesirable, low-amplitude coupled oscillation about both the yaw and roll axes that affects many swept wing airplanes. Dutch roll is minimized by the use of a yaw damper.

Dutchman shears. A common name for compound-action sheet metal shears.

dynamic pressure (q). The pressure a moving fluid would have if it were stopped. Dynamic pressure is measured in pounds per square foot.

edge distance. The distance between the center of a rivet hole and the edge of the sheet of metal.

elastic limit. The maximum amount of tensile load, in pounds per square inch, a material is able to withstand without being permanently deformed.

elevator downspring. A spring in the elevator control system that produces a mechanical force that tries to lower the elevator. In normal flight this spring force is overcome by the aerodynamic force from the elevator trim tab. But in slow flight with an aft CG position, the trim tab loses its effectiveness and the downspring lowers the nose to prevent a stall.

elevons. Movable control surfaces on the trailing edge of a delta wing or a flying wing airplane. These surfaces operate together to serve as elevators, and differentially to act as ailerons.

empennage. The tail section of an airplane.

enamel. A type of finishing material that flows out to form a smooth surface. Enamel is usually made of a pigment suspended in some form of resin. When the resin cures, it leaves a smooth, glossy protective surface.

energizing brake. A brake that uses the momentum of the aircraft to increase its effectiveness by wedging the shoe against the brake drum.

Energizing brakes are also called servo brakes. A single-servo brake is energizing only when moving in the forward direction, and a duo-servo brake is energizing when the aircraft is moving either forward or backward.

epoxy. A flexible, thermosetting resin that is made by polymerization of an epoxide.

Epoxy has wide application as a matrix for composite materials and as an adhesive that bonds many different types of materials. It is noted for its durability and its chemical resistance.

expander-tube brake. A brake that uses hydraulic fluid inside a synthetic rubber tube around the brake hub to force rectangular blocks of brake-lining material against the rotating brake drum. Friction between the brake drum and the lining material slows the aircraft.

expansion wave. The change in pressure and velocity of a supersonic flow of air as it passes over a surface which drops away from the flow. As the surface drops away, the air tries to follow it. In changing its direction, the air speeds up to a higher supersonic velocity and its static pressure decreases. There is no change in the total energy as the air passes through an expansion wave, and so there is no sound as there is when air passes through a shock wave.

extruded angle. A structural angle formed by passing metal heated to its plastic state through specially shaped dies.

FAA FSDO. Federal Aviation Administration Flight Standards District Office. An FAA field office serving an assigned geographical area staffed with Flight Standards personnel who serve the aviation industry and the general public on matters relating to certification and operation of air carrier and general aviation aircraft.

fading of brakes. The decrease in the amount of braking action that occurs with some types of brakes that are applied for a long period of time.

True fading occurs with overheated drum-type brakes. As the drum is heated, it expands in a bell-mouthed fashion. This decreases the amount of drum in contact with the brake shoes and decreases the braking action.

A condition similar to brake fading occurs when there is an internal leak in the brake master cylinder. The brakes are applied, but as the pedal is held down, fluid leaks past the piston, and the brakes slowly release.

fairlead. A plastic or wooden guide used to prevent a steel control cable rubbing against an aircraft structure.

feather (helicopter rotor blade movement). Rotation of a helicopter rotor blade about its pitch-change axis.

ferrous metal. Any metal that contains iron and has magnetic characteristics.

fiber stop nut. A form of self-locking nut that has a fiber insert crimped into a recess above the threads. The hole in the insert is slightly smaller than the minor diameter of the threads. When the nut is screwed down over the bolt threads, the opposition caused by the fiber insert produces a force that prevents vibration loosening the nut.

file. A hand-held cutting tool used to remove a small amount of metal with each stroke.

fill threads. Threads in a piece of fabric that run across the width of the fabric, interweaving with the warp threads. Fill threads are often called woof, or weft, threads.

fillet. A fairing used to give shape but not strength to an object. A fillet produces a smooth junction where two surfaces meet.

finishing tape. Another name for surface tape. *See* surface tape.

fishmouth splice. A type of splice used in a welded tubular structure in which the end of the tube whose inside diameter is the same as the outside diameter of the tube being spliced is cut in the shape of a V, or a fishmouth, and is slipped over the smaller tube and welded. A fishmouth splice has more weld area than a butt splice and allows the stresses from one tube to transfer into the other tube gradually.

fitting. An attachment device that is used to connect components to an aircraft structure.

flap (aircraft control). A secondary control on an airplane wing that changes its camber to increase both its lift and its drag.

flap (helicopter rotor blade movement). Up-and-down movement of the tip of a helicopter rotor blade.

flap overload valve. A valve in the flap system of an airplane that prevents the flaps being lowered at an airspeed which could cause structural damage. If the pilot tries to extend the flaps when the airspeed is too high, the opposition caused by the airflow will open the overload valve and return the fluid to the reservoir.

flat pattern layout. The pattern for a sheet metal part that has the material used for each flat surface, and for all of the bends, marked out with bend-tangent lines drawn between the flats and bend allowances.

fluid. A form of material whose molecules are able to flow past one another without destroying the material. Gases and liquids are both fluids.

fluid power. The transmission of force by the movement of a fluid. The most familiar examples of fluid power systems are hydraulic and pneumatic systems.

flutter. Rapid and uncontrolled oscillation of a flight control surface on an aircraft that is caused by a dynamically unbalanced condition.

fly-by-wire. A method of control used by some modern aircraft in which control movement or pressures exerted by the pilot are directed into a digital computer where they are input into a program tailored to the flight characteristics of the aircraft. The computer output signal is sent to actuators at the control surfaces to move them the optimum amount for the desired maneuver.

flying boat. An airplane whose fuselage is built in the form of a boat hull to allow it to land and takeoff from water. In the past, flying boats were a popular form of large airplane.

foot-pound. A measure of work accomplished when a force of 1 pound moves an object a distance of 1 foot.

force. Energy brought to bear on an object that tends to cause motion or to change motion.

forehand welding. Welding in which the torch is pointed in the direction the weld is progressing.

form drag. Parasite drag caused by the form of the object passing through the air.

former. An aircraft structural member used to give a fuselage its shape.

Frise aileron. An aileron with its hinge line set back from the leading edge so that when it is deflected upward, part of the leading edge projects below the wing and produces parasite drag to help overcome adverse yaw.

full-bodied. Not thinned.

fully articulated rotor. A helicopter rotor whose blades are attached to the hub in such a way that they are free to flap, drag, and feather. See each of these terms.

fungus (*plural* fungi). Any of several types of plant life that include yeasts, molds, and mildew.

fusible plugs. Plugs in the wheels of high-performance airplanes that use tubeless tires. The centers of the plugs are filled with a metal that melts at a relatively low temperature.

If a takeoff is aborted and the pilot uses the brakes excessively, the heat transferred into the wheel will melt the center of the fusible plugs and allow the air to escape from the tire before it builds up enough pressure to cause an explosion.

gage (rivet). The distance between rows of rivets in a multirow seam. Gage is also called transverse pitch.

galling. Fretting or pulling out chunks of a surface by sliding contact with another surface or body.

gasket. A seal between two parts where there is no relative motion.

gear-type pump. A constant-displacement fluid pump that contains two meshing large-tooth spur gears. Fluid is drawn into the pump as the teeth separate and is carried around the inside of the housing with the teeth and is forced from the pump when the teeth come together.

gerotor pump. A form of constant-displacement gear pump. A gerotor pump uses an external-tooth spur gear that rides inside of and drives an internal-tooth rotor gear. There is one more tooth space inside the rotor than there are teeth on the drive gear.

As the gears rotate, the volume of the space between two of the teeth on the inlet side of the pump increases, while the volume of the space between the two teeth on the opposite side of the pump decreases.

gram. The basic unit of weight or mass in the metric system. One gram equals about 0.035 ounce.

graphite. A form of carbon. Structural graphite is used in composite structure because of its strength and stiffness.

greige (pronounced "gray"). The unshrunk condition of a polyester fabric as it is removed from the loom.

ground effect. The increased aerodynamic lift produced when an airplane or helicopter is flown nearer than a half wing span or rotor span to the ground. This additional lift is caused by an effective increase in angle of attack without the accompanying increase in induced drag, which is caused by the deflection of the downwashed air.

guncotton. A highly explosive material made by treating cotton fibers with nitric and sulfuric acids. Guncotton is used in making the film base of nitrate dope.

gusset. A small plate attached to two or more members of a truss structure. A gusset strengthens the truss.

gyroscopic precession. The characteristic of a gyroscope that causes it to react to an applied force as though the force were applied at a point 90° in the direction of rotation from the actual point of application.

The rotor of a helicopter acts in much the same way as a gyroscope and is affected by gyroscopic precession.

hardwood. Wood from a broadleaf tree that sheds its leaves each year.

horsepower. A unit of mechanical power that is equal to 33,000 foot-pounds of work done in 1 minute, or 550 foot-pounds of work done in 1 second.

hot dimpling. A process used to dimple, or indent, the hole into which a flush rivet is to be installed. Hot dimpling is done by clamping the metal between heating elements and forcing the dies through the holes in the softened metal. Hot dimpling prevents hard metal from cracking when it is dimpled.

hot-wire cutter. A cutter used to shape blocks of Styrofoam. The wire is stretched tight between the arms of a frame and heated by electrical current. The hot wire melts its way through the foam.

hydraulic actuator. The component in a hydraulic system that converts hydraulic pressure into mechanical force. The two main types of hydraulic actuators are linear actuators (cylinders and pistons) and rotary actuators (hydraulic motors).

hydraulic fuse. A type of flow control valve that allows a normal flow of fluid in the system but, if the flow rate is excessive, or if too much fluid flows for normal operation, the fuse will shut off all further flow.

hydraulic motor. A hydraulic actuator that converts fluid pressure into rotary motion.

Hydraulic motors have an advantage in aircraft installations over electric motors, because they can operate in a stalled condition without the danger of a fire.

hydraulic power pack. A small, self-contained hydraulic system that consists of a reservoir, pump, selector valves, and relief valves. The power pack is removable from the aircraft as a unit to facilitate maintenance and service.

hydraulics. The system of fluid power which transmits force through an incompressible fluid.

hydroplaning. A condition that exists when a high-speed airplane is landed on a water-covered runway. When the brakes are applied, the wheels lock up and the tires skid on the surface of the water in much the same way a water ski rides on the surface. Hydroplaning develops enough heat in a tire to ruin it.

hypersonic speed. Speed of greater than Mach 5 (5 times the speed of sound).

ICAO. The International Civil Aeronautical Organization.

icebox rivet. A solid rivet made of 2017 or 2024 aluminum alloy. These rivets are too hard to drive in the condition they are received from the factory, and must be heat-treated to soften them. They are heated in a furnace and then quenched in cold water. Immediately after quenching they are soft, but within a few hours at room temperature they become quite hard. The hardening can be delayed for several days by storing them in a subfreezing icebox and holding them at this low temperature until they are to be used.

inch-pound. A measure of work accomplished when a force of 1 pound moves an object a distance of 1 inch.

induced drag. Aerodynamic drag produced by an airfoil when it is producing lift. Induced drag is affected by the same factors that affect induced lift.

induction time. The time allowed an epoxy or polyurethane material between its initial mixing and its application. This time allows the materials to begin their cure.

ingot. A large block of metal that was molded as it was poured from the furnace. Ingots are further processed into sheets, bars, tubes, or structural beams.

interference drag. Parasite drag caused by air flowing over one portion of the airframe interfering with the smooth flow of air over another portion.

jackscrew. A hardened steel rod with strong threads cut into it. A jackscrew is rotated by hand or with a motor to apply a force or to lift an object.

joggle. A small offset near the edge of a piece of sheet metal. It allows one sheet of metal to overlap another sheet while maintaining a flush surface.

jointer. A woodworking power tool used to smooth the edges of a piece of wood.

K-factor. A factor used in sheet metal work to determine the setback for other than a 90° bend.

Setback = K · (bend radius + metal thickness).

For bends of less than 90° the value of K is less than 1; for bends greater than 90° the value of K is greater than 1.

Kevlar. A patented synthetic aramid fiber noted for its flexibility and light weight. It is to a great extent replacing fiberglass as a reinforcing fabric for composite construction.

kick-in pressure. The pressure at which an unloading valve causes a hydraulic pump to direct its fluid into the system manifold.

kick-out pressure. The pressure at which an unloading valve shuts off the flow of fluid into the system pressure manifold and directs it back to the reservoir under a much reduced pressure.

kilogram. One thousand grams.

kinetic energy. Energy that exists because of motion.

knot (wood defect). A hard, usually round section of a tree branch embedded in a board. The grain of the knot is perpendicular to the grain of the board.

Knots decrease the strength of the board and should be avoided where strength is needed.

knot (measure of speed). A speed measurement that is equal to one nautical mile per hour. One knot is equal to 1.15 statute mile per hour.

Koroseal lacing. A plastic lacing material available in round or rectangular cross sections and used for holding wire bundles and tubing together. It holds tension on knots indefinitely and is impervious to petroleum products.

kraft paper. A tough brown wrapping paper like that used for paper bags.

lacquer. A finishing material made of a film base, solvents, plasticizers, and thinners. The film base forms a tough film over the surface when it dries. The solvents dissolve the film base so it can be applied as a liquid. The plasticizers give the film base the needed resilience, and the thinners dilute the lacquer so it can be applied with a spray gun. Lacquer is sprayed on the surface as a liquid, and when the solvents and thinners evaporate, the film base remains as a tough decorative and protective coating.

laminar flow. Airflow in which the air passes over the surface in smooth layers with a minimum of turbulence.

laminated wood. A type of wood made by gluing several pieces of thin wood together. The grain of all pieces runs in the same direction.

lateral axis. An imaginary line, passing through the center of gravity of an airplane, and extending across it from wing tip to wing tip.

lay-up. The placement of the various layers of resin-impregnated fabric in the mold for a piece of laminated composite material.

L/D ratio. A measure of efficiency of an airfoil. It is the ratio of the lift to the total drag at a specified angle of attack.

lightening hole. A hole cut in a piece of structural material to get rid of weight without losing any strength. A hole several inches in diameter may be cut in a piece of metal at a point where the metal is not needed for strength, and the edges of the hole are flanged to give it rigidity. A piece of metal with properly flanged lightening holes is more rigid than the metal before the holes were cut.

linear actuator. A fluid power actuator that uses a piston moving inside a cylinder to change pressure into linear, or straight-line, motion.

longitudinal axis. An imaginary line, passing through the center of gravity of an airplane, and extending lengthwise through it from nose to tail.

longitudinal stability. Stability of an aircraft along its longitudinal axis and about its lateral axis. Longitudinal stability is also called pitch stability.

Mach number. A measurement of speed based on the ratio of the speed of the aircraft to the speed of sound under the same atmospheric conditions. An airplane flying at Mach 1 is flying at the speed of sound.

major alteration. An alteration not listed in the aircraft, aircraft engine, or propeller specifications. It is one that might appreciably affect weight, balance, structural strength performance, powerplant operation, flight characteristics, or other qualities affecting airworthiness, or that cannot be made with elementary operations.

major repair. A repair to an aircraft structure or component that if improperly made might appreciably affect weight, balance, structural strength, performance, powerplant operation, flight characteristics, or other qualities affecting airworthiness, or that is not done according to accepted practices, or cannot be made with elementary operations.

manifold pressure. The absolute pressure of the air in the induction system of a reciprocating engine.

matrix. The material used in composite construction to bond the fibers together and to transmit the forces into the fibers. Resins are the most widely used matrix materials.

mean camber. A line that is drawn midway between the upper and lower camber of an airfoil section. The mean camber determines the aerodynamic characteristics of the airfoil.

MEK. Methyl-ethyl-ketone, an organic chemical solvent that is soluble in water and is used as a solvent for vinyl and nitrocellulose films. MEK is an efficient cleaner for preparing surfaces for priming or painting.

mercerize. A treatment given to cotton thread to make it strong and lustrous. The thread is stretched while it is soaked in a solution of caustic soda.

microballoons. Tiny, hollow spheres of glass or phenolic material used to add body to a resin.

Micro-Mesh. A patented graduated series of cloth-backed cushioned sheets that contain abrasive crystals. Micro-Mesh is used for polishing and restoring transparency to acrylic plastic windows and windshields.

micron ("micro meter"). A unit of linear measurement equal to one millionth of a meter, or one thousandth of a millimeter, or 0.000 039 inch. A micron is also called a micrometer.

Micronic filter. The registered trade name of a type of fluid filter whose filtering element is a specially treated cellulose paper formed into vertical convolutions, or wrinkles. Micronic filters prevent the passage of solids larger than about 10 microns, and are normally replaced with new filters rather than cleaned.

MIG welding. Metal inert gas welding is a form of electric arc welding in which the electrode is an expendable wire. MIG welding is now called GMA (Gas Metal Arc) welding.

mil. One thousandth of an inch (0.001 inch). Paint film thickness is usually measured in mils.

mildew. A gray or white fungus growth that forms on organic materials. Mildew forms on cotton and linen aircraft fabric and destroys its strength.

mist coat. A very light coat of zinc chromate primer. It is so thin that the metal is still visible, but the primer makes pencil marks easy to see.

moisture separator. A component in a high-pressure pneumatic system that removes most of the water vapor from the compressed air.

    When the compressed air is used, its pressure drops, and this pressure drop causes a drop in temperature. If any moisture were allowed to remain in the air, it would freeze and block the system.

mold line. A line used in the development of a flat pattern for a formed piece of sheet metal. The mold line is an extension of the flat side of a part beyond the radius. The mold line dimension of a part is the dimension made to the intersection of mold lines and is the dimension the part would have if its corners had no radius.

mold point. The intersection of two mold lines of a part. Mold line dimensions are made between mold points.

moment. A force that causes or tries to cause an object to rotate. The value of a moment is the product of the weight of an object (or the force), multiplied by the distance between the center of gravity of the object (or the point of application of the force) and the fulcrum about which the object rotates.

Monel. An alloy of nickel, copper, and aluminum or silicon.

monocoque. A single-shell type of aircraft structure in which all of the flight loads are carried in the outside skin of the structure.

MSDS. Material Safety Data Sheets. MSDS are required by the Federal Government to be available in workplaces to inform workers of the dangers that may exist from contact with certain materials.

multiple-disk brakes. Aircraft brakes in which one set of disks is keyed to the axle and remains stationary. Between each stationary disk there is a rotating disk that is keyed to the inside of the wheel. When the brakes are applied, the stationary disks are forced together, clamping the rotating disks between them. The friction between the disks slows the aircraft.

nailing strip. A method of applying pressure to the glue in a scarf joint repair in a plywood skin. A strip of thin plywood is nailed over the glued scarf joint with the nails extending into a supporting structure beneath the skin. The strip is installed over vinyl sheeting to prevent it sticking to the skin. When the glue is thoroughly dry, the nailing strip is broken away and the nails removed.

nap of the fabric. The ends of the fibers in a fabric. The first coat of dope on cotton or linen fabric raises the nap, and the fiber ends stick up. These ends must be carefully removed by sanding to get a smooth finish.

naphtha. A volatile and flammable hydrocarbon liquid used chiefly as a solvent or as a cleaning fluid.

neutral axis (neutral plane). A line through a piece of material that is bent. The material in the outside of the bend is stretched and that on the inside of the bend is shrunk. The material along the neutral plane is neither shrunk nor stretched.

neutral flame. An oxyacetylene flame produced when the ratio of oxygen and acetylene is chemically correct and there is no excess of oxygen or carbon. A neutral flame has a rounded inner cone and no feather around it.

Nomex. A patented nylon material used to make the honeycomb core for certain types of sandwich materials.

nonenergizing brake. A brake that does not use the momentum of the aircraft to increase the friction.

normal shock wave. A shock wave that forms ahead of a blunt object moving through the air at the speed of sound. The shock wave is normal (perpendicular) to the air approaching the object.

    Air passing through a normal shock wave is slowed to a subsonic speed and its static pressure is increased.

normalizing. A process of strain-relieving steel that has been welded and left in a strained condition. The steel is heated to a specified temperature, usually red hot, and allowed to cool in still air to room temperature.

nose-gear centering cam. A cam in the nose-gear shock strut that causes the piston to center when the strut fully extends. When the aircraft takes off and the strut extends, the wheel is straightened in its fore-and-aft position so it can be retracted into the wheel well.

oblique shock wave. A shock wave that forms on a sharp-pointed object moving through the air at a speed greater than the speed of sound. Air passing through an oblique shock wave is slowed down, but not to a subsonic speed, and its static pressure is increased.

oleo shock absorber. A shock absorber used on aircraft landing gear. The initial landing impact is absorbed by oil transferring from one compartment in the shock strut into another compartment through a metering orifice. The shocks of taxiing are taken up by a cushion of compressed air.

open angle. An angle in which sheet metal is bent less than 90°.

open assembly time. The period of time between the application of the glue and the assembly of the joint components.

open-center hydraulic system. A fluid power system in which the selector valves are arranged in series with each other. Fluid flows from the pump through the center of the selector valves, back into the reservoir when no unit is being actuated.

open-center selector valve. A type of selector valve that functions as an unloading valve as well as a selector valve.

Open-center selector valves are installed in series, and when no unit is actuated, fluid from the pump flows through the centers of all the valves and returns to the reservoir.

When a unit is selected for actuation, the center of the selector valve is shut off and the fluid from the pump goes through the selector valve into one side of the actuator. Fluid from the other side of the actuator returns to the valve and goes back to the reservoir through the other selector valves. When the actuation is completed, the selector valve is placed in its neutral position. Its center opens, and fluid from the pump flows straight through the valve.

orifice check valve. A component in a hydraulic or pneumatic system that allows unrestricted flow in one direction, and restricted flow in the opposite direction.

O-ring. A widely used type of seal made in the form of a rubber ring with a round cross section. An O-ring seals in both directions, and it can be used as a packing or a gasket.

ornithopter. A heavier-than-air flying machine that produces lift by flapping its wings. No practical ornithopter has been built.

oxidizing flame. An oxyacetylene flame in which there is an excess of oxygen. The inner cone is pointed and often a hissing sound is heard.

ozone. An unstable form of oxygen produced when an electric spark passes through the air. Ozone is harmful to rubber products.

packing. A seal between two parts where there is relative motion.

paint. A covering applied to an object or structure to protect it and improve its appearance. Paint consists of a pigment suspended in a vehicle such as oil or water. When the vehicle dries by evaporation or curing, the pigment is left as a film on the surface.

parasite drag. A form of aerodynamic drag caused by friction between the air and the surface over which it is flowing.

parent metal. The metal being welded. This term is used to distinguish between the metal being welded and the welding rod.

parting film. A layer of thin plastic material placed between a composite lay-up and the heating blanket. It prevents the blanket from sticking to the fabric.

Pascal's law. A basic law of fluid power which states that the pressure in an enclosed container is transmitted equally and undiminished to all points of the container, and the force acts at right angles to the enclosing walls.

pilot hole. A small hole punched or drilled in a piece of sheet metal to locate a rivet hole.

pin knot cluster. A group of knots, all having a diameter of less than approximately $1/16$ inch.

pinked-edge tape. Cloth tape whose edges have small V-shaped notches cut along their length. The pinked edges prevent the tape from raveling.

pinking shears. Shears used to cut aircraft fabric with a series of small notches along the cut edge.

piston. A sliding plug in an actuating cylinder used to convert pressure into force and then into work.

pitch (aircraft maneuver). Rotation of an aircraft about its lateral axis.

pitch (rivet). The distance between the centers of adjacent rivets installed in the same row.

pitch pocket (wood defect). Pockets of pitch that appear in the growth rings of a piece of wood.

pitot pressure. Ram air pressure used to measure airspeed. The pitot tube faces directly into the air flowing around the aircraft. It stops the air and measures its pressure.

plain-weave fabric. Fabric in which each warp thread passes over one fill thread and under the next. Plain-weave fabric typically has the same strength in both warp and fill directions.

planer. A woodworking power tool used to smooth the surfaces of a piece of wood.

plasticizer. A constituent in dope or lacquer that gives its film flexibility and resilience.

plastic media blasting (PMB). A method of removing paint from an aircraft surface by dry-blasting it with tiny plastic beads.

plastics. The generic name for any of the organic materials produced by polymerization. Plastics can be shaped by molding or drawing.

ply rating. The rating of an aircraft tire that indicates its relative strength. The ply rating does not indicate the actual number of plies of fabric in the tire; rather it indicates the number of plies of cotton fabric needed to produce the same strength as the actual plies.

plywood. A wood product made by gluing several pieces of thin wood veneer together. The grain of the wood in each layer runs at 90° or 45° to the grain of the layer next to it.

pneumatics. The system of fluid power which transmits force by the use of a compressible fluid.

polyester fibers. A synthetic fiber made by the polymerization process in which tiny molecules are united to form a long chain of molecules.

Polyester fibers are woven into fabrics that are known by their trade names of Dacron, Fortrel, and Kodel. Polyester film and sheet are known as Mylar and Celenar.

polyester resin. A thermosetting resin used as a matrix for much of the fiberglass used in composite construction.

polyurethane enamel. A hard, chemically resistant finish used on aircraft. Polyurethane enamel is resistant to damage from all types of hydraulic fluid.

polyvinyl chloride. A thermoplastic resin used in the manufacture of transparent tubing for electrical insulation and fluid lines which are subject to low pressures.

potential energy. Energy possessed in an object because of its position, chemical composition, shape, or configuration.

pot life. The length of time a resin will remain workable after the catalyst has been added. If a catalyzed material is not used within its usable pot life, it must be discarded and a new batch mixed.

power. The time rate of doing work. Power is force multiplied by distance (work), divided by time.

power brakes. Aircraft brakes that use the main hydraulic system to supply fluid for the brake actuation.

Aircraft that require a large amount of fluid for their brake actuation normally use power brakes, and the volume of fluid sent to the brakes is increased by the use of deboosters.

power control valve. A hand-operated hydraulic pump unloading valve.

When the valve is open, fluid flows from the pump to the reservoir with little opposition. To actuate a unit, turn the selector valve, and manually close the power control valve. Pressurized fluid flows to the unit, and when it is completely actuated, the power control valve automatically opens.

precipitation heat treatment. A method of increasing the strength of heat-treated aluminum alloy. After the aluminum alloy has been solution-heat-treated by heating and quenching, it is returned to the oven and heated to a temperature lower than that used for the initial heat treatment. It is held at this temperature for a specified period of time and then removed from the oven and allowed to cool slowly.

prepreg. Preimpregnated fabric. A type of composite material in which the reinforcing fibers are encapsulated in an uncured resin. Prepreg materials must be kept refrigerated to prevent them from curing before they are used.

pressure. Force per unit area. Hydraulic and pneumatic pressure are normally given in units of pounds per square inch (psi).

pressure manifold (hydraulic system component). The portion of a fluid power system from which the selector valves receive their pressurized fluid.

pressure plate (brake component). A strong, heavy plate used in a multiple-disk brake. The pressure plate receives the force from the brake cylinders and transmits this force to the disks.

pressure vessel. The strengthened portion of an aircraft structure that is sealed and pressurized in flight.

primer (finishing system component). A component in a finishing system that provides a good bond between the surface and the material used for the topcoats.

profile drag. Aerodynamic drag produced by skin friction. Profile drag is a form of parasite drag.

pump control valve. A control valve in a hydraulic system that allows the pilot to manually direct the output of the hydraulic pump back to the reservoir when no unit is being actuated.

Pureclad. A registered trade name for clad aluminum alloy.

pusher powerplant. A powerplant whose propeller is mounted at the rear of the airplane and pushes, rather than pulls, the airplane through the air.

quartersawed wood. Wood sawed from a tree in such a way that the annual rings cross the plank at an angle greater than 45°.

quick-disconnect fitting. A hydraulic line fitting that seals the line when the fitting is disconnected. Quick-disconnect fittings are used on the lines connected to the engine-driven hydraulic pump. They allow the pump to be disconnected and an auxiliary hydraulic power system connected to perform checks requiring hydraulic power while the aircraft is in the hangar.

rack-and-pinion actuator. A form of rotary actuator where the fluid acts on a piston on which a rack of gear teeth is cut. As the piston moves, it rotates a pinion gear which is mated with the teeth cut in the rack.

radius dimpling. A process of preparing a hole in sheet metal for flush riveting. A cone-shaped male die forces the edges of the rivet hole into the depression in a female die. Radius dimpling forms a round-edged depression into which the rivet head fits.

rectangle. A plane surface with four sides whose opposite sides are parallel and whose angles are all right angles.

rectification (arc welding condition). A condition in AC-electric arc welding in which oxides on the surface of the metal act as a rectifier and prevent electrons flowing from the metal to the electrode during the half cycle when the electrode is positive.

reducing flame. *See* carburizing flame.

reinforcing tape. A narrow strip of woven fabric material placed over the fabric as it is being attached to the aircraft structure with rib lacing cord. This tape carries a large amount of the load and prevents the fabric tearing at the stitches.

rejuvenator. A finishing material used to restore resilience to an old dope film. Rejuvenator contains strong solvents to open the dried-out film and plasticizers to restore resilience to the old dope.

relative wind. The direction the wind strikes an airfoil.

relief hole. A hole drilled at the point at which two bend lines meet in a piece of sheet metal. This hole spreads the stresses caused by the bends and prevents the metal cracking.

relief valve. A pressure-control valve that relieves any pressure over the amount for which it is set. They are damage-preventing units used in both hydraulic and pneumatic systems.

In an aircraft hydraulic system, pressure relief valves prevent damaging high pressures that could be caused by a malfunctioning pressure regulator, or by thermal expansion of fluid trapped in portions of the system.

repair. A maintenance procedure in which a damaged component is restored to its original condition, or at least to a condition that allows it to fulfill its design function.

restrictor. A fluid power system component that controls the rate of actuator movement by restricting the flow of fluid into or out of the actuator.

retarder (finishing system component). Dope thinner that contains certain additives that slow its rate of evaporation enough to prevent the dope blushing.

retread. The replacement of the tread rubber on an aircraft tire.

retreating blade. The blade on a helicopter rotor whose tip is moving in the direction opposite to that in which the helicopter is moving.

retreating blade stall. The stall of a helicopter rotor disc that occurs near the tip of the retreating blade. A retreating blade stall occurs when the flight airspeed is high and the retreating blade airspeed is low. This results in a high angle of attack, causing the stall.

return manifold. The portion of a fluid power system through which the fluid is returned to the reservoir.

reverse polarity welding. DC-electric arc welding in which the electrode is positive with respect to the work.

rib tread. A series of circumferential grooves cut into the tread of a tire. This tread pattern provides superior traction and directional stability on hard-surfaced runways.

ribbon direction. The direction in a piece of honeycomb material that is parallel to the length of the strips of material that make up the core.

rivet cutters. Special cutting pliers that resemble diagonal cutters except that the jaws are ground in such a way that they cut the rivet shank, or stem, off square.

rivet set. A tool used to drive aircraft solid rivets. It is a piece of hardened steel with a recess the shape of the rivet head in one end. The other end fits into the rivet gun.

roll (aircraft maneuver). Rotation of an aircraft about its longitudinal axis.

rosette weld. A method of securing one metal tube inside another by welding. Small holes are drilled in the outer tube and the inner tube is welded to it around the circumference of the holes.

rotary actuator. A fluid power actuator whose output is rotational. A hydraulic motor is a rotary actuator.

roving. A lightly twisted roll or strand of fibers.

ruddervators. The two movable surfaces on a V-tail empennage. When these two surfaces are moved together with the in-and-out movement of the control yoke, they act as elevators, and when they are moved differentially with the rudder pedals, they act as the rudder.

saddle gusset. A piece of plywood glued to an aircraft structural member. The saddle gusset has a cutout to hold a backing block or strip tightly against the skin to allow a nailing strip to be used to apply pressure to a glued joint in the skin.

sailplane. A high-performance glider.

sandwich material. A type of composite structural material in which a core material is bonded between face sheets of metal or resin-impregnated fabric.

satin-weave fabric. Fabric in which the warp threads pass under one fill thread and over several others. Satin-weave fabrics are used when the lay-up must be made over complex shapes.

scarf joint. A joint in a wood structure in which the ends to be joined are cut in a long taper, normally about 12:1, and fastened together by gluing. A glued scarf joint makes a strong splice because the joint is made along the side of the wood fibers rather than along their ends.

scissors. A name commonly used for torque links. *See* torque links.

segmented-rotor brake. A heavy-duty, multiple-disk brake used on large, high-speed aircraft.

Stators that are surfaced with a material that retains its friction characteristics at high temperatures are keyed to the axle. Rotors which are keyed into the wheels mesh with the stators. The rotors are made in segments to allow for cooling and for their large amounts of expansion.

selector valve. A flow control valve used in hydraulic systems that directs pressurized fluid into one side of an actuator, and at the same time directs return fluid from the other side of the actuator back to the reservoir.

There are two basic types of selector valves: open-center valves and closed-center valves. The four-port closed-center valve is the most frequently used type.

See closed-center selector valve and open-center selector valve.

selvage edge. The woven edge of fabric used to prevent the material unraveling during normal handling. The selvage edge, which runs the length of the fabric parallel to the warp threads, is usually removed from materials used in composite construction.

semimonocoque structure. A form of aircraft stressed skin structure. Most of the strength of a semimonocoque structure is in the skin, but the skin is supported on a substructure of formers and stringers that give the skin its shape and increase its rigidity.

sequence valve. A valve in a hydraulic system that requires a certain action to be completed before another action can begin.

Sequence valves are used to assure that the hydraulically actuated wheel-well doors are completely open before pressure is directed to the landing gear to lower it.

servo. An electrical or hydraulic actuator connected into a flight control system. A small force on the cockpit control is amplified by the servo and provides a large force to move the control surface.

servo tab. A small movable tab built into the trailing edge of a primary control surface of an airplane. The cockpit controls move the tab in such a direction that it produces an aerodynamic force moving the surface on which it is mounted.

setback. The distance the jaws of a brake must be set back from the mold line to form a bend. Setback for a 90° bend is equal to the inside radius of the bend plus the thickness of the metal being bent. For a bend other than 90°, a K-factor must be used. *See also* K-factor.

shake (wood defect). Longitudinal cracks in a piece of wood, usually between two annual rings.

shear section. A necked-down section of the drive shaft of a constant-displacement engine-driven fluid pump. If the pump should seize, the shear section will break and prevent the pump from being destroyed or the engine from being damaged.

Some pumps use a shear pin rather than a shear section.

shear strength. The strength of a riveted joint in a sheet metal structure in which the rivets shear before the metal tears at the rivet holes.

shelf life. The length of time a product is good when it remains in its original unopened container.

shimmy. Abnormal, and often violent, vibration of the nose wheel of an airplane. Shimmying is usually caused by looseness of the nose wheel support mechanism or an unbalanced wheel.

shimmy damper. A small hydraulic shock absorber installed between the nose wheel fork and the nose wheel cylinder attached to the aircraft structure.

shock wave. A pressure wave formed in the air by a flight vehicle moving at a speed greater than the speed of sound. As the vehicle passes through the air, it produces sound waves that spread out in all directions. But since the vehicle is flying faster than these waves are moving, they build up and form a pressure wave at the front and rear of the vehicle.

As the air passes through a shock wave it slows down, its static pressure increases, and its total energy decreases.

shop head. The head of a rivet which is formed when the shank is upset.

show-type finish. The type of finish put on fabric-covered aircraft intended for show. This finish is usually made up of many coats of dope, with much sanding and rubbing of the surface between coats.

shuttle valve. An automatic selector valve mounted on critical components such as landing gear actuation cylinders and brake cylinders.

For normal operation, system fluid flows into the actuator through the shuttle valve, but if normal system pressure is lost, emergency system pressure forces the shuttle over and emergency fluid flows into the actuator.

sidestick controller. A cockpit flight control used on some of the fly-by-wire equipped airplanes. The stick is mounted rigidly on the side console of the cockpit, and pressures exerted on the stick by the pilot produce electrical signals that are sent to the computer that flies the airplane.

sight line. A line drawn on a sheet metal layout that is one bend radius from the bend-tangent line. The sight line is lined up directly below the nose of the radius bar in a cornice brake. When the metal is clamped in this position, the bend tangent line is in the correct position for the start of the bend.

silicone rubber. An elastomeric material made from silicone elastomers. Silicone rubber is compatible with fluids that attack other natural or synthetic rubbers.

single-acting actuator. A linear hydraulic or pneumatic actuator that uses fluid power for movement in one direction and a spring force for its return.

single-action hand pump. A hand-operated fluid pump that moves fluid only during one stroke of the pump handle. One stroke pulls the fluid into the pump and the other forces the fluid out.

single-disk brakes. Aircraft brakes in which a single steel disk rotates with the wheel between two brake-lining blocks. When the brake is applied, the disk is clamped tightly between the lining blocks, and the friction slows the aircraft.

single-servo brakes. Brakes that uses the momentum of the aircraft rolling forward to help apply the brakes by wedging the brake shoe against the brake drum.

sintered metal. A porous material made by fusing powdered metal under heat and pressure.

Skydrol hydraulic fluid. The registered trade name for a synthetic, nonflammable, phosphate ester-base hydraulic fluid used in modern high-temperature hydraulic systems.

slat. A secondary control on an aircraft that allows it to fly at a high angle of attack without stalling. A slat is a section of the leading edge of the wing mounted on curved tracks that move into and out of the wing on rollers.

slip roll former. A shop tool used to form large radius curves in sheet metal.

slippage mark. A paint mark extending across the edge of an aircraft wheel onto a tube-type tire. When this mark is broken, it indicates the tire has slipped on the wheel, and there is good reason to believe the tube has been damaged.

slipstream area. For the purpose of rib stitch spacing, the slipstream area is considered to be the diameter of the propeller plus one wing rib on each side.

slot (aerodynamic device). A fixed, nozzle-like opening near the leading edge of an airplane wing ahead of the aileron.

A slot acts as a duct to force high-energy air down on the upper surface of the wing when the airplane is flying at a high angle of attack. The slot, which is located ahead of the aileron, causes the inboard portion of the wing to stall first, allowing the aileron to remain effective throughout the stall.

snubber. A device in a hydraulic or pneumatic component that absorbs shock and/or vibration. A snubber is installed in the line to a hydraulic pressure gage to prevent the pointer fluctuating.

softwood. Wood from a tree that bears cones and has needles rather than leaves.

soldering. A method of thermally joining metal parts with a molten nonferrous alloy that melts at a temperature below 800°F. The molten alloy is pulled up between close-fitting parts by capillary action. When the alloy cools and hardens, it forms a strong, leak-proof connection.

solidity (helicopter rotor characteristic). The solidity of a helicopter rotor system is the ratio of the total blade area to the disc area.

solution heat treatment. A type of heat treatment in which the metal is heated in a furnace until it has a uniform temperature throughout. It is then removed and quenched in cold water.

When the metal is hot, the alloying elements enter into a solid solution with the base metal to become part of its basic structure. When the metal is quenched, these elements are locked into place.

speed brakes. A secondary control of an airplane that produces drag without causing a change in the pitch attitude of the airplane. Speed brakes allow an airplane to make a steep descent without building up excessive forward airspeed.

spike knot. A knot that runs through the depth of a beam perpendicular to the annual rings. Spike knots appear most frequently in quartersawed wood.

spin. A flight maneuver in which an airplane descends in a corkscrew fashion. One wing is stalled and the other is producing lift.

spirit level. A curved glass tube partially filled with a liquid, but with a bubble in it. When the device in which the tube is mounted is level, the bubble will be in the center of the tube.

splayed patch (wood structure repair). A type of patch made in an aircraft plywood structure in which the edges of the patch are tapered for approximately five times the thickness of the plywood. A splayed patch is not recommended for use on plywood less than 1/10 inch thick.

split (wood defect). A longitudinal crack in a piece of wood caused by externally induced stress.

spoilers. Flight controls that are raised up from the upper surface of a wing to destroy, or spoil, lift. Flight spoilers are used in conjunction with the ailerons to decrease lift and increase drag on the descending wing. Ground spoilers are used to produce a great amount of drag to slow the airplane on its landing roll.

spongy brakes. Hydraulic brakes whose pedal has a spongy feel because of air trapped in the fluid.

spontaneous combustion. Self-ignition of a material caused by heat produced in the material as it combines with oxygen from the air.

springwood. The portion of an annual ring in a piece of wood formed principally during the first part of the growing season, the spring of the year. Springwood is softer, more porous, and lighter than the summerwood.

square. A four-sided plane figure whose sides are all the same length, whose opposite sides are parallel, and whose angles are all right angles.

squat switch. An electrical switch actuated by the landing gear scissors on the oleo strut. When no weight is on the landing gear, the oleo piston is extended and the switch is in one position, but when weight is on the gear, the oleo strut compresses and the switch changes its position.

Squat switches are used in antiskid brake systems, landing gear safety circuits, and cabin pressurization systems.

SRM. Structural Repair Manual.

stabilator. A flight control on the empennage of an airplane that acts as both a stabilizer and an elevator. The entire horizontal tail surface pivots and is moved as a unit.

stability. The characteristic of an aircraft that causes it to return to its original flight condition after it has been disturbed.

stabilons. Small wing-like horizontal surfaces mounted on the aft fuselage to improve longitudinal stability of airplanes that have an exceptionally wide center of gravity range.

stall. A flight condition in which an angle of attack is reached at which the air ceases to flow smoothly over the upper surface of an airfoil. The air becomes turbulent and lift is lost.

stall strip. A small triangular metal strip installed along the leading edge of an airplane wing near the wing root. Stall strips cause the root section of the wing to stall before the portion of the wing ahead of the ailerons.

standpipe. A pipe sticking up in a tank or reservoir that allows part of the tank to be used as a reserve, or standby, source of fluid.

static. Still, not moving.

static air pressure. Pressure of the ambient air surrounding the aircraft. Static pressure does not take into consideration any air movement.

static stability. The characteristic of an aircraft that causes it to return to straight and level flight after it has been disturbed from that condition.

Stoddard solvent. A petroleum product, similar to naphtha, used as a solvent and a cleaning fluid.

STOL. Short takeoff and landing.

stop drilling. A method of stopping the growth of a crack in a piece of metal or transparent plastic by drilling a small hole at the end of the crack.

The stresses are spread out all around the circumference of the hole rather than concentrated at the end of the crack.

straight polarity welding. DC-electric arc welding in which the electrode is negative with respect to the work.

strain. A deformation or physical change in a material caused by a stress.

stress. A force set up within an object that tries to prevent an outside force from changing its shape.

stressed skin structure. A type of aircraft structure in which all or most of the stresses are carried in the outside skin. A stressed skin structure has a minimum of internal structure.

stress riser. A location where the cross-sectional area of the part changes abruptly. Stresses concentrate at such a location and failure is likely.

   A scratch, gouge, or tool mark in the surface of a highly stressed part can change the area enough to concentrate the stresses and become a stress riser.

stringer. A part of an aircraft structure used to give the fuselage its shape and, in some types of structure, to provide a small part of the fuselage strength.

   Formers give the fuselage its cross-sectional shape and stringers fill in the shape between the formers.

subsonic flight. Flight at an airspeed in which all air flowing over the aircraft is moving at a speed below the speed of sound.

summerwood. The less porous, usually harder portion of an annual ring that forms in the latter part of the growing season, the summer of the year.

supersonic flight. Flight at an airspeed in which all air flowing over the aircraft is moving at a speed greater than the speed of sound.

surface tape. Strips of aircraft fabric that are doped over all seams and places where the fabric is stitched to the aircraft structure. Surface tape is also doped over the wing leading edges where abrasive wear occurs.

   The edges of surface tape are pinked, or notched, to keep them from raveling before the dope is applied.

swashplate. The component in a helicopter control system that consists basically of two bearing races with ball bearings between them. The lower, or nonrotating, race is tilted by the cyclic control, and the upper, or rotating, race has arms which connect to the control horns on the rotor blades.

   Movement of the cyclic pitch control is transmitted to the rotor blades through the swashplate. Movement of the collective pitch control raises or lowers the entire swashplate assembly to change the pitch of all of the blades at the same time.

symmetrical airfoil. An airfoil that has the same shape on both sides of its chord line, or center line.

symmetry check. A check of an airframe to determine that the wings and tail are symmetrical about the longitudinal axis.

system-pressure regulator (hydraulic system component). A type of hydraulic system-pressure control valve. When the system pressure is low, as it is when some unit is actuated, the output of the constant-delivery pump is directed into the system. When the actuation is completed and the pressure builds up to a specified kick-out pressure, the pressure regulator shifts. A check valve seals the system off and the pressure is maintained by the accumulator. The pump is unloaded and its output is directed back into the reservoir with very little opposition. The pump output pressure drops, but the volume of flow remains the same. When the system pressure drops to the specified kick-in pressure, the regulator again shifts and directs fluid into the system.

   Spool-type and balanced-pressure-type system pressure regulators are completely automatic in their operation and require no attention on the part of the flight crew.

tack coat. A coat of finishing material sprayed on the surface and allowed to dry until the solvents evaporate. As soon as the solvents evaporate, a wet full-bodied coat of material is sprayed over it.

tack rag. A clean, lintless rag, slightly damp with thinner. A tack rag is used to wipe a surface to prepare it to receive a coat of finishing material.

tack weld. A method of holding parts together before they are permanently welded. The parts are assembled, and small spots of weld are placed at strategic locations to hold them in position.

tacky. Slightly sticky to the touch.

tailets. Small vertical surfaces mounted underside of the horizontal stabilizer of some airplanes to increase the directional stability.

tang. A tapered shank sticking out from the blade of a knife or a file. The handle of a knife or file is mounted on the tang.

Teflon. The registered trade name for a fluorocarbon resin used to make hydraulic and pneumatic seals, hoses, and backup rings.

thermal dimpling. *See* hot dimpling.

thermal relief valve. A relief valve in a hydraulic system that relieves pressure that builds up in an isolated part of the system because of heat. Thermal relief valves are set at a higher pressure than the system pressure relief valve.

thermoplastic resin. A type of plastic material that becomes soft when heated and hardens when cooled.

thermosetting resin. A type of plastic material that, when once hardened by heat, cannot be softened by being heated again.

thixotropic agents. Materials, such as microballoons, added to a resin to give it body and increase its workability.

TIG welding. Tungsten inert gas welding is a form of electric arc welding in which the electrode is a nonconsumable tungsten wire. TIG welding is now called GTA (Gas Tungsten Arc) Welding.

toe-in. A condition of landing gear alignment in which the front of the tires are closer together than the rear. When the aircraft rolls forward, the wheels try to move closer together.

toe-out. A condition of landing gear alignment in which the front of the tires are farther apart than the rear. When the aircraft rolls forward, the wheels try to move farther apart.

torque. A force that produces or tries to produce rotation.

torque links. The hinged link between the piston and cylinder of an oleo-type landing gear shock absorber. The torque links allow the piston to move freely in and out of the landing gear cylinder, but prevent it rotating. The torque links can be adjusted to achieve and maintain the correct wheel alignment. Torque links are also called scissors and nutcrackers.

torque tube. A tube in an aircraft control system that transmits a torsional force from the operating control to the control surface.

torsion rod. A device in a spring tab to which the control horn is attached. For normal operation, the torsion rod acts as a fixed attachment point, but when the control surface loads are high, the torsion rod twists and allows the control horn to deflect the spring tab.

total air pressure. The pressure a column of moving air will have if it is stopped.

tractor powerplant. An airplane powerplant in which the propeller is mounted in the front, and its thrust pulls the airplane rather than pushes it.

trammel (*verb*). To square up the Pratt truss used in an airplane wing. Trammel points are set on the trammel bar so they measure the distance between the center of the front spar, at the inboard compression strut, and the center of the rear spar at the next compression strut outboard. The drag and antidrag wires are adjusted until the distance between the center of the rear spar at the inboard compression strut and the center of the front spar at the next outboard compression strut is exactly the same as that between the first points measured.

trammel bar. A wood or metal bar on which trammel points are mounted to compare distances.

trammel points. A set of sharp-pointed pins that protrude from the sides of a trammel bar.

translational lift. The additional lift produced by a helicopter rotor as the helicopter changes from hovering to forward flight.

transonic flight. Flight at an airspeed in which some air flowing over the aircraft is moving at a speed below the speed of sound, and other air is moving at a speed greater than the speed of sound.

transverse pitch. *See* gage.

triangle. A three-sided, closed plane figure. The sum of the three angles in a triangle is always equal to 180°.

trim tab. A small control tab mounted on the trailing edge of a movable control surface. The tab may be adjusted to provide an aerodynamic force to hold the surface on which it is mounted deflected in order to trim the airplane for hands-off flight at a specified airspeed.

true airspeed (TAS). Airspeed shown on the airspeed indicator (indicated airspeed) corrected for position error and nonstandard air temperature and pressure.

trunnion. Projections from the cylinder of a retractable landing gear strut about which the strut pivots retract.

truss-type structure. A type of structure made up of longitudinal beams and cross braces. Compression loads between the main beams are carried by rigid cross braces. Tension loads are carried by stays, or wires, that go from one main beam to the other and cross between the cross braces.

turbine. A rotary device actuated by impulse or reaction of a fluid flowing through vanes or blades that are arranged around a central shaft.

turnbuckle. A component in an aircraft control system used to adjust cable tension. A turnbuckle consists of a brass tubular barrel with right-hand threads in one end and left-hand in the other end. Control cable terminals screw into the two ends of the barrel, and turning the barrel pulls the terminals together, shortening the cable.

twist drill. A metal cutting tool turned in a drill press or hand-held drill motor. A twist drill has a straight shank and spiraled flutes. The cutting edge is ground on the end of the spiraled flutes.

twist stripe. A stripe of paint on flexible hose that runs the length of the hose. If this stripe spirals around the hose after it is installed, it indicates the hose was twisted when it was installed. Twist stripes are also called lay lines.

ultimate tensile strength. The tensile strength required to cause a material to break or to continue to deform under a decreasing load.

ultraviolet-blocking dope. Dope that contains aluminum powder or some other pigment that blocks the passage of ultraviolet rays of the sun. This coat of dope protects the organic fabrics and clear dope from deterioration by these rays.

undamped oscillation. Oscillation that continues with an unchanging amplitude once it has started.

underslung rotor. A helicopter rotor whose center of gravity is below the point at which it is attached to the mast.

unidirectional fabric. Fabric in which all the threads run in the same direction. These threads are often bound with a few fibers run at right angles, just enough to hold the yarns together and prevent their bunching.

unloading valve. This is another name for system pressure regulator. *See* system pressure regulator.

utility finish. The finish of an aircraft that gives the necessary tautness and fill to the fabric and the necessary protection to the metal, but does not have the glossy appearance of a show-type finish.

variable displacement pump. A fluid pump whose output is controlled by the demands of the system. These pumps normally have a built-in system pressure regulator. When the demands of the system are low, the pump moves very little fluid, but when the demands are high, the pump moves a lot of fluid. Most variable displacement pumps used in aircraft hydraulic systems are piston-type pumps.

varnish (aircraft finishing material). A material used to produce an attractive and protective coating on wood or metal. Varnish is made of a resin dissolved in a solvent and thinned until it has the proper viscosity to spray or brush. The varnish is spread evenly over the surface to be coated, and when the solvents evaporate, a tough film is left.

varsol. A petroleum product similar to naphtha used as a solvent and a cleaning fluid.

veneer. Thin sheets of wood "peeled" from a log. A wide-blade knife held against the surface of the log peels away the veneer as the log is rotated in the cutter.

    Veneer is used for making plywood. Several sheets of veneer are glued together, with the grain of each sheet placed at 45° or 90° to the grain of the sheets next to it.

vertical axis. An imaginary line, passing vertically through the center of gravity of an airplane.

vertical fin. The fixed vertical surface in the empennage of an airplane. The vertical fin acts as a weathervane to give the airplane directional stability.

viscosity. The resistance of a fluid to flow. Viscosity refers to the "stiffness" of the fluid, or its internal friction.

viscosity cup. A specially shaped cup with an accurately sized hole in its bottom. The cup is submerged in the liquid to completely fill it. It is then lifted from the liquid and the time in seconds is measured from the beginning of the flow through the hole until the first break in this flow. The viscosity of the liquid relates to this time.

vixen file. A metal-cutting hand file that has curved teeth across its faces. Vixen files are used to remove large amounts of soft metal.

V_{NE}. Never-exceed speed. The maximum speed the aircraft is allowed to attain in any conditions of flight.

vortex (*plural* vortices). A whirling motion in a fluid.

vortex generator. Small low-aspect-ratio airfoils installed in pairs on the upper surface of a wing, on both sides of the vertical fin just ahead of the rudder, and on the underside of the vertical stabilizers of some airplanes. Their function is to pull high-energy air down to the surface to energize the boundary layer and prevent airflow separation until the surface reaches a higher angle of attack.

warp clock. An alignment indicator included in a structural repair manual to show the orientation of the plies of a composite material. The ply direction is shown in relation to a reference direction.

warp threads. Threads that run the length of the roll of fabric, parallel to the selvage edge. Warp threads are often stronger than fill threads.

warp tracers. Threads of a different color from the warp threads that are woven into a material to identify the direction of the warp threads.

wash in. A twist in an airplane wing that increases its angle of incidence near the tip.

wash out. A twist in an airplane wing that decreases its angle of incidence near the tip.

watt. The basic unit of electrical power. One watt is equal to 1/746 horsepower.

web of a spar. The part of a spar between the caps.

weft threads. *See* fill threads.

wing fences. Vertical vanes that extend chordwise across the upper surface of an airplane wing to prevent spanwise airflow.

wing heavy. An out-of-trim flight condition in which an airplane flies hands off, with one wing low.

woof threads. *See* fill threads.

work. The product of force times distance.

yaw. Rotation of an aircraft about its vertical axis.

yaw damper. An automatic flight control system that counteracts the rolling and yawing produced by Dutch roll. *See* Dutch roll.

A yaw damper senses yaw with a rate gyro and moves the rudder an amount proportional to the rate of yaw, but in the opposite direction.

yield strength. The amount of stress needed to permanently deform a material.

Zeppelin. The name of large rigid lighter-than-air ships built by the Zeppelin Company in Germany prior to and during World War I.

INDEX

Aviation Maintenance Technician Series
Airframe
Volume 1: Structures

Editing	Jennifer Trerise
Copy Editing	Janice Bultmann, Kitty Crane
Design	Dora McClurkin Muir
Illustration & Production	Dan McArdle, Cynthia Wyckoff
Additional Illustration	Glen Greenwood, Virginia Wright
Color Illustration & *Production, 3rd Edition*	Kelly Burch, Tyra Menzel, Sandi Harner

Produced at
ASA's Graphic Design & Publications Department
in Times and Helvetica Black using Microsoft Word,
Macromedia FreeHand, Adobe Illustrator, Adobe PageMaker
and Adobe Photoshop

Product names are trademarks or registered trademarks of their respective holders.

READER RESPONSE

Dear Aviation Maintenance Technician:

You have made an investment in your future by purchasing this textbook from ASA's *Aviation Maintenance Technician Series*. We hope you were pleased with your selection. Your input is invaluable to us. Please take a moment to provide us with your comments and suggestions. Include your name and address so we can thank you.

— Aviation Supplies & Academics, Inc.

Please print clearly.

NAME _____ DATE _____

TITLE *(Student, Instructor, other)* _____ EMAIL _____

BUSINESS/SCHOOL _____

ADDRESS _____

CITY _____ STATE _____ ZIP CODE/POSTAL CODE _____

COUNTRY _____ TELEPHONE *(optional)* _____

WHERE DID YOU PURCHASE THIS **AIRFRAME** AVIATION MAINTENANCE TEXT?_____

WAS THE TEXT RECOMMENDED TO YOU? _____ BY WHOM? _____

DO YOU INTEND TO PURCHASE ASA'S TWO ADDITIONAL TEXTS IN THE SERIES? GENERAL _____ POWERPLANT _____

COMMENTS AND SUGGESTIONS
Please tell us what you liked or disliked about the text: content, subject matter, ease-of-use, illustrations and figures, etc.

_____

_____

_____

_____

_____

_____

_____

MAIL THIS FORM TO:

Aviation Supplies & Academics, Inc.
7005 132nd Place SE
Newcastle, Washington 98059-3153

Please photocopy or remove this page.